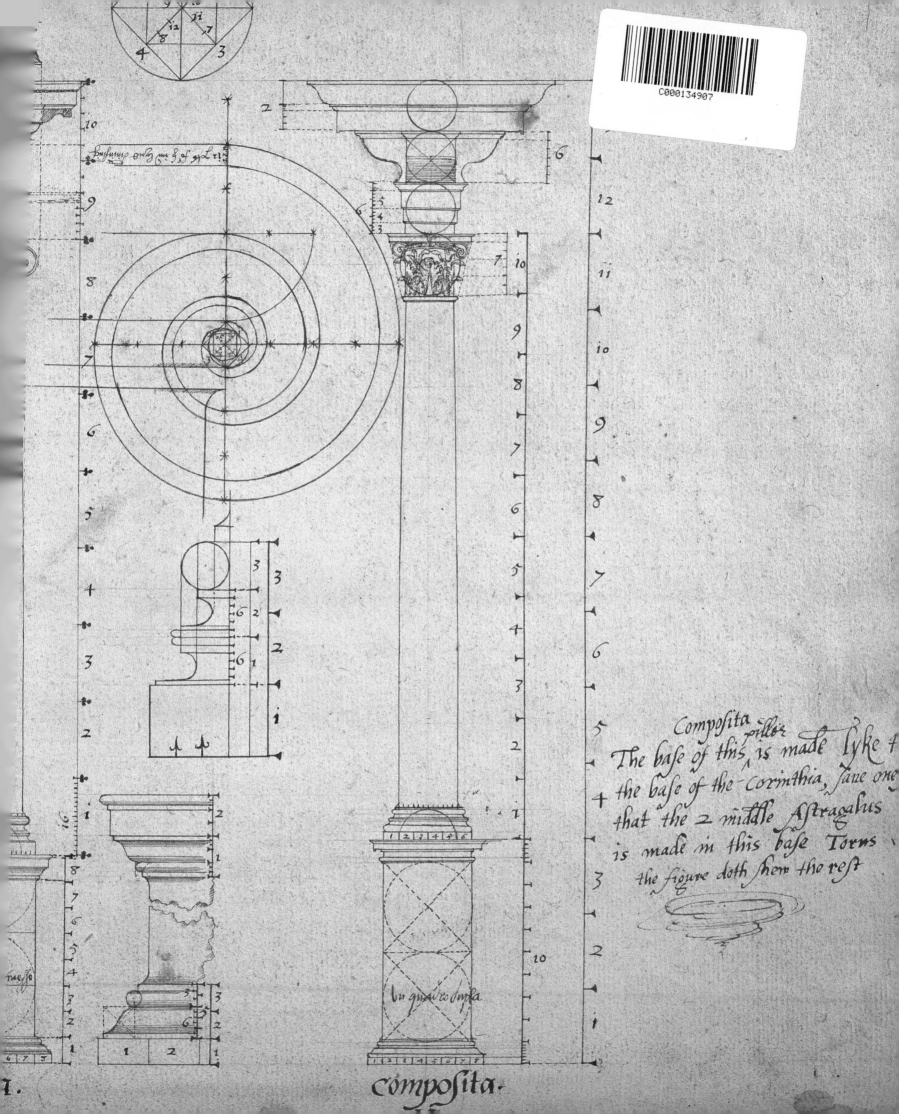

Composita pillor
The base of this is made lyke t[he]
the base of the Corinthia, save one
that the 2 middle Astragalus
is made in this base Torus
the figure doth shew the rest

In quadeo dupla

composita.

MARK GIROUARD

Elizabethan ARCHITECTURE

Its Rise and Fall, 1540–1640

Published for

The Paul Mellon Centre for Studies in British Art

by

Yale University Press

New Haven & London

Designed by Gillian Malpass

Printed in Italy by Conti Tipocolor s.p.a.

Library of Congress Cataloging-in-Publication Data
Girouard, Mark, 1931–
  Elizabethan archtecture : its rise and fall, 1540-1640 / Mark Girouard.
      p. cm.
  Includes bibliographical references and index.
  ISBN 978-0-300-09386-5 (cl : alk. paper)
  1. Architecture, Elizabethan–England. 2. Architecture,
Jacobean–England. 3. Architecture, Domestic–England.
  4. Architecture and society–England–History–16th century.
  5. Architecture and society–England–History–17th century. 1. Title.
  NA965.G57 2009
  720.942'09031–dc22

                                    2009031471

A catalogue record for this book is available from
The British Library

Endpapers   Corinthian, Ionic and Composite orders (*front*),
and Tuscan and Doric orders (*back*), as drawn by John Thorpe (T13 and 14)

Page i   Detail of the plasterwork on the ceiling of the great chamber in
Kinnersley Castle, Herefordshire, *c.*1588

Page ii   On the roof at Burghley House, Lincolnshire

Chapter frontispieces   Frontispiece of Books I and II of Sebastiano Serlio's *Architettura*
(Paris, 1545), with modern tinting

for ALICE

dear friend

Contents

Foreword

In 1955, when I decided to venture into architectural history by way of a Ph.D. thesis at the Courtauld Institute, I chose as a subject the Smythson family of mason-architects, partly on the strength of the existence of a great collection of Smythson drawings at the Royal Institute of British Architects, partly because of Robert Smythson's likely connection with Hardwick Hall, a house that I had known and loved since childhood.

Out of the thesis developed my *Robert Smythson and the Architecture of the Elizabethan Era*, published in 1966 (revised and redesigned as *Robert Smythson and the Elizabethan Country House* in 1983), and my catalogue of the Smythson drawings, published as volume 5 of *Architectural History* in 1962. In addition, my *Life in the English Country House* (1979) contained a chapter on the Elizabethan and Jacobean country house. I had long considered developing this and my Smythson books into a general study of Elizabethan and Jacobean architecture, expanding on J. A. Gotch's pioneering works early in this century and on John Summerson's all-too-short chapters in his *Architecture in Britain, 1530–1830*. But I became involved in other subjects, and it has been only in recent years that I have come round to attempting it.

When I first started research into the architecture of the period I was something of a pioneer: it was an unfashionable subject, and very few people were working on it. This situation has gradually been transformed in the intervening years, and now there is a mass of material available, and more being published all the time, in the form of both articles and books. But much of this is not easily accessible, and there is still no general history on the lines I envisaged. Although my book is in no way a pioneering study, I hope it may be useful in putting together in accessible form the results of my own researches and the published researches of others, and that it may give the general reader some idea of the wealth and excitements of the architecture of the period.

I do not cover vernacular architecture. The book is essentially concerned with high-style Elizabethan architecture and its Jacobean sequel, mainly as expressed in the more ambitious domestic buildings of the period – by no means always large, but whether large or small, always highly charged. I also deal with university and church architecture, where relevant, and occasionally with other public buildings in the towns, on the infrequent occasions when these rose above a vernacular level. I say a certain amount about church monuments because stylistically it is hard to separate them from the buildings. I deal barely, if at all, with garden design. The book is a history and anatomy of a style, not a gazetteer, and I have chosen my examples selectively, to illustrate my points.

Out of my work on this book I hope to develop a 'Biographical Dictionary of English Architecture, 1540–1640', to bridge the gap between the great dictionaries of John Harvey and Howard Colvin.

Note to the Reader

Most of the newly drawn plans are to the same scale; those on pages 114 and 117 are reproduced at 70 per cent.

In the captions to the illustrations, references in parentheses to drawings by Robert and John Smythson, (SM. DWGS), are to the number given to them in my catalogue, 'The Smythson Collection of the Royal Institute of British Architects', *Architectural History*, 5 (1962), referred to above. References in parentheses to drawings by John Thorpe, (T), are to the number given to them in John Summerson, ed., *The Book of Architecture of John Thorpe in Sir John Soane's Museum*, Walpole Society, 40, Glasgow, 1966.

Acknowledgements

The years of research and gestation have been lightened for me by the pleasure of conversations with, or suggestions and information from colleagues working in the same or related fields as mine. In addition to Andor Gomme, who, sadly, died in 2008, I must express my gratitude to Malcolm Airs, Emily Cole, Rosalys Coope, Nicholas Cooper, Tarnya Cooper, Paul Drury, David Durant, Claire Gapper, Richard Garnier, Elizabeth Goldring, John Goodall, Manolo Guerci, Karen Hearn, Paula Henderson, Richard Hewlings, Gordon Higgott, Deborah Howard, Maurice Howard, Jill Husselby, James Lawson, Peter Leach, Charles McKean, Kathryn Morrison, John Newman, Arnold Pacey, Pete Smith, Simon Thurley, Geoffrey Tyack, Anthony Wells-Cole, Adam White, Elizabeth Whittle and Lucy Worsley. Letters in the inimitably minuscule handwriting of Howard Colvin fed me information and advice up to his death in 2008; and John Harris has been a constant source of help.

Among the many owners or occupants of houses who generously allowed me access and offered hospitality and information, I should especially like to thank Cornelia Bayley, Douglas and Sophie Blain, Dick Carter, Pam Clarke, Mr J. Colville, Ed Fairfax-Lucy, Chrissie Fairlamb, Ian and Sarah Forrest, Paul and Janet Griffin, the Earl of Guilford, Caius Hawkins, Anthony Jennings, Michael Jones, Freddy de Lisle, Christopher Maclaren, Sandy McMillan, Alex Moulton, Peter and Elisabeth Prideaux-Brune, the late Lord Radnor, Robert Sackville-West, Lord Saye and Sele, Angela Scott, Mr and Mrs L. R. Stanton, Mr and Mrs J. L. Stringer, Nigel Thimbleby, Alan Urwick, the Countess of Verulam, Humphry and Katharine Wakefield, Amanda Wemyss and Tessa Wheeler. John Schofield stimulated me with information and ideas about Godolphin; the late Dickon Scarbrough and Lady Scarbrough showed me the Lumley Inventory and allowed me to photograph it.

Like all students of the period I owe an especial debt to Robin Harcourt Williams at Hatfield, John Culverhouse at Burghley and Kate Harris at Longleat. I must express my gratitude for help at Cambridge to David McKitterick at Trinity and David Watkin at Peterhouse; and at Oxford to Christopher Butler at Christ Church, Alan Bott at Merton and Chris Davies at Wadham. I thank David Adshead, Paul Holden and Mark Bradshaw of the National Trust, Caroline Stanford and Katherine Oake of the Landmark Trust, Anne Smith at Sherborne Castle, Anne Padfield at Hill Hall, David Knight at Stonyhurst College, Dawn Webster at Kiplin Hall, Edward Rooth and Bob Louden at South Wraxall, Pat Moseley at Ruperra and Eric Throssell at Hartwell. I thank also John Martin Robinson for a tour of north-western houses and for information about discoveries at Wilton; David Mlinaric for providing Angus McBean's photograph of Thorpe Hall; Christopher Gibbs for locating chimneypieces and other features; Ruth Guilding for driving me around in the later stages of my research, and for hospitality and companionship; David Cheshire for combing newspapers and magazines on my behalf, not least for examples from the strange world of neo-Elizabethan design; and Blanche and Dorothy Girouard for their encouragement and patience over the years.

The bulk of the new photography was taken by Martin Charles, supplemented with contributions by Harland Walshaw, Peter Burton, Thomas Pakenham, Mark Watson and Georg-Philipp von Pezold. I am grateful to all of them, Martin Charles above all, and have also had pleasure in using photographs by two friends now dead, Edward Piper and Fred Maroon.

Sue Neale and Liz Robinson undertook the picture research, Gemma Bryant drew the plans, Liz Manners was, as usual, invaluable in typing for me at all times, and it has been a pleasure working with my editor, Gillian Malpass, and her assistant, Emily Angus.

Finally, I must thank two institutions for support in health and sickness: the always helpful staff of the London Library, for easing my work on published sources, and the surgeons, doctors and nurses of St Mary's Hospital, Paddington, for seeing me through the illness that has delayed the publication of this book.

Prologue

By what art are we to worm our way into those strange spirits, those even stranger bodies? The more clearly we perceive it, the more remote that singular universe becomes. With very few exceptions . . . the creatures in it meet us without intimacy; they are exterior visions, which we know, but do not truly understand.

Lytton Strachey, Elizabeth and Essex (1928), part II, p. 8

Lytton Strachey came to the Elizabethan age as an outsider, and wrote on the basis of much curiosity but no very deep knowledge or research. But even today, eighty years later, when so much more has been written, and so many different facets of Elizabethan life and thought explored, the remoteness remains. The Elizabethans still seem like a race apart, looking differently, thinking differently, acting differently from anything in our experience.

In portrait after portrait the bodies of those portrayed scarcely exist, apart from pale faces and long pale hands; stiff figures, sheathed in gorgeous multi-patterned clothes, stand on patterned carpets, adjoined by magnificent coats of arms. What were they thinking or feeling? There are virtually no diaries to give a clue, and the convoluted sentences of their letters are little more revealing. Even love poems, exquisite though they often are, conceal strong personal feeling, if it existed, inside a crafted framework; and the cries of anguish or frustration that sometimes break out of the cage seem undirected to any personal object. The portraits, it is clear enough, were not designed to reveal the personality of those portrayed. They were icons, vivid images intended in endless variation on an accepted formula to express wealth, status, sometimes marriage or pregnancy. There were sometimes, it is true, inscriptions, jewels, or attributes – a bird, a flower – that gave further information about the subject, but their meaning was deliberately opaque. The Elizabethans in general follow Polonius's advice to his son: 'Give thy thoughts no tongue . . . Give every man thy ear, but few thy voice'. They did not give themselves away. Even their miniatures, the pictorial equivalents of the love poems and often even more exquisite, are curiously without intimacy.

The houses – or at least the houses of great people – can stretch a veil across the life lived inside them as beautiful and baffling as the gorgeous clothing of the portraits. In a medieval house one knew where one was. The kitchen, the great hall, the chapel, the staircases, the gatehouse, the lodgings of dependents were easily distinguished by their roofs, their windows or their doors. There is no reason to suppose that this was based on any conscious doctrine of functionalism; openings, windows and distinctive roofs were put where they were needed, and even in buildings where a degree of symmetry was imposed to make an effect, it was diluted or abandoned whenever it became inconvenient.

But in many Elizabethan houses the lovely regular mask comes first: in search of symmetry two storeys of windows are disguised as one, or two rows of windows light a single space, or completely false windows have solid stone behind their glazing; and the little pavilions at the right angles of the entrance court, the towers spaced around the main building, are there to add to the exquisitely balanced picture, not because they were needed at that particular place.

Medieval houses – indeed most medieval buildings – were designed from the inside out, Elizabethan ones from the outside in. Not all Elizabethan houses, of course, but it is with the ones that were, the intensely artificial, elaborately composed houses of great people, as artificial as

QVOMODO SC ANDIT CONRVET STATTIM

THE·WHEELE
OF·FORTVNE

WHOSE·RVLE·IS
IGNORAVNCE·

the clothes that encased their inhabitants, that this book is mainly concerned – and also with charting how these could on occasions be emulated in the houses of lesser people, and how the extremes of artificiality could be diluted for practical reasons.

A moving impulse behind Elizabethan voyages of discovery into this impractical world was the pursuit of the 'device', a word constantly used in the sixteenth century for any ingenious or original shape or concept. The idea of a building as a device is very occasionally found in late medieval England: in whole buildings, such as circular Queenborough and hexagonal Wardour castles; perhaps in building elements, such as gatehouses or kitchens. It reoccurs in the little buildings known as banqueting houses put up by Henry VIII and his courtiers, and even more in the geometric prettiness of the plans of Henry VIII's forts, which fell like starfish or grew like sea-flowers around the English coast in the 1540s, expressing a geometric elaboration that had little to do with practical problems of fortification.

But, although it may have had precursors, the idea of fashioning whole houses as devices was essentially an Elizabethan one. One can watch its slow but steady progress from the mid-century on: first the entrance front symmetrically composed, then the internal courtyard, then the whole house; finally the courtyard disappears, and the house or building becomes a single, contrived mass.

Other elements could be fed in, to add to the strangeness, originality or enjoyableness of an architectural device. It could be expressed in the language of classical architecture, using, perhaps, Sebastiano Serlio's epic-making book (the architectural bible of the Elizabethan world, itself full of suggestions for composed plans as well as composed elevations), the whole process given flavour by the belief that the classical vocabulary expressed ancient mysteries: something that had been 'withdrawen and hidden', 'kept secret and

not spoken of, as John Shute, who drew on Serlio to resurrect the Five Orders for the English, put it.

The native English tradition could also provide elements: bay windows, towers and battlements could be fed into the composition, to add to the intricacy of ground plan and elevations, and be drawn upwards to provide memorable skylines; windows could be enlarged so that houses became elaborate lanterns of glass, lit up from inside or flaming in the evening sun; even chimneys and chimneystacks could be made to play their part in the composition.

And buildings could be given secret meanings and connotations: made to express the mysteries of the Trinity, to imitate the initials of the owner, to echo the Temple of Solomon or the Church of the Holy Sepulchre in Jerusalem, articulating other cryptic codes that have never yet been cracked.

The extent, elaboration and intensity of composition varied from building to building. There are buildings where only one façade and the internal court were contrived; buildings where the front matched the back and the sides each other, but the sides were different from front and back; buildings that were identical on all four fronts. The houses had, after all, to be lived in, and extremes of artifice led to practical problems; much ingenuity was shown in fitting the standard accommodation into unlikely outlines. But even in more everyday houses the sense of composition can be sensed; and even if restrained in the main house, artifice could be let loose in little accompanying buildings, there as much for decoration as use, in pavilions, gatehouses, banqueting houses and lodges, so full of fancy and so thickly scattered over the landscape of Elizabethan architecture.

William Harrison saw what was happening and described it: 'It is a worlde to see how divers men being bent to buildinge, and haveing a delectable view in spending of their goodes by that trade, doe dailie imagine new devises of their owne to guide their workmen withall, and these more curious and excellent than the former.' That was in 1577; nearly fifty years later, when the creative fury of Elizabethan architecture was on the decline, Henry Wotton could write disparagingly: 'Design of such nature doe more ayme at Rarity than Commoditie; so for my part I had rather admire them, than commend them.'

Was he right? One can return to comparing Elizabethan to medieval architecture, or can put high-style Elizabethan buildings against vernacular ones. Medieval builders were inventive engineers. The increasing elaboration of their stone vaults, the scaffolding of buttresses needed to support these, the heroic carpentry of the roofs of their churches and halls, and the great widths that on occasions these spanned – structures like these were what excited them, and caught their imaginations, as they can still catch ours, so that even their canopied tombs were miracles of structure in miniature. The Elizabethans were interested in form, not structure. Although intrigued by the decorative shapes and patterns evolved in medieval vaulting, they were content to copy these in plaster. When they needed to bridge wide spaces, they used inherited medieval techniques, and did not improve or develop on them; in the one exception, the flat roof of the hall at Wollaton, which uses a, to England, novel technique from Serlio, the real structure is disguised and a fake medieval-style roof put beneath it, presumably because the patron liked the look of it. The one structural innovation – and that an important one – was the open-well, cantilevered wooden staircase; but this was in fact a post-Elizabethan development, first documented around 1605.

At the same time as great people in the Elizabethan world (or their hangers-on) were evolving their contrived and complex buildings, lesser gentry, yeomanry, merchants and shopkeepers were putting up quite different buildings, in half-timber construction, brick or locally quarried stone; solid, sensible and lovable. High-style Elizabethan architecture is not especially solid, not in the least sensible, scarcely lovable.

One can see this as a moral story, in old-fashioned Arts and Crafts terms: medieval architecture genuine and commendable, vernacular Elizabethan humbly carrying on a good tradition, high-style Elizabethan an abortion. Set against this the shock of delight that the carefully contrived symmetries of these Elizabethan buildings can still give to us, and quite clearly gave to their creators: 'so every part answerable to other, to allure liking', as Lord Burghley wrote of the approach to and entrance front of the huge house of Holdenby in Northamptonshire.

Elizabethans were interested by, and analysed, the differences between prose and poetry, and the intensity and urgency that rhyme, metre and the different patterns of stanzas can give to language, pulling it out of what George Puttenham called the 'common course of ordinarie speech', and giving it 'a certain noveltie, and strange maner of conveyance, disguising it no little from the ordinarie and accustomed'; or shaping unformed imaginings, as Thomas Daniel wrote of the sonnet, 'by the divine power of the spirit . . . wrought into an Orbe of order and forme'. They were doing the same with buildings; contriving a poetry of architecture.

The power of creating a compact and memorable entity is found in Elizabethan art of all kinds, not just in the buildings; it was done better in England than anywhere else in Europe. One can find it in the development of the 'air', the short and exquisite poem of carefully contrived variety and differences of rhythm, set to equally exquisite music. One can find it in the best portraits, in the intense artificiality, the single vivid image, which can still fill one with amazement both in the portraits of Elizabeth herself – which frequently carry as well different depths of allegorical meaning – and in the simpler, less coded but equally striking images of lesser people, such as those of the two Fitton sisters; two portraits of tall girls in white dresses, one with a long string of pearls, the other with a long string of rubies, standing against plain backgrounds, scarcely portraits at all, in the modern manner of revealing character, yet one sees them with a leap of the heart.

One can find it in the contents and decoration of houses, as well as in the houses themselves. These, too, could be devices, and, as in the main structure, a wide range of sources could be drawn on to create them, above all the engravings pouring off the printing presses of Antwerp. For whenever an Elizabethan wanted to embroider a dress or a cushion, decorate a gable, put together a chimneypiece, a church monument or a ceiling, engrave a bowl, inlay a piece of furniture or panelling, frame an inscription or a map, carve an allegorical figure or a scene from the classics or the Bible, he or she seldom if ever consulted thir own fancy, or modelled from the life and nature around them. Instead they went straight to whatever engravings they had acquired or could get access to, and cobbled their designs together from them.

The engravings were almost invariably foreign; and the artificers who adapted them were often foreign immigrants too, usually in retreat from religious persecution and coming from France, occasionally from Italy or Germany, and, above all, from the Low Countries. But this does not mean that English architecture and decoration of the time is made up of straightforward importations from the Continent or of secondhand, provincial and clumsy copies by English artificers of the real thing. The foreigners, as is often the case, adapted their work to suit the tastes and needs of their clients or the practices of their English colleagues. The engravings could be just a starting-point: artificers adapted, changed, combined, collaged, till the sources sometimes all but disappeared; on occasion they could pull one figure from an engraving and isolate it so that it acquired

a force and vitality lacking in the orginal. Behind everything was a native English tradition, infusing the way in which people thought and worked. The result was, at its best, a creative fusion, original, often exciting and quite unlike anything on the Continent. The fusion was perhaps most successful in the architecture but was to be found in the decoration and furnishing as well.

Hardwick is full of striking images, in plaster, stone, alabaster, embroideries and pictures. Outstanding among them are the series of hangings of Noble Women of the Ancient World, originally in the withdrawing chamber, each Woman isolated against a black background under an arch, with smaller figures of the Virtues which they epitomize, similarly under arches, well separated to either side (Figs 34, 267). All the Noble Women may derive from engravings, but only one source has tentatively been identified: an engraving of a naked Rhea Silvia, the mother of Romulus and Remus, who (just as Nicholas Hilliard took a naked Mercury, put him in Elizabethan dress, encircled him with wild roses, and turned him into one of the most famous of Elizabethan miniatures) has been abstracted from one corner of an engraving, part clothed with draperies collaged from cut-up older embroidery, and turned into Lucrecia killing herself after her rape by Tarquin, as the symbol of chastity.

The needlework queens or heroines, with their attendants, so memorably isolated in their classical framework, are accompanied at Hardwick in the plasterwork frieze of the High Great Chamber by Diana with her court, presiding over her forest kingdom of elephants, lions and deer, with scenes of the hunt across the room and Spring whipping Cupid with a bundle of flowers in the window. This forest plasterwork is in striking contrast to the Flemish tapestries below it, just as the Hardwick appliqué work and needlework contrasts with the Mannerist professionalism of the few French embroideries in the house, or with the Flemish engravings from which most of the work derives. But it is the Hardwick work, infused with a poetry that one can call naif, if one wants to, that sticks in the memory.

But the many images at Hardwick are not just there for decoration: they are there to inform and exhort. They can give us a glimpse into that mysterious world, the Elizabethan mind. The Elizabethans used visual images to trigger off information and act as guides to conduct. Hence the popularity, so difficult for us to understand, of impresas and emblems: visual images combined with a motto or concise text, which enshrined a warning, a moral truth, or a statement about the beliefs of the people who had selected them. Bess of Hardwick was in the same field, at once informing and exhorting. Arthemisia, Zenobia, Lucrecia, Penelope and Cleopatra, with their attendant virtues, show how Bess valued people who were constant, pious, magnanimous, prudent, chaste, liberal, persevering, patient, brave and just. Her especial favourite, as is made clear from other depictions at Hardwick, was Penelope, the epitome of Patience and Perseverance. She saw herself as aiming for the best and being patient in surmounting the difficulties needed to obtain it.

Hence Perseverance, in the hanging (Fig. 267), holds an eagle, who is striving for the sun. In the roofless High Great Chamber in the Old Hall at Hardwick a young man, winged on the shoulders and ankles, with one arm outstretched, appears to be leaping into the room from between two giant figures on the overmantel. He has been abstracted from an engraving of the Triumph of Patience, in which he is one of the figures pulling the triumphal car on which Patience sits; he is Studium, perhaps best translated as Enthusiasm, and he, too, in the engraving, is reaching for the sun.

Bess of Hardwick was both giving information about her own values and exhorting others to adopt them – not least her own family, and above all, perhaps, her granddaughter, Arbella, who lived at Hardwick with her, whom she hoped might one day become Queen of England, and who, as she wandered, as we know from her own letters she did, through the great empty rooms, could absorb not only the virtues epitomized by the five Noble Women, but a mass of other information, or exhortations to conduct, presented in the other carvings, pictures or embroideries that filled the house. And for use away from Hardwick the visual images could be committed to memory, for memory then was far less bombarded with information than it is today and tenacious of what it was offered as a result.

Hardwick, in fact, provided a huge visual encyclopaedia and guide to conduct, spread out over the great house in the way that Quintilian, in the first century, had suggested the imagination could conjure up a building, with pictorial objects spaced at easily recognised places in it, as triggers to memory. It was a palace or theatre of the memory made real in a casket of golden Derbyshire stone, supplying knowledge or teaching conduct to those who walked around it.

The actual fabric of the house at Hardwick also had a moral message, for it epitomized the two qualities of order and degree, which were accepted as the linchpins of society: order expressed in the symmetry of its plans and façades, and in the disposition of its six towers; degree in the way its room heights, and the windows that lit them, increased from floor to floor, from a floor for servants, a floor for the family, and a floor for state and for the entertainment of the queen, should she come. This too could equally be committed to the memory in the form of its vividly distinctive plan; and such ordered plans, exquisitely drawn out and coloured, were valued possessions of the age.

In 1570 the Crown Commissioners sent up from London to survey the lands forfeited as result of the Northern Rebellion in 1569 reported on Raby Castle: 'The Castell of Raby', they wrote, 'is a marvellous huge house of building wherein are three wards and builded all of stone and covered with leade; and yet is there no order or proporcion in the building thereof.' Raby, with its irregular congregation of great towers, was the seat of Charles Neville, Earl of Westmoreland, one of the two northern earls who had led the last serious rebellion against the Tudors; and the Nevilles had been leading figures in the troubled half-century following on the unlawful depositon of Richard II in 1399, and including the murder of Henry VI. The Tudors claimed with justification that they had brought order and respect for degree back to England again, and kept it peaceful and ordered when most of the countries of Europe were in turmoil. The irregular towers of Raby Castle seemed to epitomize the disorder of a bad time that had passed.

The concept of 'progress' developed only in the eighteenth century; the Elizabethans thought in terms of trying to go back to a good age that had been corrupted, not forward to a better age in the future. Elizabeth was celebrated by contemporary poets as Astraea, the goddess of Justice and the Golden Age, who had retreated in dissatisfaction from the corruption of the Iron Age and settled in the firmament as the constellation Virgo. Her return to Earth to bring back a second golden age had been hymned by Virgil and others in praise of Augustus, and used as a metaphor by early Christian writers.

But even those who believed in it were aware of the fragility of Elizabeth's new Golden Age. All over England the huge abandoned shells of once magnificent monastery buildings reminded them of the impermanence both of their own lives and of buildings and monuments. Ruins filled their imagination – Shakespeare's 'bare ruined choirs', Ralegh's 'broken monuments of my great desires', Daniel's apostrophe to the mysterious stones of Stonehenge, not only part shattered but their history and function forgotten:

That huge domb heap, that cannot tell us
     how, Nor what, nor whence it is, nor with
          whose hands

. . . Whereon when as the gazing passenger
Hath greedy lookt with admiration
. . . Then he turnes againe
And looks and sighs, and then admires
     afreshe,
And in himself with sorrow doth complaine
The misery of darke forgetfulness . . .

One curious accompaniment to this sense of the impermanence of worldly things is apparent in much Elizabethan architecture, especially its grander varieties. Far from underlining the solidity of their buildings, at least to give the impression that they would be lasting, Elizabethan builders emphasized their fragility. William Harrison, in his description of England, contrasted the buildings of the time of Henry VIII with those of his own age: 'Certes masonry did never better flourish in England than in his time. And albeit that in these days there be many goodly houses erected in the Sundry quarters of this island, yet they are rather curious to the eye like paper work than substantial for continuance . . .'

Harrison talks as though the buildings of Henry VIII's time were actually more substantial. In fact it was a matter of appearance. In early Tudor buildings, as in the buildings before them, windows and openings were set back behind reveals, which gave an idea of the thickness of the wall. In Elizabethan buildings they are set flush to the external line of the wall, and the reveals are on the inside. Hence the suggestion, in certain lights at least, of paper thinness, of buildings that might melt into air, like Prospero's cloud-capped towers and gorgeous palaces.

In general, whether looked at from the point of religion, of scientific knowledge, such as it was, of philosophy or of history, the lot of humanity on Earth, as seen by the Elizabethans, was not only insecure, but unhappy.

Earth and humanity on it, was permanently scarred by Adam's and Eve's fall from grace; even allowing for Redemption, the truly good times could only be hoped for after death. Life expectancy was short, teeth rotted, beauty decayed, golden boys and girls turned to dust. Far from being the centre of the universe, Earth was its sump, the lowest level beneath the purity of the stars and rotating planets, and the heavenly Empyrean above them, the domain of angels, the blessed, and God. It was the discoveries of Copernicus that gave a sense of liberation, by lifting Earth up to join the planets, but these were scarcely in circulation in Elizabethan England. For those who were Platonists, as most thinking Elizabethans were, the natural world and everything in it were pale copies of the reality of the ideal.

Even Elizabeth's Golden Age was losing its shine by the end of the decade. The high proportion of her subjects who remained openly or at heart Catholic still resented it. In spite of the euphoria following on the defeat of the Armada, England was still vulnerable to foreign invasion, several years of disastrous harvests brought famine and much misery, the uncertainty of what would happen after Elizabeth's inevitably approaching death was a nagging worry, resentment about monopolies and other perquisites was widespread, the traumatic disgrace and execution of Essex, the hero and darling of the late Elizabethan age, brought much unpopularity to the queen.

Yet the last decade of her reign saw, among much else, the writing of Shakespeare's *Hamlet* and *Midsummer Night's Dream*, of Marlowe's *Hero and Leander*. of the first and best odes of Donne and Campion, of Dowland's airs and the exquisite verses that were sung to them, of the most memorable of Hilliard's miniatures, and, in architecture, the buildings of Hardwick and Montacute at one end of the scale, and the Triangular Lodge at Rushton at the other.

The reasons for periods of high creativity are always mysterious, but high prosperity is always a help; it is hard to think of a poverty-stricken culture that has produced memorable art. In spite of seasonal ups and downs, as a whole England in the sixteenth and early seventeenth centuries was growing steadily richer. Quite apart from the wealth brought to Catholics and Protestants alike by the break-up of religious property (for the Catholics dabbled in monastic lands as much as anyone), new opportunities in trade, manufacture and exploration were boosting the economy. Increasing sumptuousness in dress, increasing lavishness in furnishing and decoration, were all expressions of it. Above all, there was a burst of domestic building, in comparative terms perhaps not equalled again in England, and expressed from the grandest houses to modest vernacular cottages. Everywhere, new buildings were going up, or old buildings were being remodelled.

The capacity of the Elizabethans for enjoyment was without end, they could even put the greatest zest into being miserable and melancholy; indeed the theory that the melancholy humour produced more intelligence and creative ability than the sanguine, choleric and phlegmatic ones made melancholia the fashionable disease for numerous young men in black cloaks with folded arms and black hats pulled down over their eyes.

Platonic idealism and religious puritanism had to struggle against delight in human flesh and beauty, in sexual pleasures, in flowers and fruit, in natural beauty, in 'Strawberries swimming in the cream / And schoolboys playing in the stream'. Spenser, with his strong puritan streak, could describe the fleshly delights of the Bower of Bliss in deeply erotic verse, but then feel compelled to smash them with as much zest as the iconoclasts of the previous generation had smashed stained glass and images. But Marlowe could revel without hang-ups in how

> Leander now like Theban Hercule
> Entred the orchard of t'Hesperides
> Whose fruit none rightly can describe but he
> That puls or shakes it from the golden tree'.

And Campion encouraged night-time love:

THE · SPEARE · OF · DESTINYE ·

WHOSE · RVLER · IS · KNOWLEDGE ·

You may do in the dark
What the day doth forbid
Fear not the dogs that bark
Night will have all hid'.

It was an age of discovery: scientific discovery, though this was in its early stages; discoveries of unknown or barely known worlds, out of which were to develop the enormous world trade and consequent wealth of England in later centuries; discoveries in literature and history, as the spread of printed books, the industry of translators and the presentation of their stories on the stage made accessible to increasing numbers of people both the history of their own country and the knowledge of both contemporary Europe and the classical world, with all their populations of memorable characters, stories and buildings.

Perhaps most important of all for the Elizabethans was the discovery of the English language and what could be done with it, how its vocabulary could be enriched with foreign words or newly minted words, into how many different forms words could be put together, what games could be played with them, how the balance of a sentence, the metre and configuraiton of a poem, the shape and rhythm of a play, could be endlessly varied. The ebullience resulting from this discovery could lead to experiments that failed, to over-rich and indigestible writing, to oppressive artificiality, but it led as a whole to a literature of extraordinary richness, vigour and variety.

Elizabethan architecture was doing much the same thing. The artificers, clients and others who built Elizabethan buildings were gleefully and inventively using a vocabulary in part inherited from the early Tudor period, in part enriched from abroad, by means of pattern books, books of the orders, and a flood of engravings of all kinds. A wealth of combinations and composition were possible, both in the making up of individual features, such as porches, chimneypieces, hall

screens and church monuments, and in the plans and façades of the buildings as a whole.

Knowledge was the key. The owner of Little Moreton Hall, as he walked to and fro in its long gallery and bucketed up and down on its undulating floor, as though on the deck of a ship at sea, came at either end to depictions based on engravings in the *Castle of Knowledge*, a book by the English pioneer of mathematics Robert Record. At one end a blindfolded and half-naked Fortune rotated the wheel that tossed the fortunes of individuals up and down; at the other, a decently clothed Knowledge, with compasses in one hand and supporting an armillary sphere of the heavens with the other, showed the way of escape from the vagaries of Fortune. Compasses stood for measuring, and the power it gave. The relationship of the stars and spheres in the heavens could be measured and plotted; the route of sea voyages could be measured out to reveal the shapes of each country and the earth's surfaces, and to show owners exactly what they owned within a country; compasses plotted out the distances and drew the curves with which to inscribe the plans from which ordered houses could rise.

But the heavens were not static; they moved in a continual dance; they were order in motion. The intricate dances of the Elizabethans were equally ordered. Buildings could not dance; but the Elizabethans, with the newly discovered art of perspective to shape their vision, cannot but have appreciated, as we do so vividly today, the way in which the static beauty of their intricately symmetrical compositions moved and changed as they moved away from the central axis; so that the six towers of Hardwick, for instance, group and regroup both as one walks around it, and from distant views all over the surrounding countryside.

It is hard not to keep returning to Hardwick, because, in addition to its quality as a work of architecture, it has retained so much more of its decoration and original contents than other houses of its period. But for a hundred years or so, all over England and Wales, other remarkable buildings were rising, in numbers, richness and inventiveness unsurpassed at any other time in the history of English architecture. Much has been destroyed, much survives only in illustrations, often inadequate, much has been lost without illustration, much is in ruins, or has been altered or stripped of contents; but what is left is remarkable enough. And behind the buildings are people: the patrons, who struggled to keep or gain power, fame and wealth, fought with the enemy or each other, broke out themselves at times into music or verse, could be variously learned, arrogant, magnificent, grasping, or treacherous; behind the patrons, the intellectuals to whom they went for ideas; and the great body of artificers who made the buildings possible, many unknown or scarcely known, many eagerly absorbing new ideas or developing ideas of their own, a few of them men of genius.

3 Chatsworth, Derbyshire. The entrance front, from a needlework picture showing it after remodelling, c.1573–80.

Chapter 1

People

The Clients

One might expect this section to begin with the queen herself. But Elizabeth, unlike her father Henry VIII or Henry VIII's contemporary and rival across the Channel, François 1, built little of importance. The greatest builder of her reign was her principal servant and trusted partner in power William Cecil, Lord Burghley, Secretary from 1558, and Lord Treasurer from 1572 until 1598, in which year the aged queen visited her even more aged minister, and fed him with her own hand in his last illness.

Not everyone liked or trusted him. A visiting German, Baron Waldstein, picked up the gossip on tour in England in 1600, two years after his death. He reported how people said of him that 'after climbing the ladder of success, he pulled it well out of everyone else's reach'.[1] In 1591, in 'Mother Hubbard's Tale', Edmund Spenser said much the same, when making one of several vicious attacks on him – admittedly not by name, but immediately recognisable, and as rash as they were courageous.

> And when he aught not pleasing would put by
> The cloak was care of thrift and husbandry,
> For to encrease the common treasures store;
> But his own treasure he encreased more,
> And lifted up his lofty towres thereby
> That they began to threat the neighbour sky,
> The whiles the Princes pallaces fell fast
> To ruine: (for what thing can ever last?)
> And whilest the other Peeres for povertie
> Were forst their auncient houses to let lie
> And their olde Castles to the ground to fall,
> Which their forefathers famous over all
> Had founded for the Kingdomes ornament,
> And for their memories long moniment.
> But he no count made of Nobilitie
> . . . Yet none durst speake, ne none durst of
>   him plaine;
> So great he was in grace, and rich through
>   gaine.

> Ne would he anie let to have accesse
> Unto the Prince, but by his owne address:
> For all that els did come were sure to faile.[2]

It was scarcely surprising that Spenser failed to get preferment in England, and was forced to spend eighteen years in what he thought of as exile, as a colonial official writing his *Faerie Queene* in a tower in an Irish bog.

But was Spenser justified? Did Burghley prosper at the expense of the queen? Did he starve the old nobility? Did his lofty towers scrape the sky, while their houses and castles decayed? Did he block all but his own creatures from promotion or royal favour?

It is true that what was seen as Burghley's favouritism was bitterly resented by those who did not benefit from it, most notably by his nephews Anthony and Francis Bacon (who referred to him as 'the old fox'). It is true, too, that the queen built nothing to compare with the two enormous houses and one considerable one that were built by Burghley; and that by the end of the century around seventeen royal houses and forty-three royal castles were in various stages of ruin or decay; and that Cobham Hall in Kent (Fig. 5) was perhaps the only important house to be built by a member of the old nobility in her reign.[3]

There is another side to the picture, however. Elizabeth, thanks mainly to her father's passion for building, was grossly over-housed. The royal houses and castles in decay were ones for which she had no use. Unlike her father, she had no especial taste for building and a strong taste for economy. As for the old nobility, one reason that they did not build was that, unlike the new men, they did not need to. They were likely already to own substantial residences, usually including a castle of some splendour. The more important medieval castles were just as much, if not more, magnificent dwellings for mighty people as places of fortification. Under Elizabeth, because of the history and tradition behind them and their

4 (*facing page*) Sir Christopher Hatton (1540–1591), Elizabeth's favourite, ultimately Lord Chancellor, and the builder of Holdenby House, Northamptonshire. From an astrological portrait inspired by his horoscope, *c.*1580.

5   Cobham Hall, Kent.
The south front.
The house was built by
William, 10th Lord
Cobham, *c.*1580–97, round
an earlier nucleus.

frequently superb situations, they retained their status undiminished: a great castle was the most prestigious form of residence. Its owner might, and frequently did, embellish it with new ranges of rooms or surround it with elaborate gardens, but it would never occur to him to rebuild it, let alone to abandon it. When Elizabeth presented her favourite Robert Dudley and his brother Ambrose with the two great castles of Kenilworth and Warwick, she was not offloading anachronisms, but making splendid gifts, the character of which they appreciated, fostered and exploited.

On the other hand, the fact that it is adequately housed already has never discouraged the aristocracy in any country from building magnificently. There is likely to be a particular explanation why the old nobility built comparatively little. Both Elizabeth and Burghley had the greatest respect for rank and lineage; but both of them, mindful of past history, were suspicious of over-mighty subjects. Encouraged to live lavishly at court rather than in the country, sent on prestigious but financially unrewarding and indeed expensive embassies, given honourable but equally unrewarding posts such as the Presidency of the

Council of the North, the Lord Deputyship of Ireland, the Lord Lieutenancy of their county, or the custody of the Queen of Scots, sweetened with grants but never too many of them, the old aristocracy were never allowed to grow too prosperous. Rather, since their expenses were large, because of the way of life that was expected of them, and which they themselves took for granted, their financial sense seldom acute, their liability to the dishonesty or exploitation of their servants considerable, their attempts at moneymaking on occasions disastrous, they were almost always in a greater or lesser degree of financial embarrassment.

Whatever the reasons, it was the new men who set the pace. And as in former and future ages, the money with which they built came from four main sources: from gifts and grants from the monarch, from office, from the law, and from entrepreneurship, whether in trade, industry, moneylending, agriculture or, on occasions, piracy.

The families who grew rich under the Tudors had common characteristics. They were mostly of modest origins, younger sons or from minor gentry or yeoman stock. They were well educated, at university or Inns of Court, or both. The great majority were, or became, Protestant. Their fortunes were based on service to the Crown, combined with prudent exploitation of financial opportunity, including advantageous buying up of monastery lands. By the time Elizabeth came to the throne in 1558, the class already existed for her to draw on; most of them had already prospered for two or three generations under her father and grandfather. The most successful had already been ennobled; of the sixty-three titled families at her accession, only twenty-eight were pre-Tudor creations.[4] The heralds were kept busy and prosperous researching or inventing pedigrees for new families of all levels.

Lord Burghley's background was typical. The Cecils (or Sitsilts) had been minor gentry on the Welsh border. Burghley's father and grandfather came to London to serve in the households of Henry VII and Henry VIII; they prospered and purchased sizeable estates in the Midlands, including the manor of Burghley. He had a solid base from which to expand. In the days of his glory the heralds produced a dubious fourteenth-century John Sitsilt, who cavorts in armour on the illuminated family tree now at Hatfield. Inevitably, the Cecils were found to descend from 'King Brute', the Trojan-descended monarch who was claimed to have reached England in 1116 BC. Another tempting suggestion was that they were by origin a noble Roman family, the Caecilii.[5]

The emoluments of office under Elizabeth seldom, if ever, bore any relationship to the official salary. This was always modest, but came with recognised perquisites, which could be large, and sometimes enormous. An office-holder could and did lend out for his own profit money on deposit in his department, sell jobs that were in his gift, and accept presents from those who hoped for favours to come or were grateful for favours received. Two of the most valuable offices were the great one of Lord Treasurer and the fruitful

one of Master of the Court of Wards. Any minor who inherited land held by knight-service automatically became a ward of the court if his father died before he came of age; the Master of the Court could assume the wardship himself or sell it to others; he or they had full use of two-thirds of the income and could dispose of the minor in marriage. The profits went, in theory, to the Crown, but the Master and his officials all took a cut.

The salary of the Lord Treasurer was £366 a year, but he was collecting around £4,000 by the early seventeenth century. The salary of the Master of the Court of Wards was £133, his income more like £3,000.[6] William Cecil became Master of the Court of Wards in 1561, Lord Treasurer in 1572, and combined the two offices up till his death in 1598. His son took over from his father in the Wards in 1598, became Lord Treasurer in 1608, and combined the two until his death in 1612. Their rewards from these two offices were still further increased as a result of a complex series of grants or leases of land, or acquisitions of minor posts, as constables of boroughs, keepers of royal parks, stewards of manors and so on. The sky-threatening masses of Burghley, Theobalds and Hatfield were the result (Figs 6, 7).

In return, the queen was lavishly entertained by the Cecils, in London or the country. Above all, both father and son were hard-working public servants. Like an American president, each created his own private office. Its members worked equally hard, but they too did well, for all approaches to the great men passed through them, inevitably with a sweetener attached. Four members of Burghley's private office built sizeable country houses: Sir Walter Cope at Holland House, just outside London; Sir Henry Maynard at Easton Lodge in Essex (Fig. 8); Sir Vincent Skinner at Thornton Abbey in Lincolnshire; Sir Michael Hickes at Ruckholt, also in Essex. All four houses have gone, or been remodelled, but

6 and 7 The
splendour of the Cecils:
(*above*) the west front of
Burghley House,
Lincolnshire, built by
William Cecil, Lord
Burghley, *c.*1558–85;
(*facing page*) the south
front of Hatfield House,
Hertfordshire, built by
Robert Cecil, Earl of
Salisbury, 1607–11.

their plans and the elevation of Easton Lodge survive, as drawn by John Thorpe (Fig. 352); and
Holland House (Figs 546–7) was to be much illustrated before it was partly burnt out in the Second
World War, and unforgivably demolished after it.

Other great officers had similar private offices,
and their servants could also do well. Trevalyn in
Denbighshire, built by John Trevor in 1576, has
the coat of arms of his master, Lord Buckhurst,
Privy Councillor, ambassador, and later Lord
Treasurer, over the entrance (Fig. 9). The arms of
the Earl of Pembroke adorn the porch of Ruperra
Castle in Monmouthshire, the house built by his

steward, Sir Thomas Morgan. Sir John Thynne,
whose great house and fortune were based on his
service to the Duke of Somerset in the mid sixteenth century, still put his old master's coat of
arms on his hall screen at Longleat forty years
later.

Apart from the Lord Treasurer, the great officers of state were the Lord Chancellor (sometimes replaced by the Lord Keeper of the Great
Seal), the Lord Privy Seal and the Lord High Admiral. Separate Lord Presidents or Lord Deputies
administered the North of England, Wales and
the Marches, and Ireland, and kept their own

courts in their mini-kingdoms. With less prestige but great power were the two Secretaries, who looked after foreign affairs and the day-to-day business of government.

There was no standing army, but a permanent armoury of cannon and firearms in the Tower of London under the Master of the Ordnance. For many years this important post was filled by the Earl of Leicester's brother, the Earl of Warwick; his nephew, Sir Philip Sidney, would have succeeded him had he lived.[7]

Customs provided a major portion of the royal revenue; they had a complicated history, some-times being farmed out to private individuals, who collected them and took a cut, sometimes administered by the government. The Lord Treasurer presided over a congregation of officers, including the Chancellor of the Exchequer, not as important then as he is today.

Most of these government offices brought in less than the Treasury and Wards, but still enough to enable their holders to build hand-somely. Sir Nicholas Bacon, Lord Keeper, built a great house at Gorhambury (Fig. 169), in Hert-fordshire, of which the sad ruins survive. The mansion of the Earl of Lincoln, Lord High

Admiral, at Sempringham in Lincolnshire, has vanished almost without record. Of the Secretaries of State, Sir William Petre built Ingestre and Thorndon Halls in Essex; Sir William Paget (ennobled in 1549) built Beaudesert in Staffordshire (Fig. 10); Sir Thomas Smith built Hill Hall in Essex (Figs 198–200); Sir Francis Walsingham built at Barn Elms in Surrey. Thorndon was rebuilt in the eighteenth century; Beaudesert was demolished in the 1930s; Hill Hall survives, but only the less impressive half of Ingestre; nothing is known of Barn Elms.

Sir Walter Mildmay, who was Chancellor of the Exchequer from 1568, largely remodelled his house at Apethorpe in Northamptonshire. Mildmay was already rich as a result of having been an official of the Court of Augmentations. This was not a court, in spite of its name, but the organisation set up to deal with the distribution of confiscated monastery buildings and lands, an undertaking that changed the pattern of land-owning in England, led to the formation of several dozen country houses in converted ab-

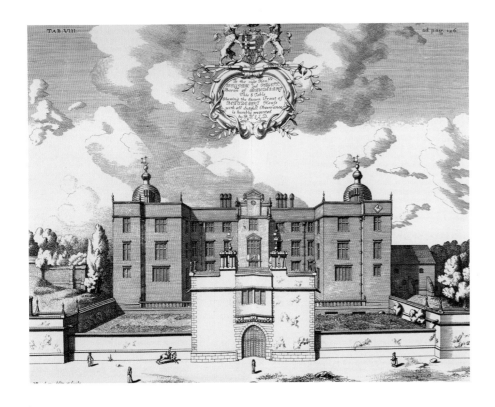

those under them could do well enough. While the Earl of Huntingdon was running into debt as Lord President in Yorkshire, his Secretary to the Council, Thomas Eymis, was housing himself lavishly at Heslington Hall, just outside York. Although Sir Henry Sidney was both Lord Deputy in Ireland and Lord President in Wales, sometimes both at the same time, he was never able to afford more than relatively modest new building, both at his own house at Penshurst and his official residence in Ludlow Castle; but a modish if not very large new house at Whitehall (Figs 90, 91), outside Shrewsbury, reflected the local prosperity of Richard Prynce, who was a member of the Council of the Marches, the principal barrister pleading in its court, and also, as Feodary of Shropshire, the local officer of the Court of Wards.[8]

10 (*above*) Government: the entrance front of Beaudesert, Staffordshire, built *c.*1576–81 for William, Lord Paget, Secretary of State. From Robert Plot's *The Natural History of Staffordshire*, 1686

bey buildings and, until the Augmentations were abolished in 1554, brought great riches to its officers. One of these was Sir William Cavendish; his house at Chatsworth in Derbyshire was the result.

Thomas Smythe, who farmed the London Customs from 1570 to 1588, built Corsham Court in Wiltshire on the proceeds. Sir William Yonge, Collector of Customs in Bristol, built a great house on the quay there, which was demolished in the eighteenth century; but his Red Lodge survives (Figs 419, 422), built by him as a sumptuous banqueting house on the hill above his house. The round-towered Walworth Castle in Durham (Fig. 11) was built about 1580 by Thomas Jennison, comptroller of works and keeper of stores for the great fortifications of Berwick.

The Lord President of the Council of the North, the Lord President of the Council of Wales and the Marches of Wales, and the Lord Deputy in Ireland were expected, as the queen's representatives, to live in semi-royal style on inadequate funds, and made little if any money, but

11 Government: Walworth Castle, County Durham, built for Thomas Jennison, Comptroller of Works at Berwick, *c.*1580.

The courts of the Lord Presidents on the Welsh borders and in Yorkshire did their best to imitate royal state and ceremony, but inevitably were pale reflections of the queen's own court, and the life that went on in and around it.

> Go tell the court it shines
> And glows like rotten wood

wrote Walter Ralegh with experience and feeling. But shine and glow it did, and a major element of its glamour was that it was a centre of power and government, as well as of ceremony and entertainment. The court of Queen Elizabeth was the most elaborate, the most formal, the most extraordinary in Europe. A continuous series of pageants, of feasts, of masques, of tourneys, were all designed to enhance the gorgeous image of the queen, and reinforce the hieratic splendour of her portraits. And behind the image was the erratic, incisive, ambiguous brilliance of her personality, and the knowledge, as in all courts, that a word and a beckoning gesture from her could lift an unknown man to fortune.

The court was presided over by the three great officers of the Household: the Lord Steward, the Lord Chamberlain and the Master of the Horse. The Master of the Horse was in charge of the hundreds of horses in the stables, the mounted gentlemen and yeomen in their finery who rode on them, the queen's own chargers, and the carriages that were made for her in increasing elaboration and splendour. The Lord Steward and Lord Chamberlain divided upstairs and downstairs between them: the Lord Steward's realm was the kitchen and halls, the feeding of the monarch, and the ceremony attached to it; the Lord Chamberlain looked after the rooms of state upstairs, and the more private chambers beyond them. Since these were the especial territory of royal life, his part was the more important and his department the larger. The Vice-Chamberlain, and the Treasurer of the Chamber who assisted him, were both officers of prestige and impor-

tance. In the inner sanctum of the Queen's Privy and Bedchamber were the Gentlemen, Ladies and Women of the Bedchamber. Under Henry VIII the male officials of the Privy Chamber had wielded great political power. But Elizabeth's mainly female Privy and Bedchamber staff were little involved in politics, though useful conduits by which petitions could get to the queen.[9] In addition to his other duties the Lord Chamberlain was responsible for the delicate and important business of assigning accommodation both in the royal palaces and in non-royal houses when the queen went on progress.

Down in Blackfriars the Master of the Revels and the Master of the Wardrobe presided over their respective departments, devising, furnishing and producing entertainments for the queen and for visiting royalty and ambassadors, and making the rumoured 2,000 dresses, each more elaborate than the last, with which the queen dazzled contemporaries.

An unassuming chamber off the Privy Gallery in the Palace of Whitehall, immediately opposite the Queen's Privy Chamber, was the nerve-centre of England. Here the Privy Council met, and effectively ran the country, in close if sometimes uneasy partnership with the queen. All the major officers of state were members, but so were all the major officers of the court; the latter moved over from running the palaces to discussing and deciding state business, at all levels from the defence of the realm and the suppression of plots to the provision of boots for soldiers.

Whitehall was the principal royal palace, in which Elizabeth spent most time; but every year she moved, along with the entire apparatus of court and government, to her other palaces in the London region: Hampton Court, Windsor Castle (especially for the Garter feasts and inaugurations) and Greenwich; and most years the whole vast cavalcade, Privy Council included, emerged from the London region to go on progress in other parts of the kingdom.

queen, was almost immediately appointed her Master of the Horse, remained close to her until his death in 1588, was created Earl of Leicester in 1564, was Constable of Windsor Castle from 1562, and Lord Steward of the Household from 1584. Christopher Hatton (Fig. 4) caught the queen's eye in his early twenties by his skill in dancing, and was rapidly promoted in the Household: gentleman pensioner in 1564, then Gentleman of her Privy Chamber, Captain of her Bodyguard in 1572, Vice-Chamberlain in 1577. Walter Ralegh took her fancy because of his good looks, Devon accent and overweening self-confidence. He had become an Esquire of the Body by 1581 and took over from Hatton as Captain of the Bodyguard in 1587. The three men heartily disliked each other.

Elizabeth expected her favourites to be more than decorative: the three were all very capable, Ralegh with a touch of genius, and all were given work to do, or took it on themselves. Leicester was put in command of the armed forces in the Low Countries in 1585, and in England at the time of the Armada in 1588. Hatton was the queen's spokesman in the House of Commons, and was made Lord Chancellor in 1587; he proved surprisingly adequate in spite of his lack of legal experience. Ralegh, as Warden of the Stanneries from 1585, was the principal government representative in Devon and Cornwall. All three were loaded with lands, gifts and perquisites – Ralegh, whose reign of favour was shorter, rather less than the others. Leicester was given Kenilworth Castle in 1563; his new buildings and remodelling and enlargement of the keep are still impressive enough, though in ruin (Figs 316, 317). Hatton replaced his modest family manor-house at Holdenby in Northamptonshire with the biggest house in England; two great arches in a field are the only memorable remains (Fig. 12). Little is left of what Ralegh did at Sherborne Castle in Dorset, which is in ruins, but the strangely turreted lodge that he built in the adjacent deer-park *circa* 1600 forms the nucleus of today's Sherborne Castle (Fig. 13).

12 (*above*) The arches, dated 1583, once to either side of the forecourt, Holdenby House, Northamptonshire.

13 (*below*) A reconstruction by J. H. P. Gibb of Walter Ralegh's Sherborne Lodge (today Castle), Dorset, before wings were added.

In general, membership of the Household was worth having less because of the perquisites, although these could be considerable, than because it brought its members into close proximity to the queen, and put them in the front rank for her bounty and attentions.

Robert Dudley, who had shared Elizabeth's tribulations and dangers before she had become

From 1572 to 1583 Elizabeth's Lord Chamberlain was Thomas Radcliffe, Earl of Sussex. He was richer in lineage than in lands or houses. In 1574 she offloaded on him one of the biggest of Henry VIII's palaces, New Hall, sometimes called Beaulieu, in Essex. It was probably not in good repair, and he replaced the main lodgings with the magnificent bay-windowed range that is all that survives today (Fig. 24).

Francis Knollys, Vice-Chamberlain under Sussex and his predecessor, erected a demolished and barely recorded house, 'fairly built of brick', at Caversham in Berkshire;[10] the mason Robert Smythson may have been working there in the 1560s. Of new-built courtier houses that survive, the most impressive is the triangular Longford Castle in Wiltshire, built by Sir Thomas Gorges and his wife, the Swedish Helena Snakenberg, Marchioness of Northampton, around 1591. The two were both creations of the court. Helena Snakenberg had been (for less than six months) third and last wife of William Parr, Marquess of Northampton, who owed his marquessate and most of his lands to his sister's marriage to Henry VIII. His widow became Elizabeth's First Lady of the Privy Chamber, her confidante, and ultimately her chief mourner. Spenser celebrated her as Mansilia:

Best knowne by bearing up great Cynthiaes
    traine:
. . . She is the paterne of true womanood
And onely mirrhor of feminitie:

Her second husband, Sir Thomas Gorges, whom she married about 1580, was a penniless younger son who became successively Groom of the Privy Chamber, Gentleman Usher and Gentleman of the Queen's Robes. He was much employed by the queen on confidential missions, and like all successful courtiers picked up a quiverful of useful jobs – enough of them, together with whatever his wife had acquired from her first husband or was given by the queen, to pay for their trian-

gular house with its chequer-board towers and porticoed entrance front (Fig. 14), rising so unexpectedly on the banks of the Wiltshire Avon.[11]

Although the principal government officers were distinct from the officers of the Household, they moved in overlapping circles, immediately around the queen, especially in the Palace of Whitehall. In contrast, the Law Courts and the legal and treasury officials were lodged in the Palace of Westminster, and formed a separate world, of lawyers and civil servants rather than courtiers.

The Elizabethan and Jacobean ages were extremely litigious, partly because the huge transferences of property on which they were based led to all kinds of difficulties about title, which encouraged people to go to law. Lawyers made at least as much as successful lawyers today, judges a great deal more than their modern equivalents, for their offices had perquisites, like all others at the time. Successful litigants were expected to show their appreciation to the judge; Francis Bacon got into serious trouble not because he accepted gifts, but because he accepted them before the case was tried. The status of a judge demanded a country house; but a number of lawyers built handsomely even before they reached the Bench.

The Elizabethan legal system was inherited from the Middle Ages, and is still recognisable today. Cases involving the Crown were tried in the Queen's Bench, civil cases in the Court of Common Pleas. Chancery tried cases by Roman, not Civil, law, and did not employ juries. The Star Chamber was essentially a committee of the Privy Council; it also used no juries, and was renowned for speed and simplicity of procedure. Litigants chose the court in which they thought they would do best. The Queen's Bench and Common Pleas heard cases in London and at county Assizes, and were each presided over by a Lord Chief Justice and three judges, as was the Court of the Exchequer. Chancery was under the Lord

14 The Court: detail from Robert Thacker's engraving of 1678 of the triangular Longford Castle, Wiltshire, built by Thomas Gorges and his wife, Helena Snakenberg, c.1591. Both were prominent at Elizabeth's court.

Chancellor or the Lord Keeper, and twelve Masters in Chancery, headed by the Master of the Rolls. The Exchequer had its own court. Maritime cases were dealt with by the Court of Admiralty. All courts had their apparatus of clerks and other officials, who did well out of fees.

Many of the country houses built out of the proceeds of the law have been demolished, although the judges or lawyers who built them are often lying in effigy, portentous in their robes, on their monuments in the adjacent parish church. The houses that survive are impressive enough. The Common Pleas produced three outstanding houses: Barlborough Hall in Derbyshire, built by Francis Rodes about 1585 (Fig. 370); Condover Hall in Shropshire, built by Thomas Owen in the

late 1590s (Fig. 15); and Blickling Hall in Norfolk, built by Sir Henry Hobart, Chief Justice, in 1616–17 (Fig. 99). Of the house at Glentworth in Lincolnshire (Fig. 17), built by Sir Christopher Wray, Chief Justice of the Queen's Bench, probably in the 1580s, only a corner and recently excavated foundations survive; Crewe Hall in Cheshire, built from 1615 by another Chief Justice, Sir Randolph Crewe, and one of the most lavish of Jacobean houses, was burnt out in the 1860s, but sumptuously 'restored' in the next decade.

From Chancery came two great houses of Masters of the Rolls built at the beginning and end of Elizabeth's reign. Melford Hall in Suffolk was built by Sir William Cordell about 1560

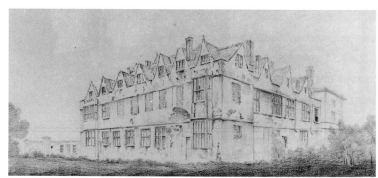

(Fig. 16), Montacute in Somerset by Sir Edward Phelips about 1600, out of the proceeds of the law, but well before he became Master of the Rolls in 1611. Of the even more magnificent house built by another Master of the Rolls, Sir Gilbert Gerard, at Gerard's Bromley in Staffordshire in 1584 (Fig. 314), only the porch survives, abandoned and overgrown in a wood (Fig. 18).

A more modest, but beautiful, product of the law is Chastleton in Oxfordshire (Fig. 19), built in the early 1600s by Walter Jones, a lawyer who also served as Town Clerk of Worcester. The starting-off point of his fortune was the money made by his father and grandfather as wool merchants in

Witney. The growing wool and textile trade was the basis of England's prosperity in the Elizabethan and Jacobean period. It flourished from the relationship between two great centres of trade and commerce, London and Antwerp. The merchants of the City of London were nearly all involved in it, gathering cloth or wool from the areas of England or Wales where it was produced, and exporting it to Antwerp, and later also to

19 (*right*) The Law: the entrance front of Chastleton House, Oxfordshire, built *c.*1607–12 by Walter Jones, lawyer and town clerk of Worcester.

17 (*facing page, top right*) The Law: Glentworth Hall, Lincolnshire, built *c.*1580 by Chief Justice Sir Christopher Wray, from a drawing of 1793.

18 (*facing page, bottom right*) The Law: the porch, dated 1584, from Gerard's Bromley Hall, Staffordshire, built by Sir Gilbert Gerard, Master of the Rolls. It was removed to Batchacre Hall in the same county when the house was demolished.

other parts of Europe, Russia and the East. In return, they imported luxury goods, tapestries and spices. London, with its congregation of potential buyers, at court, in the government, or coming up from the country to go to law or attend Parliament, became a great luxury market, which City merchants kept supplied. Inevitably, they became financiers as well, lending money to the queen, the aristocracy, the gentry and each other.

A typical pattern was for someone from an area producing wool or textiles to set up as a merchant in London, use his local contacts to build up his business, make his fortune, and invest it in acquiring an estate and building a house in his home county. In the early seventeenth century, for instance, the Lamberts, of the London Grocers' Company, built comfortable manor-houses at Boyton and Keevil in Wiltshire (Figs. 93, 21); next

door to Keevil, John Topp of the Merchant Taylors' Company built Stockton Manor, externally only a little grander, but sumptuously decorated inside (Fig. 437); the Welshman Philip Jones, a member of the Grocers' Company but also dealing in felt, bought out his impecunious elder brother and built Treowen in Monmouthshire; a little later Henry Hewett, one of a network of North Country Hewetts involved in the textile trade in London, built Shireoaks in Nottinghamshire.[12]

At the head of the commercial world, under Elizabeth and earlier, was the formidable Sir Thomas Gresham, as well known in Antwerp as in London, the mainstay of English finance and the munificent donor of the Royal Exchange and Gresham College in London. His great house at Osterley, just outside London, was rebuilt in the

perhaps as large as Gresham's, were laid under Elizabeth but matured under James, with houses to match. The remains of Sir Baptist Hickes's Campden House at Chipping Campden (*circa* 1608) are also fragmentary, but none the less memorable, especially the two exquisite banqueting houses that still face each other across what was the façade of the house (Figs 22, 324).

Hickes was a member of the Mercers' Company, but especially well known as a moneylender. Sir Arthur Ingram, perhaps the biggest and most unscrupulous financial wheeler-dealer of his day, bought Temple Newsam in Yorkshire, already a large house, in 1622, and doubled it in size, besides building a substantial hunting lodge at Sheriff Hutton, in Yorkshire, and a sizeable house in York. His contemporary, Sir William Cokayne, of the Skinners' Company (and Lord Mayor in 1619–20), was another great moneylender. One of his mortgagees was Sir Francis Tresham, son of the builder of the Triangular Lodge at Rushton. Cokayne foreclosed on the mortgage, took over the Rushton property in 1614 and passed it on to his son, who in the 1620s and 1630s nearly doubled the house in size (Fig. 23), and gave it a hall with an open hammerbeam roof, as a piece of ancestral splendour to mask his father's money-bags.[14] The house survives, as does Caverswell Castle in Staffordshire, where, in similar fashion, Mathew Cradock, 'a wool-buyer of Stafford' (or possibly his son), bought the ruins of the medieval castle and rebuilt them in a deliberately feudal fashion, with curtain walls and corner towers rising above a moat.[15]

It is often stated, and widely believed, that the great Elizabethan houses were built to entertain the queen when she went on progress. In this context the same passage is invariably quoted: Lord Burghley writing to Sir Christopher Hatton in 1579, after he had been to see Hatton's enormous new house at Holdenby, and been able to compare it to his own house at Theobalds, in Hertfordshire: 'God send us both long to enjoy

eighteenth century, and his slightly smaller house at Intwood in his home county of Norfolk in the nineteenth century (Fig. 20); his stables at Osterley survive, a good deal altered, but only his garden walls at Intwood. His Antwerp factors, Richard Clough and Thomas Dutton, built their own smaller country houses (Figs 189–90, 225) at Bachegraig and Plas Clough in Denbighshire, and at Sherborne in Gloucestershire[13] – all mostly demolished or much altered. Other City fortunes,

22 Commerce: one of the banqueting houses originally to either side of hte demolished Campden House, Oxfordshire, built *c*.1608 by the City of London tycoon Sir Baptist Hickes.

23 Commerce: aerial view of Rushton Hall, Northamptonshire, enlarged and remodelled *c*.1620–30 by the son of Sir William Cokayne, Lord Mayor and money-lender.

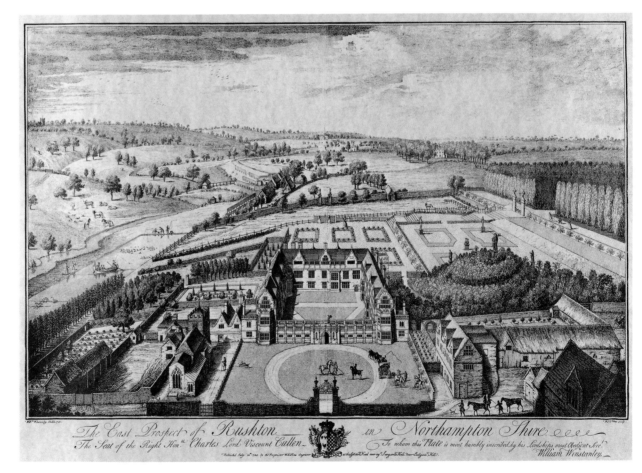

The East Prospect of Rushton in Northampton Shire
The Seat of the Right Hon.ble Charles Lord Viscount Cullen. To whom this Plate is most humbly inscribed, by his Lordships most Obedient Serv.t William Winstanley.

Her, for whom we both meant to exceed our purses in these.'[16]

But these were special cases. Theobalds, in Burghley's own words, 'was begun by me with a mean measure but encrease by occasion of her Majesty's often coming'; or, as his contemporary biographer put it: 'after he came to entertain the Queen so often there, he was enforced to enlarge it'.[17] Elizabeth came, indeed, thirteen times, often for long visits, and almost treated this house of her chief minister as an alternative palace; and he enlarged it to the size of a palace accordingly. Holdenby was also of palace size (Fig. 214), at least as big as Theobalds. (Both were in fact to be acquired as royal palaces under the Stuarts.) The only convincing explanation as to why Hatton built on such a scale was that he hoped that he would take over from Burghley as the queen's chief minister, and that Holdenby would then take the place of Theobalds. He was, after all, twenty years younger than the Lord Treasurer, and the queen's trusted favourite. In fact, he died in 1591, aged only 51. Burghley survived him for seven years, and Elizabeth never once visited Holdenby; Burghley's comment 'God send us both long to enjoy Her' could be taken to mean 'I'm not going to die yet.'

Burghley's second house at Burghley, in Lincolnshire, was also the house of a chief minister thinking royally, even if not built quite on the scale of Theobalds. Elizabeth's prime and original favourite, the Earl of Leicester, undoubtedly put up new buildings and remodelled old ones at Kenilworth in anticipation of the queen's visits. The last, and far and away the most famous and lavishly celebrated, of her visits came as the fruition of his new building in 1575; it lasted three weeks, and may have been planned by him as a demonstration of his suitability to be her husband.

Elizabeth, when visiting Gorhambury on her progress of 1572 or 1573, is said to have remarked to Sir Nicholas Bacon: 'What a little house you have gotten'.[18] By the time she returned in 1577 he had built a new wing, containing a long gallery, and probably lodgings for the queen at the end of it (Fig. 169).

Her remark and its sequel may be no more than a good story; but there is solid documentary evidence that the great range of splendid rooms built by Thomas Radcliffe, Earl of Sussex, at New Hall in Essex, probably soon after 1573, was specifically designed with the reception of the queen in mind. Elizabeth had given Sussex the royal palace of New Hall, or Beaulieu as Henry VIII preferred to call it, in May 1573. It was enormous and not in good repair. Sussex rebuilt the main range of lodgings, probably soon after the grant (Fig. 24). He had been created Lord Chamberlain in July of the previous year, that is to say, made the principal officer of the Queen's Household; his position, combined with gratitude to the queen, made it likely that he would provide a full set of royal lodgings for her reception, and, when he died in 1583, his will, and the accompanying inventory, makes it clear that that is what he had done.[19] 'My meaning', he wrote, 'hath been to have New Hall to remain honourably furnished as well for receiving the Queen's Majesty when it shall please her to come hither', and he accordingly left to his brother beds and hangings that 'at her Majesty's last being there' had furnished a full sequence of royal lodgings: great chamber, presence chamber, privy chamber, withdrawing chamber, and bedchamber and inner chamber.

Apart from this small group, the evidence for Elizabethan houses being built or enlarged in anticipation or hopes of a royal visit is thin. To which county or counties a progress would go was usually decided on at most a few months before it took place, and the actual houses to be visited could be determined at even shorter notice. In 1597 Michael Hickes heard that the queen was to stay two nights at his house in Essex only five days before she arrived.[20] In general, there was time at most to decorate a room or two, seldom if ever

24 (facing page)
The great windows of New Hall, Essex. They originally lit a series of state rooms specifically built in the 1570s to entertain the queen.

to build more than a temporary structure. At Elvetham in Hampshire, where the lavish celebrations for the visit of the queen in 1591 are described and illustrated in a contemporary publication, the modest and irregular existing house was quite inadequate, and a free-standing range of large temporary rooms was hastily run up.[21]

When on progress, the queen visited, and often stayed at, houses of all dates and sizes.[22] It is true that anyone who did build a handsome new house would know that if a progress came to his part of the world, his house was likely to be one of those chosen for a visit. The odds were high enough against it, though; Elizabeth visited only twenty-five of the forty English counties, and none of the Welsh ones; in twenty years of her reign she did not go on progress at all. A royal visit was anyway a dubious honour. Little or no correlation has been proved between a visit and the receipt of offices, grants or perquisites; very occasionally it was accompanied or followed by a knighthood. Although in theory the queen and her court paid their way, a visit was inevitably expensive, and if it went wrong could be disastrous. This did not stop some owners soliciting a visit, as the Earl of Northumberland did, unsuccessfully, in 1591; but Petworth, to which he hoped she would come, was not a new house but a large and rambling medieval one. At least seven cases are known of owners trying to get out of a visit.[23]

In terms of building, the provision to be made for a possible visit was anyway not very onerous. Elizabeth's retinue was enormous, but most of its members were normally farmed out to other houses in the vicinity of the one in which she stayed herself. Except, perhaps, at the houses of her chief ministers, the queen clearly did not expect to find a full royal suite, such as she had in her palaces or was provided for her at Theobalds and New Hall. She was satisfied with a basic provision of a presence chamber, in which to give audience; a privy chamber, in which to eat; and a bedchamber, in which to sleep. This could be

provided by the great chamber, withdrawing chamber and best bedchamber that made up the standard accommodation of all sizeable Elizabethan houses. There is no evidence of her being impressed by the size or splendour of any house in which she stayed; what she appreciated were the entertainments that were put on for her, or the gifts that she was given. The progresses all took place in summer and had a strong *al fresco* element: there was much hunting, and meals or refreshments in specially constructed bowers of leaves, flowers and boughs; most of the entertainments were put on out of doors.

If the importance of progresses as an inducement to build to accommodate the queen has been exaggerated, another aspect of them has been largely ignored. They were an important way of informing the upper classes of what was happening in the country-house world. Elizabeth took round with her the court and her government: the great officers of state, the Privy Council and a substantial section of her Household. These saw, year after year, what was being, or had been, built in different parts of England. This was especially valuable at a time when houses were not being illustrated or engraved. An eighteenth-century landowner had the advantage of the views of Kip and Knyff, the volumes of *Vitruvius Britannicus*, and the publication of individual architects keen to advertise their skills. The Elizabethans and Jacobeans had nothing (why this was so, why, in general, topographical illustrations developed so much more slowly in England than on the Continent, is an interesting question). The personal experience of those travelling on progress provided a partial alternative.

The situation under James I was somewhat different, for a number of reasons.[24] First, if he was travelling with his queen, there were now two royalties needing handsome separate accommodation. Accordingly, two and possibly three Lord Treasurers provided full-scale suites for both king and queen, the Earl of Salisbury at Hatfield and the Earl of Suffolk at Audley End in Essex; it is possible that the Earl of Dorset intended similar provision at Knole in Kent, but if so he died before it could be completed. A little later, the Duke of Buckingham, the king's favourite, and more powerful than any Lord Treasurer, at least envisaged double accommodation on the grand scale at Burley-on-the-Hill in Rutland. Second, James was so delighted at becoming a rich English king instead of a poor Scottish one that, unlike Elizabeth, he handed out grants and favours with a lavishness that appalled his ministers. A royal visit was likely to be worth it – or so, at least, those who angled for one hoped.

But the pattern of his visits was different from Elizabeth's. Elizabeth's aim, however partially accomplished, was to show herself all over her kingdom. James's main aim was to go hunting. His passion for hunting amounted to a mania. When he found a deer-park or a forest that was to his taste, he was likely to keep returning there. Many of these hunting expeditions were not state visits but holiday outings; even on full progresses hunting figured far more largely than under Elizabeth. In 1607 the Venetian ambassador commented on his hunting outings in which 'he throws off all business' and 'is more inclined to live retired with eight or ten of his favourites than openly, as is the custom of the country'.[25]

Robert Cecil equipped his new house at Hatfield for visits by both king and queen, and Cranborne Manor in Dorset for visits by the king alone. The character of the houses is outstandingly different: Hatfield (Fig. 7), in the grand manner, Cranborne (Fig. 522), a holiday house for hunting. The evidence suggests that James, brought up in Scotland, which followed the French tradition of relative informality in royal life,[26] preferred the latter, whether travelling informally or on progress. Lord Howard of Bindon built his 'little pile in Lulworth park' in Dorset at Robert Cecil's suggestion at much the same time and in the same spirit as Cranborne;

most probably, it was built with the king in mind.[27] At Kirby in Northamptonshire what was in royal terms a modest though very handsome extension (Fig. 338) was probably built to accommodate the king, who came there three times, in 1612, 1616 and 1619. He came even more frequently to nearby Apethorpe, and lodged there with Sir Francis Fane in the existing house on five different occasions, in 1605, 1612, 1614, 1616 and 1619. Then, in 1622, Fane was ordered to enlarge his house 'for the more commodious entertainment of His Majesty and his company'. A visit of a quite different nature must have been envisaged, perhaps as part of an especially grand progress to show off the Prince of Wales and his intended Spanish bride. But the marriage expedition of Prince Charles and the Duke of Buckingham to Spain in 1623 was famously abortive, for they returned without a Spanish princess, or any promise of one, and negotiations finally collapsed in 1624. None the less, Fane's large and lavish extension (Fig. 25) was duly completed in time for James to make one visit, in 1624 – and to create Fane Earl of Westmorland – before his death in the next year.[28]

Apethorpe is unique as a documented example of a house enlarged for a royal visit at royal command. In contrast are the problematic stories of Lord Zouche and the building of Bramshill, and Sir John Pakington and the building of Westwood Park.[29] In 1605 Lord Zouche, a peer of ancient lineage but encumbered estates, exchanged his inheritance of good land in Northamptonshire for several thousand acres of mainly barren heath in Hampshire. They were suitable for little but hunting. It is hard to see why he did this, except in order to be able to offer James good sport within handy reach of Windsor. If so, he set about it the wrong way, for instead of building a prettily fantastical lodge like Cranborne, he built an enormous house (Fig. 407) with at least one potential royal lodging on the grand scale. It took so long to build that it was not ready

25 The east range of
Apethorpe Hall,
Northamptonshire, built
at the command of
James I for his
accommodation, 1622–4.

for (or at least did not receive) a visit from the king until 1620, and it cost so much more than he could afford that his heirs had to sell it in 1638.

Westwood Park in Worcestershire (Figs 96, 103) has all the signs of a house created as a bait for royalty: a huge new deer-park, a house entered through a triumphal arch (the traditional entry for monarchs) with an Apotheosis of James I over its central arch (Figs 275, 386), a grand staircase leading to an enormous great chamber. The king never came; a visit by the Earl of Northampton, Lord President of the Marches, cannot have been a satisfactory alternative, even though he was the king's representative.

William Cavendish, then Earl (and later Duke) of Newcastle, provides a final sad story in the reign of Charles I. He was eager for a major post at court. He in his own words 'hurt his estate' in sumptuously entertaining Charles at Welbeck Abbey in Nottinghamshire in 1633 and at nearby Bolsover Castle in 1634. His second wife, Margaret, admittedly given to exaggeration, said that the two visits cost him £20,000. Then he waited

for the pay-off. It came in the form of the post of Governor to the Prince of Wales, a respectable position, but he must have been hoping for more.[30]

But if one can usually discount progresses, why were new country houses built? In the case of new families, the reasons were straightforward. In the sixteenth century, as in previous and subsequent centuries, those who made money almost automatically invested it in land, because of the status that this gave them. Although they occasionally bought a property with a sufficiently handsome house already on it, in the majority of cases they did not, and a new house was the inevitable result. The size and quality of this depended on the size of the estates they acquired, and the nature of their ambitions. Into what level of the upper classes were they hoping to move? Moderate commercial fortunes, such as those of the Lamberts of Boyton and Keevil, and of Philip Jones at Treowen, produced moderate gentry houses. Thomas Topp aimed a little higher at Stockton, but not to the very top. The big money produced Sir Thomas Gresham's mansions at Osterley and Intwood, Sir Baptist Hickes's many buildings at Chipping Campden, or Sir Arthur Ingram's doubling in size of Temple Newsam. Judges usually came in at a high level, and so did the principal officers in the government.

A change in status could produce a new house on old property. In the 1570s three commoners were raised to the peerage as Lord Compton (1570), Lord Burghley (1571) and Lord Cheyne (1572). Within a few years all had equipped themselves with courtyard houses on the grand scale, fitted to their rank: Lord Compton at Castle Ashby in Northamptonshire (Fig. 135), Lord Burghley at Burghley (Fig. 6) and Theobalds, Lord Cheyne at Toddington in Bedfordshire (Fig. 45). Lord Burghley could afford it; the other two probably overspent. Lord Cheyne certainly sold most of his extensive properties in Kent, and the Comptons were heavily in debt, until marriage to Elizabeth Spencer, the greatest heiress of the day, paid off the family liabilities and enabled an extra storey to be added to make the already large house even larger, in scale with the earldom that they purchased in 1618.[31]

The Artificers[32]

The first point to be made about building artificers under Elizabeth is how low they rated in the social hierarchy. In or around the 1570s Sir Thomas Smith (in a passage repeated word for word by William Harrison, in his much-quoted description of England) put them in their place, when analysing 'the division of the parts and persons of the common wealth'. He worked down through the first class of nobility, knights, esquires and gentlemen, the second class of citizens and burgesses, and the third class of yeomen, to

> the fourth sort of men . . . day labourers, poore husbandmen, yea marchantes or retailers which have no free lande, copiholders, and all arti-

ficers, as Taylers, Shoomakers, Carpenters, Brickemakers, Bricklayers, Masons & c. These have no voice nor authoritie in our common wealth, and no account is made of them but onelie to be ruled, not to rule others.[33]

To sit on juries, or to become churchwardens or constables, was the best that they could hope for. They were Quince the carpenter and Snug the joiner, brought in with Bottom, Flute and Snout for bored courtiers to laugh at, after dinner on a midsummer night.

Their lack of status was partly because of the stigma of any job that involved manual labour, however skilled, partly (the two were related) because they made so little money. John Stow summed up their situation when writing about London in 1598: 'The Private riches of London resteth chiefly in the handes of the Marchantes and Retaylers, for Artificers have not much to spare, and Laborers have neede that it were given unto them.'[34] Artificers were above the subsistence line, but seldom much more than that.

Successful 'merchants and retailers' used their wealth, in London as elsewhere, to buy or build a substantial house, acquire a coat of arms, if possible a knighthood, and establish themselves, or their children, as landed gentry. But the most that all but a tiny handful of artificers could hope for was to better themselves sufficiently to acquire, or at least rent, a farm and lift themselves into the ranks of the yeomanry. Every successful artificer expressed his success in property.

Robert Smythson, when he came to Longleat in 1568, was paid eight shillings a week, or around £20 a year, a good wage suited to a London master mason, with his own gang of five (separately paid) masons. But when, in 1572, he and Alan Maynard moved from day labour to contracting 'by the great' to erect the great new classical façades at Longleat, and their income perhaps tripled as a result, both he and Maynard promptly rented farms from Thynne, and rose in status accordingly.[35]

Successfully taking work by the great was one way in which an artificer could increase his income. Another was by being put in charge, as 'surveyor', of an entire building operation. In the years 1610–12 William Arnold was paid £1 a week for supervising the building of Wadham College, Oxford, a payment that almost certainly included the provision of drawings. Artificers providing specialist products that were especially valued could also be rewarded: at Hardwick, in the 1590s, Abraham Smith, the plasterer, and Thomas Accres, the marbler, were both kept permanently on the staff of Bess of Hardwick with a retainer and a rent-free farm, to give them yeoman status.[36] The successful provision of chimneypieces or church monuments, from a yard in London or (for alabaster) Burton upon Trent, was another way of making a living above the average. It could be even more profitable to become an entrepreneur: as owner or leaser of quarries, like the Grumbolds and Thorpes in Northamptonshire, and the Strongs in Oxfordshire; as building merchant, like Richard Wyatt, the City of London carpenter (Figs 27, 54) whose wealth, deriving from his building yard on the Thames, enabled him to endow the still existing Carpenters' Company almshouses in Godalming in Surrey; and as a property developer, like Andrew Kerwin, who seems to have made a modest fortune out of house building in London.[37] Finally, an artificer could diversify into more paying occupations. John Thorpe, brother and son of freemasons, may have been trained as one, but if so he quickly diversified, and his reputation and respectable wealth derived from his position as one of the leading land-surveyors in the country; John Smythson, trained as a freemason, was describing himself as 'architector' by the time he came to make his will in 1634, but his considerable properties probably depended more on his activities as land-surveyor, and steward and man of business, working for the Cavendish family.

One or two especially well-established artificers felt prosperous and confident enough to start to call themselves 'gentlemen'. Robert Smythson was described as one in 1601, and is so called on his monument in the church at Wollaton in Nottinghamshire; when his son John married in 1600 he was 'gentleman' in the marriage register.[38] In 1617 William Arnold signed a contract for work at Dunster Castle, Somerset, as 'William Arnold, gentleman', but in the register of his home parish, Charlton Musgrove in Somerset, he is never called more than 'yeoman'. This was indeed all that the two small farms he owned or leased entitled him to; these seem to have been the only gains of the long and busy career of one of the most successful and interesting of Jacobean artificers.[39]

Neither Arnold nor the Smythsons ever became armigerous. The seal of gentility, respectability and property ownership attained by acquiring a coat of arms from the College of Heralds was more than most artificers could hope for. The London mason William Kerwyn, who obtained a coat of arms in 1587, was exceptional. Money from property development was probably the explanation, both for the arms and for his handsome freestanding monument in St Helen's Bishopsgate, the inscription of which celebrates how he 'aedibus attalibus Londinium decoravit'.[40] The Thorpe family had assumed a coat of arms by 1618, but this probably reflected John Thorpe's activity and wealth as a land-surveyor rather than his brother Thomas's status as a freemason and quarry owner or leaser.

There was, however, one secure route to fortune, status and a coat of arms, through successful service in the Royal Works. In contrast to the great explosion of palace and fortification building under Henry VII, royal building under Elizabeth was quiescent; she was shedding palaces (she got rid of seven in her reign), not building them. But she was still fully maintaining at least thirteen royal palaces and castles, some of them enormous; wings were added, rooms remodelled or redecorated, gardens and garden buildings constructed, in addition to constant maintenance. In her reign

Wíllⁱ Portington Esq⁹ ⁹⁹ Carpenᵗ in ỹ office of his ⁹⁹aᵗⁱ buildings : who serued
in ỹ place 40. peeres ᵍ departed this life ỹ 23 of march .1623. being aged.84. peeres, who
was a well willer to this societie this being ỹ gift of Mathew Bankes who serued him 14 peeres ᵍ is at this
presentⁿ ⁹⁹ of the said companⁿ. Anno Dⁿi 1657.

26 and 27 Two
successful carpenters:
(*above left*) William
Portington (Master
Carpenter in the Royal
Works, 1595/6–1624/5) and
(*above right*) Richard
Wyatt, from portraits now
in Carpenters' Hall, City
of London.

at least £180,000 was spent on royal palaces[41] (Wollaton, for comparison, cost about £5,000, Hardwick a little less), and much the same on fortifications; in terms of amount of work, though not quality, the Crown remained far and away the biggest employer in the country, and the Royal Works employed far and away the biggest building establishment. This was based on the Surveyor, Comptroller, Paymaster, Master Mason, Carpenter and Bricklayer, Chief Joiner and Glazier, Serjeant Plumber and Painter, and a shifting number of Clerks, all based on Scotland Yard, in Whitehall. In addition, there was a sizeable organisation at Berwick, the major fortification project of Elizabeth's reign; other smaller groups at the Tower of London, Windsor Castle and Chester; and resident clerks dotted around other royal palaces.

A post in the Works brought status, security and a guaranteed income, all highly desirable in the Elizabethan building world, where on the whole there was little security and less money. As in all government posts under Elizabeth, very modest basic pay (£45. 12s. 6d per annum for the Surveyor, £18. 5s. 0d for the Master Craftsmen and the Clerks), which had been frozen since early in the century, was increased by an assortment of allowances and numerous unofficial, but for the most part tolerated, perquisites; as in the London printing trade until recent years, for instance, the senior officers did well by keeping dead personnel on their books, and drawing their wages. In 1609, when an attempt was made to get rid of the perquisites, but replace them with compensatory allowances, the salaries were readjusted, as follows: Surveyor £284. 5s. 10d, Comptroller

£145. 6s. 10d, Master Mason £103. 12s. 10d, Master Carpenter £113. 7s. 6d, and so on.[42]

These were comfortable salaries, that of the Surveyor in particular; and before the reform the more successful or unscrupulous officers were probably pulling in considerably more than even the revised scales. Moreover, the officers were free to take on outside work, and the pressure of royal work was low enough to give them plenty of opportunity to do so.

The Surveyor was the unchallenged head of the building world. He and his senior colleagues in the Works establishment wore gowns and chains of office, and walked in royal processions; all the Surveyors and a number of other senior officers acquired estates and coats of arms. It was not surprising that, even if its great days seemed over, the Works continued to attract personnel of high quality. On the other hand, from 1578 onwards, artificers had the galling experience of seeing the plum job of Surveyor going to individuals who were not artificers by training, as was the case with at least four of the seven Surveyors who filled the job between then and 1643.[43]

The Building Trades

Under Elizabeth and James almost all incorporated towns (that is, towns with a corporation granted by royal charter) had their trade guilds or companies, which represented their various disciplines or 'mysteries', oversaw the taking of apprentices by individual members, and regulated and supervised standards of work and conduct. The most important were, not surprisingly, in the bigger towns: London, Bristol, York, Exeter, Norwich and Newcastle upon Tyne. The London building guilds were especially important both because of the size and status of London, and because of their links with the Royal Works: the officers of the Works were often also wardens or heads of the guilds, and the Works recruited heavily, though certainly not exclusively, from their members.

Lengths of apprenticeship could vary, but seven years was the most usual. On concluding his apprenticeship and paying a fee, the artificer automatically became a full member of the guild and a freeman of the town or city. Surviving apprentice rolls, which normally give the place of residence and occupation of the father, make it clear that only a minority of the apprentices came from the town in which they enrolled, or were the children of artificers.[44] Every guild had an upper level, the equivalent of aldermen in the city government, and a group of officers, perhaps warden, sub-warden and treasurer – the names varied. The artificers' guilds did not rank high in the hierarchy of their respective towns. The pecking order – literally – in London is shown in the list of 'messes', that is, portions of food, served to members of the sixty City guilds at the annual dinners in the Guildhall.[45] At the top of the list were the City aristocracy: Mercers (five messes), Grocers, Drapers, Brewers, Ironmongers, Merchant Haberdashers and Fishmongers (four or four and a half messes), and Goldsmiths, Skinners, Leathersellers, Butchers and Merchant Taylors (three messes). The Aldermen and Lord Mayor were recruited exclusively from these top twelve guilds. At the bottom were the guilds served only one mess, amongst them all the building guilds except the Carpenters, who rated two messes. The London Carpenters were probably considered more important than the others because of the greater extent of their work: the City consisted mainly of timber-framed structures, which were built or rebuilt in large numbers during the sixteenth century (as happened, too, in Bristol, if on a smaller scale).

The guilds maintained a monopoly of work within the city boundaries (usually defined by the city walls) and in addition could be extensively employed in surrounding areas. London artificers, for instance, are documented working in Middlesex, Essex, Surrey and Hertfordshire. But all towns had suburban areas that grew up outside the boundaries or small areas within the boundaries that were, for various historical reasons, free, over which the corporation and guilds had no control. In Bristol, for instance, the area around the castle was free of City control; when it was finally amalgamated with the City in 1629 at least four building artificers were working there.[46] These outsiders were resented by the guilds, because even if they could be kept out of the towns, they competed for work in the surrounding areas. There was not much that the guilds could do about it, apart from ineffectively petitioning the Privy Council or some other central body.

The largest, most successful and (by native artificers) most resented settlements of outsiders or 'strangers' were around the City of London: in Westminster, in and around Smithfield, and, above all, across the river in Southwark, notable for three settlements of those who wanted to be free of City control: actors, prostitutes and immigrant craftsmen, especially joiners and tombmakers. The members of this Southwark colony were ideally situated to get work that the London companies would like to have monopolised for themselves. Their workshops were on or close to the river, with easy access to water transport; they were close to the numerous wealthy patrons, especially lawyers, courtiers and Members of Parliament, who settled and built houses in Westminster, the northern slopes, and as far west as Kensington and Chelsea, but also frequently owned country houses as well. They were mostly, and perhaps all, refugees from religious persecution, especially in the Low Countries, and included many highly skilled craftsmen, knowledgeable in the latest Continental fashions. They could, and usually did, take out denization and become naturalised English citizens;[47] but foreign-born artificers were never admitted into the London companies, nor did they ever become officers in the Works or Revels, though these two organisations often employed them. The guilds in towns other than London were less exclusive; Bristol guilds, for instance, were open to any craftsmen who were prepared to pay the entrance fees, though in fact only a few of these (such as Robert Trunckye in Bristol and Bernard Dininghoff in York) were foreigners.[48]

But under Elizabeth and James I the most important and prestigious building was going on outside the towns, at the great new or newly enlarged country houses. The artificers involved in these, although sometimes trained in, and members of, town guilds, were working free of control by them, frequently settled in the country, and were able to take apprentices independently, though the extent to which they did this is hard to establish owing to lack of documentation. These out-of-town artificers included some of the most able and interesting of the period, Robert Smythson, coming from London, amongst them. Country houses attracted the cream of the artificers, and their best and most original work. But they attracted them in different ways. Sometimes artificers sent out drawings, or dispatched chimneypieces or church monuments, or came out themselves to work on site, but remained town-based, at the yard and offices of the Royal Works in Whitehall and elsewhere, or in their own workshops or building yards, in or around the City of London or in Bristol, York, Exeter and other provincial cities. Henry Hawthorne and John Symonds, both in the Works, sent out drawings to Burghley and Theobalds in the 1570s, but may never have gone there in person;[49] a constellation of Works artificers worked alongside foreigners at Hatfield;[50] and Knole was remodelled and refurbished by them – by William Portington, the Master Carpenter (Fig. 26), by Cornelius Cure, the Master Mason, by Richard Dungan, the Master Plasterer, by Thomas Mefflin, the Chief Glazier, all probably working under the supervision of Simon Basil, the Surveyor.[51] All three clients were Lord Treasurers, and in a strong position to obtain the services of Works personnel.

At a less exalted level, the Kettle family, with a mason's yard in Aldersgate in London, had a line in chimneypieces, probably of stone, which they could supply out of London, or in it, on demand. In 1604 they supplied Ashley Park in Surrey with three chimneypieces, modest ones for the hall and gallery chamber, a more expensive one for the great chamber. These were sent up the river and then overland, probably from Walton-on-Thames; they did no other work in the house, and possibly never went there.[52] In Bristol, the two Fryndes and the Byrd family, freemen of Bristol and members of its Freemasons' Guild, made sumptuous chimneypieces for rich Bristol merchants, but also exported them to accessible neighbouring country houses, most notably to South Wraxall Manor in Wiltshire; they may also have been responsible for the Tower of the Orders that forms the porch of Old Beaupre in Glamorganshire.[53] John Gildon of Hereford, who worked in both stone and wood, provided church monuments of stone (Fig. 28) in Herefordshire, Worcestershire and Gloucestershire, and obligingly signed and dated them. One would expect him to have worked in country houses as well, though his work there remains to be identified.[54] Nicholas Baggett, freeman of Exeter, made elaborately panelled entrance doors for the Guildhall, and for private houses in his own city, and can be credited with the richly Corinthian screen (Fig. 472) in the hall of Bowringsleigh in Devon.[55]

Sometimes an artificer arrived to work for a patron and stayed on to work for life, or for substantial periods, in his service. Robert Leminge, a London carpenter, played an important part in the building and design of Hatfield, and in 1616 moved on to become 'architect and builder' of Blickling Hall in Norfolk, as the Blickling parish register put it when he died there in 1628. In Essex William Petre seems to have enjoyed shopping around for craftsmen, and a series of London artificers came and went to work for him on different parts of his new house, Thorndon Hall, in the 1570s and 1580s; one of them, Walter Madison of the London Carpenters' Company, settled there permanently, or for a long period, as the surveyor and organiser of the new building.[56] Another London carpenter, Richard Kirby, played a similar role under Sir Thomas Smith, of Hill Hall, who expressed a wish in his will that Kirby should act as 'cheefe Architecte overseer and Mr of my workes', to finish off the house.[57] Robert Smythson, of the London Masons' Company, went to work for Sir John Thynne at Longleat, and then entered the service of Sir Francis Willoughby at Wollaton, arriving in 1580

28 The monument to Richard Harford at Bosbury, Herefordshire, made and signed by John Gildon, 1578. It carries the arms of the Marquis of Winchester, whose servant Harford must have been.

29 The old Ouse Bridge, York, built by the mason Christopher Walmesley in 1566.

and staying till his death in 1615; his long-time associate at Longleat, Alan Maynard, continued to live on Thynne property until his death in 1598.[58] Longleat and Wollaton became the centres of little colonies of artificers, living in the house or nearby, just as Bess of Hardwick acquired the permanent services of a French painter, John Balechouse, and the English artificers Abraham Smith, carver and plasterer, and Thomas Accres, marble-carver. After her death, Balechouse's son stayed on to build and run the Hardwick Inn, at the bottom of the hill below the great house; and the account-book of her son, William, records his attending the funeral of Thomas Accres in 1605.[59]

Other artificers worked and lived independently of patrons and free of guild control, in small towns or out in the countryside, sometimes their place of birth, sometimes coming from outside, usually of unidentified origins. The precise background of the gifted William Arnold is not known (though his father had worked at Longleat in the 1550s), but he and his brother were based from the late sixteenth century in the village of Charlton Musgrove, in Somerset, where William died in 1637.[60] Walter Hancock, background also unknown, was living at Much Wenlock in Shropshire when he made his will in 1599, but actually died at Madeley nearby, where the parish clerk glowingly described his all-round abilities in the register.[61] In Shropshire he worked at Madeley Court, Condover Hall and Shrewsbury Market Hall, and he and his assistants carved the fine monument of Margaret Herbert at Montgomery in Wales. The bridge-building Christopher Walmesley, who was brought in by York Corporation to rebuild the Ouse Bridge there, and to span the river with one mighty arch (Fig. 29), lived and had a farm in the remote village of Bolton by Bolland in the North Riding.[62]

When Sir John Strode built his new house at Chantmarle in Dorset, started in 1612, he employed Gabriel Moore, freemason, from Somerset but possibly by then based in Exeter, as surveyor; a plasterer, Robert Easton, from Stogursey in Somerset to install the decorative plasterwork; and Joseph and Daniel Rowe, from Ham Hill in Somerset and possibly quarry leasers or workers there, as masons. The Rowes came to Chantmarle from Wadham College, Oxford, where they had gone to work under William Arnold.[63]

Quarry workers form a distinct group. More research needs to be done into Elizabethan and Jacobean quarries, their ownership, and the way in which they operated. They normally belonged to local landowners, but were rented or leased out to artificers. These were sometimes described simply as 'quarrymen', and supplied stone in bulk, but not worked, measured by the ton. But often they were freemasons, who shaped stone at the quarry and could provide details such as mullions and transoms for windows ready-made, sometimes to be erected by others at the building site, though sometimes they were prepared to come and erect them themselves. The quarries at Weldon, in Northamptonshire, for instance, belonged to Sir Christopher Hatton, but were drawn on by Sir Thomas Tresham when he was building the Market House at Rothwell and the New Bield at Lyveden. Pifford, described as the

designed, perhaps, to advertise his skills, and adorned with his initials (Fig. 30).

Stone could travel considerable distances, especially to areas that had no building stone of their own but could be linked to the quarry by water. Carting or dragging stone overland was much more expensive than carrying it by water. Cambridge, without stone of its own, drew on the Kingscliffe and Weldon quarries, among others, from at least the late fifteenth century; the supply route was first by land, to the River Nene near Wansford, and then by the Nene, Ouse and Cam for the rest of the journey. The Kingscliffe stone used for windows, doors and other details in the otherwise brick-built Blickling Hall in Norfolk in the years 1619–23 must have come almost entirely by water: up the Nene to the Wash, round to the east coast of Norfolk, and then up the Bure to within a mile of the house. Thomas Thorpe of Kingscliffe, who supplied the stone, also worked on site as chief mason.[67] Kingscliffe stone made an even longer journey by river and sea to London, to be used in the rebuilding of Aldgate in the City of London in 1607, once again with Thomas Thorpe involved at either end.[68]

In 1581 Purbeck stone, probably for use as paving, came by sea from Dorset to a wharf on the Thames, at Grays Thurrock in Essex, from which it was carted ten miles or so inland for use at Sir William Petre's Thorndon Hall. Petre's surveyor, Walter Madison, brought the mason Thomas Kettle down from London to measure it at the wharf.[69] In the 1630s both Purbeck stone and black and white marble were coming by way of London up the Thames to Abingdon and overland to Oxford, for use as paving at St John's College, Queen's College and probably Christ Church.[70] In 1603 Thomas Garret, of Headington outside Oxford, was providing both stone in bulk and cut stone from Headington quarries, for 'doors, crests, vynialls [finials] and piramides [obelisks]', for the building of Ashley Park, near Walton-on-Thames in Surrey. He sent Whitt-

'quarryman', supplied stone in bulk for the main walls of the latter, but the windows and other details were supplied and set up by William Grumbold and Thomas, his son, also of Weldon; William had already been used by Tresham on the Market House at Rothwell.[64] The Grumbold family continued active at Weldon into the late seventeenth century, and another family, the Frisbys, were also working there, possibly in a different quarry, from at least 1560–61, when William Frisby provided 22 tons of freestone for Trinity College chapel, Cambridge, until the mid-seventeenth century.[65] Humphrey Frisby, who died in 1624, also had an interest in the famous quarries at Kingscliffe in Northamptonshire, where the dominant quarry family were the Thorpes, four generations of whom are commemorated on a monument in the church, erected in 1623. Both Lord Burghley and Sir Walter Mildmay, and later his son Anthony, owned quarries at Kingscliffe.[66] The initials of Arthur Grumbold, and the date 1654, are on a house in the main street of Weldon; a younger Humphrey Frisby built himself the eccentric Haunt Hill House, just outside the village, in the years 1636–43, a piece of elaboration in miniature,

more, his mason, to install them; this Headington stone was coming down the Thames from Oxford at the same time as the Kettle family's stone chimneypieces were coming up the Thames from London.[71] In the years 1637–40 Richard Boyle, Earl of Cork, employed John Ken, a Bristol freemason who had interests in the Dundry Hill quarries, just outside Bristol, to provide and ship pre-cut windows for his house at Gill Abbey, in County Cork, and paid him the substantial sum of £310 for doing so.[72]

The lessees or owners of the Dundry Hill and Headington quarries, being as these were just outside Bristol and Oxford, were likely to be members of the Masons' guilds of those cities. Artificers working quarries away from the bigger towns – the oolite quarries of Northamptonshire, the Hazelwood quarries in the West Riding, the limestone quarries at Burford and Taynton in Oxfordshire, the quarries at Beer in Devon and Ham Hill in Somerset, the Tottenhoe quarries in Bedfordshire, the Kentish Rag quarries around Maidstone (much used for buildings in London) – worked independently of the guild system, and, if they took apprentices, took them on their own terms. Such apprenticeships are little documented and were perhaps not all that common, for most quarrymen seem to have operated family businesses, passing from father to son. But Stephen Mason or Maison, who owned a quarry at Boughton Monchelsea in Kent, took as apprentice Thomas Chafyn (d. 1572), and later left him the quarry, as we know from Chafyn's will. Chafyn did not work the quarry himself, however. He had been 'appointed by force and aucthorite of our said soveraigne Lady the quenes Majesties commission and in her name comanded to travaile into the, parties and domynyons of Russia beionde the seas there to serve in the workes of the Emperour of Russia in the science and arte of masonry, wherein I have been traded and brought up'.[73]

There are no other known examples of so extensive a migration; but there was certainly coming and going between Ireland and England. A good number of apprentices of Bristol artificers came from County Cork, and in 1617 the Earl of Cork commissioned Alexander Hylles, 'tomb maker' of Holborn, to make him the elaborate monument still in the church at Youghal in that county for £217.[74] Hylles, who had already provided sundials for erection in Cork, came over from London to install the tomb (and repair another one), and seems to have remained in Ireland; a mason of that name, living in County Clare, is listed among the Protestants who took refuge in Ballyallia Castle in that county during the Catholic uprising of 1642.[75] About 1610 Sir Thomas Ridgeway is said to have employed masons from his native Devon to build his fortified house (now known as Spur Castle) at Augher in County Tyrone; its star-shaped plan suggests that he knew of the similar plan of the Star Castle in the Scilly Isles, built in 1593–4.[76] In 1628 William Parrott, possibly a London freemason by origin, contracted with the London Irish Society to erect what is now St Columb's cathedral in Londonderry for £3,400; an inscription commemorates the rebuilding: 'If stones could speak then London's prayse should sounde, who build this church and cittie from the grounde.'[77]

In 1617 Richard Cobb, of the London Plasterers' Company, went up with another plasterer, Robert Whitehead, to install ceilings in Holyrood Palace in Scotland.[78] But English artificers, other than plasterers, are not known to have adventured north of the border, though examples may well come to light.[79] Inside England and Wales, however, they were freely mobile; they went wherever work was available. 'Brinsmead', for instance, is a rare enough surname for there to be a presumption that artificers of that name, working in Dorset, Staffordshire and Lancashire, were related: John Brynsmede was the principal

31 Alexander Brinsmead built the staircase at Borwick Hall, Lancashire, in 1595, and carved his name on it.

nally from Maidstone in Kent.[81] Arnold Goverson, and William and Godfrey Goverson, alias Arnold, ultimately of Charlton Musgrove in Somerset, must have been related to a younger Arnold Goverson, who is documented at Oatlands in Surrey *circa* 1616–18, and was working quarries at Ketton in Rutland in 1621, when he supplied stone for the building of Raynham Hall, in Norfolk.[82] Sir Henry Savile, Warden of Merton College, Oxford, brought down from his native Yorkshire two freemasons, John Akroyd and John Bentley, and a carpenter, Thomas Holt, to work on the new quadrangle that he built at Merton in 1609–10. These Yorkshiremen stayed on permanently in Oxford, to work on the Schools Building and (probably) the Bodleian Library; Holt also provided roofs for the hall and library at Wadham College in 1612.[83] But Akroyd's son-in-law, John Clarke or Clark (*circa* 1585–1624), who was in Oxford by at least 1616, when he built the Carfax Conduit, moved on to London and was a member of the London Masons' Company by 1620.[84] The large gang of artificers whom William Arnold brought up with him from Somerset to work on the building of Wadham College in 1609 seem all to have gone back to the West Country when the work was finished, or at least did not stay in Oxford.

John Rodes and his son or younger brother Christopher, very skilled (though illiterate) freemasons, worked extensively in the Midlands between 1574 and 1595, at the Turret House at Sheffield, Wollaton, Hardwick New Hall, and no doubt elsewhere; it must have been a temporary cessation of local work that brought Christopher south to work at the Tower of London in 1586–7[85] – or just possibly empressment at royal command, such as brought John Lewis up from Longleat to work on the great roof of the Middle Temple Hall in 1562.[86] The surprising appearance of Richard and Gabriel Royley, of Burton upon Trent, prolific suppliers of alabaster tombs in the 1570s and on into the 1580s, as ordinary freemasons working

mason for the reconstruction of Beaudesert, Staffordshire,[80] *circa* 1576–81; 'Alexander Brinsmead, Mason, 1595' is carved on the stone parapet at the top of the staircase at Borwick Hall, Lancashire (Fig. 31), the only known example of an Elizabethan mason signing a building, as opposed to a church monument; Roger Brinsmeade or Brinsmeade, was the master mason for the building of the school-house at Sherborne, Dorset, in the years 1606–8, and died in Sherborne in 1623; Gregory Brinsmeade supplied paving for the Earl of Bristol at Sherborne Castle and the Earl of Cork at Stalbridge House, Dorset, in and around 1638.

Robert Smythson's progress, from London to Wiltshire by way of Oxfordshire or Berkshire, and from Wiltshire to Nottinghamshire, has already been discussed. John Hill or Hilles, who accompanied him on the same route, came origi-

at Wollaton Hall in 1582,[87] suggests that, as was the case, their particular style of work was beginning to go out of fashion.

The building artificers' companies inevitably included masons, carpenters, joiners, bricklayers and glaziers. In small towns they could be amalgamated in various combinations. Tilers and plasterers were often put in with the bricklayers, but as plasterers grew in importance they set up their own guilds. London had a Company of Turners, separate from carpenters and joiners, and a Company of Marblers, curiously combining work in alabaster and other 'hardstones' and the provision of memorial brasses; it fell on hard times, and went in with the Masons in 1585.[88]

Since joiners and carpenters both worked in wood it was possible for the same man to combine the two trades, a situation recognised by the amalgamation of the two trades into one guild in York.[89] But the distinction between the work they did was clear enough.[90] Carpenters were concerned with structure: they provided floors, ceilings, roof-structures, staircases and complete frameworks for half-timbered buildings. Joiners were concerned with lining and decorating; they provided panelling, chimneypieces, door-cases and carved woodwork of all kinds, as well as furniture. They could collaborate with carpenters: the larger and more elaborately carved hall screens of the period, for instance, were provided by joiners on a framework put up by carpenters, and joiners embellished with decorative elements the carpenters' staircases and open-timber roofs.

The full title of the Joiners' Company in London was the 'Company of joiners, seelers and carvers'. 'Seeling' was the contemporary term for panelling. 'Carving' is an interesting term, because it involved crossing the boundaries between the trades. A skilful carver was prepared to work in different mediums: wood, stone, marble and even plaster. So one finds Robert Pinckney, a leading member of the London Joiners' Company, carving a great stone chimneypiece and overmantel for the gallery (today part of the Royal Library) at Windsor Castle in 1583 (Fig. 32); and in the seventeenth century Garrett Christmas and his sons Matthias and John, all members of the London Joiners' Company, carved the elaborate wooden bows and stem of royal warships, but also produced and designed a series of church monuments in marble and alabaster.[91]

Freemasons, who had skills in ornamental stonework or panels of sculpture for overmantels,

32 The stone chimney-piece carved by Robert Pinckney in 1583 for Queen Elizabeth's new Long Gallery (now part of the Royal Library) at Windsor Castle.

could also call themselves carvers, and are also found carving in wood as well as stone. Nicholas Stone, a member of the London Masons' Company, is best known for his church monuments, but he also provided chimneypieces, garden ornaments and individual sculptures; he (or his assistants) also worked as freemasons at a number of locations. All this was in stone, alabaster or marble, but in 1616 he fitted out the Chapel Royal at Holyrood with wooden wainscot and carving (he was described as Nicholas Stone, carver, in the contract).[92]

The work of other 'carvers' was equally varied. In 1608 the Flemish-born Maximilian Colt, who had made his English reputation with Queen Elizabeth's monument in Westminster Abbey, was appointed Master Carver or Master Sculptor, a new post specially created for him. His documented or convincingly attributed work includes monuments and chimneypieces in alabaster and marble, and carvings in wood on royal barges and in the chapel at Greenwich Palace.[93] The documented work of the Cure family, variously described as 'freemasons' or 'carvers', includes fountains for Sir Nicholas Bacon at Redgrave in Suffolk and the Earl of Leicester at Wanstead in Essex, chimneypieces for Lord Burghley at Burghley or Theobalds and the Earl of Dorset at Knole, and the monument of Mary, Queen of Scots in Westminster, besides a large corpus of attributed works of all kinds.[94] Garret Hollemans was described as 'a dutch carver' by Sir Edward Pytts of Kyre Park in Worcestershire when he bargained with him in 1592 to make two chimneypieces depicting the stories of *Mars and Venus*, and of *Susanna*; in 1594 he went on from Kyre to work for Richard Barneby of Bockleton in the same county, probably on the fine stone monument still in Bockleton church; its distinctive style enables a series of other monuments to be confidently attributed to him, along with the woodcarving from Holdenby House, now incorporated in the screen in the church there, and probably the elaborate chimneypieces known to have been at Holdenby, but long since disappeared.[95]

Since the decorative elements of plasterwork, especially if involving repeated motifs, were made in carved wooden moulds, the line between joiners and plasterworkers was also blurred. John Symonds, a joiner by training (but also carving in stone), was appointed Master Plasterer in the Royal Works in 1585; in the north the joiners or carvers Francis and Thomas Gunby were responsible for the elaborate woodwork of St John's, Leeds, and the screen in what is now Wakefield cathedral, but also for the decorative plasterwork at Gawthorpe Hall, Lancashire, and in the roof of St John's; in York, John Burridge was working in both plaster and wood for Sir Arthur Ingram in 1624–5; at Hardwick, Abraham Smith worked in stone and plaster.[96] It is possible that outside London, where the individual guilds jealously guarded their particular patches, such mixed roles were more common. An extreme case was that of 'old Veale of Bodmin', if Richard Carew is to be relied on in his *Survey of Cornwall*: '. . . without a teacher he is become very skilful in well-near all manner of handicrafts: a carpenter, a joiner, a millwright, a freemason, a clock-maker, a carver, metal-founder, architect and quid non? . . . yea, a surgeon, physician, alchemist, etc.'.[97]

In addition to one or more apprentices, a successful master craftsman usually took on a number of qualified artificers who worked under or with him, and travelled round with him, if he travelled. Robert Smythson arrived at Longleat in 1568 with five masons, called 'his men'.[98] Thomas Collins, the principal mason and carver of Bristol, had six masons working with or for him when he died in 1594.[99] When William Arnold came to Oxford in 1610, as surveyor for the building of Wadham College, he arrived with twenty-six men, probably all masons, whom he had recruited in the West Country. Only three of them, however, were described in the building accounts as his own men.[100] It seems likely that the Elizabethan building world was essentially atomic, made up of small permanent or slowly changing groups or gangs of artificers that would coalesce on occasions on a big job, under the direction of a surveyor, or be taken on as temporary labour by a master craftsman.

Large buildings could go up over a number of years with a comparatively small workforce, perhaps especially if ready money with which to pay the wages was in short supply. But on occasions, when money was ample and speed important, much larger numbers were employed. A huge company of artifcers is said to have worked on the building of the Royal Exchange in London in 1566–7. Up to 124 masons worked on its intended rival, the New Exchange on the Strand, in 1608–9.[101] The at least sixty different masons' marks that have been identified on the grand new extension added to Apethorpe in Northamptonshire in and after 1623 suggests the speed at which this was run up, perhaps to get it ready for a royal visit in 1624.[102]

Payments made for task work to a single artificer must often conceal the names of the other artificers who were working with him. This is obviously true in the case of large building works, but even church monuments are likely to be the work of several hands, and one need not necessarily assume that the work of the highest quality was the responsibility of the master artificer who was paid for them. The will of the Shropshire mason Walter Hancock, made in 1599, shows that other artificers had worked with him on the monument put up by Margaret Herbert, George Herbert's mother, to the memory of her husband, Lord Herbert of Cherbury, in the church at Montgomery.[103] In 1568 the London carver-joiner Robert Pinckney had living with him in Southwark as 'servants' two Brabant-born joiners, John Boyon and Simon Wiltyns.[104] A flood of Low Country craftsmen, many exceedingly able, were arriving as refugees in England in the mid-six-teenth century, and enterprising English-born craftsmen could take advantage of their skills.

Most of the artificers working in the sixteenth and early seventeenth centuries were illiterate. Illiteracy did not preclude success. John Roods and his brother Christopher, who were responsible for most of the stonework at Wollaton and Hardwick, could sign only with their mark, yet they were able to take on and successfully execute stonework at Hardwick valued at £890 – including rough and ashlar walling, cornice frieze and architrave all round the exterior façades, doors, windows, and fireplace surrounds and the great stone staircase.[105]

It is worth comparing them with the Beane family, masons probably from Yorkshire, who started to work in a similar capacity at Hardwick in 1591, but were for some reason displaced by the Roodses. In 1586–7, when, among other work, they built a 'great Baye window' for the Earl of Rutland at Belvoir Castle, Thomas Beane could manage to sign only with his initials, but his son Christopher signed with his full name.[106] The progress over two generations was perhaps not untypical of the period. Certainly, literacy must have been an advantage; all the leading artificers discussed in this book – for example, the officers of the Works, the Smythsons, the Arnold-Goversons, Alan Maynard, Robert Leminge, William Collins and the Fryndes – were literate.

Two skills, related to literacy, were also valuable, and possibly essential, for ambitious artificers: measuring and the making of drawings. A senior artificer was often used to measure the work done by others, who were working 'by the great', that is, being paid by quantity of work done, not by time. All master carpenters, the elements of whose structures were usually made off site, needed to be able to measure them accurately to be sure that they would fit, and masons similarly had to check the measurements of the building elements that they fabricated at the quarries. The plan of a proposed building needed to be accurately laid out by measure on the site.

Measuring was the subject of a manual of instruction written by Leonard Digges, and first published in 1556: *A Boke named Tectonicon*. This, as expounded in the preface, showed

> how to measure truly and very speedily all manor land, timber, stone, steeples, pillers, globes, board, glasse, pavement, and c., without any trouble, not pained with many rules, or obscure tearmes, nor yet with the multitude of Tables . . . ye shall by this booke understand the whole making and comely handling of the Carpenters Ruler.

Digges explained how artificers or others could make their own Rule or Ruler, and described the uses of another instrument, 'the profitable Staffe'. His book, he claimed, was most conducible for 'Surveyors, Landmeaters, Joyners, Carpenters, and Masons'.

It proved to be one of the bestsellers of its time. Nine editions had appeared by the end of the century, and another nine by 1656.[107] In 1585 the London printer and bookseller Roger Warde had five in stock in his branch shop in Shrewsbury (and no books on architecture).[108] In 1658 John Martyn, in his *Mensuration Made Easy*, described what he claimed to be a better rule, on the grounds that as a result of being transcribed from rule to rule over a century, Digges's ruler had become inaccurate. An improved rule had also been devised by Thomas Bedwell in 1574, but according to Martyn its use involved a knowledge of mathematics 'far beyond ordinary capacities'.[109] Both Digges and Bedwell (but especially the latter) were drawn on by the London carpenter Richard More in his *The Carpenter's Rule* (1602 and 1616), but this ran only to two editions. Digges reigned supreme.

Measuring involved above all knowledge of arithmetic; the making of reliable plans, and the drawing out of the orders, involved both arithmetic and geometry. The first book of Serlio's *Architecture* deals with geometry, and starts with an encomium on its importance.

> How needfull and necessary the most secret Art of Geometrie is for every Artificer and Workeman, as those that for a long time have studied and wrought without the same can sufficiently witnesse, who since that time have attained unto any knowledge of the said Arte, doe not onely laugh and smile at their owne former simplicities, but in truety may very well acknowledge that all whatsoever had bene formerly done by them, was not worth the looking on.

English artificers could not read this in English before 1611, when Robert Peake published a translation,[110] and in his preface to the First Book repeated Serlio's views and his own wish to 'convey unto my Countrymen (especially Architects and Artificers of all sorts) these Necessary, Certaine, and most ready Helps of *Geometrie*: the ignorance and want whereof, in times past (in most parts of this Kingdome) hath left us many lame Workes, with shame of many Workemen'. But the importance of geometry for artificers had already been stressed in John Shute's *First and Chief Groundes of Architecture* (1563) and Dee's preface to Billingsley's translation of Euclid (1570); and the geometrical base of the columns, capitals and mouldings of the orders are clearly set out in Shute's plates. It should be stressed, however, that there was nothing new about all this; the importance of geometry for master masons was just as much emphasised in the Middle Ages, and medieval tracery and vaulting could scarcely have been constructed without it.

An Elizabethan or Jacobean artificer could most obviously learn to draw, and acquire knowledge of geometry, from the master to whom he was apprenticed. If his master lacked the skills himself, or if his ex-apprentice wanted to improve on whatever he had learnt from him, Richard

More in *The Carpenter's Rule* (1602) had two suggestions, as far as concerned geometry: he should
study Euclid in Sir Henry Billingsley's English
translation of 1570, or attend the weekly lectures
on geometry at Gresham College in London.
These had started in 1597, and were given by
Henry Briggs, a leading mathematician and, later,
astronomer, of his day; he lectured in Latin in the
morning, and in English in the afternoon.[111]

The architectural drawing with the most
elaborate geometrical base to have survived from
the Elizabethan period is by John Smythson (Fig.
33). It is a 'Draughte For the Platte of a rounde
windowe Standinge in A Rounde walle', dated
1599.[112] The complicated method of setting this
out is carefully shown on the drawing; it has not
been traced to any published book. The likelihood of such a combination being needed in an
Elizabethan building is remote (though not
impossible), and the drawing has the air of being
more a demonstration than a design intended to
be executed.[113] It and two other Smythson drawings for round windows, undated but clearly of the
same period, seem, however, to relate to the
smaller window of the same pattern of tracery
actually built at Heath School, Halifax, *circa* 1598–
1601, in a flat wall; part of the land on which it was
built was given by the 7th Earl of Shrewsbury, son
of Robert Smythson's old patron at Worksop.
Since both Smythsons are known to have travelled down to London, it is worth surmising
whether the more elaborate window developed
out of one of Briggs's lectures (Briggs, incidentally, came from Halifax).[114]

An artificer or other individual engaged in
making architectural drawings needed the same
instruments as a geometrician; allegorical figures
of *Architecture* and *Geometry* display identical
tools (Fig. 34). An engraving dated 1599 from the
Italian Giovanni Pomodero's *Geometria Practica*
illustrated no less than sixteen instruments. But
for normal purposes in England, and probably
elsewhere, only five were used: compasses, scorer,

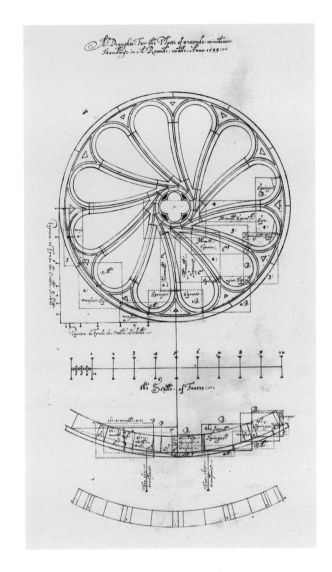

square, rule and pen – rule for straight lines,
square for right angles, compasses for curves,
compasses or scorer for measuring out, pricking
and marking lines on the paper or vellum used,
pen for the final inking in.[115] The salient points
were marked out with pricks on the blank sheet
and then joined with scored lines. Compasses
were what would be called today dividers, with
two sharp points; curves were scored with compasses in the same fashion as straight lines marked
with scorers. The pricks and scored lines can be
clearly seen on drawings of the period if they are
brightly lit from the side. It was not till the pricking and scoring were completed that the final
inking in took place.

34 (*right*) An allegorical
figure of Architecture
from an embroidery at
Hardwick Hall,
Derbyshire.

35a and b (*facing page*)
Designs, possibly by
Lawrence Bradshaw, for a
house in the form of a
cross, *c.*1560–70 (Hatfield,
CPM I/ 7,8).

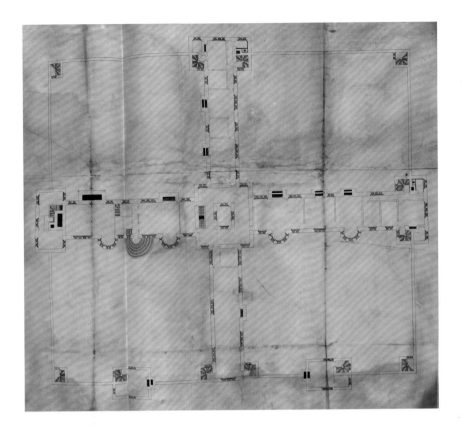

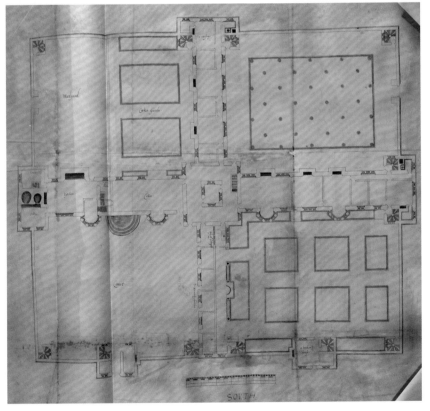

As a refinement for more finished drawings, shading and colouring were added: shading made either with crossed or closely parallel inked lines or with lumps of graphite, colouring with a brush, confusingly called in the sixteenth century a pencil. The development of a 'lead pencil' with a sharp point, which could be used as an alternative or supplement to the scorer, appeared in English architectural drawings only at the very end of the sixteenth century or early in the seventeenth. John Thorpe's plan of a house for 'Mr Taylor at potters bar', conveniently dated 1596, is still based on scoring, with pencil (in the modern sense) used only for shading. But in the course of the seventeenth century pencil lines gradually took over from scored ones as providing the usual basis for the final inking in.[116]

Between 1540 and 1640 around fifty English artificers are documented as providing drawings, mostly 'platts', or 'platforms' for plans, but occasionally 'uprights' for elevations. In the case of around thirty of these fifty, actual drawings survive, which can definitely or convincingly be attributed to them. Inevitably, there are further drawings (around a dozen, individually or in sets) that remain anonymous.

Most of these drawings are by craftsmen working (or who had worked) in the Royal Works, or based on, or originating from, London. The Works had a tradition of fine draughtsmanship that went back to early Tudor times, if not earlier.[117] Some of the drawings are of considerable beauty. One can cite plans, perhaps by Lawrence Bradshaw (Surveyor 1547–1560), for William Cecil's house in the Strand (*circa* 1560), and for a house in the shape of a cross (Fig. 35), the idea, but not the style of draughtsmanship of which derives from Jacques Androuet du Cerceau; and the lovely unexecuted elevation of 1562 (Fig. 36), almost certainly by John Revell (Surveyor 1560–63), for a new spire for St Paul's cathedral, intended to replace the one destroyed by lightning in 1561.[118]

36 (*right*) A design of 1562 for a new spire (never built) at St Paul's cathedral, London, probably by John Revell.

37 (*facing page*) Unexecuted design by Cornelius Cure for a monument for Edward vi, *c.*1580.

All these are show drawings, carefully finished and coloured. Plenty of other competent drawings (mostly plans), made for use rather than show, by artificer members of the Works survive. Among them are the survey of Ampthill in Bedfordshire, showing proposed additions, made by Richard Rowlands and John Vincents in 1567; plans by Henry Hawthorne for a new wing at Windsor Castle (1576); undated plans by John Symonds for the Cursitor's office in London (?1570s); an elevation by him for a gateway at Theobalds (1577); and plans of 1595 by Symonds and William Spicer for a house (later Beaufort Hall) for Robert Cecil in Chelsea.[119]

Two groups of London-derived drawings, not necessarily connected with the Works but possibly to be grouped with them, deserve looking at: a small group by Cornelius Cure, and a much larger group by Robert Smythson. The Cure drawings have survived because, with one exception, they entered the collection of Lord Burghley, for whom Cure was working from at least 1587.[120] Their subjects are varied: designs for an unexecuted tomb for Edward vi (*circa* 1580) and an executed but long-since demolished fountain at Hampton Court (*circa* 1584) (Fig. 173); designs for a doorway and chimneypiece for Lord Burghley; and a design for a little pavilion, probably also for him (Figs 396–8). In addition, on grounds of style and the known connection of the Cures with Nonsuch, it is tempting to attribute to Cornelius Cure the well-known series of drawings in the 'Lumley Inventory', made in 1590 and showing fountains (Fig. 172), tables and other features at Nonsuch and Lumley Castle, although these are survey drawings, not original designs.[121]

The sensitively coloured and drawn designs for Edward vi's tomb (Fig. 37) are perhaps the most attractive of surviving Elizabethan architectural drawings; and the others are all of high quality. But where did Cornelius Cure learn to draw? Was it from his father, William Cure, who was at Nonsuch with Nicholas Bellin and later worked

for the Duke of Somerset? He was probably related to, and possibly the son of, 'Guglielmus Cuer' of Gouda in Holland, whom Guicciardini listed in 1567 as among the outstanding 'sculptors and architects' in the Low Countries.[122] This suggests a background for William Cure in the world of early Flemish classicism, in which high drawing skills certainly existed. But no drawings by him have been identified.

Robert Smythson (as will appear in chapter 7) was trained in London, and may have been apprenticed to Humfrey Lovell, Master Mason in the Royal Works, who sent him to Longleat in 1568. His and his son's drawings survived in the Smythson family until the early eighteenth century, when they were acquired by the Byrons of Newstead Abbey, and ultimately ended up in the RIBA Drawings Collection.[123] Along with the drawings of John Thorpe (to be discussed later in this chapter), they are one of the two largest surviving collections of Elizabethan and Jacobean architectural drawings. They include show drawings, both plans and elevations, carefully drawn and coloured, and clearly intended for the eyes of an employer or potential client, and a variety of unfinished drawings of all types, probably for the Smythsons' own use or for the use of the artificers working for them. The style of draughtsmanship of the show drawings is already in evidence in an elevation[124] that must have been made by Robert shortly after he came to Longleat, and is in the Works tradition (Fig. 38); he must have learnt to draw in London. Later drawings pick up a few conventions of shading or stippling that seem to derive from engravings in Serlio's *Architecture*, to which he certainly had access. The show drawings are not, perhaps, quite up to the standard of Revell's St Paul's spire or Bradshaw's plans; but they are handsome and decorative objects none the less.

Drawings by artificers outside the Works circle differ, not surprisingly, very much in quality. At the top end of the scale are the handsome draw-

ings by Alan Maynard (Fig. 40), the Frenchman who worked with Smythson and others at Longleat.[125] Maynard had presumably learnt to draw in France; but although he and Smythson worked in partnership neither seems to have been influenced by the drawing style of the other. At the bottom end come the plans and elevations of Ralph Simons and Gabriel Wigge for St John's College, Cambridge, of 1598 (Fig. 39), and of Richard Wilson for Sheriff Hutton, of 1619: all drawn crudely enough (though gaily coloured, in the case of the Cambridge ones), probably just with a square and rule, without the aid of a compass.[126]

In between there is a good deal of variety. The designs by William Browne for a custom house at Hull (1573) are engagingly adorned with depictions of cranes and merchandise on the quayside (Fig. 41), and neatly drawn to an unusual convention in which all four elevations are stretched out in a single line.[127] What may be William Arnold's

38 (*left*) Design for a window by Robert Smythson, *c.*1568, related to those built at Longleat (SM. DWG 1/16).

39 (*above*) Design for St John's College, Cambridge, by Ralph Simons and Gabriel Wigge, 1598.

40 Design for an unidentified façade by Alan Maynard, the French mason who worked at Longleat from 1563 to 1598.

only surviving drawings (Fig. 134), plans for Cranborne Manor, Dorset (*circa* 1609), are no more than respectable.[128] Plans by the glazier Bernard Dininghoff for Sheriff Hutton, Yorkshire, are chiefly remarkable for their fancy lettering, reminiscent of the inscriptions with which he decorated his heraldic windows; his elevations are very crude.[129] Designs for monuments by the Flemish tomb-makers Maximilian Colt and

Garrat Johnson[130] have none of the quality of Cornelius Cure; they make clear that foreign artificers were not necessarily better draughtsmen than English ones such as Simon Basil (Fig. 42). What must have been important designs by Robert Leminge for Hatfield (*circa* 1611) and Blickling Hall (*circa* 1618) have been lost. All that survives is his lively but somewhat crude drawing for a garden seat at Blickling (Fig. 43);[131] Leminge

43

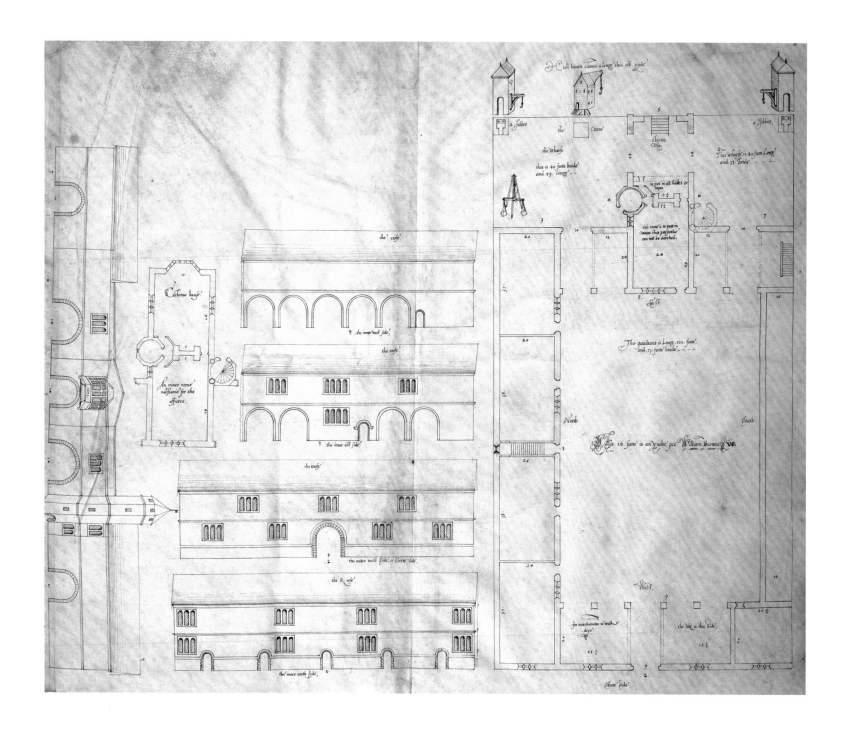

41 Design, probably unexecuted, by William Browne for a custom house at Hull, 1573 (Hatfield, CPM 2/3).

apologised to his patron, Sir Henry Hobart, for its being drawn 'very roughly and my tyme very short'.

Designs were not necessarily drawn on paper. At Acton Court in Gloucestershire, about 1550, detail drawings for the base of an oriel and the head of a roof truss were inscribed in the plaster of a wall, compass and rule being used; they are still there.[132] There must have been many similar

examples of what were, in effect, working drawings being so inscribed on site. It was a convenient way of working, with a long tradition behind it, exemplified by a celebrated floor in a room over the chapter-house passage at York Minster, still confusingly covered with a mass of inscribed drawings of the fourteenth century.

Walter Gedde, in his *Book of Sundry Draughtes principaly serving for Glasiers* published in 1615,

44

42 Elevation by Simon Basil, probably for Little Salisbury House, London, 1590.

THE UPRIGHTS ON THE GARDEN SYDE

43 (*below*) Robert Leminge's design for a garden seat at Blickling Hall, Norfolk, *c.*1620.

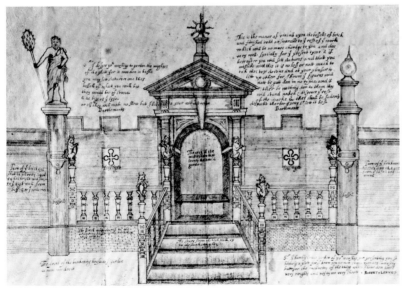

describes how his designs should be first drawn out on what he calls 'the table', and then individual pieces of glass cut to fit, ready for soldering together with strips of lead. His designs, many extremely elaborate, are grouped in two parts, depending on whether or not they needed a compass to draw them out. Only an artificer with some knowledge of geometry could have worked out the latter, or similar examples of fanciful glazing.

The title page of Gedde's book goes on to say how his draughts are 'not impertinent for Plasterers and Gardiners'. They were certainly used to provide some of the elaborate geometric designs that became such a feature of Elizabethan and Jacobean plasterwork.[133] Such designs must have been first drawn out or incised on the plain plaster of the ceiling, perhaps on the basis of an initial drawing (if Gedde was not used); such a drawing, for a ceiling long since demolished at Ramsbury in Wiltshire, survives at Longleat. An ordinary compass would, of course, have been much too small for inscribing on the ceiling; a much larger compass, with grips for the hands halfway down, is shown in the portrait of Ralph Simons at Emmanuel College, Cambridge.

Important elements in the building process, the making of which also needed some knowledge of geometry, were 'moulds'. These were distinct from cavity-moulds, into which plaster or other fluid material could be poured or pressed in order to be given shape. They were what would be called today 'templates', profiles cut, probably in wood, from which masons could work when cutting window, door or stair details, or elements of the orders. They were normally made by joiners, who must have drawn them out on the wood before cutting, possibly, but not necessarily, on the basis of a drawing. There are some drawings for moulds at the beginning of John Thorpe's book: 'rayle mould for a stayre', 'a good Jambe mould', and so on (Fig. 44).[134]

The provision of moulds frequently features in building accounts. When Sir Thomas Tresham, for instance, was building his Triangular Lodge at Rushton in 1594, Thomas Greene and his brother, joiners in nearby Rothwell, made moulds for crockets and chimney mouldings, and also for the 'Doric Cornice'; the Greenes apparently did not feel competent to make the moulds for the 'Dorick architrave', and these were provided by the masons at the quarry in nearby Weldon.[135] This suggests that quarry masons, in addition to providing, on demand, details pre-cut at the quarry, were prepared to supply moulds from which other masons could work on site.

In addition to working from drawings or moulds, artificers could also work from books or engravings. These were a principal means by which knowledge of unfamiliar styles and details came to artificers. Serlio's *Architecture*, in particular, was in frequent use; many examples will occur in later pages. Architectural books may have belonged to the artificers themselves, but they were expensive, and documented examples are rare. They are mentioned in a handful of wills, and Nicholas Stone's signed copy of Jean Martin's French edition of Vitruvius is now in the British Library.[136] It was probably more common for books to be supplied by employers. There is a documented example of this. Sir Edward Pytts, of Kyre Park in Worcestershire, died in 1618; his son and heir mentioned after his death that Pytt's chief mason, John Chaunce of Bromsgrove, 'hath in his keeping one booke of Architecture of myne'.[137] At Wollaton, architecturally the most learned house of its time, Robert Smythson may have relied entirely on the library of his employer, Sir Francis Willoughby, who owned one of the biggest collections of architectural books and prints, and related works, recorded in this period. But it is possible that he also had books of his own, which may have passed to his son, John, and been among the undifferentiated 'books' that featured in the latter's will in 1634.[138]

William Cure, the carver, also left just 'bookes' to his son Cornelius in 1579; Robert Stickelles, freemason and clerk in the Works, left 'bookes' in 1620; Francis Carter, carpenter and also in the Works, left 'bookes of architeckter' in his 'cabinet' in 1630.[139]

Tools, both for working and drawing, drawings and possibly engravings, and books, were valuable elements of the stock in trade of an artificer, and are mentioned accordingly in their wills. Working tools feature frequently, as one would expect, drawing instruments, drawings and books much less often because far fewer artificers had them to leave. William Cure left 'plots and modells' as well as tools in 1579.[140] In 1594 Thomas Collins, the leading freemason in Bristol in the late sixteenth century, left his working tools to be divided among the five freemasons working for him. In addition, to John Frynde or Frende, the most important of them, he left his pen and inkhorn and all his drawing tools. Finally, he left 'my bookes of byldinge unto John Frynde and Anthony Frynde, freemasons, with my draught plottes to be devided according to the discrecion of John Frynde or my owne selfe'.[141] In 1597 John Symonds left John Allen, carver, joiner and plasterer, 'sometyme my servant', 'thone halfe of all my tooles belonginge to my occupation as well for free stone as for hard stone and thone halfe of all my platts, my best case of yron compasses with all the other tools in the same case, my finest pensell guilded which was my Mr Stockettes and my Geometricall square of latten for measureing of lande'.[142]

In addition, he left him his 'backe' sword and second dagger, his 'sky collored gowne', his 'rugge goune', his 'damaske Jackett with sleeves garded with velvet' and his 'sylke grograyne doblett being cutt with longe cuttes'. These were just a portion of the extensive legacies of clothes left by Symonds, who would seem to have been the most foppish and dressiest of Elizabethan artificers, and able to indulge in this expensive taste, more probably on the fruits of property development than from his earnings as a craftsman.

Non-Artificers

Knowledge of geometry and the ability to draw and measure were accomplishments that it was important for ambitious artificers to acquire, but they were not confined to them. They were to be found fairly widely distributed among professionals, academics and gentlemen, courtiers or otherwise; and anyone who had them, especially if he had access to the relevant books as well, was likely to feel able to adventure into the design of buildings. Such non-artificer designers are among the most interesting features of Elizabethan and

Jacobean architecture, but also the most elusive, for a known reputation is very seldom accompanied by any attributable designs, and because they were often unpaid they do not feature in accounts.

A number of officials of the Works were not trained as artificers. Several of these, however, seem to have been appointed because they were good managers, or had good connections, not because they had skills in design or drawing. Robert Adams, who was appointed Surveyor in 1594, was different. His father was an engraver and schoolmaster to the royal pages; he himself had made his reputation as a map-maker and a deviser (and probably engraver) of sundials before going on to survey and design fortifications when he entered the service of the Earl of Leicester in the 1580s. He died after less than a year as Surveyor; a star-shaped castle in the Scilly Isles and the citadel at Plymouth are the only works he is known to have designed.[143] But his clerk, Simon Basil, also a non-artificer, whom he had brought into the Works with him, stayed on after his death and ended up a Surveyor from 1606 to 1615. Inigo Jones, who followed as Surveyor from 1615 to 1643, was a painter and designer of masques, and after him, with the insignificant exception of the Cromwellian plumber John Embree (Surveyor 1653–1660), none of the Surveyors of the Royal Works had trained as artificers.

The most interesting non-artificer in the Elizabethan Works establishment was John Thorpe;[144] but he is interesting because of what he did outside it. His father, his grandfather and his two brothers were masons, but, perhaps as the clever one of the family, he seems to have set out to better himself in a non-manual job. He entered the Works in 1582, aged sixteen or thereabouts, and stayed till 1600 or 1601. He was employed as storekeeper, bookkeeper and clerk at various locations, and probably also as a draughtsman; certainly he acquired drawing skills, and probably measuring ones. In the mid-1590s he began to

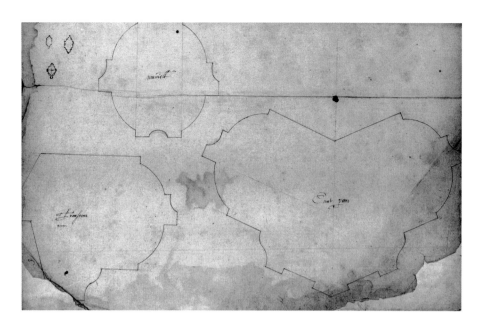

44 Designs for window moulds by John Thorpe (T3).

bird's-eye perspective view of Toddington Manor, Bedfordshire, in his survey of 1581,[145] is one of the more sensitive of Elizabethan depictions of a building (Fig. 45), there is no evidence that he was involved in making new designs. Similarly, although the prolific Essex surveyor John Walker (*circa* 1550–1626) called himself 'architector' or 'architector and surveyor' on a number of surveys made by him in the 1580s, no architectural work by him has been identified.[146] On the other hand, Ralph Treswell, who made detailed surveys of Sir Christopher Hatton's properties at Holdenby, Kirby and Corfe Castle in the 1580s, is documented in the years 1614–17 as supervising and possibly designing substantial new building at the royal house of Easthampstead, Berkshire, and in the royal park at Theobalds; there is no mention of the making of 'plots', by him or anyone else, but his detailed survey plan of the buildings of Corfe Castle shows that he was capable of it. It is just possible that Hatton employed him in a designing as well as a surveying capacity.[147]

Painters had skills that could be turned to devising buildings or their decoration, and so, in an age that filled its buildings with heraldry, could heralds, who were often trained as painters. On the Continent painters (and to a lesser degree sculptors) played a major role in introducing classical architecture derived from Roman remains to the countries in which they operated. In England they were far less important, though their role is not without interest. Two mid-century Italians who worked in England, Antonio Toto and Nicholas Bellin, were painters by origin but prepared to try other lines. Toto was credited by Vasari with designing palaces for Henry VIII, but there is no evidence for or likelihood of this; Bellin was mainly of importance as a plasterer, but his influence did not last. John Shute, of the London Painter-Stainers' Company, returning from Italy to publish his *First and Chief Groundes of Architecture*, might possibly have followed the Continental pattern if his patron had not been

provide 'platts' for houses on his own independent account. In 1600 he put in unsuccessfully for the reversion of one of the major offices. It was probably this failure that induced him to leave the Works. On the basis of his acquired skills he then set up, with great success, as a land-surveyor, but continued to provide 'platts' as a sideline well into the 1620s. More than 250 of his drawings, bound up in a book together, came into the collection of the Earls of Warwick at Warwick Castle in or before the eighteenth century; they were bought by Sir John Soane in 1810, and are now in the Sir John Soane Museum in London. They include what appear to be copies of drawings by others, to which Thorpe perhaps had access in the Works, but also numerous plans and elevations by Thorpe. Some of these are survey drawings but many (how many is debatable) are his own original designs. More will be said about him in chapter 7.

Since land-surveyors needed knowledge of geometry, and measuring and drawing skills, and were likely to have to produce surveys of buildings as well as of land, one might have expected some of them to pursue the opposite route to Thorpe's and diversify from surveying to providing 'platts' for new projects. But, although Ralph Agas's

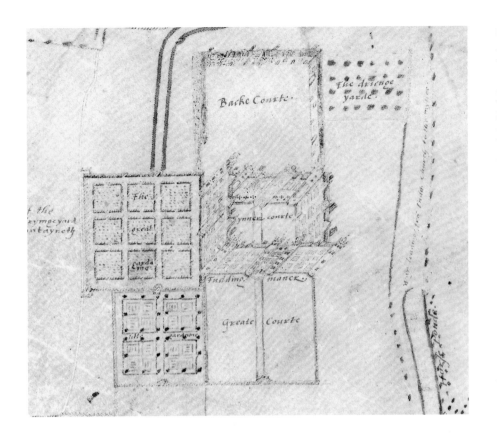

45 Bird's-eye view of Toddington Manor, Bedfordshire, from a survey by Ralph Agas, 1581.

selves to putting a classical column as a studio prop in the backgrounds of their portraits.[148]

The heraldic decorations, in stained glass and probably also plasterwork and panelling, that must have made the great chamber of Shrewsbury House, on the Thames in London, one of the most remarkable of Elizabethan interiors were devised jointly in 1578–9 by Robert Cooke, the Clarenceux Herald, and William Jones, mysteriously described as 'the finisher'. The equally magnificent (and still surviving) heraldic decorations of the great chamber at Gilling Castle in Yorkshire (Figs 269, 482) seem to have been the result of collaboration in the 1580s between Robert Glover, Somerset Herald, and Bernard Dininghoff, a heraldic glass painter. In 1630 Richard Boyle, Earl of Cork, 'gave mr Leveret, the purcevant at Armes, 40s. for drawing the Module of my dear wives tombe'.[149]

In addition, there is a sizeable group of people in other occupations who made designs, or were credited with the ability to make them. Sir Thomas Cawarden, the powerful Master of the Revels from 1544 to 1559, was said to have been 'skilfull and delighting in matters of devise', though this does not necessarily mean that he made drawings. Leonard Digges, whose muchreprinted *Boke named Tectonicon* (1556) has already been referred to, was described by Fuller in his *Worthies* as 'the best Architect in that age, for all manner of buildings, for conveniency, pleasure, state, strength, being excellent at fortifications'. None has been identified; but his son Thomas was involved with the fortification of Dover harbour, as adviser and surveyor, from 1581 to 1584, and some drawings by him survive.[150]

In the 1570s John Osborne, probably a young Cambridge graduate, entered the service of Sir Nicholas Bacon. Bacon employed him as a draughtsman on designs for Stiffkey Hall in Norfolk (1576–7) and for the porch of his intended new chapel for Corpus Christi College, Cambridge (1579). His design for this survives, adorned

executed and he himself died young. In 1582–3 Sir George Gower, Elizabeth's Serjeant Painter, filled three courtyards of Greenwich with, apparently, *trompe-l'œil* decorations of 'Cornisses, Architraves, gable endes, porches, dores, Balasters, Railles, Peristalles and boultelles'. In the 1590s and later John Balechouse, a French painter, was in charge of the building operations at Hardwick. In 1611 Robert Peake, one of the most gifted of Elizabethan and Jacobean portraitpainters, published an English translation of Serlio's *Architecture*. William Cavell, 'Lymner', who had worked in the Guildhall at Bath in 1627, made an elaborate design for an altarpiece in Gothic style for Exeter cathedral, which was erected in 1638–9. Edward Pierce (or Pearce), senior, was described as 'A good History and Landskip Painter, in the reign of King charles the First and II. He also drew Architecture, Perspective, etc. and was much esteem'd in his time.' In 1640 he published a book of very capable designs for friezes. But in general painters confined them-

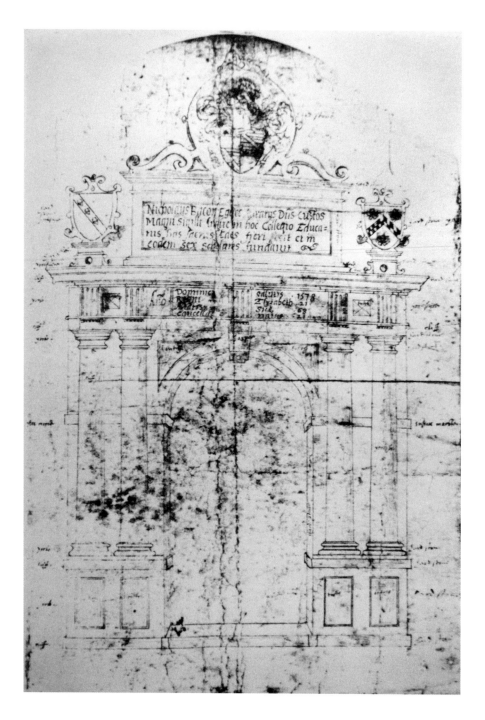

46 Design, probably by John Osborne, for the porch of the chapel of Corpus Christi College, Cambridge, 1579.

(More will be said about these remarkable designs in chapter 6.) It would be satisfying if the two John Osbornes were the same person, but the evidence is against it.[151]

Among clergymen, the Catholic priest Hugh Hall worked on garden designs in the 1560s and 1570s for Sir Christopher Hatton, who was said to favour Catholics, and for Lord Burghley, who did not favour them at all. The manuscript of 'Mr Halles a priestes discourse of gardening applied to a spiritual understanding' is in the British Library, and includes two simple garden designs and drawings of garden instruments, with spiritual interpretations attached.[152] The Protestant clergyman John Layfield, described as 'skilled in architecture', worked on the King James Bible, and advised on the translation of the passages on the Tabernacle and Temple in Jerusalem; he was probably involved in planning the circular almshouses at Beamsley in Yorkshire, erected in 1593 by Margaret Clifford, Countess of Cumberland, whose spiritual adviser he was.[153] Another Catholic priest, George Gage, who travelled in Italy and was painted there by Van Dyck, was described as 'the Architect of Tart-Hall', the idiosyncratic but not very Italianate house built by Alethea, Countess of Arundel, in St James's Park in London, *circa* 1636–9.[154]

Sir Walter Ralegh's half-brother, Adrian Gilbert, alchemist and astrologer, lived at Ralegh's country estate of Sherborne Castle in Dorset, in the 1590s, supervising the new buildings and laying out the gardens. He constructed a watercourse in Lord Burghley's garden at Theobalds, and later became one of the 'learned and ingeniose persons' who made Wilton House what John Aubrey called 'a college' under the Countess of Pembroke; again according to Aubrey, he 'made the curious wall about Rowlington-parke' next to Wilton.[155] Arthur Gregory, born at Lyme Regis in the 1550s, was a skilled cryptographer, made musical instruments, contrived fire ships, and was skilled at 'plotting, surveying, architec-

with some elegant humanist script, which shows his education (Fig. 46). At the turn of the century a John Osborne, who held the important post of Lord Treasurer's Remembrancer, installed a Serlian classical room, inspired by the Pantheon, in Chicksands Priory in Bedfordshire. About 1609 he made surviving drawings for a classical portico in the garden of Salisbury House in the Strand.

ture or what else' (all this according to Fuller's *Worthies*). He made an unexecuted plot for a fort near Harwich, and was responsible for the remodelling of Upnor Castle, Kent, in the years 1599–1601. When Robert Adams, Surveyor of the Works, died in 1596 Gregory unsuccessfully petitioned Burghley for the job. His non-artificer background was somewhat similar to Adams's; but in the end the Surveyorship was given to a long-established artificer, William Spicer.[156]

Richard Haydocke, Fellow of New College, Oxford, engraver and physician, published his translation of Giovanni Lomazzo's *Trattato dell'arte della pittura, scultura et architettura* in 1598; in 1601 he was to present his copies of Lomazzo in the Italian, Vasari and Serlio to the Bodleian.[157] Around 1615 Francis Bacon employed the elder William Dobson, Master of the Alienation Office and father of William Dobson, the painter, to assist him in designing and building his ingenious lodge at Verulam.[158] This miscellaneous collection can end with the Dutchman Balthazar Gerbier (1592–1663), 'courtier, diplomatist, miniature painter and architect', as Colvin's *Dictionary* puts it, whose work for the Duke of Buckingham in the 1620s included architectural work at York House in the Strand and New Hall in Essex.

The last, but not the least interesting, group, are the owners themselves. How many of them were capable of making designs for buildings?

Whether a gentleman could respectably be a painter was a matter of controversy. Aristotle commended the art and Baldassare Castiglione made it one of the accomplishments of his courtier; Sir Thomas Hoby, who translated Castiglione, can be presumed to have agreed with him. His brother-in-law, Sir Henry Killigrew, was himself an amateur painter, hopefully described as 'a Durer for proportion . . . an Angelo for his happy fancy, and an Holbein for oyl works'.[159] But John Stow wrote of the art in 1592: 'sure I am, it is now accounted base and mechanicall, and a more mestier of an artificer, and handy craftsman.

Insomuch as fewe or no Gentleman or generous and liberall person will adventure the practising this art.'[160]

On the other hand, to make plots for buildings was acceptable, perhaps because it could be seen as an offshoot of geometry, which was a liberal art – or because it was connected with the science of fortification, which was a fashionable interest for a gentleman.

In 1580 Philip Sidney, giving his friend Sir Edward Denny a suggested timetable and reading list, wrote: 'your books of the art of soldiery must have another hour, but before you go to them you should do well to use your hands in drawing of a plot, and practice of arithmetic'. In 1598 another friend of Sidney's, Peregrine Bertie, Lord Willoughby d'Eresby, newly arrived as Governor of Berwick, used his hands in just such a way and drew a bird's-eye view and a 'plot' to show what needed to be done to the town's fortifications: the respectable results can still be seen in The National Archives.[161]

In 1560 Thomas Wilson, in his *Arte of Rhetorique*, had treated of both painting and drawing as acceptable, when describing ways of praising a noble personage: 'Againe, I may commend him for playing at weapons, for running upon a great horse, for charging his staffe at the Tilt, for vaulting, for playing upon instruments, yea and for painting, or drawing of a Plat; as in old time noble Princes much delighted therein.'[162]

There is little evidence as to how many gentlemen acquired drawing skills; one would guess not very many. A distinction needs to be made between devising and plotting. Devising meant having an idea; plotting involved drawing it out. The two activities could be split between two people, often an employer and an artificer. The combination is already made clear in the case of Henry VIII in 1513: 'The King signed the platte that he will have of his chapel, which is the platte that was made according to his first device.' There are other examples of his signing platts, but none

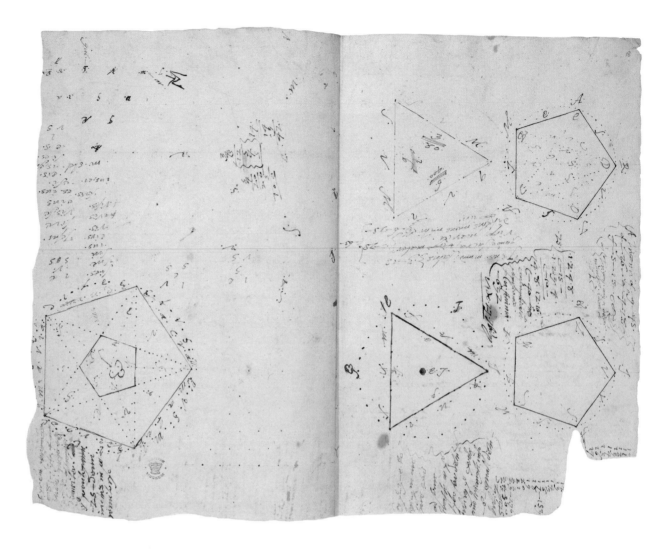

of his making them; but William Harrison could write in 1577 of his palaces 'such as he erected after his owne devise (for he was nothing inferiour in this trade to Adrian the Emperor and Justinian the law-giver)'.[163]

When in 1559 a 'new piece of building at Longleat' was 'to be erected acording to a platt thereof made and signed by the said Sir John Thynne and Willm Spicer', and when, about 1570, Lord Hertford asked Thynne to send 'the platt of my howse devised by you and O. Lovell', one can be fairly confident that the 'platts' were actually drawn by the two masons, Spicer and Lovell. But Thynne does not always seem to have relied on others for drawings; in his will, made in 1580, he orders a tomb to be built for him and his wife 'accordynge to A plott thereof made and signed

with my owne hande', with no mention of collaboration with an artificer.[164] And around 1612 Sir John Strode wrote of his new house at Chantmarle in Dorset: 'Gabriel Moore, my surveyor . . . had of me 20s monthly, with his dyet, for his paines only to survey and direct the building to the forme I conceived and plotted it.'[165]

Two features might seem to encourage an owner in the making of architectural drawings: the ownership of architectural or related books and engravings, and the ownership of drawing instruments. The evidence for both together is usually lacking, but can never be precluded. The largest known collections of architectural books in Elizabethan and Jacobean England belonged to Sir Francis Willoughby, Sir Thomas Tresham, Henry Percy, 9th Earl of Northumberland, Sir

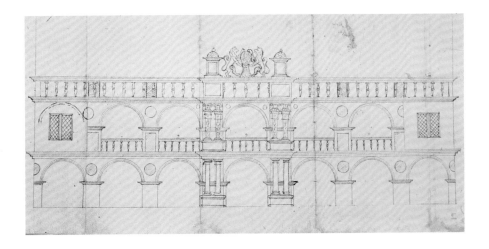

48 and 49 Designs, probably of the 1570s, for (*top*) Theobalds House, Hertfordshire (Hatfield, CP 143/42), and the north front of Burghley House, Lincolnshire. Both might be drawn by Lord Burghley himself.

Thomas Knyvett and Sir Robert Cecil (based on books inherited from his father). To this list could perhaps be added Sir William Pickering, on the strength of 'my papers of Antiquities that are pasted together of the monuments of Rome and other places', probably collected by him when he was travelling in Italy and Germany in 1554–5. Pickering also owned a 'library', of which, unfortunately, no inventory survives.[166]

When Tresham was imprisoned, as a Catholic, at Ely in or around 1590 he had his room embellished with elaborate symbolic decorations, and his many pages of explanation of these are illustrated with diagrams that show that he could at least make simple drawings of geometrical figures and circles, and must have owned compasses (Fig. 47). Indeed, a compass and square are among the many objects shown in the remarkable engraved portrait of him, made in 1585 (Fig.

281).[167] For Pickering's drawing skills there is implicit evidence, for when he died in 1574, he bequathed to his friend Lord Burghley, whom he named the supervisor of his will, 'a case of my best compasses and Sesers Bridge [*sic*] and any soche other instrument as shall best please his Lordshippe to like of'.[168]

In 1591 Burghley wrote to Sir William More of Loseley: 'Sir, this other daie my being at Guildford, when I viewed the Priorie theare, I made a rude tricke thereof, in a manner of a platt with mine owne hand, at wcvh time a servant of yors or Mr Wolleis being present, and being a mason, as I remember, he offered him to make the same more parfitlie.' Burghley could draw a platt then, however 'rude'. Two crudish little drawings for windows, one endorsed in Burghley's distinctive Italian hand as 'a pattern for the wydd of the great chamber', have been supposed to be examples of his capabilities.[169] But Pickering's legacy suggests that already by 1574 he either had more advanced drawing skills or was hoping to acquire them.

There are in fact three other, more elaborate, drawings that can be tentatively attributed to him: an elevation of the gallery on the inner side of the first court at Theobalds, inscribed by Burghley 'Inward side of my gate-house. voyd' (Fig. 48); an elevation of the arcaded wing built out into the garden at Theobalds, endorsed by him 'upright of the gallery garden', with copious annotations in his hand; and an elevation of the north front of Burghley (Fig. 49), not quite as built, without inscription.[170]

One reason for attributing these drawings to Burghley is because they are so bad. It is scarcely conceivable that officers of the Works such as Hawthorne and Symonds, with their organisation's traditions and standards of draughtsmanship, could have produced drawings of such low quality for the most powerful man in England. But, as drawings by Burghley himself, to show what he wanted, and to be given to artificers to be drawn up 'more parfitlie', they make sense.

Sir Thomas Smith was another member of this group of patrons with drawing skills. John Strype in his late seventeenth-century life of him describes a letter that he wrote in 1572 to Sir Francis Walsingham, then in France,

to procure him ... a case of mathematical instruments, directing him to the place where they were sold, that is, at the palace in Paris. He meant that it should contain two compasses or three, a square, a pen of metal, and other things. He had two already; but he was minded to have another of the biggest size, with the case a foot long.

This sounds like the large-size compasses being held by Ralph Simons in his Cambridge portrait. Walsingham sent him a case, but it contained far more instruments than he expected – perhaps something approaching Pomodero's sixteen, referred to earlier. 'Smith himself understood not them all, nor looked for so many, nor of that sort. But this was proper employment for him; and at his leisure he intended to find out the property and use of them.'[171]

Smith certainly made drawings of some kind for his seminal house, Hill Hall in Essex (see p. 177 below). But he made them in collaboration with his carpenter-surveyor Richard Kirby; in his will he refers to 'the plott and disigne which I made by Richard Kirbies advice' and appointed him to be 'the cheefe Architect overseer of pfecting my house according to the plott'.[172]

In the early seventeenth century Lord Burghley's son Robert called himself 'a good Architectour', and his contemporary Sir Charles Cavendish (Bess of Hardwick's second son) was called a 'good architect' by his son William in 1659,[173] but although there is ample evidence of the interest that both of them took in architecture, no reference has come to light of their making drawings, though the possibility cannot be ruled out. The most explicit reference by Charles Cavendish suggests the distinction between devising and plotting already discussed. In 1607, when Cecil was collecting ideas for his intended new house at Hatfield, Cavendish sent him a 'plat', with accompanying explanation, by way of his brother-in-law Gilbert Talbot, Earl of Shrewsbury. He had clearly not drawn this himself, however, for he apologises for 'something mistaken by the drawer in my absence'.[174] The 'drawer' was likely to have been either Robert or John Smythson. On the other hand, there is one drawing in the Smythson collection that one could conceive of as being by Charles. It is one of a pair, related to the vanished Cavendish house at Oldcotes in Derbyshire, but not as built. A rather roughly drawn and scarcely worked out (no windows or fireplaces shown, etc.) but ingenious four-way geometrical plan (Fig. 51), the style of draughtsmanship of which does not relate to drawings by either of the Smythsons, has had its curves translated into right angles and been turned into a realisable building, in an exquisitely drawn elevation (Fig. 50). The elevation is certainly by Robert Smythson; the plan could be by Charles Cavendish.[175]

The section can end with two possible architect earls, Henry Howard, 1st Earl of Northampton, and Henry Percy, 9th Earl of Northumberland. Of these, Henry Howard, younger son of the poet Earl of Surrey, was much the oldest, but the disgrace and execution of his elder brother, the 4th Duke of Norfolk, in 1572 blasted the family fortunes, and he had little if any money to spend on building during the reign of Elizabeth, who disliked and distrusted him. She had good reason for doing so, for this 'sinister bachelor don', as he has been called, was as treacherous as he was clever, and through Elizabeth's reign was conducting a secret correspondence with both Mary, Queen of Scots and her son, James, and drawing an equally secret salary from the King of Spain. When Elizabeth died, his intrigues paid off, and he was largely responsible for bringing the Howard family back into power and favour under James I. His nephew Thomas Howard

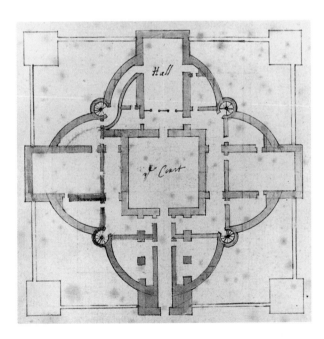

was created Earl of Suffolk in 1603, he himself
Earl of Northampton in 1604, and the huge ducal
estates, confiscated in 1572, were largely divided
between them. Lord Suffolk's gigantic house at
Audley End and Lord Northampton's grand
London mansion, later Northumberland House,
overlooking the river at the west end of the
Strand, were the result.

Northampton's claim to be an 'architect' rests
entirely on one statement, made in 1650, that 'he
assisted his nephew, the Earl of Suffolk, by his
designing and large contribution to that excellent
Fabrick, Audley-End'. The statement was made
soon enough after the event to be worth taking
seriously; and it is also just worth wondering
whether a reference to a visit by James I to his new
banqueting house in Whitehall in 1607 could
refer to Northampton (if not, to whom else?):
'when he came into it he could scarce see by

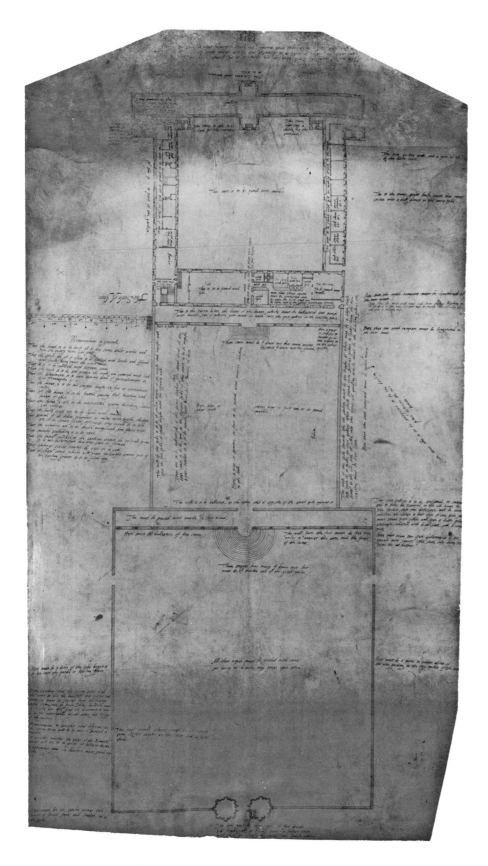

reason of certaine pillars which are sett up before the windowes and he is nothing pleased with his Ld Architect for that device'.[176]

The Earl of Northumberland's interest in architecture is better documented. 'The Wizard Earl' is known more for his interest in astrology and astronomy than in architecture, and for his sixteen years imprisonment in the Tower of London, with three tame scientists in attendance. But he took architecture seriously; he built up one of the best architectural libraries of his time, and collected room measurements from houses all over England before beginning to remodel Syon House in Middlesex in the years 1604–6. When in the Tower he consoled himself by getting out designs for an enormous new house (never to be built) at Petworth; a photograph of the plan survives (Fig. 52), covered by his copious annotations, and very possibly also drawn by him.[177]

Out of this diverse pattern of clients, artificers professionals and amateurs, the Elizabethan and Jacobean buildings emerged. The ways in which they did so could vary greatly. Anyone planning to build had first to collect a team of artificers, and put someone in charge as 'surveyor' of them, either one of the artificers or one of his own household. But then how to decide what form the building was to take? A 'platt' and possibly an 'upright' could be obtained from outside, picked up on a visit to London, perhaps, from an artificer with a reputation like Robert Stickells, or a non-artificer like John Thorpe; or alternatively from a local man, like Robert Smythson living at Wollaton or Walter Hancock living at Church Stretton. The provider might never come to the building site. Alternatively, one or more of the artificers on site might have drawing skills, or might simply be sent to a neighbouring building and be told to copy it. But elements of a building – the roofs, the panelling, the hall screen, the chimneypieces, the staircases – were very probably designed by the craftsmen who executed them, and these may not have been part of the main building team but have been brought in from outside just for the one job. These craftsmen might have drawing skills, and their own books or engravings, from which to get ideas, or the client might have his own books, to show them and to tell them 'copy that'. Judging from results, chimneypiece, panelling and plasterwork in a room were often designed separately, by separate artificers, with no concern about producing an integrated whole.

Examples of many different approaches will occur in the course of this book. So will examples of clients or artificers with such enthusiasm for architecture or outstanding capabilities that they, singly or in partnership, were able to impose their personality on entire buildings, or the entire decoration of individual rooms. There was nothing especially new about this: it was one possible situation among many, and had existed, if not very often, since medieval times. But a, for England, new word began to be attached to it: 'architect'.

The Architect

In 1563 John Shute, described as 'paynter and architect', published his *The First and Chief Groundes of Architecture*. This is the first known appearance of 'architect' as an English word; the consciousness of pioneering was perhaps the reason why Shute (unlike Serlio, Palladio and Philibert de l'Orme) displayed the description on his title page.

In his text Shute writes both about architecture and the qualities necessary to an architect. Architecture he defines as 'the arte and trayde to rayse up and make excellent edifices and buildinges'. He goes on to say:

suche is the amplitude and largnes (I may well say perfection) of this facultie, that without sum acquaintaunce with many other artes ye shall not enter into ye depe secretes: for it hath

a natural societie and as it were by a sertaine kinred and affinitie is knit unto all the Mathematicalles which sciences and knowledges are frendes and a mayntayner of divers rationall artes: so that without a meane acquaintance or understanding in them neyther paynters, masons, Goldsmythes, embroderers, Carvers, Joyners, Glassyers, Gravers, in all maner of metalles and divers others moe can obtayne anye worthy praise at all.[178]

In his section 'What the office and Duetie is of hym that wyll be a Perfecte Architecte or Mayster of buyldings', he lists the various 'sciences and knowledges' that it is necessary to have. He derives his list, like many writers who preceded him, from the celebrated first chapter of the first book of Vitruvius's *Ten Books of Architecture*. Vitruvius's list was again paraphrased in 1570 in John Dee's preface to Billingsley's translation of Euclid:

an Architect (sayth he) ought to understand languages, to be skilfull of Painting, well instructed in Geometrie, not ignorant of Perspective, furnished with Arithmetike, have knowledge of many histories and, diligently have heard Philosophers, have skill of Musike, not ignorant of Physike, know the answeres of Lawyers, and have Astronomie, and the courses Coelestiall, in good knowledge.[179]

Dee, unlike Shute, does not mention Vitruvius's qualification of this formidable list of skills, that 'although he be not parfaict in them or every of them, yet he should have some knowlaig in them'. And neither of them mentions the statement with which he starts his treatise: an architect should be skilled as an artificer as well as intellectually accomplished ('opera ea nascitur et fabrica et ratiocinatione'). According to Vitruvius, an architect who relies on manual skills without education can never acquire authority; and one who relies on letters and reason alone is pursuing the

52 (*facing page*) Unexecuted plan for Petworth, Sussex, annotated by Henry Percy, 9th Earl of Northumberland, and probably drawn by him. From a photograph of a lost original.

shadow, not the substance: 'umbram non rem per-secuti videntur'.[180] This aspect of Vitruvius was quietly dropped in the Renaissance, and scarcely emerged again before Arts and Crafts days. The most that Shute and Dee can allow for is that an artificer can improve himself by acquiring the intellectual equipment needed to raise himself to the level of an architect.

Dee, again unlike Shute, moves on from Vitruvius to the Renaissance theorist Leon Battista Alberti. Alberti thought that Vitruvius's list of necessary qualities was ridiculous.[181] Dee does not reveal this; but he treats at some length Alberti's own definition of the necessary qualities. Alberti saw the essence of an architect as the ability to conceive an entire building in the abstract and embody and work out his concept by drawing it in lines and angles:

> . . . I ought to expresse, what man I would have to be allowed an Architect. For, I will not bryng in place a Carpenter: as though you might Compare him to the Chief Masters of other Artes. For the hand of the Carpenter, is the Architectes Instrument. But I will appoint the Architect to be that man, who hath the skill . . . both in Minde and Imagination to determine: and also in worke to finish . . . The whole Feate of Architecture, in buildyng, consisteth in Lineamentes, and in Framyng . . . And it is the property of Lineamentes, to prescribe unto buildynges, and every part of them, an apt place and certaine number: a worthy maner, and a semely order . . . Lineamente, shalbe the certaine and constant prescribyng, conceived in mynde: made in lines and angles: and finished with a learned mynde and wyt.[182]

'We thanke you Master Baptist', writes Dee, 'that you have so aptly brought your Arte, and phrase thereof, to have some Mathematicall perfection: by certaine order, number, forme, figure, and Symmetrie mentall: all naturall and sensible stuffe set apart.' And he goes on to cite and expand on Plato: 'Plato affirmeth, the Architect to be Master over all, that make any worke. WherUpon, he is neither Smith, nor Builder: nor separaely, any Artificer: but the Hed, the Provost, the Director, and Judge of all Artificiall workes, and all Artificers.'[183]

Alberti was heavily influenced by Plato; and the influence of Plato in Elizabethan England was considerable. For a Platonist not only was there an idea behind every building, which was quite independent of the materials of which it was made, but this mental idea was also independent of, and more important than, the material building. What Dee called the 'mentall' attributes of 'number, forme, figure' were distinct from 'natural and sensible stuffe'. A few years later Henry Wotton was to expand on this. The architect's 'glory' is to conceive an idea, and make 'the Form which is the nobler part . . . triumph over the matter'.[184]

Building, in fact, was a matter of conceiving or 'devising', leading to drawing or 'plotting', and then to making. Devising was 'mentall', making was 'material'. Drawing was the link between the two. Devising and drawing went together as the activities of an architect, but devising was the superior of the two; it was perhaps because of this that a man who devised for another to draw could be called an architect, as may have been the case with Robert Cecil and Charles Cavendish.

But in terms of the spread of the word 'architect', neither Shute nor Dee had much apparent effect. While the term proliferated in the Low Countries from at least the 1540s, only three or four English uses of the word have been identified in the rest of the century. When Sir Thomas Smith, in his will in 1576, appointed Richard Kirby to be the 'cheefe Architecte overseer and Mr of my workes for the pfecting of my howse', he seems to be using the word in a Vitruvian sense, but since he owned five copies of Vitruvius he was in no need of outside influence.[185] In 1581 John Baret, in his Latin, Greek, French and

53 A triumphal arch designed by Stephen Harrison, called 'Joyner and Architect', in 1603 for the state entry of James I into the City of London which, owing to the plague, was delayed until 1604.

the word (and that metaphorically). It occurs in *Titus Andronicus* (*circa* 1594):

> Behold this child
> Of this was Tamora delivered
> The issue of an irreligious Moor
> Chief architect and plotter of these woes.

If, as seems likely, Shakespeare was not using 'plotter' in the usual modern sense, but in a contemporary sense of 'maker of plottes' (i.e., drawings), he was giving the word 'architect' a sense not so far removed from Alberti's.

Even if the word 'architect' was slow in coming into use, both Shute and Dee must have been read and appreciated by appreciable numbers of people, artificers included. The concept of a building all designed by one person, and of that one person not necessarily being an artificer and indeed having a range of intellectual equipment beyond the powers of most artificers, may have encouraged the appointment of non-artificer Surveyors of the Royal Works, from Robert Adams onward. Certainly, when Robert Stickells, a freemason by training, put in for promotion in the queen's service about 1599, he emphasised his range of non-manual skills, and asked to be tested 'in the mathematicall sciences, or in the rules of architecture, of shipbuilding, or of fortifying, house-building, or any such ingenious causes'.[187] He still did not get his promotion. But Dee's quotations from Alberti and Plato must also have inspired other ambitious artificers to acquire skills and capabilities in order to lift themselves into a superior rank, and escape from the stigma of being mere 'mechanics'. Robert Smythson, for instance, almost certainly had access to both Shute and Dee in the library of his employer Francis Willoughby at Wollaton. One can surmise how much Dee's quotation from Plato would have meant to him: 'neither Smith nor Builder; not separately any artificer: but the Hed, the Provost, the Director, and Judge of all artificiall werkes, and all Artificers'. And Wol-

English dictionary, does not include 'architect' as an English word. He translates the Latin, French and Greek *Architectus*, *Architector* and *Architecton* as 'a deviser in building', the 'contriver of any work' and 'master of the works', in a sense that follows Vitruvius, but also in a more limited sense, as 'maister mason', 'maister carpenter' or 'principall overseer'.[186] It is not clear what the land-surveyor John Walker meant by calling himself 'Architector' in 1584 and adjacent years. Perhaps most revealing is Shakespeare, in his one use of

laton, and Smythson's relationship to it, embodies Alberti's ideas as much as any Elizabethan building.

In the forty years after 1600 the use of the term 'architect' in England became commoner, with at least nineteen people so describing themselves, or being so described, as opposed to three in the forty preceding years. Two of these were visiting foreigners: the Italian Constantino de' Servi, called 'architect to our late Prince Henry' in 1614, and Isaac de Caux, called 'the French architect' in 1638. Two were gentlemen: Robert Cecil, calling himself 'a good architectour' in 1602, and the mysterious 'my lord architect' in 1607. One, Moses Glover, was a painter-stainer by training, but in 1635 signed as 'Moses Glover, architect' the huge map of the Hundred of Isleworth, which hangs today at Syon.[188]

Fourteen of the nineteen were artificers. Of these, the description of Stephen Harrison, who published a book of illustrations of the triumphal arches erected for the entry of James I to London in 1603 (Fig. 53), is the most explicit: he is called 'Joyner and Architect' on the title page, and the text describes how 250 artificers were employed on constructing the arches 'over whom Stephen Harrison, Joyner, was appointed chief; who was the sole inventor of the Architecture, and from whom all directions, for so much as belonged to Carving, Joining, Molding and all other works in

those five Pageants of the Citie (Paynting excepted) were set down'.[189]

Seven artificers are described as 'architectus', 'architecter', 'architector' or 'architect' on their monuments, in their wills or in parish registers: John Bentley (d. 1613), Robert Smythson (d. 1614), John Scampion (d. ?1622), Thomas Holt (d. 1624), Robert Leminge (d. 1628), John Smythson (d. 1634) and Matthew Morgan (d. 1635). In 1631 Robert Stickells was called 'the excedllent Artichect of our time' in Stowe's *Chronicles*.[190] The use of the term suggests more than the ownership of drawing skills, but perhaps not much more. The term was still mainly a status symbol, a claim that the man who carried it was a level above an artificer.

None the less, in the course of the early seventeenth century the word 'architect', by becoming current, had, as often happens when a new word appears, given substance to something that was not entirely new, but had not been named in England before: the concept of a man who could conceive and get executed an entire building, down to the details; the concept of someone whose intellectual skills lifted him above artificer status, even if he might be an artificer by origin. Once the word was there, more people were going to try to live up to it; but the idea of an independent profession of being an architect was a long way into the future.

54 Richard Wyatt and his family, as redrawn from the brass in the chapel of the almshouses at Godalming, Surrey, which he endowed.

Chapter 2

Catering

for a

Lifestyle

The Elizabethan house – in the same way as the early Tudor house and the medieval house – was planned round the stomach. The preparation of meals, the serving of meals, the eating of meals, provided the framework of the life lived in them, and whatever there was of household ritual – very considerable in the larger houses.[1]

Four rooms served as the pivots: the kitchen, the hall, the great chamber and the parlour. The kitchen and hall were the original couple, going back to the days when the whole household ate in the hall, with the family and principal guests on the raised dais at one end of it. By the end of the fifteenth century, in all the larger houses, the family had ceased to eat there except on special and rare occasions. They ate in a room usually situated on the first floor, known as the great chamber, or in a room on the ground floor, known as the parlour. The great chamber was a room for state, the parlour for informality. The head of a great household – a peer, normally – ate in state most days. The laying of his table and the bringing up of his food from the kitchen to the great chamber was a ceremony. It came in procession from the kitchen, went through the hall, where everyone stood up in its honour, and was carried up flights of stairs, the more handsome and spacious the better, to the great chamber on the first floor.

The numbers to be fed varied considerably. An earl living in style was likely to have around 100 or more of his own household sitting down to meals, exclusive of himself and his family. The Earl of Derby, famous for the splendour of his lifestyle, had around 130 in 1587; the Earl of Dorset had 111 in 1613. The Earl of Huntington was relatively modest, with 75 in 1564. Lord Berkeley, only a baron but an ostentatious one, had a household of approximately 130 before 1560; he got into financial difficulties and had to reduce it to around 90 in 1560 and to 70 in 1574. 'Bess of Hardwick', Countess of Shrewsbury, only a widow but a formidably rich one, had a household of around 65 at Hardwick in 1598: the servants of her granddaughter, Arbella Stuart, who lived with her, and her eldest son, William, who was often in residence at Hardwick, probably lifted it towards 90; this was the size recommended early in the seventeenth century by the unidentified 'R. B.' in his *Some Rules and Orders for the Government of the House of an Earle*.

The numbers being fed could be greatly increased by visitors. There were always a substantial number of these coming and going in a big household, of all ranks and coming for business or pleasure. An earl visiting another earl, for instance, could arrive with an entourage of at least twenty people, and all would be fed. And on great occasions – weddings and funerals, or Christmas festivities – the numbers swelled. At the funeral of the Earl of Shrewsbury in 1560, 320 'messes' – that is, portions of food that could feed more than one person – were served indiscriminately 'to all manner of people who seemed honest'.

A common arrangement in the hall was to have a high table on a dais at one end, for the steward and upper servants, and three or more long tables down below it, probably at right angles to the dais, as in the halls of Oxford and Cambridge colleges or Inns of Court today. Sometimes, later on in the sixteenth century, there was no high table, and the upper servants ate in the parlour. In the great chamber there could be two tables, one more prestigious than the other; in one early example they were referred to as 'the lord's table' and 'the knights' table'. Guests were seated at one or other of these, or on the high table or down in the body of the hall, according to rank, or to the favour or disfavour that the lord or his steward wished to show them. Much resentment or gratification could be evoked in this way.

Lesser rooms collected round the main ones. The kitchen (Fig. 56) had its pantry, for baking, its scullery, for washing up, its dry and wet larders, for storing different types of food, and a 'surveying' or 'serving' place, into which food was passed

55   A banquet and masque given by Sir Henry Unton (?1557–1596). Detail from a picture showing scenes in his life.

62

57 and 58   Two closets, the inner sanctums of their owners: (*right*) at Walter Ralegh's Sherborne Lodge (today Castle), Dorset, *c.*1600; (*far right*) at Holcombe Court, Devon, *c.*1570.

56 (*facing page*)   The mid-sixeenth-century kitchen, Burghley House, Lincolnshire.

through a hatch from the kitchen to the waiters waiting to carry it to the hall, parlour or great chamber. The hall had its pantry, for storing and cleaning plate, and its buttery, in which beer was served out to the servants, brought up by a stair going down from it to the beer cellar in the basement. Lodgings for family, servants and guests congregated round the great chamber and parlour, or round the courtyard, if there was one, or up under the roof. Lodgings varied from one to three rooms. The owner and the most important guests were likely to have a bedchamber, an inner chamber or closet for prayer or study (Figs 57, 58), and a withdrawing chamber for private meals and reception. People of some standing had two rooms – a bedchamber and an inner chamber. Lesser people and upper servants had one chamber only; lower servants or unimportant guests were put in two or more to a chamber.

Although the basic function of the hall, the great chamber and the parlour was eating, it was by no means the only one. There was no feeling that a room should be kept for one class or one use. The hall was the room where the servants ate, but also where they sat around in the intervals between meals, and where inferior people who had come on business sat and waited. It was the entrance hall through which visitors of all ranks passed on their way to the rooms beyond it. It could also be used for the putting on of plays or masques; the servants would then be cleared out or kept in the background, and the gentry, nobility, and even the monarch, took their place. In 1613, when Queen Anne of Denmark was entertained with a masque in the hall of Caversham House in Berkshire, she sat in her chair of state with 'many Lords and Ladies' on the dais around her, and the sides of the hall were built up with

59, 60 and 61 Three types of hall: (*facing page*) two-storey with open timber roof, at Deene, Northants, early 1570s; (*above left*) two-storey with flat ceiling, at Heslington Hall, York, *c.*1565; (*above right*) single-storey, at Montacute House, Somerset, *c.*1600.

scaffolding to provide seating for 'beholders of worth'.[2]

Because of its long-established status, its function as the entry to the house and its occasional use for grand functions, the hall remained a dignified and well-appointed room. The traditional entry to it by way of a screen passage was the normal one well into the seventeenth century, and the screens and chimneypiece were always handsome and sometimes elaborate. But, in terms of importance, in decoration as well as status, it was steadily losing out to the great chamber. Single-storey halls became more and more common (Fig. 61); under James I only a few two-storey ones were built, and these were in the greatest houses, as at Hatfield and Audley End; Aston Hall, Warwickshire (1618), compromised with one and a half storeys.

As early as the 1560s the two-storey halls at Holcombe Court in Devon and Heslington Hall in Yorkshire (Fig. 60) had flat ceilings, with another storey over them, instead of the gabled open-timber roofs of the traditional halls (Fig. 59). Such flat-ceilinged two-storey halls became common; the great hall at Burghley (1578) was perhaps the last completely new hall in a private house (as opposed to a hall in a college or Inn of Court) to be given its own independent roof (Fig. 210). A hall with a storey of rooms above it could of course no longer be heated with the traditional open hearth, with a louvre in the roof above for smoke. The arrangement continued to be used in Oxford and Cambridge colleges, and in the Inns of Court, as at Trinity College, Cambridge (1604); here and in other colleges the open hearth survived into the early nineteenth century.[3] The hall

62 and 63 Elizabethan interiors as presented in early Victorian lithographs published by Joseph Nash and S. C Hall: (*right*) the great chamber of *c.*1590, once at Boughton Place, Kent; (*facing page*) the parlour of *c.*1590 in one of the round towers of Longford Castle, Wiltshire. The nude goddess was removed from the chimneypiece later in the nineteenth century.

in the Duke of Somerset's Somerset House in London had an open hearth, still shown as in use in Thorpe's early seventeenth-century plan. The arrangement may have continued in a few domestic early Elizabethan great halls, as (possibly) at Deene in Northamptonshire; but it was not found at Theobalds and Burghley, and must have quickly gone out of use.[4]

It was the great chamber that was now the cynosure of the house (Fig. 62). It was hung with tapestries, if its owner could afford them, or otherwise richly panelled; it usually had the most sumptuous chimneypiece in the house, and often a rich plasterwork frieze and ceiling. Apart from being the room where the owner of the house and his or her guests ate in state and ceremony, it could be used in the same way as the hall for the putting on of masques and plays. It was very frequently used for dancing, after the tables had been cleared. When the owner died, he or she was

laid out in state there, for the tenantry and local gentry to come and pay their respects and be refreshed with wine. In the intervals of meals or events it was used by guests as a kind of common room, but the servants attached to the great chamber also sat around in it and played cards or backgammon there when they were not on duty. In 1609 regulations for the Earl of Huntingdon's Ashby-de-la-Zouche laid down that no yeoman was 'to play at cards, tables, or checks' there, 'and that such gentleman waiters as shall play in the afternoon do it at the sideboard'. But at Berkeley Castle around 1570 Lord Berkeley himself used to play at 'tables' (that is, backgammon) with his yeoman servants in the great chamber.[5]

The parlour was less grand than the great chamber (Fig. 63), and never used for formal events. Meals were served in it, but it was also used for games, music, gossip and recreation. In the grandest houses it was more a common room for the

upper servants than a family room, though the family came into it on occasions to mix with the upper servants, who were often related to them. In houses of all sizes the mistress often sat there with her upper women servants, who were as much companions as servants.

Larger houses often had more than one parlour. Especially common was a winter parlour, its use obvious from its name, usually smaller than the main parlour, next or close to the kitchen and often immediately under the family bedrooms in what, in the winter, was kept as the warmest end of the house.

Houses of medium size echoed, in scaled-down form, the pattern of the bigger ones. The men who built them had often seen service in great households and imitated what they saw. Hall, kitchen, great chamber and parlour were the staple elements. Sometimes the hall was scaled down to a single storey in height; sometimes the

great chamber served as the best bedchamber, and eating was confined to the hall and parlour. Withdrawing chamber and gallery could be omitted.

In bigger houses, the most distinctive development in the Elizabethan period was the growth in popularity of the gallery – or long gallery, as such rooms became called, though the term was not used (and then at first only rarely) until the early seventeenth century. Galleries as such were not a new invention.[6] They had appeared in England in the early sixteenth century, perhaps in imitation of comparable rooms in France. They became, in particular, a feature of royal palaces. Some of the royal galleries were very large: the Queen's Gallery at Hampton Court, for instance, built in the years 1533–7, was around 170 feet long and 20 feet broad, and with its lavish glazing and bay windows was a clear prototype of the Elizabethan galleries.[7]

But galleries in most non-royal houses in the mid-sixteenth century were neither all that frequent nor all that large. The gallery at The Vyne in Hampshire, the earliest surviving example (*circa* 1530), is about 85 feet long and 15 feet broad; the gallery of the 1560s above the two-storey hall of Holcombe in Devon is 65 feet long, and its low ceiling makes it a modest and intimate room (Fig. 64).

It may have been Nicholas Bacon's new gallery added to his house at Gorhambury (Fig. 169), perhaps as a result of Queen Elizabeth's visit in 1572, that helped to set off a fashion for grander galleries in non-royal houses.[8] It was a little over 100 feet long, and 20 feet broad, on the first floor over an open loggia, in what was to become a popular combination. It must have been seen by all the crowds of officials and courtiers who attended Elizabeth on her second visit to Gorhambury in 1577. It may have pre-dated Lord Burghley's galleries at Burghley (124 ft) and Theobalds (about 122 ft): Theobalds was ultimately to acquire no less than three of them.

Sir John Thynne's gallery at Longleat, envisaged in the mid-1570s, would have been 160 feet long, but there is some uncertainty as to whether it was ever constructed; if it was, it could have been seen by the entourage of Queen Elizabeth, who visited Longleat on her western progress in 1574. The gallery of Lord Hunsdon's great suburban house at Hackney (demolished as late as the 1950s) was about 150 feet long, and can be dated by the heraldry of its ceiling plasterwork to *circa* 1578–83. On grounds of style and size this is a likely date for Thomas Heneage's superb gallery at Copped Hall in Essex, 174 feet long, 28 feet broad and 24 feet high; it was demolished in the eighteenth century, but its appearance is preserved in drawings (Fig. 66). All these were eclipsed by the Earl of Shrewsbury's gallery of 1585 at Worksop Manor in Nottinghamshire. It was 212 feet long and 36 feet broad, and filled the entire second floor.[9]

There was competition among owners over galleries. In 1607, when Sir George Chaworth visited the great house that the Earl of Dunbar was building at Berwick, Dunbar's servants, who showed it to him, boasted that 'Worksopp gallerye was but a garrat in respect of the gallerye that woold there be'.[10] Dunbar died in 1611, possibly before his house and its gallery had been finished; it was demolished not long after, when the house may still have been a shell. But Worksop was also being eclipsed at much the same time by Lord Suffolk's gallery at Audley End, 220 feet long and 32 feet broad. This marked the culmination of the age of great galleries; in the 1620s James I's adored and all-powerful Duke of Buckingham seems to have been content with a gallery of about 180 feet at Burley-on-the-Hill in Rutland, and by the mid-seventeenth century galleries were going out of fashion.[11]

But from the 1570s till the 1620s every new house of any importance had to have a gallery no less than 100 feet in length and often much longer. When fashion changed, many of these great rooms were to be demolished, as at Audley End, or cut up into smaller rooms, as at Burghley,

64 (facing page, top) The gallery of the 1560s above the two-storey hall at Holcombe Court, Devon.

65 (facing page, bottom) The long disused gallery of c.1605 over the hall at Knole, Kent.

or virtually abandoned, as was the upper gallery at Knole (Fig. 65). The grandest survivor is at Hardwick; it is 166 feet long, 22 feet wide and 26 feet high, and is further increased in width by two great extensions into the towers. The longest survivor is at Montacute, and is 172 feet long.

Galleries had two main functions. They were used for exercise and for hanging pictures, especially portraits. Exercise, for health reasons, was taken seriously: in fine weather it took place along a terrace in the garden, or on the roof, if it was flat; in wet but not too cold weather it could be taken in an open gallery or loggia; in cold or bad weather it was taken under cover in the long gallery. The closed gallery was not infrequently positioned above the open one, and below a roof-walk. Pictures were hung in galleries as an obvious way of filling their often vast spaces; they supplemented the view from the windows as an extra for promenaders to look at. Portraits could be of famous people, especially kings and queens, of family friends, the more influential the better, and of members of the family. In 1609 Lord Howard of Bindon asked Robert Cecil for the gift of his portrait, in order to place it in the gallery at Bindon Abbey in Dorset, which 'I lately made for pictures of sundry of my honourable friends'. Having it, he said, 'will greatly delight me to walk often in that place where I may see so comfortable a sight'.[12]

The Bindon gallery has long since gone; the gallery at Hardwick is still there (Fig. 67). Thanks to the survival of an inventory and letters one knows exactly who was walking in it, and how it was furnished, on the afternoon of 7 January 1603.[13] Its tapestries and over half of the thirty-seven pictures which they surveyed as they walked are still hanging in it, among them portraits of the three walkers, Elizabeth, Countess of Shrewsbury – 'Bess of Hardwick' (Fig. 68) – her eldest son William Cavendish and her granddaughter Arbella Stuart (Fig. 69): the tough octogenarian widow, black dress, huge multiple strings of

pearls, dyed red hair; her son, dutiful, cautious and mean; her clever, neurotic grandchild – three small figures walking up and down in the huge gallery, which must have been icy cold, even if fires were blazing in the two chimneypieces, pausing by the fires to warm themselves, waiting for the arrival of the queen's emissary, Sir Henry Brunker, who was coming from London to look into Arbella's misdeeds – while at the end of the gallery the portrait of the queen herself surveyed her subjects, in one of her amazing dresses, rich with pearls, lace and embroideries of animals and flowers.

The possibility of reconstructing a moment such as this in a surviving room is all too rare.

There is no wealth of descriptions in diaries and letters such as illuminate domestic life from the later seventeenth century onwards. Something can be pieced together from inventories and building accounts. To get an overall feel of life in a grand house one can go, however, to George Whetstone's *Heptameron of Civill Discourses* (1582).[14] This is not a description of something that happened but an imaginary account of a week of celebration and discussions held at Christmas in a great house. It is ostensibly set in Italy, in the house of a 'Signor Philoxenus', and the house party is clearly inspired by Castiglione's *Courtier*, which Hoby's translation had introduced to English readers. But the way of life

68 and 69   Portraits of
Elizabeth, Countess of
Shrewsbury and her
granddaughter, Arbella
Stuart, hanging in the
gallery (*facing page*) of
Hardwick Hall,
Derbyshire.

described by Whetstone, the rooms in which
his events take place, the richly ceremonious
atmosphere that envelops them, is in fact that
of a great English house, and each individual
element can be backed up by references in
English sources.

Whetstone's narrator, having been amazed
by his first sight of the splendour of Signor Philoxenus's house, arrives in front of it, to be greeted
by Signor Philoxenus himself, 'accompanied with
divers Gentlemen of good quallytie'. He is led by
way of the magnificent hall screen into the
'Stately Hall', and on (and probably up) into 'a
faire great chamber richly hung with tapistries:
Ye Roof wherof was Allablaster plaister, embost

wt many curious devises in gold and in sundrie
places in proper colours was ingraved his device,
which was a Holly Tree, full of red Berries, and
in the same a fluttering Mavis fast limed to the
bowes, with this posie in French "Qui me nourit
me destruit".' Here he 'imbraced the salutations
of such a brave troupe of Gentlemen and Gentlewomen as the honour of the householde might
well given envie unto some Princes Court'.

After polite speeches have been made, the narrator is escorted by servants to his lodging 'to be
dispoiled of my riding attyre'. He finds himself in
'a Bed Chamber, so well acomodated with every
necessarie pleasure, as might have served for the
repose of Cupid and his lover Ciches: having a

fayre prospect into a goodly Garden'. From this he goes to join the company at supper, where he is gratified that 'for my place at the Table, I had the pryveledge of a Stranger, set above my degree'.

Philoxenus's sister Aurelia is appointed by him to be the queen of the company; she announces the week's programme and proclaims her laws. Every gentleman has to choose a mistress 'uppon paine to bee turned into the great Hall among the Countrie Trulles ye whole Christmas'. The division of each day is to be as follows: 'the forenoone to be bestowed in the service of God: after dinner two houres to be intertained in civell discourse and disputations; the rest till supper at pleasure and after supper to spend a time in daunsing, masking, or other like pleasures'.

And so the week proceeds. Every morning 'Phoebus golden rayes . . . peared through every small passage into Signor Philoxenus Pallace; and glimering in the young Gentlemens faces wakened them'. Then 'the tinkling of a small bell gave them warning of a sermon' and summoned them to the chapel. While prayers took place 'the tables were covered with a most stately Order, and with the sound of trumpettes were furnished with so many several daintie Dishes, as the Rialtie of the Feaste might have pleased Heliogabalus'. The company was in its 'most sumptuous weedes'; there was 'much pleasant table talke'. Dinner on New Year's Day was especially splendid, for New Year, not Christmas, was the customary day for extra festivity and the giving of presents. So 'the trumpets, drumes and Flutes sounded through every small passage'; the company

> in their most brave and sumptuous araye . . . made the Great Chamber resemble a fayre Garden in Maye, in the imbroderies of whose Garments, Flowers and fancies were so naturally and artifically wrought: some of Pearle, some of golde, some of Bugle, every one according to their humour: More over every Gentlemans head was armed with his Mis-

tresses favour, and every Gentlewomans hart was warmed with her servants affection.

Each day after dinner a 'chosen company', having 'paused a time by the Fire to put their wittes in order', retired with Philoxenus and Queen Aurelia into another room for their two hours of 'discourse and disputation'. On most days this took place in a 'fayre withdrawing chamber'; but once it was held in a 'most delycate Banqueting House'. On another afternoon Queen Aurelia is sick and 'keeps her chamber'; there is no discussion, and Philoxenus takes the narrator into 'a very beautifull Gallerie', where there are pictures of all Christian princes, heathen rulers, learned men and grave magistrates, as well as maps of the world.

After supper and 'a little time bestowed on the hearing of sweete musique', each evening is filled with different forms of entertainment. On the first night 'the Musicke summoned the yonge Gentlemen and Gentlewomen to daunsing for (this night) they expected no other pastime unless it were dicing, carding, or such like unthrifty sports'. On the second night a masque is put on by five gentlemen, who come unexpectedly into the great chamber while the others are dancing, each preceded by a page carrying a torch, wearing their mistress's colours and carrying devices. They present these to Queen Aurelia, choose ladies to dance with, and finally depart: 'which done, the Gentlemen and Gentlewomen began to shrinke out of the great Chamber, as the starres seem to shoote the skie, towardes the Breake of Daye'. On another night a 'mountebank' is brought in to amuse the company with performing snakes; on another an impromptu play is put on.

All these activities take place in the great chamber; but on the last night the 'country trulles' are displaced from the great hall, and the company come into it to enjoy an especially elaborate masque, featuring a 'high mountain' decorated with trees, fruits, little animals and 'an arbour of sweet eglantine' in which Diana sits on a 'stately thron' accompanied by the Nine Muses. The 'monster Envy' then makes an entry, and is killed by Queen Aurelia; Diana rewards her with the gift of her shield, and the Muses descend to crown her with garlands of roses; finally, 'a stately Almain is danced'.

The week's activities are threaded with music. In addition to the trumpets, drums and flutes that sound out to announce the serving of meals, each afternoon's discussion is preceded by the singing of a 'sweet lay' and the masque by a 'consort of sweet musicke'. Some, at least, of the company have their own instruments. The narrator comes in early one morning to find the great chamber, which the evening before had been filled with 'earthly goddesses' and 'attired like a second paradise', desolate and empty except for 'sundry savage beasts, portrayed in the tapestry hangings'. Overcome with melancholy, he takes up his cittern, and to its accompaniment sings a sad song 'to recomfort my throbbing heart'.

The various celebrations and events of this week are paralleled in the many accounts of festivities put on for visits of Queen Elizabeth or the early Stuart monarchs. The eminence of royal guests made it likely that a record would be kept of these visits. But similar events certainly occurred when no royalty was involved. The masque staged at a banquet given by Sir Henry Unton and his wife is shown in the unique strip-cartoon of his life now in the National Portrait Gallery (Fig. 55).[15] As in Whetstone's narrative, Diana is there, with her attendants; so are pages carrying torches; six musicians sitting in a circle provide the 'consort of sweet musique'. Six more musicians are painted in a frieze of the 1580s in the great chamber at Gilling Castle in Yorkshire. A description survives of a masque put on in 1607 in the great chamber of Ashby-de-la-Zouche Castle in Leicestershire, for the visit of the Dowager Countess of Derby to her daughter the Countess of Huntingdon; it is remarkably close to those of Signor Philoxenus, both in its elaborate nature and in the language in which it is described.[16] Directions for a masque centring round the children of the Fane family, put on in or around 1625, probably at Apethorpe in Northamptonshire, describe how '8 little fairies bring in a little bower with the 3 little children, and dance round about them, then the horns shall Winde, which shall scare them away, and Diana with her nymphs shall come and dance . . .'.[17]

It was common enough for great people to employ musicians, either working as such full time or combining music with services as an upper servant, as was the case with Thomas Whythorne, who describes such service in his autobiography.[18] John Maynard, who published a book of airs for viola da gamba, lute and voice in 1611, was probably the son of Sir John Thynne's French mason, Alan Maynard, and had worked in the Thynne household.[19] The Earl of Dorset (d. 1608) left each of his household musicians an annuity of £20 on the grounds that they had 'often given me, after the labors and paynefull travells of the day, much recreation and contentacon with their delightful harmony'.[20] Other servants could have musical skills without being professional musicians – as, very often, had their employers. Four of Bess of Hardwick's upper servants, James Starkey (the chaplain), John Good, Francis Parker and Richard Abrahall, were able to provide celebratory music when she moved into her new house at Hardwick in 1597.[21]

We know of discussions by a 'chosen company' held at Sir Matthew Arundell's Wardour Castle in Wiltshire about 1595, and at Sir George Trenchard's Wolfeton Manor in Dorset in 1593, and in both cases we know who took part.[22] The company at Wardour included Shakespeare's loving patron the Earl of Southampton, and Queen Elizabeth's lively godson Sir John Harrington; a prosaic but interesting result of their discussions was the world's first water-closet. The company at Wolfeton included Sir Walter

Ralegh, and accusations that their discussions were of an atheistic nature were to lead to the sitting of an ecclesiastical court of inquiry, and permanent and probably unjustified damage to Ralegh's reputation.

The Plan

Apart from the efflorescence of the gallery, the standard accommodation of large Elizabethan houses had already been developed in the fifteenth century, and earlier. But the way in which it was arranged changed considerably. There was a move towards greater symmetry, greater height and greater compactness.

The move had been anticipated in medieval and early Tudor architecture, in a small but interesting group of houses that are symmetrically disposed. The series starts with castles, but develops into what Leland called 'houses built castle-wise', in which the castle element, at least in terms

of serious fortification, grew weaker and finally disappeared. The commonest arrangement, pioneered at castles like Harlech and Beaumaris, was based on a rectangular mass, usually but not always built round a courtyard, articulated by external towers, square or round, at the corners and sometimes symmetrically arranged on the intermediate façades. The plan was found both in entire castles and in residential free-standing towers within the castle enclave, as at Tattershall. There were variant plans as well: cross-shaped at Warkworth, hexagonal at Wardour, a circular ring of towers at Queenborough. The aim in all of these, including 'houses built castle-wise', was perhaps to impress, overawe or express status.

Although a symmetry of general massing (never of internal planning) was common to all the group, symmetrical fenestration, except on the entrance façade, was much rarer. Indeed, West Wickham in Kent (see pp. 84–5), built by Sir John Heydon about 1470, was (if Thorpe's plan is to be relied on) perhaps unique: a four-towered building built round a tiny courtyard, a light well only, with four identical façades, including a central door on each façade, no moat, and only a few token arrow-slits.

Outside this group, the pattern of domestic architecture was different. The bigger houses were much more loosely grouped, in free-standing units in earlier centuries, later in continuous ranges round a courtyard, with numerous irregular appendages; symmetry, if in evidence at all, was confined to the entrance façade or a gatehouse. Symmetry in the courtyard was rare enough, but in the early sixteenth century was impressively developed, on three sides at least, at Cowdray in Sussex and at Wolsey's Hampton Court. Both houses had grand symmetrical entrance fronts, but otherwise irregular external façades.

Cowdray follows the traditional way of arranging accommodation in the house of a great man in four ranges round a courtyard, with entry into the court through an archway or prominent gate-

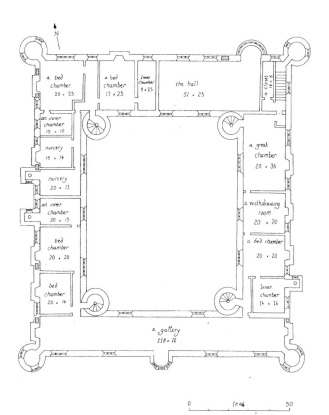

70 and 71 Two courtyard houses: (*right*) re-drawing of a plan made about 1573 for Stiffkey Hall in Norfolk; (*facing page*) the first-floor plan of a house for Lord Sheffield in the Smythson drawings (SM. DWGS 1/18(2)).

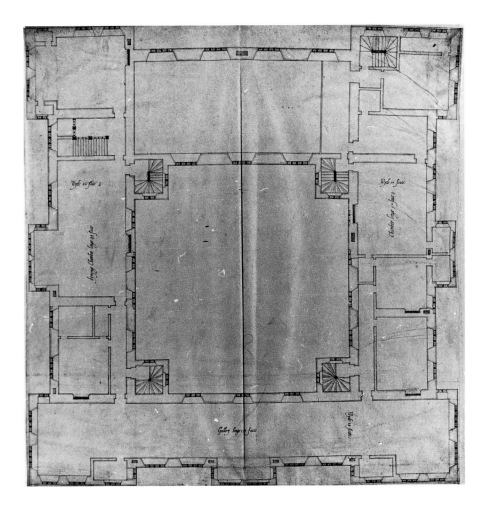

fill the east range of the courtyard and provide the accepted sequence of rooms, great chamber (over parlour), withdrawing room, bedchamber and inner chamber, in that order. The family lodgings are reached more modestly by a newel staircase beyond the screens end of the hall, one of four in turrets in the angles of the courtyard. The owners' bedchamber is in the north-west corner of the house, snugly over the kitchen, with its inner chamber and two nurseries running along the west range beyond it. Further lodgings, for subsidiary family use or less important visitors, are fitted in to either side. East and west ranges are joined by a gallery, filling the south, entrance range. When the house was built, from 1576 onwards, the gallery range was left out, probably for economy, and the east and west ranges slightly curtailed, by omitting the 'withdrawing room'.

The Stiffkey arrangement of family and best lodgings is to be found well before the sixteenth century, and remained common in the Elizabethan period. The gallery filling the entrance range was a specifically Elizabethan feature, of which nine or ten examples are known, not all of them executed (Fig. 71). The earliest of these is in a plan of 1560, for a house projected but never built by Lord Paget at Burton upon Trent.[24]

The arrangement was an alternative to the one, traditional in the grander houses, of having a gatehouse in the centre of the entrance front, with large rooms above the entrance passage and smaller rooms in turrets to either side. The two arrangements could in fact be combined, but combination led to difficulties. At Burghley in 1575 the gallery was driven right through the gatehouse (Fig. 207b), but this meant that the ashlar side walls of the top floor of the gatehouse had to be carried over the void of the gallery – a considerable problem, though not an insurmountable one. But gallery-fronted houses often did without a gatehouse, as at Stiffkey; and in general, even with no gallery, the gatehouse was often omitted, as at Gorhambury, perhaps partly for economy,

house and the hall normally on the opposite side of the courtyard to the entry. The arrangement is found at least from the fifteenth century, and went on into Elizabethan days and beyond. A typical early Elizabethan example is shown in the plan made about 1573 for Stiffkey Hall in Norfolk, a house paid for by Sir Nicholas Bacon but built for his son Nathaniel (Fig. 70). The plan is useful because the rooms are named; but unfortunately it shows the first floor only. From an inventory of 1622–3 we know, however, that on the ground floor the kitchen was in the north-west corner, and that there was a 'great parlour' below the great chamber.[23]

The house is divided into a side for family lodgings and a side for best lodgings, with the hall in between. The principal staircase leads up from the dais end of the hall to the best lodgings. These

72 and 73
Asymmetrical and
symmetrical arrangements
of the hall: (*above*) at
Hoghton Tower,
Lancashire, 1561–5; and
(*facing page*) Kirby Hall,
Northamptonshire.

partly because one was considered too preten-
tious for all but the grander families, partly
through preference for a classically adorned entry
rather than a traditional one. But incorporated
gatehouses with turrets continued to be built well
into the Elizabethan age, as at Chatsworth in
(probably) the 1560s (see Fig. 3) and Toddington
in the 1570s; perhaps the last was at Brereton Hall
in Cheshire, dated 1586 (Fig. 373). Stonyhurst in
Lancashire, built *circa* 1592–5, has a turreted gatehouse on the courtyard side, but, perhaps in the

course of building, it was replaced by a 'Tower of
the Orders' on the entrance front.[25]

These courtyard houses were inward-looking;
the main façades were round the courtyard, and
on the entrance front, as leading up to them. The
other external façades were usually utilitarian and
irregular. The courtyard façades tended to be
symmetrical, and the side façades in it to match
each other. This kind of symmetry had already
been exploited at Cowdray in Sussex, in the 1530s,
and, in a royal context, in the first court of

78

Hampton Court in the 1520s. But at Cowdray the formidable symmetry to the courtyard of the entrance range and side façades dissolved on the hall façade; this was completely irregular, though grand in scale and detail. The problem, here and elsewhere, was the two-storey great hall and its bay window; how could this be fitted into a symmetrical scheme? Builders in the early Tudor period, who appreciated symmetry but were not obsessed by it, were quite happy to abandon it when it was inconvenient (Fig. 72). The Eliza-

bethans, with their delight in symmetry and obsession with 'order', were more worried, and tried to get round the problem: one solution, as at Kirby Hall in Northamptonshire in the 1570s, was to mirror-image the hall with fake giant windows, lighting two storeys, with the centre lights filled with stone instead of glass (Fig. 73).

In the later Middle Ages and the early Tudor period, chambers for servants and less important visitors were frequently provided in ranges with rows of individual doors, sometimes leading onto

74 Single-range centres
with wings:

a. Great Chalfield Manor,
Wiltshire, late fifteenth
century

b. Eastbury Manor,
Barking, Kent, c.1570

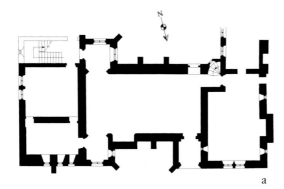

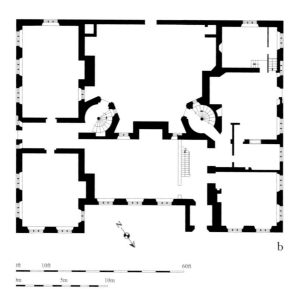

a

b

0ft 10ft 60ft

0m 5m 10m

staircases supplying similar small lodgings on the first floor. The arrangement was taken over for Oxford and Cambridge colleges, where it is first found in the fourteenth century and has remained in use up to the present day. The side façades in Elizabethan courtyard houses were sometimes arranged in this way, as is shown in an eighteenth-century engraving of the demolished great court at Sissinghurst in Kent (Fig. 195) and is still to be seen in the courtyard of Kirby Hall.

The court at Sissinghurst was in fact open on one side except for the gatehouse, as at Stiffkey as it was built; but at Sissinghurst the arrangement was probably adopted deliberately from the start. These open-sided courtyards became quite common: fine late examples are found at Rushton Hall in Northamptonshire, as it developed in the

1620s, and at Lanhydrock in Cornwall, as late as the 1630s, with the gatehouse placed well out in front.

Such plans are an intermediate form between full courtyard houses and houses planned as a single range with, perhaps, shallow protruding wings. Houses of the latter kind were obviously suited to the more modest landowners. A good example is found as early as the late fifteenth century, at Great Chalfield Manor in Wiltshire. It is planned with an approximate symmetry: great hall in the centre, with a gabled bay window more or less matched by the gabled porch, and larger gables to either side over the great chamber and family chamber, each with oriels.

The pattern of Great Chalfield was to recur, with numerous variations, throughout the sixteenth century and well on into the seventeenth (Figs 74, 76). At Great Chalfield the kitchen was originally in a detached building at the rear, in a not uncommon medieval arrangement, but in later examples it was always incorporated in the main body of the house. Such houses offered the same kind of accommodation as a courtyard house, but to begin with in reduced form, usually with no gallery, often with no withdrawing chamber and only one parlour, and obviously with fewer bedchambers. But the plan could be expanded or contracted, from modest convenience to considerable splendour. By extending the wings and by adding a second storey, a withdrawing chamber and winter parlour could be included, and a gallery incorporated into the second floor.

More and more often the hall was only one floor high, and in this case the great chamber was often above the hall instead of above the parlour. There were normally two principal staircases, at the family and 'best' ends; in earlier examples these took the form of round or octagonal newel stairs; the octagonal turrets containing them are placed in the re-entrant angles on the entrance front at Grove Place in Hampshire (Fig. 77), East-

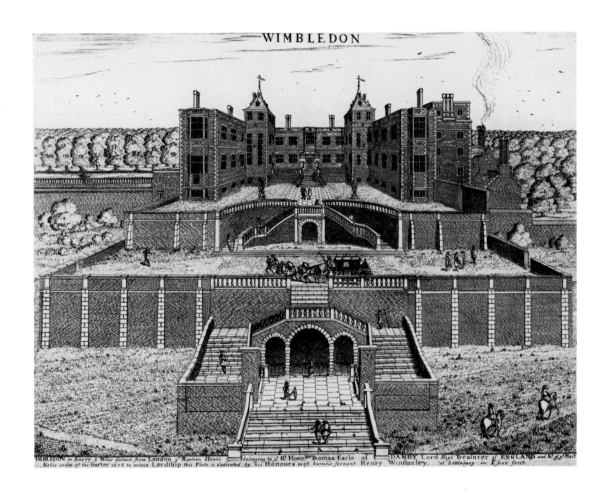

75 and 76 Single range with wings on the grand scale. The entrance front and plan of the demolished Wimbledon House, Surrey, dated 1588.

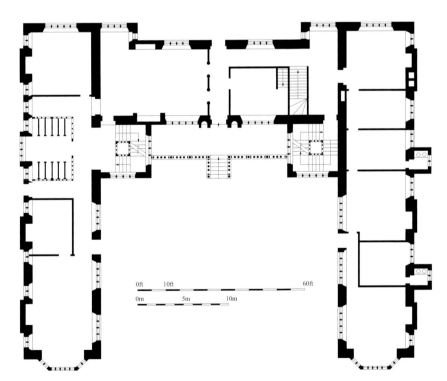

bury Manor, Barking (Fig. 74b) (both *circa* 1570), and elsewhere, with agreeably symmetrical effect. Later on the stairs were usually larger, and taken up in square turrets around a square (and sometimes hollow) newel, often paired like the earlier ones on the front or back of the house, as at Wimbledon House in Surrey (1588, on the front) (Fig. 75) and Montacute in Somerset (*circa* 1600, on the back). The hall was almost always in the middle, and if it were two storeys high, questions of sym-

metry could be dealt with by pairing off the porch and bay window; in earlier examples, starting with Poundisford Park in Somerset (*circa* late 1550s), symmetry is broken by the archway of the porch still being visible on the front, but by the late sixteenth century the entrance was usually moved round the corner so that from a full frontal view total symmetry was preserved.

Single-range houses may originally have been built by owners who wanted to combine gentry

78 Ground, first and second floors of Montacute House, Somerset, with room uses based on an inventory of 1638.

1 Kitchen
2 Study
3 Lobby by kitchen
4 Buttery etc.
5 Hall
6 Parlour
7 Lobby by parlour
8 Parlour chamber
9 Kitchen chamber
10 Larder chamber
11 Middle chamber
12 Butler's chamber
13 Lobby to Little dining Room
14 Little dining room
15 Best chamber
16 Withdrawing room
17 Garden chamber
18 Lobby without dining room
19 Dining room
20 Wainscot chamber
21 Gallery
22 Blue bedchamber
23 Primrose chamber
24 White chamber
25 Chamber at top of great stairs
26 Later corridors

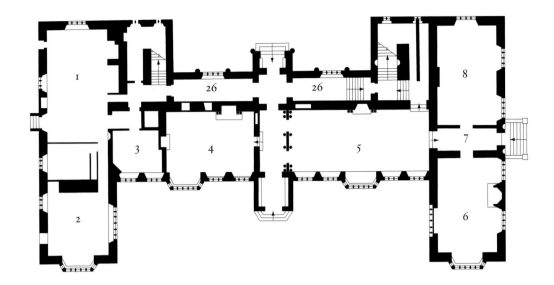

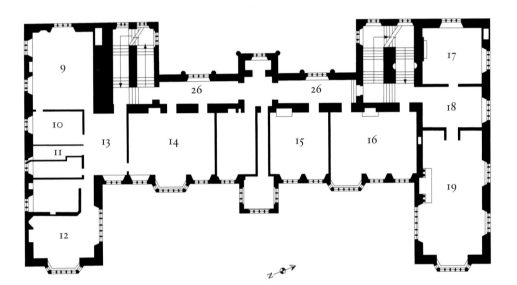

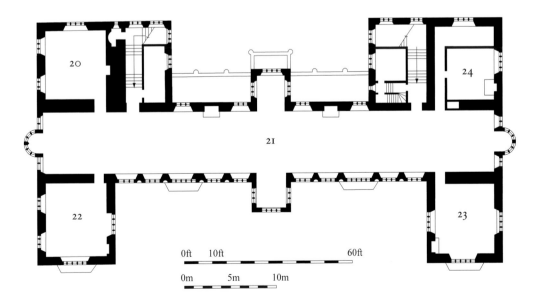

dignity with modest accommodation. But Montacute has almost exactly the same amount of accommodation that Stiffkey would have had if the full courtyard had been built, and is much more commanding in its architecture (Fig. 78). Such a single-range house in the grand manner had been anticipated, less grandly but imposingly enough, as early as the late 1560s by Thomas Eymis, Secretary to the Council of the North, at Heslington Hall, just outside York. Here there was a very large two-storey hall, the lofty bay window of which was paired by a 'fake' giant bay, lighting two storeys, but treated as though it were lighting one; there was a second storey above the hall, which may have contained a gallery.[26] By the late sixteenth century the single-range house, in fact, was competing for favour with the courtyard house. There may have been social reasons of supervision behind this: the activities in a single-range house with just two entries were easier to control than in a courtyard one where there were many semi-independent doorways. But the primary reason was probably an aesthetic one: the concentrated impact of a great unified block rising up from its curtilage of walls and gardens proved hard to resist, and from within the house the views out to countryside and gardens must have seemed preferable to looking in onto a courtyard, however grand its architecture might be.

The changeover from the inward-looking to the outward-looking house is one of the outstanding developments of the Elizabethan period. The single-range house is only one expression of this transition: compact outward-looking courtyard houses also need to be considered (Fig. 79) and, even more, the various combinations of double-pile, triple-pile or multi-pile houses – 'double-pile', etc., being used to describe houses in which two ranges of rooms are placed parallel to each other, to either side of an internal wall.

Compact outward-looking courtyard houses had been anticipated in the remarkable plan of Wickham Court, at West Wickham in Kent,

built in the late fifteenth century by Sir John Heydon (Fig. 79a). This was (and, a good deal altered, still is) a compact block with four octagonal corner towers, built around a very small internal court; entry to the hall is from the outside façade. Thorpe was sufficiently interested by this to draw a plan of it,[27] and his book contains four later plans of compact outward-looking houses round slightly larger courts, two of them (one for 'Mr Tayler at potters barr 1596' (T225, 22; Fig. 79d)) dating from the 1590s, the other two probably from the early seventeenth century. A fine early seventeenth-century example survives at Chastleton in Oxfordshire (Fig. 79b). Similarly compact courtyard houses had already been built at Eastington Manor in Gloucestershire in 1578 (Fig. 318), and at the twins, Barlborough Hall in Derbyshire (Fig. 360) and Heath Old Hall in Yorkshire, in the 1580s.[28] These three houses can be linked with Longleat, Eastington on stylistic grounds, the others because of their likely connection with Robert Smythson, who came up from Longleat to the Midlands in 1580. Among the Smythson drawings are designs for two houses of the same plan-type, dating from the late sixteenth or early seventeenth century, which may not have been executed (Figs 79c, 344), and one for Burton Agnes in Yorkshire (1601–10), which still exists.[29] Behind the whole group lies Longleat itself, remodelled round three internal courts from 1572 onwards, as an outward-looking house in the grandest manner.

The possibilities of gaining compactness by making houses, or portions of houses, two rooms thick had barely been exploited in the later medieval period. It was taken for granted that the different ranges of any buildings would only be one room thick. One good reason for this was practical problems of drainage. If the double thickness was to be covered by a single roof, it would have to be uncomfortably and expensively high; if by two roofs in parallel, the result would be a valley gutter and all the problems of drainage

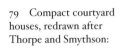

79 Compact courtyard
houses, redrawn after
Thorpe and Smythson:

a. Wickham Court, Kent,
*c.*1470, as improved by
John Thorpe

b. Chastleton House,
Oxfordshire, *c.*1605–12

c. A plan by Robert
Smythson

d. 'Mr Tayler at potters
barr', as drawn by John
Thorpe, 1596

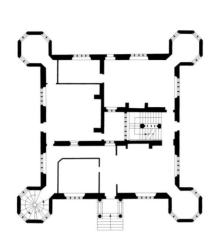

a

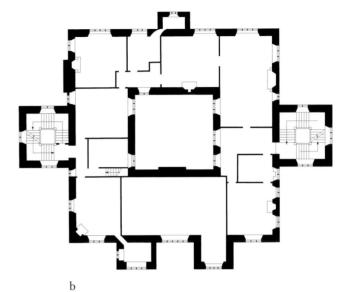

b

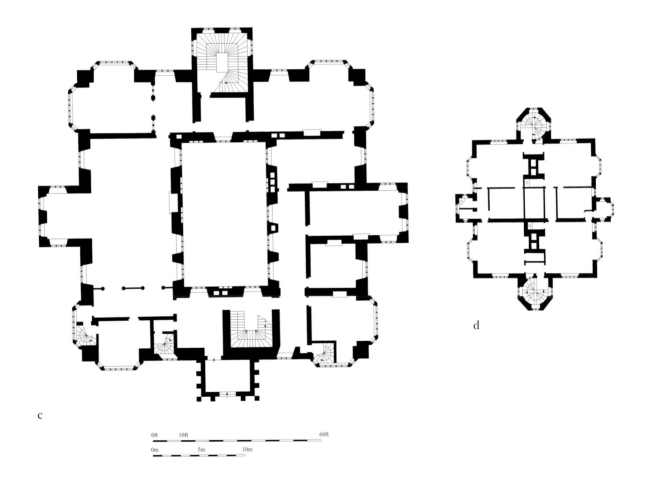

c

d

0ft   10ft   60ft

0m   5m   10m

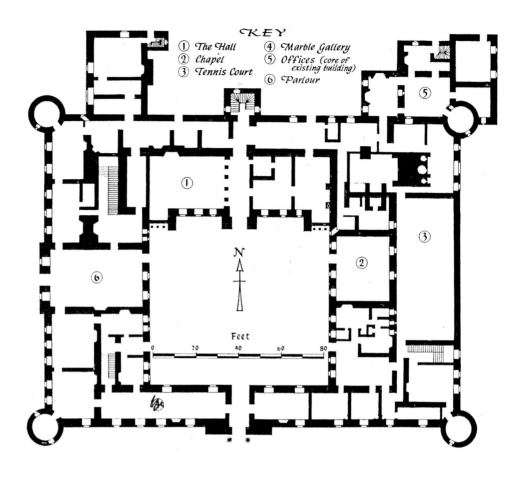

① *The Hall*　　④ *Marble Gallery*
② *Chapel*　　　⑤ *Offices (core of existing building)*
③ *Tennis Court*　⑥ *Parlour*

80 The first floor of the demolished Toddington Manor, Bedfordshire, built *c*.1575, as redrawn from an eighteenth-century plan, when the bay window lighting the parlour and great chamber above it had been removed.

that that involved. These problems must have seemed to obviate the practical advantages of the double pile: that it was cheaper to build, with three parallel walls needed, instead of four, and cheaper to heat, because the fireplaces and flue could be in the central spine wall, and the heat from the flues kept in the house rather than being wasted into the outside.

But the increasing exploitation of the flat, or relatively flat, leaded roof pointed the way to how to deal with the problem of the double pile. Lead could be laid in shallow steps, or to a very modest camber. In the mid-sixteenth century flat leaded roofs became popular with those who could afford them because of the Tudor passion for walking up and down on the 'leads' for exercise, or to enjoy the view. The technique had been known since medieval times, but the drawback to lead was its expense. Only the rich could afford to use it in large quantities. But prosperity was

growing under Elizabeth, and in addition large quantities of lead at competitive prices (or as gifts by royal grant) became available as a result of the dissolution of the monasteries and other religious foundations. Sir John Thynne, for instance, got lead from Amesbury Abbey in 1547, and in 1573 William Cecil bought it at a good price from the dissolved college of Fotheringay in Northamptonshire for use at Burghley House.[30]

In the mid-sixteenth century flat leaded roofs were all on single-pile ranges. But double-pile ranges under leaded roofs appeared on a grand scale at two houses, Sir Christopher Hatton's Holdenby in Northamptonshire (*circa* 1578–81) and Lord Cheyne's Toddington in Bedfordshire (in or before 1581) (Figs 80, 322, 81).[31] One must have influenced the other, for both have the same feature of a great chamber on a very grand scale carried through the double pile, and lit by elaborately profiled bay windows; at Toddington it was

81 The ground-floor plan
of Holdenby, Northamp-
tonshire, as redrawn from
a plan by John Thorpe.
The great chamber was on
the first floor above the
centre of the range shown
at the bottom of this
illusration.

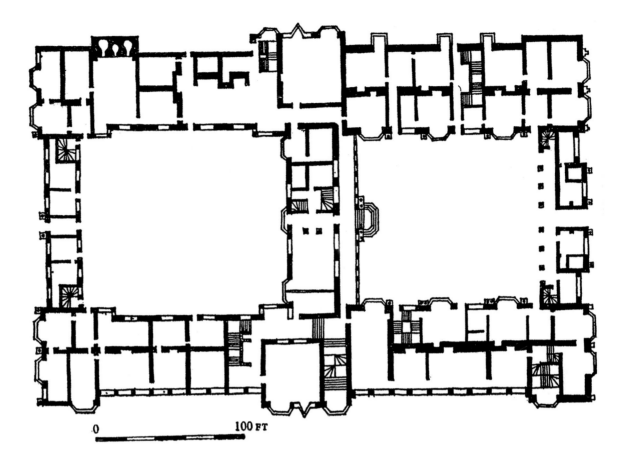

.0   100 ft

above a parlour of the same size. But at Toddington only two sides of the courtyard were given
double-pile treatment. The far bigger Holdenby
was built round two courts, and all but two of its
seven ranges were double pile (Figs 81, 214) . In
1578 a new range containing a new and grander
great hall and kitchen was added alongside the
existing east range of the courtyard at Burghley,
turning it into a double pile.

In 1580 Robert Smythson, newly arrived in the
Midlands from Longleat, devised an ingenious
and striking plan for the new house built at
Wollaton by Sir Francis Willoughby (Fig. 292).
The plan was not in fact a new invention, but
inspired by the remarkable early Tudor lodge at
Mount Edgcumbe in Cornwall, which Smythson
certainly knew of. By enclosing the hall in four
ranges of buildings, all with flat leaded roofs, and
lighting it by a clerestory, the problem of fitting
it into a symmetrical building was dealt with;

access to the screens end of the hall was by an L-
shaped corridor leading from the door at the
centre of the entrance front.[32]

But when Smythson supplied the plan for
Hardwick New Hall in 1590 he adopted a different solution (Fig. 82). The house is a very large rectangular double pile, embellished with six turrets;
it is covered with a flat leaded roof on the grand
scale (Bess of Hardwick had her own lead mines).
But the centre of the spine wall of the double pile
is pierced to allow a hall to be driven through it.
The hall, in fact, is rotated 90 degrees from its traditional position so that the dais and screen ends
are placed in the centre of the rear and front elevations, and symmetry is neatly preserved.

This Hardwick 'through hall' could have been
suggested by the through great chambers at Holdenby and Toddington. Alternatively, the arrangement may have been derived from centrally
placed *salles* or *sale* in plans in Palladio (Bess of

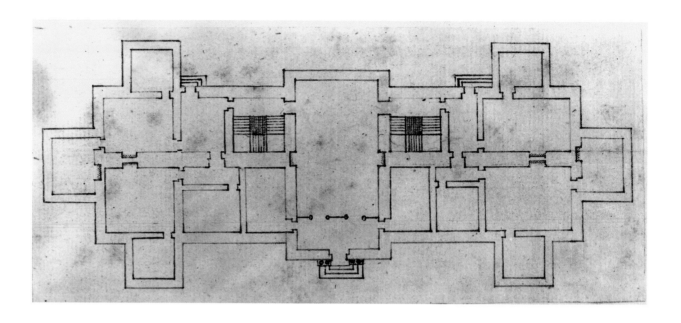

82 Robert Smythson's first plan for Hardwick Hall, Derbyshire, not quite as executed (SM. DWGS I/8).

83 and 84 John Thorpe and Palladio: (*right*) a plan by Thorpe (T141), and the plan in Palladio's *Quattro Libri* (*below*), on which it is based.

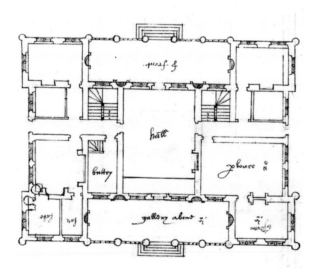

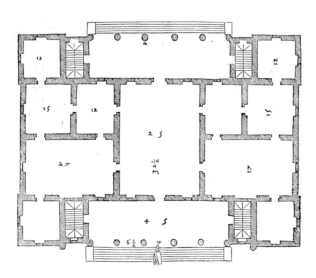

85 (*facing page, top*). Thorpe's plan and elevation (T182) of the banqueting house, Holdenby, Northamptonshire, possibly built *c.*1608.

86 and 87 (*facing page, centre and below*). Thorpe's plan (T202) of Somerhill, Kent, *c.*1613, is based on Palladio, but there is nothing Palladian in Somerhill's exterior.

Hardwick's daughter Grace owned a copy) or Du Cerceau (an undoubted adaptation of a Du Cerceau plan is in the Wollaton archives).[33] Whatever its origins, the arrangement, unlike the Wollaton plan, caught on and was copied, in Derbyshire in a house designed by Smythson (but perhaps never built) at Blackwell in the Peak, and at Tissington and Renishaw Halls, possibly in Yorkshire at Constable Burton and Sandbeck, and in Nottinghamshire at Manor Lodge, Worksop (but here the hall is pierced through a single pile).[34]

Meanwhile, in the south and perhaps quite independently, John Thorpe was drawing out plans for houses with through halls that were definitely inspired by Palladio, for two of them have plans copied direct from his *Quattro Libri* (Figs 83, 84), and others are clearly linked to these.[35] When Christopher Hatton's nephew, for instance, inherited from his uncle the embarrassing legacy of a house so large that he could not conceivably afford to live in it, and which he sold, no doubt with relief, to James I in 1608, he kept a stake in his ancestral property by enlarging a banqueting house at the corner of the garden into a comfortable residence for himself (in which his widow continued to live after his death in 1619).

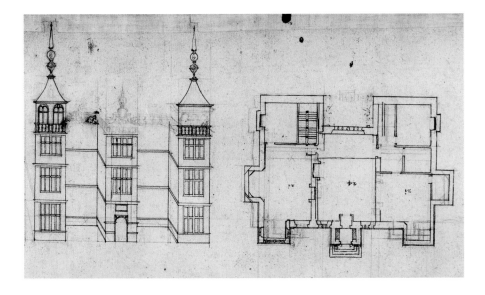

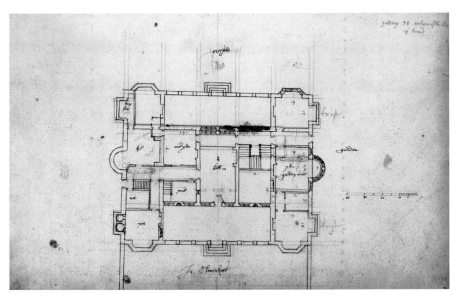

The plan and elevation, with a through hall in the Palladian manner, are drawn by Thorpe (Fig. 85), who almost certainly also devised them, for Palladio's original from which the plan is adapted (a version, not exactly copied, of his Villa Augurano) is drawn in pencil under the design that derived from it.[36]

The through hall was at least as popular in the south as in the north. In addition to the unidentified house plans drawn by Thorpe, some nine examples, in or near London or clearly London-inspired, can be identified: Eagle House in Wimbledon, Charlton House in Greenwich (partly influenced by Hardwick) and Plas Teg in North Wales are fine surviving examples. All these houses, in and out of Thorpe, have elevations that are purely Jacobean, rather than Palladian, in style.

Of the nine Palladio-copied or Palladio-inspired plans drawn by Thorpe, only one has survived (Figs 86, 87). It is Somerhill in Kent, built about 1613 for the Irish Earl of Clanricarde and his wife; previous to her Irish marriage she had achieved the remarkable double of marrying both Philip Sidney and the Earl of Essex, the two *preux chevalliers* of their day. No one looking at the house would suspect its Palladian origin.

But centrally placed through halls by no means swept the board. Numerous double-pile houses were still being built with a traditional hall in the traditional position; and there were a few triple-pile houses, and variations of all kinds. One possibility was to put a long gallery along the back of the hall, an arrangement found as early as the late 1570s at Trerice in Cornwall (Fig. 88a), and later at, for example, Condover Hall, Shropshire (1590s) (Fig. 88b), Hatfield House, Hertfordshire (1607–12), and Aston Hall, Birmingham (1618). At Easton Lodge, Essex, and Worcester Lodge, Surrey (Fig. 88d), the staircase was in the middle, with a through hall to one side.[37] At two interesting and innovative houses, Francis Bacon's Verulam House in Hertfordshire (finished in 1615) and

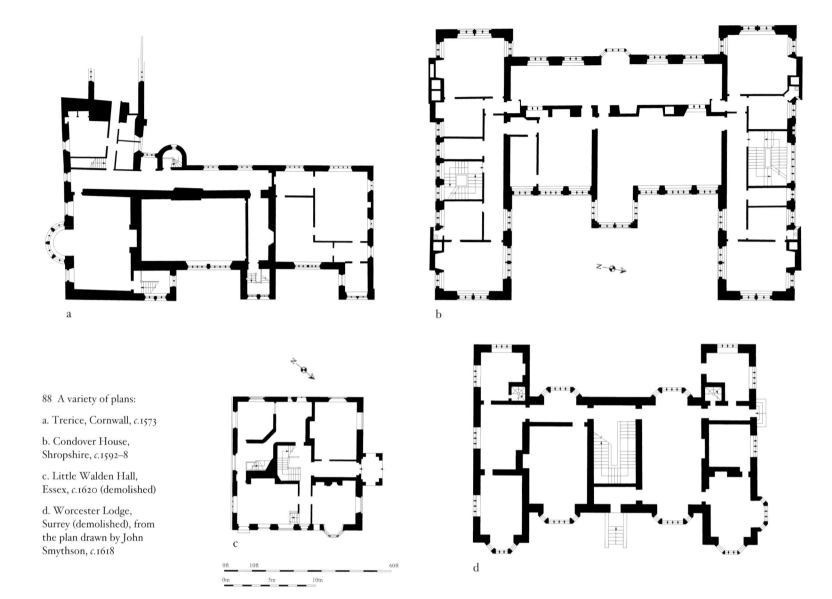

88 A variety of plans:

a. Trerice, Cornwall, *c*.1573

b. Condover House, Shropshire, *c*.1592–8

c. Little Walden Hall, Essex, *c*.1620 (demolished)

d. Worcester Lodge, Surrey (demolished), from the plan drawn by John Smythson, *c*.1618

0ft   10ft   60ft

0m   5m   10m

the Earl of Suffolk's Little Walden Hall in Essex (*circa* 1620) (Fig. 88c), the centre of the house was filled by an enclosed top-lit open-well staircase.[38] There are a couple of similar designs for unidentified houses in Thorpe;[39] this central-staircase plan is to be found in occasional houses later in the seventeenth century, and proliferated in the eighteenth century.

In a handful of houses the traditional plan with a screens-entered hall was abandoned, and a hall without screens was entered in the middle of its long side. A house of which the plan is in Thorpe's book and which can be identified as Rusholt Hall in Essex (Fig. 89), was possibly built before 1604.[40] Then came Holland House, London (*circa* 1610) (Fig. 546), Westwood, Worcestershire (1613), Wothorpe, Northamptonshire (now Cambridgeshire; *circa* 1615) (Fig. 551), and possibly Barningham Hall, Norfolk (1612).[41] But the force of tradition led to screens-entered halls being built into the middle of the seventeenth century. In general, the accommodation and arrangement of Jacobean houses remained much the same as in Elizabethan days, though, since the hall was now usually single storey, the great chamber was often over it rather than over the parlour. A good ascent

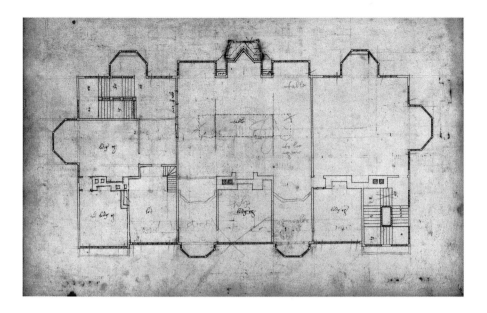

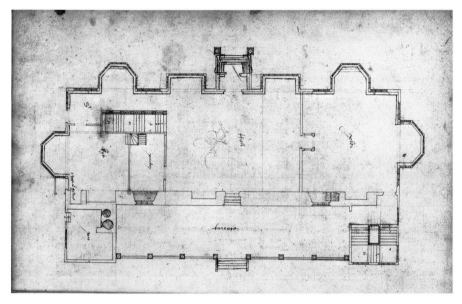

89a and b   Plans by John Thorpe (T98, 97) for 'Mr Hicks', probably for Rusholt Hall, Essex (demolished), perhaps c.1603.

to the great chamber was as important as ever, and the new development of the open-well timber staircase could make it resplendent with painting or carving.

Great chamber, withdrawing chamber and gallery were frequently grouped together, but often the bedchamber that had been the accepted end-room of the succession in Elizabethan days was omitted; they were becoming reception rooms, rather than 'best lodgings'. In a small, but impressive, group occurring sporadically between the 1570s and the 1620s, the grand rooms were up on the second floor. More will be said about these in chapter 5.

Although the vogue for flat leaded roofs may have encouraged the adoption of double-pile and other compressed plans, by no means all such houses had them. Patrons who were unwilling to afford leaded roofs still wanted the double pile. It was a heyday for leadwork, and for inventive plumbers and glaziers, busily engaged in making conduits for water-supply and fountains, in devising fancy glazing for windows, and in supplying the down-pipes and often elaborate rainwater heads that were beginning to replace the traditional spouts to take water off roofs. They became adept at devising systems of graded valley gutters, or if necessary taking gutters through the attics to get the water out of spaces entirely enclosed by roofs. Some of the resulting houses are so elaborate, and their outlines so complex, that little if any economy could have resulted from the compressed plans. Even those based, like Hardwick, on a simple double-pile rectangle are normally embellished with towers or other projections to give them consequence.

But at the same time as these high-flyers were being built, another form of house was developing, which in the long run was to have a more numerous progeny. This was the plain square or rectangular double-pile (or sometimes triple-pile) house, with few or no frills in the way of turrets or bay windows (Fig. 90).

Such a house had already been built in 1567 at Bachegraig in North Wales, as is to be described in chapter 3 (Figs 189–91). It was a plain square or near-square in plan, with just one bay window at the back, all sheltering under one lofty roof, without gables. The waste of space that this roof would otherwise have involved was obviated by filling it with two storeys of rooms, lit by dormer windows. It was a Flemish arrangement, and the form of the house, and some of its materials, were an importation from Flanders. There is no certain evidence as to its plan.

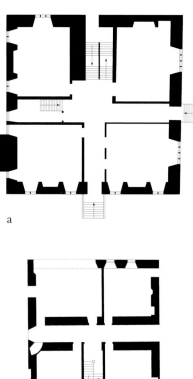

a

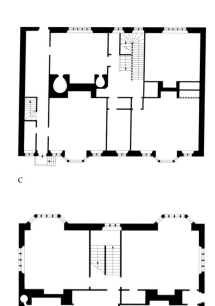

c

b

d

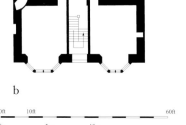

But Bachegraig, in its remote position, had no obvious influence in England. Or did it? On the edge of Shrewsbury, in the years 1578–82 Robert Prynce built Whitehall (Figs 90a, 91), another remarkably early deep-plan house, in the form of an unadorned square, which has long intrigued architectural historians. It has certain resemblances to Bachecraig, which is not all that far away, but instead of Bachegraig's Flemish roof it has twelve very English gables – but from the middle of them projects a little banqueting house in the form of a cupola, as at Bachegraig.[42]

An interesting building that comes in date between Bachegraig and Whitehall, and that has certain resemblances in plan to them, which may or may not be coincidental, is the Old Hall in Buxton in Derbyshire (Fig. 90b). This was built in 1572–3 by the Earl of Shrewsbury, as a lodging-

92 Dowsby Hall, Lincolnshire, today. About one third of the house was demolished in the eighteenth century.

cer in the Royal Works, who served as Comptroller from 1556 and joint Comptroller and Paymaster from 1578 until his death in 1595. For many years, as Surveyors came and went, he was effectively running the Works. In 1565 he bought three tenements on the Strand, which at some stage he demolished and replaced by the single house, the plan of which Thorpe drew (commenting on his drawing: 'London house of 3 bredths of ords tenemts'). Fowler had lived in the house himself, and was proud of it; he left a stipulation in his will that Lord Burghley or Sir Robert Cecil should be given the opportunity of leasing it. It must have been prominent on the Strand, three storeys high above a basement, with a terrace walk, a covered gallery and servants' rooms in a fourth storey at attic level. It was a double-pile house, and the chimneys were all concentrated in two groups along the spine.

Thorpe must have realised that town-house plans, necessarily compact because of their position, had capabilities for use in country houses. Another plan of his,[45] showing three square double-pile houses in a row, is captioned '3 howses for the cytty or for a country howse'. He used the plan of the Fowler house, with its concentrated chimney stacks, in a number of variations, some more embellished than others. They all have the chimneys in the spine wall.[46] One example survives, at Dowsby Hall in Lincolnshire, built *circa* 1600 for Sir William Rigden (Figs 90d, 92). A third of it has been demolished; but what is left is very interesting. The plan was close to Thomas Fowler's house, and probably modelled on it. It was a plain double-pile rectangle, unadorned on the two short sides, and with two shallow and unassertive bay windows on each of the main fronts. The chimney stacks were all along the line of the spine wall, as in Thomas Fowler's house. There were originally at least eight of them, rising high in a long straight row, prominent from a distance and still impressive enough in the two-thirds of the house that remains.

house for visitors who came to take the waters – a rather grand lodging-house, since the visitors included Mary, Queen of Scots, Lord Burghley and the Earl of Leicester. It was enlarged and remodelled in the eighteenth century, but the basic plan and structure survive remarkably intact. It was a near square, four storeys high. It had a flat leaded roof. There were no embellishments, apart from Shrewsbury's arms framed in his Garter, very large on one front. In plan it was a triple pile, for it contained two lots of lodgings on each floor, divided by a corridor; there was a similar arrangement in the basement, at least, at Whitehall.[43]

Compact rectangular plans were also being developed in the south. Thorpe gives the plan of a house on the Strand,[44] lived in by Sir Thomas Lake when he drew it, but built by Thomas Fowler (Fig. 90c). Fowler was an important offi-

93 Boyton House, Wiltshire, completed 1618. A detail of the entrance front.

Red Hall, Bourne, is six miles from Dowsby, and was built a few years later, by Gilbert Fisher, newly risen into the gentry. It is clearly modelled on Dowsby, and has a similar but reduced plan; all the chimney stacks are in the spine wall, eight in all in groups of four, but unlike Dowsby each is joined to its neighbour by an arch, to form two aerial arcades. There are no bay windows; a classical porch and the chimney stacks are the only adornments.[47]

The standard town house, in the fifteenth and sixteenth centuries and later, was built on a deep narrow plot, in a long row of similar plots. Houses had to be deep and high, if they were to be of any size. Sufficiently prosperous people acquired two or three plots and joined them together, as did Thomas Fowler. We know how Thorpe adapted the sizeable but conveniently deep and compact plan that resulted for free-standing houses because his drawings survive. But he was not unique. Other surveyors and artificers were doing the same thing, and it is impossible to say who was

94 and 95 Gainford Hall, Durham (*right*), and Gaythorne Hall, Westmorland (*facing page*), early seventeenth-century houses of almost identical plan.

imitating whom, or who was working out the plan independently.

Bird's-eye views of London by Wenceslaus Hollar and others show a scattering of compact free-standing houses on its outskirts. Similar houses were built in Bristol and Bath, perhaps in York and Norwich. Other houses are scattered in the country all over England. They did not all have their chimneys in the spine wall. They did not all necessarily imitate urban models, but they have a family resemblance. Thomas Lambert, son or grandson of a London grocer, building his new house at Boyton in Wiltshire (Fig. 93), produced something similar to the Bristol merchant John Dowel setting up house at Over Court, Almondsbury, in Gloucestershire.[48] The plan-type spread (Figs 94, 95) because such houses were suitable for prosperous but serious people, merchants or country gentlemen, who avoided the expense or the show of the more fanciful Jacobean style.

For those who did not want to run to the cost of a leaded roof, draining the roofs of deep houses must always have presented a problem, and been likely to cause trouble. Then, in the 1620s and '30s, the hipped roof began to make its appearance, enabling a house to be covered with a single roof structure, all draining outwards, possibly equipped with a flat walk at the top and a cupola

by which to get out onto it.[49] Like the roof at Bachegraig, the form was probably introduced from the Low Countries, but unlike the Bachegraig example, it caught on. Jacobean fantasy went out of fashion and rectangular houses with hipped roofs and no bay windows were to dominate for the next hundred years, and be built by grand families as well as modest ones.

Gatehouses, Banqueting Houses and Lodges[50]

Elizabethan and Jacobean country houses did not stand in parkland, with grass rolling up to their walls in the Capability Brown manner. They rose more like a keep in a castle behind its defences, screened by high walls, courtyards, pavilions and gatehouse, as one can still appreciate at Hardwick and comes across vividly in an eighteenth-century painting of Glemham Hall in Suffolk (Fig. 109).

But in all too many cases later generations swept the original setting away, often unrecorded.

In a number of his plans Thorpe shows the standard arrangement; what he shows is backed up by contemporary surveys. A large house normally opened out onto an entrance court, a woodyard, a garden and (less invariably) an orchard, all walled. Of these the woodyard was always next to the back door, giving access to the kitchen, service rooms and cellars; it contained piles of wood ready for burning, as its name suggests, and probably much other functional clutter, on its way in or out of the house. The garden usually adjoined the side of the house containing the great chamber and parlour. The orchard could be on the fourth, remaining side; in Elizabethan and Jacobean days it was a semi-formal garden, not the utilitarian space that the name suggests today.

Somewhere in the curtilage outbuildings, both utilitarian and decorative, had to be fitted in:

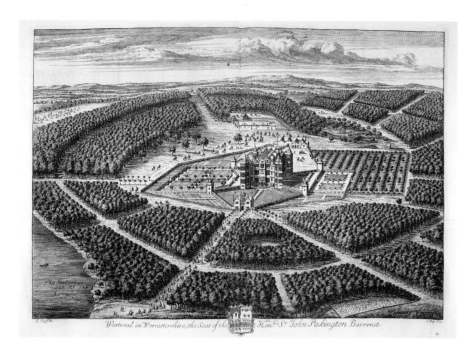

Westwood in Worcestershire, the Seat of the Hon.ble S.r John Pakington Barronet.

96 A bird's-eye view of Westwood Park, Worcestershire (begun 1613), from Johannes Kip and Leonard Knyff's *Britannia Illustrata*, 1716, showing it after wings had been added to the main building.

stables, dairy, brewhouse, laundry, and perhaps farm and dovecote, on the one hand; often banqueting houses and an aviary and garden seats on the other; and a gatehouse, which was between the two.

A few attempts were made to fit these elements into a symmetrical whole around the house. The most elaborate was at Wollaton in the 1580s, as shown in a Smythson plan.[51] In this (Fig. 292) the house fills the central square of nine squares, or near squares, with ranges of buildings opposite its four façades on the perimeter of their squares: the gatehouse opposite the entrance front; dairy and laundry at the opposite extremity across the garden; bakehouse and brewhouse across the woodyard; stables across what may have been intended as an orchard. This dispersion of the service buildings would have been impressive, but scarcely convenient. Even so, something like the arrangement was executed, but possibly with seven instead of nine squares, and with the service buildings concentrated across or around the woodyard.

In 1613 Sir John Pakington set the very grand hunting lodge, which he began to build in that year at Westwood in Worcestershire, in a layout

that was as impressive as that designed for Wollaton, rather more convenient, and certainly all carried out, though only half of it survives (Fig. 96). The lodge, compact and very tall, formed the joining point of two diamond-shaped courts, an entrance court and a woodyard. The outer corners of the diamonds were joined to provide gardens or orchard. The huge hexagon that resulted had the gatehouse at the bottom angle, the stables and possibly other service rooms in a five-gabled range at the top angle, and four lofty pavilions at the other four angles, as miniature echoes of the house. Outside all this was a great deer-park. The lodge, the gatehouse and two of the pavilions remain; the logic of the layout was so powerful that when the lodge was enlarged, perhaps about 1660, the enlargement took the form of four wings set diagonally along the courtyard walls.[52]

Sometime between 1607 and 1625 Laurence Eyton, a minor landowner but an extravagant one, rebuilt his house at Brockhall in Northamptonshire (Fig. 97). The house was modest in its architecture, but ambitious in its formality. It was planned symmetrically, inside and out; the four courts were symmetrically disposed around it; the entrance court was flanked by twin free-standing ranges, one containing 'dayrie, stables & c.', the other 'bakehouse brewhouse & c.'. The arrangement was drawn by John Thorpe, who may have devised it.[53]

In 1623 outbuildings similarly flanking the courtyard, but architecturally more elaborate, with Flemish gables instead of Brockhall's plain ones, were built in front of the recently completed Blickling Hall, the façade of which they still frame in a memorable composition (Fig. 99). The architect of these outbuildings, as of the house, was Robert Leminge. The arrangement, complete with Flemish gables, was repeated at Wothorpe Lodge in Northamptonshire (now Cambridgeshire) in about 1620 (Fig. 98), and Stratfield Saye in Hampshire, probably in the 1630s.[54]

But formal arrangements of the service buildings were not common. What became almost invariable, however, was a formal treatment of the entrance court, with a gatehouse, or at least an architecturally treated archway, opening centrally and often aligned on the hall porch; the forecourt was always walled, and sometimes the walls were closed at the corners with turrets or pavilions, to make a formal composition with the gatehouse. Occasionally, there were terraces on either side of the court, as shown in the Wollaton plan and surviving at Biddulph Old Hall in Cheshire.

Elizabethan and Jacobean gatehouses come in all shapes and sizes (Figs 100–10, 111). Much care and ingenuity went into devising them, the small as well as the large. They formed the introduction to the house, and gave a foretaste of its quality. Even the simplest exudes a sense of occasion. Some rise up three or four storeys high, and are turreted in the manner of their early Tudor precursors, as at Shute in Devon and Sissinghurst and Lullingstone in Kent (though Lullingstone may be just pre-Elizabethan). At Sissinghurst (Fig. 196) the gatehouse is four storeys high, and the turrets are set back at the sides, making the central projection extraordinarily slender and elegant. At

97–9 Three houses with symmetrical forecourt ranges.

97 (*top*) Brockhall Hall, Northamptonshire, *c.*1610. From the drawing by Peter Tillemans.

98 (*above*) Wothorpe Lodge, Cambridgeshire, *c.*1615, as shown in a drawing by John Haynes in 1755, before its dismantling and the demolition of the wings

99 (*right*) The entrance front of Blickling Hall, Norfolk, 1618–29.

100–03 The gatehouse as
introduction to the house.

100 (*right*)
At Hardwick Hall,
Derbyshire (*c.*1595).

101 (*centre*)
At Doddington Hall,
Lincolnshire, *c.*1593–1600.

102 (*bottom*)
At Charlecote Park,
Warwickshire, *c.*?1580.

103 (*facing page*)
At Westwood Park,
Worcestershire, *c.*1613.

104–7 Four gatehouse variations.

104 (*above left*)
At Trevalyn Hall, Denbighshire, 1576.

105 (*above right, top*)
At Madeley Court, Shropshire, *c*.1560–70.

106 (*above right, bottom*)
At Hamstall Ridware, Staffordshire, *c*.1600.

107 (*facing page*)
At Bradstone Manor, Devon, early seventeenth century.

Tixall in Staffordshire it is of three storeys with higher corner turrets, but is broader than early Tudor examples, giving scope for the sumptuousness of the Doric, Ionic and Corinthian orders between the towers (Fig. 221).

But sometimes the gatehouse shrinks to two single-storey pavilions or turrets joined by an

arch; at Hamstall Ridware in Staffordshire and Toddington in Bedfordshire these have, or had, little domes; at Hardwick and Cranborne (Figs 100, 527) they are set at 45 degrees to the axis of the house; at Hamstall Ridware (Fig. 106), Hardwick (Fig. 100) and Toddington there is delicate cresting over the central arch, and at Hardwick this is continued on the turrets, and in simplified form all round the walls of the entrance court, and is echoed by the cresting on the turrets of the house, all 'as though splintered by the lances in a tournament', as Mrs Ratcliffe put it. There was classical ornament, as grand as at Tixall, on the demolished gatehouse at Clifton Maybank in Dorset (Fig. 528); and not so grand, but handsome enough, on the four-turreted gatehouses at

Charlecote in Warwickshire and Burton Agnes in Yorkshire. A full apparatus of Doric, Ionic and Corinthian, somewhat naively detailed, survives at Lostock, in Lancashire (Fig. 108). The two-turreted gatehouse at Madeley Court in Shropshire (Fig. 105) has classical entablatures and classical roundels. Single turrets set back to either side, to contain staircases, as at Sissinghurst, are also found on the ruined gatehouse at Baconsthorpe in Norfolk (Fig. 161). The sumptuous three-storey gatehouse at Glemham Hall in Suffolk had continuous glazing all the way round, and a cupola over all (Fig. 109). Some gatehouses have shaped gables, as at Merton in Norfolk, Westwood in Worcestershire (Fig. 103) and Stanway in Gloucestershire, the last perhaps the most exquisite of

English gatehouses; at Westwood the two two-storey gabled pavilions of the gatehouse were joined by the Bromsgrove carpenters Thomas and Richard Bridgen with a transparent screen of woodwork incorporating the armorial stars of Sir John Pakington, who built it (Fig. 110).

The primary function of medieval gatehouses had been security and supervision. Security, as provided by arrow-slits, gun embrasures and machicolations, had become largely symbolic even by late medieval times. Under the Elizabethans

109 (*above*) An early eighteenth-century painting of Glemham Hall, Suffolk. The house was remodelled and the gatehouse and pavilions demolished in the eighteenth century.

110 Looking through the wooden screen that joins the turrets of the gate-house at Westwood Park, Worcestershire.

high walls and a sturdy door, which could be closed and barred at night, provided all that was felt necessary. Supervision remained important, and was provided by the porter in his lodge; two rooms for the porter continued to be the basic element of gatehouses into Jacobean days. In 1601 the little two-roomed gatehouse at Hardwick contained two feather beds, a bolster, two blankets, a coverlet, a board and two halberds.[55] The smallest gatehouses did not even have a porter's lodge: the miniature marooned gatehouse at Butt House, King's Lyon, in Herefordshire just has a room over the arch, accessible only by a ladder.[56]

Just how the rooms were used in the bigger gatehouses, and who occupied them, remains a problem, as in earlier gatehouses. They often

contained at least one large room; at Combe Florey in Somerset this has a ceiling of elaborate plasterwork.[57] It is possible that they sometimes provided semi-independent lodgings for a member of the family, a widow or an elder son, or perhaps for the steward: semi-independent because their accommodation almost never included a kitchen. Sometimes the big room may have served as a banqueting room, with further access to the leads on top for the view. But their size was perhaps more a matter of status than of use.

Gatehouses were especially vulnerable when fashions changed, and the surroundings of the house were opened up. Hundreds must have been demolished; perhaps not more than fifty remain. Occasionally, however, the house has gone and the gatehouse survives, turned into a house, as at Malton in Yorkshire, Lostock in Lancashire

(Fig. 108) and Leighton Bromswold in Hunting-donshire.[58]

The combination of gatehouse and corner pavilions, which must have been so sensational at Glemham Hall, survives at Shute in Devon (Fig. 112), where the house has gone, and, with minia-ture pavilions, at Hardwick in Derbyshire. At Montacute the gatehouse has gone but the pavil-ions are still there (Figs 305, 516). They are exquis-itely designed, with ogee roofs and little semi-circular projections; the courtyard walls are also exquisite, for the standard stone wall of most entrance courts is opened up with balustrades, obelisks and circular lanterns of Doric columns; the gatehouse must have been equally fanciful, but no depiction of it has survived. At the Little Castle at Bolsover in Derbyshire there was no gatehouse, but small pavilions given battlements and gun embrasures in mock-castle style.

How the corner pavilions at Montacute and elsewhere were intended to be used remains as problematic as the use of the rooms in the gatehouses. The pavilions at Glemham, with their huge windows, were perhaps intended as

banqueting houses; other pavilions may have contained lodgings for servants, or for visitors when the house was full, or been used as storage space for the gardeners. It is likely that many pavilions were first built for effect, and a use found for them later.[59]

112 (*right*) The gatehouse and corner pavilions of *c.*1590, part of a largely demolished house at Shute Barton, Devon.

113 (*facing page, top*) The banqueting house that grows from the roof of the Oak House, West Bromwich, Staffordshire. From the lithograph in S. C. Hall's *Baronial Mansions*, 1848.

114 (*facing page, bottom*) Banqueting houses of the 1560s built by Robert Smythson on the roof of Longleat House, Wiltshire.

A banquet was not a great feast, as the word is generally used today. It was a dessert course of spices, wine and sweetmeats, often served after dinner but in a separate room; the dons who leave High Table in Oxford and Cambridge colleges today to take dessert in the Senior Common or Combination Room are continuing a tradition that has existed since Jacobean days, if not earlier. Banquets could, in fact, be served at any time of the day, and to any number of people, from two to twenty, but perhaps seldom as many, for they were usually more intimate functions.

Banqueting rooms or independent banqueting houses varied accordingly in size and location; a location with a good view was clearly found desirable. They were often in turrets up on the roof; the great room in the octagon tower that rises above the courtyard at Melbury in Dorset was probably built as an early banqueting room in the 1530s; the tiny octagonal room in a turret of the 1550s approached by a rooftop walk at Lacock Abbey in Wiltshire (Fig. 154) still retains its octagonal stone table on which the banquets were served (Fig. 111). What seems to have been a round banqueting house of the 1570s, in a turret on the roof at Chatsworth, was panelled, and decorated with 'Alablaster, blackstone and other devices of carving', according to the inventory.[60] At the Oak House, West Bromwich in Staffordshire, a little timber banqueting house sprouts unexpectedly from the gables of the half-timbered house (Fig. 113). There were eight, and still are seven, square or octagonal turrets on the roof at Longleat (Fig. 114), at least four of them having 'lytle starres won fro the roofe so as they may serve an banketting houses', according to a specification of 1568 or 1569.[61] At Hardwick one of the six turrets on the roof served as a banqueting room, and has a plasterwork frieze and ceiling of some elaboration.

Banqueting houses were often built in the garden. At Montacute there was one at the end of the west walk, at Wimbledon House in Surrey an

Banquets could also be combined with hunting and fishing. The towers or pavilions known as stands or standings, from which the hunt was watched, were normally equipped with a banqueting room. The stand, now known as the Hunting Tower, high on the hill above Chatsworth, takes the form of a four-storey tower (Fig. 116), with four round and domed towers rising a storey higher, forming tiny pavilions, with delicate plasterwork on their ceilings; these may have served as banqueting houses, along with the upper room in the tower below. A little two-storey building in the park at Althorp in Northamptonshire carries the inscription 'This staning was made by Robert Lord Spencer. 1612 et 1613'. It is still there, though its wall paintings of hunting scenes, described in 1822, have gone.[65]

The building now known as Bourne Mill, on the banks of the Bourne stream or river, on the

115 (*above*)
The banqueting house or stand built in 1632 by the vanished great house at Swarkestone, Derbyshire.

116   The Hunting Tower or Stand, probably built in the 1580s, on the hill above Chatsworth, Derbyshire.

elaborately geometric one as a central feature facing the house, at Chatsworth one on the mount, containing an alabaster table.[62] These have all gone, but the octagonal banqueting house, perhaps of the 1570s, in the garden at Melford in Suffolk is still there, though it has lost the marble table described in the inventory of 1635.[63] A banqueting house at Swarkestone in Derbyshire was built above a loggia in 1632 to survey the bowling green and provide refreshment for the bowlers; it still stands between two little turrets, one of which contains a staircase that gives access to it and continues up to the terrace of the roof (Fig. 115).[64]

106

(Fig. 117). Another fishing-cum-banqueting house, now no more, is shown, in an engraving by Kip (Fig. 118), rising out of a square pond at Sundridge Manor in Kent.[66] It had accommodation for pigeons above, ducks below, and humans in the middle, in a banqueting room with access onto a cantilevered balcony from which to fish. A geometrically exceedingly elaborate 'little wooden banqueting house' was projected by Richard Carew to rise out of an island in his 'fishful pond' at Antony in Cornwall, but was never built. Banqueting houses, like gatehouses and even more so, were often based on ingenious and unusual plans. More will be said about these in chapter 4.

Lodges are the third of the lesser building types associated with the great families of the period. A lodge was originally a residential building in a deer-park, forest or rabbit warren, secondary to the main house or houses where the family lived. Such parks or warrens were by no means always, or even often, next to the main house; the idea that a country house should be set in a park was an eighteenth-century one.

Lodges were of two grades, those for the owners and those for their employees, especially keepers and warreners. The latter type were normally modest buildings, but not always, because they sometimes doubled up as banqueting houses. The warrener's lodge at Rushton is one of the most elaborately decorated and best known of Elizabethan buildings (Figs 276–80), but this was not in deference to the warrener but to his employer, Sir Thomas Tresham: the warrener lived and skinned and stored his rabbits on the bottom two floors; the top floor was a banqueting room. The tiny Rodminster Lodge in the park at Longleat was carefully designed in 1585 for Sir John Thynne by his French mason Alan Maynard; here again the bottom room was probably for the keeper, and the top room for banquets.[67]

In a park belonging to a great family or to the Crown there was often a ranger or keeper who supervised it; he was a person of standing, and

edge of Colchester in Essex, is dated 1591. It was built as a banqueting house and fishing pavilion attached to St John's Abbey, which the Lucas family had converted into a private house. The eccentric and endearing Margaret, Duchess of Newcastle, who was a Lucas and was brought up there, must have disported herself with her tribe of sisters beneath its extravagantly shaped gables

118 (below) A fishing
pavilion, once at
Sundridge Manor in Kent,
as depicted in a detail
from an engraving by
Johannes Kip.

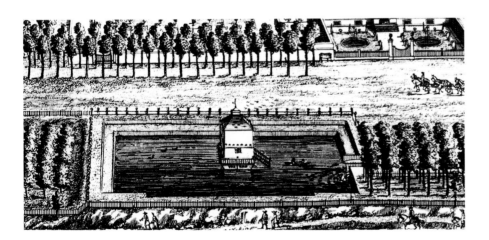

occupied a lodge that was a substantial building and in which it was perhaps assumed that the owner of the park and his hunting party would, at times, be entertained and even accommodated. The keeper or ranger of the Earl of Shrewsbury's parks at Worksop in Nottinghamshire was Roger Portington, of a good Yorkshire gentry family; the ranger of the royal Richmond Park was Sir Thomas Gorges, the builder and owner of Longford Castle; the ranger of Nonsuch Park was the Earl of Worcester, the owner of Raglan Castle.

119   The towering Manor Lodge, at Worksop, Nottinghamshire, completed 1595, was originally even higher, probably with a flat roof and parapet.

All built, or had built for them, substantial lodges in their parks; the amazing Manor Lodge at Worksop is the only survivor (Fig. 119).[68]

A new type of lodge appeared at the end of the sixteenth century, built not for hunting but as a retreat from the formality and responsibilities of a big house. Sir Thomas Tresham started to build such a lodge or 'New Bield' at Lyveden in 1594, but never completed it (Figs 255, 282); around 1615 Francis Bacon built a lodge at Verulam, a few hundred yards from his big house of Gorhambury;[69] at much the same time, the Earl of Exeter built a lodge at Wothorpe in Northamptonshire. It was described by Thomas Fuller: 'Wothorpe must not be forgot (the least of Noble Houses and best of Lodges) seeming but a dim reflection of Burghley, whence it is but a mile distant. It was built by Thomas Cecil, Earl of Exeter, to retire to (as he pleasantly said) out of the dust, whilst his great house at Burghley was 'a sweeping' (Figs 98, 307).[70]

But whether to hunt, meditate, relax or keep a mistress (according to Aubrey, Sir Nicholas Poyntz built Newark Park in Gloucestershire 'to keep his whores in',[71] and the 6th Earl of Shrewsbury took Eleanor Britten with him to his lodge at Hanwell, in Yorkshire, as a consolation and refuge from the formidable Bess),[72] lodges were places for escape, retreat and pleasure (Figs 119–24). They were holiday houses for rich people, designed for fewer servants and less ceremony. Their architecture is one of fantasy and enjoyment, not ostentation. They have certain common characteristics. They are built to compact plans, never courtyard ones. They are often built high, with a flat roof from which to watch the hunt or enjoy the view. There is no 'lodge plan', because they set out to be different; what they have in common is their variety.

Most lodges had the normal accommodation of a gentry house: a hall with screen, a parlour and a great chamber, not necessarily a withdrawing chamber and gallery, always fewer bedchambers.

120 and 121 Grand and
modest lodges in their
parkland setting at (*above*)
Wootton Lodge,
Staffordshire, built *c.*1610,
and (*right*) Hardington,
Somerset, dated 1581.
The lodge at Hardington
has been made habitable
in recent years.

122 and 123 Two
appendages of *c*.1600
to Weston Hall, West
Yorkshire: the banqueting
house in the garden (*right*)
and the remains of Dob
Park Lodge, high up on a
remote adjoining hillside.

In the lodge of King Basilius described in Philip
Sidney's *Arcadia*, no servants sleep in the house;
they must have slept in separate service buildings,
and there cannot have been many of them.[73]
When the Earl of Derby retired from his great
houses to keep what was called 'secret house' in
his lodge at Lathom in Lancashire in the 1580s, his
own sons waited on him at meals.[74]

Some lodges are tiny, but still with a sense of
presence; even the biggest are never enormous.
The lodge at Beckley Park in Oxfordshire (*circa*
1560) was one of the earliest and smallest, but it
still had room for a parlour and great chamber and
even, possibly, for a gallery on the top floor;
its three gabled turrets rising above the water
garden, perhaps developed from the medieval
moats of an earlier building, make it one of

110

124 Beckley Park, Oxfordshire, built, probably in the 1560s, as a hunting lodge on the edge of Otmoor.

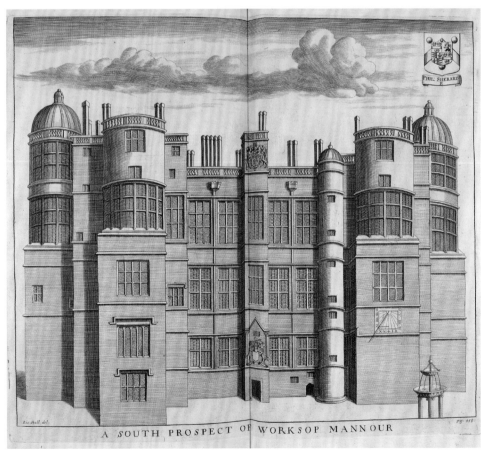

125 Worksop Manor, Nottinghamshire, originally one of the largest of lodges, built in two stages by the Earls of Shrewsbury, *c*.1550–90, as engraved for Robert Thoroton's *The Antiquities of Nottinghamshire* in 1677.

A SOUTH PROSPECT OF WORKSOP MANNOUR

126 (*facing pag, top*) Plan of the royal lodgings at Havering, Essex, based on the survey by John Symonds, 1578.

the most memorable of all Elizabethan lodges (Fig. 124).[75] The biggest known lodge was what became known as Worksop Manor in Nottinghamshire (Fig. 125). It owed its size to the fact that the 6th Earl of Shrewsbury added an extra floor to the lodge built by his father, to accommodate the newly fashionable gallery; but even so it is unlikely to have had more than half a dozen good bed-chambers.[76]

There is an obvious architectural influence running from Worksop to Hardwick. But Worksop was a single-pile house; by doubling the thickness at Hardwick, it was possible to produce enough bedchambers for the full-time residence of what Horace Walpole called 'a costly countess'. Worksop was equally clearly the model for Doddington Hall in Lincolnshire;[77] this was also single-pile, but the length of the gallery was curtailed and the length of the side wings increased so as to provide enough accommodation for the principal residence of a prosperous lawyer. It is probable that the fashionable glamour of lodges helped to increase a preference for high, compact plans, rather than courtyard ones, for use in houses that were full-scale country houses, not lodges.

Lodges also helped create what was to become one of the most lasting and powerful images of the country house: the house set well away from village, town or parish church in the secret world of its own park. The pleasures of lodge life proved such that in a generation or two from their being built they often became the principal residence of the family that built them and were enlarged if necessary to enable the conversion, as at Sherborne Lodge and Westwood. The 'Parks' and 'Lodges' that so often feature in the names of eighteenth- and nineteenth-century country houses were usually so called because they were rebuildings or remodellings of earlier lodges.

Palace Planning

Neither Elizabeth nor James I ever built a palace, and Elizabeth, as far as is known, never even contemplated building one; nevertheless, palace planning during their reigns is an interesting subject.

The necessary accommodation for royalty, under Henry VIII, is clearly set out in the plan drawn up to show how the Exchequer Building in Calais was to be converted in 1532 to accommodate a meeting between Henry VIII and François I. His wife, Katherine of Aragon, was accommodated too. The three royal apartments are made up, in sequence, of watching chamber, dining chamber, raying chamber, bedchamber and inner chamber, together with private oratories or closets, and stool chambers.[78]

Something like this accommodation was clearly provided at Nonsuch in the 1540s, as described in contemporary accounts and confirmed by excavation, even though no plans or building accounts have survived. Here there were just two sets of royal lodgings, for the king and his queen. Unlike the arrangement in Henry VII's royal lodgings at Richmond Palace, where king and queen were placed one above the other, the Nonsuch lodgings were on either side of a court, joined at the far end of each set by a gallery that filled the fourth side.[79]

A similar arrangement of two lots of five principal rooms plus chapels round a courtyard, but without the Nonsuch gallery, is shown in a plan for a projected royal palace at Waltham in Essex, probably to have been built for Mary and Philip of Spain.[80]

In 1578 John Symonds made a survey of the royal palace at Havering in Essex (Fig. 126), an irregular assembly of medieval buildings, but one quite frequently resorted to by the queen when on progress. The plan is useful because it names the rooms in the royal lodgings. There are five principal rooms, as in the earlier plans, but the names have changed. They are now great chamber

127 (*facing page, bottom*) Plan by Henry Hawthorne for the first floor of proposed additions to Theobalds, Hertfordshire, 1572.

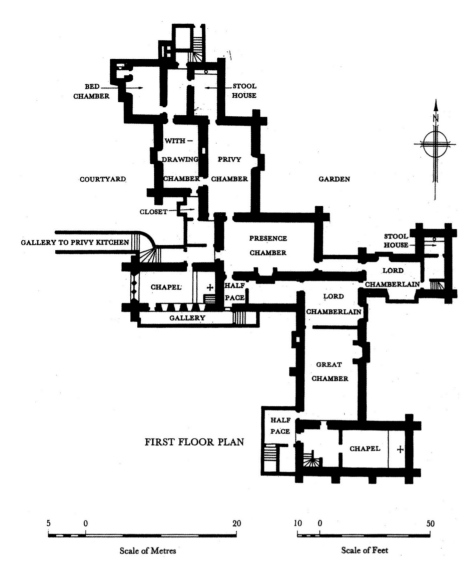

BED CHAMBER

STOOL HOUSE

COURTYARD

WITH — DRAWING CHAMBER

PRIVY CHAMBER

GARDEN

CLOSET

GALLERY TO PRIVY KITCHEN

PRESENCE CHAMBER

STOOL HOUSE

LORD CHAMBERLAIN

CHAPEL

HALF PACE

LORD CHAMBERLAIN

GALLERY

GREAT CHAMBER

HALF PACE

FIRST FLOOR PLAN

CHAPEL

N

5　0　　　　　　　　20　　　　10　0　　　　　50

Scale of Metres　　　　　　Scale of Feet

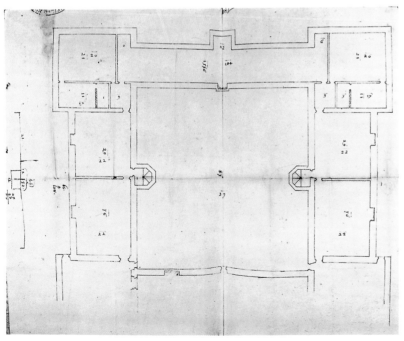

(instead of watching chamber), presence chamber (instead of dining chamber), privy chamber (instead of raying chamber), withdrawing chamber (instead of inner chamber) and bedchamber. Two rooms for the Lord Chamberlain, whose job it was to administer the queen's lodgings, are infiltrated in the sequence.[81]

The names remained the standard ones under Elizabeth and James. The great chamber, like the watching chamber, was a guardroom. The presence chamber was the room where the monarch gave audience and made proclamations, enthroned under a canopy, and sometimes ate with the senior members of the court on great occasions. But Elizabeth, unlike earlier monarchs, often ate alone and without great ceremony in her privy chamber. In 1599 Platter described how her meal was served with splendour to a splendidly appointed table in the presence chamber at Nonsuch, set out as though the queen were sitting at it, and then carried through for her to eat in the privy chamber.[82] Her withdrawing chamber and bedchamber were used as in non-royal houses.

When it became clear to Lord Burghley that Elizabeth was going to be making regular visits to his house of Theobalds, and that the existing accommodation was inadequate, he added on an extra courtyard for purpose-built royal lodgings. The first plan for this, drawn up for him by Henry Hawthorne in 1572, survives, and is remarkable (Fig. 127). It shows identical 'his and her' lodgings, each of four rooms, to north and south on either side of the courtyard, joined by a gallery, as at Nonsuch; the existing hall provided a great or guard chamber.[83]

There seems only one explanation for this. Burghley must have been anticipating a royal marriage. We have become so used to the image of the 'Virgin Queen' that it is easy to forget that in the first half of her reign it was taken for granted that Elizabeth would marry. The only problem was to whom. Between 1570 and 1582 (with a break when the St Bartholomew's Massacre in 1572 aroused strong anti-French feeling) the French

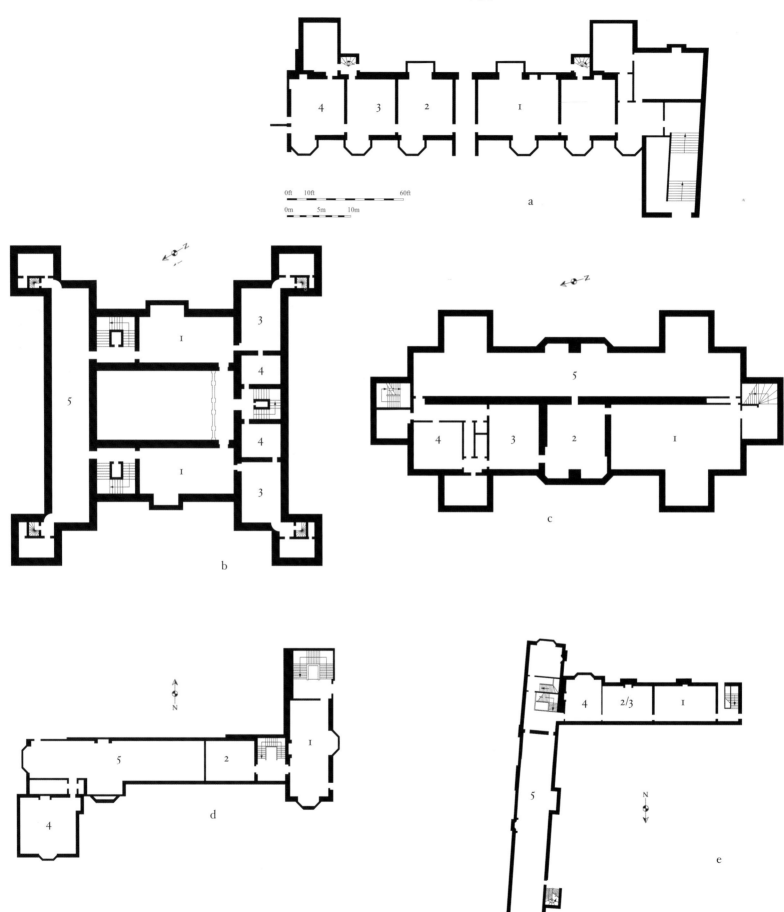

0ft   10ft   60ft

0m   5m   10m

a

b

c

d

e

128 (*facing page*)
Potential royal lodgings in non-royal houses:

a. New Hall, Essex, *c.*1573

b. Wollaton Hall, Nottingham, 1580–88.

c. Hardwick Hall, Derbyshire, 1590–97

d. Knole, Kent, *c.*1604–8

e. Apethorpe Hall, Northamptonshire, started 1622

1   Presence chamber
2   Privy chamber
3   Withdrawing
    chamber
4   Bedchamber
5   Gallery

dukes of Anjou and Alençon were the leading candidates, supported by Burghley and apparently favoured by the queen, though strongly objected to by some of her subjects. Marriage articles were actually drawn up in 1581.

In support of this explanation is the fact that when the new court was gradually built, more or less as in Hawthorne's plan of 1572, though with modifications, the northern royal lodgings were left as a blank.[84] With the exception of the north-west pavilion, which could not be truncated without spoiling the important west elevation to the privy garden, only the ground floor of the north range was built, finished off with a flat terrace walk at first-floor level, where the royal lodgings would have been.

This curious story of the non-materialising consort and his lodgings has one other odd possible sequel. Sir Francis Willoughby's Wollaton, started in 1580, two years before the final collapse of the negotiations, has identical 'his and her' lodgings on either side of the central great hall (Fig. 128b). Each are of three main rooms only; but as discussed in chapter 1, Elizabeth when on progress seems to have been content with lodgings of three rooms, rather than four. The double set is very odd. Willoughby, unlike Burghley, had no close connection with royalty, no apparent political ambitions, no government position, and did not even go to court. He was neurotic and obsessive, and architecture was one of his obsessions; it may be that he was thinking in terms of an ideally balanced plan, without other connotations.[85]

It seems improbable that magnificent four-room royal lodgings were not incorporated into the huge mass of Holdenby, presumably behind the long façade on the garden side; but in the lack of any but a ground-floor plan and the absence of any clear description of the interior, how it was arranged can only be surmised. At Burghley, Thorpe's plan of the first floor shows that four-room lodgings of great splendour could easily have been accommodated; but the planning of Burghley presents problems that there is no room to discuss. There are, however, two straightforward examples of a four-room sequence on the grand scale, simply arranged in sequence: at Longleat and Hardwick.

With Sir John Thynne at Longleat one has the same problem as with Sir Francis Willoughby at Wollaton: why should he provide such a grand set of lodgings? He was as detached from court life and politics as Willoughby. A search for the ideal may again be the explanation: the continuous creation and re-creation of Longleat was the passion of his life. In fact, unlike Wollaton, the queen did come to Longleat, in the summer of 1574, to Thynne's dismay, because the final remodelling of the house was still incomplete. The queen may never have occupied the lodgings clearly shown in the plans of Longleat that Burghley acquired, perhaps after her visit.[86]

The Longleat rooms have been redecorated. But if one wants to get the feel of the scale and the splendour of an Elizabethan royal lodgings, one can get it overpoweringly at Hardwick. Here, in sequence, are potential presence chamber, privy chamber, withdrawing chamber and bedchamber,[87] a sequence 166 feet long and backed by a magnificent gallery of the same length, with the presence chamber, privy chamber and gallery rising higher than the rest, up to a formidable 26 feet (Fig. 128c). The presence chamber is considerably larger and higher than the one at Theobalds, as enlarged at the request of the queen.

Again, why? There might seem no great likelihood of the ageing queen coming as far as Derbyshire in the 1590s. But at Hardwick one is faced with the problem of Arbella. Thanks to the marriage of Bess of Hardwick's daughter to Charles Stuart, Earl of Lennox, grandson of James IV of Scotland and his wife, Margaret, the sister of Henry VIII, Arbella Stuart, who was her only child, had a claim to the succession of the English throne, in rivalry to that of Mary, Queen of Scots' son James. As early as 1584, Mary had complained that 'nothing has alienated the Countess of

Shrewsbury from me more, but the vain hope, which she has conceived, of setting the crown of England on the head of her little girl, Arbella'.[88] As with Elizabeth's marriage, which never took place, Arbella's abortive succession can easily be dismissed, because with hindsight we know that her cousin James was to succeed smoothly and without opposition to the English crown in 1603. But in 1590, when the New Hall was started, the succession was still up for grabs; serious negotiations were in progress, apparently backed by Burghley, for the marriage of Arbella to Rainutio Farnese, son of the formidable Duke of Parma, the commander-in-chief of the Spanish army with which England was then at war. It was to be a political deal, peace to be signed with Spain in return for recognition of Arbella's claim to the English throne.[89] All this must have been heady stuff for Bess, who had left Hardwick as a minor squire's penniless daughter fifty years before.

In October 1591, a year or so after the building of the New Hall had started, Bess travelled with Arbella in grand style for an eight-month visit to London, and to the court. It is tempting to surmise that one of the aims of the visit was to pave the way for a visit by Elizabeth to the completed Hall, at which Arbella's marriage plans would be finalised, and her claim to be Elizabeth's successor recognised. In fact, negotiations fizzled out when Parma unexpectedly died in November 1592, and Rainutio's political importance died with him. Arbella never became queen; Elizabeth never came to Hardwick; Charles I, when Prince of Wales, dined in the High Great Chamber in 1619, but George V was the first and last monarch to sleep there.[90]

The accession of James I led to a change in the planning of royal lodgings.[91] Two sets in a single house now became an actuality, not a possibility, and in any house planned for a special relationship with royalty, suitable double provision needed to be made. The results can be seen in five (or, as will appear, possibly four) houses or palaces, three of which were built, while the other remained in plan. Not surprisingly, all five were enormous.

The first plan was produced by the Works, to be built by and for the king and his queen. There are two versions of this, a variant recorded by John Thorpe, and possibly designed by him, and one preserved at Hatfield. It was for a royal house to be built at Ampthill in Bedfordshire, and the letter from the Lord Treasurer, dated 3 August 1605, specified a house in which the king 'may be lodged, though not in state, yet sufficient to serve for the enjoying of his pleasures of hunting and hawking'.

The Works response to this request for something modest was to produce plans for a palace on the scale of Holdenby and Theobalds. It was planned round a large court of entry and two smaller internal courts divided by a cross hall, serving as a great or guard chamber. Double staircases to either side of this led up to king's and queen's lodgings, made up of the usual succession of four rooms, round two sides of the internal courts, with the royal bedchambers letting onto king's and queen's galleries, each 125 feet long and filling between them the entire garden front. To either side of the entrance court double-pile ranges were filled with lodgings for courtiers. It was all on the grand scale, unimaginative, and not very interesting. A similar, equally unimaginative plan is in the Thorpe drawings. Neither, not surprisingly, was ever built.[92]

The Cecils and the Howards dominated the first years of James's reign. Robert Cecil, long the trusted aide of his father, Lord Burghley, and a formidable personality in his own right, had engineered James's smooth succession. Both in reward for this and in justified tribute to his abilities he was created Earl of Salisbury in 1605 and Lord Treasurer when Dorset died in 1608. In 1607, one can surmise to his relief, he engineered the exchange with the king of the monstrous pile of Theobalds, which now became a royal palace, for a nearby property in Hertfordshire, on which he erected Hatfield House. This was large enough, but nowhere near as large as Theobalds.

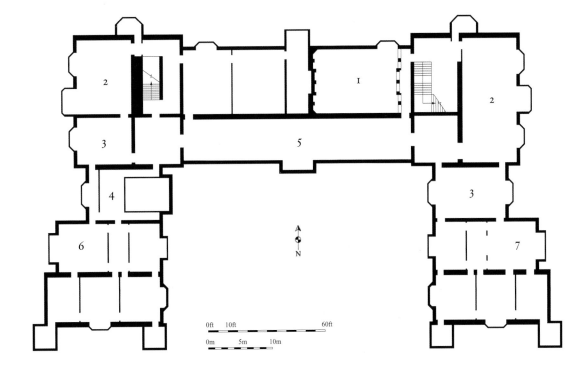

129 Plan of the first floor of Hatfield House, Hertfordshire, with room use based on an inventory of 1611.

1 Upper part of hall
2 Great chamber
3 Withdrawing chamber
4 Upper chapel
5 Gallery
6 Queen's bedchamber
7 King's bedchamber

Like Theobalds, however, it catered for royalty. There were lodgings for the king and queen forming east and west wings to either side of a great hall (Fig. 129). It is possible that Salisbury originally intended to join them together by a gallery at the bedroom end of the lodgings, enclosing a court; but in the event the gallery was built along the back of the hall, an unusual position in terms of conventional royal accommodation but making much more sense in terms of a house for a commoner – and getting rid of the courtyard plan, which was going out of fashion. James I came there once, in 1611, before Salisbury died of cancer in 1612.[93]

A feature of James's early reign was the resuscitation of the Howard family. It had been in the shade since the execution of the Duke of Norfolk in 1572, and the confiscation of his enormous properties. Norfolk's brother, Henry Howard, had been one of James's principal supporters before his succession; the Howards now came back into full royal favour: Henry Howard was created Earl of Northampton, and his nephew Earl of Suffolk, and much of the sequestered Norfolk property, was divided between them.

They were ready to supplant Robert Cecil, or to replace him when he died. And indeed, when this happened, the Lord Treasurership was first placed in commission between Northampton and Suffolk, and then granted outright to Suffolk when Northampton died in 1614. Meanwhile, in 1613, Suffolk had engineered a dubious divorce for his daughter and remarried her to the king's pretty Scottish favourite, Robert Carr.

In the early years of the reign, probably before Robert Cecil started work at Hatfield, Suffolk, encouraged and aided by his uncle, began to build a house as big as Theobalds at Audley End in Essex (Fig. 131).[94] Its plan was a variant on the Ampthill ones. The royal lodgings were deployed round a very large internal courtyard instead of two small ones; the hall was conventionally placed in the front range; two elaborate porches to either side of it gave entry to the king's and queen's lodgings (Fig. 130). Across the courtyard from the hall a chapel and (possibly) a council chamber over a privy cellar were placed at either end of a very long gallery, not, apparently, subdivided, but linking the king's and queen's lodgings. There was an immense arcaded forecourt of courtiers' lodgings,

A General Prospect of the Royal Palace of Audlyene

H. Winstanley at Littelbury fecit

131 A bird's-eye view of Audley End, Essex, built c.1605–14, from views and plans by Henry Winstanley, published c.1688–95.

130 (facing page) The two porches at Audley End, designed as separate state entries for the king and queen.

larger, probably, than was originally envisaged, and lower than the main building.

The whole enormous complex was finished, bar the great staircase to the king's lodgings, ready for James I's first visits to his new Lord Treasurer in 1614. He never returned. Suffolk had none of the character or capabilities of Robert Cecil or his father; his wife was corrupt and avaricious; his son-in-law had been disgraced and ostracised; in that year James had fallen for a handsomer and more determined young man, George Villiers, who was no friend to the Howards. In 1618 Suffolk was impeached for embezzlement and dismissed from the Lord Treasurership. He lost his job but kept his house, an appalling burden on his family until his grandson managed to unload it on Charles II in 1666 as a royal palace. In 1701, by when its architecture was completely out of fashion, William III returned it to the unhappy

Howards, whose only option was to demolish all but a third of it; but that third, which remains today, is large enough.

Meanwhile, George Villiers had gone on to become Duke of Buckingham and the most powerful subject of both James and Charles I. He embarked on an enormous house in his turn, on property that he bought at Burley on the Hill, Rutland, about 1620. Two, and possibly three, projects for it are recorded by Thorpe.[95] Something like them seems to have been built, but was perhaps never completed, and was demolished without adequate record later in the century.

The fourth design for a great new royal or private palace is also in the Hatfield papers (Fig. 132). It carries the date September 1605, and no other inscriptions.[96] The date suggests it was an alternative project for Ampthill, but it could have been a first project for Audley End. It comes as a

119

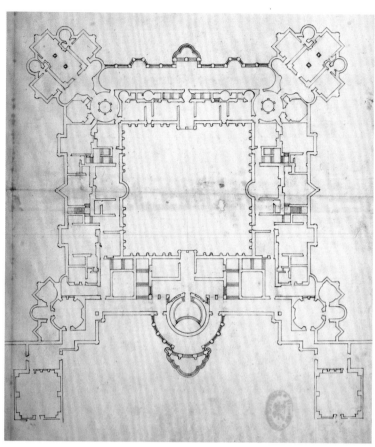

132a and b Plans dated
1605 for a projected royal
palace, probably at
Ampthill, Bedfordshire
(Hatfield CPM 2/8, 17).

relief after the other designs, for it is the most
inventive and enjoyable palace plan ever produced
in England – admittedly a country not distinguished for palace planning. It is a witty and ingenious conflation of English, French and Italian
plan forms, carried out with the greatest panache.

The dominant elements are a domed central
chapel or council chamber, with curved entrance
arcades wrapped round it, and four corner pavilions, in which the plan of a domed Italian centralised church is imposed at 45 degrees on a
square plan so as to produce the canted bay
windows favoured by the Jacobeans. Two of these
contain the royal bedchambers, and other inner
royal accommodation, grouped round a circular
lobby; two contain circular top-lit privy kitchens.
King's and queen's withdrawing chamber, privy
chamber and presence chamber, ingeniously
switched from side to side of double-pile wings,
link the bedchamber end to grand staircases on

either side of the central rotunda. There are king's
and queen's galleries back to back on the garden
front, and two great kitchens in the two wings
(only partially shown) enclosing the forecourt.
Who was responsible? A case can be made out for
John Thorpe, but only by explaining away his pro-
duction of two such totally different designs
within the same year, or couple of years. No other
name suggests itself.

After these plans other projects for royal accommodation come as an anti-climax, but one
not without interest.

At James I's accession in 1603, Thomas Sackville, Lord Buckhurst and soon to be created Earl
of Dorset, had been Lord Treasurer since 1599. In
the early 1600s John Thorpe had provided him
with plans for the rebuilding of his house at Buckhurst in Sussex (Fig. 133). They were on an enormous scale, and clearly designed for the full-scale
accommodation of royalty in the manner of

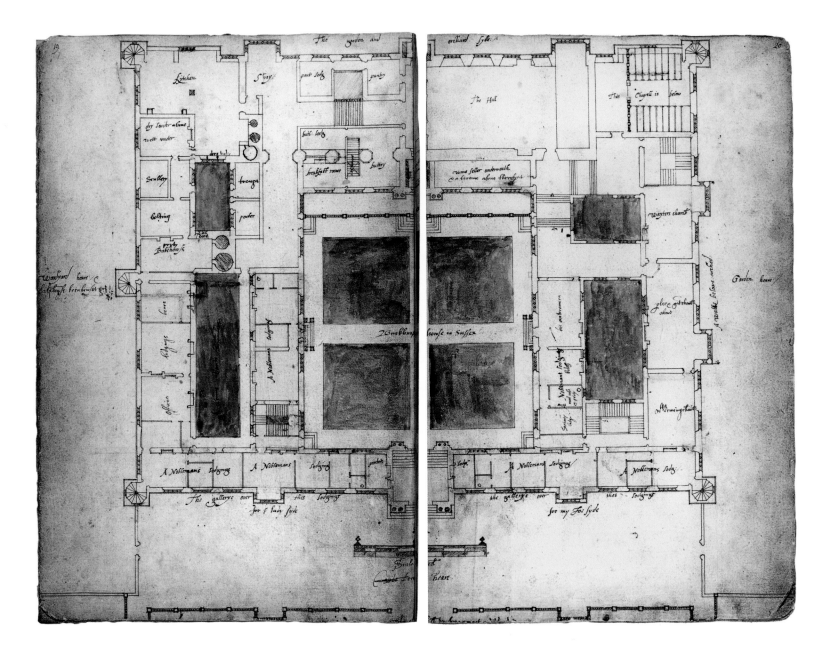

The handwritten labels on the plan include:
Kitchen, Stray, The garden and, orchard syde, The Hall, dry Larder a Cone nwell under, pant lody, panty, Waytars cham, Scullery, dreg bat, bruga, breakfast room, butry, buth lody, The Chapell is below, Colting, powter, pantry, Woodyard have Coltehoufe brenhoufes, hure, A Nobtemans lodging, Wine seller vnderneath & a terrene abone throghout, Garden have, Lodgyngs, glere girthalt aboud, M Drawing cha, Offices, A Nobteman sodyng, A Nobtemans sodyng, A Noblemans sodyng, A Noblemans sodyng, A Nobtemans sodg, The galleryc over thes lodgyng for ł laus syde, the gallerye over thes Lodgyng for my Ios syde

133 Plan of c.1603 for the first floor of a projected house at Buckhurst, Kent, adaptable for royal visits by king and queen. From a drawing by John Thorpe (T19, 20)

Theobalds. Curiously enough, there is no mention of royal accommodation in the annotations to the plans; the matching 'his and her' galleries are annotated as 'for my lords side' and 'for ye lady side'. The explanation, in this and other lodgings in non-royal houses, may be that it was inappropriate to give royal names to rooms except when the monarch was actually in residence; the only exception was perhaps for bedchambers, and these only when the monarch had slept there, after which, one can surmise, they were reserved for royal use.[97]

The house at Buckhurst was never built: in 1604 Thomas Sackville obtained possession of Knole in Kent and transferred his attentions to it. There was already a sizeable medieval and later house there, and he set about remodelling and enlarging it on the grand scale. He has been described as 'an old man in a hurry'; even so, he died in 1608, when his work was incomplete, and before any royal visit had been made. King's lodgings were formed along one side, to the southwest of the hall. The two doors at either end of the entrance loggia before the hall, seeming like

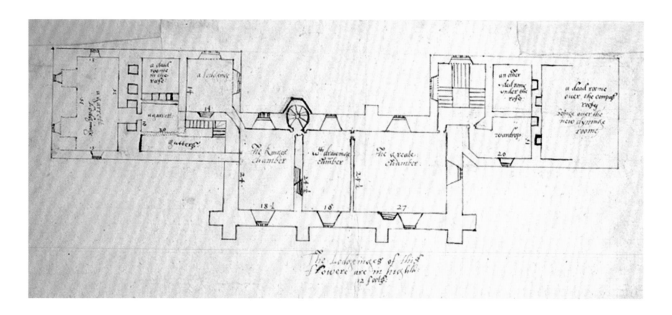

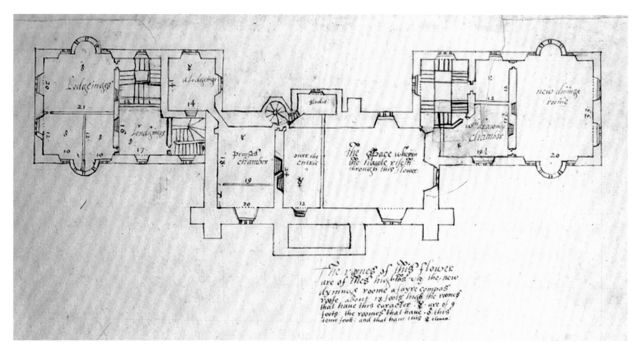

modest precursors of Audley End's great porches, suggest that matching queen's lodgings were contemplated, but if so they were never carried out. A forecourt of lower lodgings was formed on an earlier basis and to either side of an earlier gatehouse, to create an arrangement similar to that at Audley End, but on a smaller (but still considerable) scale.

The potential king's lodgings consisted of a very large presence chamber, a privy chamber, a gallery doubling up as a withdrawing chamber, and a bedchamber. Dorset used the artificers of the Works to decorate them, along with the hall and staircases by which they are approached. The artificers went on to work on Anne of Denmark's remodelled and extended lodgings at Somerset House, lavish and expensive interiors that were to be demolished without visual record. The Knole rooms, above all Cornelius Cure's exquisite fireplaces (Figs 434, 438), give some idea

135 A winter view of the south front of Castle Ashby House, Northamptonshire, built in the 1570s, the top storey added c.1624–35.

of what must have been their outstanding quality.[98]

The Scottish monarchs had lived in the French fashion, with far less formality and in far less extensive suites of lodgings than the English.[99] When he came to England James took on the full apparatus of English courtly life, but was anxious enough to get away from it when he could. His escape valve was to go hunting, on informal outings attended by (in contemporary terms) the minimum of servants and officials. In fact, he spent so much of his reign hunting as to arouse hostile criticism that he was neglecting the duties of his position. On many of these expeditions he stayed with his subjects. A plan of Robert Cecil's Cranborne Manor Lodge in Dorset is marked up for a royal visit and shows how inconsiderable was the accommodation that satisfied him: in effect, privy lodgings rather than state ones. He is given a modest great chamber, a small withdrawing

chamber and a bedchamber above the hall; there was no gallery (Fig. 134). The 'Prince' – probably Charles – had a chamber on the floor below, with a little staircase won through the medieval wall to a tiny 'studie' charmingly situated over the porch.[100]

One of James's favourite hunting grounds was Grafton Forest in Northamptonshire. When in this area he stayed frequently with the Hattons at Kirby and the Fanes, earls of Westmorland, at Apethorpe. The extension to the south-west corner of Kirby, with its two great compass windows (Fig. 338), was probably built to accommodate him.[101] He may have been similarly accommodated at Apethorpe; but in 1622 (as discussed in chapter 1), after five visits, for some reason Fane was ordered to enlarge the house 'for the more commodious entertainment of his Majesty and his company at his repair unto these parts for his princely recreation there'. The king gave him 100 trees from the royal forest to help him on his way.

A new west wing was accordingly added to the house (Fig. 25), and richly decorated rooms in the usual sequence were formed, in part on the basis of what was there before, ending in a large gallery. Entry to these lodgings bypassed the old great hall, and was by way of an arcaded 'white hall' on another side of the courtyard, with its own entrance, surmounted by a statue of the king. Anne of Denmark had died in 1619, so there was no need for queen's lodgings.[102]

But in the next reign lodgings for Charles I and possibly for the queen may have been provided between 1624 and 1635 at nearby Castle Ashby.[103] William, Lord Compton, had maried the daughter and heiress of the immensely rich Lord Mayor of London, Sir John Spencer, and was raised to the peerage, as Earl of Northampton, in 1618. He

was in the mood for aggrandisement: the existing house was raised by a second floor of rooms (Fig. 135) on a grander scale than those below them, on either side of the courtyard. Elaborate staircases were provided in both wings, each approached by independent access from the courtyard; the eastern one was rebuilt after a fire, but the west one retains its sumptuous balustrades and grand doorcases, the grandest of them at the head of the stairs on the second floor, clearly to give access to the lodgings of importance. There has been so much alteration and destruction in subsequent years that it is unclear whether these east and west lodgings – in a completely unfashionable position according to later tastes – were ever completed. But the ghost of them survives, hovering above the house, as a memento of the ambitions of those who responded to the existence, the illusion or the hopes of a special relationship with royalty.

136 Three of the family ancestors on the 1633 wing of Stapleford Park, Leicestershire

Chapter 3

Learning a
Language

The Arrival
of Classicism

Gillam Angram, of Dorchester, Mason. Married to a French woman. 9 children. In England 19 years.

Andrew Baudwyn, joiner. Born Normandy. In England 38 years. Aged 55. Married a Englishwoman of Kinsbury, Somerset.

Robert Lamberd, Frenchman, working on Nonsuch clock.

John Coke, joiner. Born Normandy. Aged 30. Has dwelt at Lewes with Mr Gage, controller of the Kings household, 12 years.

Ferawte Bazyn. Born Normandy, aged 60, Mason. In England 20 years.

Extracted from a return of Frenchmen, 1 July 1544

A return of Frenchmen in England, made in 1544 and certainly not comprehensive, revealed more than a hundred artificers, mainly masons, joiners and carpenters, scattered over the south and south-west of England. Most of them came from Normandy and Brittany; many had been in England since at least the 1520s.[1]

There is no reason to suppose that all these artificers could provide ornament in the new manner, but some of them certainly could. They were amongst the first wave of immigrant craftsmen who were to bring Continental fashions to England throughout the sixteenth century and into the seventeenth. Some (especially later on in the sixteenth century) came to escape religious persecution; more perhaps were just looking for work in a prosperous country that was free of the wars and massacres that troubled northern Europe, and was well supplied with clients greedy for new fashions. Some worked for royal or noble patrons, but by no means all did. A group of Dorset manor-houses, for instance, mostly quite modest, have stone panels of *circa* 1550 carved with Renaissance ornament, probably by one or more of the fourteen foreign artificers listed in the county in 1544.[2]

Returns of foreigners include few Italians, an indication of their failure to take root in England. Italian artists, artificers and engineers had in fact been coming and going since Pietro Torrigiano and three assistants came over from Florence to work on Henry VII's tomb and the adjacent high altar in Westminster Abbey in 1511. Torrigiano

returned to Italy in 1520; his skill in modelling was beyond English emulation at the time, but the device of a wreath flanked by cupids, which he used on the end of the Westminster tomb chest, was to be copied into the 1570s by Midlands alabaster workers on their monuments, his shapely cupids becoming rustic infants with bolster-like arms and legs in the process.

In 1521 Giovanni da Maiano provided the terracotta roundels of emperors now at Hampton Court for Cardinal Wolsey; in 1527 he was working on court entertainments. His roundels were to be much imitated in England, but he himself had returned to Italy by 1530. In 1524 Benedetto da Rovezzano came to England to work on a tomb for Cardinal Wolsey; in 1527 Henry VIII purloined him and whatever he had so far achieved for his own prospective monument, on which Rovezzano seems to have worked until he left England in 1543. Work on the monument, as magnificent in conception as it proved to be abortive in execution, continued in fits and starts until it finally petered out in the 1580s. All that survives today are the four bronze candelabra that have ended up at St Bavon in Ghent, and the marble sarcophagus originally made for Wolsey, which contains the body of Nelson in the crypt of St Paul's cathedral.[3]

Antonio Toto del Nunziata, who had come to England from Florence as one of Torrigiano's assistants in 1519, stayed longer and achieved more than most of the other Italians. He was a painter, but like most of the Italians was proba-

137 (*facing page*) A detail from the tomb chest of the Dormer monument at Wing, Buckinghamshire.

138 Design for an
unidentified building,
perhaps by an Italian
working in England,
c.1540.

They included the mysterious John of Padua, variously described as musician, architect, artificer, engineer and deviser of buildings, who was drawing £36. 10s. a year from 1543 to 1557, for services that have never been identified. About the rest of the funeral contingent, including five 'masters of building', nothing is known whatsoever. A drawing of *circa* 1540 in the British Library (Fig. 138), showing the elevation of a quite elaborate classical building, might be an unexecuted design by an Italian.[6]

What were the reasons for the failure of most of the Italians? Was it difficulties of language or religion, or was it that, on the whole, only the second- or third-rate ventured across the Channel? Whatever the reasons, French and Flemings, including those listed in 1544, achieved more, with less pretensions.

In England early (for this country) Renaissance ornament was called at the time 'antique work'. It was a delicate and distinctive style of decoration, usually in low relief (if cast or carved), and small in scale, deriving from painted Roman decorations as disinterred in Rome and adapted by Raphael for his loggias in the Vatican; from Rome it moved into northern Italy and was taken up with enthusiasm all over northern Europe. Its nature was vividly, if somewhat patronisingly, described in 1606 by Henry Peacham, writing when its vogue was on the wane:

> An unnatural and unorderly composition for delight sake, of men, beasts, birds, fishes, flowers & c without (as we say) Rime or reason, for the greater variety you show in your invention, the more you please ... You may, if you list, draw naked boyes riding and playing with their paper-mills, or bubbe-shells upon Goates, Eagles, Dolphins & c: the bones of a Rammes head hung with stringes of beads and Ribands, Satyres, Tritons apes, Cornucopias, Dogges yoackt & c. drawing Cowcumbers, cherries & any kind of wild trail or vinet after your own

bly ready to adventure into any of the arts. From 1523 to 1530 he disappears from the accounts, and perhaps returned for a time to Italy; but from 1530 until his death in 1554 he was steadily employed by the Crown, painting pictures, supplying heraldic pennons for tents and funerals, and devising and painting appurtenances for masques. In 1544 he was appointed Serjeant Painter and took out a coat of arms; in 1551 he was at the head of one of the two teams of painters that decorated the banqueting house erected in Hyde Park for the visit of the French ambassador. One of his daughters married Sir Charles Calthorpe, later Attorney General in Ireland; his descendants might still be traceable.[4]

All this time other Italian artists and military engineers were coming and going, and making little mark. In Henry VIII's funeral procession in 1546, an Italian contingent, fitted out in black at royal expense, included nine Italians described as 'artificers', 'engineers' and 'masters of building'.[5] Apart from Nicholas Bellin of Modena, about whom more will be said later on in the chapter, they were a shadowy and possibly forlorn group.

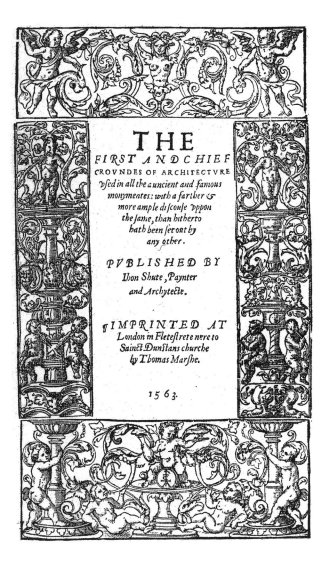

painting 'anticke worke' in rooms at Belvoir Castle, Rutland, in 1541, were foreigners; they both came from Leicester, and their names suggest that they were English.[8]

Engraved sources were the other route by which this European fashion came to England. Antique work was as suitable for embellishing books and prints as buildings; it could be used to make pretty borders, chapter heads and title pages (Fig. 139), and was lavishly so used in books printed on the Continent, and soon in books printed in England, some, but by no means all, by printers of foreign origin. Such books, wherever they came from, were freely raided by artificers or their patrons looking for ideas for ornament.

This kind of 'antique work' continued to be used in decorations up to the end of the sixteenth century and beyond. But it ceased to be in the van of fashion; its place was taken by a new, more robust or at least rumbustious style of decoration, described sometimes as 'cartouche' work but also, confusingly, as 'antique work'. It was popularised in England in the second half of the sixteenth century by Flemish engravings, but first introduced there by way of Fontainebleau at the great royal palace of Nonsuch in Surrey.

Nonsuch[9] was built and embellished for Henry VIII between 1537 and his death in 1546. It became the most celebrated English building (outside churches) of the sixteenth century, and remained so throughout the century (Fig. 140). William Camden, in *Britannia* (1586), his topographical and historical account of Great Britain, gave it the longest and most enthusiastic of his short accounts of individual buildings. It was (to quote him in part, from Holland's translation of his Latin text)

> built with so great sumptuousness and rare workmanship, that it aspireth to the very top of ostentation for shew; so as a man may think, that all the skill of Architecture is in this one piece of work bestowed, and heaped up

invention, with a thousand more such idle toyes, so that herein you cannot bee too fantastical.[7]

The word 'antic' derives from it.

Antique work could easily be incorporated in, or applied to, traditional late Gothic features such as tombs, window transoms and mullions, or open timber roofs; this was done frequently, and clearly with no feeling of a clash of styles. In England some, and perhaps most, of this work was produced by foreign craftsmen, but native-born artificers picked it up, either by learning from the foreigners or by copying engravings. There is no evidence, for instance, that Adrian Poole and John Wright, who were paid for

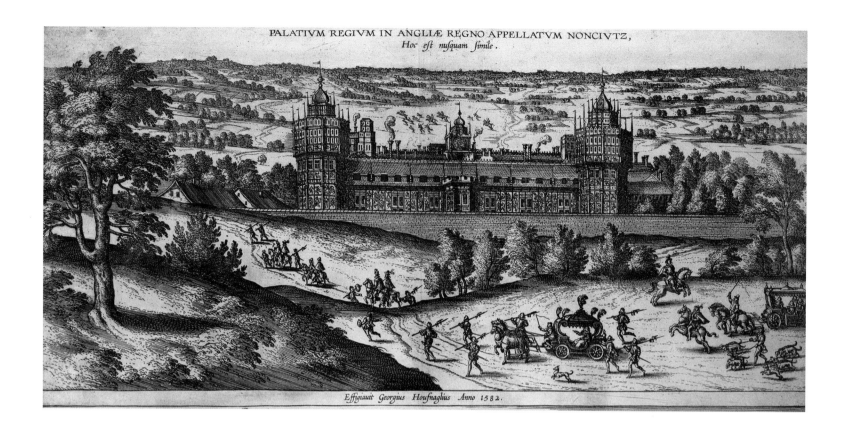

Effigiauit Georgius Houfnaglius Anno 1582.

140   Engraving of Joiris
Hoefnagel's view of
Nonsuch, Surrey, 1568.

together. So many statues, and lively images there are in every place, so many wonders of absolute workmanship, and workes seeming to contend with Romane antiquities, that most worthily it may have, and maintaine still this name that it have of Nonesuch.[10]

Nonsuch was designed as a place for retirement and pleasure, not as a seat of government; Henry VIII was influenced by his French fellow-monarch, rival and artistic exemplar, François I, whose way it was to transform the summer camping sites where he stopped on his hunting expeditions into pleasure-palaces large and small, culminating in the gigantic fantasy of Chambord (where he spent only sixty nights, or an average of three or four nights a year).[11] Nonsuch was a fantasy too, but in timber, slate and plaster, not stone. It was (apart from a stone gatehouse) a traditional English timber-framed structure, perhaps the biggest ever built in England, with two towers at the outer angles of its courtyard

rising up into cantilevered belvederes and turrets, the skyline alive with an army of little lions holding gilded standards, in the traditional Tudor manner. But all the timber framework, both inside the courtyard and on three of the external façades, was covered with carved and gilded slate, and the spaces between the timbers were filled with hundreds of plaster reliefs, depicting gods, heroes and scenes of classical mythology.

In 1670 Charles II gave Nonsuch to one of his mistresses, the Duchess of Cleveland, and she subsequently let it be demolished for the value of its materials. The few surviving depictions of its exterior give only a sketchy impression of its decoration; but the hundreds of fragments that came to light when it was excavated in 1959, combined with a design for an interior for Henry VIII, now in the Louvre,[12] and with all too little documentary evidence, make it clear that its decorations derived from royal buildings in France, above all from what is now known as the Galerie François Ier at Fontainebleau.

The walls of the gallery were sumptuously decorated in the 1530s by Italian painters and workers in stucco, led by Rosso and Primaticcio. The resulting decoration was more three-dimensional, larger in scale and more figurative than the low-relief manner of antique work. A series of big rectangular mythological paintings were linked by a stucco framework involving (along with a good deal else) smaller mythological scenes, boldly modelled life-size figures of cupids, gods and goddesses, luscious swags of fruit, profile heads of satyrs, and the leathery scrolls that came to be known as 'strapwork', all deployed and combined with variety and resourcefulness.

The timber structure of Nonsuch was erected by English artificers and its construction was supervised by a local office of the King's Works based on Hampton Court. But much, and perhaps most, of the decoration was by foreigners. Three names are known, in addition to Robert Lambert, the Frenchman who worked on making the clock: Giles Gering, certainly a foreigner, but it is not known from where, was granted an annuity of £20 in 1545 as 'the moldemaker of Nonsuch'; he was described in 1545 as involved in the king's 'white worke' there, was still drawing his annuity in 1548, when he was working for the Duke of Somerset, but then disappears and may have returned to the Continent.[13] William Cure, usually referred to as 'carver', the first of three generations of carvers or sculptors of distinction to work in England, was described in 1571 as 'in England thirty years, sent for hither when the King did byulde Nonesutche'.[14] Nicholas Bellin of Modena was an Italian who had worked at Fontainebleau.

Bellin was almost certainly the dominant stylistic influence at Nonsuch. He was gifted but dishonest. He first appears working at Fontainebleau with Primaticcio in 1533, on the king's chamber and the early stages of the gallery. In 1534 he was found out in some scheme to defraud the king and fled, ultimately, to England. François put pressure on Henry VIII to repatriate him to

France for punishment, but Henry was not going to give up so gifted and up-to-date an artist. Bellin was in royal service in England from at least 1537, first, probably, at Whitehall, and then at Nonsuch. He was allotted an annual pension of £10, which was later increased to £20. He took out letters of denization in 1541: they allowed him to take on two apprentices and four servants, of any nationality. At Whitehall he worked on a banqueting house, and a large chimneypiece of plaster in the privy chamber; on the latter he was assisted by seven 'Frenchmen'. He is known to have made other 'antike' plaster chimneypieces, either at Whitehall or Nonsuch. He was at Nonsuch by at least 1541, when he and five assistants were working on carving the slate decoration. He almost certainly worked on the plaster decoration there as well.[15]

In 1544 he was moved over to work on the tomb of Henry VIII. He had three French assistants, and possibly English ones as well, and was given accommodation and a workshop in what was known as the 'tombe house' in Dean's Yard, Westminster.[16] He was expelled from this, for unknown reasons, in 1551, but later reinstated. Early in 1547 he worked for the Revels on the 'mount', of mixed joinery and plaster of Paris, which featured prominently in a masque of *Orpheus*, put on for Edward VI's coronation festivities. It was dismountable and possibly moveable, and its decoration included twenty-four 'heddes', and an unspecified number of 'Antique boyes'. The moulded work was provided by Bellin and twenty-two 'other Carvers', unfortunately not named. At least twenty-seven joiners were also involved, working night and day for three or four days, amongst them Lewis Stocket, a future Surveyor of the Works, and his assistant John Symonds, both to play an important role under Elizabeth. The whole unwieldy structure, with masquers disporting on it, was probably pulled at the relevant moment into the great hall at Whitehall or Westminster.[17]

141 Portrait of Henry Howard, Earl of Surrey, c.1546. The surround is in the Fontainebleau style associated with Nicholas Bellin.

The Revels were under the direction of Sir Thomas Cawarden.[18] He was a crucial figure in patronage at the period, 'skilful and delighting in matters of devise' according to the diarist Henry Machyn. He was Keeper of Nonsuch from 1544, its leasehold occupier from 1550 until 1557, and Master of Tents and Revels from 1544 until his death in 1559. At the Revels workshop, located in his town house at Blackfriars, he provided lavish employment to foreign artificers; as a powerhouse of those in the vanguard of design it must have acted as a kind of Tudor Bauhaus. But the coronation mount, with its 'antique boys', the 'venus pageant' presided over by 'an ymage of Cupid', the 'Maske of Greke worthies' with headpieces 'of paste and cement moulded lyke Lyons heddes', the 'chariat, canapie and other properties' made for the Lord of Misrule in the Christmas season of 1551–2, all this and much else devised by Antonio Toto and Cawarden himself, made by Nicholas Bellin, by the Frenchman John Caron, the Low Countryman Robert Trunquet and others, has gone without visual trace.[19]

Bellin did more work for the Revels in 1548 as a 'moulder'; in 1550 he appears briefly and unimportantly in the accounts as a 'property maker'.

142 (facing page) Chimneypiece overmantel attributed to Nicholas Bellin, Broughton Castle, Oxfordshire, c.1555.

Then he disappears from both the Revels and the Works accounts, and although he continued to draw his pension and was given a New Year's gift of 40s. by Elizabeth in 1561, his career is without other documentation until his death in 1569.[20]

He is variously described as 'peintre', 'sculpteur', 'faiseur des masques' in his French period, and 'carver', 'moulder' and 'property-maker' when he came to England. Like other Italians he could work in a number of mediums. As a painter he can with some confidence be credited with the ornamental surround of the posthumous portrait of the Earl of Surrey (Fig. 141), until recently in the collection of the Duke of Norfolk and possibly painted in 1547, for this is a confident and swaggering exercise in the Fontainebleau style.[21] But his importance in England must mainly have derived from his skill as a 'moulder', modelling in the latest fashion in gypsum plaster or plaster of Paris, a technique and material previously unknown in England. Unlike the softer, more malleable and slower-setting lime plaster traditional in England, but before the middle of the sixteenth century used without ornament for rendering walls and ceilings, plaster of Paris set quickly and extremely hard, could be polished to a brilliant white, and needed quick modelling, which could be touched up by carving.[22]

All Bellin's work for royal patrons has long since disappeared, but one piece of work survives that must be his. It is in the somewhat unlikely setting of Broughton Castle in Oxfordshire. Here, in what is now an upstairs bedroom, a ring of Dryads dance hand in hand round a tree in a cartouche flanked by elegant naked boys and allegorical figures, all forming part of an overmantel, securely dateable to the years around 1555 (Fig. 142). Without doubt it derives from Fontainebleau: the dancing dryads, illustrating a passage in Ovid's *Metamorphoses*, are closely modelled on a fresco by Rosso in the Galerie François 1er, which was engraved at the time, as was the design for the cartouche. The quality of execution is from

QVERCVM·ERISICHTO
[·]IIALI·DRYADES·CIN[·]C
XÉRE·CHOREIS

143 An overmantel at Lyme Park, Cheshire, similar in style to the Broughton Castle chimneypiece.

fine overmantel in the drawing room (Fig. 144), though this owes more to Flemish than French sources. There is no documentation for the work of this period at Lyme Park; perhaps *circa* 1555–65 is the best one can offer.

One other member of the Nonsuch–Bellin–Revels circle needs to be mentioned: Robert Trunquet, Trunquette, Trunckey, Trunckye, Trunkwell, Trunkewell, joiner (all the spellings occur), sometimes referred to as Robert Arras, presumably because Arras was his home town. When Bellin died in 1569, Trunquet petitioned unsuccessfully for his pension to be transferred to him, claiming that Bellin was his 'master', and that Henry VIII had promised him a pension anyway. In his petition he gives a list of the works that he had carried out for Henry: a new 'preaching place' at Whitehall, equipment for the army at Boulogne, a banqueting house and 'Tower of Babylon' at Hampton Court, and another banqueting house in Hyde Park, built for a visit of the French ambassador. For Queen Mary he had 'wroughte . . . sondrie and straunge peces of work' on the strength of which Philip of Spain had tried to entice him out of England; later he had worked for 'manye right honerable and worshipfull personages', including the Earl of Leicester, in connection with Queen Elizabeth's visit to Kenilworth in 1566 or 1568.[24]

Trunquet was employed extensively by Cawarden at the Revels. His name occurs frequently in the accounts from 1547 until Cawarden's death in 1559. He is described as joiner, carver, or property or pattern maker, makes many accessories for masques, and the Lord of Misrule's chariot and canopy, and draws out devices for masques 'devysed by the Master' and sometimes possibly by himself. He was clearly trusted and favoured by Cawarden; Cawarden's successor dropped him, and he vanished from the Revels accounts, except for a brief reappearance in 1572, making 'patternes' and 'plottes' for the masque put on in Whitehall for the visit of the Duc de Montmor-

Fontainebleau as well; no English artificer at the time would have been capable of it.[23]

Even further afield from Nonsuch, the same distinctive cartouche reappears on the overmantel of the great chimneypiece now in the long gallery at Lyme Park in Cheshire (Fig. 143). It was probably once in a different and higher room, such as the great chamber, for the cornice has been removed to fit it into the gallery. It is a magnificently robust design, but lacks the refinement of the Broughton overmantel, and is perhaps by a less accomplished member of the Nonsuch team. The same artificer was clearly responsible for the

Cawarden from 1547 until his death in 1559, and he is said to have lived there with some magnificence.[27] The Reigate chimneypiece (Figs 145, 146) carries the royal arms, and probably came from his great chamber; it was common enough for chimneypieces in great chambers to be so adorned in non-royal houses, as a sign of loyalty.

The Reigate chimneypiece is joiner's work at its most elaborate and accomplished, translating the plaster curves of Fontainebleau into more angular shapes suitable to wood, with alcoves and canopies inspired, perhaps, by church work in the north of France, but with two winged and naked youths in the full Fontainebleau manner holding a crown over the royal arms.

This work at Broughton Castle, Lyme Park and Reigate Priory is the only surviving example of Nonsuch-style decoration. It is likely enough that other work in the same style has been destroyed; early in the eighteenth century, for instance, Daniel Defoe visited the 'decayed magnificence' of the great house of Lord Clinton (later Earl of Lincoln) at Sempringham Priory in Lincolnshire, shortly before it was demolished, and described how 'the plaster of the ceiling and walls in some rooms is so fine, so firm, and so entire, that they break it off in large flakes, and it will bear writing on with a pencil or steel pen, like the leaves of a book. This sort of plaster I have not seen anywhere so very fine, except in the palace of Nonesuch in Surrey.'[28]

But even allowing for destruction, Nonsuch and its decoration seems to have been more admired than emulated. Surviving examples of hand-modelled figurative plasterwork are not found again until the 1570s, and not much of it before the 1580s; figured plasterwork on exteriors not until the very end of the century. Plaster of Paris, or its equivalent 'alabaster plaster', made with powdered alabaster instead of gypsum, continued to be used on occasions.[29] But the type of plasterwork decoration that caught on was in a different style, material and technique: soft,

ency. Somewhat mysteriously, in May 1562 he became a freeman of Bristol. He took no apprentices there, and there are no payments to him in the City of Bristol archives.[25]

Trunquet's œuvre is as elusive as the work of all the others in the circle. But, as Cawarden's favoured joiner, one outstanding piece of work can be attributed to him with some confidence. This is the great wooden chimneypiece, now at Reigate Priory in Surrey, but according to John Evelyn, who saw it in 1655, brought there from Bletchingley, a few miles away.[26] The manor-house at Bletchingley belonged to Sir Thomas

145 and 146 (*facing page and right*) A chimneypiece now at Reigate Priory, Surrey, probably removed from Bletchingley Manor nearby, the home of Sir Thomas Cawarden, Master of Tents and Revels. It is attributed to the Flemish joiner Robert Trunquet.

slow-setting lime plasterwork, moulded not by hand but repetitively in wooden moulds made by joiners or carvers, or made by pulling shaped scrapers across the wet plaster to produce elaborate patterns of ribs, sometimes on extrusions built out in timber or metal from the ceiling and plastered over to form pendentives. The inspiration derived from late Gothic stone vaulting by way of ribbed timber ceilings, as in the Watching Chamber at Hampton Court.

It may be that the technical difficulties of modelling by hand quick-setting plaster of Paris was an obstacle to its spread. It is possible, too, that character defects in Nicholas Bellin, who has claims to have introduced it to England, worked against it. Bellin's flight from France, his expulsion, even if only briefly, from his quarters in Westminster, the slow progress of Henry VIII's tomb, the fact that he seems to have been dropped from employment at both the Revels and Works, suggest an unsatisfactory personality.

The Five Orders

Intriguing though the story of Nonsuch and its influence may be, in the 1540s and '50s the English discovery of the five orders, and of the Roman buildings in which they were used, was more important. The long reign of Tuscan, Doric, Ionic, Corinthian and Composite, still going strong today, had begun.

It is hard for us, who take the orders for granted, to realise how exotic and interesting they must have seemed to Englishmen in the mid-sixteenth century. England had a long and lively tradition of native architecture, but it was an architecture without rules, and without written treatises, even if with secrets of construction and proportion enshrined within the mysteries of the masons' guilds. At first the 'antike maner' had seemed merely an agreeable new kind of ornament that could be used to enrich traditional construction. But then came the gradual recognition of these five architectural entities, each with their own individuality, each with their own rules, each with a long pedigree going back to ancient days, endowed with the authority that that gave for people who thought less in terms of new inventions than in the rediscovery of ancient wisdom.

There were three main ways of becoming acquainted with the orders, by direct experience of Roman remains in Italy or France, by learning from others who knew about them, or by learning from books, engravings or drawings.

Although travel to Italy from England was increasingly discouraged in the course of the sixteenth century, and licence to make it had (in theory, at any rate) to be given by the Privy Council, a significant number of visits are recorded, some under licence, others made more or less permanently by Catholics in retreat from religious persecution. Visiting Rome was viewed with especial suspicion; visiting Venice was more acceptable, because Venice was intolerant of papal authority.[30]

But although English tourists might visit Roman remains and modern buildings, and write about them with appreciation, as did William Thomas in his *Historie of Italie* (1549), it was difficult to apply the knowledge gained in any meaningful way without bringing back drawings, books or engravings from which to work. Thomas Hoby's autobiographical description of his Italian visit in 1548–9 is full of enthusiastic descriptions of what he saw; but when he returned to England and collaborated with his brother to remodel and add to the monastic buildings at Bisham Abbey in Berkshire, the modest pedimented windows and respectable classical chimneypiece in the great hall, attractive though they are, are combined with traditional Tudor features and could have been created (as such features were) by patrons who had never been near Italy.[31] Twenty years or so later, in 1574, Robert Corbet, Sir Philip Sidney's old school fellow and friend, met up with him in Venice, and was entrusted by Sidney with his portrait by Veronese, to take to Sidney's mentor Hubert Lanquet. On his return, as Camden puts it, 'carried away with the affectionate delight of Architecture [he] began to builde in a barraine place a most gorgeous and stately house, after the Italians modell; But death prevented him, so that he left the new work unfinished and the old castle defaced.' But it would not occur to anyone not knowing the background to see direct Italian influence in the lively Elizabethan classicism of the ranges that he did put up at Moreton Corbet in Shropshire (Figs 220, 222, 223).[32]

Although there may well have been others, only two examples have come to light of English visitors apparently bringing back graphic material from Italy at this period; in both cases whatever they brought back has disappeared. Of the 'trikes and devises' collected in Italy in 1550 by the protégé of the Duke of Northumberland, John Shute, more will be said later on in this chapter. In 1554–5 Sir William Pickering, who had been ambassador in France from 1551 to 1553, travelled for a year in Germany and Italy. When he died in 1575 he left to his 'good frinde and old acquaintance' Lord Burghley 'all my papers of Antiquities that are pasted together of the monuments of Rome and other places as appeareth better by a paper booke of the same'. It is probable that these were collected on his visit of 1554–5.[33]

Some of the artificers who came to England from abroad in the mid-century must have been acquainted with the orders. Occasional columns feature in the Galerie François 1er, though more as part of the decoration than its framework; and the Fontainebleau overmantel at Broughton Castle incorporates fluted Ionic pilasters and entablature. The Reigate Priory chimneypiece includes a handsome order of four Corinthian columns.

But the main source from which the orders in mid-sixteenth-century England derived was from publications.[34] They featured in illustrated editions of Vitruvius, by Jocundus in 1511, by Cesariano in 1521, by Barbaro in 1556. Editions of Vitruvius certainly came to England in the sixteenth century,[35] but, as sources for the orders, three other publications were more important: the Third and Fourth Books of Sebastiano Serlio's *Architettura*, first published in 1540 and 1537 respectively; Hans Blum's *Quinque Columnarum exacta descriptio atque delineatio cum symmetria*, published in Zurich in 1550; and John Shute's *First and Chief Groundes of Architecture*, published in London in 1563. Serlio was first in the field, and included, in addition to the five orders (Fig. 147), engravings of Roman remains, and of his own classical designs. Blum illustrated only the orders

(Fig. 148), but illustrated them in folio rather than (as Serlio and Shute) in quarto, with careful engravings of high quality, which were easy to work from, and inspired frequent new editions, published in German, French and Dutch throughout the century (but in English not until 1601). Shute also illustrated only the orders, and had the advantage of writing in English; new editions were published in 1579, 1584 and 1587. Inspired by what Vitruvius and Serlio had written about the characteristics of the orders – Doric masculine, Ionic and Corinthian feminine – and by the somewhat tentative way in which Serlio had accordingly introduced female figures into his Ionic and Corinthian chimneypieces, Shute accompanied each order by a full-scale human figure or caryatid, very competently drawn: Atlas for Tuscan, Hercules for Doric, Diana or Juno for Ionic (Fig. 149), Vesta or 'some lyke virgin' for Corinthian, Pandora for Composite. The use of Atlas and Pandora seems to have been his own invention; the others derive from hints in Vitruvius or Serlio.[36] Thus personalised, the five orders joined the other groups with which the Elizabethans liked to humanise or make vivid abstract qualities or historical eras: the Seven Liberal Arts, the Three Graces, the Four Cardinal Virtues, the Nine Worthies, and so on.

Serlio's Third and Fourth Books were momentous publications. For most Elizabethans the engravings in the Third Book were the first and usually the only way in which they got to know the classical monuments in Rome and elsewhere, in plan, elevation, section and detail: among them the Colosseum and other theatres or amphitheatres, the triumphal arches of Titus, Septimius Severus and Constantine, Trajan's Column, the Pantheon and other temples. The Third Book, and later the Fourth and Fifth, not only gave details of the individual orders but also expanded on them, and on ideas derived from classical buildings, to show how the classical style could be applied to contemporary needs, and produce ele-

147, 148 and 149 Three versions of the orders: (*right*) an Ionic capital, from the Fourth Book of Sebastiano Serlio's *Architettura*, 1537; (*below*) the Five Orders, as adapted by John Thorpe (T13) from Hans Blum's *Quinque Columnarum Exacta Descriptio*, 1550; (*far right*) the Ionic Order, as illustrated in John Shute's *First and Chief Groundes*, 1563.

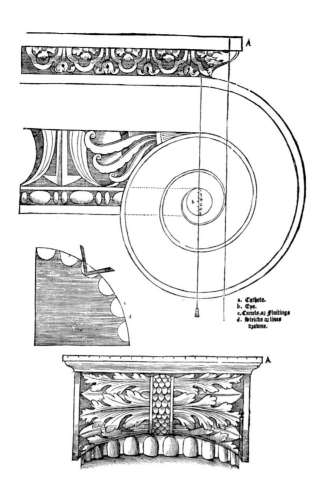

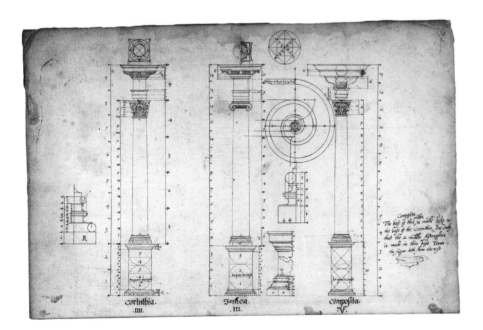

ments for which there was no classical precedent, such as domestic buildings, churches, chimney-pieces, ceilings, balustrades, window surrounds and altarpieces. For a hundred years and more they were to be a fruitful crib for whole buildings or details of buildings, in England as elsewhere in northern Europe. The cribs, however recognisable, were seldom exact; the inexactitude had Serlio's blessing, for he stressed the importance of 'invention', and made it clear that the Romans themselves frequently diverged from the rules laid down by Vitruvius.[37]

The extent to which English users read Serlio's text, in addition to using his engravings, is debatable, for the first English edition appeared only in 1611. What he wrote must, however, have been accessible both to the sizeable number of foreign artificers working in England and to educated

English patrons, for there were editions available in Italian, Latin, Dutch, French and German. Serlio's publication history is in fact prolific and exceedingly complicated[38] – a tribute to his popularity. The Third and Fourth Books first appeared in Venice in 1540 and 1537. The First and Second Books, on geometry and perspective, were published jointly in Paris in 1545, in French and Italian. The Fifth Book, on 'Temples' – that is, churches – also first came out in Paris, in the same two languages, in 1550. A book of designs for doorways, first published in Lyons in 1551, was incorporated with the first five books in one volume, printed in 1566 in Venice. The Seventh Book, on buildings for irregular sites, appeared only posthumously, at Frankfurt in 1575. All the books had subsequent editions, in various languages. For England those published in Antwerp by Pieter Breughel's stylistically unlikely father-in-law, Pieter Coecke of Alost, were the more important, probably more so than Serlio's originals. Coecke was one of the generation of Flemish painters and sculptors who travelled to Italy, and especially to Rome, in the first decades of the sixteenth century, fell in love with classical buildings, and displayed their love, on or before their return, in paintings of Roman, mythological or biblical scenes against a classical background, in panoramas of entire classical cities, and in designs for actual classical buildings, archways, chimney-pieces, tombs and tapestries.[39] Coecke had been to Rome in the 1530s, and even beyond it to Istanbul; but his especial contribution was to publish pattern books of classical architecture, first his own modest *Die Inventie der colommen* (1539), inspired by Vitruvius, then, from 1539 onwards, his editions of Serlio, and finally, in 1550, his handsome folio book of engravings of the triumphal arches and other decorations put up to celebrate the visit of Philip of Spain to Antwerp in 1549.

This early (for northern Europe) classicism, of which Coecke was one of the leading protagonists but by no means the only one, was to be over-shadowed by later developments in the Low Countries. Most of its products, including the royal palaces of Boissu, Binche and Mariemont, have been demolished; and the second half of the century saw the development, often under those who had been the leaders of the earlier manner, of a new vocabulary of Mannerist classicism, of distorted or exaggerated forms enriched with lavish strapwork and other ornament, which took it a long way from its Roman origins. This was made accessible by a flood of engravings, and was taken up in England with such enthusiasm that the influence there of early Flemish classicism has been largely forgotten.

Coecke was a shameless plagiarist who, to Serlio's fury, produced his unlicensed Flemish version of the Fourth Book in 1539, two years after Serlio's Italian first edition. He followed it up with French and German translations in 1542, and Flemish translations of the Third Book in 1546, and of the First, Second and Fifth Books in 1553. But he was a man of gifts; his editions, however dubious his methods, were well produced, his reproductions of Serlio's illustrations were of at least as good quality as the originals, and he was learned enough to amend the text in the light of his own study of Vitruvius.

Since England's connections with the Low Countries, especially with Antwerp, were much closer than those with France or Italy, and since Antwerp was burgeoning as the centre of the book trade in northern Europe, it is likely that Serlio reached England at least as often via Coecke as by other routes. When the first four books were finally translated into English in 1611, they were based on Coecke's editions, not Serlio's.[40]

Whether originating from Venice, France or Antwerp, designs from Serlio were used in England from 1540, if not before. Ceiling designs appear, possibly on the cove of the screen at King's College chapel, Cambridge, of about 1536, certainly on the ceiling of the Chapel Royal in St

James's Palace, London, dated 1540. Then comes the extraordinary drawing of a multi-storey archway designed as an apotheosis of Henry VIII, dated 1546, and signed by Robert Pyte or Pytt. Nothing is known of him, except that on 17 March 1550 he was granted the office of engraving coinage dies for the Royal Mint at the Tower of London, and by June 1552 was dead. The design incorporates elements of one of Serlio's Composite chimneypieces in its upper sections, and its Ionic order probably derives, with variations, from Serlio.[41]

If this problematic drawing was ever intended to develop into an actual structure, it almost certainly failed to do so. But between about 1547 and 1551 the first English building to be conceived in terms of the orders rose up on the Strand: the long street range of the Lord Protector and Duke of Somerset's Somerset House, all that he achieved of an intended rebuilding of this courtyard house

before he fell from power and was subsequently executed in January 1552 (Figs 150, 151).

The site was a prominent one, on the main thoroughfare joining the City of London to the palaces of Whitehall and Westminster. Elements from it were to be much imitated. As an exercise in classicism it was a good deal more serious than the strapping of bastard pilasters with which one of two new gatehouses at Whitehall had been encased at the same time or a little earlier.[42] But it is easy enough to pierce the classical disguise and see the traditional Tudor entrance façade behind it: classicised bay windows at either end, a classicised gatehouse in the centre, small classicised windows in between.

Unfortunately, almost all contemporary documentation, including the building accounts of the entrance range, have disappeared, and all that one has to go on for evidence of what artificers were involved is the payment of debts outstanding at the time of Somerset's fall, made to men who were not necessarily working on Somerset House: to Gering and William Cure, both probably Flemings, who had also been working at Nonsuch; to the English masons Humfrey Lovell, who was to become the Queen's Master Mason in 1564, and John Hill, who later reappears at Longleat; and to the English carpenter John Revell, who was to become Surveyor of the Royal Works in 1560.[43] In addition, in 1549 Somerset's right-hand man Sir John Thynne had sent down what his West Country steward described as a 'lewd company' of drunken French masons to work on an intended house at Bedwyn Broil in Wiltshire, a project that seems never to have got beyond the foundations; and these may well have been working at Somerset House.[44] Thynne's name should be added to the various artificers, for his total commitment to building was to be shown in subsequent decades at Longleat.

In spite of the lewd masons, and what has been written about Somerset House (by me amongst others), there is not much sign of stylistic influ-

150 (below) The Strand front of Somerset House, Westminster, c.1547–51, as drawn by John Thorpe (187).

151 (bottom) The Strand front of Somerset House, from an eighteenth-century drawing.

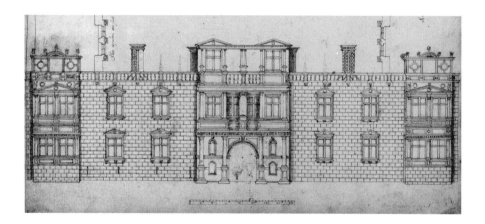

152 The triumphal arch put up by the English merchants in Antwerp in 1549 to celebrate the entry of Philip of Spain. It was designed by the Antwerp painter Lambert van Noort. From Cornelius Scribonius, *Spectaculorum in susceptione*, 1550.

153 An eighteenth-century measured drawing of the chimneystacks on the Strand front, with ornament derived from Serlio.

triumphal arches put up at the expense of the Spanish, English, Florentine and German merchants to celebrate the entrance of Philip of Spain to Antwerp in 1549 (Fig. 152). These accomplished designs, made by Lambert van Noort and others, drew heavily on Serlio and were engraved (probably with improvements) in the handsome record of the entry published in Flemish, French and German by Coecke in 1550, with a text by his friend Cornelius Grapheus, the town clerk of Antwerp.[45]

At Somerset House there were direct quotations from Serlio on the chimney stacks, where traditional Tudor ornament was replaced, somewhat inappositely, by ceiling coffering taken from Serlio (Fig. 153), and in the flaming grenades, much fancied by Serlio, that topped the two bay windows. The classical features of the gatehouse were inspired by, but did not copy, Roman triumphal arches as recorded in Serlio's Third Book, and by Serlio's own designs for gateways in his Fourth Book.

The female Victories, who hold wreaths that filled the spandrels of the entrance arch and were to catch the fancy of English artificers, derive from the similar figures in the spandrels of the Arch of Constantine in Rome, but apparently

ence from France on its Strand front. Rather, the general composition follows the English Tudor tradition, and the classical detail relates to Serlian classicism as retailed in Antwerp, especially in Coecke's edition of his books, and in the series of

by way of the Antwerp arches in which they featured; for Serlio, although he engraved the Roman arch, did not show its sculptural embellishments. From the Antwerp arches, too, come the panels of linked circles and rectangles on the Somerset House bay windows, a device that was to be constantly repeated in England.

Another feature of the Strand façade, as depicted by Thorpe, were classical roof balustrades, taking the place of the battlemented parapets traditional in England. Such balustrades also

derived from Serlio, and (if the engraving is to be relied on) one crowned the grand arch erected by the English merchants in Antwerp in 1549 (Fig. 152). They were an invention of the Renaissance, an expansion on the single balusters used in Roman times to support candelabra or funerary urns.[46] In Italy in the late fifteenth and sixteenth centuries they marked off terraces, loggias or floor-deep windows; they were sometimes used to crown churches or public buildings, perhaps never (and never in Serlio) as parapets for domestic

155 The monument to Sir Robert Dormer, carrying the date 1552, at Wing, Buckinghamshire. John Shute is suggested as the possible designer.

Two of the most remarkable productions of the mid-sixteenth century in England are Bishop Stephen Gardiner's chantry in Winchester cathedral and Sir Robert Dormer's tomb at Wing in Buckinghamshire. Gardiner died in 1555, but the chantry may have been erected before his death. Dormer's tomb carries the date 1552, the year of his death, but was probably erected a few years later.[47] The Winchester work is an impressive outburst of robust and competent classicism, enclosed, in a way that seems odd to us but may not have seemed odd to contemporaries, in a rich setting of Gothic tracery and vaulting. The Wing tomb is equally splendid, both in the scale and richness of its four Corinthian columns and the Corinthian entablature of the canopy that they support (Fig. 155), and in the tomb chest under the canopy, sumptuously adorned with ox-skulls and swags (Fig. 156). Fussy later additions in the wall behind the tomb detract only marginally from the noble gravity of the whole.

The round-headed alcoves and figurative sculpture of the Winchester work suggest a relationship to the Antwerp arches, and possibly to similar arches erected in London by the Genoese and Florentine merchants for the coronation of Mary in 1553, of which no illustrations survive.[48] One might posit a similar background for the Wing tomb, but a tempting alternative is worth considering. Could it be the one surviving design of John Shute, the author of *The First and Chief Groundes of Architecture*?

Shute was a member of the Painter-Stainers' Company in London, and had been sent by the Duke of Northumberland to Italy in 1550. In his own words, to quote from the oddly punctuated dedication to Queen Elizabeth in his book,

. . . being servant unto the Right honorable Duke of Northumberland. 1550. It pleased his grace for my further knowledge to maintaine me in Itailie ther to confer with the doings of ye skilful maisters in architectur, and also to

buildings, which usually had low-pitched roofs extending to the eaves. At Somerset House they were used pioneeringly as protection for domestic roof-top walks. They were copied almost immediately at Lacock Abbey (Fig. 154) to crown the tower and probably to protect the walk that led up to it, although its existing parapet is a later replacement. From then on, for the rest of the century and beyond, they featured prominently in the grander domestic buildings in England.

156 The tomb chest of the Dormer monument.

157 A Roman sarcophagus in the Museo dei Conservatori, Rome.

view such aincient Monumentes hereof as are yet extant, whereupon at my retourne, presenting his grace with the fruites of my travailes, it pleased the same to shewe them unto that noble king Edward the VI. Your maiesties most deare brother of famous memorie, whose delectation and pleasure was to see it, and suche like. And having the sayde trikes and devises aswell of sculpture and painting as also of Architecture, yet in my keeping, I thought it good at this time to set fourth some part of the same for the profit of others, especially touching Architecture.

It is not known in what year Shute returned from Italy, or what, if anything, he did for Northumberland or Edward VI. Presumably he envisaged, and possibly started on, a publication on architecture, to be dedicated to one or other of them, as William Thomas had dedicated his *Historie of Italie* to Northumberland (then Earl of Warwick) in 1549. But in July 1553 Edward died; and in August Northumberland was executed, having failed to put Jane Grey on the throne instead of Mary Tudor.

A few portrait miniatures of no great importance are attributed to Shute. In 1561, more interestingly, he designed a masque for the Merchant Taylors' Company to celebrate the inauguration of Sir William Harper as Lord Mayor of London; the masque featured David (a pun on Harper) accompanied by Orpheus, Amphion, Arion and Iopas. *The First and Chief Groundes* (the figures in which are suggestive of masque designs) finally came out in 1563; the text suggests that further volumes were in contemplation, but Shute died in the same year.[49]

It would be surprising if Shute's Italian expertise, drawing skills, knowledge of architecture and collection of Italian material (whatever the 'trikes and devises' may have consisted of) was not put to further use during the ten or more years after his return to England. There are two grounds for considering the possibility of his involvement with the Dormer tomb: Dormer's connections with the Sidney and Dudley families, and the nature of the monument.

Robert Dormer's son, William, who probably put it up, had been married to Mary, daughter of Sir William and sister of Sir Henry Sidney. Henry Sidney was married to Mary, the daughter of the Duke of Northumberland and sister of Robert Dudley, later Earl of Leicester. The Sidneys were proud of the Dudley connection; in 1584 Henry's son Philip Sidney was to write 'my chiefest honour is to be a Dudley'.[50]

In the 1550s a good many people would have been capable, especially on the basis of Serlio, of producing the grand Corinthian order of the Dormer tomb. The tomb chest is a different matter. It relates to nothing in Serlio, and is inspired by Roman altars and sarcophagi (Fig. 157), of which no contemporary engravings have been identified.[51] Could such a drawing have been

among the 'trikes and devises' that Shute brought back from Italy?

Mid-century Classicism

In the years between 1550 and 1570 no attempt (with the exception of some wholesale imports from Antwerp, to be discussed later) seems to have been made to go even as far as at Somerset House, tentative though that was, in giving a comprehensive classical treatment to a whole façade. In the typical mix found in buildings in this period, individual features – door openings, porches, chimneypieces, balustrades, sometimes windows – are classically designed, often drawing on Serlio and incorporating classical columns; but the buildings as a whole are in the Tudor Gothic tradition. They have gables, octagonal staircase-turrets, hood-moulded windows, arched window lights, and door and fireplace openings with mouldings and four-centred arches in the traditional manner. Perhaps more façades are symmetrical, or nearly so, than earlier in the century, and more windows have square-headed lights. The impression given is of different artificers or sets of artificers at work, Englishmen still working in the old manner on the main fabric, often but by no means invariably foreigners supplying fashionable individual features. The end result is seldom, if ever, distinguished, but often agreeable. The period, anyway confused enough, is made even harder to write about because so often there is no documentation, and both dates and the names of the artificers involved are matters of conjecture.

The oriel window in the centre of the entrance front at Broughton Castle (Fig. 159) is at least firmly dated 1555 on the fabric. It is an enterprising attempt to translate the traditional English many-lighted mullioned-and-transomed window into the classical language by the simple expedient of turning the mullions into columns and the

159 An oriel window
dated 1555 at Broughton
Castle, Oxfordshire.

transoms into entablatures. It was a sporting
effort, with considerable charm, but can scarcely
be called a success because the need to keep the
divisions slender led to odd proportions and over-
simplifications of both columns and entablatures.
It bred no known imitations, with the possible
exception of the curious undated window now re-
set, with blocked lights, into the east front of
Deene Park in Northamptonshire; in this plain
transoms are strapped across the middle of attenuated Ionic mullion-columns.[52]

The naivety of the Broughton window, and the
assurance of the contemporary Fontainebleau-
style overmantel inside the house, make an odd

158 (*below*) The centre-
piece on the entrance
front of Lyme Park,
Cheshire, *c*.1555–60.

combination, and are an obvious example of two
lots of artificers working in independence. There
is a similar combination and contrast at Lyme
Park, between the Fontainebleau-inspired overmantel in the gallery and the centrepiece on the
entrance front, both undated but both perhaps
carried out not so long after the work at Broughton. The centrepiece (Fig. 158) is clearly inspired
by the gatehouse and bay windows at Somerset
House; it elides the two and climbs up in four
stages of Tuscan, Doric (pedimented like the
Somerset House windows), Ionic and Corinthian
with different spacing and arrangements on the
different floors, the whole ending up as a composition with more liveliness than sophistication.

The lumbering porch at Dingley Hall in
Northamptonshire, dated 1558, appears even
more amateurish, though this may partly be due

Three widely scattered porches, in Suffolk, Warwickshire and Wiltshire, have in common their competent classicism and the fact that there is no adequate documentation by which to date them: one is reduced to saying '*circa* 1560' and accepting that they might be a little earlier, or up to ten years later.

The simplest is at Melford Hall, in Suffolk (Fig. 16), a house built or remodelled by Sir William Cordell, the Master of the Rolls: very respectable Ionic above Doric pilasters, and over all one of the shell-shaped lunettes that first appeared in England in the 1550s, but remained in fashion into the 1570s. But Melford is more remarkable for its six wonderfully slender towers (Fig. 160), possibly Continental late Gothic in inspiration, but finished off with little classical cupolas, of elegantly carved stone; the turrets are clearly related to similar ones on either side of the gatehouse at Baconsthorpe in Norfolk (Fig. 161).[54]

There are more shell lunettes on the parapet of the so-called Holbein porch at Wilton House in Wiltshire (Fig. 162). Here one is on firmer ground,

160 (*above*)   Towers, probably *c.*1560, on the garden front of Melford Hall, Suffolk.

161   A related tower on the ruined porch of Baconsthorpe Castle, Norfolk.

to alterations or omissions made when it was moved and re-erected, possibly in the late seventeenth century. Whoever built it (it may have been the mason Thomas Thorpe, father of John)[53] had access to Serlio, however, for the ornamental device of rosettes set in squares, which fills the space around its first-floor window, derives directly from the engravings of ceiling coffering in Roman buildings in his Third Book. To misapply coffering in this way suggests a purely visual choice by someone who was unable to read the foreign text.

162 (*above left*) The so-called Holbein porch, Wilton House, Wiltshire, built *c*.1559–61, probably by John Chapman. It was originally the entry porch to the house.

163 (*above right*) The vaulted interior of the porch.

although there is no documentation; one can at least attribute it fairly convincingly to a known artificer, and suggest a likely date. In the eighteenth century it was taken down and re-erected as a feature in the garden, but it was originally built as the entrance porch to the house that William Herbert, 1st Earl of Pembroke, had formed out of the former religious house that he had been granted in 1544. In plan, it was very similar to the two-storey porch that Sir John Thynne had added to Longleat in the years 1556–8, but which was removed in the seventeenth century. John Chapman, William Sharington's gifted and much sought-after mason and carver at Lacock, came over to Longleat to work on this, and it is likely that he went on to work on the Holbein porch, perhaps in or around 1559–61.

Holbein certainly had nothing to do with it; the attribution was a piece of eighteenth-century myth-making.

The ornament on the porch, and its idiosyncratic vault (Fig. 163) and heraldic lions, relate closely to Chapman's work at Lacock, as does the outstanding quality of the workmanship, though Lacock's grinning satyrs have been replaced by portrait roundels of Herberts and their mythical ancestors. But instead of the early Renaissance delicacy and shallow pilasters incised with arabesques of Sharington's monument and gallery chimneypiece at Lacock, a bold array of coupled Ionic above Doric columns projects on all three sides of the porch. The explanation here and at Longleat must be, as so often is the case in England, the arrival of Serlio, and the intimations

150

of Roman grandeur that his engravings gave to English patrons.[55]

The porch that Sir Thomas Lucy built at Charlecote in Warwickshire is, probably by accident, a scaled-down version of the Holbein porch: just two pairs of Corinthian columns, bracketed out over pairs of Ionic pilasters (Fig. 164). The fish-scaled console brackets come out of Serlio, as does the balustrading; the window over the archway has ovolo mouldings, which are unlikely to have been used before the mid-1560s.[56] The placing of columns above pilasters may have been for reasons of economy, although the recurrence of a similar top-heavy effect in a number of Elizabethan and Jacobean chimneypieces (see pp. 332–5 below) suggests that it was found attractive.

In general, as one moves on into the 1560s from the mixed bag of the 1550s, the bag remains mixed, in terms of the lack of relationship between houses as a whole and their individual elements, but less mixed in terms of the quality of the classical detail. Immigrant craftsmen of quality were still arriving from both France and the Low Countries to supplement those already there, and both were dispersing over the country; and some, at least, English artificers were working with confidence in the classical style. Serlio was still frequently drawn on (or his influence can be surmised); so was Somerset House; so, less often, were other engraved sources, German, Flemish or French.

There is little sign of this in the agreeably traditional and only approximately symmetrical exterior of Loseley Park in Surrey, built by Sir William More from 1561 to 1569.[57] The excitement is inside, in the form of the chimneypiece in the great chamber (Fig. 165). This is a kind of anthology of engraved sources, most of which have been run to earth by Anthony Wells-Cole:[58] four engravings by the German Virgil Solis, one (for the terms) by the Frenchman Jacques Androuet du Cerceau, a console with lion's feet misplaced from Serlio's Doric chimneypiece (Figs 166, 167), interfaced ornament and Vitruvian scrolls also from Serlio; others remain to be disinterred. The result is ebullient and extraordinary, if barely under control: a world away from the exterior. The explanation is probably the familiar one: the main fabric is the work of Mabbanke (Christian name unknown), More's chief mason, English and probably local; the chimneypiece and other elements of the decoration are by three carvers or joiners who were almost certainly French: 'Gyllane', 'Perowe' and 'Brykleton'. To them should be added the name of Sir William More, the client; not for nothing was he the friend and executor of Sir Thomas Cawarden, the Master of the Revels.[59]

At houses such as Broughton, Lyme and Dingley there has been much external alteration, so that the original relationship of central features to façades is uncertain. At Gorhambury, in Hert-

164 A detail of the porch (c.1560–70) at Charlecote Park, Warwickshire.

166 (*right*) A giant
console by a window in
the great chamber,
Loseley Park, Surrey.

167 (*far right*)
The chimneypiece in the
Fourth Book of
Sebastiano Serlio's
Architettura, 1537, from
which the console derives

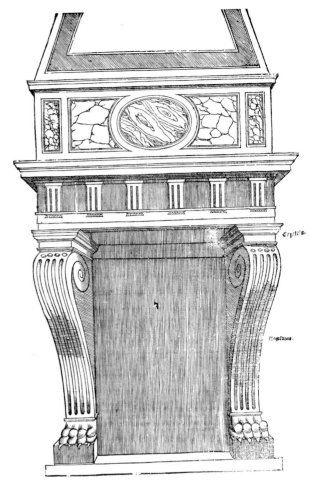

165 (*facing page*) The
chimneypiece in the great
chamber at Loseley Park,
Surrey. Probably the work
of French carvers, *c.*1565.

fordshire, although what remains is fragmentary, there is plenty of pictorial evidence to show how it originally looked; the work is dated, and the name of one of the artificers can be surmised with some confidence.[60]

Gorhambury was built by Sir Nicholas Bacon, Lord Privy Seal and one of Queen Elizabeth's most trusted counsellors. The original building accounts have been lost, but an abstract survives, sadly without names of individual craftsmen. It was built between 1563 and 1568, at a cost of £3176. 11s. 9¾d., exclusive of timber (felled in Bacon's woods) and reused stone from St Alban's Abbey.[61] It was allowed to fall into ruin after the present Gorhambury House was built in the years 1777–90.

The house was typical of its date (Fig. 169). It was built of rendered brick, with windows and door-cases in stone, on a courtyard plan, one room thick. Entry was through a central archway into a courtyard. Across this and immediately opposite the entrance was the hall porch, in an asymmetrical façade, with the windows of the two-storey great hall to the left, and two storeys of windows to the right. The other courtyard façades were probably symmetrical, as was the gabled entrance façade, framed by octagonal battlemented turrets rising high above the rest. All the other external façades were irregular. Beyond the hall a chapel protruded out of the quadrangle; to one corner of this a very lofty octagonal clock and bell-tower was attached. The windows were in a mixture of square and arched lights, with cavetto mouldings.

Only two features in this very traditional whole were classical: the arched entrance, which has

169 Gorhambury House, Hertfordshire, built by Sir Nicholas Bacon, 1563–8, the wing added in the 1570s, largely demolished in the eighteenth century.

168 (*facing page*) The porch of Gorhambury House, with the new house that replaced it in 1777 in the background.

been demolished, somewhat modestly so, and the porch, surviving but sadly decayed (Fig. 168), an ambitious and accomplished structure, bearing little relationship to the façades to either side of it. It was of two storeys, a correctly detailed Doric and Ionic, and was built of different stones carefully selected for colour contrast, with inset panels of black marble, veined with white. In the spandrels of the entrance arch were white marble roundels of profile heads of emperors; to either side of the window above the porch were alcoves containing statues in Roman armour; panels above the windows on all three sides were extended up to small surmounting pediments; the panel on the main front contained the royal arms, and under the window an inscription in good Roman lettering commemorated the building of the house. At the corners of the porch, to either

side of the central pediment, were wooden figures, probably of angels blowing trumpets. Although angels and Roman figures have long since mouldered away, one of the marble roundels survives, and is of outstanding quality. As a whole the porch in its delicate scale and variegated colouring is more like a piece of cabinetwork than a work of architecture. Trumpeting angels, royal arms and Roman sentries waited for the inevitable visit of Queen Elizabeth, who must have passed through the porch when she came to Gorhambury in 1572 and 1577.

The porch can confidently be attributed to William Cure, probably working with his son Cornelius. William Cure, as has already been discussed, had been at Nonsuch and was almost certainly the Cure who was later working for the Duke of Somerset at the time of his disgrace in

170 A chimneypiece
from the old house,
re-erected in the hall of
the new one at
Gorhambury.

younger William Cure between 1606 and 1613. On the basis of a little documentation (including of the Mary, Queen of Scots monument), and some surviving drawings (Figs 37, 173, 396–8), one of them annotated as by 'Cure', a corpus of work by the Cure workshop was first put together by John Summerson, and convincingly extended by Adam White with many attributions of monuments, based on strong stylistic resemblances.[63]

In 1561 William Cure tried to join the Marblers' Company in London. There is no evidence that he succeeded, and it is likely that he was rejected because of his foreign birth. His English-born son, Cornelius, however, became a Marbler, and went on to join the bigger and more prestigious Masons' Company when the Marblers were absorbed into it in 1585.[64]

The Cures' feeling for colour and their propensity for insetting small panels of different coloured marbles into their works relates to their background as marblers, but also to William Cure's origins in Flemish classicism. A chimneypiece in different coloured marbles from the old house at Gorhambury, re-erected in the hall of the new one (Fig. 170), is obviously William Cure's work. Monuments attributed to the Cure workshop and erected in the same period have detail relating to the Gorhambury porch, such as the distinctive festoons suspended from rings, which occur over the Gorhambury royal arms and above the arches on the memorial to Sir Richard Blount (d. 1564), in the chapel of St Peter ad Vincula in the Tower of London (Fig. 171).

The gap between William Cure's payment in 1552, for work done for the Duke of Somerset, and his appearance working for Nicholas Bacon in and before 1568 was probably filled in part by work at Nonsuch for Henry FitzAlan, Earl of Arundel. It was Arundel who sponsored Cure for the Marblers' Company in 1561.[65] Arundel had bought Nonsuch from Queen Mary in 1556. The elaborate fountain that he erected in the court-yard there (Fig. 172) features among the survey

1552. On 13 September 1568 Nicholas Bacon wrote from Gorhambury to his son, in connection with the fountain that he was having put up at one of his other houses, at Redgrave in Suffolk: 'Sonne I have appointed that this bearer Cure whoe is the workman that made my fountain and is now come downe to set it up and his servauntes should be lodged and boarded with you.'[62] This Cure was most likely William. The fountain has long since vanished, but the Gorhambury porch survives and can be attributed to him, with confidence, as the project on which he had worked immediately preceding the fountain.

The porch ties in with a remarkable and stylistically consistent group of tombs, fountains and chimneypieces, carried out from the later sixteenth century on into the early seventeenth, by three generations of Cures, William, Cornelius and William the Younger. It culminated in the monument to Mary, Queen of Scots in Westminster Abbey, executed by Cornelius and the

171 The monuments to Sir Richard (d. 1564) and Sir Michael Blount (d. 1592) in St Peter-ad-Vincula, Tower of London, both attributed to the Cure workshop, the second probably erected some years after the first, but duplicating it.

drawings in the celebrated 'Lumley Inventory'.[66] It is likely that William Cure worked on it, and acquired a reputation for fountains that remained in the family, and led to further fountains at Redgrave, Wanstead, Hampton Court (Fig. 173), Greenwich and probably elsewhere.

Arundel was a leading Catholic, Bacon a leading Protestant. Differences in religion did not necessarily set up a barrier between enthusiasts for classicism, whether in literature or building. In the mid-1570s Bacon added a wing to Gorhambury, containing a long gallery above a loggia. Along the inside of the loggia were painted 'sentences' and

devices, later to be seen and admired by John Aubrey. Bacon sent a book containing copies of the sentences (mostly in Latin) to Arundel's Catholic daughter and heiress Jane, married to the equally Catholic Lord Lumley. He had the sentences illuminated, decorated and inscribed in a fine Italian hand, probably by Petruccio Ubaldini, an Italian calligrapher much patronised by Arundel. The introductory page reads: 'Sentences painted in the Lorde Kepars gallery at Gorhambury and selected by him owt of divers authors, and sent to the good ladye Lumley at her desire.'[67]

172 (*right*) The fountain erected *c.*1560 by Henry Fitzalan, Earl of Arundel, in the courtyard of Nonsuch House, Surrey, as depicted in the Lumley Inventory.

173 (*far right*) A design by Cornelius Cure, *c.*1584, for a fountain at Hampton Court Palace (Hatfield, CPM I/11).

Jane Lumley was a highly educated Renaissance woman; her translations from Greek into Latin, and Greek into English, survive in manuscript in the British Library. Bacon's wife Anne was equally learned. She was one of the four formidable blue-stocking, and more than blue-stocking, daughters of Sir Anthony Cooke, of Gidea Hall in Essex:[68] Mildred, married to Lord Burghley; Anne, married to Sir Nicholas Bacon; Elizabeth, married to Sir Thomas Hoby (the translator of Castiglione's *The Courtier*); and Katherine, married to Sir Henry Killigrew.

Mildred Burghley was one of the best Greek scholars of her time; according to Roger Ascham she spoke Greek as fluently as English. In 1564 Anne Bacon translated her friend Bishop John Jewel's *Apologia pro Ecclesia Anglicana* into clear and forceful English. When Elizabeth Hoby's husband Thomas died relatively young in 1566 she wrote long epitaphs in Greek, Latin and English for his monument, which she set up in the church at Bisham jointly to her husband and her brother-in-law, Sir Philip Hoby. The monument is convincingly attributed by Adam White to the Cure workshop, as is the monument to Sir Anthony Cooke (d. 1576), father of the learned sisters, at Romford in Essex.[69] Katherine Killigrew, the youngest of the sisters but the first to die, is also described as proficient in Greek, Latin and Hebrew.

This learned world can be followed to Cambridge, the university where, with Lord Burghley as an active chancellor, classical studies continued to flourish in the second half of the sixteenth century, if not as much as they had in the first. The ancient and decaying Gonville College had already been revived and re-founded, as Gonville and Caius College, by Dr John Caius (pronounced Keys) in 1557. Caius was a Catholic, but this did not prevent his being a friend of Matthew Parker, the Archbishop of Canterbury. Both were learned men; Caius was a doctor of great distinction. Caius's new buildings at his college were started in 1565 and completed in 1575, after his death in

174   The Gate of Virtue, Gonville and Caius College, Cambridge, erected c.1569, probably with Humfrey Lovell as master mason.

1573, but according to designs approved by him. The buildings followed the usual mid-century mixture, though with an extra element of symbolism: unassuming traditional buildings with mainly small windows, arched lights and octagonal staircase turrets, into which were infiltrated three classical elements. These were the three celebrated gates, of Humility, Virtue (and Wisdom) and Honour. The student pursued a symbolic route through the college: entering by the modest gate of Humility, continuing through the gate dedicated to Virtue on one side and Wisdom on the other, and leaving to collect their degrees through the Gate of Honour.

The freemason working on the Gate of Virtue in 1569 (as mentioned in a couple of Caius's letters) was called 'Humfrey',[70] and can probably be identified as the Humfrey Lovell who had been working for Somerset in 1551 and had been created Master Mason of the Royal Works in 1564. The gate is a simplified version of the gateway at Somerset House, like it a 'Tower of the Orders', but made up of pilasters, not columns (Fig. 174). It rises in three diminishing stages: Ionic, Corinthian and Composite, and the archway spandrels are decorated with Victories, as at Somerset House.

The Gate of Honour[71] was on the south side of the court, otherwise kept open, for reasons of health. This delicious little building (Fig. 175) is a simplified variation on the archway erected by the Spanish merchants, probably to designs by Pieter Coecke, for the entry of Philip of Spain into Antwerp in 1549 (Fig. 176). It is about one third of the size; its miniature scale is part of its charm. The Spanish arch, in its turn, derived from a design for a Corinthian temple in Serlio's Fourth Book (Fig. 177). It is possible that the Gate of Honour draws on both sources. Serlio's temple is placed on a platform bounded by a balustrade; in the gate, temple and balustrade are elided. The gate contains much Serlian detail, but the source of the playful aedicules between the Corinthian

columns has not been established. In general, the classical detail is sufficiently accomplished to make one believe that the appearance of pointed arches and Gothic detail on the entrance is deliberate, rather than incompetent.[72]

The Spanish arch takes the form of a temple above a triumphal arch, and so, in miniature, does the gate. But the Antwerp temple is round, the Cambridge one rectangular. The Gate of Honour, in fact, incorporates the only known temple fronts in Elizabethan architecture. It is likely that the Elizabethans, unlike the Georgians, would have thought it unseemly to use a temple portico as an entrance to a secular building. A free-standing pavilion, such as the gate, was a different matter. The temple incorporated in the Spanish arch was designed as a Temple of Janus, in Roman days closed in peace and open in war. The fact that the temple on the gate, being solid, cannot be opened is perhaps a deliberate conceit, chiming in with Caius's crest, the dove of Peace, that originally surmounted it.

The Gate of Honour is so much more inventive and accomplished than the Gate of Virtue that one suspects a different mind at work. One would like to know whose, for someone has had a great deal of fun devising it. It was erected after Caius's death in July 1573, but said to have been built 'according to the very form and figure which Dr Caius in his lifetime had himself traced out for the architect'. A new arrival at Caius, probably shortly before Caius's death, was the German or Fleming Theodore Haveus, described as an outstanding craftsman and distinguished professor of architecture, who came to Cambridge, perhaps by way of King's Lynn, to construct a sundial in the courtyard at Caius, and work on Caius's festive alabaster monument in the chapel.[73] A creative partnership between Caius and Theodore is perhaps the most likely explanation of both gate and monument. This too was erected after Caius's death, but according to directions that he had left behind him.

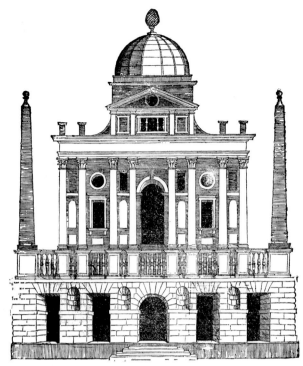

176 and 177 One of the gates (*right*) erected for the entry of Philip of Spain to Antwerp, 1546, and (*far right*) a design in the Fourth Book of Sebastiano Serlio's *Architettura*, 1537.

175 (*facing page*) The Gate of Honour, Gonville and Caius College, erected after the death of Dr John Caius in 1573.

The gallery wing of the President's Lodge at Queens' College, Cambridge, is described in *The Buildings of England* as 'one of the most picturesque of English timber-framed structures, its beauty being one of irregularity and happy accident, rather than plan'. But if one ignores its half-timbering, uncovered in the early twentieth century to delight watercolourists in search of the picturesque, and looks at it more than superficially, one can appreciate it as a building carefully designed as a whole, and one of the most successful examples of the mid-century mixture of modern Gothic and antique classic. The façade to the cloister court is all but symmetrical, a projecting central bay window, with smaller windows to either side, lighting the gallery, between further staircase projections in the angles of the courtyard (Fig. 178). The three main projections, all cantilevered out over a brick cloister (which may be earlier), were originally carried up as three turrets, receding in Nonsuch fashion; these are prominent in the Loggan print, though since decapitated (Fig. 179). The smaller windows are pedimented with sills supported on consoles,

as at Somerset House, but projecting further, owing to their timber construction. These consoles are probably Serlio-inspired, and very elegant; nicest of all, on the more irregular rear façade another staircase gives out onto the President's garden by way of a little pedimented doorway of wood, with Ionic pilasters and gay miniature Victories in the spandrels of the opening (Fig. 180).

The building is not well documented, and usually described as erected *circa* 1540, a date that is scarcely possible. It is more likely to date from *circa* 1570, and to have been erected by William Chaderton (President 1568–79), a protégé of Burghley, chaplain to the Earl of Leicester, and married to a daughter of John Revell, Surveyor of the Royal Works – in fact, with all the right connections. Revell had died unexpectedly of the plague in 1563, but owing to the relationship Chaderton was likely to have had contacts with the officers of the Works.[74]

With Sir John Thynne at Longleat one moves into a different, but related, world. Thynne had not been to university and was not a scholar, nor

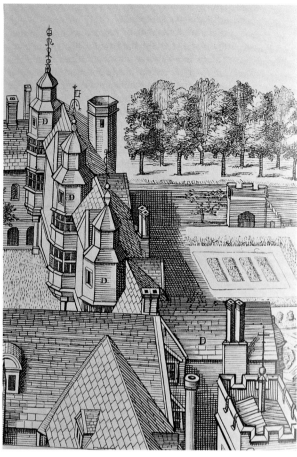

178 (*above left*)
The gallery wing of the President's Lodge, Queens' College, Cambridge, perhaps built *c.*1570 on an earlier base.

179 (*above right*)
The gallery wing from the air, a detail from Loggan's view of Queens' College.

180 A Victory in the spandrel of the door leading from the President's Lodge at Queens' College, Cambridge to his garden.

is he ever known to have travelled outside England and Scotland. But as the steward and right-hand man of the Duke of Somerset, he not only made himself a substantial fortune by no very scrupulous means but was also in touch with the highly educated Protestant elite that ruled England under Edward VI and re-emerged to rule it under Elizabeth. Above all, he had become obsessively interested in architecture, first while supervising Somerset's own building projects, and then while creating his own home round the kernel of the small religious house at Longleat in Wiltshire that he had acquired in 1541.

The building history of Longleat is well documented but extremely complex. By the end of the 1560s, after frequent additions and alterations and one disastrous fire, it had developed into something not unlike other buildings previously discussed in this chapter: a gabled courtyard

181 and 182 Two chimneypieces attributed to Alan Maynard at Longleat House, Wiltshire.

house with stair-turrets in the corners of the main courtyard, enriched with classical elements, including a porch, bay windows probably inspired by those at Somerset House, and, inside, a number of classical chimneypieces.[75]

But Longleat is more interesting at this stage for the craftsmen employed there. Thynne had built up a formidable team, which was to stay with him till his death. The longest established was the Englishman, John Lewis, the head carpenter, who had arrived in 1554. Adrian Gaunt, the head joiner, a Frenchman, naturalised in 1567, was there by 1565, and possibly by 1563. Alan Maynard, free-mason and carver, another Frenchman, natu-ralised in 1566, was there by 1563. Robert Smyth-son, freemason, an Englishman, arrived in 1568, sent by Humfrey Lovell, the Queen's Master Mason.[76]

The two Frenchmen are the only uncontested French building craftsmen of importance known to have been working under Elizabeth – if one discounts Gyllane and Perowe at Loseley, whose identification as French is not certain, and John Caron,[77] an undoubted French carver very active in the Revels but not known to have worked outside them.

Gaunt, in these early years, is especially inter-esting because, when Longleat was part destroyed by fire in 1567, he made a model for the rebuild-ing, the only architectural model known to have been made in England under Elizabeth. Alan Maynard's main work, in his first years at Long-leat, seems to have been the provision of chim-neypieces; three of these had been carved by 1566. Three of his chimneypieces (not necessarily the same) survive at Longleat (Figs 181, 182), on the strength of which a number of others elsewhere, and a number of church monuments, can be at-tributed to him, most notably two chimneypieces at Woodlands Manor, Mere, also in Wiltshire (Fig. 183). A remarkable, probably unexecuted, design by him, also at Longleat, may date from the 1560s (Fig. 40).[78]

Since Maynard continued active until at least 1585, and lived at or near Longleat until his death in 1598, giving dates for his work is harder than making attributions. Whatever their dates, the surviving group of chimneypieces, some of which may belong to the 1560s, are lovely in their vigor-ous and sumptuous classicism. They are French in character in their use of scrolls, swags and urns; the terms with which some of them are carved

183 A chimneypiece,
probably by Alan
Maynard, at Woodlands
Manor, Mere, Wiltshire.

184 The entrance front of Grafton Manor, Worcestershire, 1567–9.

185 (*below*) Pavilions built by Robert Smythson, 1568–9, on the roof at Longleat House, Wiltshire, to serve as banqueting houses.

show the influence of Du Cerceau, whose *Exempla Arcuum* (1549) was certainly drawn on for the terms with twisted double tails in his

drawing. Maynard presumably owned, or had access to, this.[79]

Robert Smythson had served his apprenticeship in London, possibly under Humfrey Lovell, who sent him to Longleat; it is chronologically possible that, as a young apprentice, he had worked on Somerset House. A drawing by him, probably for windows at Longleat, derives from the Somerset House bay windows, as do the flaming grenades with which his windows are surmounted – unless these came direct from Serlio. In his first years at Longleat his main works, still happily surviving, were the little pavilions with their fish-scale domes and miniature classical lanterns (Fig. 185), built at the top of the staircase towers to serve as banqueting houses, which were accessible only from the roof.[80]

By the end of the 1560s Longleat, although the main achievements there were still in the

186 and 187 The court-
yard and exterior of the
Royal Exchange, London
(1566–7), from engravings
attributed to Franz
Hogenberg.

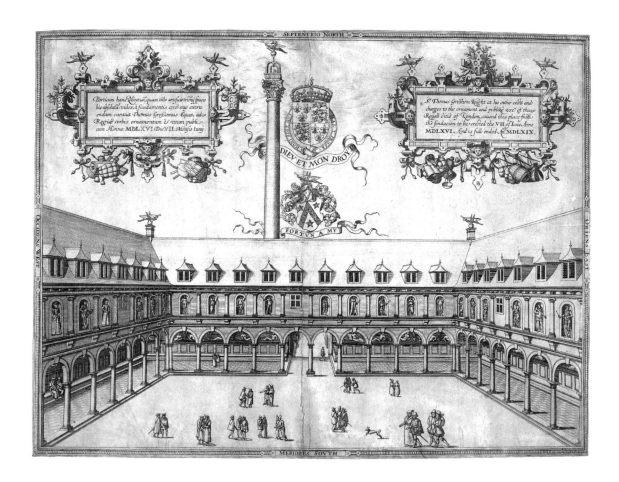

188 The town hall at Antwerp, built 1561–5 to the designs of William van den Broecke and Cornelis Floris. From the engraving by Hans Vredeman de Vries, 1565.

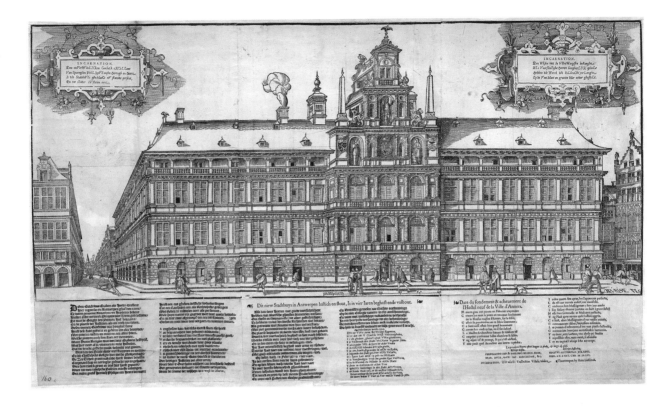

future, was already a remarkable place. Thanks to Thynne's sensitive eye for quality and obsession with architecture, it was becoming a school or magnet for talent, the influence of which was to spread over the country. Already in the 1550s John Chapman, the carver of the remarkable Renaissance tables at Lacock, had been working there. William Spicer learnt his trade there from 1557 to 1569, when he quarrelled with Thynne and went off to work at Kenilworth for the Earl of Leicester, and later to become Surveyor of the Works. Thynne's carpenter John Lewis was lent to the Middle Temple in 1562, and worked on the great hammerbeam roof of its hall, late Gothic in shape but enriched with classical detail. Bess of Hardwick and Sir William Cavendish were begging, perhaps unsuccessfully, for the loan of his plasterers in 1555 and 1560. Between 1567 and 1569 a freemason, John Fortune, went from Longleat to work for Sir John Talbot at Grafton Manor, in Worcestershire. The house (Fig. 184) has a typical mix of traditional features and classical detail, on the porch and elsewhere; the likelihood is that the

former were provided by a local mason, Stephen Merryman, and the latter by Fortune. And, much later, Robert Smythson was to leave Longleat and transfer his skills to the Midlands.[81]

Thynne was married to the sister of the great Sir Thomas Gresham, the man who dominated English finance and Anglo-Flemish trade from at least 1551 until his death in 1579. With Gresham the Low Countries came back into the story, for Gresham's many imports from Antwerp included architectural detail and one entire building. This was the Royal Exchange in London (Figs 186, 187), built in 1566–7 under the supervision of an Antwerp mason, Henryk van Paesschen, but perhaps to designs by Cornelis Floris.

Pieter Coecke had died in 1553. Floris, a sculptor by training, had worked with him on the Antwerp triumphal arches in 1549. Aesthetically, Floris had a double personality. The triumphal arches erected by the townspeople in Antwerp in 1549, in contrast to those erected by the foreign merchants, had little if anything to do with Serlio, and were one of the first places in which was dis-

189 and 190 Two views
of Bachegraig,
Denbighshire, built in
1567–9, from watercolours
by Moses Griffith.
'A miniature Flemish
country house in remote
country in Wales'.

191 A detail of the blocked loggia in the surviving wing of Bachegraig.

title page. Cornelis Floris was probably responsible for all these: certainly, this kind of ornament filled his acknowledged *Veelderleij Niewe Inventien van Antyksche*, published in 1557.[82]

But the designs with which he and the painter William Paludanus (or Van den Broecke) won the competition for Antwerp Town Hall (built 1561–5) had none of this extravagance (Fig. 188): it was a grave and monumental exercise inspired by Serlio and with at least one direct quotation from him.[83] Its centrepiece was a kind of extended triumphal arch or Tower of the Orders, rising high up above the roof; to either side identical ranges of windows divided by pilasters ran round all four façades.[84]

Floris and Paludanus, according to the Antwerp master masons, were incapable of dealing with the practical problems of building the Town Hall, and two of the mason fraternity, Hendrik van Paesschen and Jan Daems, were brought in to help them out. Van Paesschen seems also to have collaborated with Floris on the Hanseatenhuis (1564–8), the huge headquarters of the Hanseatic merchants in Antwerp. This was a more utilitarian building than the Town Hall, but what ornament it had was soberly classical.[85]

Between 1566 and 1568 Van Paesschen was spending much time in England as the surveyor or master mason in charge of building Gresham's Exchange; the references are only to 'Henryck' in surviving correspondence of the period, but there is no doubt of the identification. Stylistically, the Exchange came somewhere between the Antwerp Town Hall and the Hanseatenhuis. Its most prominent feature was its internal court, a classical version of the late Gothic courtyard of the Antwerp Exchange, with its covered arcades for merchants to do business in.[86]

Although van Paesschen is usually credited with being the designer of the London Exchange, there are no contemporary references to him or anyone else providing designs. It is possible that they came from Cornelis Floris; a passing joint

Prætorium de Oudenhove.

192 The castle of Oudenhove, as depicted in Antonius Sanderus's *Flandria Illustrata* (1641–2).

played the elaborate strapwork, and the imps and grotesque figures entrapped in it, that were to become the distinctive Antwerp form of decoration. The same kind of ornament figured on the

reference in English correspondence to 'Henryk' and 'Floris' being consulted about sending material to England gives some support to the suggestion.[87]

The features of the Exchange that had most influence in England were the arcades. These, in which round arches were superimposed directly upon columns without an intervening section of entablature, owed nothing to Serlio and derived from early Renaissance arcades in Italy. Such arcades had become common enough in northern Europe, and may also have featured in the courtyard of the Hanseatenhuis; but they were new to England. Columns, along with wainscoting and other material, were sent over to Gresham by van Paesschen, and also to William Cecil, who incorporated them into arcades at Theobalds and possibly Burghley.[88] The arcades of this type that still exist in the courtyard at Burghley may not be the

original ones of the 1560s, but, if not, they are their descendants. Once introduced, such arcades were to reappear constantly in England, on into the seventeenth century.

The oddest result of Gresham's Antwerp connection was the importation of a miniature Flemish country house into remote country in Wales.[89] Gresham's Antwerp factor and right-hand man, Richard Clough, came from Denbighshire, and built himself a house there in the years 1567–9. A Welsh poet wrote at the time:

> At Bachegraig he reared a stately pile
> Of strong materials, which he brought from
> Antwerp.
> Thence, too, his mansion's marble pillars
> came.[90]

Surviving views of the house support the poem (Figs 189, 190). The house was of brick, which was likely to have been made locally, but timber, panelling and stone may well have been imported. The main building took the form of a pavilion, completely in the Flemish manner, just one main floor above a basement, and then a high Flemish roof with two tiers of little dormers, surmounted by a belvedere. It belonged to a small Low Countries group of compact square buildings with high roofs, such as the weigh house of Amsterdam (1563–5) and the little Flemish château of Oudenhove (Fig. 192).[91] Next to the house was a separate building, containing warehousing and stables, and this, unlike the house, was later converted into a farmhouse. It survives, complete with its arcade, although the latter has been filled in; the wide spacing of its Tuscan columns is made possible because the entablature is made up of wooden beams (Fig. 191), an arrangement that may also have been found at Burghley.[92] In July 1774, just before the house was demolished, it received an unlikely visitor in the person of Dr Johnson, coming with his friend Mrs Thrale, to whom it then belonged. He commented: 'the house was less than I seemed to expect . . . the addition of

193   The monument to Richard Jervois (d. 1563) in Chelsea Old Church, London.

170

another story would make an useful house, but it cannot be great'.[93]

Gresham and Clough were prominent members of the Mercers' Company in London. The Mercers dominated trade with the Low Countries, and whenever a Mercer is involved a Low Country connection can be suspected. A Dutch or Flemish workman was perhaps responsible for the curious little monument to Richard Jervoise (d. 1563) in Chelsea Old Church (Fig. 193), which takes the form of a miniature triumphal arch,[94] and for the monument to Thomas Mason (d. 1559) in Winchester cathedral, the surviving fragments of which have similar detail and figurative sculpture derived from a Flemish engraving.[95] Jervoise was both the son and son-in-law of a Mercer, and Thomas Mason's father, Sir John, though a diplomat, not a Mercer, had served in Brussels from 1553 to 1556.

One half of a house surviving at Bassingthorpe in Lincolnshire (Fig. 194) shows Low Countries influence. Unlike many buildings of the period it is conveniently dated on the fabric, 1568. It was built by Thomas Cony, a prosperous merchant and a member of the Mercers' Company, married to a Mercer's daughter, trading to Calais, Bruges and Antwerp in cloth and in wool from the 847 sheep grazing in the meadows round Bassingthorpe. The particular form of the stepped gables of his house suggests the Low Countries, as does the distinctive oriel window; and its window mouldings, concave on the outside, in the traditional English manner, are on the inside an early example of the ovolo profile, which is to be found on Antwerp Town Hall, and was to become, inside and out, the most popular profile for window mouldings in England on into the seventeenth century.[96]

The distinctive mixture of tradition and novelty of the 1560s continued, in many cases, to be found in the 1570s. Before considering the startling transformation that took place in that decade, it is worth looking at one more example of the old manner, in which, however, one can sense a forecast of something new.

This is, or was, the great house at Sissinghurst in Kent,[97] built on a very large scale by Sir Richard Baker, and perhaps finished in a hurry in order to entertain Queen Elizabeth there in 1573 (Fig. 195). With its skyline of gabled dormers and chimney stacks, its profusion of bay windows and its lofty towered gatehouse, it was in some ways a traditional building. But the courtyard was orchestrated with care as a unified composition by the rectangular rhythm of its repeated porches and bay windows, but also by no less than seven classical doorways, repeated at intervals around its three façades. It is sad to have lost this great courtyard, which Horace Walpole, no great admirer of the Elizabethans, described as 'perfect and very beautiful' in 1752;[98] but one must be grateful for the gatehouse that survives (Fig. 196). In one way this is one of the last and most beautiful in the great native sequence of lofty turreted gatehouses; but at the same time the

194 Bassingthorpe Manor, Lincolnshire, built by Thomas Cony, a merchant trading to the Low Countries, and dated 1568.

SISINHERST KENT the Property of Sᴿ HORACE MANN Barᵗ

195 Sissinghurst Castle, Kent, *c.*1570, as depicted in Edward Hasted's *The History and Topographical Survey of the County of Kent*, vol. III, 1778–9.

ways in which it is exquisitely set off by a crisp contrast between rectangles and octagons, by the rectangular section of its mullions and by its two stages of pilasters are all signs of a new spirit.

The English Classical House

In the 1570s a determined effort was made to create English classical houses – as opposed to traditional English houses with classical bits added. Nothing was written about this at the time; it has to be deduced from the buildings.

No one then knew what Roman houses had been like, the Italians no more than the English. The recognisable remains were of temples, triumphal arches, city gates, theatres, amphitheatres and public baths. There were almost no

known Roman windows, no chimneypieces, balustrades, chimney stacks or staircases, no ceilings other than the soffits of porticos. Modern classical houses had to be made up, by adapting the known classical vocabulary to contemporary needs, and extemporising where necessary. The starting-off point was inevitably the lifestyle and tradition of domestic architecture in each country. Italian Renaissance *palazzi* were created by taking Gothic *palazzi* and translating them into the classical language, replacing machicolations by giant bracketed-out cornices, and Gothic windows by round-arched windows on slim classical columns, or later, by pedimented aedicules. *Palazzi* in towns were seldom free-standing; for free-standing houses in the open the concept developed of a single unified design, with a consistent treatment running round all four façades. This could be achieved by repeating a *palazzo*

172

196 The gatehouse at Sissinghurst which survived when the main house was demolished.

197 A design in J. A. du Cerceau's so-called *Petites Habitations* (1545).

Italian ones. Italians were building for a hot, dry climate and wanted small windows, to keep rooms cool and soften the bright external light, and a liberal supply of loggias and open galleries, as a retreat from the sun. English clients were increasingly demanding big windows, to give as much light as possible, and wanted fewer arcades, and those more to provide protection from the rain than the sun. For an Italian, a flat roof was likely to be a heat-trap rather than a pleasant viewing place; for the English, flat roofs, if one could afford the necessary leadwork, were the ultimate luxury, even if good sense suggested that steep rain-shedding roofs were more practical. The English liked bay windows, for which there was no tradition in Italy, and preferred fireplaces set into the wall to the hooded chimneypieces favoured by Italians.

The idea of unity, and the way to achieve it by using the orders as the unifying element, was all there in Serlio, but expressed in plans with separate elevations, without perspective drawings to show how façade related to façade. It is possible that the publication of Jacques Androuet du Cerceau, starting with his so-called *Petites Habitations*, apparently published as early as 1545, had more influence in presenting the idea to Englishmen. A copy of the former was certainly in England by 1580, and possibly earlier.[99] Du Cerceau's designs vividly, if somewhat crudely, suggested by perspective drawings how French needs and tastes could be classicised and given unity by the application of the orders, whether expressed explicitly, with columns or pilasters, or implicitly, by the extension of one or more entablatures all round the building (Fig. 197).

Antwerp Town Hall, which was engraved and must anyway have been well known to many Englishmen, also showed how unity could be imposed and Northern needs supplied in classical language. Individual house fronts in Antwerp and elsewhere repeated the formula of glazing between columns or pilasters. The Royal Ex-

façade four times, or by devising new formulae, of which Palladio's invention of four repeated temple porticoes is the best known. Hints came from Roman amphitheatres, in which arches between superimposed Doric, Ionic and Corinthian columns were carried all round the exterior. Jacopo Sansovino adapted the arrangement for his Library in Venice, but such continuous arcades were not needed in a domestic context; in his Villa Garzoni, south of Padua (*circa* 1536), he used the amphitheatre formula to provide two storeys of loggias in the centre, but for the façades to either side simply extended the entablature, without an order. Such houses bore no relationship to the rambling, one might even say picturesque, planning of Roman villas; but before the days of excavation Roman villa architecture remained almost unknown.

Serlio had included a number of designs for palace façades in his Third and Fourth Books, as well as engravings of the free-standing Poggio Reale at Naples, and of his own more elaborate variation on it. In addition, he had provided many designs for details of all kinds. All this must have been full of interest for the Englishmen who turned his pages. But English needs were not

change demonstrated the attractions of a unified classical design in the heart of London.

The concept of a distinctive northern classicism, which is implicit in English buildings of the period, but never specifically stated in anything written that has come to light, was clearly expressed in a Flemish context by Hans Vredeman de Vries in his *Architectura*, first published in 1565. The 'Antique Italian' style, he wrote, was adapted to the mode, custom and fashion of Italy, where there was no need for large windows or abundance of light. The opposite was the case in the North, especially on the constructed sites of cities, which led to high buildings on narrow streets where maximum glazing was an essential. He praised Flemish designers such as Jacques Dubroeucq, Cornelius Floris and Willem Van den Broecke (Latinised as Paludanus) – all leading pioneers of classicism – for having realised this and 'adapted their art to local conditions and needs'.[100]

Indeed, just as Italian town *palazzi* of the Renaissance were classicised versions of late Gothic ones, Flemish classical buildings, both private and public, developed out of their Gothic predecessors. These had also been heavily glazed; de Vries's argument about the need for extensive glazing in high narrow streets may or may not have been a starting point, but extensive glazing had become just as much a feature of buildings on large open market squares or along spacious quaysides or canals.

Cornelius Floris's Town Hall at Antwerp is a classical version of Flemish late Gothic town halls – 'casket Gothic', they have been called, mostly on free-standing, or near free-standing, sites, with a lush Flamboyant framework enclosing the extensive glazing. This was replaced in Antwerp by a grand Doric, Ionic and Corinthian framework, running without variation round all four sides, and by continuous glazing in between.

There was, however, a significant difference between England and the Low Countries. Flemish classicism was launched by painters and sculptors, who had no connection or training within the traditional structure of the artificers' guilds. They went to Italy, came back with all the prestige of their knowledge, and found powerful patrons to commission designs from them, which the artificers executed. They published their designs, and moved with confidence in court and academic circles. There were considerable tensions between the two groups.[101]

There was nothing like this in England. John Shute was the only known Englishman to follow the Flemish pattern, and any influence he might have exerted was aborted by his early death. As noted in the first chapter, there are examples of painters or sculptors making designs for English buildings, but before Inigo Jones they were of minor importance.[102] The Elizabethan classical house was created by English artificers working directly with English patrons, on the basis of engravings and books, or very limited direct experience of buildings on the Continent. Foreign-born artificers were sometimes responsible for details or individual elements, especially chimneypieces or church monuments, but everything that is most impressive or moving about Elizabethan classicism was home-made.

A fascination with classicism combined with much less knowledge of it than was available on the Continent; a strong reaction combined with a great deal of improvisation; a respect for authority tempered by enormous vitality; a pride in England's own past combined with limitless curiosity about the past of others; out of this mixture emerged the Elizabethan classical house.

Four great English houses, created at much the same time, drew on Flemish, French and Italian examples to pioneer the idea of English needs given unity derived from the orders: Hill Hall, Kirby Hall, Longleat and Burghley.

Hill Hall, in Essex, came first, if with a somewhat patchy history (Figs 198–200). Sir Thomas Smith, who built it, belonged to the inner circle

198   The courtyard of
Hill Hall, Essex, built by
Sir Thomas Smith,
1567–77.

of highly educated Protestant functionaries that effectively ran England: friend of Cheke and later Cecil, protégé of the Duke of Somerset, benefactor to Queens' College, Cambridge, when Chaderton was the President, Greek scholar, Cambridge don, Secretary of State, twice ambassador in Paris, author of a book on the English constitution.[103] In 1567–8, back from his first stint as ambassador, he started to rebuild his brick and timber-framed courtyard house at Hill Hall. He began with its north and west ranges, and lined their courtyard fronts with three storeys of columns, Doric, Ionic and (for dormers above the eaves in the French manner) Corinthian. Then he went back to France, and on his return rebuilt the remaining two ranges in 1572–3, with the same arrangement on the courtyard side, though of slightly better quality, but with the novel, and for England remarkable, feature of a giant Doric order on high pedestals on the external façades. He may have intended to continue this order round the two earlier façades, for when he died in 1577 his house was still unfinished.[104]

In the 1560s a giant order had featured in Jean Bullant's work at the châteaux of Chantilly and Ecouen, which Smith may have known of. Alternatively, he could have seen its use in Philibert de l'Orme's *Premier Livre d'Architecture*, published in 1567 (Fig. 201); in 1568 William Cecil wrote to Paris for a book on architecture that he had seen 'at Sir Thomas Smith's', and this was probably the *Premier Livre*.[105] When the books in the gallery at Hill Hall were listed on 1 August 1566, the only architectural books among them were five differ-

199 A detail of the exterior of Hill Hall.

200 (*below left*) The chimney piece in the hall at Hill Hall.

201 (*below right*) Façade with giant order from Philibert de l'Orme's *Premier Livre d'Architecture*, 1567.

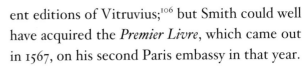

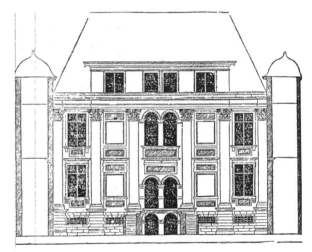

ent editions of Vitruvius;[106] but Smith could well have acquired the *Premier Livre*, which came out in 1567, on his second Paris embassy in that year.

Smith's formula produced a classical house by the single-minded application of columns and entablatures and not much else; there is otherwise very little ornament, and the windows are of standard Tudor form. For his interiors he employed a competent painter who, on the basis of engravings, covered the walls with spirited versions of paintings by Raphael and others. For the outside he could draw on his copies of Vitruvius and, probably, de l'Orme, and on the services of Richard Kirby, a member of the London Carpenters' Company,[107] as surveyor or clerk of the works; in the absence of local stone his columns were of plastered brick. He almost certainly knew what he wanted; he owned drawing instruments

and could probably draw it out himself, however crudely. The result is much more naive than the paintings, the Ionic columns painfully stumpy, the way the entablatures are carried beyond the columns very clumsy. Even so, there is a monumentality and single-mindedness about the courtyard that leaves a strong impression.

Kirby Hall, in Northamptonshire, was built at much the same time as Hill Hall; like it, it shows French influence and uses a giant order; like it,

its orders or entablatures run right round the courtyard and along two sides of the exterior. Otherwise, the two houses could scarcely be more different. Kirby could benefit from the golden local stone and from Northamptonshire masons skilled in laying and carving it; one can sense a creative hand, still to be identified, at work: it exudes a richness and a sense of celebration and delight lacking in the single-minded architecture of Hill Hall.

It is firmly dated by the inscription on John Thorpe's plan of the ground floor: 'Kerby whereof I layd ye first stone A[nno] 1570', and by the dates of 1572 and 1575 carved on the house. As John Summerson established, Thorpe must have been a child of about five in 1570; it is highly likely that his father, Thomas Thorpe of Kingscliffe, was the master mason at Kirby.[108]

Kirby was built by Humphrey Stafford, but bought by Sir Christopher Hatton on Stafford's death in 1579.[109] It was to be much and sensitively embellished, by the Hatton family, but in Stafford's time all the splendour was in the courtyard. The dominant feature of this was the giant order of Ionic pilasters, carried round all four sides, but with different rhythms: on the entrance side (Fig. 203) conditioned by the arches of the ground-floor loggia, on the hall front spaced wider to accommodate the towering windows of the great hall (Figs 73, 202), on the side façades spaced wider still, to carry the pilasters across subsidiary ranges. The three windows of the hall were mirrored on the other side of the porch, in order to achieve symmetry, although there were two storeys on this side, masked by the windows; two storeys also in the solidly glazed extrusions in either corner. But the porch was expressed by two storeys of smaller orders, corresponding to the screens and the gallery over it in the hall: Ionic pilasters on the ground floor, Corinthian columns bracketed out on consoles on the first floor. The Ionic entablature reappeared on either side of the great windows to divide the two floors of the east

and west façades, and go over the arcade of the loggia; the Corinthian entablature was carried all round the top of the courtyard, so that it became the entablature of the giant Ionic pilasters, though scaled (not too happily) to its smaller order. The two entablatures appear again on the outside of the house, running all the way along the north and west façades, but not the south and east ones. These façades must originally have been very plain: the west front, until it was embellished with strapwork gables, perhaps about 1600, was without ornament, though given character by its great projecting chimney stacks; the north entrance front may have been equally plain, but was remodelled in the middle of the seventeenth century.

Kirby, unlike Hill Hall, is rich with carving, on friezes, pilasters, consoles, parapet and gables. The carving incorporates dates, and the crests and initials of the Staffords and related families, but much of it is purely ornamental, and always delightful. The gable over the porch is concealed by a run of seven little Corinthian columns (Fig. 202), supported on consoles, and continued by one further column around each corner. This festive array is crowned by concave scrolls leading up a semicircular lunette, all filled with low-relief carving; and there are related, but plainer, gable fronts to either side.

As a way of adding importance to the porch, this becolumned top-piece was as original as it was successful; there is no known prototype for it. The source of the embellishments of the giant order in the centre of the opposite front has been traced. The 'antique' ornament of cherubs, scrolls and balusters that fills the two pilasters and their bases comes from an engraved framework much used on English title pages in the mid-sixteenth century, including the title page of Shute's *First and Chief Groundes of Architecture* (Fig. 139).[110] The two capitals, with lively horse's heads in place of the volutes, are very free adaptations of a capital in the Basilica del Foro Transitorio in Rome, as

202 (facing page)
The central feature on the north side of the courtyard of Kirby Hall, Northamptonshire, built 1570–75.

engraved by Serlio.[111] From Serlio also may come the 'Vitruvian scroll' along the top of the parapet on the hall façade, and the fan-shaped shells on the surmounting lunette. The sources of the other ornamental motifs have not been traced, though, as in any Elizabethan building, one suspects that engravings have been extensively drawn on.

The courtyard plan and great windows of Kirby are thoroughly English, but about the general character of the decoration there can be no doubt. It comes from France; the concept of richly embellishing the elements of the orders with delicate ornament is distinctively French, as had been pioneered most obviously in Lescot's façade at the Louvre. The loggia on the inside of the entrance front is a French feature too (Fig. 203); the great depth of the Kirby loggia exactly follows the arrangement at the château of Ecouen. The façade of the loggia range appears to

be a simplified version of the façade of the entrance range in the base-court of the Château de Charleval.[112]

Charles x's huge château at Charleval was probably designed by Jacques Androuet du Cerceau; most of it was never built, though the executed portions seem to have included this base-court range. But the château was started in 1570, at the earliest, that is to say it was exactly contemporary with Kirby; and it was not to be engraved until it featured (along with Ecouen) in the second volume of Du Cerceau's *Les Plus Excellents Bastiments de France* in 1579 (Fig. 204). How did its influence percolate to Kirby?

The actual carving at Kirby may have been the work (as attributed at Dingley) of Thomas Thorpe.[113] But there is something at Kirby beyond the capability of a Northamptonshire mason; what Thomas Thorpe (if it was he) got up to on his own can be seen, apart from Dingley itself,

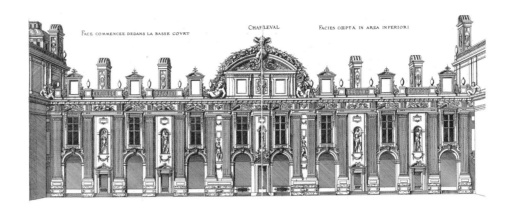

204 The courtyard at the Château de Charleval (started 1570), as depicted in J. A. du Cerceau's *Les Plus Excellents Bastiments de France* (vol. 2, 1579).

in the gay but undisciplined monument to the Griffins of Dingley in the nearby church at Braybrooke.[114] Humphrey Stafford himself is a shadowy figure: a local gentleman, member of a junior branch of the great medieval family of the Staffords, dukes of Buckingham, but himself with no known court, humanist or foreign connections, and not especially active even in his own county.

The explanation may lie in his uncle, Sir Robert Stafford. In 1544 he was one of the numerous men (Philip Hoby and Thomas Cawarden among them) who were knighted at Boulogne by Henry VIII, ebullient after his capture of the town. He was in Italy in 1549, when Thomas Hoby met him in Siena and Rome. In 1551–2 he features as one of the challengers in a tilt, part of the festivities of the Lord of Misrule, designed by Toto del Nunziata and put on by Cawarden and the Revels to amuse Edward VI in the Christmas season. In 1556 he was in France, where his quarrel with his cousin, Thomas Stafford, was reported to the Privy Council, and he fought a duel with Brian Fitzwilliam on the bridge by Notre-Dame in Paris. Toward the end of the 1560s he was in France again, involved in some mysterious negotiation involving both Elizabeth and Catherine de Médicis; he lost money by this, and attempts, backed by Elizabeth, to get Catherine to pay him what he was owed were abortive. It was perhaps in compensation that he was appointed Elizabeth's Serjeant Porter in January

1569, and given a substantial grant of land in 1572. He provides a likely link between France and Northamptonshire.[115]

In 1572 Sir John Thynne started on the final remodelling of Longleat.[116] Work was approaching completion when he died in April 1580, and was finished off by his son. The existing ground plan seems not to have been touched; the main feature of the remodelling was the re-facing of all the external façades. This external work was almost entirely carried out by a team of masons led by the Frenchman, Alan Maynard, and the Englishman, Robert Smythson, working in partnership. Each façade was enriched by shallow rectangular bay windows, regularly spaced, four on the entrance façade, three on each of the others. Each bay window was identically treated with three storeys of pilasters on high pedestals, Doric, Ionic and Corinthian, each with their entablatures; and the entablatures, but not the pilasters, were continued across the intervening façades (Fig. 205).

The work was carried out in two stages: first the Doric and Ionic storeys, and then, from 1575 or 1576, the final Corinthian storey, replacing or masking the gables of the earlier building. Alan Maynard drew a large elevation, much faded but still one of the most remarkable of surviving Elizabethan architectural drawings, showing all three storeys; this suggests, although it certainly does not prove, that the complete arrangement was envisaged from the start.

The detailing at Longleat is more restrained than at Kirby, but of the highest quality. The friezes are left plain, apart from the necessary Doric triglyphs and metopes and a touch of delicate fretwork at the corners of the Ionic frieze. But the windows are more carefully integrated into the scheme of decoration than at Kirby. They are framed with classical mouldings; underneath each window is a very simple but elegantly shaped apron between fluted consoles. On the Ionic and Corinthian stages of the bay windows this is replaced by a different arrangement, no apron or console but roundels edged with a gadrooned moulding, clearly intended to contain sculpture, though what sculpture there is is a late seventeenth-century insertion. The mullions and transoms have what have been called tramline mouldings, thin rectangular strips round each opening instead of the Flemish ovolos as at Kirby; but this type of moulding (there had been similar ones on the Strand front of Somerset House) also came from Flanders.[117]

Piling three orders one on top of the other always presents a problem. All correctly scaled columns or pilasters reduce, and are thinner at the top than the bottom. If the scale of the orders is kept the same, the upper one, with its base in proportion, appears uncomfortably top heavy. In his earlier bay-window drawing (Fig. 38) Smythson had dealt with this by placing somewhat clumsily widening projections above the lower order. The solution recommended in 1550 by Hans Blum in his *Quinque Columnarum* (though often ignored by the Elizabethans) was to reduce the columns or pilasters in each stage, as had been done in the Gate of Virtue at Caius College.[118] This meant that the storeys progressively reduced in height too, which was acceptable at Caius, where the upper floor was of little importance, and that the spaced-out pilasters in the third stage could seem very skimpy. At Longleat the pilasters were closer together, and the space in between filled with windows, so it looked all right; but the planning

of Longleat called for the tallest windows to be on the first floor. Maynard and Smythson dealt with this very neatly: the space between the Doric pedestals accommodates the windows of the basement; the ground-floor rooms fill the height only of the Doric pilasters; the rooms behind the Ionic order fill the height of both pedestal and pilaster (Fig. 206).

In an undated letter written jointly by Maynard and Smythson to Thynne, probably in 1574 or 1575, they stated, in respect of the work at Longleat, that 'the ordenanse therof came frome us as yore worshipe douthe knowe'.[119] This is the clearest and most explicit claim for responsibility for design known in the Elizabethan period. It is clear that the two men worked closely together, but inevitably one wonders who contributed what. The detailing of the parapet, both as shown in the drawing and as executed, must be due to Maynard, for the elegant motifs that decorate it, with their shells and festoons, are adaptations from French dormer windows, but silhouetted with nothing behind them. It is likely that, in general, the correctness and refinement of the classical detail is also due to Maynard. There is nothing especially French, however, about the general disposition of the orders, with the spaces between the pilasters filled largely by windows bigger than any to be found in France. The same arrangement occurs in Antwerp Town Hall, and in this respect the influence at Longleat seems more likely to be Flemish than French classicism.

The bay windows, however, are English, by way of Somerset House. But at Somerset House there were only two of them and they were modest affairs, compared to the great Longleat bays. It was partly an accident of its development that ended up in Longleat being an outward-looking house; but the final result, the compactness, the unity, the thirteen bays linked by their entablatures marching round the house, was like nothing ever built before in England. The fact that the bay windows were on a rectangular plan, that the

205 The south front of Longleat House, Wiltshire, remodelled by Robert Smythson and Alan Maynard, 1572–76.

orders were of pilasters not columns, fitting the building like a skin, rather than projecting from it, that the house was finished with a parapet not gables, that the window grids were all square and the tramline window mouldings were of square, not ovolo, section gives the house a predominant rectangularity. It was impressive from an angle, both from the rhythm of the windows and because the setting of the bay windows away from the corner produced a bold effect of stepping; this effect was echoed in miniature on the bay windows, by stepping the entablature at their corners, which suggests that it was deliberate, not accidental.

183

Enough of these features were to be repeated in later buildings, where only Smythson was involved, to make one see his hand in them.

Burghley House in Northamptonshire has a history as complicated as Longleat, and there are few accounts and not enough in the way of documentation to illuminate it.[120] An exhaustive structural analysis of the fabric might help to elucidate its history, but this still has to be made. There must be a strong element of hypothesis in any account of it, including the one that follows.

Like Longleat, it is a remodelling of an earlier building, in its case not a religious one but the sizeable courtyard house built by William Cecil's father in the 1540s. When Cecil inherited it in 1552 he at once began to alter it; a certain amount of correspondence between him and his employees about this in the 1550s and '60s survives, but it is difficult to make much sense of it. It was in this period that Henryk van Paesschen may have been supplying architectural detail.[121]

In 1572 Cecil was raised to the peerage as Lord Burghley; in 1573 he was given the Garter and appointed Lord Treasurer; he was now indisputably the first person in the kingdom, after the queen, and his income was enormous. From at least 1573 building work was going on, perhaps in fits and starts, perhaps continuously, until in 1587 his son, Thomas Cecil, was able to write to him expressing the hope that 1588 would see the 'perfection of your long and costly buildings'.[122]

It is difficult to point to any element of Burghley today and date it confidently to before 1570, with the possible and problematic exception of the round-arched arcades in the courtyard. It is more likely that the house was almost entirely remodelled and enlarged between 1573 and 1588, to be in keeping with Burghley's new status and to serve, as his contemporary biographer put it, as 'the seat of his barony'.[123] The remodelling, according to his own account, was on the basis of the old courtyard house; it probably amounted to rebuilding. The main enlargement consisted of an additional range to the east, butting against the east range of the courtyard, and containing a new and larger hall and kitchen. The west range can be documented as built in 1575–8, the north range, or most of it, as dating from 1587–8. There is some evidence that the great hall was built, or in building, in 1578. There is no good evidence for the date of the south range, which contains the main apartment, but it was perhaps rebuilt in the early 1580s. The great 'Tower of the Orders' in the courtyard was added in front of an earlier porch, and may only have been built in 1585, if the date inscribed on its uppermost stage is the date of the whole.[124]

Plans in John Thorpe's book for the ground and first floors at Burghley (Figs 207a, b)[125] do not show the Tower of the Orders and must date from before 1585 (or, more probably, be copies of plans that date). But they show the north range, and its grand central feature (Fig. 319), which was only built in 1587. They must be more than survey drawings; the question is, how early were they (or their originals) made? Perhaps earlier rather than later, in which case the final form of Burghley, or something very like it, was envisaged at least in the late 1570s, and probably earlier.

Lord Burghley seems to have had two aims at Burghley, which led to a more complex message than that put across by Longleat as remodelled at the same time. He wanted to assert his status as a baron and Knight of the Garter (Thynne was neither), and the antiquity of his lineage; he had had a family tree, still at Hatfield, drawn up for him in which a medieval, if genealogically dubious, Cecil was shown cavorting as a mounted knight in armour.[126] But he also wanted to build a modern classical house, of the most splendid nature.

The front and the great hall and kitchen at Burghley assert tradition (Figs 208, 210, 56). The west front has a turreted gatehouse, corner towers and bay windows, in the late Gothic manner; the hall has a magnificent hammerbeam

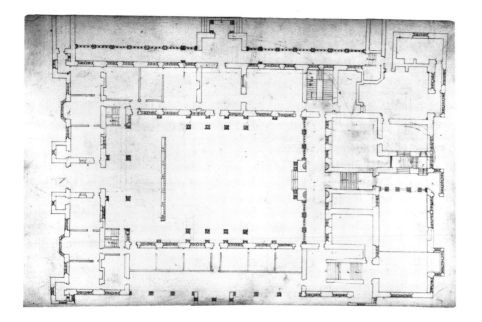

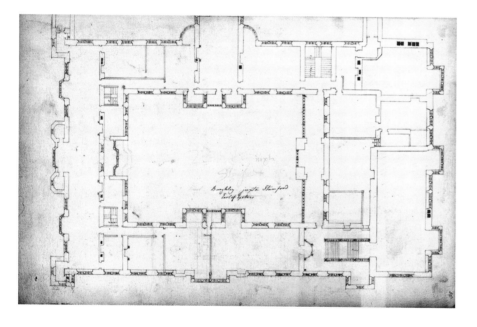

207a and b   Plans by John Thorpe (T57, 58) of the ground and first floors of Burghley House.

in, in 1587 or 1588, the entablatures were found to be several feet out of alignment, but this was clearly not intended). Against the persistent and unifying background accompaniment of the entablatures the different moods of the different façades are played out, using different combinations of the same range of classical motifs: scrolls, coffering, roundels, shell-filled lunettes or alcoves, obelisks, consoles, lion's heads, windows of ovolo section, and everywhere, large and small, the motif of linked squares and circles that originated in Antwerp, and came to England by way of Somerset House.[127] The orders are used sparingly on the outer façades, more extensively in the courtyard, and appear on the roof in the splendid form of giant chimney stacks shaped as Tuscan columns (see p. ii).

The west front (Fig. 208), however feudal it may look, does not contain a single Gothic detail. Only in the great hall and kitchen are pointed arches allowed, in the vault of the kitchen (but the mouldings are classical), and in the window tracery and the arch of the hammerbeam roof of the hall (Fig. 210); but the Burghley classical vocabulary proliferates over this as well, and the chimneypiece is adapted from Serlio.

The courtyard (Fig. 209) is dominated by the Tower of the Orders leading to the hall, and by great twin centrepieces in the façades to either side, each penetrated by deep arched and coffered recesses: the parapets above are enlargements of the parapets above the Somerset House bay windows. Jill Husselby has made the attractive suggestion that these flanking features and the Tower of the Orders were conceived as, in effect, grandstands, from which to watch events (a masque, a tilt?) in the courtyard;[128] the first-floor arch of the tower is flanked by roundels of the Emperor Charles v and the Sultan of Turkey, an ideal accompaniment to Queen Elizabeth in person in the archway; the roundels on the archway below show Paris and Aeneas, who by way of King Brutus were ancestors of Elizabeth

roof, and the kitchen is elaborately vaulted. The courtyard, on the other hand, is the grandest classical ensemble of the period surviving in England.

But in fact the two moods are carefully melded. There is a consistent language of classical detail that runs all the way through Burghley. Three classical entablatures, above ground, first and second floors, run remorselessly round all the external and courtyard façades (it was perhaps inevitable, given the surveying technology available at the time, that when the final link was put

208 The west front of
Burghley House,
Lincolnshire, built 1575–8,
probably to an elevation
supplied by Henry
Hawthorne.

(and Burghley as well), according to popular genealogy, which some scholars endeavoured to explode, but which Burghley supported.

One can even wonder whether Lord Burghley
planned to give a Garter feast at Burghley, on the
lines of the five-day Garter feast and tournament
given by Sir Rhys ap Thomas at Carew Castle in
Pembrokeshire in 1507.[129] Burghley, like Thomas
a man of relatively modest origins, was inordi-
nately proud of his Garter: there is some evidence
that the main first-floor rooms at Burghley were
decorated to celebrate the Order.[130] But all this is
just surmise, however tempting: Elizabeth never
came to Burghley, and Burghley himself came
there seldom enough, if a little more frequently
than Sir Christopher Hatton to Holdenby.

By virtue of his position as Lord Treasurer he
had easy access to the artificers employed in the

Works, including Henry Hawthorne and John Symonds. Hawthorne was a carpenter by training who had been in the Works since at least 1570–71. He had provided a 'platt' for the inner court of Theobalds in 1572, and it was probably he who provided an 'upright' for the west front of Burghley in 1575. In 1576 he was making drawings for an important new wing at Windsor.[131] He died soon after, and in place of him Burghley employed John Symonds. Symonds had been an apprentice of Lewis Stocket, and was a joiner and carver, apparently working in wood, plaster, stone and marble, who made a surviving design for a gateway at Theobalds in 1577, and in 1578 provided a 'platt' for the hall at Burghley.[132] To these two the name of Cornelius Cure should perhaps be added. He had been working for Lord Burghley since at least 1587. There are existing designs made for Lord

Burghley and attributed to him, for a doorway and chimneypiece (Figs 397, 398). Lord Burghley's fine monument in St Martin's, Stamford, though not documented, is almost certainly by Cure (Fig. 211). The obelisks and scrolls that surmount it echo the obelisks and scrolls on top of the Tower of the Orders at Burghley; the coffered vault, a favourite Cure motif, is similar to the coffered vaults in the courtyard there.[133] But the coffered vault of the north staircase (Figs 247, 249) is in a different manner altogether, and probably by a different and as yet unidentified hand.

The west front and possibly general designs by Hawthorne; the hall, possibly further designs, and possibly carving, by Symonds; possible contributions by Cure; almost certainly, in view of the size and long building history of Burghley, an input from other craftsmen; no doubt an input, proba-

A number of other houses or buildings, erected or started in the decade ending in 1580, follow the development inaugurated at Hill Hall and Kirby, and carried to fulfilment at Longleat and Burghley. Like them, they are given unity by use of the orders, either explicit or left implicit except for their entablatures. Two of these are as important as anything built under Elizabeth, but unfortunately our knowledge of them is fragmentary: Lord Burghley's other great house, the 'Princely Seat'[134] of Theobalds in Hertfordshire, and Sir Christopher Hatton's equally enormous house at Holdenby in Northamptonshire.

Theobalds[135] was continuously in building from about 1567, till, probably, Burghley's death in 1598. Unlike Burghley, it was within easy reach of London, and Elizabeth came there constantly. To accommodate her court and her wishes, Burghley kept adding to and altering it, until it ended up sprawling over the landscape round four court-yards, with an open two-storey gallery projecting into the gardens, which were also of enormous size and elaboration (Fig. 212). The courtyard containing the main rooms was rebuilt from 1572, on the basis of a 'plat' provided by Hawthorne, with four great rectangular corner pavilions, and another gallery or loggia to the garden.

For all this we have the ground and basement plans, as given by Thorpe,[136] some descriptions, and a few drawings, including a design for a modest gateway, by Symonds, and elevations of two subsidiary façades (Fig. 48), the draughts-manship of which is so amateurish that it has been suggested, in chapter 1, that they could have been drawn by Burghley himself.[137] This is not enough by which to judge its quality. It was certainly an amazing building, and amazed contemporaries; but one suspects that it never acquired the unity that is so impressive a feature of Burghley. Even so, so remarkable and much visited a house must have been influential.

Its silhouette was dominated by the four great angle pavilions of the courtyard of 1572, each with

211 The monument to Lord Burghley (d. 1598) in St Martin's, Stamford, Lincolnshire, attributed to Cornelius Cure.

bly important, by Burghley himself and his son Thomas, who unlike his father spent much time at Burghley and seems, on and off at least, to have supervised the building work there – this is the best one can do for this extraordinary house. If Hawthorne was responsible for the general concept as well as the west front, he needs to be ranked as an *éminence grise* of Elizabethan architecture.

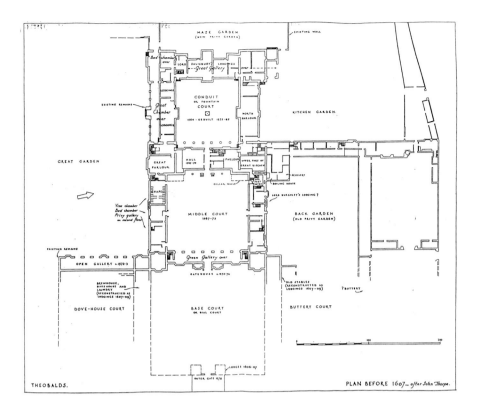

212 (*above*)
A reconstruction of the
plan of Theobalds House,
Hertfordshire, based on a
plan by Thorpe. It was
started in about 1567 and
built and altered in
ensuing decades.

213 (*right*) A room in the
palace of Binche,
in the Low Countries
(as depicted in 1549) on
which the great chamber
at Theobalds was
part-modelled.

turrets at the corners. These pavilions were to
be imitated, amongst other houses, at Holdenby
in the 1570s and Audley End around 1605; and
the house's five loggias, the earliest built from
elements sent over by Henryk van Paesschen

from Antwerp, must have served to establish the
popularity of the loggia in English houses of
the period. The sixteen turrets on the four pavilions, each surmounted by a lion-supported
weather vane, and supplemented by further turrets over gatehouse and hall, combined with chimney stacks and ornamental parapets to produce
a roofscape as tangled and exciting as that of
Burghley.

The lavish decoration of the interior, lovingly
described by visitors from the Continent, inevitably bred imitations. The influence of the heraldic decorations of the green gallery, with shields
hanging from enfilades of trees, survives in the
great chamber of Gilling Castle in North Yorkshire; real trees, or branches, enclosed in plaster
to decorate friezes, are still to be found in the
High Great Chamber at Hardwick.

There was a curious and puzzling example of
Low Countries influence in the decoration of
the great chamber, as remodelled and probably
enlarged in the mid-1580s; it was much commented on at the time but was swept away when
James I took over Theobalds in 1607. In 1584 Sir
John Yonge of Bristol sent Lord Burghley a load
of the sparkling quartz known as St Vincent's
Rock, to adorn the grotto that dominated one
wall of the great chamber;[138] above it the ceiling,
as described by Rathgeb in 1592, was decorated
with the Twelve Signs of the Zodiac. Grotto and
ceiling were quite clearly inspired by the similar
features in one of the great rooms of the palace of
Binche in the Low Countries, designed by Jacques
Dubroeucq and shown in illustrations of the fêtes
held there in 1549 (Fig. 213). But this room is said
to have been swept away when the palace was
sacked and part-demolished later in the century
and before the 1580s.[139]

Holdenby, or at least its ruins, survived a little
longer than Theobalds. There is a ground plan
by John Thorpe (Fig. 81), some early eighteenth-
century drawings and engravings of the ruins, and
surviving fragments, including the two arches of

191

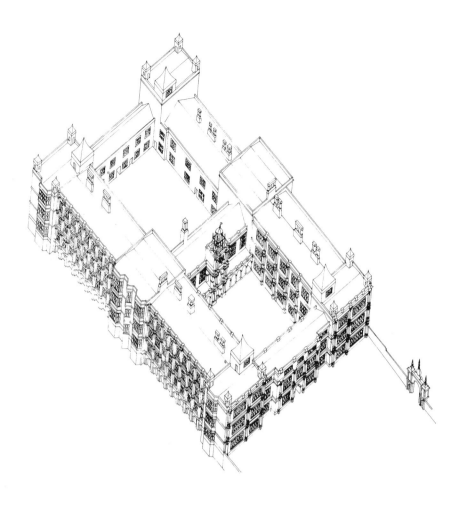

courtyard, culminating in the tower of paired columns of the hall porch; a nice drawing of this, when in ruins, by Sir James Thornhill survives (Fig. 215). The columns were linked by continuous entablatures, as in the other houses, and there may have been bay windows, distributed between the columns. It is by no means certain that either entablature or orders were carried around the corner along the 380 feet of the garden façade; more probably, it was articulated by the curious pilaster strips, linked by mouldings, still to be seen on the two forecourt arches, themselves very free adaptations from Serlio.

214 (*above*) A bird's-eye reconstruction of Holdenby House, Northamptonshire, based on a plan by Thorpe and later drawings of the ruins.

215 (*right*) A drawing by Sir James Thornhill of the hall porch, Holdenby.

216 (*facing page*) The screen in the church at Holdenby, probably moved from the chapel in the house.

the forecourt (Fig. 12), a screen removed from the house into the church, and a portion of the service wing, enlarged and converted in the nineteenth century, all of which give one some idea of it – but not enough.[140]

The scale of Holdenby, as depicted in Thorpe's plan, is staggering.[141] Looking at it one is tempted to wonder whether, like Longleat, Burghley and Theobalds, it grew in stages, watered by Elizabeth's never-ceasing flow of generosity to her favourite, and whether a house built one room thick round one courtyard perhaps in the early 1570s was greatly enlarged in the second half of the decade by the addition of a second court and the doubling in width of the side wings (Fig. 214).

The end result, however achieved, was articulated with three orders, rather sparingly distributed along the entrance front and round the first

The fine classical screen (Figs 216, 217) now fitted into the church can be attributed with some confidence to the Flemish or Dutch carver Garret Hollemans. He was probably also responsible for at least some of the elaborate chimneypieces that the house is known to have contained.[142] The beautiful monument to Hatton's relatives the Saunderses in the nearby church at Harington

217 (*right*) A detail of the church screen at Holdenby.

(Fig. 218) is almost certainly by Hollemans, and can give some idea of their likely quality. The enormous gardens were designed by Hugh Hall, a Catholic priest, who also worked at Burghley, and is sometimes referred to as 'Hatton's priest': Hatton, though not a Catholic himself, was well disposed to Catholics.[143] But there is no evidence as to who provided 'plats' for the plan and elevation of the house: Hatton, in a letter to Burghley of 1579, frustratingly refers to 'the Surveyor', but does not name him.[144]

Perhaps specifically in order to build Holdenby, Hatton acquired a quarry at Weldon, where some of the best Northamptonshire oolite was quarried. In the 1570s he presented his neighbour, Sir Thomas Tresham, with stone from Weldon,

with which to build a market house in Rothwell. Tresham reminded him of this, in a letter written in 1583; the building, he wrote, was 'a witness of the bounty of happy Holdenby to ruinous Rushton'.[145] It was built by a family of Weldon masons, the Grumbolds; in July 1578 William Grumbold, the eldest of them, signed a contract for it which refers to 'a plot . . . drawn by the said William, showed unto the said Sir Thomas Tresham'.[146] It is possible that the Grumbolds also worked at Holdenby.

The market house is one of the earliest known examples in England of unifying orders applied all round a building, if a small one, and is of interest because of that (Fig. 219). But the engaging naivety of its skimpy Doric and Ionic pilasters

218 The monument to
the Saunders family at
Harington, Northampton-
shire. Attributed, like the
screen at Holdenby, to
Garret Hollemans.

suggests that Hatton's surveyor was not involved, even if his masons were, and that Tresham himself had not attained to the architectural expertise (or access to it in others) that his buildings were to show later on in the century.

Another smaller classical building of this period, the gatehouse at Tixall in Staffordshire (Fig. 221), is more accomplished than the Rothwell market house. Its exact date is not known; it was built by Sir Walter Aston, who inherited in the late 1560s and died in 1583. It stood in front of a half-timbered house, built by his father, which has been demolished. One is tempted to surmise a connection with Charlecote, for Sir Walter's son and heir married Sir Thomas Lucy's daughter about 1580; the gatehouse at Charlecote is a simplified version of that at Tixall.

The Tixall gatehouse is dominated by identical three-bay, three-storey orders of coupled Doric, Ionic and Corinthian columns on both façades, under a classical balustrade; between each central pair, above the archway, is a shallow two-storey bay window, reminiscent (if Thorpe is to be relied on) of the arrangement at Holdenby. The orders are correctly detailed and proportioned, and handsomely carved; in the spandrels of the arches are voluptuous Victories on one side and warriors on the other. At the four corners four octagonal turrets, with elegantly shaped stone domes, rise above the balustrade: one of them contains a staircase and gives access to the flat roof, which is paved with stone and was clearly designed for the enjoyment of the view. The entablatures are not continued round the turrets, and their junction with the centre is a little clumsy; even so, the gatehouse fully deserves its near-contemporary description, by Sampson Erdeswicke, local gentleman and antiquary, as 'one of the fairest pieces of work made of late times, that I have seen in all these countries'.[147]

Moreton Corbet (Fig. 220) – too fragmented a ruin, but a beautiful one – was, as has already appeared (p. 138), built but left unfinished by

221 The front of the gatehouse at Tixall in Staffordshire, probably built in the 1570s. It was desribed by a contemporary as 'one of the fairest pieces of work made of late times'.

219 (*facing page, top*) The Market House, Rothwell, Northampton-shire, built by the Grumbold family for Sir Thomas Tresham in and after 1578.

220 (*facing page, bottom*) The west end in the south range of the ruined remains of Moreton Corbet Castle, Shropshire, *c.*1578–83.

Robert Corbet, 'smit with the love of architecture . . . in the Italian style' as Camden inaccurately put it. The L-shaped building was to have consisted of an east wing, containing a great hall, and a south wing, containing the principal rooms. It carries the date 1579 on the south wing, but was probably projected before Robert Corbet's father died in 1578; it had not been finished when Robert died of the plague in 1583. The hall wing was then only half built, and was probably never roofed; the south wing was structurally complete and roofed, but unglazed, and it was left to Robert's son Vincent to fit it up. The building fell into decay in the eighteenth century, but early drawings reveal much that no longer exists and show the long south front, so shattered today,

complete (Fig. 222), though in not unromantic decay.[148]

The parish clerk, entering Robert Corbet's death in the parish register, enthused about his career: 'was of grate estima'on w'the the Queens majestie and the nobyllytie, because he could speacke perfectly soondry forraigne langag's bye reason of hys longe absence in hys youthe owt of Englande and especiallye trayned up as it wer in the Emperors court'. It was probably of more immediate importance for the architecture of Moreton Corbet that he had been on an embassy to Antwerp in 1573, sent by Lord Burghley.[149]

But what is notable about Moreton Corbet is not that it is Italian classical, or French classical, or Imperial or Antwerp classical, but that it is

197

222 The south façade of
Morton Corbet Castle,
drawn when still complete
in the eighteenth century.

essentially English and Elizabethan classical, borrowing with confidence and playing English variations with assurance and enjoyment around its basic classical framework. This is of two storeys, Doric and Ionic, with columns on the main, south front (Fig. 222) pilasters on the west front and the linking entablatures continued round the long north front without an order. But more than half of the façade is glazed and the rhythm of the great windows is as important as the orders. The main front is symmetrical and carefully composed on an *a bbb a bbb a* rhythm: three lots of big five-light-wide windows, slightly projecting from the façade, and in between two groups of three-light windows, two of them truncated at the bottom to allow for the introduction of symmetrically matching doorways. The groups of three windows

are articulated by columns, and fill the space between them in the manner of Antwerp Town Hall; but the big five-light windows, where one might expect columns, are framed by curious pilaster strips, and are widened out by consoles at top and bottom. At the top they are carried up above the entablature to shaped gables, containing small pedimented windows inspired by those on the Strand front of Somerset House.

The north front, most of which has disappeared, was built to a different and much less complex rhythm:[150] an enfilade of seven identical windows, five lights wide, with pediments alternately straight and curved, incorporated into the entablature that linked the first-floor windows; four dormer windows above the bays with curved pediments combined with the three dormers on the south front to give staggered light to the gallery, nearly 160 feet long, that ran the whole length of the range under the roof.

The orders, entablatures and other classical detail are of very respectable quality, but enlivened by some enjoyable extempore carving, most notably the scrolls on the window consoles and the winged beasts that replace the pedestals of the corner orders. Very little interior detail survives: confusing evidence in eighteenth-century depictions (Fig. 223) suggests that a giant order was to have been incorporated on the east front;[151] there are remains of a strapwork overmantel, and some shallow plaster rustication that derives from Serlio's Third Book;[152] it is likely that the detailing of the orders comes from Serlio too, and perhaps the idea of alternating straight and curved pediments. But the way of incorporating windows with the main entablature, although inconspicuously shown in one engraving by Serlio, is more likely to be inspired by the publications of Du Cerceau.[153]

Moreton Corbet is put together with such care, and even sophistication, that one inevitably finds oneself wondering who was responsible. Robert

223   Moreton Corbet from the south east, detail from an eighteenth-century painting.

Corbet, of course; the extent of his input can only be guessed at, but must have been considerable; it is likely that he owned books by Serlio and Du Cerceau. But who was the Smythson or Maynard to his Thynne? Can the same hand or team be found at work on other buildings?

There is one answer to the last question, at least: the huge vanished house of Gerard's Bromley, in Staffordshire (Figs 18, 314), but only fifteen miles or so from Moreton Corbet, and built around 1584 (the date on the porch), only a year or two later. The enfilade of giant windows on its entrance façade gives it a place in chapter 5, but prominent above these windows was a row of pediments incorporated in a continuous entablature – all straight-sided, admittedly, if Plot, our only authority, is to be relied on. The play of windows resulting from the contrast between solidly glazed centre and small windows in the wings also suggests Moreton Corbet, and makes it tempting to surmise that Sir Gerard, the lawyer-builder of Gerard's Bromley, did more than send his own mason over to Moreton Corbet to get ideas.[154]

At much the same time, in Wiltshire and adjacent counties, the Longleat craftsmen (to whom the work can confidently be attributed) were working out ways of building classical houses for those who baulked at the expense of Longleat's elaborate apparatus of the orders. At Corsham Court, in Wiltshire,[155] started, probably, soon after 1575 and finished in 1582, the Longleat bays are reduced and simplified, with entablatures but no pilasters and with surmounting pediments. Four of these bays and a porch projecting in the same fashion give a rhythm to a half-H-shaped entrance front; unity comes by continuing the entablatures over the intervening façades. The only use of the orders is in the Doric of the entrance porch; the porch is surmounted by a semicircular lunette, hot from the press, so to speak, because it derives from a design in Jacques Androuet du Cerceau's *Livre d'Architecture*. But

Both are handsome and dignified buildings: but more ambitiously, at Sherborne in Gloucestershire, Thomas Dutton, possibly the same man as the Thomas Dutton who was for a time one of Thomas Gresham's factors in Antwerp (and to whom he married the mother of his illegitimate daughter), started to re-front his house with the whole Longleat formula, bays and all, on a smaller scale but with columns instead of pilasters (Fig. 225); his work was never completed, perhaps because of his death in 1581, but was finished off forty years or so later by his son, with rather different detail. A connection with Smythson and/or Maynard can be surmised, and the earlier work may even anticipate the remodelling of Longleat.[157]

Scattered all over England and Wales is more classical work of (or attributable to) the 1570s: gateways, tombs, fountains, chimneypieces and porches, often, as in the previous decade, isolated

224 and 225 The entrance porch (*above*) of Shaw House, Berkshire, *c.*1575–81, and (*right*) a window at Sherborne House, Gloucestershire, reconstructed but perhaps originally built *c.*1570.

the linking entablatures feature only on this entrance front; the other three façades were unpretentious and the third floor has traditional gables with hood-moulded windows, as there had been at Longleat before the Corinthian order was extended over them. Shaw House in Berkshire, built *circa* 1575–81 (Fig. 224), has a similar ordonnance, including the gables, a porch with Ionic pilasters but no bay windows; but here the entablatures were continued right the way round the house.[156]

226 (*above left*) The stone door-case at the head of the stairs at Wolfeton House, Dorset, almost certainly carved by Alan Maynard, *c.*1580

227 (*above right*) A door-case, probably by Robert Smythson, inserted into the fourteenth century Wardour Castle, *c.*1576.

228 A chimneypiece, possibly by Alan Maynard or Thomas Collins, as removed to Broomwell House, near Bristol, from an earlier house. Detail from a drawing by W. H. Bartlett.

features in buildings of a traditional nature, varying a good deal in quality, but with common characteristics of a freshness and directness in their use of the classical vocabulary which makes it a pleasure to come across them.

Alan Maynard, thanks to his distinctive detail, can be traced all through the 1570s and on into the 1580s, at church monuments at St Peter's, Bristol, Bishop's Canning, All Cannings and Nunney in Wiltshire, and at Sherborne in Dorset, in a chimneypiece ornamented with a grandly simple Vitruvian scroll at Upper Upham in Wiltshire, possibly in at least one chimneypiece in Bristol (Fig. 228), and in the lovely stone staircase with a delicate Corinthian door-case at the head of it at Wolfeton Manor in Dorset (Fig. 226).[158] A classical entablature caps the exquisitely understated

229 The chimneypiece, probably of the 1570s, in the hall of Lumley Castle, Durham.

façade of the work of this period at Wolfeton. Another runs all round the equally plain outer courtyard at Sudeley Castle in Gloucestershire; this, unlike the work at Woodlands, is firmly dated 1572 on the fabric, but was probably the work of William Spiar rather than of Maynard.[159] There is reasonable evidence that it was Robert Smythson who brought Wardour Old Castle up to date with door-cases, alcoves and tablets in the years 1576–8.[160]

The grave Doric order and splendid lion's masks of the doorway in the courtyard there (Fig. 227) is paralleled, with the same robustness but rather less sophistication, in the huge chimney-piece that Lord Lumley (creator of famous gardens at Nonsuch) introduced into his great hall at Lumley Castle in Durham at much the same peri-

od (Fig. 229), drawing on Serlio for the interlacing ornament above the fireplace opening.[161] In 1578 Lady Lumley's penfriend Sir Nicholas Bacon commissioned a drawing of a Doric porch for the chapel he proposed to donate to his old college, Corpus Christi, at Cambridge; the drawing, possibly by his servant and draughtsman, the enigmatic John Osborne, survives (Fig. 46). The design was executed by the Cambridge mason John Martin. The chapel itself was in the Gothic style; chapel and porch have been demolished. Osborne may also have been involved in the design of the long Doric loggia of the wing (Fig. 169) that Bacon added to Gorhambury some time between 1572 and 1577.[162]

The gardens at Nonsuch were the most famous of their age in England, and although they were

231 The fountain of
c.1577, originally in the
courtyard of Wilton
House, Wiltshire,
as re-erected with alter-
ations in the gardens.

noted that Arundel had brought water to the house 'which King Henry could not find'.[163]

A smaller fountain originally in the courtyard of Wilton was moved, somewhat altered, to the garden, where it survives; it can be dated by the heraldry to 1577 or later (Fig. 231). Other fountains in gardens or in courtyards (a favourite place for them) have gone without known illustrations or inadequate ones, including a great royal fountain at Richmond and an even more elaborate one at Kenilworth. A notable survivor is the fountain of 1601–12 in the Great Court of Trinity College, Cambridge (Figs 232, 233).[164] What can be identified as the 'garden seat' built, like the fountain, for Queen Elizabeth's visit to Kenilworth in 1575, survives also, or at least the frontispiece does, removed to one side of the gatehouse (Fig. 230). It is an accomplished combination of Doric pilasters and shell-head alcoves, with Leicester's ragged staff and five-leafed rosettes instead of the usual roundels and ox-heads in the metopes.[165]

An unidentified carver at Burford in Oxfordshire clearly had access to both Serlio and Flemish engravings. A series of monuments to the Sylvester and Bartholomew families in the church, starting perhaps in the late 1560s and going on into the 1580s, repeat the same model, a skilful adaptation of the Ionic chimneypiece in Serlio's Fourth Book (Figs 234, 235). A more ambitious monument, dated 1569, to Edward Harman, married to a Sylvester and the owner of famous local quarries, has charming reliefs of his children in frames of interlacing Serlian ornament and Corinthian columns and a pediment above, which encloses a strapwork panel adapted from an engraving by Cornelis Bos. The same carver probably worked on chimneypieces in Harman's house, Burford Priory, and on its columned central feature.[166]

There is a similar collection of work of the 1570s in Sussex, and here the name of the carver or mason of at least some of the work is known, though not his first name. 'Flynte' is identified by

destroyed in the late seventeenth century, the appearance of their fountains, columns and obelisks is recorded in the 'Lumley Inventory' made in 1590. Most of their embellishments were erected by Lord Lumley after he inherited Nonsuch from his father-in-law, the Earl of Arundel, in 1580. But the grandest of the fountains was put up by Arundel, and stood in the main courtyard of the house, not in the gardens (Fig. 172); it was probably erected between FitzAlan's purchase of Nonsuch in 1556 and 1565, in which year the Spanish ambassador visited and

232 and 233 The fountain of 1601–12 in the Great Court of Trinity College, Cambridge.

the will of Richard Covert of Slaugham as the carver of his beautiful Corinthian tomb in the church there (Fig. 236), with its delicately festooned heraldry and deliciously reducing depictions of his children.[167] The same carver was clearly responsible for an equally delicate chimneypiece at Cuckfield House, nearby, dated 1574.[167] He must be a candidate for the loggia at Slaugham Place itself, which survives in ruins today as almost all that remains of the great house of the Coverts (Fig. 237): possibly also for the remains of chimneypieces, one quoting from Serlio, that with other fragments are now built into a wall of

what was the Shirleys' house at Wiston in Sussex (Fig. 239).[168]

In Northamptonshire, the little archway to the courtyard at Winwick (Fig. 238), and the panelling, dated 1571, at the end of the hall at Deene (Fig. 59) are both, in their different ways and materials, attractive exercises in the Doric order.[169] Down in Cornwall Sir John Arundell, who had been in the household of the Earl of Arundel at Nonsuch, filled his house at Trerice with respectable, if slightly clumsy, classical chimneypieces and friezes, all in plaster, and conveniently dated them 1572 and 1573.[170] In 1576–7 at Plas

205

Mawr in Wales, next to Conwy Castle, Robert Wynn, who had been in the household of Sir Philip Hoby, decorated the earliest wing of his house with pedimented and consoled windows (Fig. 240) directly copied from Somerset House.[171] At the other end of Wales, the Earl of Worcester, who had acquired a copy of Hugues Sambin's *L'Oeuvre de la Diversité des Termes* (1572) – a change from Serlio) – probably when on an embassy to Paris in 1573, had four of the terms adapted for the great stone chimneypiece in his new long gallery at Raglan Castle (Figs 241, 242).[172]

234 and 235 One of the monuments (*above*) to the Bartholomew and Sylvester families in the church at Burford, Oxfordshire, and (*right*) the chimneypiece in Fourth Book of Sebastiano Serlio's *Architettura*, 1537, from which they derive.

236 (*far right*) The monument to Richard Covert (d. 1573) at Slaugham, Sussex, carved by 'Flynte'.

206

237 A loggia in the ruins of the Covert family's great house at Slaugham, Sussex.

238 An archway, probably of the 1570s, at Winwick Manor House, Northamptonshire.

in the originally free-standing Turvey monument the arch that covers the effigies has Victories in the spandrels. But what is significant about these monuments is that they draw freely from engravings in Cornelis Floris's *Veelderleij Niewe Inventien*, published in Antwerp in 1557 (Fig. 246).[174] This was one of the founding sources of the Flemish Mannerism into which the Serlian classicism of Pieter Coecke developed in Antwerp and elsewhere. Floris popularised, and possibly invented, variations on a bulging sarcophagus motif, sometimes used for actual (or ostensible) sarcophagi, sometimes as replacements or additions to the frieze or cornice of the entablature. The motif, for better or worse, was to become popular in England. In the Mordaunt tomb it is used only for the tomb chest; in later monuments in the group it features prominently above the entablature.

239 (*above*) Part of a chimneypiece derived from Serlio, built with other fragments, probably of the 1570s, into a wall at Wiston Park, Sussex.

240 A window derived from Somerset House at Plas Mawr, Conwy, Wales.

One of the most impressive products of the 1570s is a group of church monuments, all of stone from the Totternhoe quarry in Bedfordshire, and yet again by an unidentified carver.[173] The earliest of them is the fine monument to the 1st Lord Mordaunt in Turvey in Bedfordshire (Fig. 243). The group works through various combinations of Doric order, terms and sarcophagi (Figs 244, 245), always with a plain surmounting pediment;

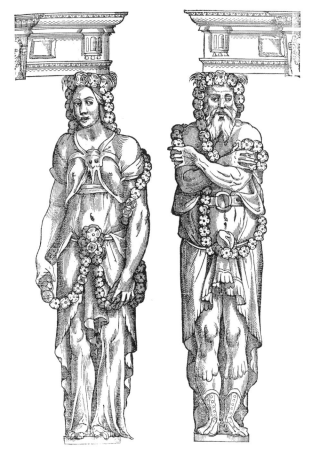

241 and 242   The remains (*right*) of the chimneypiece (*c*.1575) in what was the Long Gallery, Raglan Castle, Monmouthshire, and (*far right*) the design in Hugues Sambin's *L'Oeuvre de la Diversité des Termes dont on use en architecture* (1572) from which it derives.

A significant example of the way in which taste was moving is to be found on the noble stone-vaulted staircase at Burghley (Fig. 247). In its general concept this seems to have come out of Italy by way of France. But the detail of the ornament on the barrel vault is of different origin. It takes the motif of linked circles and squares devised perhaps originally, as we have seen, by Pieter Coecke, and elaborates on it (Fig. 249). The links are made more complicated; the squares are filled with shallow diamond faceting; and the whole network is incised with small round holes, as though they had been punched in leather, not stone. The motif is found in engravings by Jan Vredeman de Vries (Fig. 250) whose many publications were to make him even more influential in England than Floris.[175]

The great house at Wollaton in Nottingham-shire (Fig. 248), built by Sir Francis Willoughby,

is in some ways the apogee of the Elizabethan classical house. It is all of a piece, conceived and built in eight years, between 1580 and 1588. It is a single entity, a great concentrated block, with no internal court, placed on a hilltop, to be seen by all. Three orders, Doric, Ionic and Corinthian, run all the way round its four façades. As originally designed (and perhaps carried out, at least in part), the towered mass of the house was set in a symmetrical layout of eight courtyards (Fig. 292), with four pavilions looking across to the four façades of the house from the four central court-yards.[176] The plan of the house itself had a rigor-ous symmetry, two matching staircases to either side of the hall, leading up to two matching great chambers (Fig. 128). The hall itself (Fig. 251) is perhaps the first Elizabethan hall to be designed as a whole, with the Doric frieze of the screen carried round the rest of the hall, and matching

243–5 Members of a
group of monuments by
an unidentified workshop
active in the 1570s.

243 (*right*)   To the First
Lord Mordaunt, Turvey,
Bedfordshire.

244 (*below left*)
To Alexander Denton,
Hilllesden, Bucking-
hamshire.

245 (*far right*)
To Elizabeth d'Arcy, 1578,
Hornby, Yorkshire.

246 (*below right*)   One of
the designs by Cornelis
Floris on which the
monuments draw.

247 (*facing page*)   The
stone-vaulted staircase,
*c.*1570–80, at Burghley
House, Lincolnshire.

248 Flemish mannerism
rampant. Wollaton Hall,
Nottinghamshire,
1580–88.

249 (*below left*) A detail
of the staircase vault at
Burghley.

250 (*below right*)
A Vredeman de Vries
design for column bases.

251 The hall at Wollaton, from an early nineteenth-century engraving.

doors, alcoves and chimneypieces to either side. The patron, Francis Willoughby, was a highly educated Cambridge graduate, and owned an impressive library, architectural books included.[177] His surveyor and principal mason was Robert Smythson, who brought with him all of the exper-

tise and several of the craftsmen that he had acquired at Longleat.[178]

But Longleat's stylistic mixture of Flemish and French classicism has been almost completely replaced by Flemish Mannerism. Vredeman de Vries is the presiding genius behind the detail;

252 Hardwick Hall, Derbyshire, 1590–97. 'The supreme achievement of Elizabethan classicism, and one secret of its supremacy is its reticence.'

253 (*facing page*) Looking through the screen to the hall at Hardwick. The screen is one of the few internal features at Hardwick possibly to have been designed by Robert Smythson.

even the Doric chimneypiece in the hall, which is adapted from Serlio's Fourth Book, has two Vriesian pendants suspended from its triglyphs. Elements derived from Longleat have constantly been translated into the language in which de Vries aimed to liven up the classical vocabulary. So the plain pilasters of Longleat have enclosing rectangular blocks around their centres; the simple Longleat roundels are given elaborate strapwork settings; the dormer motifs used in silhouette on the Longleat parapet have swollen to gables, equally in silhouette, richly embellished with strapwork scrolls and obelisks; more strap-

work, in low relief, fills the panels of the hall screen; the conventional rosettes of the Serlian Doric frieze have been encircled with strapwork too; the open timber roof of the hall is closely modelled on that at Longleat, and was constructed by the younger John Lewis, son of Thynne's head carpenter, but the suspended Doric capitals and Serlian consoles of Longleat have been replaced with grotesque heads and the goitrously swelling silhouettes beloved by Vredeman; even the elegant wasp-waisted Serlian balusters originally on the Longleat parapet have been replaced with gently bulging Vriesian ones.

214

But the bold stepping planes that give depth to Wollaton's façades owe something to Longleat but nothing to Vredeman; the enfilade of glass provided by the great windows goes beyond anything in the Low Countries; the looming central feature, whatever its symbolism, and the silhouette of the four towers leading up to it is as much an expression of Elizabethan romanticism as the tangled roofscape of Burghley.

The same artificers and the same controlling mind moved on in 1590 to build Hardwick Hall, Robert Smythson's masterpiece (Figs 250, 252). The sense of order, the all-round unity, the feeling for movement and silhouette at Wollaton are still there. But as though at the wave of a magician's wand all Vredeman de Vriesian ornament, and almost all the apparatus of the orders, has van-

ished. One can wonder if this was simply economy on the part of the formidable octogenarian who paid for it, but hope that it was not. For Hardwick is the supreme achievement of Elizabethan classicism, and one secret of its supremacy is its reticence. Classical detail on the exterior is confined to the four levels of entablature on main storeys and towers, to the consoles under the window sills, to the balustrade, and to the plain Tuscan porticos, originally intended to run all round the house. It is enough.

There are other memorable features: most notably the six-towered plan and the famously enormous windows. Both relate to other aspects of Elizabethan architecture, as important as classicism, which deserve their separate chapters.

254   The Sidney porcupine carved on the fountain at Wilton House, Wiltshire.

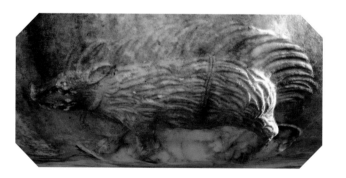

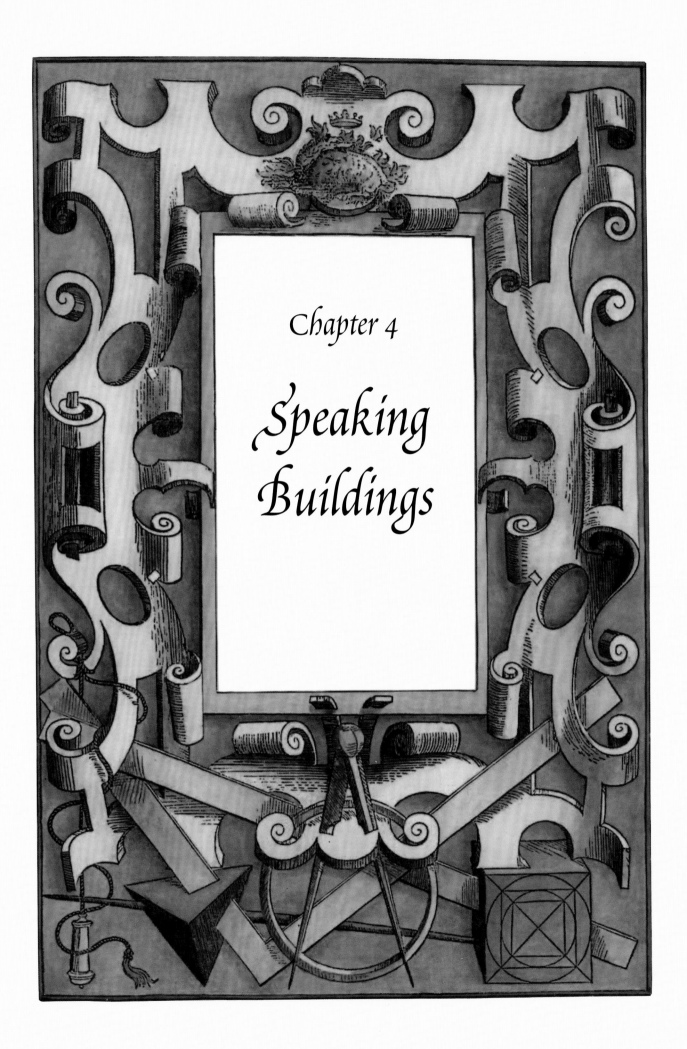

Chapter 4

Speaking Buildings

Elizabethan and Jacobean houses are full of messages, designed to inform, to exhort, to encourage, to delight or to mystify. They share this quality with those portraits of the period that tell of more than the physical appearance of the persons portrayed, and give hints about their background, their family, their emotions and their point of view. Sometimes these are mystifying too: and the problems that they posed delighted the contemporaries who saw them and tried to penetrate their meaning. Who can forget Marcus Gheeraerts's painting, never yet identified or explained, of the melancholy girl in Persian dress, standing in the shade of a nut-tree on which a swallow perches, laying a chaplet of flowers on the head of the young but weeping stag at her side, her own sorrows expressed but not clarified by a framed sonnet, the couplets of which stay in the mind:

The restless swallow fits my restless minde,
In still revivinge still renewinge wronges;
Her just complaints of cruelty unkinde,
Are all the Musique, that my life prolonges . . .[1]

But the picture is no more problematic or moving than was the panelled room from Chicksands Priory, moved to the Victoria and Albert Museum and now, alas, dismantled, the elements of which transported one into a mysterious but tranquil world: the serene classical architecture of the panelling, inspired by that of the Pantheon in Rome – but why? – the doves or halcyons covering – but, for what reason? – the ceiling, the Latin poem on the overmantel exhorting the reader, in exquisite Roman lettering, to live for others and die to himself.[2]

The most straightforward way in which buildings could give a message was by means of inscriptions, perhaps of a verse or a quotation from the Bible, carved on an overmantel or over the entrance, or by longer inscriptions in the external entablature, informative along the façade of Lady Abigail Sherard's new wing at Stapleford in Leic-

estershire (1633), religious in the inscriptions that run all the way round Sir Thomas Tresham's buildings in Northamptonshire. A series of panels dated 1582 in the frieze of Hesketh End, a little manor-house at Chipping in Lancashire, give a potted history of England from Roman to contemporary days. One use of the gallery at Apethorpe in Northamptonshire is expressed in an overmantel (Fig. 256) inscription:

Rare and ever to be wisht maye sounde heare
Instruments wch fainte sprites and muses
    cheere
Composing for the Body Soule and Eare
Which Sickness Sadness and Fowle Spirits
    feare

In the early seventeenth century a fashion was started for silhouetting inscriptions in parapets, with the cut-out letters taking the place of balusters. The hint may have been given in the 1590s, at Hardwick, where Bess of Hardwick's initials ES under a coronet are silhouetted eighteen times on the parapets of the six towers. Soon after James I's accession, the Earl of Northampton ran a parapet inscription along the length of the prominent Strand façade of his new London house, and probably round the courtyard too. Similar inscriptions followed at Audley End in Essex (circa 1606), Felbrigg in Norfolk (circa 1620) (Fig. 257), the gatehouse of Skipton Castle, Yorkshire (circa 1628), Castle Ashby in Northamptonshire (1624–35), Temple Newsam in Yorkshire (circa 1630), and along the walls of the entrance court of Trentham in Staffordshire (1630s) (Fig. 258).[3]

Elizabethan architecture is richly embellished with figures, human or animal, featured singly or in groups, in stone, alabaster, marble (much more rare), wood and plaster, to be found in or on friezes, ceilings, chimneypieces, overmantels, hall screens, cartouches, porches and parapets, in addition to the tapestries and painted walls that have too often disappeared. What messages

255 (facing page) An aerial view of Lyvedon New Bield, Northamptonshire.

The figures that enrich the architecture derive from four main sources: the Bible, classical history and mythology, allegory and heraldry. They were, perhaps almost without exception, based on Continental, especially Flemish, engravings; but the way in which these were adapted and changed is a source of curiosity or delight.

In decorative schemes before 1600 the Bible meant the Old Testament. The great Protestant surge of iconoclasm in the mid-sixteenth century was powered by hatred of idolatry: the worship that should have gone direct to God was being diverted to religious images. So, in buildings for the rest of the century, images of Jesus, Mary, Joseph, the Apostles, Evangelists and still more the post-New Testament saints all but disappeared; even in Catholic houses they were kept to private inner chambers, as in the case of the dramatic coloured relief of the Crucifixion (Fig. 260) that still survives in what was the private closet of Sir Thomas Tresham at Rushton Hall in Northamptonshire.[4] Only in the seventeenth century, under the influence of the Arminian movement and with the softening of English Calvinism, did they begin to reappear, especially in stained glass.

But Old Testament scenes were acceptable; so, and perhaps even more popular, were themes and figures drawn from the classics; but most popular of all was the whole world of allegory. Personifications of the Five Senses, the Four Elements, the Four Continents, the Four Seasons, the Three Theological Virtues, the Seven Cardinal Virtues, the Seven Liberal Arts, the Seven Planets, the Seven Acts of Mercy, took the place of the rows of saints on medieval screens and façades; to which can be added the Nine Worthies, though these were historical characters. And in addition to single figures were more elaborate groups: the Triumph of Death, of Fame, of Love, of Patience, of Time, of Time over Fame.

Decoration could express the uses of individual rooms, or the qualities owned by, or thought appropriate to, the owners. Celebrations of music

256 The chimneypiece in the gallery at Apethorpe Hall, Northamptonshire, c.1622–5.

these are meant to convey is sometimes obvious, sometimes can be guessed at, sometimes are not obvious at all; in a few cases it is possible to work out, or guess at, a consistent scheme over an entire room or building; too often one suspects that the patrons chose at random from the sheaves of engravings that the artificers offered them.

220

257 Felbrigg Hall, Norfolk, built to the designs of Robert Leminge, *c.*1621–4.

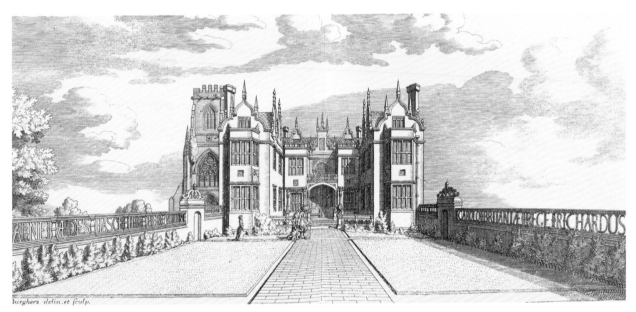

258 Trentham Hall, Staffordshire, built in the 1630s, as depicted in Robert Plot's *Natural History of Staffordshire*, 1686.

were suitable for great chambers and galleries, as, probably, with the reliefs of Apollo and the Muses formerly at Chatsworth and Toddington (Fig. 259),[5] or with the David with his harp still in the long gallery at Apethorpe (Fig. 256). Statues of Justice and Charity, as on the chimneypieces in the gallery at Hardwick (Fig. 510), personified the essential qualities of any landowner, especially a Justice of the Peace; the qualities of the wise judge were also epitomised by reliefs of the Judgement of Solomon, as at Fountains Hall (Fig. 440). An individual skill could be commemorated by the relevant figure or group: an interest or skill in architecture by a figure of Geometry, as found, along with Arithmetic, on the chimneypiece of the great chamber at South Wraxall Manor (Fig. 424); skill in needlework by the figure of Penelope, who featured for forty years in the houses of Bess of Hardwick. Religious beliefs could be

shown in concealed depictions of the Crucifixion, as in the closet of the Catholic Thomas Tresham, or by the Death of Jezebel (Fig. 436), as originally at Heath Old Hall in Yorkshire, Jezebel being the accepted personification of Rome and the Scarlet Woman. In similar vein, at Lord Burghley's Theobalds was an overmantel depicting 'Minerva, driving away Discord, overthrowing idolatry, and restoring true Religion' – although one wonders whether the early nineteenth-century description of this lost overmantel was right about Minerva.[6]

Sometimes there is a consistent scheme in a room, but one does not know why. At Lanhydrock in Cornwall a huge slain Goliath sprawls across the wall at the end of the long gallery (Fig. 261), and on the two overmantels are depictions of Saul's attempting to kill David, and David's sparing Saul's life (probably 1630s). One would like to know the reason why John Robartes, heir

259 A relief of Apollo and the Muses, c.1575, originally at Toddington Manor, Bedfordshire.

the (relatively speaking) modern Arthur, Charlemagne and Godfrey of Boulogne. They had a revival in late Elizabethan England, and between the 1580s and the 1620s can be found in many different materials and in at least sixteen different localities. Stone Worthies stand in alcoves between the windows of the top floor at Montacute (Fig. 262), are deployed on balustrades and on the entrance gate at Fountains Hall, and surmount, in a crumbling row, the terrace wall before the hall porch at Chillingham Castle in Northumberland. They climb in wood up the staircase at Hartwell House in Buckinghamshire (Fig. 263), and process in plaster round the frieze of the Great Chamber at Aston Hall in Birmingham. Just one survives in marquetry at Weston Hall in Yorkshire, and all nine are painted in a row above the dais of the hall at Great Binnall in Shropshire.[7]

260 (*top*) A relief of the Crucifixion, dated 1577, at Rushton Hall, Northamptonshire.

261 (*above*) The death of Goliath, as depicted at one end of the long gallery at Lanhydrock, Cornwall, *c.*1630.

262 (*right*) Two of the Nine Worthies carved along the top floor at Montacute House, Somerset (*c.*1600).

of his father's tin and wool fortune, adopted the David theme; as one of the opponents of royal power in parliament did he see himself as David fighting against a monstrous royal prerogative?

Exploration of sermons and devotional writings of the period might sometimes cast light on the iconographies adopted in decoration. One curious feature is the popularity of the Nine Worthies. These were of medieval origin, and were made up of three lots of three warriors: the biblical David, Joshua and Judas Maccabeus; the classical Hector, Alexander and Julius Caesar;

The Worthies were the subject of the only English pattern book of the sixteenth century, apart from Shute's *Architecture*. In 1584 'Richard Lloyd, gentleman' published *A briefe discourse of the most renowned actes and right valiant conquests of those puissant Princes, called the Nine Worthies*, with engravings of each of them. But the publication seems an early expression of the fashion, not its cause, for with the possible exception of Great Binnall the engravings from which English *Worthies* are copied, are, where found, all Continental ones.

The Worthies would have been suitable enough for the houses of military men, but there was nothing military about Phelips at Montacute or Proctor at Fountains. It may be that their biblical, classical and modern backgrounds appealed to a culture that drew creatively on all three sources.

The most ambitious surviving piece of sculpture in a house of the period is the four-tiered reredos (for that is in effect what it is) that fills the wall behind the dais in the hall of Burton Agnes in Yorkshire (Fig. 264). This seems to show a kind of Pilgrim's Progress of Sir Henry Griffith, who built Burton Agnes about 1601–10. In the lowest tier he stands among, and perhaps is inspired by, the Four Evangelists, and is then led by an angel by way of the Twelve Apostles in the second tier to a kind of Heavenly Jerusalem in the third one.

The reredos is the culmination of an unequalled wealth of allegorical subjects at Burton Agnes,

264 The stone-carving behind what was the dais end in the hall at Burton Agnes Hall, Yorkshire.

carved on screens, arches and overmantels. But even Anthony Wells-Cole, who has worked out the engraved sources for most of them, can offer little more than 'an overtly moralistic purpose' as a theme.[8] He can do more at Hardwick, where the abundant iconography in the decoration is supplemented, unlike at Burton Agnes, by surviving tapestries, embroideries and painted hangings. He sees an underlying theme as being covertly introduced, in a very Elizabethan way, by the great winged figure striding out of the overmantel in the Forest Great Chamber in the Old Hall (Fig. 265). This (as described in the Prologue) derives from the figure of 'studium' or desiderium' in a Flemish engraving of 1559 depicting the Triumph of Patience: Patience, seated on a char-

iot, has conquered Fortune, who is tied to the back, and is being pulled along by Spes and Studium/Desiderium – by Hope and what perhaps can best be translated as Enthusiasm (Fig. 266). Bess of Hardwick identified herself with Patience, as can be seen by the constant appearance in her house of Penelope, the patient and faithful wife of Ulysses, who stayed at home working at her weaving or embroidery while her husband strayed (Fig. 267). One can see Hardwick as itself a celebration of Patience, a final flowering around an old woman in her seventies, secure in her wealth and reputation after a lifetime of stress and drama.[9]

Heraldry, with all its concomitants of shields, crests, supporters and mottoes, was another way

225

265 The overmantel (*c.*1591) in the Hill Great Chamber at Hardwick Old Hall, Derbyshire.

266 The engraving of *The Triumph of Patience* after Martin Heemskerk, from which the figure over the Hardwick overmantel derives.

of conveying information, and announcing status in doing so. It was the great age of heraldry in England; heraldic displays, expanding on and exaggerating their medieval predecessors, were

not to be equalled again until the nineteenth century. Both ages had the common factor of many new families anxious to show that they were not as new as all that, or at least to display their newly acquired coats of arms, and of old families anxious to put the new families in their places. In numerous publications young men were urged, far more urgently than they were recommended to study architecture or even geometry, to acquire a knowledge of heraldry, and to be able to recognise the more prominent achievements of arms.[10] Heraldry was carved in stone over entrances and on parapets, in plaster on walls or ceilings, in wood on panelling and screens, in stained glass in windows, in stone, wood or plaster on overmantels. Sixty-one shields (with twelve blank ones ready to be filled in) of the Zouche family and

267 Penelope flanked by Perseverance and Patience, as depicted in a hanging of *c.*1575 at Hardwick Hall, Derbyshire. Bess of Hardwick identified herself with Penelope, the patient wife of Ulysses.

268 The heraldic screen in the hall at Bramshill House, Hampshire, *c.*1610.

269 The great chamber at Gilling Castle, North Yorkshire, decorated c.1585. Today it is the home to St Martin's Ampleforth preparatory school.

their connections cover the screen at Bramshill in Hampshire (Fig. 268); the family tree of the 1st Lord Montague, with the shields of the different generations linked by fluttering tendrils, fills an overmantel at Boughton in Northamptonshire. The glowing but variegated colours of heraldry, the strange beasts and devices associated with it, exactly fitted Elizabethan and Jacobean tastes.

The most glorious outburst of Elizabethan heraldry to have survived to the present day is in the great chamber of Gilling Castle in Yorkshire (Figs 269, 354, 482). Its three huge windows are all but solid with the enamelled shields of the Fairfax family, successive generations of which installed it from about 1585, and of their connections; their

crests dot the plasterwork of the ceiling; the royal arms preside (as they often do in great chambers) from high up in the overmantel, with the Fairfax arms (rather larger) below them; and all round the walls, an orchard or forest of painted trees are hung with the shields of Yorkshire gentry – well over 400 of them on twenty-two trees.[11]

These displays of coats of arms of local families, and the way in which they are depicted, were not unique to Gilling. Thomas Tresham had the shields of Northamptonshire gentry carved in a frieze round the outside of his market hall at Rothwell, where they are still to be seen, and Sir Christopher Hatton covered two obelisks at the entry to the hall at Holdenby with them; they rise

228

forlornly in the ruins in early eighteenth-century depictions by Thornhill and Buck. Sampson Erdeswick lined his long gallery at Sandon with the shields of the Staffordshire gentry,[12] and, to either side of royal arms and commemorative verses, the shields of the Kentish gentry ran round the great chamber of the circular medieval castle of Queenborough, installed there in 1593 by Sir Edward Hoby, the constable of the castle.[13] The last two have long been demolished, without illustration or detailed description. The shields may have been depicted hanging on trees, like the Gilling shields; the convention derives from medieval tournaments, where a tree by the tilting ground would be hung with the shields of the competing knights.

The convention was certainly followed at Theobalds in what became known as the Green Gallery. This filled the entrance range of the first court. Its heraldry was on a national, not county basis. An account of 1602 describes 'all England represented by 52 trees, each tree representing one county. On the branches and leaves are pictured the coats-of-arms of all the dukes, earls, knights and noblemen residing in the county; and between the trees, the towns and boroughs, together with the principle mountains and rivers'.[14] The heraldry was in place by 1583; the Gilling decoration was probably inspired by it.

Burghley House must have been as rich in heraldry as Theobalds, but much has gone in the almost total redecoration of the interiors in the succeeding centuries. Even so, a good deal remains. The coffered vaults of the stone staircase and the first floor of the central feature in the courtyard are filled with the crests of the Cecil family connections and the local aristocracy and gentry respectively. There is heraldic stained glass still in the windows of the hall, and although the stairs from the hall to the great chamber, decorated with arms of the Garter knights, have been demolished, Burghley's own Garter still encloses an armorial clock in the tower above the courtyard, supported to either side by huge heraldic lions, silhouetted against the sky.

At Hardwick much more has survived from the sixteenth century, and there heraldry is everywhere, not only in every kind of variety and combination on chimneypiece overmantels but also constantly introduced in the embroidery and furniture inlay; and on the skyline the royal arms and the family arms rise above the parapet on the east and west fronts. Above all, the Hardwick stag, with its necklet of five-petalled eglantines (or wild roses), is omnipresent. Three eglantines also feature on the Hardwick coat of arms; the stag was the Hardwick crest, but it may have been Bess of Hardwick's own idea to give it its eglantine necklet. One reason for doing so is mysteriously inscribed in the inlay of the great table now in the High Great Chamber (Fig. 270): 'The redolent sme[ll] of eglantine We stagges exauet to the devyne'. The eglantine was also one of the favoured devices of Queen Elizabeth: the verse, in addition to honouring the Hardwicks, expresses their loyalty to the queen. In somewhat similar fashion Bess of Hardwick's third husband, Sir William Cavendish, had devised his own crest and motto, and it too is much in evidence at Hardwick (and still in use as the family crest). A knotted snake is accompanied by the punning motto: *Cavendo Tutus* ('safe by taking precautions'). The spectator is left wondering: is it William Cavendish who is kept safe by being on the look-out for poisonous enemies? or is he learning caution from the example of the wise snake, who has wrapped itself into a knot so as to make it impossible for birds to swallow it?[15]

The combination of stag and verse, or snake and motto, make up what was called at the time an impresa. Similar to the impresa was the emblem, technically distinct from it, but also combining a distinctive visual image with, usually, a piece of verse. Both were often referred to as 'devices'. Emblems, impresas and devices filled contemporary life and thought, and are to be found in architecture and decoration as well as everything else.[16]

Emblems were general, impresas particular and personal. The Scottish poet William Drummond defined the difference in about 1630.

> Emblems serve for a demonstration of some general thing, and for a general rule, and teaching precepts to everyone as well for the author and inventer, as for any other . . . An impresa is a demonstration and manifestation of some notable and excellent thought of him that conceived it and useth it; and it only belongs to him.[17]

An individual adopted an impresa either to express his attitude to life or to fit a particular situation, as the knights did each year when they jousted in the tournaments held on the queen's birthday; the shields with their impresas were subsequently hung at Whitehall, in the Shield Gallery.[18] Emblems, on the other hand, were

teaching tools; they embodied, in compressed and memorable form, a truth or axiom of conduct; the way of thinking and general attitude of Elizabethans and Jacobeans were conditioned by the emblems that they had read or studied.

The distinction between impresas and emblems was often blurred. Impresas were called emblems, and both could be referred to as 'devices'. It is as 'devices' that Shakespeare, in *Pericles*, describes the impresas on the shields of the knights taking part in a Triumph or Tournament before the King of Antioch:

> And the device he bears upon his shield
> Is a black Ethiop reaching at the sun;
> The word, *Lux tua vita mihi*

But when the Earl of Rutland commissioned a shield for a tournament in 1613 and 1616 from Shakespeare (who thought up the idea) and his partner Richard Burbage (who painted and made it), he paid 'to Mr Shakspeare in gold about my

270 A detail from the inlaid table of *c.*1567 now in the High Great Chamber at Hardwick Hall, Derbyshire. It includes an early version of the Cavendish knotted snake.

271 An emblem in the ceiling of the gallery at Blickling Hall, Norfolk.

Tresham, of the Triangular Lodge, owned at least seven of them. And they were constantly transferred from books into the decoration of buildings.[20] Sir Henry Hobart and his family, as they walked up and down the gallery at Blickling Hall in Norfolk, could (at the expense of a stiff neck) contemplate in the plasterwork of the ceiling twenty-one emblems adopted from Henry Peacham's *Minerva Britannia; or, A garden of Heroical Devises, furnished and adorned with Emblemes and Impresas of sundry natures* (1612) (Fig. 271), and be reminded of what they had to teach about such topics as the power of love, the majesty of kings, the need to trust God, and the importance of avoiding hypocrites;[21] the Hobarts would have been already familiar with the book, which they certainly owned, and with Peacham himself – who may have taught Sir Henry's son Miles, to whom he dedicated one of his emblems. Lady Drury, sitting in her closet at Hawstead Place in Suffolk, could be edified by being encased in forty-two emblems, derived from at least seven emblem books and painted in glowing colours in each division of the panelling (Fig. 272).[22]

The gallery ceiling at Blickling also contained the Hobart coat of arms, with its five-pointed star, regularly repeated. It was already a well-established family coat, but Sir Henry Hobart turned it into a personal impresa by adding his own motto to it, also repeated down the ceiling: 'my word that I chose and use under my coate of arms',[23] as he put it. This motto *quae supra* expanded (as the perceptive would realise) on the symbolism of the star, being a compression of St Paul's admonition, 'Set your affection on things above, not on things on the earth.'

Impresas, with or without their mottoes, were featured in buildings as well as emblems, sometimes surrounded by mystery, as was their point. As Thomas Tresham wrote, the harder a device is to interpret, the more commendable it is 'so as (it being discovered) it be perspicuously to the purpose'.[24]

Lorde's impreso Xliiii s' (in 1613) and 'Richard Burbage for my Lorde's shelde and for the embleance' £4.18s. (in 1616).[19]

'Device' was a more general term, not always used in this specialist fashion. In its widest sense it meant any mental concept, thought up in order to be embodied in physical form; more commonly it was applied to a concept that was seen as especially ingenious or original, not necessarily containing a message further than its own originality.

Emblems and impresas were easily accessible, because books of them were published in very large numbers: around a thousand on the Continent and fifty in England by 1700. Sir Thomas

NVNQVAM MINVS SOLA

QVAM CVM SOLA

272 One wall of the early
seventeenth-century
closet originally at
Hawstead Place, Suffolk,
and now in Christchurch
Museum, Ipswich.

1560s, did Thomas Hoghton place a carving of Hercules Killing the Nemean Lion over the archway of his gatehouse at Hoghton Tower, in Lancashire (Fig. 274)? A marigold opens in fine weather and closes in rain or storm, and can clearly serve as a metaphor for the human condition; but why, in the 1580s, were open and closed marigolds carved all the way round the gallery at Haddon Hall in Derbyshire (Fig. 418)? Were they the personal impresa of Sir John Manners, who built the gallery, and if so, what did they signify? And why, in 1613, did Sir John Pakington have a crowned figure, riding on an eagle and holding a sword and the scales of justice, carved over the porch of his house at Westwood in Worcestershire (Fig. 275)? Here, at least, one can provide an explanation: the carving is an apotheosis in miniature of James I, in the manner of the statue of the Emperor Charles V, similarly accoutred and mounted, that was put up in the 1530s over the entry of the Coudenberg Palace in Brussels.[25]

Most interesting of all are the entire buildings that serve as architectural equivalents to emblems or impresas because they contain coded messages. The best-known members of this group are Sir Thomas Tresham's Triangular Lodge, Rushton, and Lyveden New Bield, both in Northamptonshire; not only are they the most elaborately worked-out examples, but unlike the others they are well documented – though many of the puzzles that they deliberately present are still unsolved.

Sir Thomas Tresham (Fig. 281) was a rich Catholic landowner who suffered considerably for his religion. In 1593 he emerged from a twelve-year period in which he had been almost continuously either in prison or under house arrest in London, and immediately set to work planning and building two buildings that would epitomise his religious beliefs, especially his devotion to the Trinity, the Mass, the Virgin and the Crucifixion; but as he was a careful manager he made them fulfil a practical function. He was also prudent.

But why, over the entrance to Redgrave Hall in Suffolk, is Sir Nicholas Bacon's motto *Mediocria firma* ('security in the middle way') accompanied by a carving of a heavenly hand, coming out of a cloud to write on a (very Elizabethan, and certainly very firm) table (Fig. 273)? Why, in the

273–5 Three impresas in stone.

273 (*above left*) The carving originally over the entrance of Redgrave Hall, Suffolk.

274 (*above right*) Hercules killing the Nemean lion, on the gate-house of Hoghton Tower, Lancashire.

275 (*right*) A monarch riding an eagle, over the entrance of Westwood Park, Worcestershire.

He would perhaps have liked to carve the exteriors of his buildings with depictions of Jesus, Mary and the Three Persons of the Trinity; but it would have got him into trouble. He had to content himself with having the Crucifixion in his closet, and externally to confine himself to cryptograms. There is no reason to suppose that he did not get enjoyment out of devising these.

The Triangular Lodge was probably planned in 1593 but was built in 1594–5.[26] It served the functions of a lodge for the warrener in Tresham's lucrative rabbit warren, within sight of his main house, Rushton Hall; but above the two floors used by the warrener was a more highly finished room, for use by Tresham as a banqueting room or a retreat for meditation. The building is very precisely an architectural impresa, in that the key to the puzzles presented by the building is given by the motto over the entrance: *Tres testimonium dant* – 'threes bear witness'. What they bear witness to is the mystery of the Trinity, expressed and extolled in the building by countless threes, groups of three, measurements made up of multiples of three, or triangles (Figs 276–80): each side of the triangular building, for instance, measures

233

33 feet and contains three groups of three windows and is topped by three gables; over all rises a triangular chimney with three smoke vents on each side. The windows on the basement and first floor are trefoil-shaped, those on the ground floor made up of trefoils affixed to the end of a

cross (the resulting openings, incidentally, are too small for access by robbers tempted by valuable rabbit skins). Tresham's name was sometimes spelt *Tres-am* – 'I am three'. The family coat of arms included two groups of three trefoils within triangles and its crest was a boar's head holding

281 An engraved portrait of Sir Thomas Tresham, the builder of the Triangular Lodge and Lyveden New Bield, dated 1585. It shows him between the attractions of his youth and later life.

a trefoil in its mouth. These coincidences (although he would not have thought them coincidences) quite clearly delighted Tresham, and crest and coat were incorporated freely in the building.

But the buildings contain more than symbols of the Trinity: there are emblems and numbers, all in groups of four, carved in the gables and elsewhere, the meanings of which are only beginning to be elucidated. The Lodge seems to have been designed to extol the Catholic Sacrifice of the Mass as well as the Trinity; but whereas the mystery of the Trinity was accepted by both Catholics and Protestants, the Mass was not: it was proscribed and heavily penalised in Elizabethan England, and the allusions to it are less obvious, probably deliberately so.[27]

Tresham almost certainly made drawings of some kind for the Lodge himself, though he also had help from a Cambridge mathematician, astronomer and astrologer, John Fletcher. The masons for most of the work were members of

282 Lyvedon New Bield, Northamptonshire, started by Tresham in 1594 and left unfinished at his death in 1605.

the Tyrrell family, who lived in the village, and the bulk of the stone, of two different colours, was quarried in the immediate vicinity. Some ashlar stone, however, came from the Weldon quarries, some miles away, and the more elaborate carvings were the work of 'Paris', probably the Andrew Parris who was working at Trinity College, Cambridge, in 1600–01, and died there in the course of his work.[28]

The Triangular Lodge is remarkable because of its symbolism, but it is also architecturally brilliant. It is an exquisite toy. The high quality of stonework, carving and lettering, the razor sharpness of the angles, the gaily inventive patterning and stripes of the façades, the vivid silhouettes of the skyline, all suggest extreme visual discrimination on the part of Tresham. The same discrimination is shown, in a very different way, in Lyveden New Bield (Figs 282, 283).

Work on this started in 1594, but owing to financial worries and further religious persecution, including another spell in prison, it pro-

284 Roland Stickell's
unexecuted design for a
lantern for the New Bield.

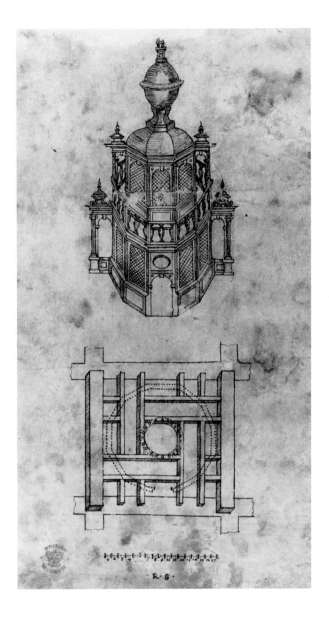

283 (*facing page*) Lyvedon
New Bield from the
adjoining Elizabethan
water garden.

ceeded much more slowly than the Lodge, and was still unfinished at the time of Tresham's death in 1605. It has stood in the fields, a romantic and evocative shell, ever since.[29]

It was planned as a lodge for Tresham himself, with the full complement of gentry rooms, including a gallery on the upper floor, which was never built;[30] even the walls of the floor below were not quite completed. The main masons employed were the Grumbold family, who had interests in the Weldon quarries, from where the stone came; the ornamental carving was probably by Paris, as at the Triangular Lodge.[31] An otherwise unknown Roland Stickells sent moulds for the

Doric order and made a design, which survives, for a wooden lantern, to be erected over the crossing on the top floor (Fig. 284); but the building never got that far. He was perhaps related to Robert Stickells, the eccentric but able Clerk in the Royal Works at Richmond.[32]

The main theme of the New Bield was the Crucifixion, and the salvation of the world that resulted from it, celebrated both by the cross-shaped plan and the carving of the Instruments of the Passion in the metopes of the Doric frieze that runs round above the ground floor. Like the Lodge, it works as an impresa, with the theme carved in the inscription over the entrance: *Jesus, Mundi Salus, Gaude, Mater Virgo Maria* – 'Jesus, the Saviour of the world: rejoice, Mary, Mother and Virgin'. Further inscriptions, which are carried all round the building, continue to celebrate Jesus as Saviour and Mary as his blessed and rejoicing mother. The building, in fact, was designed to celebrate Mary as well as her Son; it is possible that carving in the frieze of the unbuilt upper floor would have had a Marian theme, as a counterpart to the Instruments of the Passion below (the basement, typically of Tresham, was designed to commemorate the Tresham family and its connections, in a continuous row of shields, which were left uncarved when building work was abandoned).

The other triangular building of the period is Longford in Wiltshire – called Longford Castle today, but Longford House until the nineteenth century. It was built by Sir Thomas Gorges and his wife, the Marchioness of Northampton, and is a few years earlier than the Triangular Lodge; it carries (or carried) the date 1591,[33] and was probably started in the 1580s, after Gorges returned from an embassy to Sweden in 1582. It was considerably altered in the eighteenth century and extensively added to and then partly put back again to what it had been in the nineteenth; but its original appearance is shown in a drawing by Thorpe (Figs 285, 286) and, with a few

late seventeenth-century trimmings, in Robert Thacker's exquisite engravings of 1678 (Fig. 14).[34] It is of three ranges round a triangular court, joined by big round towers. Thorpe has a plan of it[35] (in fact, for a building slightly larger than what was built) and has drawn in the centre of the courtyard the symbol of the Trinity, well known since medieval times: three outer circles, *Pater*, *Filius* and *Spiritus*, joined by links inscribed *est* to a central circle, *Deus*. This may just be Thorpe's interpretation of the plan, but it seems likely to express the intention of Gorges and Lady Northampton. There may have been a fountain in the centre of the courtyard, to represent *Deus*. A fountain in this position is shown in a variant triangular plan drawn by Thorpe (Fig. 287);[36] in his plan of Longford itself the centre is covered by the Trinity symbol, so no fountain could be shown. If there was one, it had gone by the time of plans made in 1678: these just show three channels leading to a central drain, an unhappy arrangement in terms of symbolism.

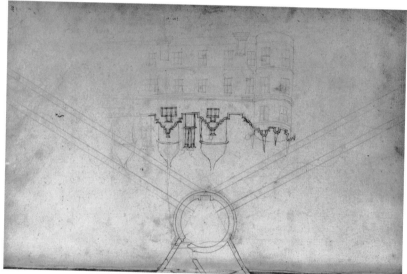

285 and 286a and b (*left*) John Thorpe's elevation and plan (T158, 156, 155) of Longford Castle, Wiltshire, built *c*.1582–91.

287 (*below*)   A related design by Thorpe (T161).

288 (*facing page*)   Looking up the hill to Wollaton Hall, Nottinghamshire.

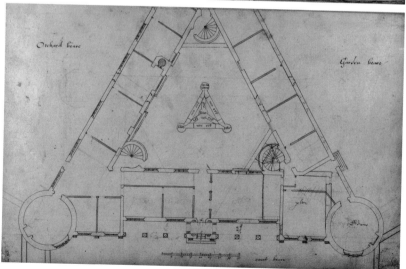

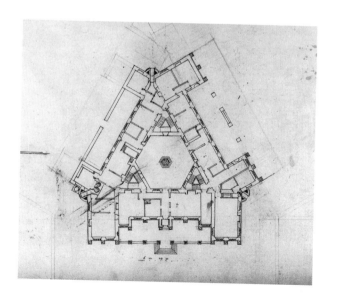

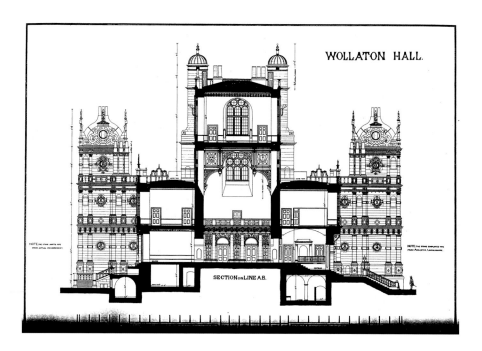

WOLLATON HALL.

SECTION on LINE A.B.

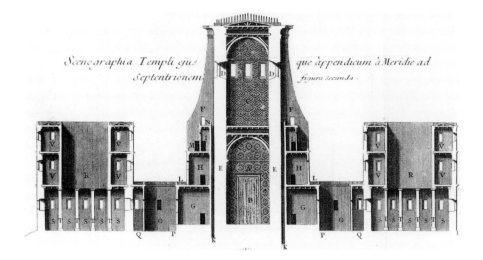

Scenographia Templi eius-
Septentrionem

que appendicum à Meridie ad
figura secunda.

289 (*top*)   The section of
Wollaton Hall.

290 (*above left*)
The section of the
Temple in Jerusalem, as
reconstructed by Bernard
Lamy, 1720.

291 (*above right*)   A bay of
the Temple sanctuary, as
reconstructed by Anton
Koberger, 1481.

Apart from the Thorpe drawings there is no contemporary documentation of Longford, and nothing to show why Trinity symbolism was chosen. The strangely memorable monument to Gorges and his wife in Salisbury cathedral, with its four barley-sugar columns and complex decoration of texts and emblems, suggests that symbolism attracted them; but it was erected in 1635, forty years or so later. Almost every detail of Longford itself is unusual: the stubby towers, unlike anything else in England, may be inspired by those of Gripsholm Castle in Sweden, which Gorges visited in 1582; the great two-storey fron-

tispiece and hanging vault of the great chamber may also have been influenced by his northern European travels; the famous astronomer Tycho Brahe, whom Gorges may have visited at his island observatory in the Baltic, possibly contributed suggestions.[37] Unusual though everything is, there is no apparent allusion to the Trinity or religious symbolism of any kind in anything except the plan.

Wollaton Hall is, in its own way, as extraordinary as Longford, and it is tempting to surmise that, like Longford, it contains a coded message; but, again like Longford, there is no inscription

242

and nothing in the surviving decoration to give a clue, and unlike Longford its plan has no obvious symbolic origin.

The house (Fig. 288) presents two especial puzzles. First, what is the *raison d'être* of the

The upper room at Wollaton appears to be an extravagant folly. It was much later to be known as the Prospect Room; in an inventory of 1601 it is just called 'the high chamber over the hall'.[38] Its entire contents then – 'certain mattes' and

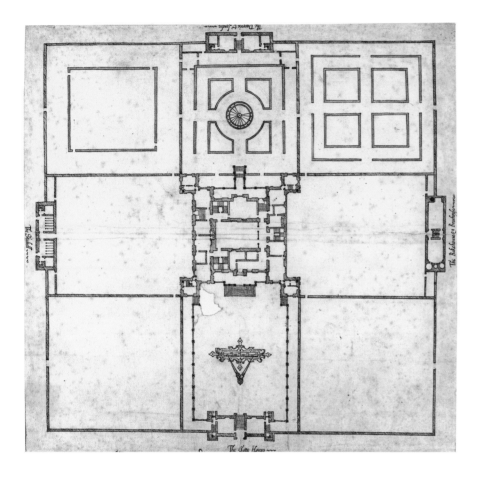

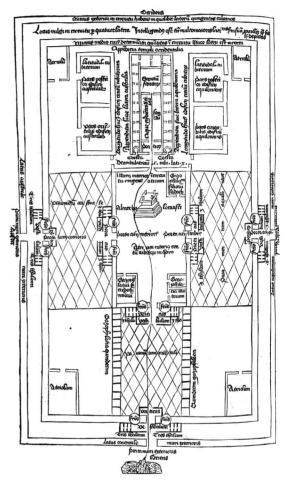

292 (*above left*) Robert Smythson's plan of house, courts and outbuildings at Wollaton.

293 (*above right*) The plan of the Temple as reconstructed by Anton Koberger, 1481.

huge room perched above the great hall and dominating the building and its skyline? Second, why is this room and the hall beneath it treated architecturally in an uncompromisingly and even uncomfortably different manner from the rest, with turrets and traceried windows, instead of Flemish gables, mullions and transoms, and the orders? These contrasting elements derive from Vredeman de Vries, for the traceried windows were inspired by designs for an ecclesiastical building in the Corinthian section of his *Architecture*.

'one joyned stool' – suggest how little used and usable it was. It does indeed have a superb prospect through its ten great windows, and as such is reminiscent of the octagon lantern at the top of its tower at Oatlands (Fig. 312) and the similar tower room at Melbury in Dorset. But it is nearly three times the size of the Oatlands lantern, and higher in proportion. As a prospect room it is absurd overkill; as anything else it is useless, for it has no fireplace and no rooms adjoining, and is accessible only by newel staircases with steps that are 2 feet 6 inches wide, which Elizabethan ladies in full rig would have had difficulty in negotiating.

It is worth making a suggestion, which, though unprovable, is at least intriguing. Could the inspiration of Wollaton be Solomon's Temple at Jerusalem? Could the hall and high chamber, with their traceried windows, be a re-creation of the towering Temple sanctuary? And could the lower ranges, with their very different character, stand for the administrative rooms and quarters for the priests that enclosed it?[39]

Odd though such an endeavour might seem today, to Willoughby's contemporaries it would have seemed a 'device' both ingenious and praiseworthy. What better model could there be than the Temple, which God had certainly approved and even (according to some accounts) designed? What more admirable than that Man, whom God had made in His own image, should make a house for himself in the image of the House of God?

The complex history of the Temple in Jerusalem (built by Solomon, sacked by Nebuchadnezzar, restored or rebuilt by Zerubbabel and again by Herod, finally destroyed by the Romans), the confusing and complicated descriptions of it, and the lack of any contemporary depictions known to medieval or Renaissance Europe, led to wide divergences in the numerous attempts to reconstruct its appearance. Most notably, opinion was divided as to whether the sanctuary was one, two or three storeys high. But all reconstructions (Figs 289–91) had one element in common: they showed the sanctuary as the dominating element, rising high above the subsidiary buildings that enclosed it.

If one takes the clearest and most consistent description, Josephus's account of Solomon's Temple, and of the Temple as restored by Herod, in his *Antiquitates Judaicae*, and the most elaborate reconstruction in circulation in Francis Willoughby's time, first published in Anton Koberger's multi-volume Latin Bible in 1481, and frequently reprinted, and attempts to combine

them, one gets something remarkably reminiscent of Wollaton.[40] Josephus is listed in the earliest surviving library catalogue of Wollaton;[41] Koberger could be one of the numerous undifferentiated bibles in the same catalogue.

Josephus unequivocally described a two-storey sanctuary. In Solomon's Temple this was enclosed, but 'the upper part had no buildings about it'; similarly, in Herod's Temple 'the whole structure . . . was on each side much lower, but the middle was much higher, so that it was visible to those that dwelt in the country for a great many furlongs'. This could just as well be a description of Wollaton. And the Temple, being on a hilltop, was approached by flights of steps, starting with a flight in the gateway to the main courtyard (as in the Smythson drawing), and finishing at the level of the sanctuary; at Wollaton two long flights of steps lead up from the courtyard to the level of the hall. Access to the great upper room of the sanctuary was the same as access to the High Chamber at Wollaton: 'the king devised access to the upper part of the temple by inserting a newel staircase [*coclea*: literally a snail] for this purpose in the thickness of the wall'. Unlike the lower sanctuary, which was approached by a 'grand portal', the upper sanctuary was entered by 'small doors from the sides' – again like the High Chamber.

Koberger differed from Josephus in making the sanctuary three storeys high, and placed the Temple building at the end of the temple enclosure, unlike Josephus, who put it at the centre. But apart from this, his plan of the enclosure is remarkably similar to the Smythson plan for Wollaton and its surrounding courts (Figs 292, 293); he too has cocleae (two instead of one) giving access to the upper rooms of the sanctuary; he shows the sanctuary with traceried windows and turrets.

But Josephus clearly describes the two rooms of the sanctuary as being of the same height, whereas the upper room at Wollaton is much

294 Beamsley Hospital, West Yorkshire, built by the Countess of Cumberland as an almshouse for women in or soon after 1593.

lower than the hall. Neither the dimensions nor the orientation of Wollaton correspond to descriptions of the Temple. There is nothing at Wollaton that bears any relationship to the Holy of Holies, which was at the heart of the Temple. And there are other discrepancies. Even so, allowing for the creative rather than scholarly manner in which the Elizabethans treated their sources, and given a learned amateur like Willoughby, a gifted but little-educated artificer like Smythson, the need to produce something moderately workable as a house, and the decision to imitate the Temple – Wollaton could have been the result.[42]

There could be no greater contrast than that between the scale and lavish stylistic splendour of Longford and Wollaton, and the minimal size and modestly vernacular detailing of Beamsley Hospital in Yorkshire (Fig. 294). But this homely and charming little building was erected on a geometric plan as remarkable as Longford's, and one for which a convincing explanation can be offered, even though again there is a lack of contemporary evidence.

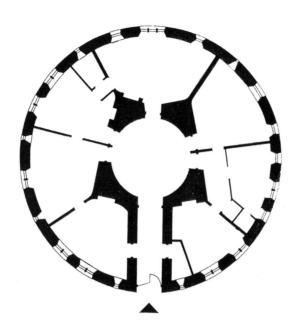

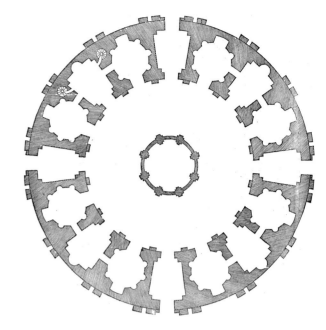

Beamsley Hospital is circular, planned as a circle within a circle (Fig. 295). The charity was founded in 1593 (but the building probably followed a few years later) by Margaret, the wife of George Clifford, Earl of Cumberland, as an almshouse for women. It retained its function until the 1970s. The plan is practical as well as unusual: a central rotunda, lit from a clerestory, served as the chapel, and round it rotated seven rooms for six old ladies and their 'Mother'. A passage from the one entrance led to the chapel, which also gave access to most of the rooms, providing 'a daily encouragement to piety', as the handbook to the Landmark Trust, which has taken over the Hospital, puts it.

Margaret Clifford's daughter, Anne, Countess of Dorset, Pembroke and Montgomery, is better known than her mother, but the latter was remarkable too,[43] a learned and pious lady, interested in alchemy, a projector of mines, moving in a circle of learned hangers-on and admirers, including the poet Samuel Daniel, who came to Skipton Castle as tutor to Anne in the late 1590s; John Layfield, one of the collaborators on the Authorized Version of the Bible, who seems to have been her spiritual adviser; and Richard

Candish or Cavendish, MP and author, who was her partner in one of her mining ventures, and to whom, in 1600, she erected a memorial in Hornsey parish church, Middlesex, with a verse inscription that she composed herself:

> . . . Adornde with vertuous and heroick
>   partes,
> Most learned, bountiful, devout and sage,
> Graced with the graces, muses, and the
>   artes . . .[44]

Richard Candish's father, also Richard, was a military engineer of distinction under Henry VIII, and his son may have learnt drawing skills from him: he is said to have translated Euclid's *Geometry*, although if he did, his translation was never published. He was a friend of John Dee, and one of the ingenious geometric poems in the *Paradise of Dainty Devices* has been attributed to him. John Layfield was chosen to revise the early books of the Bible, because 'Being skilled in architecture his judgment was much relied on for the fabric of the Tabernacle and Temple'.[45]

John Aubrey describes Wilton House in the time of Philip Sidney's sister, Mary, Countess of Pembroke, as 'like a College, there were so many learned and ingeniose persons'.[46] There would seem to have been another such a group round the Countess of Cumberland at Skipton Castle or in London, one product of whose ingenious and learned discussions was the little building at Beamsley. Its main inspiration must have been the round medieval churches of the Holy Sepulchre, with their higher centres, especially the Temple Church in London and Holy Sepulchre in Cambridge; as Rector of St Clement Danes, a few hundred yards from the Temple Church, and a Fellow of Trinity College, Cambridge, Layfield would certainly have known both of them. It is not known whether the chapel at Beamsley was dedicated, and if so to whom, but the Sepulchre would have seemed suitable for old people, preparing for death in hopes of a joyful resurrection.

An alternative, or, more probably, supplementary source for the plan and section of Beamsley is a design 'della forma de tempio rotondo' in Book Three of *I quattro primi libri di Architettura* (Venice, 1554) by the Sienese architect Pietro Cataneo. This has the same basic organisation as Beamsley, but whereas in the medieval churches the central rotunda is surrounded by a continuous ambulatory, in Cataneo's plan this is replaced by separate chapels and porches – sixteen in all, instead of the eight at Beamsley, but the principle is the same (Fig. 296). Cataneo was certainly known in England; Sir Thomas Knyvett of Ashwellthorpe had a copy in 1608, and Tresham's copy is now in the Sir John Soane Museum.[47]

At much the same time as Beamsley Hospital was being built in a then remote part of Yorkshire, another group of circular or circular-cum-polygonal buildings was rising in the suburbs of London, and forming one of the most novel and distinctive additions to the London skyline: the five or so theatres, starting with The Theatre in Shoreditch in 1576, and followed by the Rose (1587), the Swan (1595), the Globe (which was The Theatre, moved and re-erected south of the river

in 1599) and the Hope (1614), all in Southwark (in contrast, the Fortune Theatre was built in 1600 on a square plan). The evidence for the appearance of these London theatres is famously inadequate and inconsistent; but it seems likely that (with the exception of the Fortune) their auditoria were all circular, and their external walls circular, hexagonal or octagonal; the Rose, the only one to have been excavated, was circular inside and out.[48]

There is little reason to doubt that the theatres were built as conscious imitations or re-creations of Roman theatres. They were certainly seen as such by foreigners coming to London. A visitor in 1600 describes seeing a comedy acted in a theatre 'that follows the ancient Roman plan'. Johannes de Witt, whose crude sketch of the Swan (Fig. 297) is the only known depiction of the auditorium of an Elizabethan theatre, said that he drew it 'since its form seems to approach that of a Roman structure'.[49]

The auditoria of Roman theatres were in fact semicircular, and are rightly understood and clearly depicted as such by Serlio and Palladio. But the descriptions in Vitruvius are confusing, and some reconstructions made them circular. Cesare Cesariano's reconstruction in his 1521 edition of Vitruvius shows a circular building (Fig. 298); it, or Gianbattista Caporali's 1536 Italian translation of it, could well have been the model adopted, in simplified form, for the London theatres. Cesariano shows the audience accommodated in three tiers, the upper two under cover in arcades, the lowest on tiered seats, in the open apart from protection from the sun by the *velaria* stretched overhead. London weather made such tiered seats impractical, and the lower circle was also (at least as shown by de Witt) seated under cover, in galleries like the other two; the open centre was for standing only. In London, half of the stage, or 'proscenium', was covered by a pentice known as the 'heavens', because its underside was painted with a representation of the sky;

247

297 (*right*) The Swan Theatre, Southwark, built 1595. A copy of a lost drawing by Johannes de Witt.

298 (*far right*) Cesare Cesariano's reconstruction of a Roman theatre, from his 1521 edition of Vitruvius.

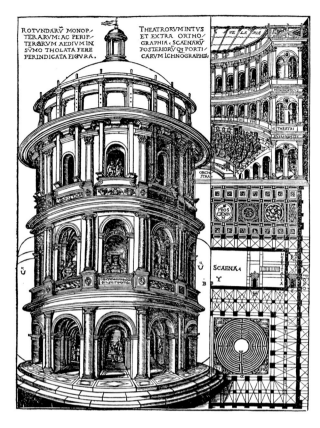

this was clearly a reduced version of the classical *velaria*, which Alberti, following Vitruvius, described as covered with stars.[50]

The London theatres were built mainly or entirely of wood, as were some of the Roman ones, according to Vitruvius. The carpenters who built them, where known, were all prominent members of the London Carpenters' Company.[51] They were not ignorant. There is every probability that they, or the actor-managers who commissioned them, owned or had access to Vitruvius. At least five people living in London or nearby in the late sixteenth or early seventeenth century are known to have owned copies. Robert Cecil's copy of the Cesariano edition, which he probably inherited from his father, is still at Hatfield. Sir Thomas Smith, who owned five copies of Vitruvius when he died in 1579, was employing Richard Kirby of the London Carpenters' Company as his surveyor and trusted collaborator in the building of his house, Hill Hall in

Essex. Smith directed in his will that Kirby should be employed as 'the architect' to finish the house after his death.[52]

The quaint exercises in half-timbering shown in some reconstructions of the Globe are unconvincing. We know from the contract for building the Fortune Theatre in 1600 that the timber framework was plastered over, inside and out.[53] De Witt describes the Swan Theatre as 'supported by wooden columns, painted in such excellent imitation of marble that it might deceive even the most prying'. The contract for the Fortune Theatre, which descends to details only when these differ from the Globe, on which (with the big exception that it was square in plan) it was modelled, specifies that the 'posts' should be 'square and wrought palasterwise'. This suggests that the posts in the Globe were 'round and wrought columnwise' and were similar to the marbled columns of the Swan; De Witt shows the gallery supports with summary scrawls, but the

pentice as supported by Corinthian columns; and if Cesariano and normal Elizabethan practice were followed, one would expect the gallery 'posts' or columns to have been Corinthian on top of Ionic on top of Doric.

These smart and prettily painted evocations of classical Rome were just as such sufficiently unusual and ingenious to be considered 'devices' at the time. But they went a step further, and contained cosmological allusions, as microcosms of the world, waiting to be penetrated by the initiated. The round plan suggested this; so did the name of the Globe; so did the flag flying from it, which Shakespeare himself may have devised, to serve as the theatre's impresa. It showed Hercules supporting the round universe, with the motto *totus mundus agit histrionem* – 'the actor's concern is the whole universe' – 'all the world's a stage', implying the counterpart: 'the stage absorbs all the world'.[54]

Chilham Castle in Kent (Fig. 299) has a plan as unusual as that of Longford, but its symbolic significance, if any, is much less obvious. It is pentagonal (Fig. 300) and built round a hexagonal court, with one side of the court left open. Inscribed over the entrance is the date – 1618 – the names of the builders – Sir Dudley Digges and his wife, Mary – and the text, adapted from Psalm 31: 'The Lord is my house of defence and my castle.'[55]

299 (*above*)
The pentagonal Chilham Catle, Kent (dated 1618), photographed from a balloon.

300 (*right*)
An anonymous contemporary plan of Chilham Castle.

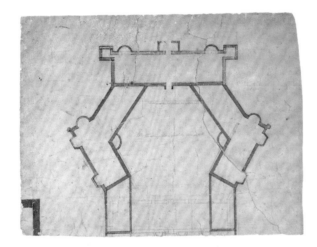

Immediately next to the Jacobean house is the thirteenth-century castle. It was already dismantled or in ruin by the time Digges built his house, apart from its octagonal keep, which still survives. The significance of the inscription would seem to be that Digges put his trust in God, not in earthly fortifications; the crumbling castle next door showed what happened to those.

But oddly enough the new Chilham Castle, although there is no hint of a castle, or any castle allusions, in its façades, is based on the plan of one of the most unusual of late medieval castles: Wardour Castle in Wiltshire, built round a hexagonal courtyard in the 1390s (Fig. 301). The resem-

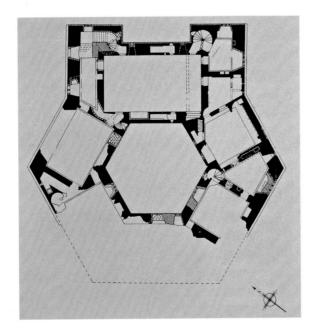

301 The plan of the fourteenth-century Wardour Castle, Wiltshire.

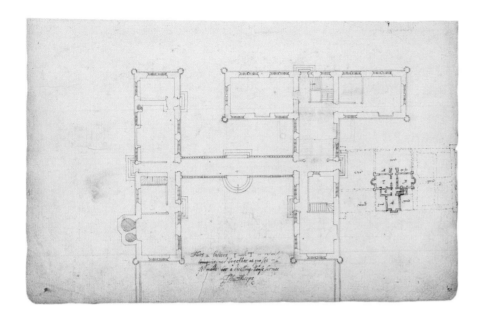

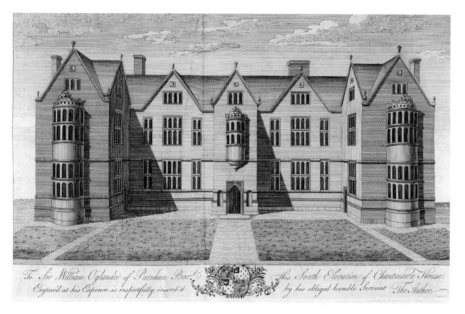

302 (*top*) John Thorpe's design (T30) for a house on the plan of his initials.

303 (*above*) Chantmarle House, Dorset, completed 1623 on an E-shaped plan, to symbolise Emanuel. From John Hutchins, *The History and Antiquities of the County of Dorset*, vol II, 1774.

blance is unmistakable with the one significant difference that the Wardour courtyard was closed on all six sides. To use a castle plan, but to open it up, so as to make it defensively useless, could be an expansion of the sentiment expressed in the inscription over the door.

A contemporary plan of Chilham (Fig. 300) shows the open side of the courtyard flanked by parallel wings, which seem never to have been built.[56] The plan is an outline one only, and could have been drawn by Digges himself, who as the

son and grandson of the mathematicians and scientists Leonard and Thomas Digges is likely to have learnt drawing skills. The surveyor at Chilham, as the parish registers show, was 'Mr Smith', possibly William Smith, a leading member of the London Masons' Company;[57] but the plan is as likely as not to have been devised by Digges. The octagonal keep next door, and the remarkable circular castle of Queenborough, 20 miles or so away, built for Edward III in the years 1361–77, may have set him thinking geometrically;[58] Wardour could have been known to him through possible contacts with Thomas Arundell, who was living there in 1618, and who, like Digges, had interests in the East.[59]

John Thorpe's well-known design on the plan of his initials ('Thes 2 letters I and T . . . joyned together as you see Is mete for a dwelling house for mee') is an 'ingenious device', a *jeu d'esprit*, for a house that Thorpe could not conceivably have afforded (Fig. 302); a sketch in a margin for a modest T-plan-only house could have been within his reach in his prosperous later years, though there is no evidence that he ever built it.[60]

The intention of the more elaborate design could scarcely have been mistaken; but perhaps no one who was shown a view of Chantmarle in Dorset (Fig. 303), a straightforward if charming manor-house built to one of the commonest of Elizabethan and Jacobean plans, would have guessed the symbolism behind it if the builder, Sir John Strode, had not provided the key: *Constructa est in forma de littera E, sc[iliced] Emanuel, id est Deus nobiscum in aeternum* ('It was built in the shape of the letter E, standing for Emanuel, that is God be with us for ever').[61] There is, incidentally, no contemporary evidence for the belief, commonly held, that houses on an E-plan commemorate Elizabeth.

Buildings, in fact, that seem straightforward may conceal unexpected meanings, and contrariwise, buildings that look as though they conceal a

I carried once a purpose to build a little wooden banqueting house on the island in my pond, which because some other may (perhaps) elsewhere put in execution, it will not do much amiss to deliver you the plot as the same was devised for me by that perfectly accomplished gentleman the late Sir Arthur Champernowne.[62]

The island is square, with four rounds at the corners, like Mount Edgcumbe. This should first have been planched over, and railed about with balusters. In the midst there should have risen a boarded room of the like fashion but lesser proportion, so as to leave sufficient space between that and the rails for a walk round about. This square room should withinside have been ceiled [panelled] roundwise, and in three of the places where the round joined with the square, as many windows shold have been set; the fourth should have served for a door. Of the four turrets shut out by this round, one should have made a kitchen, the second a storehouse to keep the fishing implements, the third a buttery, and the fourth a stair for ascending to the next loft; which next loft should have risen on the flat roof of the lower, in a round form, but of a lesser size again, so as to leave a second terrace like the other. And as the square room below was ceiled round, so should this upper round room be ceiled square, to the end that where the side walls and ceiling joined, three windows and a door might likewise find their places. The void spaces between the round and square he would have turned to cupboards and boxes, for keeping other necessary utensils towards these fishing feasts.

If there had been any symbolism behind the banqueting house, Carew, in this detailed account, would surely have mentioned it.

There are a great many fanciful Elizabethan and Jacobean plans (Figs 305, 306), executed and unexecuted, for buildings large and small:

304 Fancifully shaped buildings: A sheet of sketch plans, not drawn to scale.

meaning may express no more than a pleasure in geometric ingenuity.

Richard Carew of Antony, in his *Survey of Cornwall* (1602), describes a fishing pavilion that he planned to build, but never built, at Antony in the 1570s:

305 and 306 Fancifully shaped buildings: (*above left*) a pavilion at Montacute House, Wiltshire (*c.*1590); (*above right*) 'Diana her House' at Amesbury Abbey, Wiltshire, dated 1600.

circular, cross-shaped, octagonal, star-shaped, x-shaped, L-shaped, and so on. The outline plans illustrated in Figure 304 give a selection. Many, but not all, were designed as lodges or banqueting houses. In many cases, it is likely that, as at Antony, they contain no hidden meaning; but one can never be sure. The x- and L-shaped plans could conceivably stand for something: Christos in Greek, perhaps, or an initial or surname. Some of the plans derive from pattern books; that for a very large cross-shaped house (Fig. 35), now at Hatfield, follows very closely a plan by Du Cerceau;[63] Wothorpe Lodge, near Burghley, is

clearly imitating cross-planned, four-towered, Italian Renaissance churches (Fig. 307). What reason the Earl of Exeter, who built it in or after 1615, had for deriving a house from a church, other than pleasure in the plan, remains mysterious.[64]

One of two polygonal banqueting houses at Amesbury Abbey in Wiltshire has over the door the mysterious inscription 'Diana her house' (Fig. 306). The necklace of towers at Walton Castle in Somerset (Fig. 593) appears to be based on the medieval Queenborough Castle in Kent. The star-shaped plans of Star Castle in the Scilly Isles and Spur Royal Castle in Northern Ireland[65] are

252

307 Fancifully shaped buildings: Wothorpe Lodge, Cambridgeshire (*c*.1615), based on a Greek-cross plan, with towers in the angles. From an old photograph. The ruin has been restored and consolidated in recent years.

clearly inspired by the greater and lesser lodges of King Basilius in Philip Sidney's *Arcadia*, both 'built in the form of a star', the lesser at the end of a 'riding' from the greater 'so that the lodge seemeth not unlike a fair comet whose tail stretcheth itself to a star of lesser greatness'. Sidney's lodges in their turn were probably inspired by the star-shaped Hvězda Pavilion at Prague (Fig. 308), which he is likely to have seen when he was there in 1575 and 1577.[66]

As a fortification the Star Castle was notably ineffective. In 1624 Henry Wotton wrote critically about Basilius's lodge, and in doing so rang out the Elizabethan and Jacobean ages: he disparaged

Sir Philip Sidney who well knowing that Basilius did rather want some extraordinary Formes to entertain his Fancie, than roome for Courtiers, was contented to place him in a Star-like Lodge; which otherwise in severe Judgment of Art had been an incommodious figure . . . Designs of such nature doe more ayme at Rarity than Commoditie; so for my part I had rather admire them, than commend them.[67]

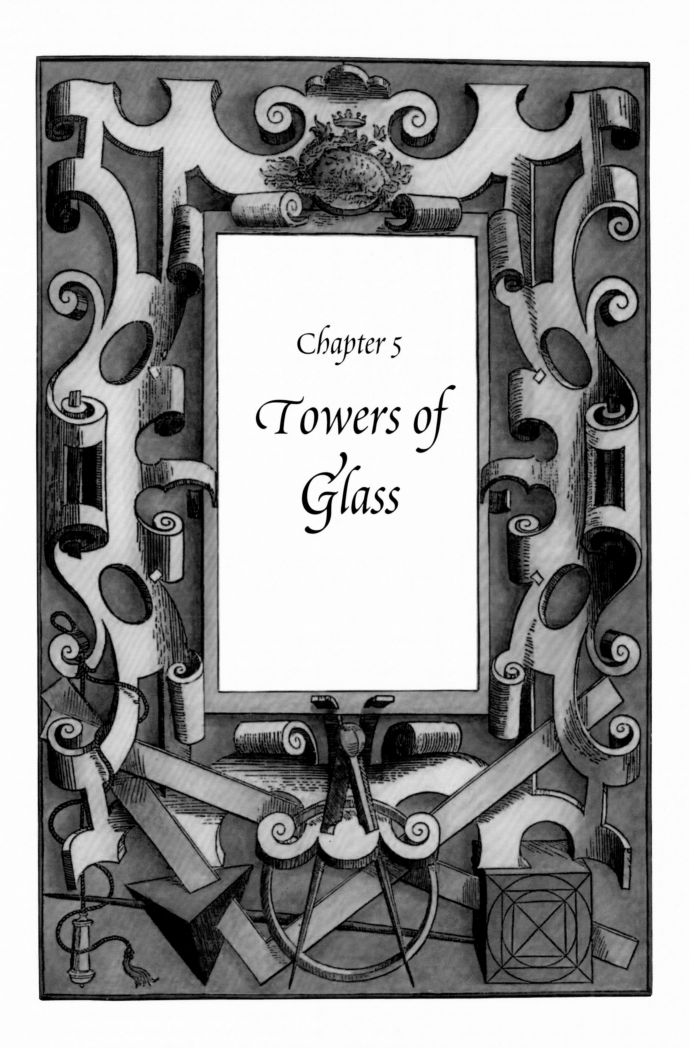

Chapter 5

Towers of
Glass

Verses written by the E. of Bristol in time of his trobles on the ocation of the sunns
bright shining on the great glass window of Sherburne Castle –

Not to doe ill is a well waled cort
Not to be guilty is a Tower of Brass
Not to deserve and suffer is a sport
But to be great is but a Tower of glasse.

The which although it dazel doth our eyes
And whilst the sunn shines out sparckles and glitters,
Yet if a storme of hayle and wind arise
Tis rent and shivered to a thousand flitters.

But Inocence it is a well built tower,
And though that ivye hide or moss orgrow it,
And it look ould, yet neyther hayly shower
Hath force to breake, nor wind to overthrow it.[1]

John Digby, Earl of Bristol, wrote his poem in 1624 or soon after, when he was living in retirement and disgrace in his house on the hill above Sherborne in Dorset (the Sherborne Castle of today) after his abortive embassy to arrange the marriage of the Prince of Wales with the Infanta of Spain. He wrote it, probably, sitting in his second-floor study (Fig. 57) looking down the hill to the Old Castle, and watching how the evening sun lit up the shattered hulk of its 'tower of glass', a huge and elaborate bay window three or four storeys high, which Walter Ralegh added to the keep shortly after he had acquired the castle in 1592.[2]

By 1624 great glass windows were beginning to go out of fashion; it was in that year that Francis Bacon wrote in his essay 'On Building': 'You shall have some-times Faire Houses, so full of Glass, that one cannot tell where to become to be out of the Sunne or Colde'. Digby had abandoned the Old Castle, and its Elizabethan improvements, for the more manageable lodge; Ralegh may have already left it,[3] before his own fall, imprisonment and ultimate execution in 1618, more lasting and dramatic than Digby's disgrace. Contemplating the great window in its decay, and meditating on its fall from fashion, and the reversals of fortune that had destroyed Ralegh and blasted his own

career, Digby saw it as a symbol of the fragility of greatness, and wrote his melancholy verses.

Most of the old castle, and Ralegh's improvements with it, were demolished at the end of the Civil War, but the base of the window survives, and enables it to be reconstructed with some confidence. It was built to a rectangular plan, about 24 feet broad and 10 feet deep; but it was given individuality by the prominent semicircle of glass that projected from the centre of the rectangle. It must have risen at least three storeys to the parapet of the keep, and may even have risen a storey higher, to provide a banqueting or look-out room, with access from the roof. It was indeed a 'tower of glass'; and it was sufficiently admired to inspire at least two other windows, or sets of windows, perhaps built by the same masons. A twin pair formed the most prominent feature of the long wing that Sir Edward Seymour ran out from his castle at Berry Pomeroy in Devon along the crest of a steep hill, probably later in the 1590s.[4] As at Sherborne, only the bases of these remain; but one can savour their effect, and that of the Sherborne window, from the façade of the Hall at Bradford-on-Avon, built by John Hall about 1600 and surviving complete.[5] Its bay windows are somewhat smaller, and probably a

309 (*facing page*) The south front of the Hall, Bradford-on-Avon, Wiltshire, built *c.*1600.

310 The plan of
Henry VII's Chapel,
Westminster Abbey,
as drawn by John Thorpe,
1609 (T69).

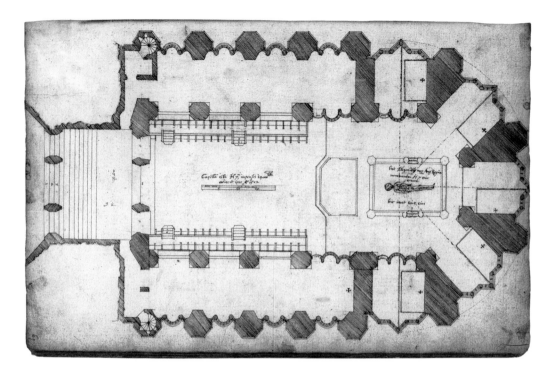

storey lower than their Sherborne prototype: but there are two of them, joined by a central façade of lavish glazing, so as to make a brave and arrogant show as they rise from terrace and rows of sculptured urns high above the Wiltshire Avon (Fig. 309).

These great windows were built at the height of the mania for glass that consumed so many Elizabethans and led to the Derbyshire and Northamptonshire sayings 'Hardwick Hall, more glass than wall'[6] and 'it shines like Holdenby'. Lavish glazing combined with a dramatic array of towers and turrets are memorable features of ambitious Elizabethan and Jacobean houses. In this they owed nothing to the architecture of Italy, let alone that of classical times, or what was known of them. There was probably some influence from heavily glazed buildings in the Low Countries, but the English did not need to cross the Channel for inspiration: the glass grids of Perpendicular churches, still much admired, were everywhere around them, and, although on the average domestic buildings in the early sixteenth century did not have large windows and were only

two storeys high, a few royal residences or houses of great people were built up to an impressive height and incorporated large windows, sometimes of fanciful plan.

The turreted gatehouses by which many of the bigger courtyard houses were entered are one example; they were by no means always heavily windowed, but some of them were, most notably the gatehouse at Layer Marney in Essex: eight storeys of low rooms or staircases in the turrets, and in between two great windows, each of twelve lights, giving onto the main rooms above the archway. At the gatehouses built by Henry VIII in the great yard at Whitehall Palace, and at New Hall in Essex, a different combination appeared: the windows between the towers were comparatively small; the towers were glazed like lanterns.[7]

Windows of fanciful plan, based on triangles and segments of circles, the domestic counterpart of the windows that angle and ripple round the aisles of Henry VII's Lady Chapel at Westminster Abbey (Fig. 310), light or lit the apartments of the Duke and Duchess of Buckingham at Thornbury Castle in Gloucestershire (the duke's above those

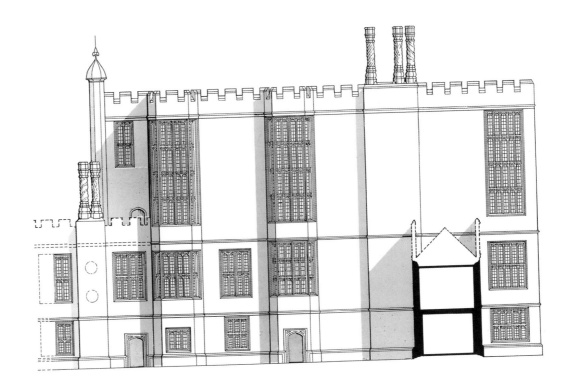

311 The Royal Lodgings built by Cardinal Wolsey at Hampton Court Palace, Middlesex, c.1528–9, before they were decapitated in the eighteenth century.

of the duchess and considerably grander). They were inaugurated by the windows of the block of lodgings built by Henry VII at Windsor Castle,[8] and had a final flowering in the complex oriel window over the entrance to the courtyard at Hengrave Hall in Suffolk.

Henry VII's lodgings at Richmond Palace were three storeys high, the king's above the queen's on the first and second floors. The inadequate surviving evidence suggests that the king's lodgings had higher ceilings than the queen's, but that the windows were not especially large or elaborate.[9] The Richmond lodgings were imitated and exaggerated in the royal lodgings that Cardinal Wolsey built in what became the Clock Court at Hampton Court (*circa* 1528–9): its rooms, lit by bay windows, grew higher storey by storey, and the second and by far the taller storey, which Wolsey must have intended as the king's, towered above the surrounding ranges (Fig. 311). Like Wolsey's equally towering gatehouse in the adjacent Base Court, these lodgings (which one can see as ancestors of Hardwick) were decapitated in the eighteenth century.[10]

It may well have been to them that John Skelton was referring when he wrote (in no friendly spirit) of Wolsey's Hampton Court:

With turrets and towers,
With halls and with bowers,
Stretching to the stars
With glass windows and bars.[11]

And perhaps Spenser, whose Faerie Queen was modelled on Elizabeth, had the lodgings in mind when he wrote of the Red Cross Knight marvelling at the 'stately buildings' of the heavenly Jerusalem with its 'lofty towres' extending 'into the starry sphere':

Till now, said then the knight, I weened well
That great Cleopolis, where I have beene,
In which that fairest Faerie Queene doth dwell,
The fairest Citie was, that might be seene;
And that bright towere all built of christall cleene
Panthea, seemed the brightest thing that was:
But now by proofe all otherwise I weene
For this great Cities that does, far surpas

And this bright Angels towre quite dims that toure of glass.[12]

But Spenser might also have been thinking of the great timber lantern tower, built for Henry VIII in 1538, that rose unexpectedly out of the irregular rear courtyard at Oatlands Palace in Surrey (Fig. 312): a slender octagonal shaft four storeys high, flowering out at the top into a cantilevered octagonal prospect or banqueting room, about 30 feet wide and continuously glazed all the way round.[13] Like Ralegh's tower of glass at Sherborne, this had twin offspring – the only slightly smaller and lower towers memorable in silhouette at either end of the garden front of Henry VIII's Nonsuch.

Tall single towers, asymmetrically attached to a house, had been a feature of domestic building in England since at least the early sixteenth century. They functioned as bell-towers, or prospect towers, or landmarks for ships or travellers, perhaps above all as status symbols. There may have been some influence from the Low Countries, where such towers were a feature of a

number of royal palaces, and, in more modest form, often no more than a slender shaft, were attached to burger or gentry houses in the towns.[14] The fashion for these Flemish towers may have come from Burgundy, where, for instance, the tower of Philip le Bon at Dijon, built in the years 1455–60, rose, and still rises, eight storeys, with a windowed room at the top, which was later used as an observatory.

The octagonal prospect room at Oatlands was imitated in stone within a year or two at Melbury in Dorset, and in the early 1550s at Lacock Abbey in Wiltshire. The great octagon at Melbury rises out of the roof of the main house; the smaller, but exquisite banqueting and prospect room at Lacock (Fig. 112) forms the top storey of a semi-detached octagonal tower, as at Oatlands but without the cantilever.[15] At much the same time Lord D'Arcy added a formidable tower to his converted abbey buildings at St Osyth in Essex;[16] and Sir John Champneys, Lord Mayor of London, built a high tower of brick onto his house in Mincing Lane. This, according to Stow, was 'the

first that I ever heard of in any private man's
house, to overlook his neighbours in this city. But
this delight of his eye was punished with blindness
some years before his death.'[17]

The most striking and romantic of these single
towers, at Freston in Suffolk (Fig. 313), may date
from as early as 1550.[18] It rises, tall and solitary,
eight storeys high on a slope above the Orwell
estuary. It is of brick, with mainly pedimented
windows and a single room to each floor. The
uppermost room is higher than the others, has
bigger windows, and was clearly intended as a
look-out room; the roof, with easy access from
the turret staircase, and with an elaborate
balustrade, was equally clearly a look-out platform. The brickwork on one side, at the bottom
of the tower, suggests that it was originally attached to a house, long since vanished.

The two bay windows at Little Moreton Hall in
Cheshire, built by the carpenter Richard Dale in
1559 (as the inscription on them announces),[19] are
jostled together, as though Dale (or his client) had
shrunk and elided the two corner belvederes at
Nonsuch and joined them like Siamese twins to

produce corner bay windows for his courtyard. At
Gorhambury in Hertfordshire in the 1560s Sir
Nicholas Bacon built a tall thin tower of brick
onto one side of his new house (Fig. 169); it seems
to have been a clock- or bell-tower, but one of the
surviving illustrations suggests a look-out or
prospect room at the head of the staircase.[20]
There may have been such a room in the massive
'great tower' shown by the surviving accounts to
have been built in 1577 as part of Lord Petre's new
building at Thorndon Hall in Essex; the accounts
are not clear.[21]

By then such single towers were going out of
fashion, and when the great age of Elizabethan
glass began in the 1570s it took a different form.
It was splendidly introduced, like much else, at
Kirby Hall in Northamptonshire in 1570 (Fig. 315).
The hall end of Kirby's courtyard is filled with a
succession of lofty windows, four lights high by
four wide in the centre, five by four to either side.
To the right of the entrance porch these great
windows rise the full height of the hall; to the left
they are deceptive, for in fact the central row of
lights are blanks, to conceal the fact that on this

261

316 (*above*) Kenilworth Castle, Warwickshire, from the east, from a seventeenth-century painting. The twelfth-century keep is to the right, Leicester's Building to the left. The lower range joining them, also probably built by Leicester, has been demolished.

315 (*facing page*) The hall front in the courtyard of Kirby Hall, Northamptonshire, built in 1570–75.

317 (*right*) The west façade of Leicester's Building, added to Kenilworth *c.*1570–74 by the Earl of Leicester. It was built under William Spicer, and probably designed by him.

side of the façade there were two storeys. This kind of deception, adopted for symmetry and effect, was never one to bother the Elizabethans; there must have been a similar arrangement at two other hall-front walls of glass, at least as impressive as Kirby's, but known only from engravings: at Gerard's Bromley in Staffordshire (Fig. 314), where the porch (all that is left of the house today) is dated 1584, and at Dunham Massey in Cheshire, which probably dated from the 1590s.[22]

On the other courtyard façades at Kirby the proportion of window to wall is much smaller, and on the external façades it is smaller still. The next stage can be seen in three great houses remodelled or enlarged a little later in the 1570s: at Longleat (Figs 205, 501), where the external

318 (below)
Eastington Manor,
Gloucestershire (c.1578), as
depicted by Johannes Kyp
in Robert Atkyn's *Ancient
and Present State of
Gloucestershire*, 1712.

319 (right)
The central feature, dated
1587, on the north front
of Burghley House,
Lincolnshire.

320 (right)
A reconstruction of the
garden front of Holdenby
House, Northampton-
shire, as built in the 1570s.

321 (facing page)   Carew
Castle, Pembrokeshire.
The north range added to
the castle c.1588, seen
across the Cleddau
estuary.

façades were rebuilt between 1572 and 1580; at Burghley (Fig. 208), where remodelling of the exterior started in 1573 and was carried on in slow stages up to 1588; and at Kenilworth Castle, where what became known as Leicester's Building (Figs 316, 317) was finished in time for Queen Elizabeth's protracted visit in 1575.

A continuous series of large windows, including bay windows of different types and sizes, runs round all four of the external façades of Longleat and Burghley: and, unlike most earlier houses, they are three rather than two storeys high. At Longleat there were thirteen bay windows, all identical and rectangular in plan, regularly spaced round the façades; at Burghley there was much more variety; the height of Kenilworth, and the long vertical strips of its bay windows, seem directly inspired by Wolsey's royal lodgings at Hampton Court, except that the tallest windows were on the first, not the second floor. This was in order for them to be latched onto the great first-floor rooms of John of Gaunt's adjoining building, so as to provide an especially grand royal apartment for Elizabeth.

There had been nothing quite like these houses anywhere before in England – or anywhere else, for that matter. They were lantern houses, and as such dazzled their contemporaries. In 1575 Robert Laneham described Leicester's building at Kenilworth as follows (and its proportion of window to wall was somewhat less than that at the two others):

the rare beauty of bilding that his Honor has avaunced; all of the hard quarry stoen: every room so spacious, so well belighted, and so hy roofed within: so seemly too sight by du proportion without: a day tyme, on every syde so glittering by glass; a nights, by continuall brightnesse of candel, fyre and torch-light, transparent thro the lyghtsome wyndz az it wear the Egiptian Pharos [the famous ancient lighthouse at Alexandria] relucent untoo all

the Alexandrian coast: or els (too talke merily with my mery freend) thus radiant az thoogh Phoebus for his eaz woold rest him in the Castle, and not every night so travel doown into the Antipodes.[23]

George Whetstone, in his *An Heptameron of Civill Discourses* (1582), describes a visit to the imaginary palace of Philoxenus and how 'after I had jornyed the space of an hower, in a sweete Groave of Pyne Apple trees, mine eye fastened upon a stately pallace, ye brightness wherof glimmered through the braunches of the younger woodde, not unlyke the Beames of the Sonne through the Crannelles of a walle'.[24] He could well have been part inspired by a first sight of Burghley, for his wife's family house was at Barnack on the edge of its park, and he himself had a house in Stamford.[25] But he could equally have had in mind Kenilworth Castle, where his friend George Gascoigne (whose life he wrote and who died in his house) wrote the entertainments provided for Elizabeth in 1575; or the slightly later (*circa* 1577–83) Holdenby in Northamptonshire, built by Sir Christopher Hatton, to whom he dedicated his *Heptameron*, and the garden front of which, 350 feet long, was glazed solid for almost its whole length (Fig. 320).

Bay windows were to proliferate for the next forty years or more, in every variety of shape and size. They could be angled, of either two, three or five sides; square, as at Longleat; semicircular; or complex, based on combinations of the other figures. Angled windows were usually described as 'cant' at the time, semicircular windows as 'compass', though on occasions 'compass' seems to have been applied to angled windows as well.

Square bay windows, certainly or probably inspired by those at Longleat, appear in a group of Gloucestershire and Wiltshire houses: those at Sherborne in Gloucestershire (?1580s) were adorned with columns and closely modelled on Longleat (Fig. 225); simpler versions are at Cor-

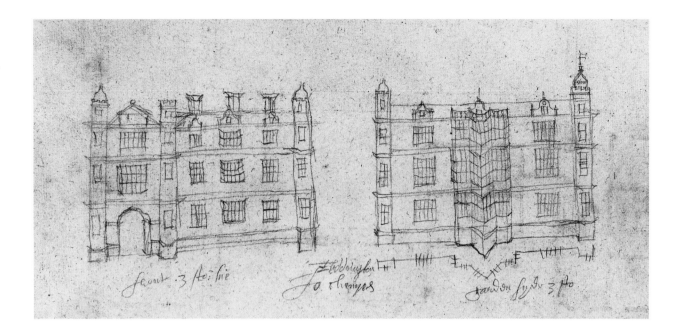

sham Court in Wiltshire (*circa* 1575–82) and Stanway (*?circa* 1590) in Gloucestershire, and there were demolished Gloucestershire examples at Eastington Manor (*circa* 1578) (Fig. 318) and Sapperton Manor (1580s).[26] There are other examples, but the type was never as common as the cant bay windows, which proliferated everywhere. Compass windows became especially popular in the late sixteenth and early seventeenth centuries; perhaps the earliest securely dateable examples are those on the north front of Burghley, dated 1587 (Fig. 319), and those at Carew Castle in Pembrokeshire (Fig. 321), of 1588 or shortly after.[27] At Carew the semicircular towers, used for fortification on the perimeter of medieval castles, have been pierced and opened up into lanterns of glass, to glitter above the waters of the Cleddau estuary; the conceit was perhaps deliberate.

An imposing three-storey 'complex' window, based on a square plan with two-sided angular or canted projections at the centre, was in the centre of the garden front at Toddington Manor in Bedfordshire by 1581, when it is shown in a bird's-eye view on a survey by Ralph Agas (Fig. 45). It intrigued John Thorpe so much that he

made one of his rare sketches of it (Fig. 322).[28] The great house at Toddington has long since been demolished, but a similar window still exists at Barlborough Hall in Derbyshire (1583–4), probably built in imitation of Toddington, and sufficiently impressive, though only two storeys high.

Both these windows may have been anticipated at Kenilworth Castle. The base of a window of the same plan is corbelled out from the ruinous wall on the south side of John of Gaunt's White Hall or great chamber. There is not enough left to show whether this was extended up to light the vanished second floor above it; but it must be an addition to the original fourteenth-century building, possibly made for Elizabeth's visit in 1575, so that the queen could look out through it from her presence chamber to the encircling waters of the castle's Great Mere.

The windows of complex plan at Sherborne Castle, Berry Pomeroy, and the Hall at Bradford-on-Avon, which followed in the 1590s, are variants, with a compass instead of a canted centre. An alternative to both types were windows in which the outer sides were splayed, not right-angled. A notable example of this, built of wood, with a semicircular central projection, long looked

323 (*right*) Sir Paul Pindar's House in the City of London (*c.*1600), photographed before the façade was re-erected in the Victoria and Albert Museum.

325 (far *right*) Sketch by John Thorpe of a house at 'the hither end of Holborn' (152).

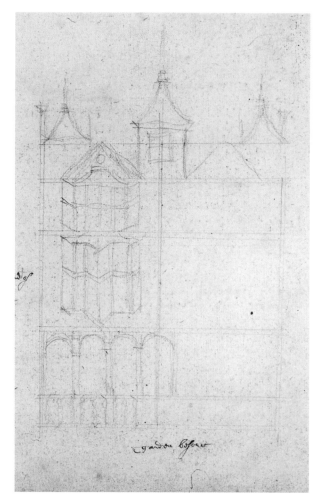

324 (*below*) An eighteenth-century bird's-eye view of Campden House, Gloucestershire (*c.*1608), probably a redrawing of an earlier survey.

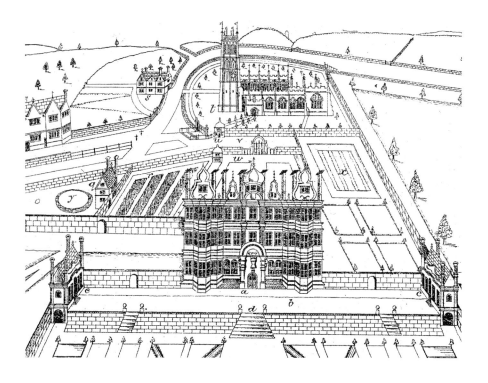

down forlornly on the shop in the Victoria and Albert Museum. It is the re-erected front of what became known as Sir Paul Pindar's house in the City of London (Fig. 323), built, in fact, by his father, in or shortly before 1600.[29] Sir Baptist Hickes's Campden House in Gloucestershire may have had similar windows (Fig. 324).[30] Another timber example in London is shown in one of Thorpe's drawings: two windows jettied out above a loggia on the garden front of a house at 'the hither end of Holborn' (Fig. 325). According to Thorpe again, there was a stone example (probably designed by Thorpe himself about 1618) in the centre of the garden front of Aston Hall in Warwickshire, built to light its great chamber; it had gone by the early nineteenth century, and probably earlier.[31]

326a and b and 327
Houses in Bristol (*right*)
and Bath (*below*), as shown
on the borders of late
seventeenth-century town
plans.

The window at the Paul Pindar house was jettied out from first-floor level. This was an obvious and easy way of enriching timber-framed buildings, and jettied windows of all shapes and depth of projection, single storey or running up through several storeys, proliferated in Bristol, Bath, Exeter and other provincial towns (Figs 326a and b, 327), as well as London, from the late sixteenth century onwards, filling the streets with variety and fantasy.[32] Not many survive. Along with medieval stone oriels (notably the one over the entrance of Hengrave Hall), these contemporary timber windows may have been the inspiration of the elaborate stone oriels that dominated the entrance façade of Northampton House on the Strand in London, as built by the Earl of Northampton from about 1605 onwards (Fig. 351). There were three of these, a simple semicircular one over the entrance, and very much more elaborate and fanciful ones at either end of the façade; and there were simpler angled oriels, of two sides only, along the side façades of the internal courtyard. All but the oriel over the entrance were swept away in the eighteenth century.[33]

Similar oriels over the hall porch at Chilham Castle in Kent and Bramshill in Hampshire (Fig. 407) may be imitating those at Northampton House, and its façade clearly influenced that of Hartwell House in Buckinghamshire (Figs 328, 329). This was simplified in the eighteenth century when shaped gables and central scrolly pilasters like those at Northampton House were removed, but it still has the combination of central and side oriels, the side one not tricky, like the Northampton House ones, but shallow, a very large 'compass'.[34]

Large windows and bay or oriel windows were not cheap, and not for ordinary people, except in their most modest form. There were always so many variables that one cannot be dogmatic, but, as a rule of thumb, one can say that (in a stone building) tripling the proportion of windows on a façade doubled the cost; and bay windows were

even more expensive. Yeomen and minor gentry were likely to be deterred by the expense, by the inhibition that to indulge in such features would be building above their station, and by the inconvenience (potentially another aspect of cost) as underlined by Francis Bacon: 'one cannot tell where to become, to be out of the Sunne or cold'. Heating them was likely to be both expensive and ineffective. The cold of Hardwick is vividly demonstrated in its 1601 inventory: in addition to the ordinary curtains – 'too curtins of red cloth

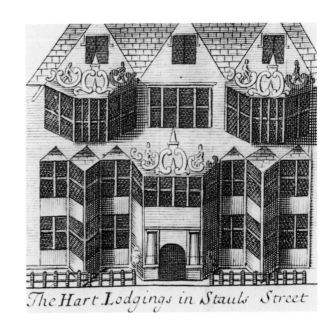

for the windowes' – Bess of Hardwick's bed-chamber had 'three coverletes to hang before a windowe' and 'a Coverlett to hang before a Dore'.[35] In fact, later generations of Cavendishes gave up any attempt to inhabit Hardwick during the winter. One of the reasons for the failure of the upper classes to keep a traditional Christmas of open hospitality in the country, in spite of frequent royal ordinances to the contrary from Elizabeth and James I, may have been their desire to escape from the cold of their fashionable new houses into snugger quarters in London.

The contrast between the two approaches to building is concisely expressed by Gervase Markham. In his *The English Husbandman* (1613) he gives a specimen sketch plan of 'A plain man's country house', a simple H-shaped building, with a hall in the centre, a parlour in one wing, a kitchen in the other, small windows and no frills (Fig. 330). 'Yet if a man would bestow cost in this modell', he adds,

the faire inward corner of the hall would be convenient for four turrets, and the four gavell

330 (below) 'A plain man's country house' as depicted in *The English Husbandman* by Gervase Markham, 1613. Rooms are as follows:

A   Great hall
B   Dining parlour
C   Inner closet
D   Strangers' lodging
E   Staircase
F   Staircase
G   Hall screen
H   Cellar/larder
I   Buttery
K   Kitchen
L   Dairy house
M   Milk house

[gable] ends being thrust out with bay windowes, might be formed in any curious manner; and where I place a gate and a plaine pale might be either a tarriss, or a gatehouse, of any fashion whatsoever; besides all those windows which I make plaine might be made bay windowes, either with battlements or without; but the scope of my booke tendeth only to the use of the honest *husbandman* and not to instruct men of dignitie.[36]

It is with buildings put up by men of dignity that this book is mainly concerned. Surviving examples, representations of what has been demolished and plans drawn by Thorpe and others make clear that Markham was less making suggestions about what might be done than describing what had been and was being done, by men of dignity, in houses all over the country. There are, or were, numerous examples of basic H-shaped plans embellished in the manner he describes. But similar treatment could be given to courtyard plans, or simple rectangular or square plans, or plans of unusual shape. Much of the pleasure and excitement of Elizabethan and Jacobean architecture derives from the way in which a variety of basic shapes are embellished with different combinations of windows, towers and gables. The potential variations were endless, and exploited with endless ingenuity and zest.

Symmetry, projection with recession, and outline whether of silhouette or plan, are ruling features of these houses. There are examples where lavish glazing is combined with an asymmetrical plan, but they are the exceptions. On the whole, Burghley's comment on Holdenby must have expressed a general feeling: 'I found a great magnificence in the front or front pieces of the house, and so every part answerable to other, to allure liking.'[37]

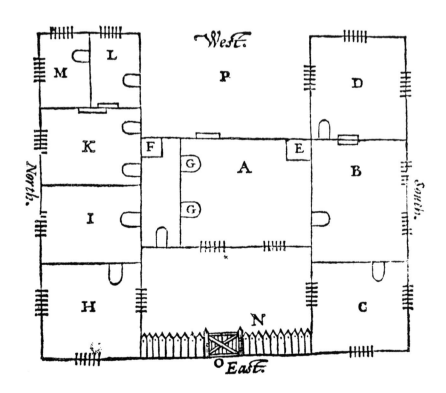

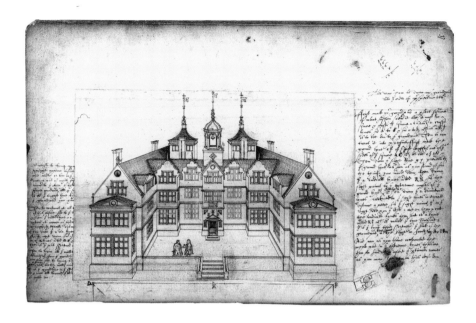

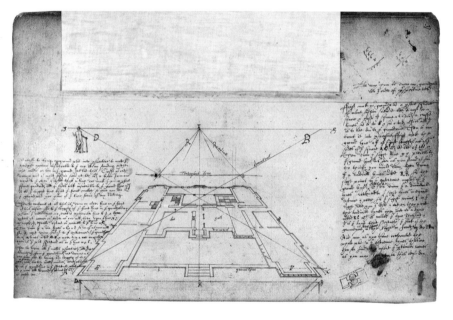

(Figs 333, 334); but it has to be said that most of the few surviving contemporary English perspectives of buildings are taken from a central viewpoint, and even when Thorpe, for instance, moves off the axis, he usually does not move far.[38] On the other hand, Robert Smythson's one surviving perspective drawing, made *circa* 1580, twenty years or more earlier than Thorpe's, though also drawn from an axial position, is taken from one in which the notional viewer is much closer to the buildings than in Thorpe's perspectives (Fig. 336); as a result, the drawing gives a bolder feeling of projection and recession, and suggests that the sensational off-centre groupings of Hardwick may have been consciously exploited.

One is perhaps on safer ground when one talks about contemporary awareness, when looking at a building, of the ground plan from which it rose. Surviving examples of plans, especially as drawn out by Robert Smythson or surviving among the Hatfield drawings, are clearly designed to be in themselves objects of beauty, intended to entice or impress a client, and to imprint themselves on his memory (Fig. 335). They show delight in a plan as a piece of formal geometry, carefully and accurately drawn out with compass, square and rule (and, often, with a compass prominently drawn as an attachment to the scale). Reading these plans must have led, not only to reading from the plan to the building, or, when viewing it, from the building back to the plan, but also to pleasure in doing so, if the plan was an ingenious one.

That the Elizabethans appreciated silhouette is self-evident from what is going on in the skyline of their buildings: the towers rising above gable or parapet, the cut-out silhouette of parapet inscriptions, the statues of persons or beasts rising from them, the dramatic size and shapes of chimneys in the form of piers or columns.

Another way in which 'men of dignity' could impress was by building high. In the early sixteenth century, and the first decades of Elizabeth's reign, the main ranges of a house, however

In addition, contemporary interest in what was, for England, the new science of perspective (Figs 331, 332) altered the way that people looked at buildings and created a new awareness of how the different planes of a building advanced and retreated, diminished and increased, not only as the viewer approached or retreated on the centre axis, but also, one can surmise, when he moved away from it. It is tempting to surmise this because the buildings of the period group so effectively and often dramatically form an angle

333 and 334 The angled view, at (*above left*) Hardwick Hall and (*above right*) the Hall, Bradford-on-Avon.

grand, were usually only two storeys high, though perhaps above a basement and embellished with higher corner towers and gatehouse, and sometimes with attic rooms under the roof and behind dormers or gables. A similar combination remained common enough from the 1570s; but rooms tended to be higher, and more and more houses were built a full three storeys high, with towers and gables rising higher still; and the upper storey, far from being given over to minor rooms, could contain the principal rooms of the house, behind great windows, as at Hardwick. In a few houses the change in taste was shown by an extra storey or storeys being added: probably, at Chatsworth, Castle Ashby (Fig. 135) and Little Moreton Hall (Fig. 366), certainly at Bramhall Hall, Raglan Castle and Worksop Manor (Fig. 125).[39]

And as the end result come the high-style Elizabethan and Jacobean houses, in all their splendour and variety, as they develop from the

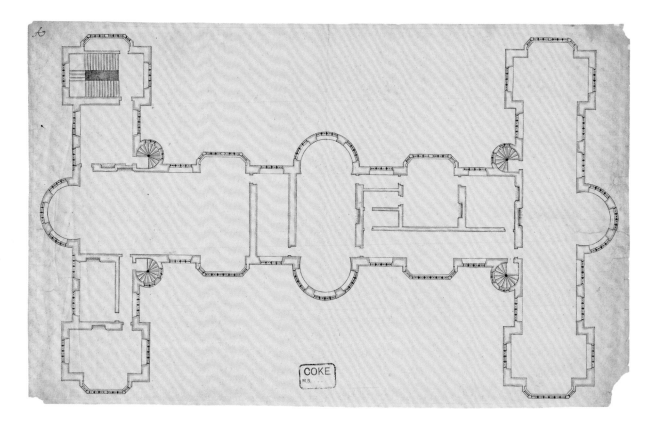

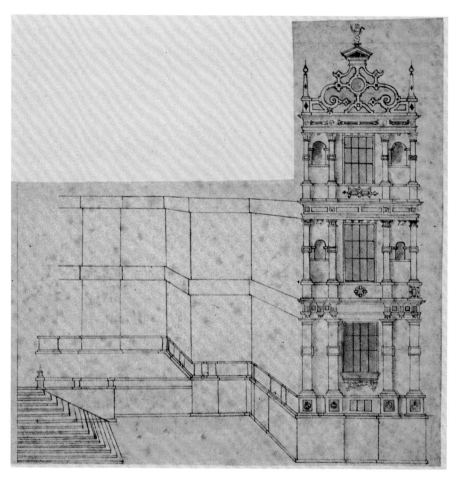

magnificent simplicity of Hardwick to the gay prettiness of Holland House (Fig. 547). Many options were available. Some houses were embellished with towers alone, some with bay windows and gables without the towers, some with gables and towers without the bay windows, many with different combinations of all three. Sometimes bay windows were run in enfilade along one façade, as in the east front at Blickling Hall in Norfolk, in the cannonade of five at New Hall in Essex (Fig. 339), especially splendid because of their close spacing and grand scale, and in the shallow ripple in alternation with gables along the front of Postlip in Gloucestershire (Fig. 340); sometimes they were paired, as in the magnificent twins that still swell out under Flemish gables at Kirby Hall (Fig. 338), and in a similar pair once at Newburgh Priory in Yorkshire (Fig. 341), shown in a seventeenth-century painting. The entrance front of Moyns Hall in Essex is made up, with artful simplicity, of three bay windows between four gables, two wide and two narrow (Fig. 337).

At Fountains Hall, in Yorkshire, the façade recesses in three steps: outer towers, bay windows under gables, and then, inset and deep-recessed in the centre, a projecting semicircular bay window (Fig. 509). There is a similar, but simpler, arrangement at Ludstone Hall in Shropshire, in two steps only; at Plas Teg in Flintshire (Fig. 543) there is dramatic recession in three steps from corner towers, but no bay windows.

Many houses have one show façade only, whether for reasons of expense or because no more than one 'platt' had been obtained from an outside surveyor. Ingestre Hall in Staffordshire, Howsham Hall in Yorkshire and Astley Hall in Lancashire have entrance fronts magnificent in bay windows and glass (Figs 343, 342), but the other façades are very modest. Sometimes the show façade is extended round the immediate corners with further bay windows. At Burton Agnes in Yorkshire there are compass windows on the main front, canted ones round the corner (Fig. 504), at Wootton Lodge in Staffordshire

(Fig. 503) the opposite; at both houses the remaining façades are less carefully contrived, and at Burton Agnes they are a storey lower. At the Hall, Bradford-on-Avon, all the splendour is on the entrance front, but the side façades were carefully detailed (though the less important of the two detailed in rendering, which has been removed, not stone);[40] the rear façade is completely utilitarian.

But a number of houses were carefully detailed on all four façades. Three sets of Smythson plans, none of which may have been executed, have four identical façades, each with a rectangular central projection (in at least one case carried up to four towers) between canted bays (Fig. 344). There seems to have been a similar arrangement at the lodge that Francis Bacon built for himself at Verulam around 1615; Kiplin Hall has identical façades, but with towers and no bay windows (Fig. 375).[41]

At other houses the façades are different, but all designed with care. Montacute has a gentle

339 (*above left*) Looking along the front of New Hall, Essex, built *c*.1575.

340 (*above right*) The south front of Postlip Hall, Gloucestershire, built *c*.1614.

338 (*facing page*) The two bow windows, perhaps of *c*.1605, at the south end of the west range at Kirby Hall, Northamptonshire.

341 (*right*) The great windows on the garden front of Newburgh Priory, North Yorkshire, *c*.1590. A detail from a late seventeenth-century view of the house.

342 Astley Hall, Lancashire, probably c.1600.

343 The early seventeenth-century Howsham Hall, East Yorkshire.

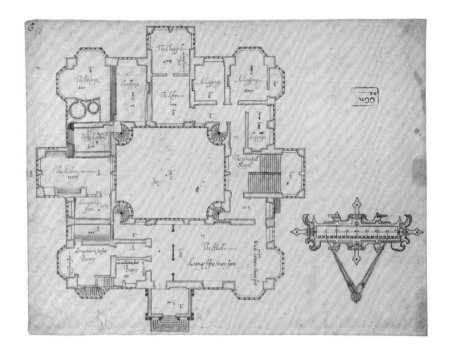

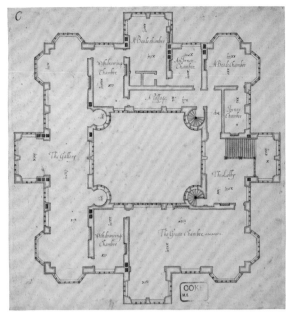

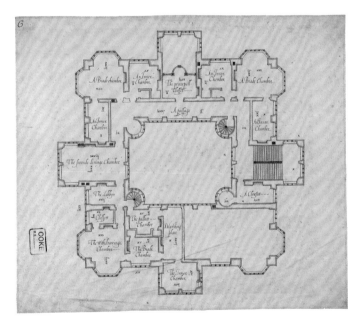

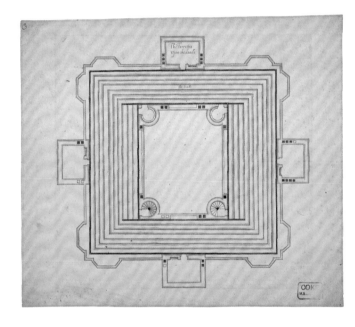

344a–d Plans by Robert
Smythson, perhaps dating
from the 1590s, for a
three-storey house with
bay windows and four
towers (SM. DWGS 11/2).

enfilade of bay windows under shaped gables on
the original entrance front (Fig. 516); the side
façades have a single lofty oriel (Fig. 363), high up
on the second floor, lighting either end of the long
gallery; the rear façade has neither bays nor oriels,
but is still symmetrical, and given character by the
different window arrangements in the two staircase towers, which follow the slope of the stairs.
Condover Hall in Shropshire has two differing

show façades, front and back (Figs 15, 539); the
side façades, identical to each other, are simpler
but still made impressive by staircase towers
rising between paired chimney stacks. Chimney-
stack projections were sometimes used for architectural effect in this way, as at Quenby in
Leicestershire, and Newton Surmaville in Somerset (Fig. 345); but the tendency in later Elizabethan and Jacobean days was to put the fire-

places in the cross walls, an arrangement that was both more efficient in terms of heat retention and kept the façade free for a show of windows.

So many games could be played, with window patterns of different sizes and sill levels, with bay windows of contrasting shapes, with combinations of bays with gables, with shallowness or depth of recession, that it must have been tempting to give up the expense of entablatures, or classical adornment, except on the porch, as was the case at Burton Agnes, Chastleton, Quenby and elsewhere; at Doddington and perhaps Worksop, only the cupolas of the turrets had entablatures. In general, there was a movement away from unity towards diversity, epitomised by the contrast in plan between William Cecil's Burghley – itself by no means the most unified of High Elizabethan houses – and Robert Cecil's Hatfield (Fig. 346). In terms of detail the original entrance front at Hatfield has the full panoply of classicism, but it is abandoned on the side and rear façades; the contrast between lushness in front and grand bleakness behind (Fig. 347) has been accentuated by later alterations, but was perhaps deliberate. In general, play and contrast with windows and changing taste led to a less overpowering weight of glazing than had been found at Holdenby, Hardwick and elsewhere.

The extreme flights of Jacobean fancy, cats' cradles of timber or filigree boxes of glass, were most easily built in wood but could be transferred to solider materials. The searching eye can sometimes find a classical framework as their basis, but often it has been abandoned. The results look as insubstantial as a house of cards, and indeed all too little survives, or if it does, survives with the more fanciful and fragile features removed. The market hall of Hereford rose like a mirage in the centre of its main street around 1600, but lost its turreted upper floor in the later eighteenth century, and was finally demolished in the nineteenth. The London triumphal arches erected in honour of James I in 1603/4, wild but not neces-

345 (*facing page, top*) Chimneystacks at Newton Surmaville House, Somerset, built *c*.1602–12. The left hand one was apparently always false, and built for tthe sake of symmetry.

346 (*facing page, bottom*) Hatfield House, Hertfordshire, built 1607–1611, from the air.

347 (*right*) The north front of Hatfield House.

348 (*below left*) Great St Hugh's, Great Baddow, Essex, probably erected in the early seventeenth century by London artificers. It has been demolished.

349 (*below right*) One of the London arches erected for the entry of James I, 1604, as depicted by Stephen Harrison.

sarily degenerate descendants of the Antwerp arches of 1549, were never meant to be permanent (Fig. 349). The delicate prettiness of Holland House did not long outlive its battering in the war of 1939–45; the filigrees of Great St Hugh's in Great Baddow, Essex (Fig. 348), surely the work

of City of London carpenters, quietly disappeared in or around the 1950s; not one of the merchant fantasies depicted in the borders of eighteenth-century town plans of Bath and Bristol have survived.

Today, perhaps the best place in which to get a feeling for the extremes of Jacobean fancy is not in a house or a town hall but in the billowing and crocketed dome, arabesque minstrels' gallery, miniature arcades and star-painted ceilings of the

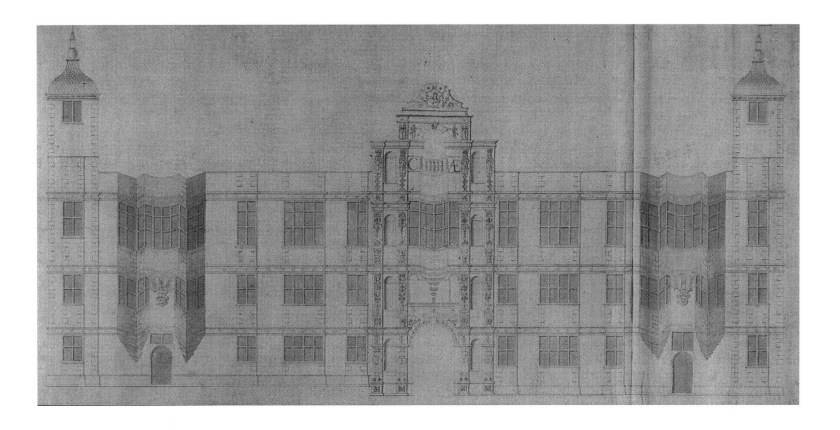

two great covered pews at Rycote chapel in
Oxfordshire (Fig. 350), perhaps put up for royal
visits to the vanished house of the Norris family
next door.

The Strand façade of Northampton House and
two of the best known of Thorpe's designs (Figs
351–3), epitomise the way in which Jacobean architecture developed – or, perhaps, the way in which
it was anticipated in the case of the Thorpe drawings, which may be just pre-Jacobean.

The façade of Northampton House (Fig. 351)
was, in its framework, that of an Elizabethan
classical house, with a 'Tower of the Orders' in the
middle, the entablatures of which are continued
across the rest of the façade, and with the
windows modelled in the Du Cerceau manner,
with gentle projections carried through the
entablatures. But its classicism is submerged. The
orders are almost totally dissolved in ornament;
repose is shattered by the gigantic oriel windows
at either end, elaborate fantasies inspired by
Gothic models; and the simple window rhythms

and huge expanses of glass of High Elizabethan
houses have been modified into windows of different sizes and spacing, and a higher proportion
of wall.[42]

The Thorpe drawings[43] are both highly finished
in the same style, must have been made at the
same period, and are almost certainly Thorpe's
own designs, and not just surveys. They perhaps
date from *circa* 1600, or a little earlier. Both are
for half-timbered houses. One is for Easton
Lodge in Essex, built for one of Lord Burghley's
secretariat, Henry Maynard (Figs 352, 8).[44] The
other design (Fig. 353) has been identified as for
Campden House in Kensington, but for various
reasons this is unlikely. The lions with outstretched tails that decorate its cove are the distinctive crest of the Howard and Percy families.
It seems most likely that it was designed for one
of the Howard family, to be built (if it was built)
in Essex or Suffolk.[45]

Both designs are carefully and elaborately
crafted all the way round, like exquisite pieces of

cabinetwork; they give a vivid feeling of the enjoyment that Thorpe must have had in drawing them. Classicism has shrunk to a minimum, confined to the porch and inconspicuous loggias. The result is window, sky and turret architecture. The second, and more elaborate design has six canted bay windows, of two or five sides; a compass window, built over the porch, is extended by further glazing to either side; continuous glazing joins the porch to the canted windows on the entrance front on the ground floor, and on the first floor they extend into little turrets glazed like lanterns, which join on to the towers at either end. A varied and picturesque pattern of glazing results; and all these features have little roofs of fish-scale tiles, in the French manner. There are covered loggias at the sides and at the rear; the main staircase is carried up above the roof to an open rooftop belvedere, from which to survey the unlikely view of six chimney stacks, each crafted like a human figure.

The drawing is unusual, in that it shows the glazing. Most of the windows are glazed with small diamond-shaped panes in the usual manner; but the central compass window is filled with panes of variegated shapes, combined in elaborate geometric patterns.

A good deal of such patterned glazing survives, and there was probably much more demolished or replaced by simpler glazing in later times. The earliest example, if it is contemporary with the windows (but is it?), is in the bay windows of 1559 at Little Moreton Hall; and there is much more in other parts of Little Moreton. The glazing in the

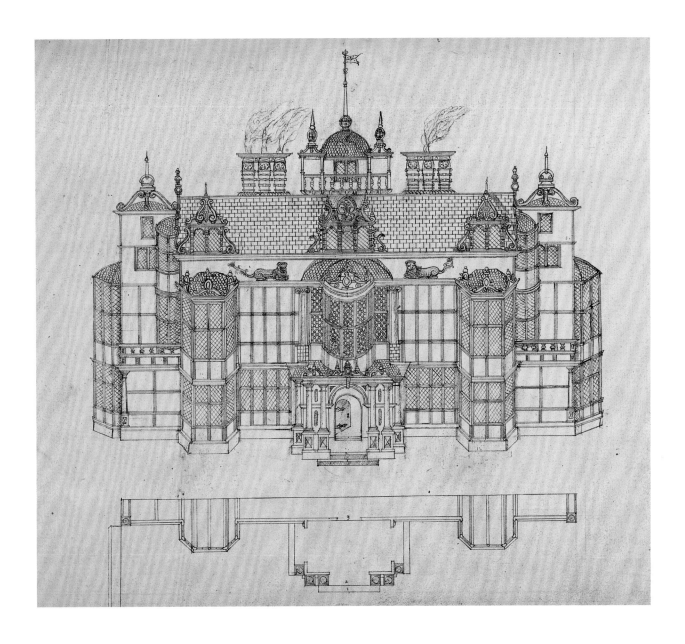

great hall windows at Collacombe in Devon (Fig. 360) dates from about 1578 (the date on the plasterwork), and that in the great chamber of Gilling Castle in Yorkshire is dated 1586 (Fig. 354). The glazing of the Hall, Bradford-on-Avon (Fig. 309), appears to date from the nineteenth century, when the Hall was extensively refaced and restored; but the pattern of the glazing is found in Walter Gedde's *Booke of Sundry Draughtes, Principaly serving for Glasiers* (1615), and the present glazing may copy whatever survived of the original.

Gedde gives 103 pages of designs, some based on rectilinear patterns, to be laid out with a rule,

some 'Circular or Compas draughts', to be laid out with a compass. The designs were to be drawn out on what Gedde calls 'the table', and the glass then carefully cut to fit, before it was leaded. The technique could have been managed only by an artificer with skills in drawing and measuring, and a good grasp of geometry, as well as with knowledge of glazing techniques.

Gedde is enthusiastic about his art. 'As the principall beautie and countenance of Architecture', he writes, 'consistes in outwarde ornament of lights, so the inward partes are ever opposite to the eies of the beholder, taking more delight in

354 Some of the heraldic
glass installed from about
1585 in the great chamber
at Gilling Castle, North
Yorkshire.

the beauty therof, being cunningly wrought, than in any other garnishing within the same.' The leading patterns in glazing, as he rightly says, are effective not only from the outside, but even more when seen in silhouette against the light from the inside. Such glazing was striking at night too, when lit from the inside and seen, again in silhouette, as Laneham described it at Kenilworth. The effect could be increased, outside and in, if heraldic glass was incorporated (Gedde's book included a section on 'The Maner Howe to Anneile or Paint in Glas').

Heraldic glass has a history going back to the Middle Ages, but the Elizabethan passion for heraldic display brought about its golden age. The

best-known and most resplendent example is at Gilling Castle (Fig. 354), where the arms of the Fairfax family and its connections were installed in the great chamber by Bernard Dininghoff, a Flemish glass painter who had settled in York; one panel is signed and dated by him 1585, which is perhaps when work started, but shields continued to be added for a decade or more, until the bay window and adjacent window that lit the great chamber were almost entirely filled with an efflorescence of heraldry, on a background of patterned glazing.[46]

The arms of the Hoby family, dated 1609 and also on patterned glazing, fill the window of the Hoby chapel at Bisham in Berkshire (Fig. 355); the

work . . . anywhere in England to be found'.[48] By May all was finished, and Jones claimed that the result was 'the fayreste great chamber as is in England'. He describes how the Earl of Surrey 'with other Lords' had come to see the new rooms and how 'the Queenes majestie was on the Thamys two or three nyghtes togeather agaynste Sherwsbury housse and stayed there with musi[ci]ons playing', presumably to enjoy the effect of light shining through glass and heraldry from the great chamber.[49]

An advantage of bay windows as far as interiors were concerned was that they provided little rooms within rooms, which could be retired into for private conversations. Francis Bacon may have had reservations about excessive glazing as a conductor of heat and cold, but he commented that 'For Inbowed windowes, I hold them of good use . . . For they bee Prettie Retiring Places for Conference'.[50] Gilbert Talbot, in another letter, describes how he and his father retired into a window to talk in privacy;[51] and when the government official Sir Henry Bronker was sent up to Hardwick in 1603, to sound out Arbella Stuart's desperate and unsuitable plots to find a husband, and (as he describes it) he took her to the other end of the gallery to talk to her away from Bess of Hardwick, one can surmise that they would have withdrawn also into one of the two great bays letting off the main gallery, for additional protection from her grandmother's beady eyes.[52]

In 1579 Lord Burghley congratulated Sir Christopher Hatton on the 'largeness and lightsomeness' of his great chamber.[53] The light that came pouring in through great windows was certainly one of the features that sold lavish glazing to the upper classes: but 'lightsomeness' could also be accentuated in another way. It is not coincidence that the efflorescence of Elizabethan glazing coincided with an efflorescence of Elizabethan plasterwork; there was good reason for the full title of Walter Gedde's treatise: *A Booke of Sundry Draughtes, Principaly serving for Glasiers: and not*

arms of the Beaupre family originally filled a window at Beaupre Hall in Cambridgeshire and are now in the Victoria and Albert Museum. There are fine displays at Fountains Hall in Yorkshire, probably also by Dininghoff,[47] and at Montacute in Somerset; and numerous scattered examples of a few coats, possibly all that survives of more comprehensive schemes.

A good contemporary description of the effect of new glazing at Shrewsbury House, on the river in the City of London, is to be found in letters written by William Jones and Gilbert Talbot to the Earl of Shrewsbury in 1579. William Jones, somewhat mysteriously describing himself as 'the finisher', was responsible for redecorating a set of rooms there, including the great chamber. Redecoration included a new ceiling, heraldic glass in the windows, and possibly enlargement of the windows as well. The heraldic glass was designed and commissioned by Robert Cooke, the Clarenceux Herald, who also designed heraldry to be incorporated in the plasterwork of the ceiling. In February Talbot told his father-in-law that Clarenceux's glass 'will be the fairest glass

impertinent for Plasterers and Gardiners: besides sundry other professions.

Ceilings plastered white, sometimes with a little embellishment of brightly coloured heraldic shields, increased the lightness of even low rooms (Fig. 356), and the fashion for having them was sweeping the board from the 1570s, as an alternative to the open timber roofs in the tradition of medieval great halls, or panelled wooden ceilings, which had been the most prestigious form of covering for rooms of smaller size. Some open timber roofs continued to be constructed, for reasons of tradition or prestige; but it was symptomatic of changing fashion that at Plas Mawr, in Conwy in Wales, a new and, for the times, rather grand open timber roof installed about 1580 must

288

359 and 360 (*above*) The
hall, dated 1574, and
glazing of the hall window
at Collacombe Manor,
Devon.

356 (*facing page, top*) The
great chamber at
Monaughty,
Denbighshire, c.1570.

357 (*facing page, bottom left*)
Maenan Hall, North
Wales, where the wood-
work of the medieval hall
was disguised with lavish
plasterwork, probably in
the 1580s.

358 (*facing page, bottom
right*) The Lumley
Chapel, Cheam, Surrey, in
fact the chancel of an
otherwise demolished
church *above* which a
ceiling of plasterwork was
installed in 1592.

have seemed too dark, and was almost immediately concealed by a ceiling of decorative plasterwork; and the same plasterers moved up the
Conwy valley to cover walls and ceiling of the
medieval great hall at Maenan Hall with a riot of
plaster decoration, of what must originally have
been dazzling whiteness (Fig. 357). The timber
roofs of a number of medieval churches were similarly disguised; most examples of this were
removed by Victorian restorers who wanted to
get back to the medieval woodwork,[54] but there is
an attractive survivor at Cheam in Surrey, dated
1592 and installed by Lord Lumley when he
remodelled the chancel of the church to make it
a fitting receptacle for his family tombs (Fig. 358).
Today the chancel alone survives, as the Lumley
chapel, next to the new church built in the nineteenth century.

Plaster ceilings could be arched, as at Cheam,
and this form became especially popular for great
chambers and long galleries; but more often they
were flat, as in the majority of smaller rooms and
the great halls of Trerice in Cornwall, Heslington
Hall, York, Collacombe in Devon and Parham
in Sussex. Collacombe (dated 1574), where the
ceiling is lit up by a wall of near-solid windows
which retain their original elaborate glazing
patterns, gives an especially vivid feeling of the
new fashion for lightness in these rooms (Figs 359,
360).

In the early days of Elizabethan plasterwork
there were two ways of decorating ceilings, both
derived from early Tudor wooden prototypes:
thin shallow ribs and pendentives. Since plaster
was much more flexible than wood, a much
greater variety of rib patterns was possible,
some copying early Tudor wooden prototypes,
some derived from Gothic vaulting patterns,
some from Serlio, some original designs worked
out with a compass and rule. All types are to be

361 The ceiling of the hall at Heslington Hall, York, probably dating from the 1560s.

found in Gedde's books, the designs of which, as his title page rightly proclaims, were as adaptable for plasterwork as for leadwork.[55] Plaster patterns could not, of course, be silhouetted like lead ones, but side light from the windows lit them up in vivid relief.

Pendentives could vary considerably in size, and either be dispersed at nodal points in the rib decoration or fill the entire ceiling, as they do so splendidly in the ceiling of the (sadly dismembered)[56] great hall at Heslington Hall outside York (Fig. 361); this almost certainly dates from the 1560s, and is one of the earliest surviving of the more elaborate plaster ceilings.

One of the advantages of big windows was the views that could be enjoyed from them, especially on the upper floors. A long gallery situated on the top floor, as many of them were, was designed for viewing as well as exercise. The famous gallery at Worksop (Fig. 125), one of the largest in England, was glazed almost continuously down one side, and opened out at either end into circular viewing spaces, glazed like lanterns all the way round. The gallery at Montacute ends, more modestly but in the same spirit, with semicircular viewing bays continued with further glazing to either side (Figs 362, 363). At Raglan Castle in Monmouthshire, William Somerset, 3rd Earl of Worcester, built a long gallery on top of one of its medieval ranges in the 1570s; it ends with a huge semi-hexagon of windows, projecting outside the circuit of the

362 and 363   Inside and out one of the great windows at either end of the gallery at Montacute House, Somerset, c.1600.

medieval curtain wall in the form of a bastion, open to the sky today but still fitted with stone benches for viewing; from them long vistas could be enjoyed over the broad lands of the Somerset family to the Welsh hills (Fig.364). At much the same time, and probably inspired by it, his brother-in-law, Sir Edward Mansel, built a long gallery on top of Oxwich Castle in Carmarthen-shire (Fig. 365). The house is a ruin, and all that survives of the gallery are the lower stubs of its

364 Looking up at the ruined end of the Elizabethan gallery at Raglan Castle, Monmouthshire.

365 (*below*) A reconstruction of Oxwich Castle, Glamorganshire, where a long gallery was built on top of the house, perhaps in the 1580s.

mullions, protruding like teeth along its silhouette; but it is still easy enough to imagine what an extraordinary place it must have been, suspended above the sweep of Oxwich Bay.[57]

Owing to the mechanics of timber construction, galleries in half-timbered houses could be continuously glazed all the way round; all that was needed was to fill the spaces between the upright timbers with glass instead of plaster or brick. The resulting long strips of window run almost from end to end of the gallery at Little Moreton Hall, high up above the rest of the house, and give an extraordinary sense of being in a look-out when one is inside the room, walking up and down its floor, which undulates owing to the uneven shrinkage of the timbers (Figs 366, 367). The demolished timber gallery at Bramhall, also in Cheshire, must have been even more remarkable, for the windows there were higher and larger.[58]

A major disadvantage of Elizabethan rooms as look-outs, however heavily glazed, resulted from the technology of Elizabethan glazing. Since this could produce only small panes of glass, the view had to be enjoyed through a netting of leadwork (and the glass itself was usually discoloured). A window or windows could be opened, of course, but technology also limited their size. It was necessary to get out of doors to get a clear view. The popularity of flat leaded roofs in the grander Elizabethan houses was largely due to their convenience as look-out terraces. The devisers of the most inventive Elizabethan houses worked out attractive combinations of indoor and outdoor space.

As early as 1568 the roof of Longleat was scattered with little square and octagonal turrets, which were designed as banqueting houses (Fig. 368). At Burghley House the magnificent arched and coffered staircase was continued right up to the roof; and a walk across the extraordinary roofscape (see p.ii) led to rooms on the top floor of the gatehouse, probably also used for banquets. The roof was one of the recognised assets of the house, and was shown to visitors as part of the tour. In

366 and 367 Inside and out the long gallery (*c.*1580) at Little Moreton Hall, Cheshire.

the house under (to judge from the external elevations) an arched plaster ceiling; above this was another rooftop promenade, leading at either end into circular domed banqueting houses, entirely surrounded by glass. All went up in flames in the eighteenth century; but more modest domed pavilions, clearly inspired by Worksop, survive off the rooftop walk at Doddington Hall in Lincolnshire (Fig. 369).

At Hardwick the northernmost of the six turrets on the roof contain the upper flights of the house's second staircase, which is carried up to give spacious and easy access to the roof; this provides another 'promenade or gallery with a leaden floor', leading the length of the house to a banqueting room with ornamental plaster frieze and ceiling in the southern turret. Down at first-floor level, there are further external walks along the top of the two loggias (musicians were placed here in 1619 to serenade the Prince of Wales as he was given refreshment inside the house).[60] The loggias, here and in many other houses of the

368 (*above*) A rooftop view at Longleat House.

369 (*right*) Rooftop pavilions at Doddington Hall, Lincolnshire, *c*.1595–1600.

370 (*facing page, top*) Barlborough Hall, Derbyshire, dated 1583–4, where the bay windows are carried up to provide little rooms accessible from the roof.

1600 Baron Waldstein, a young nobleman from Moldavia, was taken up there; he commented on the 'promenade or gallery, with a leaden floor, from which you get a most beautiful view'.[59]

At Worksop Manor in Nottinghamshire in the 1580s, the 6th Earl of Shrewsbury (William Jones's patron at Shrewsbury House, but at Worksop employing Robert Smythson) added two lofty storeys on top of a modest early six-teenth-century hunting lodge, already two storeys high; the upper storey was almost completely filled by the great gallery, running the length of

At Barlborough Hall in Derbyshire and the demolished Heath Old Hall, its twin in Yorkshire, the bay windows were carried up to provide four little rooftop rooms or gazebos (Fig. 370). At Lulworth Castle in Dorset a staircase came up by means of a central tower to give access to the roof, with views of the sea on one side and the deer-park on the other, and across the roof to rooms in the four corner towers. At Verulam an elaborate central staircase gave access both to the roof and to the richly decorated room that Aubrey called Francis Bacon's 'summer house'.[61] At Apethorpe in Northamptonshire a rooftop walk alternates between open views and views through windows in the gables, with stone alcoves to sit in at regular intervals (Fig. 371).

An unusual and effective combination of indoor and outdoor space used to exist at Brereton Hall in Cheshire (Figs 372, 373). Here one of the two towers of the gatehouse, which is dated 1586, contained a newel staircase and was originally carried up high above the main body of the gatehouse to a domed turret. This gave access to a bridge, carried in one arch across open space above the gatehouse. The bridge led to a banqueting house in a matching turret above the other tower; the top of the bridge also served as a terrace from which to enjoy the view. The bridge is still there, but the two domed turrets were lopped off early in the nineteenth century.[62]

These rooftop terraces and banqueting or summer houses could be used for the pleasure of enjoying a prospect or catching the breeze on a hot summer evening; they could also be viewing platforms from which to watch the hunt in an adjacent deer-park. Such viewing points, if built as a separate structure rather than incorporated in the main house, were known as 'stands'. A stand, later named the 'hunting-tower', survives on the hilltop above Chatsworth (Fig. 116), in the form of a tower of four lofty storeys, with round corner turrets, all richly glazed; the turrets are carried up at the corners to domed pavilions, as at Brereton;

371 (*below*) A rooftop walk of *c.*1622 at Apethorpe Hall, Northamptonshire.

time, provided further external space, for exercise or enjoyment, covered to give protection from the rain or retreat from a too-hot sun.

372 and 373 (*right and below*) The gatehouse at Brereton Hall, Cheshire, dated 1586, as it is today, and as it was before removal of the turrets, as depicted in George Ormerod's *History of the County Palatine and City of Cheshire*, 1819.

374 (*facing page*) Looking down from the upper roof at Wollaton Hall, Nottinghamshire.

one contains the stairs that give access both to the roof and to little rooms under the cupolas: all of these have delicate plaster decoration in their vaults, for the delectation of Elizabethan ladies and gentlemen.

The rooftops of Theobalds included an 'Astronomers Walk', according to Baron Waldstein, who was on the roofs in 1600.[63] Their convenience as unimpeded viewpoints of the heavens at night was one of the attractions of roof terraces. The top room of the Tower of the Five Orders in the Schools quadrangle at Oxford (Fig. 577) was used by the University Astronomer, and he must have continued up its newel staircase to the roof of the tower to set up his telescopes.[64] Sir Francis Willoughby of Wollaton was interested in astronomy: 'astronomicall talk' formed part of the conversation with his sister Margaret Arundell when his servant visited her in London.[65] One can wonder if the great platform provided by the rooftop of the Prospect Room at Wollaton, nearly 90 feet up from the base of the house, which itself was on the summit of a high hill, was used by him for astronomical observations (Fig. 374).

In 1605 Francis Bacon described how some men searched for knowledge as 'a couch whereon

375 Kiplin Hall, West
Yorkshire, built in the
early 1620s. Detail from a
painting of 1780 by
George Cuit the elder.

to rest a searching and restless spirit; or a terrace for a wandering and variable mind to walk up and down with a fair prospect; or a tower of state, for a proud mind to rest itself upon'.[66] 'For there my Pallace royall shall be placed', declaimed Marlowe's Tamerlane, 'whose shining turrets shall dismay the heavens.'[67] Such metaphors vividly evoke the great Elizabethan houses, and the state of mind of the people who created and used them. But the desire for aerial terraces and towers of state evaporated in the course of the seventeenth and eighteenth centuries, along with the related desire for huge and fanciful windows, loggias to parade up and down in and high-ceilinged state rooms jacked up onto the second floor.

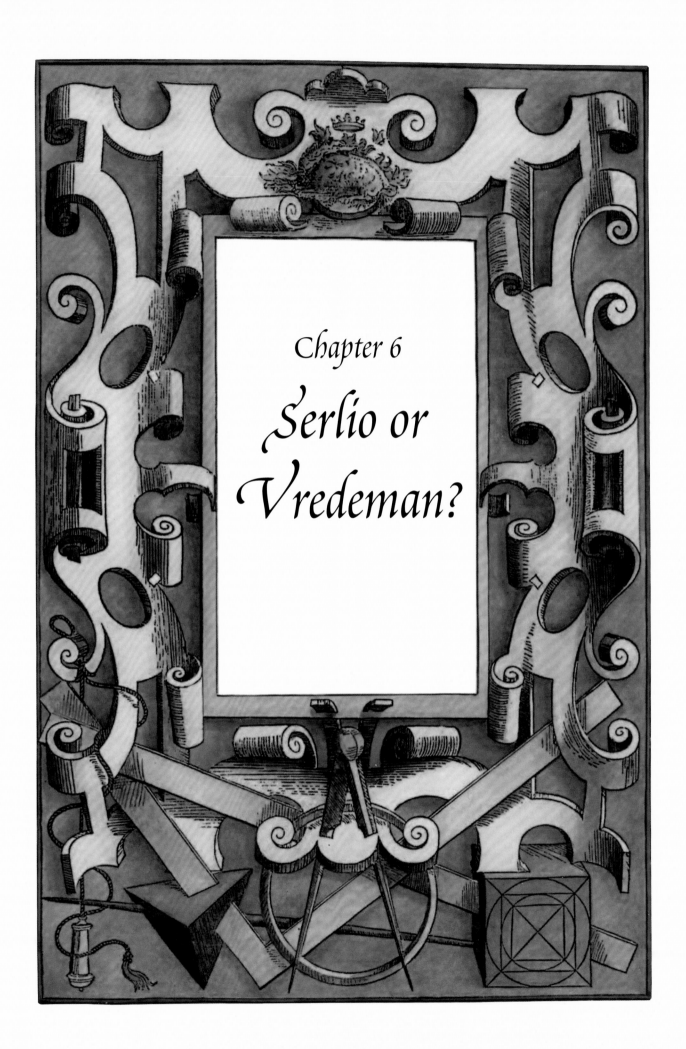

Chapter 6

Serlio or

Vredeman?

All through the sixteenth century the printing presses of Antwerp were pouring out engravings of architecture and ornament, bound up in volumes or published in separate sheets. In the second half of the century the city was far from peaceful. Protestant iconoclasts ran amok in 1566, smashing sculpture and ornament in Catholic churches. The Duke of Alba moved in as governor in 1567, and for seven years ruthlessly persecuted the Protestants. Spanish troops massacred and looted in 1576. In 1577 Antwerp broke away from Spain, and joined the northern provinces. Eight war years followed, but in 1585 Philip II's commander, the Duke of Parma, retook the city. In the four years that followed all Protestants were forced to leave, and the population, already down from its mid-century summit, was reduced from 80,000 to 42,000.

In spite of and all through the troubles, the printing houses continued to publish; only as a result of the mass exoduses of the 1580s did the primacy of Antwerp begin to be threatened by other cities, in the Netherlands and Germany especially. On the other hand, persecution led to the emigration of numerous Protestant artificers, to Germany, the Baltic States and cities in central Europe, and in large numbers to England. They arrived, in all probability, with their own supplies of books and engravings to supplement those that were exported to booksellers and printsellers, especially in London. The emigration of 1585–9 was similar, if on a smaller scale, to the emigration of French Protestants after the revocation of the Edict of Nantes in 1685. The cumulative result was that Flemish-inspired ornament in England was much more abundant in the late sixteenth and early seventeenth centuries, even though the engraved sources used often date from the 1550s and 1560s.

The resulting ornament dominated the applied and decorative arts: it appeared on title pages, and in embroideries and metalwork; it embellished the scales and inscriptions on portraits or land

surveys; and in architecture and architectural ornament was to be found everywhere, on church monuments, porches, gables, chimneypieces, staircases, panelling and ceilings, in stone, wood, stained glass and plaster.

This architectural ornament was above all inspired by the numerous publications of Hans Vredeman de Vries (Figs 250, 378, 554), supplemented by those of the Floris family.[1] It made popular a number of devices, which transformed the straightforward classicism illustrated in the publications of Serlio and other Italians. These included strapwork in all its forms; scrolled gables; columns embellished in numerous different ways, sometimes all the way up, sometimes just in the lower portion; cornices bracketed out on consoles or given a prominent bulging section, often with features resembling consoles wrapped round them, some with a distinctive beaked profile; grotesque or animal masks and faces; and terms and caryatids of every variety, sometimes armless or with their arms ending in scrolls, sometimes imprisoned in blocks of heavy masonry. Almost all these devices were to be found, as has already been discussed, at Wollaton in the 1580s, where such ornament made, not its first, but its first mass appearance in England.

The rich Vriesian embellishments of Wollaton in the 1580s (Fig. 199) were followed in the 1590s by the frontispiece of Longford (Fig. 377): altered in the eighteenth century, restored to something like its original state by Salvin, with considerable variations but still giving a vivid approximation of its original appearance as drawn by Thorpe and Thacker. This frontispiece, which, other than the date of 1591 on the upper arcade, is without reliable documentation, is unique in England, and would seem more at home in front of a Flemish town hall than an English country house. With its terms and gables it is clearly influenced by Vredeman de Vries, especially by the designs in his *Architectura* of 1577; but there is no close copying, unlike, for instance, Thorpe's 'a front or a garden

376 (*facing page*) The end of the north-east wing of Lyvedon New Bield, Northamptonshire, left unfinished in 1607. Its pure Elizabethan classicism shows no sign of the influence of Vredeman de Vries.

300

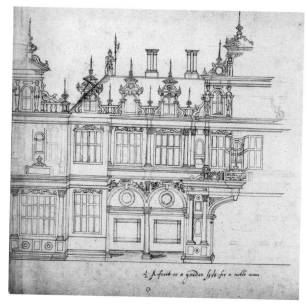

377 (*above*) The entrance front of Longford Castle, Wiltshire, 1591 It 'would seem more at home in front of a Flemish town hall than an English country house.'

378 'A front or a garden syde for a nobleman' by John Thorpe (T24) dated 1600 and closely copied from a design by Vredeman de Vries.

379 (*facing page*) A detail from Wollaton Hall, Nottingham, distilled from *Variae Architectura e Formae* and other books by Hans Vredeman de Vries.

syde for a nobleman', dated 1600, which is a close copy of one of the Corinthian façades in de Vries's *Architectura* (Fig. 378). The Doric columns of the first-floor arcade at Longford are recessed in an Italian Mannerist manner not found in Vredeman. The court connections of its builders, Sir Thomas Gorges and the Marchioness of Northampton, make it likely that the designs emanated from the Works, but one cannot discount the possibility of something brought back by Gorges from his visit to Sweden and return via Germany in 1582. John Thorpe, in whose drawings it features prominently, and who was in the Works when it was built, may have had some connection with it, but one would hesitate to credit the design to him; it is certainly far removed from his designs for Condover and Babraham (Figs

380 and 382 (*right and far right*) Two chimneypieces (*c.*1586) at Brereton Hall, Cheshire.

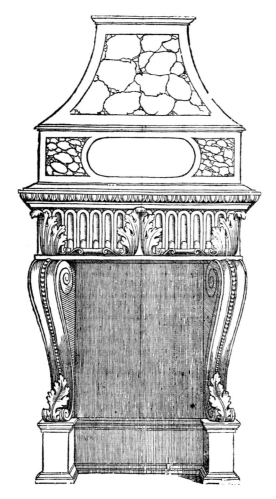

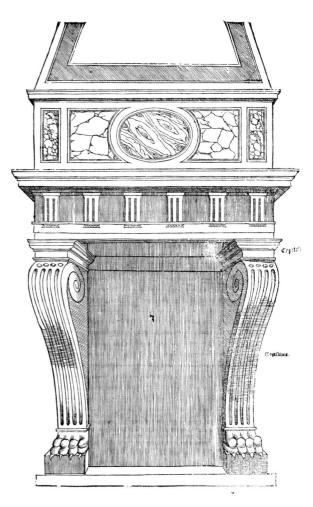

381 and 383 (*right and far right*) The chimneypieces in the Fourth Book of Sebastiano Serlio's *Architettura*, 1537, from which the mantlepieces above derive.

384 and 386 The illustration (*right*) of the Arch of Constantine in the Third Book of Sebastiano Serlio's *Architettura*, 1537, from which the porch (*far right*) at Westwood Park, Worcestershire (*c*.1611), derives.

385 (*below*) Another Serlian derivation, at Whittington Court, Gloucestershire (1580s).

538, 540), which were made at much the same time.

But it was not the case in England that Serlio went out by one door as Vredeman de Vries and his fellows came in by the other. Serlio continued to be used well on into the seventeenth century, often making it difficult to date Serlio-inspired ornament as a result. Serlio and Vredeman could be used in the same building. As has already been pointed out, amid all the welter of Vredeman de Vries elements at Wollaton, the hall chimney-piece comes out of Serlio (though given a few Vriesian trimmings), and the internal windows

387 and 388–90
Wothorpe Lodge,
Cambridgeshire (*c.*1615)
and (*facing page*) the
illustrations from Serlio on
which it draws.

classical language, Lyveden New Bield, still incomplete in 1605, is a singularly pure example of English classicism expressed with moving simplicity (Fig. 376). Tresham did, indeed, adjust his Doric order, but he altered it not to admit Mannerist elements, but to Christianise it; in an interesting letter to his steward he explains how the ox-masks of Roman metopes, symbols of pagan sacrifice, are to be replaced by the instruments and symbols of the Passion.[3]

The grand stone chimneypiece (?1580s) at Whittington Court in Gloucestershire enlarges on one of the Doric chimneypieces in Serlio's Fourth Book (Figs 385, 381); the entrance porch of Westwood Park in Worcestershire (*circa* 1611) is a variation on the engraving of the Arch of Severus in his Third Book (Figs 386, 384); Wothorpe Lodge, now in Cambridgeshire, combines a church plan and design from his Fifth Book with distinctive windows and doors from his Fourth Book (Figs 387–90).

The most remarkable examples of pure classicism inspired by Serlio are due to the amateur designer John Osborne, a protégé of Lord Burghley, who inherited from his father the important and rewarding post of Lord Treasurer's Remembrancer in 1592. He had a good humanist background. His father, Peter Osborne (1521–1592), was related by marriage to Lord Burghley and to Sir John Cheke, the great humanist (who died in his house); he was brother-in-law of the Regius Professor of Greek at Cambridge, and had served as Keeper of Edward VI's Privy Purse, before moving to his Treasury post.[4]

In 1609 or thereabouts, John Osborne made designs for an open gallery or 'porticus' to be erected on the edge of the Thames at the bottom of the garden of Lord Salisbury's house on the Strand. His very detailed specification survives, together with the biggest, and one of the finest, of surviving Elizabethan and Jacobean architectural drawings, 85 inches (217 cm) long and 16 inches (43 cm) high (Fig. 391).[5] The specifica-

at first-floor level in the hall have extended Ionic volutes, derived from Serlio's Ionic chimneypiece. At Brereton Hall in Cheshire, the gatehouse, dated 1586, is embellished with ornamental features derived, rather modestly, from Vredeman de Vries; inside the house are straightforward and careful copies of two of Serlio's chimneypieces (Figs 380–83).[2]

Moreover, there were some patrons, designers or artificers who avoided Flemish Mannerism altogether, into the seventeenth century. There is not a hint of it in the buildings of Sir Thomas Tresham; and if the Triangular Lodge owes more to geometry and religious symbolism than the

tion, for a 'porticus', is annotated as by 'Mr Osborne', and is in John Osborne's distinctive handwriting. The porticus was to have been of stone, 70 feet long, and of two rows of sixteen Corinthian columns, supporting a riverside terrace with a balustrade, the fifty balusters of which were crowned by fifty 'halcyons', each with a sprig of foliage in its mouth. The ends were to have been of two storeys of four Corinthian and four Composite columns, the Composite pairs finishing off the riverside walk and surmounted by pediments. The dimensions were all carefully worked out, as explained at length in the specification, on the module of the Corinthian column, following Vitruvius, with acknowledgements also to Serlio and (confusingly) Vredeman de Vries. The idea may have been derived from Pliny's description of a porticus in one of his letters. There is no hint of Vredeman in the architecture, the source for which is probably the porticoes of the theatre at Pula in Croatia and of the 'Athenian Council Chamber', illustrated in Serlio's Third Book (Fig. 392).[6]

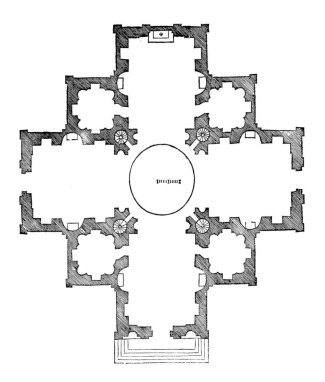

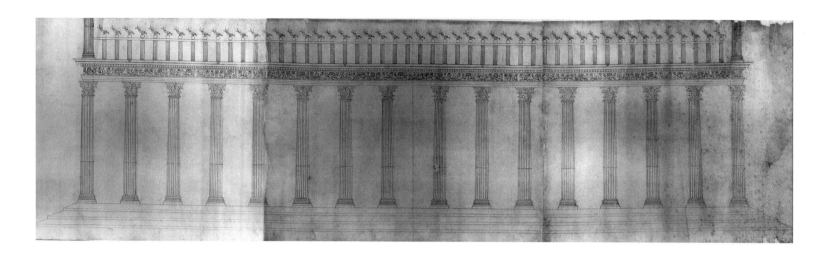

391 Design for a 'porticus' for Salisbury House, Westminster, designed by John Osborne, *c.*1609, to support a riverside walk, but never built (Hatfield, CPM Supp. 89).

The uncompromising simplicity of Osborne's porticus is unlikely to have been to Salisbury's taste, and it was almost certainly never built. But in his own house Osborne could please himself. At some undocumented date he inserted a panelled room or gallery into Chicksands Priory in Bedfordshire. This became known as the Haynes Grange Room (Fig. 394), because it was removed

to that house from Chicksands, probably in the early eighteenth century; the dimensions may have been altered in the process. The room (of which only a corner can now be seen, erected in the British Gallery of the Victoria and Albert Museum) originally took the form of a gallery, and the inscription over the chimneypiece, exhorting the reader, in beautiful Roman lettering, to die to earthly things in order to attain eternal life, suggests that it was meant for meditation. The room exuded a sense of peace and tranquillity. What are probably halcyons, though without sprigs in their mouth, covered the ceiling. The grave architecture of the panelling derived from engravings of the Pantheon in Serlio (Fig. 395): room-high Corinthian pilasters alternate with pedimented Corinthian aedicules.[7]

392 (*right*) The Serlian model for the porticus.

393 (*facing page*) One of the two Tuscan porticoes at Hardwick Hall, Derbyshire.

John Osborne, acting jointly with his father, Peter, had bought Chicksands in 1576; but legal problems then arose, leading to lawsuits, and they only got possession in 1587.[8] The obvious connection in design between the room and the porticus could suggest that the two are close in date to each other, and this may be the case. It lands one, however, with the problem of a civil servant, rising 60, making extraordinary designs, with nothing apparently to lead up to them. The proportions of the orders in the room have a certain wilfulness lacking in the porticus, and the incised ornament on the friezes and underside of the

394 (*above left*) A corner of the 'Haynes Grange Room', orginally installed, perhaps *c.*1590, to the designs of John Osborne at the Osbornes' Chicksands Priory, Bedfordshire.

395 (*above ight*) Serlio's engraving of a detail of the Pantheon, Rome, on which Osborne drew.

entablatures, though very unobtrusive, all come from Vredeman de Vries. This suggests that the room is the earlier of the two. A date of 1587 or soon afterwards would put it into the last years of Peter Osborne's life; and indeed the message of the inscription seems especially suitable for an old man, preparing for death.

Inevitably, one looks around for other buildings with which John Osborne could be connected. It would be satisfying if he could be identified with Sir Nicholas Bacon's protégé, also John Osborne, who may have designed the classical porch for the chapel of Corpus Christi College, Cambridge, in 1578 (Fig. 46), and could also have been involved in Bacon's classical loggias

at Gorhambury (*circa* 1575) (Fig. 169) and at his house in London; but the weight of the evidence seems against it.[9]

The classicism of Osborne's porticus and of the Haynes Grange Room have aroused excitement as 'anticipating Inigo Jones', but in fact they do not bear much relationship to Jones's earlier work or to his more complex and modelled classical style. It is perhaps more apposite to see them as the culminating refinement of the pure Serlian style that is to be found as an element running through English architecture from the mid-sixteenth century, with the porticus as a grander Corinthian development of the Tuscan colonnades of Hardwick (Fig. 393).

It is a very far remove from Osborne's single-minded intensity to the coloured confections of the Cure workshop, but in their own way the three generations of Cures, William, his son Cornelius and Cornelius's sons, William Junior and Edward, maintained a consistently independent house style for sixty years or so, from around 1560 to 1620, expressed in porches, chimneypieces, door-cases, fountains, minor buildings (Fig. 396) and church monuments. Something has already been said in chapters 1 and 3 about Cornelius Cure's drawings and William Cure's work at Gorhambury and elsewhere.[10] The distinctive features of the workshop are sensitive combinations of alabaster and coloured marbles, coffered barrel vaults carried on simple but handsome

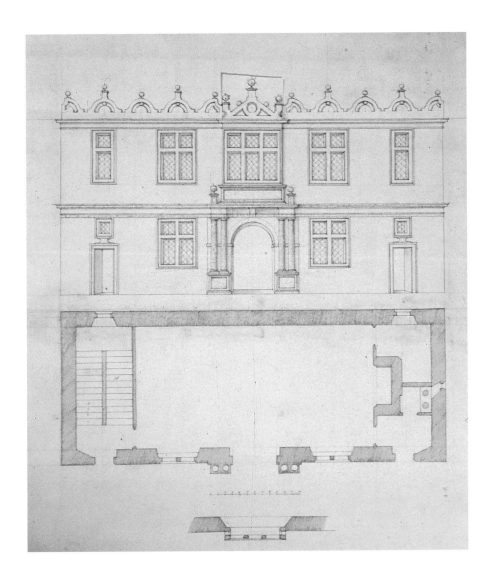

396 Another design attributed to Cornelius Cure (Hatfield, CPM 2/11).

columns and entablatures, and, especially in domestic work, delicate embellishments of swags, garlands, consoles, balusters and trophies of arms or musical instruments; although there are occasional elements taken from Vredeman, and, in one case, from Du Cerceau,[11] these are kept subordinate to the workshop style. This is expressed in the coloured classicism of the Gorhambury porch and chimneypiece and a design for a door-case for Lord Burghley (Fig. 398); the more sumptuous richness of another chimneypiece design for Burghley (Fig. 397) and of the chimneypieces at Knole (Figs 434, 438); and the rich sobriety of monuments to Edward VI (Fig. 37), Mary, Queen of Scots, Sir William Cordell, Lord Burghley himself (Fig. 211), and (on convincing attributions) many others.

But in general Serlio was giving way before the increasing influence of Flemish pattern books and engravings, with an occasional input from Du Cerceau or the German designs of Wendel Dietterlin. The progress can be watched in the treatment of the 'Towers of the Orders', the compressed and piled-up combinations (in effect, vertically extended triumphal arches) of the Doric, Ionic, Corinthian and sometimes also Tuscan and Composite orders, which became fashionable in late Elizabethan and Jacobean England.

In those Roman buildings that were decorated with the orders in different stages it was by no means an inevitable or even usual convention for each stage to be expressed with a different order, in hierarchy from Doric or Tuscan upwards; but it was a device employed with prominence at the Colosseum and the Theatre of Marcellus in Rome, both engraved by Serlio. The device was taken over for the façades of Italian palaces and villas and imitated in a number of French buildings; it was the most prominent feature of the Town Hall at Antwerp, and was recommended by Hans Blum and others.

The stages of the gatehouse of Somerset House were Corinthian on Ionic on Doric, and so were

399 (*facing page, top left*)
A 'tower of the orders'
dated 1575, at Ightham
Court, Kent.

401 (*facing page, top right*)
The centrepiece at
Waterston Manor,
Dorset, dated 1586.

397 and 398 (*below left and
right*) Designs by
Cornelius Cure for a
chimneypiece and
doorway for Lord
Burghley (Hatfield, CPM
2/55, CP 141 f.73).

those of the centrepieces at Lyme Park and later Waterston Manor (Fig. 401), of the Gate of Virtue at Caius College, Cambridge, of the bay windows at Longleat, and of the gatehouse at Tixall. But in all of them the orders were dispersed with some complexity or were part of a general composition. To concentrate them into a single compact tower, islanded in otherwise plain façades, called for a different approach. The result seems more an exercise in teaching. The orders show their attributes like allegorical figures displaying the attributes of Charity, Justice or Geometry.

In England, the sequence of these towers starts innocently and in an unexpectedly provincial context, in embryo at Woodbridge Abbey in Suffolk in 1561, and was more developed at the modest house of Ightham Court in Kent in 1575 (Fig. 399). Here four storeys, each of four evenly spaced and mostly rather stumpy columns on high bases, end up with a somewhat rudimentary Composite order under a plain pediment.[12] More pro-

fessional examples, all with paired columns, followed at Holdenby (*circa* 1578), of three storeys (Fig. 215); at Walworth Castle, Durham, of three storeys, part submerged by later additions, and probably dating from *circa* 1580; at Burghley, of three storeys, dating from 1585 at the latest, and earlier if the top storey of 1585 is an addition (Fig. 402); and at Stonyhurst (Fig. 404), of four storeys, an afterthought added to the forefront of the gatehouse *circa* 1592–5.[13] All these are straightforwardly classical. Vredeman's influence appears quite modestly at Old Beaupre (three storeys) in Glamorganshire, dated 1600 and perhaps carved by Bristol masons (Fig. 406); at Burton Agnes, Yorkshire (three storeys, single columns only), dated 1601; and more prominently at Merton College, Oxford (four storeys) (Fig. 403), Wadham College, Oxford, Hatfield House (three storeys), and paired in the wings of the entrance courtyard at Audley End (three storeys). All these were built at very much the same time, around

1610–12. At Hatfield and Audley End the towers are set in arcaded façades, as at Anet in France (Fig. 400). Flemish influence is especially strong on the decorated drums and bases of the Hatfield frontispiece (Fig. 405), and equally abundant on the towering mass of the Schools frontispiece at Oxford, dating from 1613–20, and the only one of the sequence to feature all five orders (Fig. 577).

The series reached a final flowering and almost literal dissolution in the frontispieces at Northampton House in London (*circa* 1607) (Fig. 351) and Bramshill in Hampshire (*circa* 1610) (Fig. 407), where one has to penetrate the froth of ornament to see that these are Towers of the Orders too, however thoroughly and, to contemporary taste perhaps, deliciously disguised. They show the inspiration, and in places the direct imitation,[14] of Wendel Dietterlin (Figs 408, 410), whose *Architectura*, published in Strasbourg in 1598, was divided into sections covering each of the five orders, but played games with them beyond anything that Vredeman de Vries had envisaged. Some artificers in England were clearly fascinated, though they did not succeed in reaching, or perhaps wish to reach, their particular pitch of nightmarish ingenuity (Figs 409, 411).

400 (*below*) The Chateau of Anet. A detail from the engraving by J. A. du Cerceau, 1579.

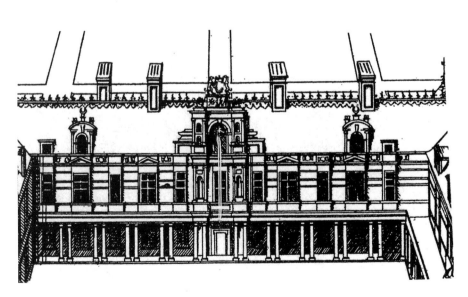

402–6   Five 'Towers of the Orders'.

402 (*facing page, top left*) Burghley House, Lincolnshire, 1585?

404 (*facing page, top right*) Stoneyhurst, Lancashire, *c.*1592–5.

403 (*facing page, bottom left*) Merton College, Oxford, 1608–10.

405 (*facing page, bottom right*)   Hatfield House, Hertfordshire, dated 1611.

406 (*right*)   Old Beaupre, Glamorganshire, dated 1600.

The obvious prototype for the towers is the three-storey one built at Anet in 1550 or earlier.[15] The motif never caught on in France, and had no French imitations. It was not engraved until (and then quite inconspicuously) it appeared in the second volume (1579) of Du Cerceau's *Plus Excellents Bastiments de France*, which certainly circulated in England (Fig. 400). At Burghley the Lord Treasurer seems to have drawn on the Anet engravings and the much larger engraving of the two-storey frontispiece at Ecouen, illustrated in the same volume; the pyramidal top-piece of Burghley is inspired by the chapel tower at Anet.[16] The Burghley frontispiece, easily accessible just off the Great North Road, could have been the parent of most of the English towers; Sir Henry Savile, who paid for the Merton one, and Sir Thomas Bodley, who, along with Savile, was the main patron at the Schools, were his friends and protégés. But Ightham, Walworth and Holdenby are all likely to have been pre-Burghley and earlier than the *Plus Excellents Bastiments*. One is left wondering whether there was an unrecorded common prototype in London, perhaps derived from direct knowledge of the tower at Anet.

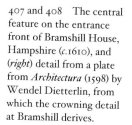

407 and 408   The central feature on the entrance front of Bramshill House, Hampshire (*c.*1610), and (*right*) detail from a plate from *Architectura* (1598) by Wendel Dietterlin, from which the crowning detail at Bramshill derives.

316

409 and 411 (*right and far right*) Dietterlin watered down, perhaps for the best. A chimneypiece and doorcase at the Charterhouse, London, the former carved by Edmund Kinsman in 1614.

410 A related plate from Dietterlin's *Architectura*.

Ornament

The frontispieces can serve as an introduction to late Elizabethan and Jacobean ornament in stone, marble, wood and plaster, a field so vast as to be unmanageable. Some of the artificers who produced it worked in wood, stone and possibly also plaster; others confined themselves to one medium; many did domestic work in addition to providing church monuments. One can pick out influences from Serlio, Du Cerceau, Vredeman and Dietterlin; many of the figurative elements derive from engravings by other Flemings, but on the whole artificers select, combine and invent, rather than straightforwardly copy. Much of this work is crude, some is overpoweringly ostentatious; but at its best there is an ebullience, a variety and a freedom of invention about the ornament of this period that is a continuous source of pleasure.

One can start off with two groups by carvers identifiably working in both wood and stone. Garret Hollemans the Elder has been discussed in chapter 3. On the strength of documentation of his vanished work at Kyre Park in Worcestershire and of his leaving there to work for Richard Barneby, probably on the Barneby monument at Bockleton in Worcestershire, he can be assigned both a group of inventive and distinctive church monuments,[17] and the related woodcarving from Holdenby House, now re-erected in the church (Figs 216, 218).[18] His work at Kyre included an overmantel of the story of *Mars and Venus*, and there are likely to have been other figurative overmantels by him at Holdenby.

No certain name has been found to attach to a group of highly individual church monuments in the Midlands, and to related domestic work; for convenience, it can be assigned to 'the Bottesford carver'. The monuments are to Henry Manners, 2nd Earl of Rutland, at Bottesford in Leicestershire, almost certainly set up well after his death in 1563 (Fig. 412); to Sir Thomas St Pol (d. 1582) and his wife at Snarford in Lincolnshire (Fig. 413); to Richard Whalley or Waley (died *circa* 1583) at Screveton in Nottinghamshire, erected, according to the inscription, by his wife in 1584 (Fig. 415); and to Edward Burnell, at Sibthorpe in Nottinghamshire, inscribed 'made anno domini 1590'. Both Burnell and Whalley had links with the Manners family.[19]

These monuments are so individual that they must be from the same workshop.[20] They provide a refreshing contrast to the products of the Southwark tomb-makers. They show a fondness for fish-scale ornament, scalloped arches and little finials, charmingly naive but far from incompetent figure sculpture, and above all inventiveness in devising variations on columns, pilasters and capitals, the latter embellished with fruit and flowers, and the end results only distantly related

to the conventional orders; the variations seem individual to this workshop and to owe little to pattern books, Flemish or otherwise.

The Bottesford monument incorporates columns with bulgy swellings in their centres, as are never otherwise found in contemporary monuments, but are common in furniture of the period.[21] This suggests a carver working in wood as well as alabaster; that this was indeed so is shown by fragments of woodwork from Screveton Manor, now re-erected at nearby Flintham Hall (Fig. 414), which include the same individual fish-scaling and fruit-and-flower capitals as on the monument in Screveton church. The same workshop must have provided the elaborate wooden chimneypiece at Baggrave Hall in Leicestershire (Fig. 416); this is so idiosyncratic that it has been accepted as interesting neo-Jacobean work of the mid-eighteenth century,[22] but in fact it has all the

412 (*facing page*) Monument to the 2nd Earl of Rutland, *c.*1580, at Bottesford, Leicestershire.

413 (*right*) Monument to Sir Thomas and Lady St Pol, *c.*1583, at Snarford, Lincolnshire. Both monuments are attributed to the unidentified 'Bottesford carver'.

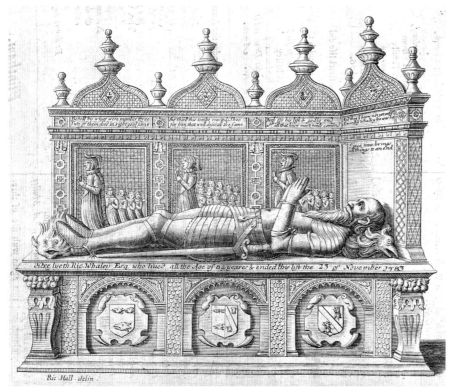

414–18　More
'Bottesford carver'
attributions.

414 (*facing page, top left*).
Woodwork from the
demolished Screveton
Hall, now at Flintham
Hall, Nottinghamshire.

416 (*facing page, top right*).
Chimneypiece, probably
of the 1580s, at Baggrave
Hall, Leicestershire.

415 and 417 (*facing page,
bottom left and right*)
Monument to Richard
Whalley at Screveton,
Nottinghamshire, erected
1584, as engraved in
Robert Thoroton's
*The Antiquities of
Nottinghamshire*, 1677, and
a detail of it.

418 (*right*)　A detail of the
panelling in the Long
Gallery at Haddon Hall,
Derbyshire, installed in
about 1589.

419 and 421 (*above left and right*) The exterior of the Red Lodge, and a design in the Fourth Book of Sebastiano Serlio's *Architettura*, 1537, from which it draws.

420 (*right*) Cartouche after Hans Vredeman deVries, from his *Multarum variarum'que protractionum . . .*, 1555.

422 (*facing page*) The chimneypiece of the 1580s in the great chamber of Red Lodge, perhaps carved by William Collins and his workshop.

SIC AMAVIT DEVS
MVNDVM, VT·FILIVM
SVVM VNICVM DEDERIT,
VT QVISQVIS EI FIDEM
HABEAT, NON PEREAT,
SED VITAM OBTINEAT
SEMPITERNAM. Iõ.3.

423 (*above*) A chimney-piece (*c.*1580s), perhaps from the Collins workshop, now in the Assize Courts, Bristol.

424 (*facing page*) A chimneypiece of *c.*1600 in the Great Chamber of South Wraxall Manor, Wiltshire, attributed to the Frynde workshop.

marks of the 'Bottesford carver'. Finally, and perhaps most intriguingly, it is irresistible to assign to him the lovely and highly individual panelling with which the long gallery at Haddon Hall was fitted out for Sir John Manners, brother of the 2nd Earl, in the late 1580s, with its peacocks, fish-scale pilasters and creative variations on the Corinthian capital (Fig. 418).[23]

The decorative work that poured out of the Bristol workshops is more conventional, but impressive in its abundance and competence.[24] It has a strong individuality and is easily identifiable. It can give an idea of what was lost in the Great Fire in London, for Bristol became London's only commercial rival, as its merchants grew in opulence and ostentation on the back of their bur-

324

geoning trade, to Europe, Ireland, and more and more to America. John Whitson, whose great chimneypiece is now in the Red Maids' School at Bristol (Fig. 430), which he founded, commissioned the celebrated *Mayflower*, though he had sold it before it set sail for New England; Robert Aldworth, whose fretted and plastered house, later St Peter's Hospital, went up in flames in the war of 1939–45, had three of his ships carved sailing across the base of his tomb in the adjacent St Peter's church.

Houses first stone-built but later of more and more fantastic jettied and carved timber-frame construction were filled with chimneypieces that grew in elaboration too, along with the panelling and plasterwork that set them off. In later centuries, as the rich of Bristol moved out of the centre, the houses became schools, warehouses, newspaper offices and tenements, or were demolished; their chimneypieces had been sold and scattered before most of the houses were blown up in 1939–45; of the twenty or so identifiable

examples only the one at the Red Lodge is in its original position. Some were moved to new locations in Bristol; more went wider afield, to country houses near and far, at least one to a London hotel, and at least two to America, where others are probably to be found.

The names of the artificers can be recovered from the Burgess and Apprentice Rolls, and some chimneypieces tentatively attributed to individuals. The records suggest two main workshops of freemasons, that of the childless Thomas Collins, who was in Bristol by 1571, taken over at his death in 1594 by John and Anthony Frynde, and John's son Nathaniel; and that of the three Birds: John the Elder and Younger, and Thomas. The elder Fryndes were active until at least 1625; the elder John Bird first appears in Bristol in 1581–2 and Thomas was working till at least 1629.

But it is Thomas Collins who can be seen as the founder of the Bristol school. He came from London, probably by way of Wilton in Wiltshire, arriving in Bristol in or before 1571, when he

became a freeman by purchase. His will shows
that he owned 'books of building' and drawing
instruments, and that he made plots; when he
died in 1594 there were six other freemasons in his
workshop and he had four deposits of Bath or
Dundry stone and two chimneypieces in store in
various parts of Bristol.[25] He was clearly the
leading mason in the city. The great classical
chimneypiece in Red Lodge (Fig. 422), erected in
the 1580s for Sir John Young, Collector of
Customs in Bristol and a friend of both Burghley
and Leicester, can convincingly be attributed to
him.[26] Its decorative cartouches derive from
Flemish engravings, which have been identified;[27]
its Corinthian entablatures and other details are
freely adapted from Serlio; a Serlio design seems
also to have provided the inspiration for its exterior, with its loggia and level roof-line (Figs 419,
421).[28]

Another chimneypiece, of noble proportions,
originally in a house in Small Street, but now only
partially surviving, and that part half-obscure

behind court fittings in the Assize Courts (Fig.
423), is quite clearly from the same workshop as
the Red Lodge chimneypiece, probably close to it
in date, and possibly even earlier; but the mastery
and brilliant under-cutting of its carving surpasses
anything at the Red Lodge, and suggests that a
carver of top quality was passing through the
workshop at the time.

The Red Lodge and Assize Court chimneypieces lead on to a dozen or so other late Elizabethan, Jacobean or early Carolean chimneypieces and at least one church monument, which
developed, with a great deal of variety, a related
but somewhat different vocabulary; the earliest of
these perhaps dates from Collins's lifetime, the
later ones can be attributed to two generations of
Fryndes: John and Anthony, and John's son
Nathaniel. John was the most important of Collins's legatees, followed by Anthony.[29]

These chimneypieces, like the first two, are all
handsomely classical, but with a strong infusion of
Flemish elements, notably terms and cartouches;

neypiece, suggesting several hands at work. A related, but separate, group have details in common, but their fireplace openings are of the conventional late Gothic type; these may possibly be products of the Bird workshop.[30]

The fireplaces were the showpieces of the houses in which they were installed. They were status symbols for opulent merchants, or for local landowners who were not going to be outdone by new men. The two most sumptuous were erected, probably within ten years of each other, by a leading Wiltshire landowner of a long-established family, Sir Walter Long, and by one of the richest Bristol merchants, John Langton. The Long chimney piece at South Wraxall Manor in Wiltshire is probably the earlier, by ten years or more (Figs 424, 425); the Langton chimneypiece was originally in a half-timbered house on the Welsh Back in Bristol (Fig. 429), but in 1906 was re-erected, along with the rest of the room, equally sumptuous in panelling and plasterwork, at New Place, Shedfield, in Hampshire.[31]

The upper stage of the South Wraxall fireplace incorporates figures of Justice and Prudence, suitable for a magistrate and landowner, and also, less obviously appropriate, of Arithmetic and Geometry, suggesting, perhaps, that Sir Walter Long had drawing skills, and may have contributed to the design, or at least the iconography, of his great chimneypiece. Prominent, in between these four symbolic figures, is a goat-legged faun or satyr – perhaps Pan, god of flocks, who would be appropriate for Long, who was a grazier on a large scale. Below are four hulking great terms, imprisoned in blocks of stone; the head of the fifth has got, as it were, detached, and supports an Ionic column, and the satyr above it, over the fireplace opening. There is a similar device, with two heads instead of one, at New Place.

These chimneypieces perhaps beat the big drum too loudly; the less overpowering products of the workshop are easier to appreciate. At South Wraxall there are no less than four others

but never with the bulging Flemish-style entablatures or brackets found elsewhere in England. Their fireplace openings are always square-headed and surrounded with rich classical mouldings; they often incorporate running acanthus ornament; small roundels or rosettes (an expansion from Serlio) are frequently distributed at intervals along otherwise plain friezes (Figs 424, 429). The figurative sculpture can be of good quality, but is variable, even on the same chim-

cathedral. At this stage he had not worked out his own distinctive style. This appears in the second of his two documented works, a monument to Henry Berkeley in the church at Berkeley in Gloucestershire, made in 1615. This is so idiosyncratic that on the strength of it a sizeable group of work can be attributed to him.[33]

Baldwin was not a Bristol man, and was not apprenticed there. He moved around various Gloucestershire locations. In 1608 he was living at Nether Lypiatt, and was described as 'joyner'. In his 1615 contract for the Berkeley monument he is 'carver', and living at Stroud.[34] At some stage after this he moved to Gloucester, where he stayed until his death in 1645. In the burial register of St Nicholas, Gloucester, he is described as 'stone cutter', and on his memorial tablet in the church as 'carver, whose workes in severall partes (without flattery) speak his praise'. He would seem to have been one of those 'carvers' who could work in both wood and stone, although no joinery by him has been identified. The fact that he was Surveyor of Defences during the siege of Gloucester by the Royalists in 1643, and in December 1644 was appointed General Surveyor of City Works, suggests that he may on occasions have acted as surveyor for whole buildings, and even have designed them.

His domestic *chef-d'oeuvre* is the chimneypiece at Ampney Park in Gloucestershire (Fig. 431).[35] This incorporates a number of features found in other monuments or chimneypieces attributed to him, and mostly deriving from Vredeman or other Flemish engravings: cartouches enriched with strapwork, garlands, swags and animals; columns with the lower portion of their drums decorated; and bracketed-out entablatures. This work is always of stone, but embellished with roundels or other small-scale details of polished black jet, set like jewels into the whole.

Baldwin combined all these features in an original manner, for he had a gift for creative design. The central relief of the Ampney chimneypiece (Fig. 432), for instance, is closely copied from an

431 and 432 (*above and facing page top*) Chimney-piece at Ampney Park, Ampney Crucis, Gloucestershire, *c.*1615, attributed to Samuel Baldwin.

433 (*facing page, bottom*) The monument to Giles Reed (d. 1611) and his wife at Bredon, Worcester-shire, attributed to Baldwin.

of outstanding quality (Figs 427, 428), the earliest dated 1598, so varied in their design, indeed, that one wonders if they all came from the same work-shop.[32]

Another identifiable West Country craftsman, Samuel Baldwin, produced both chimneypieces and church monuments in considerable quanti-ties. He first appears in 1606, making a monu-ment for John Yonge and his two wives in Bristol

engraving after Maarten de Vos of *Miles Christianus*, the Christian Knight. But though the carving of the figures in the relief is somewhat naive (notably more so than the symbolic figures between Corinthian columns to either side), the way in which they are framed against plain ashlar, and in which the Knight himself and the lascivious nude (representing the World and the Flesh) on whom he is trampling are brought forward by the colonette that leads the eye up to them, make it considerably more effective than the overcrowded engraving.[36]

Similarly effective is the way in which two of the most sumptuous of the monuments attributed to him play a counterpoint between the lower order of pilasters, which frames kneeling figures to either side, and the Corinthian columns and entablatures of the centre, set in front of them and rising from a higher level (Fig. 433). In the 1620s and 1630s (probably) chimneypieces that can be attributed to Baldwin become quieter: handsome compositions of two storeys of Corinthian columns framing coats of arms sometimes surrounded by laurel wreaths, from which Vriesian elements have largely vanished (Fig. 435).[37]

Another group of classical chimneypieces, together with other features internal and external, can be associated with the Somerset mason William Arnold, though he did not necessarily carve them. They will be discussed in more detail in chapter 7, but one can look in passing at their distinctive features (Fig. 437): straightforward paired columns in the lower stage; shell-headed alcoves, on their own or between columns in the upper stage; Vriesian cartouches, filling the centre of the upper stage and above the fireplace opening in the lower stage; outsize egg-and-dart ornament and curious minuscule nudes – all this in plain stone, with no embellishment of jet or alabaster.

These Arnold chimneypieces can serve as an introduction to a large but miscellaneous selection, only a minority by documented craftsmen or with convincing attributions. They can be roughly

in the ways in which the framework can be treated. It is at its most straightforward and splendid in the great Corinthian chimneypiece dated 1585, originally in Heath Old Hall, West Yorkshire (Fig. 436), but removed to Hazlewood Castle after the scandalous demolition of the Hall in 1961. Accomplished and more elaborate later

examples are the two chimneypieces in the long gallery at Hardwick (*circa* 1595) (Fig. 510) and Cornelius Cure's chimneypieces at Knole (Fig. 439).[38] A variation was produced by setting the outer columns or terms back behind the inner ones, as was done with superb *braggadoccio* in a chimneypiece at Cobham Hall, Kent, dated 1599 (Fig. 438), one of a magnificent series in the house probably carved by the Flemish Giles de Witt,[39] and with more restraint in the chimneypiece in the library at Hatfield, which may be by Maximilian Colt.[40]

Another highly effective category consists of what might be called top-heavy chimneypieces.

434 (*above left*).
The chimneypiece in the great chamber or ballroom at Knole, almost certainly made and designed by Cornelius Cure *c.*1607.

classified under three headings, architectural (to which the Arnold group belong), sculptural and decorative.

The architectural group are all based on a secure and prominent framework of columns or terms and entablatures, but there is much variety

435 (*facing page, right*)
A later chimneypiece
once at Prinknash Priory,
Gloucestershire,
attributed to Baldwin.

436 (*above left*)
A chimneypiece carved
with the Death of Jezebel
and dated 1585, originally
at Heath Old Hall,
West Yorkshire.

438 (*above right*)
A chimneypiece, probably
carved by Giles de Witt,
and dated 1599, at
Cobham Hall, Kent.

437 (*left*) The great
chamber at Stockton
Manor, Wiltshire, as
depicted by Joseph Nash
in *Old English Mansions*,
1915 edn, with a chimney-
piece attributed to
William Arnold or his
circle.

440 The Long Gallery at
Hatfield House, Hertford-
shire, with one of its two
chimneypieces, carved by
Samuel Jenever, in the
foreground.

439 (*facing page*) The
chimneypiece in the
Withdrawing Room at
Knole, Kent, almost
certainly carved by
Cornelius Cure, *c*.1607.

In these the lower stage of pilasters supports
an upper stage of columns, or there are paired
columns in the upper stage above single ones in
the lower, or the upper stage is cantilevered out
so as to project beyond the lower. Examples of
these various treatments can be found used with
restraint in Robert Pinckney's chimneypiece of
1583 in the library at Windsor,[41] and more ebul-
liently in great Jacobean chimneypieces at
Quenby Hall in Leicestershire (Fig. 441a), Canons
Ashby in Northamptonshire (Fig. 442) and Fountains Hall in Yorkshire (Fig. 441b). The two chimneypieces in the long gallery at Hatfield are
joiners' not masons' work, but follow the same
technique of design (Fig. 440). The Fountains
Hall chimneypiece with its columns between

obelisks in the upper stage is an especially brilliant and original design, somewhat let down, as
too often at the period, by the quality of the figure
sculpture.[42]

Not surprisingly, tours de force such as these
provoked a reaction. Baldwin's later chimneypieces are an example; so, in a different vein, are
two chimneypieces at Bramshill, Hampshire,
effective exercises in strong but simple patterns
and two colours of marble: one is just of black and
white marble (Fig. 443), in the modish new combination that arrived around 1620, in reaction
against earlier Jacobean polychromy.[43]

In 'sculptural' chimneypieces, the figure sculpture is more important than the architectural
framework, if indeed there is one. Two fine exam-

441a and b Early
seventeenth-century
chimneypieces at
Fountains Hall, North
Yorkshire (*far right*), and
Quenby Hall
Lincolnshire (*right*).

442 (*facing page*) The
great chamber at Canons
Ashby, Northampton-
shire.

ples are Maximilian Colt's chimneypiece made
circa 1609–11 for Lord Salisbury's 'book chamber'
at Hatfield (Fig. 444), and the later chimneypiece
attributed to Nicholas Stone at Newburgh Priory
in Yorkshire.[44] There is an elegance and sophistication about both of these that was new to
England, and was indeed an importation from the
contemporary Low Countries, in which by this
date Vriesian Mannerism, though still going
strong in England, was outdated. Nicholas Stone
had trained in Amsterdam *circa* 1607–13 under the
Dutch architect and sculptor Hendrik de Keyser,
whose daughter he married. Although best known
for his church monuments, his notebooks list
thirty-four chimneypieces supplied by him; of
these all but that at Newburgh Priory have disappeared, though the chimneypiece in the great

chamber at Charlton House, Kent, with its two
supremely elegant caryatids, has also been attributed to him (Fig. 445). Colt was a Fleming from
Arras, who had come to England in the mid-1590s
by way of Utrecht. The book-room chimneypiece
at Hatfield and his beautiful monument to Lord
Salisbury in Hatfield church are his masterpieces,
though his chimneypiece in the great chamber at
Hatfield, dominated by a life-size figure of James
I (of stone, but painted to imitate bronze) and the
monument to Elizabeth I in Westminster Abbey,
with which he made his reputation, are handsome
enough. The chimneypieces now in the Winter
Dining Room at Hatfield (Fig. 446), and in the
hall at Cobham Hall in Kent (Fig. 447), may be by
another hand or hands, more ebullient, possibly
coarser, but undoubtedly effective.[46]

443 (*right*) A chimney-piece of *c*.1620 at Bramshill House, Hampshire.

445 (*far right*) The chimneypiece in the Great Chamber of Charlton Park, Greenwich, attributed to Nicholas Stone.

444 (*right*) The chimneypiece made *c*.1609–11 by Maximilian Colt, for what was originally the Earl of Salisbury's 'book chamber' at Hatfield.

446 (*far right*) Chimneypiece in the winter dining room, Hatfield.

447 (*right*) Chimney-piece in the hall of Cobham Hall, Kent.

448 (*far right*) Justice and Peace carved on the chimneypiece of *c.*1625 in the Little Drawing room at Apethorpe Hall, Northamptonshire.

Sculptural chimneypieces proliferated under James I, particularly in the second half of his reign, carrying on into that of his son. At Apethorpe in Northamptonshire around 1625, the gallery chimneypiece is dominated by a figure of King David, playing a harp (Fig. 256); in the little drawing room the customary terms in the overmantel stretch out their hands to pluck open a canopy, revealing figures of Justice and Peace (Fig. 448).[47] Up in the north of England an unidentified Newcastle carver, probably an immigrant Low Countryman, was prolific in the 1620s and '30s in producing, in wood and more rarely stone, lavish figurative overmantels based on Flemish engravings;[48] and there are similarly teeming overmantels of about 1610 at Burton Agnes in Yorkshire.[49]

In contrast to this northern group, two extraordinary chimneypieces at Crewe Hall in Che-

449 A chimneypiece of *c.*1620 at Crewe Hall, Cheshire, as restored after a fire in the nineteenth century.

450 The chimneypiece of *c*.1590 once in the Long Gallery, Copped Hall, Essex, as drawn in the eighteenth century.

The earliest example is the great chimneypiece, known only from a drawing, in the demolished gallery at Copped Hall, Essex; it cannot be later than 1595 (Fig. 450).[52] A few miles away, at Langleys in the same county, the two unforgettable Jacobean chimneypieces in the dining room and drawing room are survivors, not securely dated, from an earlier house remodelled in the eighteenth century (Fig. 454). They must relate to Copped Hall, if only by imitation: both, but the drawing room chimneypiece in particular, seem as though the sumptuous sea of plasterwork in the ceiling had spilled over down the walls. Two chimneypieces at Aston Hall, Warwickshire, which cannot date from before 1618, are almost as overpowering (Fig. 453).[53]

The taste that produced these tours de force can be seen, in a less extreme form, in two chimneypieces of *circa* 1610 at Charlton House, Greenwich; and one has to look carefully at the chimneypiece, installed as late as the 1630s, at Baddesley Clinton in Warwickshire to recognise, under the embellishments, a fairly close version of one of Serlio's Composite designs (Figs 451, 452) (still further disguised by the fact that, in being moved in the mid-eighteenth century, the pieces of the lower pilasters were re-set in the wrong order).[54] Externally, something of the same quality informs the frontispieces, already discussed, of Charlton House, Northampton House (Fig. 351) and Bramshill (Fig. 407).

To adopt a different approach, and consider materials rather than styles, one can take a look at joiners' work, and then at plasterwork, brickwork and carpenters' work.

shire, dating from *circa* 1620 or later, are probably by London artificers (Fig. 449), for Sir Randolph Crewe, who built the Hall, was an eminent London lawyer.[50] They could have been carved, and were probably influenced by, one of the artificers who worked on the triumphal arches erected for the entry of James I to the City of London in 1604. These seem in a different world from the contemporary sophistication of Stone and Colt; and yet, undisciplined though they may appear, they are almost the only structures of the period that can be shown to have been erected on a rigid mathematical grid.[51]

The sculpture of the arches and related chimneypieces shade off into the last class, the 'decorative' chimneypieces and their fellows, in which both architecture, if there is any, and figures are submerged in ornament. As so often in the period, these very distinctive chimneypieces developed in parallel with other types, rather than sequentially to them.

Joiners

For joiners, hall screens are a good starting-off point. These were as much status symbols as were chimneypieces. They were suitable vehicles for displays of heraldry and the family's ancestry and good connections. Some of them were of stone or

451 and 452   A chimney-piece of *c*.1580 at Baddesley Clinton, Warwickshire, and (*above right*) the Composite chimneypiece from the Fourth Book of Sebastiano Serlio's *Architettura*, 1537, from which it derives.

even marble, but the great majority were of wood, the larger and more elaborate screens on a framework provided by carpenters, but with their ornamental exteriors provided by joiners. In the nineteenth and early twentieth centuries screens of wood were frequently stained dark brown to give them an antique look. It makes them gloomily overpowering; in light coloured wood, embellished with gilding and with bright colours on the heraldic shields, they would have been much more festive.

Two screens were especially significant: the screen made for the Duke of Somerset, at Somer-set House, of which no record survives, and the screen of the 1570s and perhaps later in the hall of the Middle Temple, which is still in existence.

That the Somerset House screen was important is suggested both by the stature of Somerset himself and by the story of what happened to it. According to Stow, in his *Survey of London*, it was never set up, owing to Somerset's fall; instead, as Stow wrote when describing the enlargement of St Bride's, Fleet Street, 'the partition between the old work and the new, sometime prepared as a screen to be set up in the hall of the Duke of Somerset's house at Strand, was bought for eight

453 (*facing page*)
A chimneypiece of *c.*1620
at Aston Hall,
Birmingham.

454 (*right*)   An early
seventeenth-century
chimneypiece in one of
two sumptuously
decorated rooms at
Langleys, Essex.

Within the drawing, inscribed text reads:

A Platte
· at ·

For A Screene
· worsoPe ·

To bee Builte
manner

6½   6½

A Screen at Worsop Manner by Smithson

455 Robert Smythson's design for a screen for Worksop Manor, *c.*1580 (SM. DWGS 1/26).

score pounds and set up in the year 1557'.[55] It was burnt with the rest of the church in the Great Fire of 1666.

Stow's wording is not clear-cut, but suggests a timber screen. The sum of £160 was a lot of money for a second-hand fitting and it must have been sizeable or elaborate, and perhaps both; it is likely to have been based on a framework of columns and entablatures, and was perhaps of two stages. One can wonder whether Robert

Smythson's two-storey screen designs for Worksop (Fig. 455) and his screen at Wollaton, with its probably envisaged second storey, were influenced by it.

A classical framework, sometimes embellished but always predominating, and possibly influenced by the Somerset House screen, can be found in other hall screens from the 1570s on into the 1590s: at Seckford Hall in Suffolk (Fig. 456); Bowringsleigh in Devon (probably by the

344

456 A hall screen, perhaps of the 1560s, once at Seckford Hall, Suffolk.

were solicited from the members of the Middle Temple in 1574.[57] But its appearance suggests a more complicated history than just erection in the later 1570s. For there is not only a strong contrast in character and design between the lower and the upper stages, but also even the lower stage has a double nature.

It is based on a straightforward Doric order and entablature, punctuated by two round-arched openings with Victories in the spandrels. But between the Doric capitals and entablature an entire second entablature has been infiltrated, far less 'correct', made up of a pulvinated frieze, bulging and richly carved, under a row of dog-tooth faceting. One can only surmise whether this curious combination was envisaged from the start, or whether the extra frieze, and possibly the unassuming but lively and elegant terms between the columns, were added either during or after construction, to give the screen greater height or importance.

The upper level is a far more overpowering and complex composition, conceived in the full flood of Flemish Mannerism. It is based on an Ionic order, as was suitable for the stage above the Doric, but all that survives of Ionic columns are their capitals, perched on the heads of cross-armed terms, and the entablature bears no resemblance to an accepted Ionic one, but is swamped with brackets, miniature cartouches and masks; and between the terms are smaller figurers of goat-legged satyrs or Pans, hanging arches, and luscious cartouches derived from Antwerp engravings by Benedetto Battine, alternating with allegorical figures in alcoves.[58]

The Battine cartouches were engraved in 1553, and in general there is nothing in the Flemish Mannerist detailing of the upper stage that could not have dated from the 1570s. But, as already discussed, there was a time lag in the arrival of Flemish Mannerism in England, and it is more likely that the upper stage was added in the 1590s, though one would like to have some evidence.

Exeter joiner Nicholas Baggett) (Fig. 472); Parham and Cuckfield Halls in Sussex; Charterhouse (1571) (Fig. 457) and Grey's Inn (1570s) (Fig. 458) in London; Hardwick Hall (1590s) and Montacute (*circa* 1600) (Fig. 520) – the two last, unlike the others, of stone.[56]

The great screen in the hall of the Middle Temple is impressive and important, but also puzzling (Figs 459, 460). Only one piece of documentation for it is known: subscriptions for it

457 (*above left*) The hall screen at the Charterhouse, London, dated 1571.

458 (*above right*) Hall and screen at Grey's Inn, London. The hall, 1556–8, the screen perhaps *c.*1570.

459 (*facing page*) Looking down the Middle Temple Hall, London, to the screen. The hall built *c.*1562–5, subscriptions for the screen solicited 1574.

The hall screens of Grey's Inn and the Middle Temple were followed on somewhat later by the screen in Lincoln's Inn, still *in situ* in the Old Hall, so called because it was replaced on a different site by Hardwick's far larger Victorian hall. The screen was erected in 1624 (Fig. 461), and, as is not the case with the other legal halls, the joiner is known: he was Robert Lynton or Linton, an Englishman who was Warden of the London Joiners' Company in 1622 and Master in 1627.[59] On a stylistic basis Lynton can confidently be credited with the elaborate hall screen at Crewe Hall in Cheshire, put up at about the same time by Sir Randolph Crewe, who was a bencher of Lincoln's Inn (Fig. 462).

These screens have moved on from the architecture of the Middle Temple screen, in which the terms dominate and almost efface the orders, to an architecture in which terms and figurative sculptures are played down or omitted altogether, and are replaced by nobbles, bosses and straps, sometimes applied to columns. Prominent in each of them is an aedicule containing a false perspective in marquetry. There is a little influence, but not all that much, from Wendel Dietterlin's *Architectura*; Vredeman de Vries has all but disappeared.

The Inns of Court were not only attended by most ambitious or social young men of their day, whether they were going on to be lawyers or not, but its members also put on entertainments in their halls that were attended by government officials and courtiers, and were fashionable and much talked about. The halls were, as a result, as

346

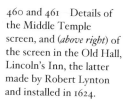
460 and 461 Details of the Middle Temple screen, and (*above right*) of the screen in the Old Hall, Lincoln's Inn, the latter made by Robert Lynton and installed in 1624.

well known as any contemporary buildings in England. The influence of the Middle Temple Hall, in particular, can be seen in a group of country house screens put up in the early seventeenth century at Knole (Figs 463, 465), Audley End and Hatfield. They are all without columns, but elaborate with terms, cartouches and grotesques, like the upper stages of the Middle Temple screen; unlike it they are also rich in family heraldry and crests. The Knole and Audley End screens could well be by the same joiner or joiners, almost certainly drawn from the artificers

employed in the King's Works, but no documentation survives. The two screens at Hatfield, at either end of its hall, are documented as carved by a German, John Buck or de Boeke, who also carved the staircase there (Fig. 494), and was employed for Anne of Denmark at Somerset House;[60] but the Knole and Audley End screens must be by a different hand.

There are other grand screens of the same period, out of London and not by London artificers, but possibly influenced by them. The earliest is the hall screen at Longleat, probably carved in 1578 by the French joiner Adrian Gaunt but not the most interesting of the Longleat work.[61] Then comes the very handsome screen (1605) in the hall of Trinity College, Cambridge, carved by the joiner-cum-carver Francis Carter, who

348

462 The hall screen at Crewe Hall, Cheshire, possibly also carved by Robert Lynton in the 1620s

possibly designed it (Fig. 464).[62] The screens of 1610–13 in the hall and chapel at Wadham College, Oxford, were made by the joiner John Bolton,[63] to whom on stylistic grounds can be assigned the contemporaneous screen in Jesus College.

These hall screens were the showpieces of their times, but they were accompanied by a mass of other joinery all over the country: panelling, chimneypieces, elaborate internal porches and embellishments to staircases in houses, and screens, pulpits, fonts and bench-ends in churches. As

with the hall screens, these can be put roughly into three stylistic groups: classical, Vredeman de Vries Mannerist and Dietterlin Mannerist. Most are undocumented, and one should be cautious about making attributions because Elizabethan and Jacobean England was awash with joiners, since the numbers of native-born ones were constantly added to by immigration. Sir John Petre, at Thorndon Hall in Essex, employed five different lots of joiners or carvers within five or six years to fit up different rooms in his house.[64]

There are obvious links between this joiners' work and contemporary stone or marble chim-

463 and 465 (*facing page, top and above*) The hall screen of *c*.1605 at Knole, Kent.

464 (*facing page, bottom*) The screen in the hall of Trinity College, Cambridge, 1605.

neypieces, not least because, if due to 'carvers', they may often be the work of the same person. But wood, being more malleable, encouraged more in the way of decoration, carved or incised, not always advantageously: there is all too much fussy mediocre joinery still surviving that one looks at with more resignation than pleasure. More interesting is the infiltration of motifs drawn from medieval sources, such as dragons, hops and grapes, and green men.

Of classical joinery the most remarkable is the 'Haynes Grange Room' already described at the beginning of this chapter (Fig. 394). In a quite different vein of Antwerpian classicism is the celebrated room of *circa* 1580 fairly recently returned to Sizergh Castle, after a long sojourn in the Victoria and Albert Museum (Fig. 466). A combination of pilasters and traceried openings on colonettes, in the manner of Vredeman de Vries church designs, is enriched with much delicate inlay; and the internal porch is finished by a little temple or rotunda, surmounted by a statue of a cherub.[65]

Sometimes an individual joiner or carver can be recognised, but all too often cannot be given a name. In the West Country, Nicholas Baggett of Exeter has already been referred to, in connection with his documented door of 1594 in Exeter Guildhall, and the screen attributed to him at Bowringsleigh (Fig. 472); two other doors in Exeter, of which only one survives, may be by his hand.[66] An anonymous joiner at work in Devon, and probably also from Exeter, was responsible for idiosyncratic work at Bradfield (Fig. 467) and Bradninch, mostly still in position, and at the Grange, Broadhembury, which has gone to America.[67] He specialised in highly decorated columns, little tabernacles on miniature columns containing figures of animals or humans, and much other gay, if naive, figurative carving. He employed a little Vredemanesque strapwork, and for his figurative overmantel panels was probably using pattern books that have not been identified. At Bradfield his work is highly coloured, and although its present colouring appears to be nineteenth century, it may well have replaced something similar. In all three houses elaborate joinery was accompanied by equally elaborate plasterwork.

In the Midlands, the tantalising work in different materials of the 'Bottesford carver' has

467 and 468 Early
seventeenth-century
internal porches at
Bradfield, Devon, and
(*above right*) Broughton
Castle, Oxfordshire.

466 (*facing page*) A room
of *c*.1580 at Sizergh Castle,
Westmoreland.

already been referred to, and so have the luscious northern overmantels of the 1620s and 1630s, probably by an immigrant carver based on Newcastle. Two immensely elaborate but grandly designed Jacobean chimneypieces, one part of a panelled room made for Rotherwas near Hereford (Fig. 471), the other last recorded in a house in King's Lynn in Norfolk (Fig. 470), look as though they had travelled east and west from the same joiner's workshop in London; the one from Rotherwas, dated 1611, is now at Amherst College in Massachusetts; the other has disappeared.[68] Three rather imposing triple-decker chimneypieces, at Levens Hall in Westmorland (Cumbria), Astley Hall in Lancashire (Fig. 469) and Gilling Castle in Yorkshire, could well be the work of one artificer, perhaps based on York.

The Gilling chimneypiece and a smaller chimneypiece in an adjacent room have the additional feature of inlay. In his book on heraldry, published in 1610, Edmund Bolton wrote: 'At St Olave's in Southwark you shall learn among the joyners what *Inlayes* and *Marquetrie* mean.'[69] Inlaying was clearly a speciality of the Low Countries immigrants who congregated in Southwark; the more elaborate examples in England relate closely enough to examples of Flemish marquetry, such as the door and surround from Antwerp Town Hall, now in the Victoria and Albert Museum.[70] Many, and perhaps most, of the relatively few examples to be found in English work of the period must have been the work of immigrant joiners. Bolton talks as though the technique was still relatively unfamiliar in England in 1610, but

in fact some outstanding Elizabethan examples survive or are known to have existed. In addition to the room at Sizergh, and the Gilling chimney-pieces, all probably dating from the 1580s, the inventory of Chatsworth of 1603 shows that room after room was filled with inlay, of which three panels (Fig. 473) and the famous 'Eglantine' table now at Hardwick (Fig. 270) are survivors;[71] one of the panels is dated 1576, and some at least of the inlay may have been the work of 'Tayler the inlayer', who was paid for work at Chatsworth in the years 1577–9.[72] There was another inlaid room at Raglan Castle, the richly inlayed over-mantel from which, perhaps late Elizabethan rather than Jacobean, is now at Badminton (Fig. 474).[73]

Tapestry was more prestigious than panelling, however elaborate, but was much more expensive. A grand Elizabethan room combined panelling or tapestry, a two-tier chimneypiece of wood, stone or marble, patterned glazing incorporating heral-dic glass, and a ceiling and possibly frieze of dec-orative plasterwork.

Plasterers

Something has already been said in chapter 3 about the Fontainebleau-inspired plasterwork of Nonsuch and Broughton, and the geometrically patterned ceilings, sometimes interspersed with pendentives, that succeeded them.[74]

470 and 471 Jacobean chimneypieces, perhaps from the same London workshop: (*facing page*, *right*) once at Rotherwas House, near Hereford, dated 1611; (*right*) once in a house at King's Lynn, Norfolk.

472 The hall screen at Bowringsleigh, Devon, attriburted to Nicholas Baggett, *c.*1600.

473 A marquetry panel of *c.*1576 from Chatsworth, now at Hardwick Hall.

474 A marquetry overmantel from Raglan Castle, Monmouthshire, now at Badminton House, Gloucestershire.

Below ceilings and friezes plasterwork increasingly offered an alternative to stone and wood, especially for overmantels, which could copy in plaster the motifs found in other materials, of terms, coats of arms and, more rarely, figurative panels. Such plaster panels are rare in the late sixteenth century, but become common enough deep into the next century, especially in the west. Many were based on engravings, sometimes interpreted and adjusted with naive charm, seldom

356

with more than that. Only at Hardwick in the 1580s and 1590s, and in a few outlying overmantels probably by Hardwick plasterers, did they reach memorable heights of invention and fancy, especially in the overmantels in the Old Hall and the forest friezes in Old Hall and New: the High Great Chamber frieze with its idyllic forest population so much more vivid than the sophisticated smoothness of the *Story of Ulysses* in the Flemish tapestries that hang below (Fig. 475).[75]

There is, in fact, a good deal of variety in quality at Hardwick. The names of Abraham Smith, John Marcer and Robert Orton occur in the accounts, but there is little to show who did what, though Smith was probably the ablest, and earliest in the field.[76] An odd feature of Hardwick is that there is so little ornamental plaster on the ceilings. But on the whole it was for what was going on on the ceilings that English plasterwork was remarkable.

Their linear patterns were endlessly inventive, as they ran their delicate network of ribs, or rippled their pendentives, over ceilings flat and arched; and soon the spaces between the ribs began to fill up equally delicately with different motifs – flowers or sprays growing out of the ribs, crests or coats of arms free-standing between them (Fig. 477). In the seventeenth century the ribs grew thicker and became broad bands of ornament; the pendentives, where they were still to be found, became more elaborate; the infill increased in size and was made up of strange animals, Vredemanesque cartouches, entire figurative scenes; the sense of linear pattern was replaced by an all-over richness, not unlike that of contemporary fabrics – including carpets and embroideries imported from the East – and probably influenced by them.

The earliest documented example of broad-rib plasterwork that Claire Gapper has discovered

475   A detail of the frieze and coat of arms in the High Great Chamber at Hardwick Hall, Derbyshire.

476 The Long Gallery at Chastleton House, Oxfordshire, c.1610.

477 The Great Chamber at Kinnersley Castle, Herefordshire, c.1590.

dates from 1582–4, and is on the ceiling of Queen Elizabeth's new gallery at Windsor Castle, now part of the Royal Library.[77] Most of the surviving broad-rib work dates from after 1600; it reached its greatest opulence in the 1620s, and went on into the 1630s. But one can look in passing at an intermediate stage, the ceiling in the long gallery at Chastleton (Fig. 476), where the ribs have only slightly thickened, interlace with each other and flow out into roses in a lovely rippling pattern all the way along 72 feet of arched ceiling.

In the ceilings of the main rooms at Knole, installed (almost certainly) by Richard Dungan, the King's Master Plasterer, between 1605 and 1608,[78] it is the varied geometric patterns of the broad ribs that dominate; the spaces in between are left blank, or contain relatively modest sprays

or crests in low relief. In the long gallery ceiling at Blickling, plastered by Edward Stanyon in 1620–21, the spaces between the ribs have filled up with strapwork and emblematic figures.[79] The Jacobean counterpane ceiling had emerged in all its lushness in the years between. Dungan may have been heading that way in his final and most ambitious work, which followed immediately on Knole: the ceiling of the short-lived second banqueting house at Whitehall, 120 feet long and 37 feet wide, enriched with forty-four pendants, large and small, with 'compartments' and 'carved boys' – perhaps little winged angels attached to the bigger pendants.[80] It all went up in flames and unrecorded in 1618.

Plasterers and patrons now had a choice between the Knole and Blickling approach; and James Lee, who succeeded Dungan as Master Plasterer in 1610, evolved a third manner, an all-over covering of broad shallow ribs in very complex patterns, but with little ornament, as in the long gallery at Hatfield.[81]

In the early seventeenth century London-style plasterwork in all its varieties spread over England and beyond (Fig. 478). One can surmise lines of communication provided by travelling Londoners, or country apprentices articled to London workshops; there is some documentation, but not enough. Stanyon went from London to Norfolk in 1620; in or before 1617 Richard Cobb, Robert Whitehead and perhaps other Londoners exported their skills and style to Scotland,[82] perhaps stopping at Chillingham Castle in Northumberland on the way, to plaster the great chamber

479 The ceiling in the former great chamber at Prideaux Place, Padstow, Cornwall, *c.*1630.

there. Something similar may have happened in the West Country.[83] The ceiling of the great chamber in a merchant's house in Barnstaple is dated 1620; the ceiling of the great chamber at Herringston in Dorset must date from between 1617 and 1623;[84] the sumptuous ceilings at Prideaux Place (Fig. 479) and Lanhydrock in Cornwall (Fig. 480) are probably a little later. These are all close enough to the full London manner, and provide the highlights of a mass of Jacobean and Carolean plasterwork in the west, to be found at all levels, in country houses, in the town mansions of rich merchants, and in modest farmhouses. But there is a sad lack of solid evidence. It has been tempting to assign too much to two known names, Robert Easton of Stogursey in Somerset and the Abbot family of Frithelstock, near Barn-

staple; though a case can be made out for John Abbot as the plasterer of the ceilings at Barnstaple, and possibly at Herringston, Prideaux Place and Lanhydrock.[85]

A feature of all four ceilings are their magnificent openwork pendants, of great size, made possible by a strengthening of metal armatures. At Herringston one of these carries little human figures, as in the observation car of a balloon. One can wonder if these were Dorset versions of the 'boys' in the ceiling at Whitehall; and whether the Whitehall boys, in their turn, were inspired by the aeronautical cherubs carved on the pendants of Henry VIII's chapel at Hampton Court.

Any ambitious Elizabethan or Jacobean interior was made up of tapestry or richly carved panelling, oriental or oriental-style carpets, cushion

480 The ceiling in the Long Gallery at Lanhydrock, Cornwall, c.1630.

added the embroidered clothes and hieratic movements of the occupants, in harmony with their setting. Pictures barely featured, except in the galleries.

Little of this survives, and often much has been added; for houses to retain their plasterwork and panelling is common enough, but in succeeding centuries pictures and soft furnishings have been brought in; the panelling has been stripped or stained; the floor covering has changed; the heraldic glass and often the leaded lights have gone. In so far as they reflect different attitudes and reactions through the centuries up to the present day, such rooms can be of abiding interest; but they do not pull one back into the Elizabethan age. Perhaps empty rooms, or even ruinous ones, are the most evocative.

The High Great Chamber at Hardwick remains unique in its power (Fig. 481). Much of this derives from its plasterwork, fabrics and furniture, close enough to what was there at the time of the 1603 inventory, or shortly after, perhaps even more from the scale and the quality of the light; and the fact that the house has been lived in only intermittently since the mid-seventeenth century means that the presence of Bess of Hardwick is still strong in it. But as a great room of state it is by no means typical: no heraldic glass, no overhead plaster; though much original paint remains on the frieze it is so faded as to give only a poignant echo of its original effect. The great chamber at Gilling Castle still (no thanks to William Randolph Hearst)[86] has its joinery, plasterwork, heraldic glass and painted heraldic frieze, making up a deservedly famous ensemble (Figs 482, 269, 354); but the contents, known from an inventory of 1594,[87] have all gone: a square table, covered with a silk carpet, and five chairs at it with needlework cushions, for Sir William Fairfax and his inner family or more honoured guests; a long table, grand enough, for the rest, of walnut 'cutt and carved', with chairs and two cupboards to match, all covered with green cloth

covers and other embroidered fabrics, ceiling and/or friezes of ornamental plasterwork, heraldic glass in the elaborately leaded windows, a great two-storey chimneypiece, usually rich in heraldry, sometimes an internal porch, not very much furniture but that massive and occasionally elaborate, including a buffet loaded with plate on ceremonial occasions; to which must be

fringed with green silk; 'long cushions' of black
and red satin, probably in the windows.

All too little research has been done on the
question of colour in Elizabethan and Jacobean
interiors. There was certainly plenty, contributed
by embroideries or other textiles, by heraldic glass
and by paint applied to panelling, to other wall
surfaces and (much more sparingly) to ceilings.
Too often, paint has been scraped away, or been
repainted with colours that cannot be relied on:
if colours have survived, they have faded, or an
entirely new colour scheme has been imposed.
Gilling is invaluable because much is inlay and

glass that have not faded, and the frieze is dominated by heraldry; but even here there seems to
have been some repainting.[88]

A precious survival is the panelling, decorated
with emblems, that was uncovered some years
ago, in its original state, in the winter parlour at
Canons Ashby (Fig. 483).[89] This, combined with
the copies of designs for tombs deposited by law
in the College of Arms[90] in the early seventeenth
century, or, for that matter, with all the sumptuous clothing and jewellery shown in contemporary portraits, make it clear that, although by no
means averse to bright colours, the Elizabethans

Whether the entire decoration of one room was ever controlled by one person is another question that there is little evidence to answer. The great chamber at Gilling Castle gives that impression; perhaps even more so the interiors of the Little Castle at Bolsover in Derbyshire (Fig. 484); and two surviving drawings by John Smythson suggest that this may be so (Fig. 485).[93] The impression is far less strong in the High Great Chamber at Hardwick (Fig. 481), wonderful room though it is; but where all the artificers were working in a common tradition, clashes were unlikely to occur, even if there was no one, overruling mind.

Another curious question is the function of a 'finisher'. In 1578–9 'William Jones the finisher' worked on the decoration of rooms at Shrewsbury House, on the Thames in the City of London, along with Robert Cooke, the Clarenceux Herald.[94] One can wonder if 'finisher' was the equivalent of today's 'decorator', but Cooke's role seems to have been more important, devising heraldic stained glass and the decoration of the great chamber ceiling, while Jones was confined to supervising and to making up other glazing, probably clear. The only other known use of the term is as applied to 'Thomas Cowk, ffinyssher', who worked with John Fletcher, joiner, on 'frettinge to chamber rowfes' at Belvoir Castle in 1587.[95]

Joiners, plasterers, carvers, heraldic glaziers and painters were concerned with decoration. Construction was the realm of bricklayers, masons and carpenters, although of course their work could have a decorative aspect as well.

and Jacobeans liked these in small sections, or broken up by diaper. They looked for effects of all-over patterning, often with results of scintillating brilliance; but unlike too much modern repainting, especially of church monuments, they were never garish.

Ceilings, as far as can be established, were usually left white, probably for maximum reflection of light;[91] but heraldic convention, not perhaps unwelcome, meant that crests and armorial coats had to be coloured. From about 1615, in some royal apartments and perhaps other rooms of great people, gold was applied.[92]

Masons and Bricklayers

Although bricks were increasingly used in the sixteenth and early seventeenth centuries, especially in areas without a good building stone, both as an alternative to timber construction and as a filling between the timbers, bricklayers did not rank

high in the artificers' hierarchy. The bricklayers were not incorporated as a City of London Livery Company until 1568. There was no Master Bricklayer in the Royal Works until 1609.[96] In London they combined with the tilers; in other towns bricklayers, tilers and plasterers could be joined together. But, unlike carpenters, bricklayers do not seem to have been entrepreneurs on a considerable scale; and their craft, unlike that of the carpenters, did not call for the complicated assembly of prefabricated elements, which encouraged literacy and organising skills.

Any client who could afford it imported stone for windows, door and fireplace openings, quoins and ornamental detail, or used plaster in imitation of stone over the brickwork. The decorative skills of bricklayers were usually confined, at best, to diapering walls, or to chimney stacks of more than simple profile; these could be very effective. But elaborate ornamental brickwork did not arrive until well on in the seventeenth century.

East Anglia, especially Norfolk and much of Suffolk, where timber was in short supply, was the one area with a distinctive brick architecture under Elizabeth and James I. This was in continuation of a tradition of brick domestic buildings in the early sixteenth century. It took over from this stepped gables, pinnacled, especially at the corners, and elaborate chimney stacks. Shaped gables did not arrive until well on in the seventeenth century. The Elizabethan contribution was pediments over windows and doors, sometimes an increase in height, and frequently bay windows. Such pedimented windows were not of

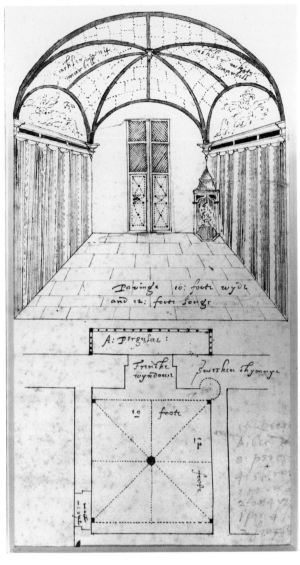

484 and 485 The Pillar
Parlour at Bolsover Castle,
*c.*1615, and (*above right*) a
design by John Smythson
for a room there
(SM. DWGS II/I(2)).

course confined to East Anglia: a good many
examples are to be found after they were inaugurated on the Strand façade of Somerset House.
But there are more of them in East Anglian
houses than anywhere else. The East Anglian
pediments were normally of brick, but often
plastered over in imitation of stone. Terracotta
ceased to be of much importance, although there
are charming classical consoles of terracotta under
the sills at Heydon Hall, Norfolk (1581–4). An
occasional feature of the early seventeenth
century are dormers extending to two storeys in
height, with sensational effect, as at Barningham
Hall, Norfolk (1612) (Fig. 486).[97]

This distinctive and lovable local style already
appeared around 1550 at Freston Tower in Suffolk
(Fig. 313), already discussed. A no doubt influential early house was Sir Thomas Gresham's long-
since-demolished Intwood Hall, Norfolk, dating,
perhaps, from the 1570s (Fig. 20), although there
is a lack of documentation.[98] Other outstanding
demolished or largely demolished examples were
Redgrave Hall, Suffolk (Fig. 487), Channons Hall,
Norfolk (*circa* 1570), and Merton Hall, Norfolk
(1613), where only the gatehouse remains.[99] But
many survive, of all sizes, often on moated sites,
as was common in East Anglia. None is more
exquisite than the miniature Thorpe Hall,

Horham, in Suffolk (Fig. 488). This property belonged to the Knyvett family of Ashwellthorpe in Norfolk, and, although there is no documentation, it is tempting to surmise that the courtier and collector of architectural books Sir Thomas Knyvett (*circa* 1539–1618) built it in the 1560s or 1570s, effectively as a lodge (though there is no record of a deer-park), before selling it later on in the century.[100]

Elizabethan and Jacobean masons were not engaged in ambitious works of constructional engineering, as in the Middle Ages. There was little vaulting outside cellars; something will be said about what there was in chapter 8, but though interesting, vaulted rooms account for only a small group in the building corpus of the period.

On the whole, masons had to take care only that their great expanses of window did not weaken walls to the extent of collapse. One example is known, though: Thornton Abbey in Lincolnshire (*circa* 1602) (Fig. 545), which, according to an account written in 1697, 'when it was finished, fell quite down to the bare ground without any visible cause, and broke in pieces all the rich furniture that was therein'.[101]

There are occasional examples of constructional ingenuity. At Hardwick the inside walls of the rooftop turrets are carried, in three cases, across the voids caused by the bays of the High Great Chamber and gallery. The walls are supported by shallow arches hidden under the roofline, and the walls of the main building to

487 *(top)* Redgrave Hall, Suffolk, 1545–54 and c.1570, from a lost seventeenth-century painting.

488 *(above)* Thorpe Hall, Horham, Suffolk, perhaps dating from the 1560s.

The Elizabethan and Jacobean carpenters were an able body of men. Most of the larger towns were built or rebuilt by them in the period, stone being reserved for a few prestigious buildings. Large areas of the country were almost entirely given over to timber-frame construction, on an increasing scale. Even buildings that appeared to be brick or stone on the outside were often built round timber-framing, and apart from the occasional vault, floors, ceilings and roofs were always of wood. Timber work was usually prefabricated, the individual elements carefully marked, lettered or numbered for correct assembly on site. For buildings of any size this was a complicated business; the master carpenter in charge of it had to be capable, certainly numerate, and preferably literate.

The carpenters, unlike the joiners, were exclusively native-born. Their craft was a traditional one. The new taste for height could lead to buildings one or two storeys higher than the medieval average, like Little Moreton Hall in Cheshire (Fig. 366), or the High House in Stafford, but they incorporated no constructional innovations, and were sometimes in trouble as a result, as the strengthening tie-beams along the gallery at Little Moreton Hall demonstrate (Fig. 367). Wide spans were also covered in the traditional way; only at Wollaton was the hall spanned by a flat ceiling, pieced together in an irregular grid on the pattern described and illustrated by Serlio: not very successfully, and necessitating the insertion of steel beams above it in modern times. A similar ceiling, on a much more modest scale, was designed for the intersection of the wings at Lyveden New Bield (Fig. 284), but never built.[102] Other examples may come to light; but most wide-span rooms were covered by gabled open timber roofs on the medieval model, even if on occasions given Renaissance trimmings. Such spans were to be found in domestic or collegiate great halls, or the

either side act as concealed buttresses. A somewhat similar arrangement supports the upper floor of the gatehouse at Burghley, where it crosses the gallery.

490 (facing page, top left)
The stone staircase at
Montacute House,
Somerset, c.1600.

491 (facing page, top right)
The staircase tower at
Canonbury Hall,
Islington, London,
perhaps dating from
the 1560s.

489   The open timber
roof in the hall of Wiston
Hall, Sussex (?1570s).

occasional large market halls, such as the two great halls built in 1558 and 1612–15 at Blackwell Hall, the London mart of the textile trade.[103] After a clutch in the 1570s (e.g., Burghley, Deene and Wiston (Fig. 489), all surviving), domestic great halls with open timber roofs became increasingly rare, but carried on into the seventeenth century with Rushton (*circa* 1630) and Lambeth Palace (1660s). The collegiate and legal roofs include Middle Temple (1562–70), Gray's Inn (1556–8) (Fig. 458), extensions to Lincoln's Inn (1583), Trinity College, Cambridge (*circa* 1600), and Wadham College, Oxford (1610–12). Remarkably late ecclesiastical examples are at Brampton

Bryan, Herefordshire (1656), and Condover, Shropshire (1660s).

The timbers of the halls at Longleat, Wollaton (Fig. 251), Burghley (Fig. 210) and Wiston in Sussex have classical embellishments, probably added to the carpenters' framework by joiners. There is little trace of classical influence in the magnificent chestnut roof at Deene (1571) (Fig. 59). The Carolean hammerbeam roof at Rushton has more-or-less Gothic tracery in the spandrels, perhaps inspired by the earlier roof at Burghley.

The only technical breakthrough made by the carpenters, but one of great importance, was the open-well cantilevered timber staircase. Earlier staircases, both of wood and stone, had been built circular or round a rectangular newel. Circular stairs were normally built with key-shaped risers of stone or wood; the circular ends were laid one above the other, to form a central newel. The more spacious square newel staircase was perhaps first pioneered in Henry VIII's palaces; there were numerous examples, for instance, at Hampton Court. If the newel was of stone, it was normally solid, though sometimes decorated with ornamental alcoves, as at Montacute (Fig. 490); in a few examples, as at Wollaton and Bolsover, it was built hollow, to contain little rooms that could be used for storage.

There is a unique and remarkable staircase in the eastern of the two octagonal staircase turrets at Grove Place, in Hampshire, where one would expect a conventional newel (Fig. 493). The staircase is open in the centre, and the string is carried up very steeply to form a kind of corkscrew column, which supports the risers rotating around a small well. The stairs are likely to be of the date of the house, which is perhaps shown by '1576', scribbled on the plaster in one of the rooms. But Grove seems to have bred no imitations, perhaps because circular stairs, whether open or closed, were going out of fashion. The future for timber stairs lay in developing the square newel type.[104]

A square or rectangular newel in a timber stair-case was of necessity hollow, built of a wooden framework, with the interstices filled with lath

492 (*below*) The open-well wooden staircase of *c.*1618 at Chilham Castle, Kent.

and plaster. A staircase of this type was in the west turret of Grove Place, until destroyed by fire in recent years;[105] and an especially fine example survives in Canonbury Tower, the remaining fragment of Canonbury Hall, Islington (Fig. 491). It perhaps dates from in or soon after 1570, the year in which the City merchant Sir John Spence bought the property. It rises in a tower to a look-out room high above the rest of the house; the newel is divided up into cupboards.

At some stage it occurred to a carpenter or his client to do without the lath and plaster, and build the stairs round an open cage of timber, fitted with balusters and a rail to prevent users falling into the central void, and giving a much lighter and more spacious effect. John Thorpe shows numerous examples, including the two matching staircases in the re-entrant angles of the entrance

369

493 The uniquely twisting staircase at Grove Park, Hampshire, probably *c.*1576.

494 The great staircase at Hatfield house, Hertfordshire, carved by John Buck (or de Baeke), c.1612.

ornamentally treated as Corinthian columns, one above the other; at Chilham these support round arches.[107]

A major step forward was made when it was realised that if the newels were discontinued between each flight, the stairs would still stand up. The earliest more-or-less dateable example of this breakthrough is at Knole in Kent, of *circa* 1605–7 (Figs 495, 496); the carpenter here was probably William Portington, the Master Carpenter of the Works,[108] and two staircases are involved, the much-illustrated main staircase, which goes only from the ground to the first floor, and the secondary stairs, between the great chamber (or ballroom) and the withdrawing chamber, which runs in a continuous cantilever through three floors around an open central well. Both staircases are separated from the main landings by arched screens.

This type of staircase may well have been pioneered in the Works; one can wonder if the staircase at the royal Woodstock Lodge in Oxfordshire, installed in 1603–4 and probably the same as the one later described as 'a fair staircase leading to the guard chamber', pre-dated Knole.[109] For a time carpenters were clearly hesitant about going over to so revolutionary and, it may have seemed, unstable a type of construction, and continuous newel stairs continued to be built; but by the 1620s the cantilevered open-well wooden stair had swept the board (Fig. 497).

These open-well staircases, leading up as they normally did to the great chamber, became status symbols. The carpenters' framework was embellished with every degree of lavishness by joiners, carvers and painters. The numerous newel heads resulting from the discontinuous newels could be surmounted by heraldic beasts, as at Knole, Theobalds and Slaugham (Sussex); by cherubs and beasts, as at Hatfield (Fig. 494); by figures of the Nine Worthies, as at Hartwell (Fig. 263); by emblematic ladies, as at Aldermaston in Berkshire; and by every variety of finial. The sides of the

front at Thomas Cecil's Wimbledon House in Surrey (Figs 74, 76). Wimbledon was dated 1588 above the entrance;[106] if the stairs were contemporary with the house, as is likely, these would be the earliest dateable examples of the type. But none of the comparatively few surviving examples of what came to be called continuous newel staircases dates from before the early seventeenth century (such as Audley End, *circa* 1605, Cranborne Manor, *circa* 1610, Chilham Castle, *circa* 1616). At Audley End the newel posts were decorated with incised ornament; at Cranborne, Chilham (Fig. 492) and elsewhere they were more

newels could be embellished with carving, the richest example of which is the great staircase at Hatfield (Fig. 494), the swags, figures and scrolling of which were carved by John Buck, who moved on to work for the queen at Somerset House.[110] Turned balusters could be replaced by more elaborate pilasters, by miniature arcades or by strapwork panels.

The main staircase at Knole is painted all over, including the walls, on which the balusters and beasts of the stairs are repeated in *trompe-l'oeil*, under and above arabesques and scenes derived from Flemish engravings, painted by Paul Isaacson, another of the Works artificers.[111] The paintings have been much repainted or overpainted; but similar work survives in its original if much

faded state at the top of the secondary stairs. These Knole staircases are the only survivors of what was a common form of decoration, which did not survive later fashions for scraping off the paint and going back to the wood, whether varnished or pickled. The Hatfield staircase was originally elaborately gilded, and probably painted too; the simple but effective painted decoration of the fine staircase at Astonbury in Hertfordshire shows up clearly in the photographs, unfortunately only black and white, in the *Country Life* article of 1910, but by the time the article was published, almost all the colouring had been stripped, as its writer laments.[112]

Elaborate carving was for the rich. Modest gentry or merchants did without it, but in their

497 Looking up the cantilevered staircase at Chastleton House, Oxfordshire, c.1610.

498 (*facing page*) Looking down the staircase of c.1620 at Treowen, Monmouthshire.

own way the resulting open-well timber staircases can be at least as impressive. They were not designed as sumptuous approaches to the *piano nobile* but rose undecorated from ground floor to attics. They were made by carpenters collaborating with turners, or carpenters also working as turners, with no frills added by joiners or carvers.

Numerous examples survive, none better than the staircase of the 1620s at Treowen in Monmouthshire, where massive turned balusters, newel posts, finials and pendants, joined by equally massive and boldly moulded rails, climb in heroic simplicity through all four floors of the house (Fig. 499).[113]

499 A perspective vista by Hans Vredeman de Vries.

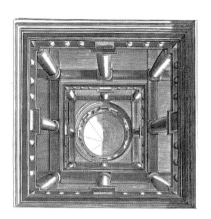

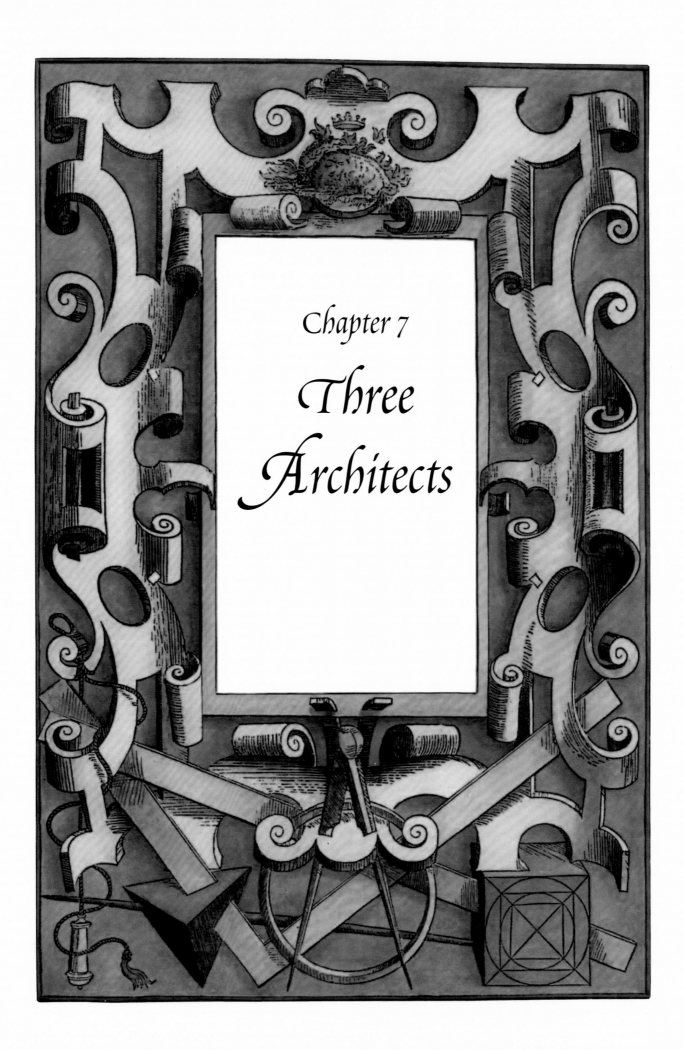

Chapter 7

*Three
Architects*

Scanning the Elizabethan and Jacobean building world, one can make a list of those about whom one would like to know more: amongst them William Spicer, Henry Hawthorne, Lewis Stocket, Alan Maynard, Simon Basil, William Collins, Samuel Baldwin, Robert Stickells, Robert Leminge, and William and Cornelius Cure. If the gaps that so tantalisingly attenuate architectural biography of the period were to be filled, they might prove to be more important, and perhaps more interesting, than had been realised; and there may be others, unknown or virtually unknown, who would grow into figures to be reckoned with. And yet one can doubt whether any of them would turn out to equal in quality and importance three men whose gifts and creative ebullience set them apart, even on the incomplete evidence that exists. These are Robert Smythson, William Arnold and John Thorpe: three remarkable men, but each very different from the others. Their names and work have appeared frequently in earlier chapters; but it is worth looking at them in isolation and attempting to estimate their achievements.

Robert Smythson

Robert Smythson[1] was much the eldest of the three, born in 1534 or 1535: that is, only a year or two after Queen Elizabeth and Robert Dudley. In the eighteenth century his descendants stated that the family had originally come from Westmorland, but it is likely that Robert himself was born, or at least brought up, in or near London.[2] He must, at any rate, have been apprenticed there to a member of the London Masons' Company, and been made free of it when his apprenticeship ended, for the Company's arms are carved on his monument in the church at Wollaton. His father was not necessarily a freemason.

His first documented appearance is at Longleat in Wiltshire. He arrived in March 1568, accompanied by five other masons, and with a covering letter from Humfrey Lovell, the Queen's Master Mason, stating that he had been working for Sir Francis Knollys, the Vice-Chamberlain. This was possibly at Caversham House, outside Reading in Berkshire. Humfrey Lovell had himself worked for the Duke of Somerset, and it would make sense, in terms of Smythson's work and career, if he had been articled to Lovell and worked under him as an apprentice at Somerset House; but this can only be surmise. It must, however, have been in the circle of London artificers, and possibly at Somerset House, that he learnt to make architectural drawings of good quality.

With Alan Maynard, Smythson was responsible for the external remodelling of Longleat in the years 1572–80. In 1576 he was involved in alterations at Wardour Castle in Wiltshire. In 1580 he went up to Nottinghamshire, where he supervised the building of Wollaton Hall for Sir Francis Willoughby in the years 1580–88. He almost certainly made plans for the remodelling of Worksop Manor for the Earl of Shrewsbury in the mid-1580s, and for the building of Hardwick Hall for Shrewsbury's estranged countess and widow during 1590–97. Among the Smythson drawings in the RIBA are plans for Burton Agnes in Yorkshire, built from 1601 to 1610, for unexecuted houses at Blackwell in the Peak in Derbyshire and Slingsby Castle in Yorkshire, probably made *circa* 1590–1600 for Bess of Hardwick's youngest son, Sir Charles Cavendish, and an elevation that seems to be a first design for Oldcotes in Derbyshire, built at Bess's expense for her eldest son, William, in 1593.

In addition, they include a number of other outstanding plans, for unidentified houses related to Smythson's other work. On the strength of his drawings and documented work, it is possible to attribute a number of other buildings to him, notably Manor Lodge, Worksop, in Nottinghamshire (1595), Fountains Hall in Yorkshire (*circa* 1600) and Wootton Lodge in Staffordshire (*circa* 1610).[3]

501 Longleat House,
Wiltshire. Robert
Smythson arrived there in
1568, and remodelled the
exterior with Alan
Maynard, 1572–80.

Robert Smythson was married by at least 1572. He had one son and three daughters living at the time of his death, which took place at Wollaton on 15 October 1614. His main legatee was his son John. John's first recorded appearance was at Wollaton in 1588, working as a junior mason. He went on to work with his father as assistant and draughtsman. Many of the inscriptions on the drawings are in his hand.[4] He features in Bess of Hardwick's account-book in March 1597, when she made presents of £1 to 'Mr Smythson the surveyor', and of ten shillings 'to his Sonne'. He was living at Wollaton in December 1600, when he married, but had left it by the time of the birth of his third daughter in 1608.

By 1612 John Smythson was surveyor for the building of the Little Castle at Bolsover, filling a role similar to that of his father at Wollaton in the 1580s. After his father's death in 1614 he remained active into the 1630s; many of the later Smythson drawings are from this period. It is likely that by the last years of their working together John Smythson was making his own contribution, and developing into more than his father's assistant.

But it is Robert who is the giant. His gift was for the creation of order. His buildings stand up and stand out as single, consistent, unified wholes (Figs 500–02). He obtained unity in a number of different ways, used individually or in combination: the full application of the orders,

502 Wollaton Hall, Nottinghamshire, built 1580–88. Robert Smythson lived at Wollaton from 1580 until his death in 1614.

treated identically on all four façades, as at Longleat and Wollaton; the similar application of an entablature only, at least above the ground floor, or on all floors, as at Hardwick; the regular background beat of huge gridded windows; and the use of towers and bay windows, square, canted or semicircular, applied with a consistent rhythm on all four façades.

At Longleat, Wollaton and Hardwick everything is square; round lanterns appeared at Worksop in the mid-1580s (Fig. 125), to be followed in later designs and buildings by semicircular or canted bay windows to soften the outlines. Four variants among the later plans all follow the same format: a rectangular bay or tower between canted bays on all four façades (Fig. 344). No building based on this plan has been traced, but the long gallery wing of Haddon Hall (*circa* 1589) seems to be a runner-up to it, on one floor and in one range only.[5] The exquisite entrance range of Wootton Lodge (Fig. 503), added to an earlier building early in the seventeenth century, follows the format on the main front, and has semicircular bays around the corners.

Smythson's apparent preference for setting his towers and bay windows away from the corners led to striking effects of stepping and recession (Fig. 504), modestly scaled at Longleat and more boldly at Hardwick. At Wollaton, where there are towers at the corners, the bold recession is in the

381

503 Wootton Lodge,
Staffordshire, *c.*1610.
Attributed to Robert
Smythson.

centre of the two main façades; there is similar recession, front and back, in one of the plans (which may be for a house at Kirkby-in-Ashfield in Nottinghamshire that Sir Charles Cavendish abandoned half-built in 1599 (Fig. 505))[6] and on the entrance front of Fountains Hall, where, owing to the house being jammed against the hill, there is effectively no rear façade (Fig. 509). The fact that the recession of Wollaton is shown in correct perspective in a Smythson drawing suggests that he appreciated the effect, and had perhaps grown to do so from learning to draw in perspective himself. It is hard to believe that he was not equally conscious of the dramatically

shifting skylines produced by his use of towers, as at Wollaton, Worksop and Hardwick, or that he did not relish the height of some of his houses, obtained by the mighty 'prospect room' over the hall at Wollaton, and by the placing of the main rooms on the second floor, as at Hardwick and Worksop, and in some of the unidentified plans – Worksop increased still more by the great gallery on the third floor.

In two known cases Smythson's plans show him extending order from the house to its surroundings: the plan for Wollaton, with its eight courts and four pavilions around the perimeter (Fig. 292), and for Slingsby Castle (Fig. 506), with its moat,

six pavilions, raised entrance court in front and secret garden behind. Something similar, simplified and adapted to the lie of the land and the existence of the Old Hall, still exists at Hardwick. All three provided an ordered approach to the houses. Order continued when the houses were entered, with a clear procession, from kitchen to hall and from hall to great chamber, and with a distinction between family and 'state' domain: all following the accepted planning of the time, but arranged with spaciousness and clarity, and fitted into the elaborate outline of the plans in such a way that (for the most part) towers and bay windows emphasised and enriched the plan and

the uses of the rooms. There is a similar clarity in all his plans.

Apart from a few drawings, all too little survives of detail that can be attributed to him. Both in drawings and attributions one can recognise the same sure sense of order. Outstanding among the drawings is the pair of screen designs for Worksop (Figs 507, 455), with their simple but satisfying rhythms of small and large arches. The courtyard entrance to the staircase at Wardour is imbued with a feeling for the strength and sobriety of the Doric order. The monumental pair of chimneypieces in the long gallery at Hardwick stands apart from the other Hardwick chimney-

505a and b   Plans by
Robert Smythson, perhaps
for Kirkby-in-Ashfield
Hall, which was
abandoned half built in
1599. These are show
plans, designed for display,
and the inscriptions and
perhaps all the
draughtsmanship,
are by Robert's son, John
(SM. DWGS 11/4(1–2)).

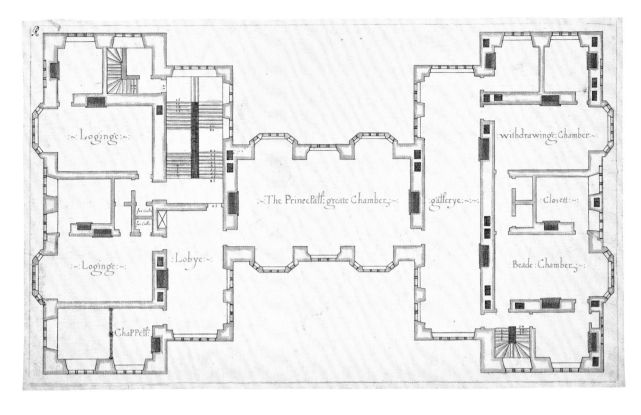

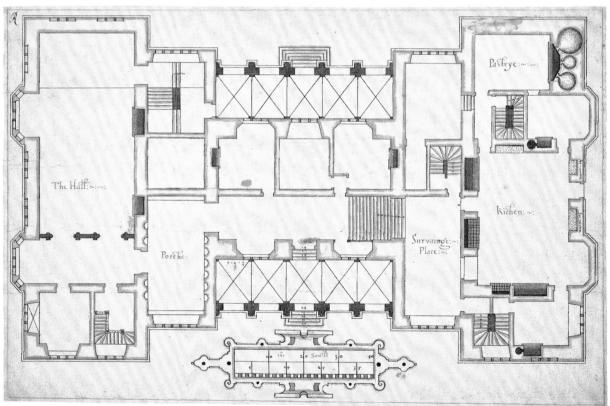

506a and b (*facing page, top
left and right*)   Robert
Smythson's unexecuted
plans, *c.*1590, for Slingsby
Castle, North Yorkshire
(SM. DWGS 1/19(1–2)).

507 (*facing page, bottom left*)
A design of the early 1580s
by Robert Smythson,
probably the first design
for a screen at Worksop
Manor, Nottinghamshire
(SM. DWGS 11/14).

508 (*facing page, bottom
right*)   Robert Smythson's
design for a gatehouse
(SM. DWGS 11/12).

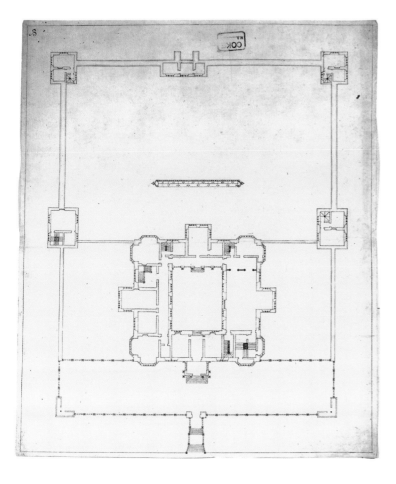

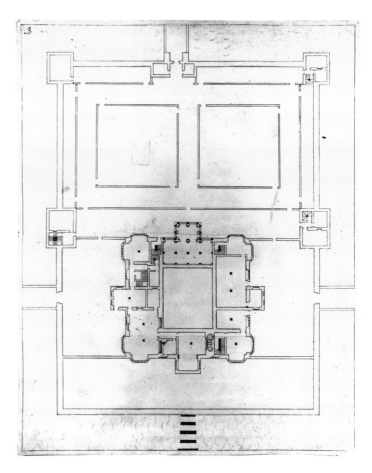

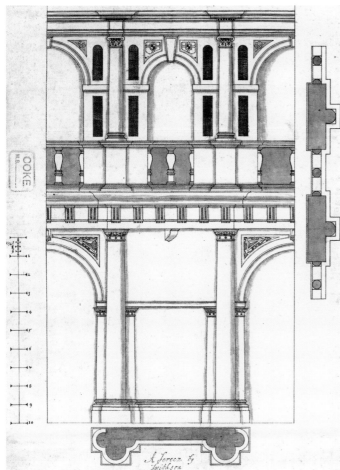

509 (*above*) Fountains Hall, West Yorkshire, built *c.*1600. The façade and ingenious plan are attributed to Robert Smythson.

510 (*facing page*) One of the two chimneypieces in the Long Gallery at Hardwick. Attributed to Robert Smythson, unlike most of the interior decoration at Hardwick.

pieces (Fig. 510). The balance between elements from Serlio and elements from Vredeman is exquisitely maintained. There is no documentary evidence that Robert Smythson designed them; but the distinctive and unusual upper entablature, with rectangular black panels between the triglyphs, is strikingly similar to the entablature of a design for a gatehouse in the Smythson drawings (Fig. 508).[7]

Among the sources on which Smythson drew for his buildings are the early Tudor lodge at Mount Edgcumbe in Cornwall; symmetrical single-range houses, as developed in the 1550s; Somerset House; the publications of Serlio, Du Cerceau and Vredeman de Vries; just possibly Palladio. He learnt from Alan Maynard, and other contemporary artificers. All his buildings inevitably had an input, greater or lesser, from his employers. He must have been influenced by the perfectionism of Thynne, the learning, library

and neuroses of Willoughby, the pride and toughness of Bess of Hardwick, the amateur enthusiasms of Charles Cavendish. He could absorb and deal with them all: a consistency of character and approach runs through his highly charged, compactly crafted, boldly profiled and always memorable buildings.

'There remains something more impalpable but all-pervading, the sense of drama. A Smythson house seems to call out for a hill-top. Who could ever forget the first distant view of Hardwick, with its six towers flashing in the evening sun? Or of Wollaton, looking across the city mark of Nottingham from its eyrie, like some immense and unlikely heraldic bird?' I wrote this in 1966, trying to express my own personal reaction to these extraordinary buildings (Fig. 511). There is a quality in them that goes beyond a feeling for order and a gift for striking composition; but with the lapse of centuries and the absence of anything written by Smythson himself, one can only grope for any understanding of what was in his own mind.

William Arnold

William Arnold is buried somewhere in the churchyard of the parish church of Charlton Musgrove in Somerset. Robert Smythson and John Thorpe are commemorated by monuments in the churches of Wollaton and Kingscliffe, but there is no monument or headstone to Arnold. A modest, half-submerged tomb chest in the graveyard, to Thomas Stretch, whoever he may have been, is carved with the nail-head ornament that William Arnold often used. An equally unassuming font cover in the church, installed in 1606,[8] could conceivably have been supplied by one of his joiners. That is all there is to suggest, at the church or elsewhere in the parish, that one of the most inventive and attractive of Jacobean artificer-designers, the creator of at least two masterpieces, Montacute House in Somerset and Cranborne Manor in Dorset, lived at Charlton Musgrove for more than forty years.

The Arnold family appears in the records, at Charlton Musgrove and elsewhere, as Goverson, Arnold alias Goverson, or just Arnold.[9] An Arnold Goverson was working as a joiner at Longleat in the years 1555–9.[10] Nothing more is known of him until he was buried at Charlton Musgrove on 4 November 1590. John and Godfrey Goverson, probably his sons, had married at Charlton Musgrove in 1580 and 1582 respectively, and numerous of their children were born and baptised there. William Goverson, later described as William Arnold, first appears in Charlton Musgrove in 1595, when his daughter was baptised there, to be followed by a son, born and buried in 1596, and another daughter, born in 1598. He must have married outside the parish, and was probably a brother of the other two. John died in 1605, but William and Godfrey lived on in the parish and died there, 'William Arnold alias Goverson' in 1636, and 'Godfrey Arnold alias Goverson' in 1637. They owned or leased small farms in the parish;[11] William served as churchwarden in 1600–01 and 1622. The two men are never described as 'gentlemen' in the parish archives. Their wills have not been traced.

On 10 February 1610 Dorothy Wadham, whose husband, Nicholas, had lately died and left her responsible for the founding of a college at Oxford, wrote to her half-brother Lord Petre, one of the overseers of the will. She urged him to 'ymploye one Arnold in the work, who is an honest man, a perfectt workman, and my neere neighboure, and soe can yeld me contynewall contentment in the same'.[12] He had, she wrote, been 'commended' to her by her 'good frend and lovinge neighboure Sir Edward Phelipps'. Dorothy lived at Merifield, near Ilminster; Sir Edward Phelipps or Phelips was the builder of Montacute. The letter, combined with the style of Montacute, make it reasonable to attribute its design and detailing to Arnold.

Following on the letter he was employed 'for drawyng of a plott and for the bylding of it', at what was to become Wadham College.[13] At least as important a consideration in his being employed as Dorothy Wadham's recommendation must have been the fact that he was already working for Robert Cecil at Cranborne Manor.

On 19 March 1610 Sir Edward Hext, another overseer, wrote to Lord Petre, reporting how Arnold's 'plott' had been seen and approved by James I, the Archbishop of Canterbury (Richard Bancroft), the Lord Chancellor (Lord Ellesmere) and the Lord Treasurer (Robert Cecil). He went on to describe how Cecil was also employing him, and how the two were discussing Cranborne together 'every day a whole houre in private. . . . Within these two dayes my Lord Threasorer sendes him to Cranborne about his workes there

512   A view of Wadham College, Oxford, built 1610–13, with William Arnold as surveyor and designer. From David Loggon's *Oxonia illustrata*, 1675.

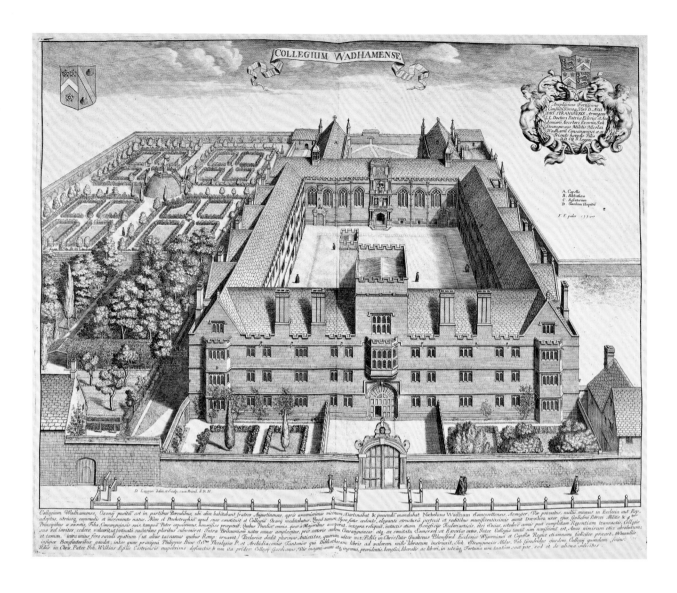

... If I had not tyed him fast to this businesse we shold hardly keepe him; he ys so wonderfully sought being in deede the absolutest and honestest workeman in England.'[14]

Arnold cannot have stayed long at Cranborne, for he arrived at Oxford in April 1610, along with twenty-six freemasons, all coming with him from the West Country. Of these, three were in his particular gang: Richard Cornish, Thomas Arnold and Edmund (or Edward) Arnold; the last two were probably his sons. Arnold supervised the work at Oxford for two years, and was paid £1 a week for this, in addition to payments for his own mason's work; he left Oxford in June 1612, when the building was approaching completion, and his

position as surveyor was taken over by Edmund, who was paid ten shillings a week.[15]

Charlton Musgrove was a good 25 miles from Dorothy Wadham's house at Merifield; it is odd, though perhaps not impossible, that his residence there should make her feel able to describe him as her 'near neighbour'. An alternative possibility is that he was in fact living at Montacute, or at one of the other two villages next to the famous Ham Hill quarries, from which Montacute House was built; he may even have had an interest in the quarries. At least two of the masons whom he brought to Wadham were from Ham Hill.[16] Perhaps he moved around from quarry to quarry, as he took on work, keeping his farm at Charlton

Musgrove as his base and family home, to give him yeoman status in his own neighbourhood, and to enable him to up himself to 'gentleman' at longer distances. It was as 'William Arnold, gentleman, of Charlton Musgrove' that in 1617 he signed a contract to make a 'plot' and 'upright' and supervise the part rebuilding of Dunster Castle in Somerset, for George Luttrell. The contract ended less than two years later in a lawsuit, brought on the grounds that Arnold had altered his original plan and exceeded his estimate; but even so Luttrell had to admit his 'great experience in architecture'.[17]

Montacute, Cranborne, Wadham and Dunster are the only four buildings with a documented link with Arnold. They each have a strong individuality but also a clear relationship with the others; they have details of overlapping idiosyncrasy; they enable a considerable number of other houses, garden buildings, churches and church monuments to be attributed to Arnold, or at least to the artificers who worked with or for him.

Arnold combined sensitivity to context with inventive fancy in detail. All designers are inevitably influenced by the demands and needs of their clients, but he had an especial gift for varying the nature of his buildings in response to their functions. And he drew on engraved sources, traditional English detail and his own invention to give porches, loggias, windows, arches, chimneypieces, alcoves and church monuments an individual and personal flavour, which mark them off from other work of the same time.

Arnold designed Wadham conservatively in the collegiate tradition (Fig. 512): it has gabled dormer windows with arched heads or tracery, a vaulted gatehouse with accommodation above it for the Warden, a traditional quadrangle with hall and chapel side by side in one range. Its most obvious model, but certainly not its only one, is St John's College, Oxford, as rebuilt from the mid-fifteenth century onwards. But it is brought up to date by a rigorously symmetrical plan, by a Tower of the Orders following the fashion set in Oxford at Merton College in 1609–10, by window tracery and gatehouse vaulting of idiosyncratic design, and by screens in chancel and hall in the best Anglo-Flemish manner.

The plan is a neat one. It is almost totally symmetrical. The entrance archway is axial to the

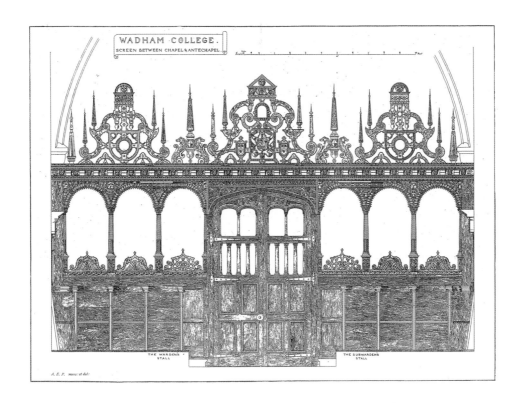

513 The screen in the chapel at Wadham College, carved by John Bolton, 1612–13, probably to William Arnold's design. From a measured drawing by Thomas Graham Jackson.

WADHAM · COLLEGE.
SCREEN BETWEEN CHAPEL & ANTECHAPEL.

THE WARDEN'S STALL

THE SUBWARDEN'S STALL

514 (*top*) Dunster Castle, Somerset, remodelled by William Arnold 1617, from a drawing by J. C. Buckler.

515 (*above*) Inside the stables at Dunster Castle.

Wadham is collegiate; in contrast, Arnold's work at Dunster[18] was designed by him for the context of a castle. It is (or was, for it was substantially remodelled in the nineteenth century by Salvin) handsome but very plain, not quite symmetrical, with two towers, and battlemented parapets instead of Wadham's dormer windows (Fig. 514). A simple classical door-case and fake gun-loops in the battlements were the only external ornament. The stables still have their original stalls, with joinery that relates to Arnold's work at Wadham and elsewhere (Fig. 515).

There are no surviving building accounts for Montacute. The date 1601 is carved above the entrance doorway on the west front; 1599 is on a plasterwork overmantel in the dining room – not in its original position, but it looks genuine; a panel of heraldic stained glass is dated 1598. The house can reasonably be dated *circa* 1596–1601.

It was devised as the seat of a successful lawyer, who was setting out to establish a county family on foundations laid by his father. It is grand, but not too grand. There is nothing innovative about it. Its plan is rather old-fashioned. Its detail mixes elements from Serlio, Longleat and Flemish engravings with English bay windows, mullions and transoms, in a manner already well established.

But many people would nominate it as their favourite among Elizabethan houses. It disputes the palm with Hardwick. The exteriors of the two houses give the same sense of one mind in control; but they have strongly contrasting characters. At Montacute the squareness and grand simplicity of Hardwick is softened and modulated. The basic rectangularity of plan and elevation is broken by gently projecting bay windows, and great oriels high up on the side façades. The long horizontals of balustraded parapet and entablatures on the entrance front are similarly broken by shaped and curved gables, by the shallow pediments over the bay windows, and by the shell-headed alcoves scooped out of the entrance front on the ground

Tower of the Orders. At St John's College hall and chapel were side by side, but to one side of the quadrangle; at Wadham they are placed to either side of the Tower of the Orders. The chapel has the T-plan, made up of ante-chapel and main chapel, that had been pioneered at Merton and Magdalen Colleges before the Reformation. The upright of the T, containing the main chapel, projects behind the quadrangle, and is paired with the kitchen, and the library above it, projecting behind the hall; a broad gallery joins them.

516 The entrance front
of Montacute House,
Somerset, built *c.*1596–
1601, probably to the
design of William Arnold.

and upper floors (Fig. 518). On the upper floor
these contain statues of the Nine Worthies, and
fill the spaces between the windows, so that the
rhythm of this floor contrasts to that of the floors
beneath it. The entrance courtyard has square
pavilions at the corners, but the rectangularity of
these, too, is softened by the double curve of their
roofs and their semicircular bay windows; and
between pavilions and house curves appear again
in the little circular rotundas with their open
coronas (Fig. 517). Unlike Hardwick, no attempt
was made to give a consistent treatment to all four
façades; instead, they contrast with each other,
probably deliberately. Finally, here and elsewhere
in Arnold's work the window mouldings are
invariably cavettos, and accordingly softer than
the rectangular 'tramlines' used at Longleat and
elsewhere, or the more assertive ovolos that
became the commonest form for Elizabethan and
Jacobean windows.

The shell-heads of the alcoves have the whorl
of the shell at the top of the arch, instead of at its
base, as found at Longleat and elsewhere. This
form derives from Serlio,[19] and became a favourite
with Arnold, almost to the extent of being his signature. At Montacute such alcoves appear inside
the house as well, on the chimneypiece in the
great chamber, and on the main staircase. The
dominant ornamental influence, however, is that
of Vredeman de Vries, and related Flemings –
but Vredeman used, as in all the best English
examples, with restraint and originality. The
screen is a fine example of Arnold's skill in adapting and of his sense of design (Fig. 520). The ram's-
head capitals of the columns come from Vredeman (Fig. 518),[20] and must have delighted Arnold's
fancy: he lifted four more of them to surmount
the playful concoction of cherubs and swags that
form the central feature of the screen: to either
side one of Vredeman's scrolled gables has been

517, 518 and 519
Montacute House,
Somerset: (*above left*) a
detail of the courtyard
walls; (*right*) a detail of the
hall screen; (*above right*)
the middle of the
entrance front.

cut in half and each half set in silhouette as a terminal feature. A similar game is played in wood at the head of the internal porch in the parlour, and was to be repeated, some years later, along the whole length of the chapel screen at Wadham.

The same fanciful spirit is at work in the forecourt, but here without obvious stylistic precedents: it has been aptly described as 'an exquisite pastiche of the fortified forecourt of a medieval house; the battlemented walls have become balustrated parapets, the turrets delicate lanterns of columns, and the towers little domed pavilions'.

520 The hall screen at Montacute.

Robert Cecil was granted the manor of Cranborne in Dorset in the late sixteenth century, and later was granted the rangership of the huge tract of royal hunting country to the north-west of the manor known as Cranborne Chase. On the edge of the village was a modest building erected in the thirteenth century by King John as a hunting lodge. Its plan and appearance are shown in a survey (Fig. 521) made by John Norden in 1605.

Cecil decided to enlarge this as a hunting lodge for himself, and a retreat from London in the hot summer months. He was an enthusiastic hunter; but there is little doubt that he was also well aware of the possibility that James I would come there, for the king's passion for hunting had become apparent to the English immediately on his accession to the throne. He was, in fact, to come to Cranborne in 1607 and 1609, and, after Robert

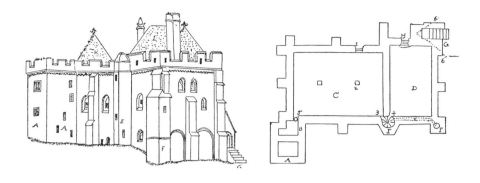

521 The original medieval hunting lodge at Cranborne, from a survey drawing by John Norden, 1605.

522 (*facing page*) The north front of Cranborne Manor, Dorset, remodelled to William Arnold's designs, from c.1605.

Cecil died in 1612, some five times more between 1615 and 1623, always in the month of August. The lodge was enlarged and remodelled accordingly. It was Arnold who was called in to do the work. The first surviving documentation is in 1608, but work probably started soon after Norden's survey in 1605.[21]

Arnold's conversion of the little medieval building into what, in German-speaking countries, would have been called a *Lustschloss* was a work of genius. It was to be a holiday house for great people, and he let his fancy play accordingly. The original house was three storeys high, with only two rooms on a floor, one small, one large, plus a small turret containing a newel staircase and a tower at the south-west corner, no taller than the rest. It had small windows, buttresses all round, and was surmounted by battlements supported on distinctive trefoil-shaped corbelling.

One might have expected the medieval house to be rebuilt, or entirely remodelled. Instead, it was made the starting-off point for a play of fancy. The newel turret was preserved, and so, by and large, were the buttresses, battlements and corbelling. Larger, mullioned and transomed windows were inserted throughout. The tower was raised a storey, and twinned with a new tower on the south-east. The medieval corbelling was copied as a capping for these. On the north front three of the original buttresses were kept, but the east end of the front, which originally projected a little, was rebuilt in the same plane as the rest, with new buttresses, battlements and corbelling,

copying the old. All the buttresses were covered with a delicate scaffolding of pilasters, doubled and in three tiers to each buttress (Fig. 522).

The culminating features on both fronts are the two loggias, one on each front. These are different from each other, but each peculiar to Arnold. The north loggia was originally the main entrance to the house, the south loggia looked out on the 'Court Garden' or 'Garden Court', the opposite of the arrangement today.[22] The south loggia is small and delicate (Fig. 523). Three gently rusticated arches on slender Doric columns support a little room on the first floor; this is the 'Prince's study' shown on the contemporary plan. Above, set into the parapet, are exquisitely carved circular representations of two of the Signs of the Zodiac, *Libra* and *Aries*; the other signs probably filled, or were intended to fill, other roundels on both façades, now empty. Inside the loggia are six of Arnold's Serlian shell-headed alcoves (Fig. 525); and the lower sections of the columns are carved with shallow rustication, also from Serlio.[23]

The north loggia is single storey, but wider and more richly decorated (Fig. 524). It, too, has three arches, but they are framed by wide piers enriched with shell-headed alcoves and strapwork ornament. There are six more alcoves within the arches, and more strapwork, in and on the parapet; but the panels joining the columns to either side of the central opening are carved with ornament of Eastern origin, perhaps derived from the engravings of arabesque ornament that were in circulation at the time. The arches have a distinctive rounded section peculiar to Arnold; and above them four jovial open-mouthed lions act as gargoyles to the terrace or balcony above the loggia.

The remodelling of Cranborne included giving it a setting in keeping: on the north an avenue leading from the Salisbury road by a bridge across the little river, a gateway and the entrance court leading up to the terrace and entrance façade; to the east a garden, an orchard and a mount; to the

396

523 (*right*) The south loggia at Cranborne Manor, as depicted on a title page in Joseph Nash's *Mansions of England in the Olden Time* (1839–48).

525 (*far right*) Inside the south loggia. The shell-headed alcoves and shallow rustication are typical of Arnold.

524 (*right*) The north loggia.

526 (*far right*) Design by Inigo Jones for Oberon's Palace, 1610.

527 (*facing page*) Looking down the approach to the gatehouse and south façade at Cranborne Manor.

528 The gatehouse, Clifton Maybank, Dorset, perhaps built in the 1590s, and demolished in the eighteenth century. Possibly an early work of William Arnold. From John Hutchins's *The History and Antiquities of the County of Dorset*, vol II, 1774.

west a wood court, kitchen garden and privy garden; south of the house the garden court, entered through a pair of little square lodges, set diagonally and framing the view of the south loggia between its towers (Fig. 527).[24]

All this fell into decay in later centuries, and the Cecils came back to live there only in 1866. The skeleton of the layout was then filled out by successive generations with what is now one of the most beautiful of contemporary gardens.

Cranborne's mixture of motifs and the way in which the house plays up to its medieval core must have been deliberately contrived. The spirit behind it was the same as that which created the masques of the period: the loggias are closely paralleled in feeling, though not in detail, to the contemporary Oberon's Palace, as designed in its first form by Inigo Jones for Ben Jonson's masque *Oberon: The Fairy Prince*, as an exquisite product of Jacobean fantasy, created in 1610, just before Jones was converted, or seduced, by Palladio (Fig. 526). One can think of Cranborne as an

enchanted palace set in Arcadia; James I's arrival there could have been greeted, as was often the case, by a masque, for which the north loggia and the backcloth of the north front behind it would have been the ideal setting: the Countess of Salisbury disguised as Diana, Queen of the Hunt, perhaps, seated with her ladies in the loggia, viols and lutes on the balcony above it, satyrs and fauns disporting on the terrace: and then Diana coming down the steps to greet the king, and give him the keys of her palace.

Robert Cecil's hour-long meetings with Arnold show the value that he put on him; one would much like to know what was discussed at them. Cecil's input must have been considerable. Cranborne as converted, with its loggias and fanciful detail, has an obvious relationship with contemporary buildings in London or the London area, especially Northampton and Holland Houses, and with Bramshill. It is likely enough that Cecil, following the practice of the times, sent Arnold to look at other buildings as examples; he could easily have taken in Bramshill on his way to Dorset. But even if such buildings showed Arnold the kind of effect that his employer wanted, what he produced was more original, inventive and enjoyable than anything in or around London.

Montacute cannot have emerged out of a vacuum. There must have been buildings with which Arnold was involved that led up to it. There are two possibilities, one modest, the other with more pretensions. The first is Edmondsham House, in east Dorset a few miles from Cranborne.[25] This was originally a tall, compact, three-storey house, with shaped gables similar to the simpler of the gables at Montacute; wings were added in the eighteenth century. The porch is

529 A chimneypiece of *c.*1600 at Wolfeton House, Dorset. One of a large group of related chimneypieces associated with William Arnold or his circle.

dated 1589. The other is the gatehouse (Fig. 528) that originally stood at Clifton Maybank, near Sherborne, in front of the great early sixteenth-century house of the Horseys. It is known only from the engraving in Hutchins's *History of Dorset* (1774). The main house was largely demolished in 1786. A portion of the façade was purchased and re-erected as the new west front to Montacute. According to the later edition of Hutchins, the gatehouse was bought in 1800 by Lord Poulett for re-erection at Hinton St George in Somerset.[26] It is not there today, and there is no evidence that it ever was there; it may simply have been bought for the ashlar stonework, and cannibalised.

The date of the gatehouse is not documented. Its most probable builder is Sir Ralph Horsey, who inherited in 1589 and died in 1612. It incorporated both types of shell-headed alcoves, and the frieze of the Ionic order of the first floor was filled with plain rectangles, in an arrangement also found on the ground-floor entablature at Montacute. These are pointers to a connection with Arnold; and so is the originality of the design. The Doric and Ionic orders on the ground and first floor projected and recessed in counterpointed rhythm: *a b a* on the ground storey, *b a b* above. To either side were turrets, rising on the second floor from a square to a circular plan, with the space between the circle and square filled with Corinthian columns.

A number of distinctive ornamental motifs appear at Montacute and Cranborne. At Montacute these are 'upside-down' shell-headed alcoves, nail-head ornament, shallow rustication (inside the porch) and a distinctive type of chimneypiece. All these recur at Cranborne, except the chimneypieces, for no Jacobean chimneypieces with overmantels survive there. In addition, Cranborne has its two highly individual loggias, incorporating two ornamental devices peculiar to Arnold: shallow rustication and a kind of bead ornament, of rounds or ovals, carved all round the medallions above the south loggia.

These motifs are also found in houses scattered over Dorset, Somerset and Wiltshire. At Wayford Manor in Somerset is a loggia, very close to the Cranborne south loggia, and a Montacute-type chimneypiece, dated 1602; if the loggia is of the same date, it pre-dates the one at Cranborne.[27] At Warmwell in Dorset, built by John Trenchard in or after 1618, is a similar loggia (Fig. 530), but of two arches only, with rounded section and decorated with beading.[28] At Wolfeton House in Dorset, as altered by John Trenchard's father, probably a few years earlier, is a round-sectioned arch (Fig. 531), a Montacute chimneypiece (Fig. 529), a rusticated doorway (Fig. 532) and a small rusticated chimneypiece.[29] At Mapperton in Dorset there are shell alcoves and a rounded-section arch; in the garden of Edington in Wiltshire (most of the house has been demolished) there are shell alcoves and a garden seat behind

two rusticated arches; at Hanford in Dorset shell alcoves and a chimneypiece that suggests Arnold; at the Hall, Bradford-on-Avon, shell arches and a Montacute-type chimneypiece; at Stockton in Wiltshire a chimneypiece with alcoves almost identical to that in the great chamber at Montacute (Fig. 437); at Poxwell in Dorset a porch with shell alcoves inside and out, as at Cranborne; at Herringston in Dorset a Montacute chimneypiece and other Arnoldian detail. There are shell alcoves in the courtyard archways at Sherborne Castle in Dorset and Keevil Manor in Wiltshire (Fig. 21).[30]

The influence of William Arnold can be surmised in all these places, and perhaps his hand; but one has to be cautious. What one does not know is whether he continued to run a tightly controlled workshop, including members of his family and other artificers working in stone and

531 and 532 Typical
Arnold details in the
staircase corridor,
Wolfeton House, Dorset.

533 (*right*) The loggia at
Warmwell Manor.

534 Arnold-type detail in the screen of the Freke chapel, Iwerne Courtney, Dorset, *c.*1610.

535 (*facing page*) The font in the church at Folke, Dorset, probably designed, like the church itself, by William Arnold.

entrance front and delicate two-arched loggia. Fitting rooms into the y was not managed with much skill; but the bonus of the plan is the lift and liveliness given to the entrance front by the gentle double kink of its two wings.

The Arnold family included William's putative brothers John and Godfrey, and his putative sons Edward / Edmond and Thomas; Godfrey's son Arnold (b. 1590), who always called himself Goverson, left the West Country early on; he was working at Oatlands in Surrey *circa* 1616–18, and had interests in the Ketton quarries in Rutland in 1621.[31]

At Wadham College, the only Arnold building for which full accounts survive, William Arnold is paid as a freemason, never as a carver; the carving work (including the unimpressive figures on the Tower of the Orders) was by William Blackshaw, who was not one of the artificers who came with the Arnolds from the West Country. On the other hand Godfrey Arnold carved a statue of Edward VI for Sherborne School in Dorset in 1614. In the years 1603–5 he was the principal mason at Lulworth Castle, where there are Arnoldian shell alcoves and lion heads under the windows, clearly related to those in the north loggia at Cranborne. But one would hesitate to ascribe the design of Lulworth as a whole to William Arnold. Since Godfrey Arnold did not go to Oxford with the other Arnolds, one can surmise that he stayed in Dorset to supervise the work at Cranborne; but this is only surmise.

The two Zodiac roundels at Cranborne are of outstanding quality. Otherwise the figurative carving on buildings in the Arnold orbit – the Nine Worthies at Montacute, the figures on the hall screen there, and on the chimneypieces in general, is clumsy. The most ambitious figures, the two life-size naked goddesses in the alcoves of the great chamber chimneypiece at Montacute, have disappeared, victims, probably, of Victorian prudery, so one cannot judge their quality.[32] What survives are chunky minuscule nudes, absurd if

wood; or whether artificers who had worked under him at Montacute, Wadham and Cranborne went on to work independently on their own, but in a similar manner.

One can posit a guess that he was in control at Warmwell Manor and that it can be added to the varied Arnold canon: a mansion, a college, a lodge, a castle and finally a manor-house, given individuality by its y-shaped plan, shaped gables on the

endearing, inserted in the strapwork of the over-mantel. There are similar little nudes on other chimneypieces in the group (Fig. 529); and they recur, reclining on their elbows, on the shelf of a monument to a lady of the Kymer family, who can be presumed to have died in childbirth, at West Chelborough in Dorset. They must be by the same carver as worked on the chimneypieces; so must the monument's full-scale effigy of the woman and her child, but here the carver's blocky technique of simplification has produced an image of moving sincerity, more akin to sculpture by Eric Gill than other work of the sixteenth century.

More conventional monuments that can be included in the group are those to Sir Edward Phelips at Montacute, to John Topp at Stockton, and to Sir John Williams of Herringston in St Peter's, Dorchester. There are examples of joinery, too: above all the screen that closes off the Freke chapel in the church of Iwerne Court-ney, Dorset (Fig. 534), where classical colonettes, Gothic tracery and Vredemanesque cresting are mixed together with brilliant success.[33]

There is a similar mix, in miniature, in the font of the church at Folke, in Dorset (Fig. 535): a stem carved with spiral fluting of late Gothic deriva-tion; a bowl that combines free-form foliage with classical fluting and Vitruvian scroll; a cover of Vredemanesque scrolls and turned finials, which seems to relate to the stalls in the stables at Dunster Castle. The church at Folke dates from about 1625–8; it is Gothic, but with idiosyncratic detail, including distinctive three-light windows, in which the central light rises higher than the other two, and distinctive capitals, supported on miniature consoles (Fig. 536).[34] There are similar capitals in the former kitchen at Cranborne; and similar windows are found in the chapel at nearby Leweston (Fig. 537), built in 1616 as the private chapel of the vanished great house of the Lewe-ston and Fitz-James families.[35]

One can surmise the hand of Arnold, not least because the Chafins of Freke, the Lewestons and Fitz-Jameses of Leweston, the Trenchards of

Wolfeton and Warmwell, the Horseys of Clifton Maybank and the Phelipses of Montacute were all linked together by a complicated web of intermarriages.[36] The lovely little chapel at Leweston is certainly worthy of his inventive genius; it has the delicate and delicious Arnold flavour.[37]

John Thorpe

John Thorpe was probably the youngest of the three men, and lived much the longest; he died, far on in his eighties, in or around 1654. He was financially the most successful, the best educated, a good arithmetician and geometrician, had some knowledge of both Latin and French, owned (probably) books by Serlio, Vredeman de Vries, Du Cerceau and Hans Blum,[38] and translated Blum's *Quinque Columnarum exacta descriptio cum symmetria* (probably)[39] and Du Cerceau's *Leçons de Perspective Positive* (certainly).[40] He travelled to Paris on at least one occasion. Unlike the other two, he was a metropolitan; he lived on the boundary between the Cities of London and Westminster, next to St Martin's in the Fields and opposite, or almost opposite, Somerset House and what later became Northumberland House. He and Thomas Graves are the only people in the building world to emerge on the printed page in the period. In 1612 Thorpe supplied a eulogistic Latin epigram in praise of Henry Peacham at the head of the latter's *The Gentleman's Exercise*, and Peacham, tutor to the children of the great, deviser of emblems and of manuals teaching the accomplishments of a gentleman, referred to him in the text as 'my especiall friend and excellent Geometrician and Surveiour, whom the rather I remember, because he is not onely learned and ingenuous himselfe, but a furtherer and faverer of all excellency whatsoever, of whom our age findeth too few'.

Thorpe's grandfather, father and brother were all freemasons, living at Kingscliffe in Northamptonshire, with an interest in the famous limestone quarries there.[41] The date of his birth is not known, but it was probably about 1565. As a child in 1570, he laid the foundation stone (as was the custom in those days) of Kirby Hall in Northamptonshire, where his father must have been the chief mason.[42] One would expect him to have had some experience of building sites and quarry work as a boy, but there is no evidence, or even likelihood, that he was apprenticed as a mason. His subsequent career suggests that he had had a good grammar-school education. At the age of sixteen, or thereabouts, he went into the Royal Works, not as an artificer, but as a clerk, employed in making inventories of stores, and probably also as a draughtsman; certainly he learnt to draw.

In 1600 Thorpe was in Paris,[43] possibly working for Sir Henry Nevill, then English ambassador to France. In that year he asked Nevill's help in recommending him for the reversion of one of the senior offices in the Works. Nevill wrote to Robert Cecil accordingly: 'in respect of some tryall I hav had of his onnest care and sufficiency in such things as he hath undertaken for mee, I am bold to satisfie his request'.[44] The recommendation turned out to be an unfortunate one, for within six months Nevill was in the Tower, accused of complicity in the Earl of Essex's abortive rebellion. Thorpe never got his promotion, and must have decided that it was time to move on from the Works. He finally left in the autumn of 1601.

The new career that he chose was one to which his skills could easily be transferred: that of a land-surveyor, measuring and plotting estates and the buildings on them. He was immediately successful, got much work both from the Crown and the Prince of Wales, and ultimately shared with John Norden the leadership of the surveying profession in England. Many of his surveys survive in the National Archives.[45] He did sufficiently well to invest £960 in buying 123 acres in Berkshire, and to assume a coat of arms, apparently without

authorisation. He also left, when he died, some 270 of his own architectural drawings, far and away the biggest collection surviving from the period. While in the Works, he must already have been supplying 'plots' to outsiders, like others of his colleagues; and he clearly continued to do so in the intervals of his second career as a surveyor. Yet outside his drawings, no reference to him as a designer of buildings, and only one possible payment for building work, have come to light. The payment is a small one for a relatively minor job at Belvoir Castle, Rutland, built in the years 1625–7,[46] and the 'Mr Thorpe surveir of ye contractinge' to whom payment was made was more probably John Thorpe's younger brother Thomas.

Thorpe's career, work and importance as a provider of designs have, accordingly, to be deduced from his drawings. This is by no means easy. There are problems of identifying them, dating them, deciding which are records of buildings by others, which copied from publications or engravings, which his own original designs, and of these last, which were made for potential clients, which as exercises for his own pleasure. The subjects of only about half of the drawings have been identified. There is the problem, too, of intention: why did Thorpe make the collection? The foundation of all work on him is John Summerson's impressive catalogue of the drawings, published by the Walpole Society in 1966, and the biographical and other discoveries that it incorporates. But Summerson would have been the first to admit that many of his conclusions were tentative. In the last forty years more identifications have been made; in the light of these, and of increasing knowledge of the period in general, it is time for a thorough reassessment. What follows is no more than an interim account.

At least twenty-one of the buildings depicted in his book were certainly not designed by Thorpe, though four or five of them contain his suggestions for alterations or additions. The

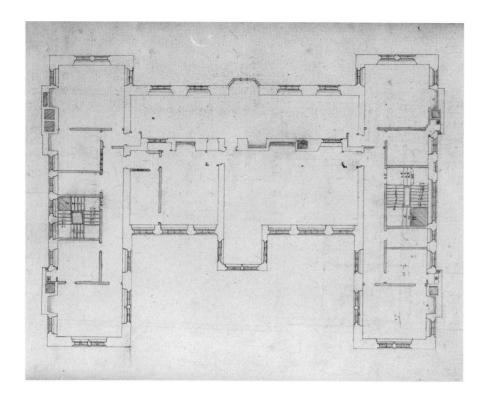

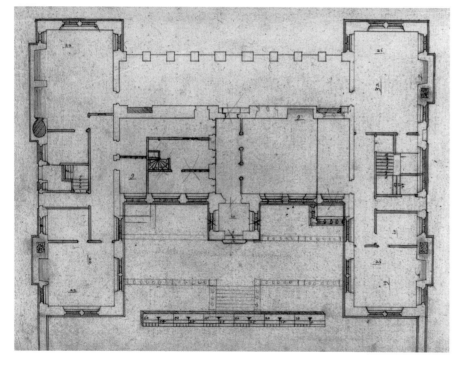

538a and b Plans by John Thorpe (T236, 235) for Condover Hall, Shropshire, built c.1590–98.

made during his period in the Works; some he may have plotted directly from the buildings themselves; for some he may have made copies of old plans, or plans made by colleagues and still kept in the Works.

The book starts with specimens of 'moulds', and a page of the five orders (Fig. 148; see also the endpapers), derived from Blum's *Architecture* (Thorpe's translation of this had been published in 1601).[47] A little later comes a demonstration, based on Serlio, of how to convert a plan and elevation into a perspective drawing. Also included are copies of designs by Vredeman de Vries, and of plans in Du Cerceau's *Plus Excellents Bastiments*. One can wonder whether Thorpe was collecting material with a view to publishing his own *Book of Architecture*, to contain building details, a section on perspective, and a collection of English 'Most Excellent Buildings' and of his own designs. His two translations and the drawings themselves show that he took architecture seriously. Perhaps he had hopes that Hans Woutmeel, who published his Blum translation, would publish such a book; if so, Woutmeel's death, before 1608,[48] would have put paid to any project that there may have been.

Enough of the remaining drawings can be accepted with certainty or reasonable probability as Thorpe's own designs to make clear his great versatility as a planner, developing or taking aboard new ideas or absorbing material from published works and existing buildings with such eagerness that one is left with the impression of a brilliant performer rather than someone keeping to a rigorously focused path, like Robert Smythson.

At least three of his own designs for actual buildings date from his period in the Works: the annotated and dated design of 1596 for 'Mr Tayler at potters barr' (T225, 226; Fig. 79d);[49] an interesting exercise in compact double-pile planning, which may never have been built; and designs for two houses that materialised: Condover Hall in Shropshire, which survives, and Babraham Hall in

buildings in this group include many of the best known of the period, among them Burghley, Theobalds, Holdenby, Wollaton, Longford, Melford, Kirby, Wimbledon and Lyveden New Bield. The bulk of these drawings was probably

539　The garden façade
of Condover Hall.

Cambridgeshire, which was rebuilt in the nineteenth century. The drawings include plans for both floors of Condover, almost, but not exactly, as executed (Figs 538a, b), but no elevations; both plans and elevations for Babraham and a number of related or variant drawings (Figs 540a, b), all of which combine to make it clear that these are Thorpe's own designs, not surveys or copies of the designs of others.[50]

Condover (Figs 15, 539) was built for Thomas Owen, a successful lawyer, from 1594 judge in the Court of Common Pleas. It may have been designed as early as 1589, but work on it seems not to have started until 1592, and was not quite completed at the time of Owen's death in 1598.[51] Babraham, which unlike Condover incorporated portions of an older house, was built for Sir Horatio Palavicino, a merchant of Genoese origin who

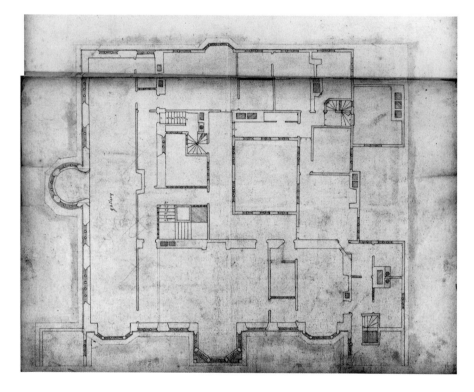

540a and b Façade (T90)
and first-floor plan (T209–
10) by John Thorpe,
probably of the
demolished Babraham
Hall, Cambridgeshire,
built in the 1590s.

ceilinged great hall, kitchen and parlour, high enough to enable a mezzanine floor to be fitted in elsewhere between ground and first floors; on the south, garden, front, this has prettily pedimented windows, below the gallery and above a loggia of piers and arches (Fig. 539). The centre of the house is double pile, with the gallery running over it behind the great chamber, as previously at Trerice and later at Hatfield. On the subsidiary façades were grand projecting chimney stacks to either side of the two staircases; these were carried up as towers. Internally, neat little privies complete with shafts were fitted in next to the chimney stacks. The towers, mezzanines and loggias gave an extra element of height and variety to an exterior that was otherwise in the manner of Shaw House, Berkshire, with plain gables and an entablature carried all round the house, though only above the ground floor. Like Shaw, the house was originally planned without bay windows; these, so prominent today, were probably added in the course of building, perhaps independently of Thorpe.

Babraham must have been designed a few years after Condover: it had bay windows, shaped gables, and a much bigger long gallery running the whole length of the garden front. The main feature, inside and out, was a central bay window letting off the gallery on a distinctive plan of two-thirds of a circle, 'quite round and large with a round table in the space of it', as an eighteenth-century description put it (Figs 540, 541). To judge from the plan, the house incorporated older building, and only the south and east fronts were by Thorpe.

A distinctive feature of the existing façades of Condover, and of the elevations of Babraham and related designs, is the use of small recessed roundels in the gables and entrance porch. In his drawings Thorpe gave these crescent-shaped shading to show their recession; the mason on the site at Condover, probably Walter Hancock,[53] carefully translated these crescents into stone.

settled in England in the 1550s, and made a considerable fortune; his house at Babraham must have been built at some time in the 1590s, before his death in 1600.[52] Owen was his friend, lawyer and executor.

Condover is a handsome, rather grand, slightly old-fashioned house suitable for a London lawyer with local roots. It was carefully and quite ingeniously planned. The first floor, containing the great chamber and gallery, was up above a high-

Jacobean equivalent of tracings, drawn to identical dimensions.[54] Only three of the ten are for identified buildings, and these are among the less close to Palladio: for Holdenby Banqueting House (Fig. 85), Brockhall in Northamptonshire and Somerhill in Kent (Fig. 86). The plan of Somerhill is very close to that of the demolished Ashley Park in Surrey, built in the years 1602–5, and probably the earliest of these southern Palladio-type plans; it is tempting to attribute it, too, to Thorpe.[55]

Neither Ashley, Holdenby, Brockhall nor Somerhill (Fig. 87), and neither of the two unidentified plans for which Thorpe supplied elevations, show any sign of Palladian influence on their exteriors. What clearly attracted Thorpe to Palladio was his use of through halls and the compactness of his planning. Somerhill conceals its Palladian plan under a gabled exterior not dissimilar to that of Condover, but with even less classical detail. The elevation of Thorpe's drawing T85, with its four corner towers and raised centre, is clearly inspired by Wollaton (Fig. 542), the exterior of which Thorpe had drawn, not very accurately, in the 1590s.[56] There seems a similar combination of Wollaton and Palladian influence in the exterior and plan of Plas Teg in Flintshire (Figs 543, 544), built for a London placeman, Sir John Trevor, perhaps about 1615.[57] This singularly beautiful house may show the influence of Thorpe, even though it is not by him, and it was certainly influenced by Ashley, of which Trevor acquired a plan.

There are other cross-hall plans in Thorpe that are less obviously derived from Palladio, and two cross-hall houses in the London area, with which he may or may not have had something to do: Eagle House in Wimbledon[58] and Charlton House in Greenwich (then in Kent). The plan of Charlton is close to that of Ashley and Somerhill, but with the individual features that the grand rooms are on the second floor, in the manner of Hardwick and Northampton House.[59]

541 The great window at Hinchingbrooke, Huntingdonshire, dated 1602. Sir Oliver Cromwell, who built it, was connected by numerous marriages with Horatio Palavacino, the builder of Babraham, where there was a similar window.

This agreeable mistake, combined with the absence of Thorpe's name in the considerable surviving archive, makes it seem likely that he never visited the site, as was probably the case with many, and perhaps most, of the 'plots' that he provided.

Early in the 1600s Thorpe acquired, or obtained access to, a copy of Palladio's *Four Books of Architecture*. The effect on his plans was considerable: no less than ten of them clearly derive from plans in Palladio's Book Two; two of these are the

411

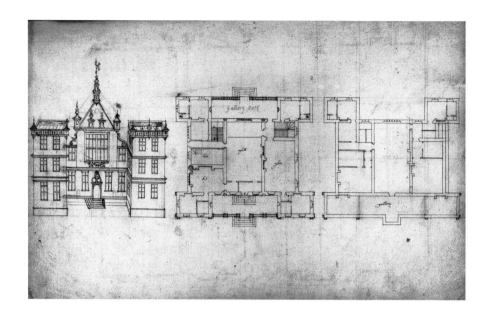

bers of Burghley's secretariat; Walter Cope (Cope Castle, later Holland House, Kensington, T93) and George Coppin (Nottingham House, Kensington, T94) were similarly employed by Robert Cecil. The houses have a great variety of plans, but all are of interest as the stylish houses of successful civil servants, without pretensions to grandeur, apart from Thornton College. All these houses seem to have had single-storey halls; those at Holland House and Ruckholt were entered from the centre, and at Easton Lodge from the corner, and all three were without screens.[60]

Thornton College was more ambitious, for Skynner had pretensions beyond his means;

542 (*top*) Wollaton-cum-Palladio: a drawing and plan by John Thorpe (T85).

543 (*above left*) Plas Teg, Flintshire, built by Sir John Trevor, perhaps *c.*1615.

544 (*above right*) The plan of Plas Teg (scale 1:350).

In the late sixteenth and early seventeenth centuries Thorpe supplied plans to a small but cohesive group of patrons (Figs 89, 352, 545, 546). They all worked in one way or another for the Cecil family: Henry Maynard (Easton Lodge, Essex, T91–2), Vincent Skynner (Thornton College, Lincolnshire, T67–8) and Michael Hickes (Ruckholt House, Essex, T97–8) had been prominent mem-

Thorpe provided him with a highly unusual plan (Fig. 545), H-shaped, but with a hall, probably of two storeys, entered through an oval lobby at the end of the cross-bar of the H, the entire cross-bar filled with what must have been a glorious gallery on the second floor, and the house buttressed all round, possibly in tribute to the adjacent ruins and gatehouse of Thornton Abbey. But the house 'when it was finished, fell quite down to the bare ground without any visible cause', and Skynner's fortunes, already overstretched, fell with it.

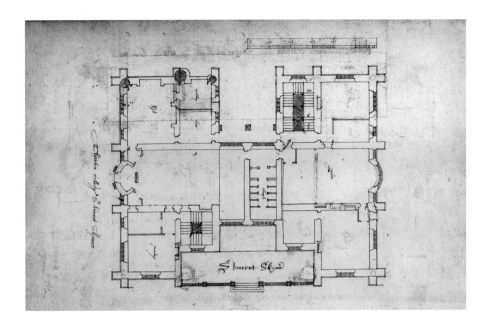

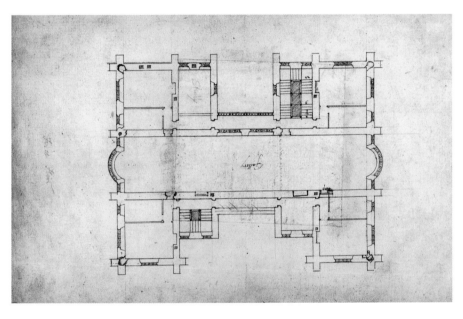

Thorpe's group of compact, unshowy, double-
pile houses, notably Dowsby Hall in Lincolnshire
(Fig. 92), has already been described in chapter 2.[61]
In striking contrast to them is a group that goes
to the other extreme, and delivers the final extravagant kick of Elizabethan and Jacobean architecture. Notable among these are designs for Leighton Bromswold, Huntingdonshire (T65–6) – perhaps the earliest[62] – the famous and often reproduced houses shown in T95–6, Holland House,
Kensington, and Aston Hall, Birmingham (T201–

5). No elevations survive for Leighton Bromswold.

All these houses have complex plans of cut-into
or pushed-out outline, shifting façades, turrets,
towers and bay windows of every variety of shape.
Perhaps timber construction was especially suited
to the manner, as is brilliantly demonstrated and
drawn in T95–6. Holland House (Fig. 547), until it
was unforgivably demolished in the 1950s,[63] shows
the manner at work in brick and stone. In fact, it
had a complex history, and was probably built in
three stages. Photographs and drawings suggest
the stages clearly enough: a compact four-roomed
block was extended and increased in height to
four storeys, and given shaped gables and terminal stair-turrets, in or around 1608; then, perhaps
in 1612, long lower wings were added to either
side, the forecourt enclosed with prettily bedi-
zened arcades, and a tall openwork porch built on
in the same style.[64] The fanciful and fretted end
result was like a pretty piece of cabinetwork; its
name, Cope Castle, expresses the playful spirit in
which it was built. A plan by Thorpe (Fig. 546) is
inscribed 'pfected p me JT', which perhaps means
that he was involved only in the third stage,
though the 'perfection' could include the second
stage as well.

Aston Hall was built a little later, in the years
1618–31, but in very much the same style. It was
slightly sobered up in subsequent decades, when
the centre was remodelled and the elaborate bay
window on the garden front removed. But the silhouette, with the three turrets and fanciful gables
of the house echoed and framed by the forecourt
pavilions (Fig. 548), remains a memorable one.[65]

Like everyone else at the time, Thorpe experi-
mented with 'devices' in the form of elaborately
geometrical or ingeniously symbolic plans. While
he was still in the Works he drew, and possibly
visited, Longford in Wiltshire, and produced his
own version of a triangular house (T161), even
larger and more elaborate than Longford (Fig.
287). Later, he drew the much-reproduced plan

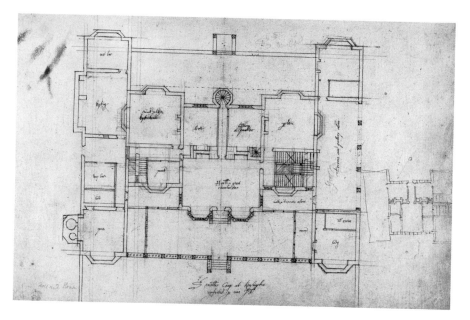

and elevation of a house based on his initials (T30, T50) (Fig. 302), as well as two versions of a simpler T plan, and an L-shaped plan (T151), perhaps for an unidentified client for whom L was the initial letter. Another odd plan, in which a square is inserted at 45 degrees into a larger square (T36), is hard to explain unless by some kind of symbolic meaning. The series culminated around 1615 in the circular house (T145–6) (Fig. 549) and the design for Wothorpe, near Burghley (T56) (Fig. 551); the circular house appears to be an alternative design for Wothorpe, for both are fitted into an identical circular platform (this, in fact, was never built).

The circular house is one of Thorpe's most ingenious and attractive designs (Fig. 549), a geometrical showpiece, basically composed of a combination of rectangles, triangles and circles, and further variegated by the three different types of bay window that project from the three rectangles; into this the standard country-house accommodation is neatly fitted. Wothorpe as built, adapted from a Greek-cross church plan from Serlio, is sufficiently unlike anything else with which Thorpe can be connected as to make one wonder whether the design is his (Figs 388, 51); if it is one can surmise the input of his patron, Thomas Cecil, Earl of Exeter, or perhaps Cecil's son William, who been in Italy in 1609.[66] It is worth noting, however, that, as built, with ogee cupolas and prominent stepped gables between the towers (Fig. 98), the house would have seemed

414

546 and 547 (*facing page, top and centre*) Thorpe's plan (T93) of Holland House, London, and its entrance front in the middle of the nineteenth century. It was built in stages, perhaps from *c.*1590, completed in *c.*1612, and largely demolished in the mid-1950s.

548 (*facing page, bottom*) Aston Hall, Birmingham, built 1618–31. There is a plan of it by Thorpe, and he probably designed it.

549 (*right*) Thorpe's design (T145–6) for a circular house.

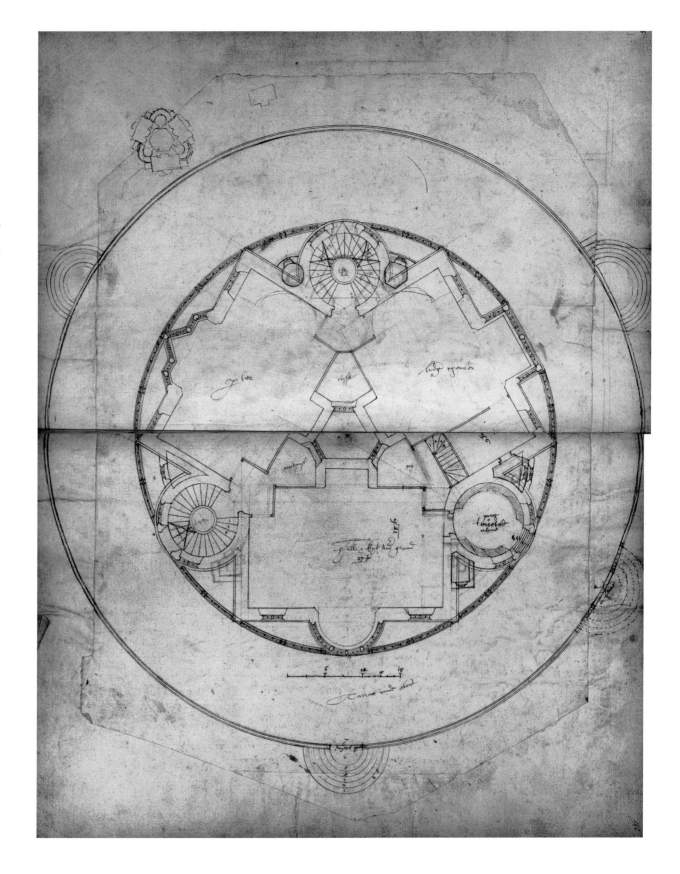

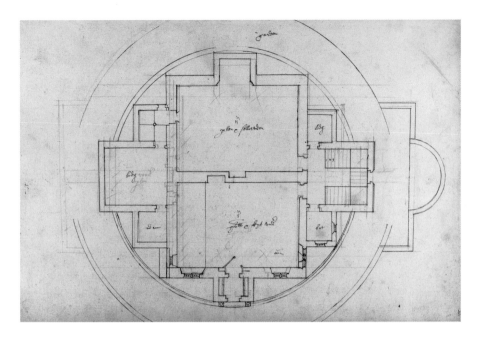

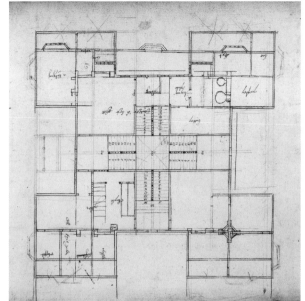

551 (*above left*) Thorpe's plan (T56) of Wothorpe Lodge, Cambridgeshire.

552 (*above right*) Plan by Thorpe (T186) of a house with an elaborate staircase.

553 (*right*) Thorpe's design (T148) for Noseley Hall, Leicestershire, dated 1606 on the drawing, with one of his distinctive cupolas.

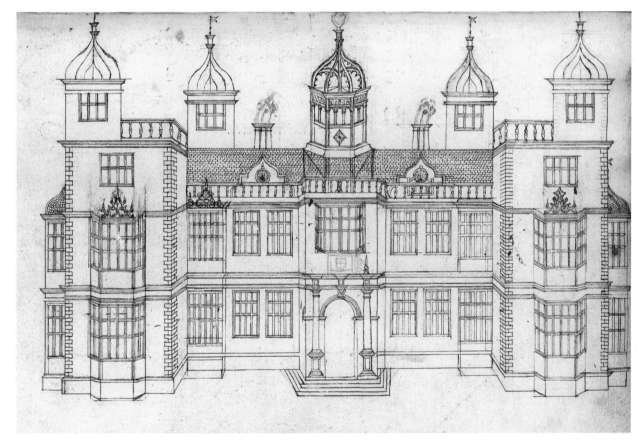

550 (*facing page*) Wothorpe Lodge, Cambridgeshire, built c.1615.

less like a stray from the Tuscan landscape than it is in ruins today (Fig. 550).

Thorpe also produced devices of another kind, in the form of staircases of unusual plan, as ingenious variants on the continuous-newel and newly fashionable cantilevered open-well types, which are also shown frequently in his drawings. The series perhaps starts with his Parisian visit in 1600, when he recorded (T162–3) an 'imperial' staircase, with a central flight dividing into two,

417

which he saw in the house of Sebastien Zamet, and suggested a variant on it, as one of two possibilities, in his plan for work at Sir Henry Nevill's house, Billingbere in Hampshire (T199). Drawing T186 shows four dog-legged stairs running up from the four façades of the house to a central lobby (Fig. 552). Drawing T190 shows a very large circular top-lit staircase, perhaps inspired by the great semicircular external staircase at Saint-Germain-en-Laye, which Thorpe had drawn on his Paris visit of 1600. In T279, the plan of Northampton House (probably not his design), he sketched in suggestions for a complex zigzag staircase, not completely worked out. This may have been done for his own amusement, and was certainly never constructed. But there is no evidence that any of his fancy staircases were built.

Another field for his ingenuity, the rooftop cupolas or lanterns that he designed in considerable and enjoyable variety (Fig. 553), must have had more chance of coming into existence; none the less, the cupola shown in Morant's eighteenth-century engraving of Easton Lodge is much simpler and more banal than the gay openwork structure that Thorpe had drawn. And did the open gallery that he had provided around the cupola of T95 (Fig. 353) ever materialise, to give viewers a near-up sight of the six chimneys in the form of rusticated terms, the fanciful rear silhouette of elaborate gables, the openwork tops of the two turrets, as a foreground to whatever more distant prospects this festive building was planned to enjoy?

554 A design by Hans Vredeman de Vries, redrawn by Robert Smythson for the screen at Wollaton Hall, Nottinghamshire

Chapter 8

Gothic

*I*n 1550 Giorgio Vasari, in his *Lives of the Artists*, launched a withering attack on Gothic architecture, as the style bought to Italy by northern barbarians. Their work was 'monstrous and barbarous, and lacking everything that can be called order... They constructed pointed arches, and filled all Italy with their abominations of buildings... their style has been totally abandoned ... May God protect every country from such ideas and style of building.'[1]

There may have been a few Elizabethan humanists who would have agreed with him; if so, their opinions have not come to light. Opinions in line with Vasari's were not to be openly expressed in England until well on in the seventeenth century.[2] The Elizabethans looked at Gothic from a different perspective. It was not something imposed from the north; it was their own way of building. Perpendicular architecture was England's especial glory. In 1564 Queen Elizabeth, on her visit to Cambridge, stood in the court of King's College and 'marvellously revising at the beauty of the Chappel, greatly praised it, above all others within her realm'. Her praises were repeated by William Camden, in his *Britannia* (1586). It was 'a Chapell, which may rightly be counted one of the fairest buildings in the whole world'.[3] As for Henry VII's Lady Chapel at Westminster Abbey, 'a man would say that all the curious and exquisite work that can be devised is there compacted'. But Gothic of all dates evoked his admiration; the west front of Wells cathedral was 'a most excellent and goodly piece of worke indeede'; Salisbury cathedral was 'a most stately and beautifull Minster'; the west front of Lincoln cathedral 'in a sort ravisheth and allureth the eyes of all that judiciously view it'.[4] And so on.

Camden, though a loyal member of the Church of England, was a conservative, who regretted the Dissolution of the Monasteries; perhaps he was enthusiastic above the average. But that Gothic should still be admired is not surprising. The whole of Elizabethan life was heavily conditioned by its medieval inheritance: its monarchy, its peerage, its laws, its system of government, its heraldry, its guilds, still followed medieval models; its church was a compromise between tradition and reform. The medieval echoes in its towers, turrets, gatehouses and huge windows have already been discussed; the Elizabethan achievement was to develop a creative merger between native traditions and needs and 'antique' forms. The use of specifically Gothic detail was less obvious, but far from uncommon, at all levels.

The traditional late medieval form of doorway and fireplace opening, with four-centred arches set within a rectangular frame, and mouldings running down the jambs to diagonally set stops, was so familiar and sensible that it is found right the way through from the fifteenth century to well into the seventeenth. Elizabethans with a little more money to spend, or wanting to be in the fashion, had square-headed openings with classical mouldings; but they were in a minority. On the other hand, windows with square-headed openings were increasingly preferred to ones with arched lights. It is a mistake, however, to try to date buildings by a simple formula: arched lights earlier, square heads later. Arched lights continued to occur here and there in a domestic context, all the way through the century. Sometimes this seems to have been for reasons of context, as in the case of the arched lights inserted into Wardour Castle in the 1570s; sometimes there is no obvious explanation, except that the employers preferred it that way.

Arched lights remained especially common in churches. The Elizabethan was not a great church-building age, less because it was irreligious than because it inherited a huge stock of churches, a high proportion of them relatively new, and in good condition. But rather more was built than is generally realised; what was done has attracted little attention because it was mostly inconspicuous. Aisles were added; churches were

555 (*facing page*) The vaulted undercroft of the chapel at Lincoln's Inn, London (1618–23). It was built by the Oxford mason John Clarke.

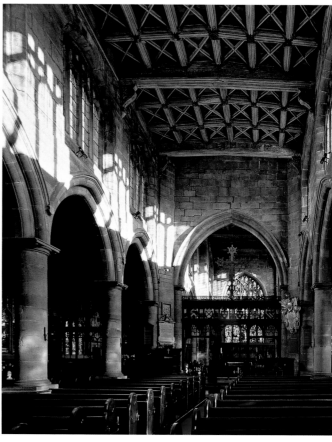

modestly rebuilt or repaired after a fire. A good many family chapels were built to contain the grand monuments that were increasingly the fashion. In this new work windows were occasionally mullioned and transomed with square-headed lights in the Elizabethan manner, but usually they had pointed heads and arched lights, to be in keeping with tradition or the rest of the church. It was all of a very low-key nature.

There were a handful of more ambitious projects. The grandest would have been the huge church that the Earl of Leicester started to build next to his castle at Denbigh in North Wales in 1578; it was left incomplete at his death ten years later, and remains a shell.[5] But the church that was successfully built and completed at Standish in Lancashire in the years 1582–4 is grand enough (Figs 556, 557). It incorporates the east end, tower and porch of a medieval church that had fallen into decay. The rest is all Elizabethan, and is an effective combination of tradition and new fashions. It has buttresses, battlements, the occasional pinnacle, and long rows of handsome windows traceried in the Perpendicular manner. The arches of the arcade are pointed, but are supported on Tuscan columns; the timbers of the roof rest on handsome classical consoles.[6]

Windows with elaborate Gothic tracery appeared in the following mid- or late sixteenth-century houses: below the half-timbered upper storeys at Tixall in Staffordshire, which carried the inscription 'Wiliam Yates made this house, 1555', one on the ground floor and two on the first floor;[7] at Harlaxton in Lincolnshire (Fig. 558) below crow-stepped gables lit by little two-light windows with steep-pointed Gothic arches, all this in what otherwise looks like a house of the late sixteenth century;[8] at Steane in Northamptonshire (Fig. 559), where two more or less matching wings had windows with reticulated tracery, and battlemented round towers attached to their outer corners – one of these may have been a genuine medieval chapel, but it seems unlikely that both were.[9] Since all three houses have long since been demolished, and documentation is sparse, it is impossible to say whether these windows were new at the time of their insertion, or were reused medieval ones; certainly such windows must have been easy to come by from the plethora of dismantled religious houses.

The commonest, and certainly the most showy, adaptations from late medieval times were those Elizabethan ceilings in which pendentives and

558 and 559   Gothic windows (*below*) at Harlaxton Old Hall (late sixeenth century?), Lincolnshire, as depicted in Joseph Nash's *Mansions of England in the Olden Time*, 1839–48, and (*bottom*) at Steane Park, Northamptonshire, from the drawing by Peter Tillemans).

ribs, which had previously been constructed in timber or stone, were executed in plaster, using patterns derived impartially from medieval sources or from Serlio. Real rib vaults in stone were much rarer. An early and remarkable example is the little octagonal vault in the lower of the two tower rooms at Lacock, which repeats in miniature the pattern of vaulting in Henry VII's Lady Chapel.[10] There is an unusual ribbed barrel vault in the Holbein porch at Wilton (*circa* 1560–?70) (Fig. 163). The vault in the circular great chamber at Longford (*circa* 1591), with its bold hanging pendants (Fig. 582), is unique, and does not look like English workmanship.[11] There are simple but handsome rib vaults supported on massive columns in the wine cellars of Castle Ashby (*circa* 1574) and Drayton (1584) in Northamptonshire, and there is a vault on a grand scale (?1570s) over the kitchen at Burghley (Fig. 56).[12] The Burghley vault is copying models of the fourteenth century or earlier, and is probably a deliberate piece of neo-feudalism; perhaps there was an element of this in the two wine cellars, for wine cellars – unlike beer cellars – were visited and admired by the gentry.

Odd little bits of surviving Gothic detail may have had similar reasons behind them. A chimneypiece once in the main buildings, but at some period moved to the gatehouse at Kenilworth Castle, is dated 1571. It is carved with Leicester's

initials, the letters being made up of the 'ragged staffs' that the Dudleys proudly, if without authority, had taken over from the medieval Beauchamps. The panels to either side of the fireplace opening are filled with blind Gothic tracery (Fig. 561). The location of the chimneypiece in Kenilworth Castle clearly influenced the design.[13] Perhaps the juxtaposition, in the mid-1580s, of the long gallery at Haddon Hall to a great fortified medieval house was similarly responsible for the surmounting feature of its brilliantly fanciful panelling: a cornice of miniature fortifications, complete with turrets and gun-loops or arrow-slits.

More full blown than the modest bits of Gothic infiltrated into the roof of the hall at Burghley is a richly traceried design (Fig. 562) annotated in Lord Burghley's own hand as for the hall louvre at Theobalds.[14] There is somewhat similar Gothic cusping in the little pseudo-vaults of the courtyard rotundas at Montacute (Fig. 563); and such cusping occurs again, together with a pointed arch, in the otherwise ambitiously classical Gate of Honour at Gonville and Caius College, Cambridge.

At the end of the sixteenth century there was a noticeable rise in the use of Gothic forms; this continued into the seventeenth century (Fig. 560), with results sufficiently distinctive to justify Horace Walpole's term 'King James's Gothic'. Various factors were at work to bring this about, among them an increasing interest in late medieval history, the growth of the High Church party in the Church of England, and the revived enthusiasm for chivalry, as especially expressed in pageants and tournaments. Something will be said about the third of these, and its effects, at the end of the chapter.

Holinshed's *Chronicles* were published in 1577 and 1586–7, and Stow's *Chronicles* in 1580, reprinted as *Annales* in 1592. Shakespeare drew on both for his historical plays, which were being produced steadily throughout the 1590s;

560 (*above*) Vault over the gatehouse entrance of Wadham College, Oxford, *c.*1610–12.

561 (*right*) Detail of a chimneypiece, probably of the 1570s, now in the gatehouse of Kenilworth Castle, Warwickshire.

Marlowe's *Edward II* was written about 1591; the Wars of the Roses (a term invented by Shakespeare) were celebrated at length in verse by Daniel in his *Civile War* of 1595, and by Drayton in his *Mortmeriados*, first published in 1596, reprinted as *The Barons' Wars* in 1603; it became a bestseller, and there were new editions at regular intervals well into the seventeenth century. His *Heroical Epistles*, many set in the Middle Ages and first published in 1597, were even more popular; his rousing *Ballad of Agincourt* was first published in 1606.

As queen, Elizabeth showed no leanings to the point of view and policy that had swept so many churches bare in the protectorate of the Duke of Somerset. The Reformation in the 1550s had removed screens in churches, but in her Royal Order of 1561 she defended them, though not the Crucifixion or Rood that they supported, and ordered that if they had been removed they should be replaced.[15] She continued to protect them for the rest of her reign, in spite of pressure

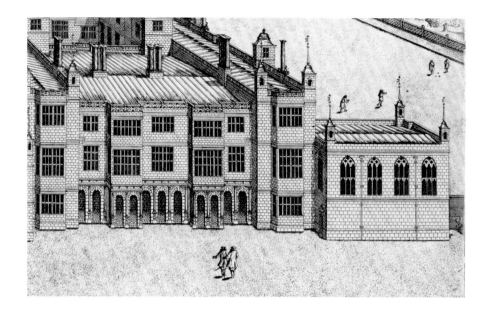

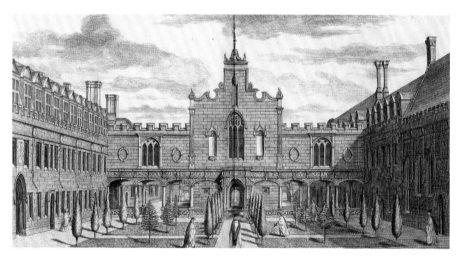

from the Puritan wing of the Church of England. She countenanced the removal of images, other than in stained glass; but she fought a long battle with the Puritans for the retention of the image of the Virgin and Child on the medieval cross in Cheapside in the City of London; when the iconoclasts smashed it, the Crown ordered it to be repaired.[16]

None the less, up till the end of the sixteenth century it was the Puritans who formed the most active and aggressive element in the Church of England, and their radicalism influenced the tone of the entire church. But in the early seventeenth century the High Church – called at the time the Arminian movement[17] – provided the new radicals, active and aggressive from an opposite standpoint, and just as controversial. In the 1630s they gained the approval of Charles I, and when Laud became Archbishop of Canterbury in 1633 they dominated the Church of England, though still arousing bitter opposition.

Instead of whitewashed churches, decorated with texts from the Bible and the royal arms, with no images and stained glass and screens tolerated only because of royal direction, instead of simply dressed clergy and free-standing unfurnished communion tables at the west end of the chancel, covered with a plain white cloth, the Arminians wanted churches furnished with carved screens, stained glass and images, clergy in vestments and altars rich with embroidery and plate placed under a canopy against the east end; they rated sacraments above sermons, and wanted ritual, not – or as well as – plain prayer. A series of bishops, occasionally supported by King James and increasingly by King Charles, led the movement, notable among them (in order of age) Lancelot Andrewes, Richard Neile, John Buckeridge, James Montagu, William Laud, Mathew Wren and John Cosin.

The Arminian movement led to the building or adornment of a considerable number of churches and chapels, and it set the tone just as the Puritans had, so that moderate Church of England

567 (*above*) Looking east
in the chapel of Wadham
College, Oxford, built
1610–12.

564 (*facing page, top*)
The chapel at Audley End,
Essex. Detail from an
engraving by Henry
Winstanley.

565 (*facing page, centre*)
The chapel of Peterhouse,
Cambridge (1623–33), as
depicted in David Loggan,
Cantabrigia illustrata, 1690.

566 (*facing page, bottom*)
The interior of the chapel
at Exeter College, Oxford
(1623–4) as depicted
before its demolition in
the middle of the nine-
teenth century.

and modern Jacobean motifs were mixed together, and occasional work that was out-and-out
Gothic.

The series starts with the Earl of Suffolk's large
and long-since demolished chapel at Audley End,
of *circa* 1605–10 (Fig. 564). It projected from the
long gallery above an undercroft, was free-standing on three sides, and had traceried windows, as
is shown in Winstanley's plans and engravings;
one can presume that it was decorated with some
elaboration, but no description survives.[18] It was
closely followed by the Earl of Salisbury's chapel
at Hatfield, of 1609–12. This was incorporated in
the main body of the house, but its presence is
made clear from the outside by windows with
round-arched heads, the east one rising through
two storeys. Unless its richness of decoration,
stained glass included, had been anticipated at
Audley End, Hatfield introduced a new lavishness
for private chapels; but there was not much of
Gothic about it.

The much more Gothic chapel at Wadham
College followed in 1610–12 (Fig. 567), and set off
a series of college and Inns of Court chapels, in
Oxford at Exeter (1623–4) (Fig. 566), Lincoln
(1631) and Oriel (1637–42), in London at Lincoln's
Inn (1618–23), in Cambridge at Peterhouse (1623–
33). All had Gothic windows with tracery, and all
were richly fitted up. The chapel at Lincoln's Inn
was above a vaulted undercroft (Fig. 555) and had
sumptuous stained glass, as did those at Wadham,
Lincoln and Peterhouse. The chapel of Peterhouse was built during the Mastership of Mathew Wren, uncle of Christopher, and later to be
Bishop of Hereford and Norwich. Its delicate
prettiness is evoked in Loggan's view (Fig. 565),
made in 1689, before irritating alterations were
carried out, especially to the flanking wings. It is
not known who designed it.[19]

A feature of the period is the appearance of
depictions of the Crucifixion, hitherto repro-
bated as idolatrous. These were no longer hidden
secretly away, as in Sir Thomas Tresham's personal closet at Rushton, but were prominent in

Calvinists also reacted from austerity in favour
of greater richness in church interiors. Modest
rebuildings, enlargements and additions for family chapels continued as before; but there were
rather more whole churches designed with some
elaboration; handsome fittings were in-stalled in
existing churches, and above all there were college
chapels and private domestic chapels far more
richly fitted up, and often much larger, than anything built under Elizabeth. The fabric of these
buildings was almost invariably Gothic, often
with traceried windows of some elaboration,
instead of the minimal Gothic windows of most
Elizabethan church work. The fittings, on the
other hand, were usually not Gothic at all, though
there were a number of examples in which Gothic

Old Testament prophets to Christ and his apostles (1616); the Crucifixion followed in 1621–22, supplied by Bernard van Linge, recently arrived in England from Emden via Paris.[21] This was the first of a series of windows by Bernard and Abraham van Linge, in Oxford and elsewhere (Fig. 568);[22] and also probably the first of a series of Crucifixion images all over England, through the 1620s into the 1630s.[23] The Puritans inevitably objected; but in 1633, when the Recorder of Salisbury, Henry Sherfield, smashed a depiction of God the Father in a window in a church in his city, his action, which would have been commended fifty, and even twenty, years previously, led to his prosecution in the Star Chamber.[24]

The chapel at Wadham had a remarkable offspring, in the form of the church at Low Ham in Somerset (Fig. 569).[25] This became a parish church but was originally built about 1620 as a private chapel, next to the house of Sir Edward Hext, which has been demolished; hence it has no graveyard, and stands alone in a field. Hext was one of the executors of Nicholas Wadham's will, and was much involved in the building of his college. His chapel is an almost archaeological reconstruction of a Perpendicular church of the late fifteenth century, complete with tower, aisles and chancel, and inside with a carefully detailed arcade and screen; one has to look carefully to realise its date. Arnold must be a possibility as its builder or designer; but it is without any trace of his individual touch, and a more likely candidate is perhaps John Spicer, the freemason who carved the windows of the main chapel at Wadham. These are straightforwardly Perpendicular in style, unlike the windows of the ante-chapel, built to match the windows of the hall with an ingenious paraphrase of Perpendicular tracery that must be owing to Arnold.

The chapel at Chantmarle (begun 1612) has been demolished, and is known only from the description of Sir John Strode, who built it; it had a plaster ceiling 'fretted over with the sun, moone,

stained glass, in principal windows of college and private chapels, and in family chapels attached to parish churches, though not at first in the east windows of their chancels.

Robert Cecil was a pioneer in commissioning New Testament scenes. He had a feeling for liturgical richness in both decoration and music; Richard Neile, later to be one of the leaders of English Arminianism, was for a time his chaplain. In his chapel at Hatfield he started by having the east window filled with scenes from the Old Testament; but the New Testament scenes that they were thought to prefigure were not illustrated, but discreetly described in script underneath them, to avoid possible accusations of idolatry. But within a year or eighteen months he had moved on and commissioned, more daringly and inevitably giving rise to controversy, eight large painted scenes from the life of Christ. The Crucifixion, however, which because of its importance in Roman Catholic devotion was especially suspect, did not feature among them.[20]

It was to be prominent, however, in the east window of Wadham College chapel (Fig. 567). Earlier windows in the chapel had moved from

569 (*above left*)
The church at Low Ham, Somerset, built as a private chapel *c*.1620.

570 (*above right*)
The interior of St Katherine Cree, City of London, built 1628–31.

stars, cherubims, doves, grapes and pomegranates, all supported with 4 angells in the 4 corners of the roofe'.[26] The little chapel at Leweston (1616) has already been illustrated (Fig. 537); it has richly carved woodwork redolent of contemporary Arminianism. The chapel added to Easton Lodge in Essex, and consecrated in 1621, is known from an eighteenth-century engraving (Fig. 8): the glass of its west window was moved on its demolition into the parish church of Little Easton.[27]

One of the earliest of the few parish churches built under James I and Charles I, is St Michael, Arthuret, in Cumberland, built from 1609 with subscriptions collected nationally. It is large and

handsome, but its low-key Perpendicular Gothic shows no sign of Arminian influence.[28] Only its east window, now removed to Whoof House, Warwick, had tracery, the simplicity of which contrasts with the sumptuous east window (modelled on the east window of St Paul's cathedral) of St Katherine Cree (Fig. 570), London, built in the years 1628–31 and consecrated by Laud in a service bitterly attacked by the Puritans.[29] The church seems to relate to St Nicholas, Rochester, largely rebuilt after a fire and dedicated in 1624 by Bishop Buckeridge, who had been Laud's predecessor and mentor at St John's College, Oxford.[30] Both churches had arcades supported on classical

columns, as in the Elizabethan church at Standish. At St Nicholas the columns support pointed arches, as at Standish; the church has been much altered but it is known that its windows were filled with tracery in the Decorated style. St Katherine Cree survived the Great Fire, and apart from unfortunate offices infiltrated into the aisles, has been little altered. Its arcades are entirely classical, with round arches supported directly on the capitals of the columns, in the Flemish manner of the Royal Exchange and elsewhere. It has apparent rib vaults, but of plaster, not stone. The windows, other than the east one, are Gothic but without tracery, of three lights with cusped heads. The middle lights rise a little higher than the side ones, in a manner reminiscent of those in the Dorset chapel and church at Leweston and Folke, already described, and attributed to William Arnold: but the Dorset buildings are earlier.

The most elaborate and sumptuously fitted-out new church built in the decades before the Civil War was St John's, Leeds (Fig. 571).[31] This was built in the years 1631–3 and consecrated by Richard Neile, Archbishop of York, in 1634. The church was paid for by John Harrison, a Leeds merchant, an Episcopalian and Royalist; it must have satisfied the archbishop's Arminian tastes. The fabric was, on the whole, Gothic, with an arcade of pointed arches and a traceried east window; but the capitals of the arcade were in a curious, though not unsuccessful, mixture of Tuscan and Gothic. The fittings are sumptuous, the screen in particular, and not Gothic at all, but an ebullient exercise, by Yorkshire craftsmen, in the De Vriesian Mannerism that had gone out of fashion in the south.

There was a good deal of re-fitting of old churches in the Jacobean and early Carolean

572 and 573 Gothic lattice-work in (*above left*) the Kederminster Pew (*c.*1613–20), Langley Marish, Buckinghamshire, and (*above right*) the screen at Cartmel Priory, Lancashire (1618–23).

period: interminable pulpits and pews, occasional fonts, font covers, screens and new roofs. On the whole all this was in the same contemporary style as the fittings at St John's, Leeds, without Gothic elements. There are occasionally exceptions, such as the former chancel screen (now moved to an aisle) at Geddington in Northamptonshire, dated 1618, which exactly copies the Decorated tracery of the fourteenth-century east window.[32] More common is a mix of Gothic and classical elements. The font cover at Terrington St Clement in Norfolk, probably of the 1630s, has a circle of paired and marbled Tuscan columns round its first stage, but from this rises up a fretted openwork Gothic spire. The painted Kederminster pew in the church of Langley Marish, Buckinghamshire (*circa* 1613–20), has pierced openwork lattices, part Gothic, part oriental, through which the occupants could peer into the church like

ladies in a harem (Fig. 572).[33] The inventive screen at Iwerne Courtney in Dorset (1610), perhaps connected with William Arnold, has already been illustrated (Fig. 534). The screens at Cartmel in Lancashire (1618–22) have a rather similar mix of elements, and are just as inventive (Fig. 573); but the immediate inspiration for their lattice-work grilles between attenuated Ionic pilasters and Corinthian columns is without doubt the similar openwork in the canopies of the fourteenth-century choir stalls at St Mary, Lancaster.[34]

The Cartmel screen was installed as part of the restoration of the church in the years 1618–23, mostly paid for by George Preston of nearby Holker Hall. This restoration included the provision of new roofs and arched plaster ceilings with Gothic detailing under them. These were removed in the nineteenth century, a common fate for such ceilings, so that only a few survive, as at

Axbridge in Somerset, dated 1636, and East Brent in the same county, dated 1637.

One of these replaced ceilings, panelled in Gothic style, was that covering the nave of Bath Abbey. The completion and repair of the abbey was the biggest restoration project of the period. The great church had been left unfinished at the Reformation, and for fifty years or so stood empty and decaying. Restoration was started in the 1590s, under the aegis of Nicholas Bellot, who had been steward to Lord Burghley, and had moved on to work for Robert Cecil when Burghley died in 1597. Sir John Harington, who was an assiduous collector of contributions towards the work from his grand friends, called him 'Saint Bellot' on the strength of it. By 1608 work on the choirs, transepts and tower was more or less completed. In 1609 James Montagu, the new Bishop of Bath and Wells, underwrote the restoration of the nave, which was still open to the skies, and this was completed, largely at his expense, by 1618. Much more was probably done than is generally realised, but the building was so worked over again in the nineteenth century and later that virtually all that remains from this period is the west door, given by Bishop Montagu's brother in 1617, and the fan vault of the crossing, put up by the freemason Nicholas Yarrington about 1608.[35]

Jacobean Gothic, with its classical admixtures, extended beyond churches and chapels, especially in the university towns. Two nice examples, modest in scale but lavish in execution, were the Carfax conduit at Oxford (1616–17) and the enlargements made to the High Cross in Bristol (1633–4).[36] Both crosses have been moved: Carfax has stood since the eighteenth century in what was the park of Nuneham Courtenay House near Oxford, its soft stone increasingly eroded by the elements (Fig. 574); the High Cross survives in a better state as an ornament at the entrance to the gardens of Stourhead in Wiltshire (Fig. 575).

Carfax was built by John Clerke or Clarke, son-in-law (probably) of the Yorkshire mason John

Akroyd; he was to go on to build the largely Gothic chapel at Lincoln's Inn (Fig. 555) in the years 1619–23. But the ebullient ornament of Carfax, fortunately recorded in a late eighteenth-century engraving, was not Gothic at all; what was Gothic was its form, an obvious re-creation of the coronas, made up of a central pinnacle supported on a flying buttress, found in St Nicholas (now the cathedral), Newcastle upon Tyne, and market crosses at Chichester, Salisbury and elsewhere. For the High Cross, on the other hand, two Bristol craftsmen, George Ewinge, 'cutter', and John Settle, freemason, sedulously extended by three stages the language of pinnacles, crockets and canopies of the fourteenth-century cross: canopied statues of Charles I and other monarchs, then a ring of cherubs supporting coats of arms, then a final pinnacle.

At Oxford, and to a lesser degree Cambridge, Jacobean Gothic proliferated. The completely new building at Wadham (Fig. 512), the extensive additions at Oriel and University Colleges and elsewhere in Oxford, and at Peterhouse in Cambridge, have already been referred to. More ambitious than any of these were the new Bodleian Library and adjoining Schools in Oxford. These were built between 1610 and 1640, initially by the freemasons whom Sir Henry Savile had brought down from Yorkshire. They formed the secular equivalent of the work on Bath Abbey, on a much larger scale of new work, but inspired by a similar pious resolve to bring life to an abandoned building: in this case the fifteenth-century Divinity School, with its miraculous fan-vaulted ceiling and Duke Humphrey's Library above it. Both had been pillaged and sacked in the first years of the Reformation, the stained glass in the Schools smashed, and Duke Humphrey's Library stripped of its books and shelves. They had stood semi-derelict since. The pious work of reinstatement led by Sir Thomas Bodley and his friend and Merton College colleague Sir Henry Savile, and enthusiastically supported by King James, not

only restored the Divinity School and the Library but also expanded them: the Library was enlarged to become one of the greatest in Europe; the Schools were increased by a spacious new courtyard dedicated, as the inscriptions over the doorways on the courtyard still announce, to the teaching of Astronomy, Geometry, Music, Arithmetic, Grammar, Rhetoric, Logic, Medicine, Jurisprudence, Theology, Moral Philosophy, Natural Philosophy, Languages and History. The additions to the Library were made at either end of Duke Humphrey's, to the east, as the Arts End, above the Proscholium, in 1610–12, to the west, as the Selden End, in the years 1634–40, with Convocation House on the ground floor below it: an H-shaped plan was the result. The Schools court-

yard was added in front of the Arts End between 1613 and *circa* 1620.[37]

Like all major Perpendicular Gothic buildings, the Divinity School was still much admired. In 1603 the judge Sir Roger Wilbraham wrote: 'The chiefest Wonder in Oxford is a faire Divinitie School with church windowes: and over it the fairest librarie.'[38] The fifteenth-century work provided the inspiration for the seventeenth-century additions. The low-relief cusped panelling that covered the façade of the Proscholium was extended, and reproduced all over the front and sides of Bodley's Arts End extension, including the stair towers at either end (Fig. 576). The traceried window in the middle of the Arts End, and its later twin in the same position at the Selden

End, were probably inspired by, and possibly copied from, traceried windows originally at either end of Duke Humphrey's Library. The end elevations of both Arts and Selden Ends were given similar big windows, but with simpler tracery. The windows in the new Schools are all square-headed, but their top row of lights has cusped heads. The crocketed pinnacles, battlements and carved corbel-table heads on Duke Humphrey's Library are continued all the way round the new work.

On the other hand, the inner side of the great crocketed, pinnacled and turreted tower that forms the entry to the Schools quadrangle is filled with a five-storey Tower of the Orders (Fig. 577). The two ends of the library are fitted up with access galleries to the upper shelves supported on thin Tuscan columns, and with classical balustrades; their panelled and cambered wooden ceilings are late Gothic in inspiration but filled with the arms of the donors in Mannerist cartouches.

The building of the Bodleian was accompanied by great activity in the provision of college libraries, either by facilitating accommodation for more books by building shelves in the new fashion to replace or supplement chained books on desks, or by enlarging existing libraries or building new ones. The medieval library at Merton College, Oxford, was improved by new shelves and fittings in 1589 and 1623, and by the building of large dormer windows to improve the lighting (Figs 578, 580). The shelves and other embellishments were 'modern Jacobean', but the windows were in the Perpendicular style. The library of 1592 at St John's College, Oxford, was approximately doubled in size in the 1630s at the expense of Archbishop Laud.[39]

At St John's College, Cambridge, a very grand new library was built in 1623–4. The new second court of St John's, built in the years 1598–1602, had been mildly Gothic, in so far as it deliberately followed the detailing of the original court of 1511–20. The library was more demonstratively

Gothic (Fig. 579), with traceried windows, buttresses and pinnacles; its internal fittings, on the other hand, were not Gothic at all.[40] The library was paid for by John Williams, Bishop of Lincoln, assisted and advised by Valentine Cary, Bishop of Exeter. Cary was an Arminian, Williams a moderate Calvinist with leanings towards ceremony; his private chapel at his palace at Buckden, in Huntingdonshire, had stained glass depicting the Crucifixion, rather daring at that date.[41] Cary wrote to the President of the College that Williams had had doubts about the Gothic windows, but accepted them when Cary argued that 'some men of judgement liked the best the old fashion of church window, holding it most meet for such

a building'. The Bodleian must have had an influence.

These libraries carry one into a world of Jacobean learning; their mixture of Gothic and classic, and the similar mix in churches of the period, can be paralleled in occasional engraved title pages of contemporary learned or religious works. Merton library as fitted up, the Bodleian as built, other college libraries of the same date, are amongst the most civilised and welcoming in the world. St Katherine Cree, even stripped of its fittings, is at least as immediately attractive as any Wren church. The 'King James Gothic' mix at its best is neither naive nor bizarre; it works. If one looks at the conjunction of the Tower of the Orders in the Schools, with its Gothic background, without presupposition that such a conjunction is ridiculous, one can appreciate how skilfully one melds into the other.

The classical elements of the Bodleian–Schools complex are still in the manner of Vredeman de Vries. Those in St Katherine Cree, or in the new Canterbury Quadrangle at St John's, Oxford, are of the next generation of Low Countries classicism, the classicism of Jacques Franquart, Hendrik de Keyser and Peter Paul Rubens, as brought to England in engravings, or by Nicholas Stone and others. The flavour of the mixture is correspondingly different, but equally effective. It reached its triumphant apogee in the porch of St Mary's, Oxford (Fig. 581), built and possibly designed by John Jackson in 1637, at the expense of Laud's former chaplain Dr Morgan Owen: a fan vault over the entry, a cusped pendant under a figure of the Virgin, and all the rest ebullient Flemish-style Baroque.[42]

578 and 580 (*above and facing page*) Modern Jacobean within, Jacobean Gothic without: the library at Merton College, Oxford, remodelled 1589 and 1623.

579 (*left*) The library at St John's College, Cambridge, built 1623–4.

earlier, far more tentative, mixtures, as in Dr Caius's Gate of Honour at Cambridge, were first steps in the same direction. But it is all surmise – likely enough, perhaps, but one would like to have some quotations to support it.

All this work gave an impetus to the building of Gothic vaults. Stone vaults had been comparatively rare under Elizabeth. Among them are the simple but handsome rib vaults in the beer or wine cellars at Castle Ashby (?1570s) and Drayton (1584) in Northamptonshire, the more elaborate vaults in the porch at Wilton (Fig. 163) and at Burghley and in the gatehouse at Charlecote (1570s). But much the most striking Elizabethan vault to survive is in the former great chamber in one of the three round towers of Longford Castle, with its dramatically hanging central pendant (Fig. 582), doing in stone what most Elizabethans

581 (*above*) The porch of St Mary's, Oxford, built in 1637 by Johhn Jackson.

582 The vault (*c.*1590) in the former great chamber at Longford Castle, Wiltshire. As a type it is unique in England.

Unfortunately, there is no evidence as to the thinking behind this kind of work. One can surmise, in the Schools for instance, a deliberate intention to express the two strands, classical and medieval, that made up university teaching, and the two languages, Latin and English, in which they were taught; and that the Tower of the Orders was seen as a more appropriate accompaniment to, for instance, the works of St John Chrysostom, which Sir Henry Savile edited in eight folio volumes (1610–13), than crockets and cusping. One can surmise a conscious pleasure in mixing the two elements. One can surmise that

A Jacobean sequence of gatehouse and corridor vaults starts off at Wadham in 1610, and carries on through the Schools, St John's, Cambridge, and other Oxford and Cambridge buildings, to the gatehouse vault in the east range of Clare College, Cambridge, of 1638–40.[44] All these are panelled fan vaults, with an admixture of William Arnold's individual detailing at Wadham (Fig. 560).

The apogee of this university fan vaulting was constructed, on one daringly slim central column, over the staircase entry to the hall of Christ Church, Oxford (Fig. 583). In its dazzling delicacy it is close enough to the fourteenth-century chapter house at Hereford cathedral (Fig. 584) to make one suspect deliberate imitation. But it is all too little documented.

Anthony Wood says that it was built 'about 1630', and that Samuel Fell 'made [it] as it is now by the help of one – Smith, an artificer from London'.[45] Fell was dean from 1638 to 1648, but his

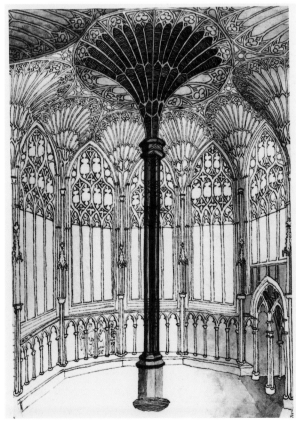

583 (*above*) The staircase at Christ Church, Oxford, built *c.*1634–5, possibly by the mason Robert Smith.

584 The fourteenth-century chapter-house at Hereford cathedral, as drawn by William Stukeley.

would venture on only in plaster. Its elaborate patterning of ribs seems to depend on no English prototypes, and the only contemporary, or near contemporary to it in the British Isles is the remarkable vault, also with deeply hanging pendants, at Bunratty Castle in County Clare. This was inserted into a top-floor room of the castle by the anglophile Earl of Thomond, perhaps around 1600, but there seems to be no documentation.[43]

'skill in contrivance of building' is said to have been made use of by Brian Duppa, who preceded him as dean from 1629 to 1638.[46] The most likely identification of '– Smith' is with a freemason, Robert Smith, possibly working with another freemason, Hugh Davies. In 1632 Smith, Davies and Richard Maude signed a contract to build what became the Canterbury Quadrangle at St John's College, Oxford.[47] They ran into difficulties and abandoned it, but probably not before they had constructed a fan-vaulted corridor to give access to the new quadrangle. Between 1625 and 1634 Davies made a series of models for a great staircase that was to have gone up to the first floor of the Bodleian Library.[48] The project collapsed, but may have inspired the Christ Church staircase, built, perhaps, in 1634–5. Robert Smith, described as 'mason' and 'privileged person' (that is, not a member of an Oxford guild), died in St Aldate's, Oxford, in 1635, apparently still in work, and across the road from Christ Church.[49]

Apart from the more prominent examples in churches, chapels and libraries, domestic windows with arched lights continued to be found from time to time. For the rooms in collegiate buildings they were still the norm, as in the previous century. When they are found in more ambitious houses, one can suspect a special reason. Their extensive use at Knole for the new work installed by the 1st Earl of Dorset from 1605 onwards was perhaps due to a wish to pay respect to the medieval house of the Fiennes family and the Archbishops of Canterbury, round the two gatehouses and other portions of which seventeenth-century Knole was developed. When the house at Chantmarle in Dorset was built by Sir John Strode 'to the form I conceived and plotted it' in and around 1611, the arched window lights that he installed throughout (Fig. 303) may have been due to his fondness for the Strode family house at nearby Parnham, where he had been brought up and which he was to inherit in 1628.[50]

This has similar windows dating from the 1540s, or thereabouts. There may have been some such reason of sentiment that led Edward Eyton to have similar windows in the new house that he built at Brockhall in Northamptonshire, some time between 1607 and 1625 (Fig. 97). It was not a provincial job: the plan, which derived from Palladio, was provided by John Thorpe, and the surveyor or freemason in charge was probably John's brother Thomas, one of the leading artificers of the period.[51]

The wing at Stapleford Park in Leicestershire remodelled by the 1st Lord Sherard and his wife, Abigail, in 1633 is in striking contrast to work of this kind (Fig. 585). It celebrates the family's ancestors, from William the Conqueror downwards, in the form of twelve statues set in a row under Gothic canopies. Some of the statues and canopies are genuinely medieval, but at least half date from the 1630s. The windows on the ground and first floors have arched heads and hoodmoulds; the central and biggest of them has three curious triangular gables of pseudo-Gothic form. Also inserted in the façade are numerous genuine medieval reliefs of religious subjects. But the building is surmounted with gables and dormer windows with pedimented tops between scrolls, of the later Flemish type introduced to England by Inigo Jones, among others, around 1620. The dormers, however, incorporate further medieval figures in niches.[52]

The fanciful architecture of Stapleford has more in common with the small but curious world of Jacobean castles and Jacobean chivalry, some discussion of which can terminate this chapter. But first it is necessary to say something about the long tradition of pageant castles.

An account of these can start with the marriage of Henry VII's eldest and short-lived son, Arthur, to Katherine of Aragon in 1501. This was celebrated by a masque in which a castle on wheels 'right cunningly devised' was drawn into the hall by 'fower great beasts with chaines of gold . . .

585 The wing at
Stapleford Park,
Leicestershire, remodelled
by Lord and Lady Sherard
and dated 1633.

There were within the same Castle disguised VIII
goodly and fresh ladyes, looking out of the windowes of the same, and in the foure corners of this
Castle were IIII turrets . . . in the which . . . was a
little child apparelled like a maiden'. The children
sang as the pageant moved up the hall, and the
castle was later assaulted by 'VIII goodly knights
naming themselves Knights of the Mount of
Love', who captured the ladies.[53]

This Mount or Castle of Love was in a line that
went back to at least the thirteenth century. In
1214, at a pageant held at Treviso in Italy, a castle,
defended by ladies armed with flowers, fruit and
nuts was attacked by similarly armed knights.[54]
Such a castle was clearly apposite for a wedding
pageant, such as for that held for Arthur and
Katherine of Aragon 300 years later. But it could
also be given a religious meaning. In the poem
'Château d'Amour' by Robert Grosseteste,
Bishop of Lincoln, which was written some time
between 1215 and 1253, the castle symbolised the
virginity of Mary, and her penetration by God.[55]
Sacred and secular versions occurred all the way
through the later Middle Ages, in literature, in art
and in pageantry. A good literary example was
published by William Neville in 1518. It is
described on the title page as: 'The Castell of
Pleasure; the conveyance of a dreme how Desyre
went to the Castell of Pleasure, wherein was
the garden of affecyon inhabyted by Beaute, to
whome he amerously expressed his love, upon
the whiche supplycacion rose grete stryfe,
disputacion and argument between Pyte and
Dysdayne.'[56]

But pageant castles were not only Castles of
Love or Pleasure; they could also serve as useful
stands for singers, musicians or the making of
speeches of welcome, for royal entries or similar
occasions; when fireworks were introduced, they
were appropriate venues from which to let them
off; they could be the objects of mock assaults for
a number of symbolic reasons.

In 1556, when Elizabeth was living at Hatfield
in her sister's reign, she dismissed a masque containing a 'devise of a castell of clothe of gold' with
the remark that she 'mysliked these folliries'.[57] It
was an attitude that she may have absorbed at the
court of her brother Edward. There is no record
of such 'folliries' during his reign. Edward's and
her tutor Roger Ascham had attacked the *Morte
d'Arthur* and 'bookes of chivalry' in general as
works in which 'these be countest the noblest

441

knights, that do kill most men without any quarrel, and commit foulest adulteries by subtlest shifs'.[58] But Malory, and chivalry in general, came back in strength in the course of Elizabeth's reign, and pageant castles with them.

It was in the tradition of the masque of 1501 that the so-called Triumph of 1581 was devised to entertain the queen and the French ambassador. Sir Philip Sidney and three others, calling themselves the Four Foster Children of Desire, unsuccessfully besieged the queen in her pavilion by the lists in Whitehall, renamed for the occasion the Castle of Perfect Beauty, and possibly embellished in keeping. Two days of jousting followed, against twenty-two other knights, who came to the defence of the castle; in the end the Four Foster Children acknowledged themselves 'overcome, as to be slaves to this Fortress for ever'.[59] The 'Triumph' was a celebration of Elizabeth's virginity, and like many other such events had political undertones: the French ambassador had come over to discuss the proposed marriage between Elizabeth and the Duke of Alençon, a match opposed by members of the war party in England, Sidney amongst them, who wanted England to lead a Protestant crusade against the Catholic monarchies on the Continent.

The celebrated Accession Day tilts were similarly political: they were designed to encourage loyalty to the queen, and grew in popularity and elaboration along with the excitement of the defeat of the Armada in 1588.[60] They had been inaugurated in the 1570s by Sir Henry Lee, the self-appointed Knight of the Crown. The tilts took place on the anniversary of the queen's accession, 17 November, in the tilt-yard at Whitehall. Her courtiers jousted in honour of their queen. Similar tilts were to be held on 24 March, the anniversary of the accession of James, up to 1621 or 1622;[61] others were held to mark special occasions, a marriage or the visit of an important foreigner, as with the Four Foster Children's challenge. The actual tilting followed medieval rules

and precedents, but it was heavily overlaid with other elements; the different knights tried to outdo each other in the elaborate decoration of their armour, the ingenuity of the devices on their shields, the fantastic outfits of the numerous attendants that escorted them. Then as later sport was given a political meaning.

As in chivalric expressions all over Europe, medieval elements were mixed with references to classical heroes and Arthurian knights. The tilts spilled over into literature, or literature spilled in the tilts. Sir Philip Sidney inserted an especially elaborate tilt into the reworked version of his prose romance *Arcadia*, published after his death in 1590.[62] Spenser's *The Faerie Queene*, published in 1590 and 1596, moved in a similar world of knights, magicians, fairies and monsters deployed in a magically unreal landscape to express moral and political meanings in allegorical forms.

In 1591 Sir Henry Lee handed over to the Earl of Cumberland. Cumberland's first tilt as Knight of the Crown in 1592 was probably the occasion for Hilliard's famous portrait miniature (Fig. 586). It shows Cumberland standing proudly in gorgeous armour speckled with the five-pointed star of his coat of arms; he holds his tournament lance; the queen's glove is pinned on his cap; his gauntlets and plumed helmet lie ready on the ground, his shield hangs on the adjoining tree, bearing his personal impresa of a thunderbolt amidst clouds and the motto *Fulmen Aquasque Fero* ('I bear lighting and water').

The miniature should be seen in conjunction with the speech that Cumberland made on this occasion. This was inspired in part by his ownership of a castle (one among many) in Westmorland, with the Arthurian name of Pendragon: he tilted as 'The Knight of Pendragon Castle'. He used what professed to be a miniature version of the castle as his pavilion. His speech resembled other speeches or challenges in tilts of the period, in the way it coated serious intent with playfulness: 'This Castle, most happy Princesse, not by

586 George Clifford,
3rd Earl of Cumberland,
from the miniature by
Nicholas Hilliard, perhaps
painted in 1592.

588 One of the pageant castles erected as part of a fireworks display on the Thames in London, in 1613.

Inchantment, but by miracle, is in one night removed from Westmoreland to Westminster . . . out of this Castle came King Arthur, and by him all his Knights, a Monument worth ye beholding for the Antiquity, ye upholding for the Honor, the Holding for ye Fortune.' Cumberland had 'resolved humbly to intreat your Hignesse to enter ye Castle, but being too homely, he durst not presume for there is nothing to be seene, but yt which this world have worne out of fashion. Excalibers Sword, ye sleeve yt Sir Lancelott bare for his Ladie, Balyns Speare, Sr Braumins smyter, Dinidans Dittie, Sr Gawains Spurres, Sir Lamoracks Gauntlett; ye Sangrealls old Sheild . . .'.[63] It is possible that his pageant castle may have served as an entry to the lists, and that the tilters

587 (*below*) The English Pavilion erected for the meeting of Henry VIII and Francois Ier at the 'Field of the Cloth of Gold', 1520.

processed into them through it. No illustration of it has survived; one can surmise that it in fact bore little resemblance to the real Pendragon Castle.

Since pageant castles were ephemeral, depictions of them are rare. Enough survive, however, to show what appears to be a consistent tradition. They were in no way imitations of real castles; they were stylised symbols of them. The illustration of a Castle of Love in the fourteenth-century Luttrell Psalter is probably based on contemporary pageant castles, and is recognisably related to the temporary pavilion erected by Henry VIII for his meeting with François I at the Field of the Cloth of Gold in 1520 (Fig. 587).[64] Because it was put up to accommodate the king and his retinue, the pavilion is much larger than the Luttrell Psalter castle, but both have battlements, and purely decorative round turrets. In the pavilion these support symbolically defensive figures – in fact statues – at the fake gun loop-holes in the turrets.

589 The keep, once known as Caesar's Tower, at Kenilworth Castle, Warwickshire, with the round arches and windows inserted by the Earl of Leicester, c.1575.

Illustrations survive of a series of little pageant forts or castles, of late Elizabethan or Jacobean date. One was erected for the queen's visit to Elvetham in Hampshire in 1591;[65] 'Oberon's Palace' was designed by Inigo Jones for the masque *Oberon the Fairy Prince* in 1611 (Fig. 526);[66] 'the Magician's Castle' and its fellow (Fig. 588) were erected on the Thames for fireworks at the marriage of Princess Elizabeth to the Elector Palatine in 1613;[67] and a rotating castle of boards was erected by Captain Robert Dover as the central feature of his Cotswold Games, some time between 1605 and 1638.[68]

All these structures had turrets and battlements. The two fireworks pavilions rose in reducing stages to a central turret, like the Luttrell Psalter Castle of Love. One of them had gunloops; so did Oberon's Palace, but its gun-looped turrets framed a fanciful classical centre. None of the buildings had any close relationship to a genuine medieval castle, or any portion of one. The references were, if anything, to Arthurian knights rather than medieval ones. The gate of Oberon's Palace opened in the course of the masque to reveal Oberon feasting with Arthurian knights 'preserved in fairyland'; they rose and emerged from the palace, not to joust but to dance.[69]

In the years 1603–5 the building of Lulworth Castle in Dorset brought this make-believe into the region of permanent structures. Up till then there had been a good deal of new building at existing castles, and such work usually paid respect to its context. Elaborate classical decoration, as at Longleat and Wollaton, was clearly considered unsuitable. Leicester's extensive work at Kenilworth was sober and simple, however grand in scale; his turreted gatehouse was reminiscent of a medieval gatehouse; the massive round arches he inserted into the keep (Fig. 589) must have been considered in keeping with its context, and the belief that the keep was in fact of Roman origin.[70] Elizabeth's additions to Wind-

590 The entrance front of Chillingham Castle, Northumberland, perhaps dating from the 1590s.

445

591 and 592   Two related castles: (*right*) at Lulworth, Dorset, built 1603–5, and (*facing page, top*) Ruperra, South Wales, dated 1626.

sor Castle were in the same vein.[71] The windows inserted for the modernisation of Wardour Castle in the 1570s had Gothic lights; classicism was confined to two door-cases, and these were soberly Doric.[72] The new range added to Chillingham Castle in Northumberland, perhaps in the 1590s, is entered by what at first sight appears to be a Tower of the Orders (Fig. 590); the fact that all three stages of the tower are Doric is likely to be due to its castle context.[73]

But Lulworth Castle (Fig. 591), although it was called a castle from the start, or at least from very early on, was not built on or near a medieval castle; and it was built in a different spirit. Lord Howard of Bindon, who built it, expressed the wish that it might 'prove pretty'; Thomas Gerard, writing about 1630, described it as 'well seated for prospect and pleasure; but of little other use'.[74] It was a lodge, if a very sizeable one, on the edge of a deer-park; its castle form was a conceit or device, as so often with lodges, and its inspiration

was more pageant than Plantagenet. With its battlements, four round towers and central turret, it was a blown-up version of pageant castles; the long arched lights of its windows were perhaps inspired by those inserted in the 1570s into Wardour Castle, but being even longer, without mullions, they had an air of elegant artificiality; lions' heads were carved under them with open mouths, as though to act as gargoyles, though they opened from nothing, and added a small extra touch of fantasy.

Ruperra Castle (Fig. 592), though 100 miles or so away in South Wales, was clearly inspired by Lulworth. It had a similar plan, battlements, corner towers and central turret; the fact that it had the same tall lights but with the extra idiosyncrasy of a higher central light, as at Leweston and Folke, suggests that an Arnold may have come from Dorset to work there. But unlike Lulworth, and perhaps inappositely, there were gabled dormers between the towers; these were later removed.[75]

446

Ruperra carried the date 1626 on the porch, and
was built by Sir Thomas Morgan (1564–1632), a
younger son who made a fortune as steward of
the Earls of Pembroke; he was knighted at
Wilton in 1623. In 1604 the Earl of Pembroke, Sir
Philip Sidney's nephew, married Alathea Talbot,
daughter of Gilbert, Earl of Shrewsbury. Thomas
Morgan was one of the trustees of the marriage
settlement. According to John Aubrey, the marriage was accompanied by a tournament at Wilton;
some of the shields of the tilters were still hanging
at Wilton in his day, 'of pasteboard painted with
their devices and emblemes, which were very
pretty and ingenious'.[76] Morgan may well have
participated; the tournament suggests, at least,
the ambience from which Ruperra emerged.

Walton Castle, at Walton-in-Gordano, Somerset (Fig. 593), was probably built shortly after 1615,
in which year its builder, Lord Poulet, acquired
the property by marriage.[77] There was no medieval castle on the site or near it. The house was
built as a lodge, like Lulworth, but was a much
more modest one; it can have been designed only
for short stays, or one-day visits. It was not for
deer-hunting, but for duck-shooting in a duck
decoy in the marshy ground along the Bristol
Channel below the castle. It takes the form of an
outer curtain wall, punctuated by round battle-

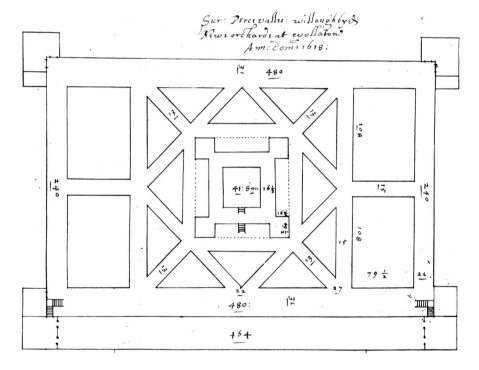

Sur: Percevallus: willoughbyes
New orcharde at wollaton
Ann: domi 1618:

480

41: Squ 16½

480:

464

595 (*above*) 'Sir Percevall
Willoughbyes New
Orchard' at Wollaton
Hall, Nottinghamshire,
designed by John
Smythson in 1618
(SM. DWGS III/16)

from which superb views could and can be enjoyed across the marshes and Bristol Channel to
Wales.

Allusions to castles, forts or fortifications occur
in a number of different contexts in the early seventeenth century. The garden walls of Audley
End, on a large scale (Fig. 594), and of Hazelbury
Manor, Wiltshire, on a small one, were varied
with bastion-like projections that gave them a
deliberately fortified air; those at Hazelbury
survive.[78] Part of the vanished garden at Ware
Park in Surrey was laid out on a plan imitating
fortifications – not, however, medieval ones, but
with the distinctive bastions of contemporary
work.[79] At Wollaton in 1618 John Smythson made
designs for 'Sir Percevall Willoughbyes New
orcharde', the central feature of which was a
mount formed fortification-wise with an outer
square with square corner bastions, and a central
square rising inside it (Fig. 595); the allusion was
perhaps both to contemporary forts and to
pageant castles.[80] It may never have been built.
Something similar seems to be shown in a miniature by Hilliard, probably of the Earl of Northumberland.[81] At Blickling around 1620 the bridge
leading to the house over the moat was decorated
with mimic gun-loops, and gun-loops and battlements were incorporated in a design made by
Robert Leminge for a garden seat there (Fig. 43),
which may never have been built.[82]

An especially inventive example of pageant
architecture turned into stone was built at some
undocumented period, but one would surmise
in the early seventeenth century, at Newstead
Abbey in Nottinghamshire.[83] It took the form of
a fountain (Fig. 596), built on the plan of a double
octagon, the smaller octagon at the top containing a water tank, a large octagon below incorporating eight alcoves, and basins into which the
water flowed. The fountain was originally erected
outside the house, but at some stage was taken
down and rebuilt in the centre of the courtyard,
the old cloister garth of the abbey. The upper

mented towers and a central tower or keep rising
from the courtyard enclosed by the curtain wall.
This is three storeys high, and has one room to
each storey; an attached staircase turret rises
one storey higher, to give access to the flat roof,

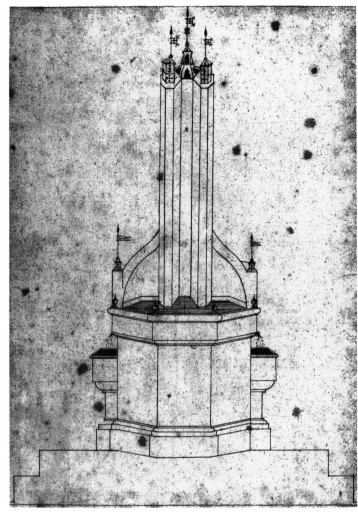

596 (*above left*)
The fountain at Newstead Abbey, Nottinghamshire, perhaps built *c.*1620.

597 (*above right*)
A design for a fountain by John Smythson (SM. DWGS 11/25(3)).

594 (*facing page, top*)
West wall of the Mount Garden, Audley End, Essex, from Braybrooke's *History of Audley End and Saffron Walden*, 1856.

stage is fancifully Gothic, pierced all the way round at the top with miniature gun-loops, and ornamented with fantastic animals at high and low level at the angles of the octagon. The lower and larger octagon starts off with battlements and quatrefoils, but then turns classical, with an entablature and shell-headed alcoves.

Two fountains designed in a somewhat similar vein by John Smythson, one certainly and the other probably for the Little Castle at Bolsover in Derbyshire,[84] can introduce that remarkable building (Fig. 598). It is deservedly the best known of Jacobean castles, but its history is not a simple one, and reflects the different personalities and aims of its two successive owners and builders, Charles and William Cavendish.[85]

The largely ruinous castle of Bolsover, on a magnificent hilltop site, was leased and then bought by Sir Charles Cavendish from his brother-in-law the 7th Earl of Shrewsbury in 1608 and 1613. In 1612 he cleared the north-west end of the site, and started to build what became known as the Little Castle. Building accounts from November 1612 to March 1614 survive.[86] They cover the building of the basement and the beginnings of the ground floor. The hall chimneypiece on the ground floor, which is an integral part of the structure, is dated 1616. Charles Cavendish died in April 1617, and was succeeded by his son William, later created Viscount Mansfield and successively Earl, Marquess and Duke of Newcastle.

Charles Cavendish's building had less in common with Lulworth and its fellows than with other new buildings on castle sites, built to be in keeping with their surroundings, as at Kenilworth, Windsor and Dunster. It was simple and solid, with conventional mullion-and-transom windows, and no external ornament. It takes its place in a line of compact tower-like structures associated with Robert and John Smythson, beginning with North Lees Hall in Derbyshire,[87] built about 1594 by a protégé of the Talbot family (Gilbert Talbot, 7th Earl of Shrewsbury, was Charles Cavendish's first cousin and greatest friend). Later examples were Carlton Hall in Yorkshire, built for Charles Cavendish's nephew by marriage, and Tipton Hall and Stydd Hall in Derbyshire.[88] Documentation is lacking, but all three were probably built at much the same time as the Little Castle; none was on a castle site.

Like Lees Hall, the Little Castle has a battlemented parapet rather than a classical balustrade, as at Hardwick. There was nothing unusual about that; battlements were in common use for buildings of all kinds. Even the corner turrets are reduced versions of the turrets that were in fashion at the time, as at Blickling, Hatfield and Northampton House. Other features, however, suggest a deliberate adaptation of the compact plan-type to give it more of a castle air: the irregular fenestration on the north-east and north-west façades, the frequent expanses of blank wall, above all the placing of the staircase tower asymmetrically at one corner, rising higher than the rest of the building, and the way in which this tower and the whole north-west façade loom sheer out of the hillside (Figs 598, 599). The effect is powerful rather than playful, as though Charles Cavendish,[89] son of a self-made man, but married to the heiress of a line of Northumbrian barons, was using the castle setting to assert the establishment of his family among the aristocracy of Derbyshire.

His contribution (aided by John and just possibly Robert Smythson) to the interior of the Little Castle was the extreme ingenuity of the planning, the vaulted rooms, and the first of the hooded chimneypieces that were to become one of its most distinctive features. Vaulted rooms were a feature of all the projects associated with him: he recommended 'fair vaults' in the letter accompanying the plan he provided for Hatfield in 1607.[90] This was for a house with no castle connections; but the context of Bolsover gave him ample reasons for indulging his taste. The basement has groin vaulting throughout; the hall (Fig. 600) and pillar parlour on the ground floor have rib vaults (Fig. 484). The vaults are supported on columns; those in the hall have pointed arches, but otherwise there are no Gothic elements, but detailing

599 (*above*) A mid-seventeenth–century drawing of the Little Castle, Bolsover.

598 (*facing page*) The Little Castle, Bolsover, Derbyshire, seen from the valley. It was built from 1611 onwards by Charles Cavendish and his son William, with John Smythson as architect or surveyor.

600 (*right*). The hall in the Little Castle.

601 and 602 Two mid-seventeenth-century drawings of the Little Castle, Bolsover, from the garden (*top*) and from the entrance court.

medieval in feel, not dissimilar to medieval hooded chimneypieces of the fourteenth century, but in fact containing no Gothic details.

William Cavendish inherited in 1617; he finished the structure of the Little Castle, if it was not finished already, and over the next fifteen years or more supplied the little building with a wealth of chimneypieces, panelling, painting and external embellishments, including balconies and classical doorways, unequalled anywhere in the kingdom for a building of its size, not only enriching but also substantially altering its character, and enabling Francis Andrewes, writing about 1640, to compare and contrast it with Welbeck, Worksop and Hardwick as 'divine', 'a pearl', 'the pendant of the eare', and 'prittie' ('. . . Hardwick is hard, Bolsover is prittie').[92] It had become a plaything.

William Cavendish's main external additions to it were two walled enclosures, one a forecourt, the other what became known as the Fountain Garden. Unlike his father he had been a tilter,[93] a companion of Prince Henry at the barriers, who would almost certainly have seen Inigo Jones's Palace of Oberon, and possibly participated in the accompanying masque. There is the same spirit visible in the Bolsover forecourt; it is punctuated with the decorative gun-loops (Fig. 605) so prominent in Oberon's Palace, but conspicuously lacking in the main building of the Little Castle. It has four little turrets, and battlements made more decorative than those of the main building by being interspersed with obelisk-shaped pinnacles. Similarly decorated battlements were carried all the way round the wall of the Fountain Garden; this is 12 feet thick, enabling it to support a broad walk, with access into the first floor of the Little Castle at one end; at intervals it is widened to contain little rooms, some with fireplaces (Fig. 604). In the garden is the fountain: busts of the emperors around the edge, urinating cherubs in the centre, and above them a plinth supporting a marble statue of a

throughout of extreme originality, presumably by John Smythson. The first design for the hall chimneypiece, for which a drawing by Smythson survives,[91] shows a hooded chimneypiece of alabaster and jet, loosely inspired by Serlio, the first in the series that was to be continued, with inexhaustible variations, throughout the rest of the Little Castle. This must have been considered too decorative for a hall, and what was built was a soberer design, of stone, and therefore more

coronet appropriate to the earldom that William Cavendish was granted in that year. He also used ornamental gun-loops to light the granary of his stables, built at Welbeck in 1625, and designed by John Smythson; Smythson used similar gun-loops in his design for stables at Clifton Hall, near Nottingham,[96] made in 1632; of his two undated designs for fountains, one has miniature sham gun-loops in the little flag-surmounted turret at the top of its central column, the other, the first design for the Venus fountain, has gun-loops ornamenting the drums supporting the cherubs; these were omitted in the fountain as it was built.

It may be that forecourt and fountain garden were two separate projects, the forecourt predating the garden; but it is just as likely that they form part of the same campaign, which could date from as late as the 1630s, and been made in immediate anticipation of the royal visit.

603 (*above*) The Venus Fountain in the garden of the Little Castle, erected *c.*1630. Statues have been added in the niches in recent years.

604 A room in the garden wall of the Little Castle.

naked Venus (Fig. 603), based on a figure by Giambologna but transposed by the sculptor into a chunky goddess, far from Italian but by no means without character – a 'Derbyshire lass', as Lucy Worsthorne has described her.[94]

The Little Castle, in fact, had become a Castle of Love. It was as such that it was visited by Charles I and his young wife Henrietta Maria when they came over from Welbeck in July 1634, and were entertained by Ben Jonson's masque *Love's Welcome at Bolsover*.[95] One can only conjecture at what stage this role for the Little Castle was envisaged. The actual fountain cannot date from before 1628, for it is carved with the

In the long wing that William Cavendish built to the south of the castle, probably in the 1630s, and in the house that his younger brother built at Slingsby Castle, Yorkshire, in the same period, castle references sank to a minimum. In the Bolsover wing the distinctive battlements of the Little Castle forecourt and garden were repeated, but its prominent feature, as at Slingsby, was its elaborate and eccentric classical detailing, partly inspired by Wendel Dietterlin. When, after the Civil War, William Cavendish, now Duke of Newcastle, came to build a new house at Nottingham Castle, on a site as superb and commanding as that of Bolsover, no attempt was made to play up to its castle background; the house was a handsome version of one of the Genoese palaces recorded by Rubens.

Epilogue

In the 1630s, as the high Elizabethan and Jacobean style petered out, and eclectic mixes of Gothic and classical went out of fashion, there was nothing obviously set to take their place; certainly no sense of excitement about something new such as had greeted the discovery of classicism by way of Serlio in the mid-sixteenth century, no fashionable fever such as was set off by the publications of Vredeman de Vries and others a few decades later. Flemish, German, French and Italian pattern books, old and new, continued to be used to give ideas for chimneypieces, monuments and entrances; seen in the mass, the result was miscellaneous in character, and variable in quality. A new feature, imported, like so much else, from the Low Countries, was elaborately modelled brickwork, often surmounted by scrolled and pedimented gables, much simplified versions of the Vriesian ones. For twenty years or so such gables became popular for buildings of stone as well as brick. They were used by Inigo Jones to surmount otherwise Italianate façades in a couple of London houses.

Jones was a giant in the world of English architecture, but too much can be made of him with the benefit of hindsight; he was laying a series of time bombs which were to explode in subsequent centuries, but his achievement and influence in his own lifetime was less than he deserved, or is often credited with. Nor, although his name is always associated with that of Palladio, did he confine himself to one vein: like most architects he was prepared to produce what his patrons wanted – scrolled gables in the 1620s, elaborate chimneypieces modelled on contemporary French work for Henrietta Maria and others in the 1630s; he presided over the complete renewal of the Gothic tracery of the choir and east end of St Paul's at the same time as he was encasing the nave and transept with low-key classical façades and adding the monumental west portico.

Jones admired Palladio because he thought that he knew more about Roman classicism than any other contemporary architect. His own discovery, analysis and recording of Roman remains in 1613–14 was the great excitement of his life and meant as much, or more, to him than Palladio's own architecture. It gave him a depth of knowledge that his English predecessors could not hope to have. His Doric temple in Covent Garden and Corinthian portico at St Paul's were the culminating result of this knowledge and owed little, if anything, to Palladio, or to contemporary architecture on the Continent; if anything, Osborne's abortive portico for Salisbury House, which Jones must have known of, offered him a prototype. In England, at the time, these two buildings were admired, but not emulated, and few of his contemporaries understood what he was up to. It took the exile imposed by the Civil War to make Englishmen look again seriously at classical architecture, forty years after Jones.

Jones can be claimed as the first English architect, on the grounds that he was the first known Englishman to control every aspect of the buildings put up under him; and as the first true English classicist, because of the extent and depth of his knowledge. Yet it could also be maintained that he was not an architect at all. He was a painter by training, a stage designer by vocation; except in the simplest situations, he could not design a convincing building in the round. He had much less feeling than, say, Robert Smythson or John Thorpe for the nuances of grouping and planning. The façade of the Banqueting House rightly amazed his contemporaries, even if John Chamberlain could say that it was too good for its purpose; but a façade is what it was, a three-bay Palladian palace façade stuck not very appropriately onto a single huge room; and the chilly magnificence of this room was a less sympathetic venue for masques than its 1609 predecessor.

The most significant feature of the middle years of the seventeenth century was the development of the plain double- or triple-pile rectangular block without frills and with a hipped roof instead of gables, the emergence of which has been described above in chapter 2, and its aggrandisement from houses suitable for minor or medium gentry to houses for great people.

Inigo Jones made a few modest essays in this vein, which may or may not have had an influence. But the seminal figure in establishing what became the ruling type in the second half of the seventeenth century was Sir Roger Pratt. Pratt had travelled on the Continent, knew Italian architecture at first hand and admired Jones. But by background he was a country gentleman and landowner; he knew what his class wanted and was interested, in a way that Jones never was, in the convenient planning of houses to fit their needs; his notes discussing this have survived, though they were not published in his lifetime.

Coteshill, Pratt's first great country house, was a building of monumental simplicity, as different as could be from the complex Jacobean houses of twenty or thirty years earlier. But it was his less heroic design for Clarendon House, prominent on Piccadilly, not tucked away in Berkshire, that was to become a seminal model. Though built for a more powerful patron, it was less monumental than Coleshill. Its friendly formula – hipped roof, central cupola, protruding wings, lack of ornamental detail apart from the entrance doorway and pediment above it – was to be copied over and over again, both in brick and stone, on into the early eighteenth century. In more modest examples the wings or the pediment could be left out. From the 1670s onwards casement windows were replaced by sash windows with small panes, usually painted white, an importation from Holland.

When, in 1667, Samuel Pepys compared Audley End with Clarendon House, to the disadvantage of the former, he was expressing the typical reaction of an educated man of his day. A time in which country houses all aimed to look much the same, and in which the emphasis was on being sensible, was not likely to see much enthusiasm for great Elizabethan or Jacobean houses, which were not at all sensible and as different from each other as their owners and designers could make them.

But Hawksmoor could say that Elizabethan Wollaton showed 'some true stroakes of architecture', and Vanbrugh's towers, forecourts, occasional bow or bay windows and dramatic skylines have elements, possibly deliberate, of the Jacobean and Elizabethan about them. So do the houses of Robert Taylor and others, in the middle of the century: they were compact Georgian 'devices' planned round top-lit staircases, as anticipated by John Thorpe around 1600, and embellished with circular and polygonal bays. It did not add up to very much. In general elsewhere Elizabethan houses were being shorn of their projections, their top storeys removed, their skylines reduced to the horizontal, their windows filled in or replaced by sashes, their top-floor state rooms abandoned, their long galleries subdivided, to make them approximate to Georgian standards.

From the late eighteenth century onwards Elizabethan architecture came back into favour at an increasing rate. A handful of neo-Elizabethan houses or additions to houses built before 1800 was followed by a larger crop in the 1820s and 1830s; and from then on, in the eclectic scene of the nineteenth century and on into the twentieth, to build buildings large and small in the Elizabethan style, or what was thought to be the Elizabethan style, was an accepted alternative to Gothic and Classical.

Architects and their clients took from Elizabethan architecture what they wanted to find in it. Their feelings about it were sentimental and historical as much as, and more than, aesthetic. They admired it for its picturesque quaintness or for expressing 'old English hospitality'. They found it 'piquant'. Hardwick was not thought much of. Horace Walpole had already written it off in 1760: 'Never was I less charmed in my life' – and even J. A. Gotch, sedulous chronicler of Elizabethan architecture and prolific designer in its style, described it in his *Architecture of the Renaissance in England* (1894) as 'an example of the less interesting houses of the period, large, symmetrical tame, and without any piquant detail'.

Large neo-Elizabethan houses were built with façades and plans of an irregularity that would never have been acceptable in the sixteenth century. Norman Shaw and others developed their 'Old English' manner with brilliant showmanship, but it had nothing much to do with the sixteenth century, or with any period of Old England. Around and after 1900 it was unshowy Elizabethan vernacular that attracted the serious middle classes, and was imitated by them. And from the 1830s onwards, at every social level, clients succumbed to the charms of half-timbering, fake or genuine.

They are still doing so today. Ignored by the architectural magazines or the glossier weeklies, half timbering, usually fake, and sub-Elizabethan in all its varieties, proliferates in the more expensive housing estates all over England. The inspiration, where recognisable, is usually vernacular. But on a more ambitious level, just as Ferdinand de Rothschild collected an anthology of details from the châteaux of France and melded them into one hilltop fantasy at Waddesdon Manor,

Christopher Moran has savoured Elizabethan country houses, selected ceilings, chimneypieces, a façade from Kirby Hall, a great fountain once at Hampton Court, brought them together, and added them to an actual hall of the fifteenth century to create a neo-Elizabethan house in the grand manner on Chelsea Embankment in London.

Only occasionally did the Elizabethan style inspire feelings or buildings of a different nature, perhaps rather closer to those of its originators. One can think of Joseph Nash's engraving of Hardwick lit up like a lantern under a full moon in his *Mansions of England in the Olden Time*; or the approach by gatehouses and pavilions to the overpoweringly symmetrical front of Harlaxton, in which Baroque and Elizabethan so magnificently clash and clang together; or move on a hundred years and find in James Stirling's delicate, piled-up fantasies in glass and glazed brick, reminiscences of Elizabethan prodigies as brilliant and impractical as they were. In these and a few other buildings, something of the high-Elizabethan spirit lives again, adventurous, strange, outrageous and beautiful.

606   James Stirling's Engineering Building, 1959–63, at the University of Leicester.

Abbreviations
and
References

Colvin
Howard Colvin, *A Biographical Dictionary of British Architects, 1600–1840*, 4th edn, New Haven and London, 2008

DNB
L. Stephen and S. Lee, eds, *Dictionary of National Biography*, 63 vols, London, 1885–1900

Girouard, *Smythson*
Mark Girouard, *Robert Smythson and the Elizabethan Country House*, new edn, New Haven and London, 1983

House of Commons, Elizabeth
The House of Commons, 1558–1603, ed. P. W. Hasler, London: History of Parliament Trust, 1981

ODNB
H. C. G. Matthew and Brian Harrison, eds, *The Oxford Dictionary of National Biography*, 62 vols, Oxford, 2004

Royal Works
H. M. Colvin, R. A. Brown and A. J. Taylor, eds, *The History of the King's Works*, 6 vols, London, 1963–82

Smythson Drawings
Mark Girouard, ed., 'The Smythson Collection of the Royal Institute of British Architects', *Architectural History*, 5 (1962)

Thorpe Drawings
John Summerson, ed., *The Book of Architecture of John Thorpe in Sir John Soane's Museum*, Walpole Society, 40, Glasgow, 1966

Wells-Cole, *Decoration*
Antony Wells-Cole, *Art and Decoration in Elizabethan and Jacobean England: The Influence of Continental Prints, 1558–1625*, New Haven and London, 1997

White, *Dictionary*
Adam White, *A Biographical Dictionary of London Tomb Sculptors, c. 1560–c. 1660*, Walpole Society, 61, 1999, pp. 1–162

Willis and Clark, *Cambridge*
Robert Willis, *The Architectural History of the University of Cambridge . . .*, ed. John Willis Clark, 3 vols, Cambridge, 1988 [a reproduction of the original 1886 edition, but not including all the plans]

*An asterisk indicates that the reference appears in the list of abbreviations on the facing page.

Chapter 1   People

1   *The Diary of Baron Waldstein*, trans. G. W. Gross, London, 1981, p. 111.

2   Edmund Spenser, 'Mother Hubbards Tale' [ll. 1170–83, 1199–1203], in *The Shorter Poems*, ed. R. A. McCabe, London, 1999, pp. 265–6. Cf. 'The Ruines of Time' (1591) [ll. 216–17, ibid., p. 173 and n., p. 587]: 'The whiles the Foxe is crept/ Into the hole, the which the Badger swept.'

3   Built *circa* 1580–94. Even Cobham Hall may have incorporated an earlier medieval building, replaced by the present central range of the 1660s.

4   The pre-Tudor peerages were those of the Duke of Norfolk; the Earls of Arundel (FitzAlan), Cumberland, Derby, Essex (as Baron Devereux), Huntingdon, Northumberland, Oxford, Rutland, Shrewsbury, Sussex (as Baron FitzWalter) and Worcester; the Barons Audley, Bergavenny, Berkeley, Bolton, Bourchier, Clinton, Cobham, Dacre of North, Dacre of South, Dudley, Latimer, Lumley, Ogle, Stourton, Windsor and Zouche.

5   John Sitsilt is illustrated in Mark Girouard, 'Burghley House, Lincolnshire, 1', *Country Life*, 191 (23 April 1992), p. 56. And cf. Richard Verstegen, *A Restitution of Decayed Intelligence in Antiquities*, Antwerp, 1605, p. 312: 'I do find very probably reason to think that . . . the honorable famillie of the Cecills . . . is originally descended from the Romans.' For contemporary embroideries on the Cecil and other Welsh family trees, see especially *Glamorgan County History*, vol. IV, ed. G. Williams, Cardiff, 1974, pp. 596–7.

6   Lawrence Stone, *Crisis of the Aristocracy*, Oxford, 1965, pp. 403–4.

7   Although Philip Sidney is often stated to have been neglected by Elizabeth, by the time of his death, aged 31, in 1586, he had already been appointed to two important diplomatic missions and given a major command in the Low Countries; as nominated successor to his sickly uncle as Master of the Ordnance, he would almost inevitably have been made a member of the Privy Council on his uncle's death.

8   For Prynce, see Penry William, *The Council in the Marches of Wales under Elizabeth*, Cardiff, 1958, pp. 173, 190. His appointment as Feodary in 1562 is in the Patent Rolls. Whitehall is discussed and illustrated on p. 92 below.

9   David Starkey, ed., *The English Court*, London, 1987, remains the best general account of the Tudor and early Stuart courts.

10   So described in the account of Thomas Campion's masque presented when Queen Anne of Denmark visited Caversham in 1613. Printed in *Campion's Works*, ed. P. Vivian, Oxford, 1909, p. 78.

11   Lady Northampton features as Marsilia in Spenser's *Colin Clout's Come Home Again*, 1595, ll. 508–15. He had dedicated his *Daphnaida* to her in 1591. There is a useful brief account of Gorges's career in *House of Commons, Elizabeth*. For his position as Gentleman of the Wardrobe, see Janet Arnold, *Queen Elizabeth's Wardrobe Unlocked*, Leeds, 1988, p. 169.

12   The Wiltshire houses are well featured in *Country Life*, 28 (20 August 1919), pp. 162–8 [Boyton]; 15 (14 May 1904), pp. 702–8 [Keevil]; 175 (9, 16 and 23 February 1984), pp. 334, 398, 466 [Stockton]. For Treowen, see *Country Life*, 128 (27 October 1960), pp. 970–74; for Shireoaks, see *Girouard, Smythson*, pp. 134–8.

13   There is no modern biography of Gresham. J. W. Burgon, *The Life and Times of Sir Thomas Gresham*, 2 vols, London, 1839, remains an invaluable, though ill-organised and un-indexed, source book, and there are good entries in *ODNB and *House of Commons, Elizabeth*. The identification of Gresham's Thomas Dutton with Thomas Dutton of Sherborne remains to be established, but seems probable. See chapter 3, note 157.

14   For Rushton, see John Heward and Robert Taylor, *The Country Houses of Northamptonshire*, Royal Commission on the Historical Monuments of England, Swindon, 1996, pp. 298, 306, in which the date of *circa* 1630 for the hammerbeam roof was first established.

15   'Caverswell Castle', *Country Life*, 29 (17 June 1911), pp. 886–95, and *Girouard, Smythson*, pp. 181–2. See Simon Degges (1669), 'Yet by country trades, in this late age, many are crept into handsome estates, as Mr Mathew Cradock's father, a wool-buyer of Stafford', quoted in *Girouard, Smythson*, p. 313 n. 29.

16   Quoted in Harris Nicolas, *Memoirs of the Life and Times of Sir Christopher Hatton*, London, 1847, p. 126.

17   Burghley, quoted in John Nichols, *The Progresses and Public Processions of Queen Elizabeth*, 3 vols, London, 1823, vol. I, p. 205 n. 1; A. G. R. Smith, ed., *The Anonymous Life of William Cecil, Lord Burghley*, Lampeter, 1990, pp. 93–4. Smith attributes the *Life* to Burghley's secretary, Michael Hickes, and dates it *circa* 1600. The *Life* was also published by Francis Peck in his *Desiderata Curiosa*, London, 1732, where this quotation is on p. 25.

18   The story comes from Francis Bacon's 'Apothegms', printed in J. Spedding, R. L. Ellis and D. D. Heath, eds, *The Works of Francis Bacon*, 14 vols, London, 1857–74, vol. VII, p. 144.

19   Tony Tuckwell, *New Hall and its School*, Kings Lynn, 2006, p. 27.

20   Alan G. R. Smith, *Servant of the Cecils: The Life of Sir Michael Hickes, 1543–1612*, London, 1977, p. 108, quoting British Library, Lansdowne MS 85, fols 47r, 49r.

21   Nichols, *The Progresses and Public Processions of Queen Elizabeth*, vol. III, pp. 101–21, including plans of the new buildings.

22   Nichols, *The Progresses and Public Processions of Queen Elizabeth*, is the main source book for Elizabethan progresses, and includes a mass of sixteenth-century material (a new edition is in prospect). For a full modern account, see Mary Hill Cole, *The Portable Queen: Elizabeth I and the Politics of Ceremony*, Amherst, Massachusetts, 1999, and for a monograph on a single progress, Zillah Dovey, *An Elizabethan Progress: The Queen's Journey into East Anglia, 1578*, Stroud, 1996.

23   For Petworth, see Gordon Batho, 'Finances of an Elizabethan Nobleman', *Economic History Review*, 2nd series, 9 (1957), p. 448. Visits were refused by the Earl of Bedford, Woburn, 1572; Sir George More, Loseley, 1576; Archbishop Parker, Canterbury, 1573; Sir Thomas Arundell, Wardour, 1600; Sir Henry Lee, Woodstock or Ditchley, 1600; The Earl of Lincoln, Pyrford, 1601; Sir William Clerk, Burnham, 1602 (Cole, *The Portable Queen*, pp. 86–93).

24   J. Nichols, *The Progresses, Processions and Magnificent Festivities of King James the First*, 4 vols, London, 1828, is the principal source book, but less comprehensive than his Elizabethan book. Emily Cole is working on a

thesis on Jacobean state apartments for the Courtauld Institute of Art.

25 Starkey, ed., *The English Court*, p. 193.

26 Neil Cuddy, 'The Revival of the Entourage', in ibid., chapter 6, has a useful account of changes under James.

27 For Cranborne, see pp. 395–400 below, for Lulworth, pp. 445–6 below; in fact, Lord Howard died in 1611, not long after Lulworth had been completed, and the first royal visit was by James I to his heir, the Earl of Suffolk, in 1614.

28 For Apethorpe, see Howard and Taylor, *Houses of Northamptonshire*, pp. 58–69, and especially *Apethorpe Hall, Apethorpe, Northamptonshire: Survey, Research and Analysis*, English Heritage Research Department Report Series, no. 82, 2 vols, Cambridge, 2006, with contributions by Peter Smith, Kathryn A. Morrison, Emily Cole, Adam White et al. (forerunner of a monograph on Apethorpe in preparation); articles by Claire Gapper and Adam White on the plasterwork and iconography of the state apartment in *English Heritage Historical Review*, vol. 3, pp. 87–101, 63–85.

29 For Bramshill, see articles by Helen Hills in *Country Life*, 178 (10 and 17 October 1985), pp. 1011, 1095; I am grateful to Pete Smith for kindly communicating his typescript 'Bramshill House, Hampshire: A Study Day Report'. For Westwood, see pp. 90, 96 below, and notes 41, 52, pp. 232, 306 below.

30 For these royal visits, see especially Lucy Worsley, *Cavalier: The Biography of a Seventeenth Century Household*, London, 2007, chapter 4, pp. 79–118.

31 For plans of Toddington, Burghley and Theobalds, see Figs 80, 207a and b, and 212. For Lord Cheyne's sale of his Kentish estates, see *House of Commons, Elizabeth, sub* Henry Cheyne.

32 The subject matter of this section is treated much more fully in Malcolm Airs, *The Tudor and Jacobean Country House: A Building History*, Stroud, 1995, but I include some material not in Airs.

33 Thomas Smith, *De Republica Anglorum* [1583, but written earlier], ed. L. Alston, Cambridge, 1906, p. 46. William Harrison, *Description of England in Shakespere's Youth* [first published in Raphael Holinshed, *Chronicles of England Scotland and Ireland*, London, 1577, and, with emendations, 1583], ed. F. J. Furnivall for New Shakespere Society, London, 1877–8, vol. 1, p. 134. Opinions dif-

fer as to who was cribbing what from whom: cf. Smith, *De Republica Anglorum*, ed. Alston, pp. XVI–XXI.

34 John Stow, 'The Singularities of the City of London', in *The Survey of London* [1598], ed. Henry B. Wheatley, London, [1912], pp. 493–4.

35 *Girouard, *Smythson*, pp. 40, 50.

36 For Arnold at Wadham, see chapter 7; for Smith and Accres at Hardwick, see D. N. Durant and P. Riden, eds, *The Building of Hardwick Hall. Part 2: The New Hall, 1591–98*, Derbyshire Record Society IX, Chesterfield, 1984, pp. LXII, LXIV.

37 For Wyatt, see J. Ridley, *A History of the Carpenters' Company*, London, 1955, pp. 55–8, with a reproduction of his portrait, now in the Carpenters' Hall, City of London.

38 In 1601 Henry Willoughby, who had been steward at Wollaton, entered into a business arrangement with 'my very loving frende Robert Smythson of Wollaton gentleman'. University of Nottingham, MI 6/171/56. For the monument and John Smythson's marriage, see *Girouard, *Smythson*, pp. 82–3, 168.

39 Arthur Oswald, *Country Houses of Dorset*, 2nd edn, London, 1959, p. 28, and information from Parish Registers and Churchwardens' accounts, Charlton Musgrove, in Somerset Record Office, Taunton.

40 For William Kerwin or Kyrwyn, see *Royal Works*, vol. III, p. 107 n., and Edward Conder, *The Hole Craft and Fellowship of Masons*, London, 1894, pp. 125–7, with illustrations of the tomb.

41 The figure, only an approximation, is obtained by adding together records of expenditure in *Royal Works*, vols III and IV, passim.

42 Elizabethan rates of pay were laid down in the patents of appointment, as recorded in the Patent Rolls; for the adjustments of 1609, *Royal Works*, vol. III, pp. 117–18; for 'dead pays', vol. III, p. 116.

43 The non-artificer Surveyors were Thomas Graves, Thomas Blagrave, David Cunningham and Inigo Jones. Robert Adams was an instrument-maker; Simon Basil's early training is uncertain; only William Spicer (Surveyor 1597–1604) was a building artificer in the traditional manner. See the relevant biographical sections in *Royal Works, vol. III.

44 See, for example, the very full publication of the Bristol Apprentice Books, 1566–93,

transcribed and indexed by Margaret McGregor, Bristol and Avon Family History Society, 4 vols, 1922–4; and the unpublished York apprentice indentures, 1573–1688, York City Archives, D12.

45 Stow, *Survey of London*, pp. 476–8.

46 Bristol Corporation Audit Book, Bristol Record Office, F/AU/I/20, John Loughton, mayor, 1628–9.

47 Many of the archival sources for foreign artificers in England have been published by the Huguenot Society, especially vol. VIII: *Letters of Denization and Acts of Naturalization for Aliens in England, 1509–1603*, ed. William Page, Lymington, 1893; vol. X: *Returns of Aliens Dwelling in the City and Suburbs of London*, ed. R. E. G. Kirk and E. F. Kirk, Aberdeen, 1900–08: part 1: 1525–1571; part 2: 1571–1597; part 3: 1598–1625 and additions, 1522–1595.

48 For Trunckye and Dininghoff, see pp. 134–5 below, and vol. 102 of the Surtees Society publications, 1899, p. 28.

49 See pp. 187–90 below.

50 See Lawrence Stone, 'The Building of Hatfield House', *Archaeological Journal*, 112 (1955), pp. 100–28.

51 Named in fragmentary surviving Knole building accounts: Maidstone, Centre for Kentish Studies, Sackville MSS U269/AI/I and A2/2. And see p. 27 in this chapter.

52 M. Blackman, 'Ashley Park Building Accounts, 1602–1607', *Surrey Record Society*, 29 (1977).

53 See pp. 326–30 below.

54 For Gildon (or Guldon), see *Woolhope Club Transactions* (1933–5), pp. 111–18; (1939–41), p. 589; Nigel Llewellyn, 'Accident or Design', in *England and the Continental Renaissance*, ed. E. Chaney and P. Mack, Woodbridge, 1990.

55 For Baggett, see p. 28 in this chapter, p. 351 below.

56 Work by Madison and other artificers for William Petre is well documented in the Petre MSS in Essex Record Office, Chelmsford, D/DP/AI9–20, and part published in *Old Thorndon Hall*, Essex Record Office Publications 61, Chelmsford, 1972.

57 His will is in Essex Record Office, D/DSH/F17/1; and see Paul Drury, 'The Development of Hill Hall, Essex, 1557–81', *Journal of the British Archaeological Association*, 136 (1983), pp. 115–16.

58 See *Girouard, *Smythson*, passim, but written before I had established the dates of

Maynard's death and of the birth of some of his children, recorded in Frome Parish Registers (available in typescript in the library of the Society of Genealogists, London).

59 Durant and Riden, eds, *The Building of Hardwick Hall. Part 2*, pp. LXII–LXX. The reference to Accres's funeral is in Chatsworth Archives, Hardwick MS 23, March 1605.

60 For Arnold, see pp. 389–406 below.

61 His will is Prerogative Court of Canterbury, 76 Kidd, made on 31 July 1599.

62 For Walmesley and the Ouse Bridge, see D. M. Palliser, *Tudor York*, Oxford, 1979, pp. 76, 172, 267; and *York Civic Records*, ed. A. Raine, Yorkshire Archaeological Society Record Series, 8 vols, [York], 1939–53, vol. VI, pp. 113–15. His will is in York Probate Registers (now in Borthwick Institute, University of York), 27, p. 235. The Corporation had to go far afield because there were no stonemasons in York itself; the local materials were brick and timber, and the Masons' Guild there, starved of work following the Reformation, was defunct by 1561 (Palliser, *Tudor York*, p. 172).

63 Oswald, *Country Houses of Dorset*, pp. 97–8. The Rowes appear in the Wadham College, Oxford, building accounts; see chapter 7, note 16.

64 In a letter to Hatton of 1 October 1583, Tresham thanked him for 'his bestowing a pit of free stone in his quarry at Weldon for the finishing of Rothwell Cross' (abstract in Historical Manuscripts Commission, *Report on Manuscripts in Various Collections*, vol. III, London, 1904, p. 38). The use of Weldon stone at Lyveden is richly documented in the Tresham papers in the British Library, especially Add. MS 58836. Tresham's contract with William Grumbold for Rothwell Cross or Market House is published in Historical Manuscripts Commission, *Report on Manuscripts in Various Collections*, vol. III, p. XXXIV.

65 *Willis and Clark, *Cambridge*, vol. II, p. 566.

66 For Burghley's quarry at Cliffe Park, Kingscliffe, see Eric Till, 'Fact and Conjecture: The Building of Burghley House, 1555–1587', *Northamptonshire Past and Present*, 9 (1997–8), pp. 323–62. Stone was 'desired' from Anthony Mildmay's quarry at Kingscliffe for the heightening of the tower of St Mary's, Cambridge: British Library, MS

Cotton Faustina CIII, fols 512–13 (old 487–8), undated, but dateable *circa* 1593–5.

67 For Thorpe at Blickling, see C. Stanley-Millson and J. Newman, 'Blickling Hall: The Building of a Jacobean Mansion', *Architectural History*, 29 (1986), pp. 1–42.

68 *Thorpe Drawings*, p. 4.

69 Petre MSS, Essex Record Office, D/DP/ A19–20.

70 Oxford, Bodleian Library, HYP B/86–87.

71 Blackman, 'Ashley Park Building Accounts'.

72 A. B. Grosart, ed., *The Lismore Papers*, 1st series: *Autobiographical Notes, Remembrances and Diaries of Sir Richard Boyle*, 5 vols, London, 1886, vol. V: diary entry for 22 June 1640; and see long and interesting letter of 1687 from Boyle's letter-book in Chatsworth MSS, fol. 244.

73 John Harvey, *English Mediaeval Architects: A Biographical Dictionary down to 1550*, 2nd edn, Gloucester, 1984, p. 50, entry for Chafyn.

74 *White, *Dictionary*, p. 60.

75 Ibid.

76 Alistair Rowan, *The Buildings of Ireland: North West Ulster*, Harmondsworth, 1979, pp. 112–13.

77 Ibid., p. 377.

78 J. Imrie and J. G. Dunbar, eds, *Accounts of the Masters of Works for Building and Repairing Royal Palaces and Castles*, vol. II: *1616–1649*, Edinburgh, 1982, pp. 47–111.

79 In 1618–19 Maximilian Colt, born in Arras but working in London from at least 1595, provided Lord Scone with a monument for his chapel at Scone Palace, Perth, together with garden stands, chimney pots and a sundial; but these are likely to have been sent up by sea from London, without Colt having to come to Scotland (*White, *Dictionary*, pp. 30, 33 n. 24, 34 n. 46).

80 H. Colvin, 'Beaudesert, Staffordshire', *Transactions of the Ancient Monuments Society*, new series, 29 (1985), p. 109, quoting Paget Papers, Staffordshire Record Office; John Newman and Nikolaus Pevsner, *Buildings of England: Dorset*, Harmondsworth, 1972, entry for Sherborne; Lord Cork's diary, quoted in Grosart, ed., *Lismore Papers*, vol. V, p. 77.

81 *Girouard, *Smythson*, pp. 49, 87, 133. His long and informative will (Nottinghamshire Record Office, PRNW) leaves legacies in Maidstone and elsewhere in Kent.

82 *Colvin, entry for William Arnold.

83 Ibid., entry for John Akroyd; Wadham College building accounts.

84 Ibid.

85 Card for Roades in John Summerson's card index for Royal Works artificers in Public Records, now held by me.

86 John Lewis's work at the Middle Temple is documented in a letter from Edmund Plowden, its Treasurer, to John Thynne, in Longleat MSS *Records of Building*, vol. II, fol. 100. He was pressed for the Works, but diverted with the queen's permission to the Middle Temple.

87 Alice T. Friedman, *House and Household in Elizabethan England*, Chicago, 1989, pp. 122–3.

88 Jon Bayliss, 'The Decline of the Marblers' Company', *Bulletin, Monumental Brass Society*, 33 (June 1983), pp. 41–2.

89 *York Civic Records*, ed. Raine, vol. III, p. 132; vol. V, p. 112.

90 Their different provinces were listed in a report delivered to the Court of Aldermen, City of London, 25 September 1632; printed in Sidney E. Lane, *The Worshipful Company of Joiners and Ceilers or Carvers: A Chronological History*, Chesham, 1968, pp. 71–7.

91 For Pinckney, see *Royal Works*, vol. IV, p. 43. For Christmas, see *White, *Dictionary*.

92 *White, *Dictionary*.

93 Ibid.

94 Ibid.

95 Mrs Baldwyn-Childe, 'The Building of Kyre Park', *Antiquary*, 21 (1896), pp. 262–3; 22 (1897), p. 25. For work attributed to him at Holdenby, see chapter 3, pp. 192–4 and note 142.

96 John Summerson, 'Three Elizabethan Architects', *John Rylands Library Bulletin* (September 1959), pp. 209–16 [Symonds]; David Bostock, 'The Jacobean Plasterwork at Gawthorpe Hall and its Sources', *Apollo*, 139 (May 1994); J. E. Stocks 'The Church of St John the Evangelist, New Briggate, Leeds', *Publications of the Thoresby Society*, 24 (1919), Appendix p. 217 [Gunbys]; West Yorkshire Archives, Leeds, TNC/2/118 [Burridge]; Durant and Riden, eds, *The Building of Hardwick Hall. Part 2*, p. LXIV [Smith].

97 *Richard Carew of Antony: The Survey of Cornwall*, ed. F. E. Halliday, London, 1953, p. 134. 'Old Veale' is presumably Thomas Veale of Bodmin, joiner, whose will, administration and inventory, 1606, are in the

Cornish Record Office, Truro, v20/1–3. No work by him has yet been documented.

98 *Girouard, *Smythson*, p. 40.

99 Legacies in his will, abstracted in *Tudor Wills Proved in Bristol, 1546–1603*, ed. Sheila Lang and Margaret McGregor, Bristol Record Society 44, Bristol, 1993, pp. 12–13.

100 'William Arnolds three men' are listed in the first payment to masons on 9 April 1610, and can be identified by later entries as Edward and Thomas Arnold, and Richard Cornish. Others of his men may have been left at Cranborne Manor. Other masons listed include 'Henry Chaffy and his man', 'Hugh French and his man' and 'Peter Plomer and his Company' (building accounts, Wadham College archives, Oxford).

101 Anne Saunders, ed., *The Royal Exchange*, London Topographical Society, 152, 1997; Lawrence Stone, 'Inigo and the New Exchange', *Archaeological Journal*, 114 (1957), p. 114.

102 Jennifer S. Alexander and Kathryn A. Morrison, 'Apethorpe Hall and the Workshop of Thomas Thorpe, Mason of King's Cliffe: A Study in Masons' Marks', *Architectural History*, 50 (2007), pp. 59–94.

103 His will, Prerogative Court of Canterbury, 76 Kidd (made 31 July 1599, proved 6 October), lists £4 19s. owed 'to William Reed which he is to receave of Mrtris Magdalen Herbert oute of that worke which he and others have done for and by my appointment at Montgomerie'.

104 *Returns of Aliens*, ed. Kirk and Kirk, part 3, p. 362.

105 Durant and Riden, eds, *The Building of Hardwick Hall. Part 2*, pp. LX–LXI.

106 D. N. Durant and P. Riden, eds, *The Building of Hardwick Hall. Part 1: The Old Hall, 1587–91*, Derbyshire Record Society IV, Chesterfield, 1980, p. 125; Durant and Riden, eds, *The Building of Hardwick Hall. Part 2*, p. 266; Rutland MSS, Belvoir Castle, Book 76, Receipts and Payments, 1586–1588.

107 Editions listed in Eileen Harris and Nicholas Savage, *British Architectural Books and Writers*, Cambridge, 1990, pp. 182–3.

108 A. Rodger 'Roger Ward's Shrewsbury Stock: An Inventory of 1585', *The Library*, 5th series, 13 (1958), p. 252.

109 Thomas Bedwell's rule was not published until after his death, in his son William's translation of L. Schonerus, *De Numeris Geometricis*. But Richard More certainly knew of it before this. Harris and Savage,

British Architectural Books and Writers, pp. 118–19.

110 Sebastiano Serlio, *The Five Books of Architecture* [1611], facsimile edn, New York and London, 1982. The dedication, to Henry, Prince of Wales, is signed by Robert Peake, but the text does not make clear whether he was personally responsible for the translation and new introduction.

111 See his entry in *ODNB.

112 *Smythson Drawings*, II/33. In my catalogue of the drawings I attributed the drawing to Robert Smythson, but it is certainly by John.

113 It might just possibly have been for a window over a semicircular porch in the unidentified Smythson house plan I/2. Round windows over porches (but these square, and never more than two storeys in height) feature in a number of mid-seventeenth-century buildings in West Yorkshire.

114 Smaller window designs in *Smythson Drawings*, II/34. The Smythson round windows, Heath School window and later Yorkshire examples are discussed by Peter Leach, 'Rose Windows and Other Follies: Alternative Architecture in the 17th-century Pennines', *Architectural History*, 43 (2000), pp. 121–39.

115 Compass, square, rule and sometimes scriber, and/or pen and plumb line, occur frequently in decoration or on the title pages of architectural books, for example, the title pages of early editions of Serlio, repeated in Peake's edition. Anthony Gerbino and Stephen Johnston, *Compass and Rule: Architecture as Mathematical Practice in England, 1500–1750*, New Haven and London, 2009, was published too late for me to make use of it.

116 *Thorpe Drawings*, T225–6 (pp. 102–3) and pl. 105.

117 For example, John Rogers's plan and bird's-eye view for the King's Manor House at Hull, 1542 (British Library, Cotton MSS Augustus I.c. 44 and I.II.13), reproduced in L. R. Shelby, *John Rogers: Tudor Military Engineer*, Oxford, 1967; and possibly the beautiful elevation for Fox's chantry, Winchester cathedral, circa 1525 (*Smythson Drawings*, IV/1).

118 The two house plans, Cecil archives, Burghley House, and Hatfield, CPM I/7–8 (9–10); the spire elevation, archives, Society of Antiquaries.

119 Ampthill, Hatfield, CPM I/14, redrawn in *Royal Works*, vol. IV, p. 42, fig. 3; Windsor, National Archives, MPF/150,254, redrawn in W. H. St J. Hope, *Windsor Castle*, 1913, vol. I, p. 276; Cursitors' Hall, National Archives, MPA/71; Theobalds, Hatfield, CP 143/47 (58); Beaufort House, rep. A. W. Clapham and W. H. Godfrey, *Some Famous Buildings and their Story*, N. C., London, [1913], chapter 6.

120 *White, *Dictionary*, p. 40, n. 5.

121 Edward VI tomb, Oxford, Bodleian Library, Gough Maps 43, no. 63; Hatfield, CPM I/13. The Lumley Inventory is in the archives of Lord Lumley's descendant, the Earl of Scarbrough, at Sandbeck Park, Yorkshire; see Lionel Cust and Mary Hervey, eds, 'The Lumley Inventories', *Walpole Society*, 6 (1917–18); *Country Life*, 180 (5 June 1986), pp. 1586–8. A new edition is being prepared for the Roxburgh Club by James Stourton.

122 L. Guicciardini, *Descrittione di Tutti i Paesi Bassi*, Antwerp, 1567, p. 101.

123 The drawings were catalogued by me for *Architectural History* (*Smythson Drawings*), and this formed the basis of the Smythson entry in the *Catalogue of the Drawings Collection of the Royal Institute of British Architects, 1969–84*. A new catalogue is needed; mine (my first publication) was inadequate, and attributed many drawings to Robert that were certainly or probably by John; see p. 380 below.

124 *Smythson Drawings*, I/16.

125 *Girouard, *Smythson*, pls 22 and 25, reproduces the two principal ones, but there are further designs for parapet details and for the little 'Rodmister Lodge' in the park in the Longleat archives. See chapter 3, note 78.

126 St John's College archives, including elevation, reproduced in *Willis and Clark, *Cambridge*, vol. II, p. 256; West Yorkshire Archives, Leeds, TN/SH/A3/1.

127 Hatfield, CPM I/2.

128 Hatfield, CPM Supplementary 85/1–5; reproduced in Royal Commission on the Historical Monuments of England, *Ancient and Historical Monuments in Dorset*, vol. V: *East Dorset*, London, 1975, pl. 41, pp. 7–12. The plans are not necessarily by Arnold, and may be later surveys drawn to show intended accommodation for James I and the Prince of Wales.

129 West Yorkshire Archives, Leeds, TN/SH/A3/2–3. Reproduced in Nicholas Cooper, *Houses of the Gentry, 1480–1680*, 1999, p. 43, pl. 29.

130 *White, *Dictionary*, pls 5, 7, 9, 13, 15, 19.

131 Reproduced in Stanley-Millson and New-man, 'Blickling Hall', p. 38, fig. 5.

132 Illustrated in Airs, *The Tudor and Jacobean Country House*, p. 91.

133 For example, a ceiling at Nutcombe Manor, Devon, illustrated in *Wells-Cole, *Decoration*, p. 126, pls 186, 188.

134 *Thorpe Drawings*, T1–5, T9, pls 1–4, pp. 43–4.

135 British Library, Add. MS 39832, fol. 36v, 1 and 8 February 1595.

136 British Library, 559* e.3 (2).

137 Baldwyn-Childe, 'The Building of Kyre Park'. The account-books, etc., on which the articles are based, are now British Library, Add. MS 62674.

138 Prerogative Court of Canterbury, Seager 110. For Francis Willoughby's library, see chapter 3, note 177.

139 Prerogative Court of Canterbury, Barkon 29, 1579 [Cure]; Prerogative Court of Canterbury, Scroope 110, 1630 [Carter].

140 Prerogative Court of Canterbury, Barkon 29, 1579 [Cure].

141 Abstracted in *Tudor Wills Proved in Bristol, 1546–1603*, ed. Lang and McGregor, pp. 12–13.

142 Will transcribed in Summerson, 'Three Elizabethan Architects', pp. 222–5.

143 *Royal Works*, vol. III, pp. 94–7.

144 *Thorpe Drawings*, pp. 1–17.

145 British Library, Add. MS 36065 H.

146 For Walker, see A. C. Edwards and K. C. Newton, *The Walkers of Hanningfield*, London, 1984.

147 Surveys for Hatton: Northamptonshire Record Office, Finch Hatton MS 272; *Royal Works*, vol. IV, pp. 77, 275.

148 For Bellin, see pp. 131–2 below; for Gower at Greenwich, see *Royal Works*, vol. IV, p. 109; for Cavell, see Bath Chamberlains Account, Record Office, Bath, and E. Croft-Murray, *Decorative Painting in England, 1537–1837*, London, 1962, p. 96 and pl. 94; for Pierce (or Pearce), see Croft-Murray, *Decorative Painting in England*, p. 206; S. Jervis 'A Seventeenth Century Book of Engraved Ornament', *Burlington Magazine*, 128 (December 1986), pp. 893–903.

149 A. B. Grosart, ed., *The Lismore Papers*, 1st series, 1886, vol. III: diary entry for 6 May 1630. For Shrewsbury House and Gilling Castle, see p. 363.

150 For Cawarden, see pp. 132–5; for Thomas Digges at Dover, see *Royal Works*, vol. IV, pp. 737, 757–9, 761.

151 For Osborne and Bacon, see Hassell Smith, 'Sir Nicholas Bacon and the Building of Stiffkey Hall', *East Anglia's History: Studies in Honour of Norman Scarfe*, Woodbridge, 2002 (suggesting that he is the John Osborne of Harkstead, Suffolk, who was granted arms in 1578). E. R. Sandeen, 'The Building of Redgrave Hall, 1545–1554', thesis, University of Chicago (copy in Bodleian Library), part published in *Proceedings of the Suffolk Institute of Archaeology and History*, 29 (1961), pp. 13 and seq. (based on Bacon MSS, University of Chicago Library).

152 British Library, Royal MS 18 C III; Paula Henderson, *The Tudor House and Garden*, New Haven and London, 2005, p. 115 and pl. 138; Eric Till, 'The Development of the Park and Gardens at Burghley', *Garden History*, 19/ii (Autumn 1991), pp. 128–35.

153 For Layfield, see p. 246 below.

154 *Colvin, entry for Nicholas Stone; *ODNB; D. Howarth, *Lord Arundel and his Circle*, London, 1985, pp. 156–8 and pl. 108.

155 John Aubrey, *Brief Lives and Other Selected Writings*, ed. Anthony Powell, London, 1949, p. 33; R. Trevelyan, *Sir Walter Raleigh*, London, 2003, pp. 212, 312; John Harington, *Nugae Antiquae*, 2 vols, London, 1804, vol. II, p. 125.

156 *Royal Works*, vol. IV, pp. 413–14, 471, 481.

157 *ODNB; K. T. Holtgen, 'Richard Haydocke, Translator, Engraver, Physician', *The Library*, 5th series, 33/1 (1978), p. 18; Harris and Savage, *British Architectural Books and Writers*, pp. 297–9, entry for Lomazzo.

158 Aubrey, *Brief Lives*, ed. Powell, p. 194. *ODNB; J. Spedding, *The Life and Letters of Francis Bacon*, vol. XIII, p. 334, quoting National Archives, SP 14, vol. XCIX. 86, August 1618, 'Paid Mr Dobson by your Lp order to discharge arrears of workmens bills left unpaid at Whittide last £100.00'.

159 *DNB, entry for Killigrew, quoting David Lloyd (1635–1692), *State Worthies*, first published 1665–70.

160 Oswald, *Country Houses of Dorset*, p. 97.

161 Alan Stewart, *Philip Sidney: A Double Life*, London 2000, p. 110, quoting Oxford, Bodleian Library, MS Don.d152; *Royal Works*, vol. IV, p. 663 (drawing, National Archives, MPF 222 [1 and 2]).

162 *Wilson's Arte of Rhetorique, 1560*, ed. G. H. Mair, Oxford, 1909, p. 13.

163 Historical Manuscripts Commission, *Report on Manuscripts in Various Collections*, vol.

164 *Girouard, *Smythson*, pp. 45, 68.

165 Oswald, *Country Houses of Dorset*, p. 97.

166 For Elizabethan and Jacobean architectural libraries, see the appendix 'Books on Art, Perspective and Architecture in English Renaissance Libraries, 1580–1630', in Lucy Gent, *Picture and Poetry, 1560–1620* Leamington Spa, 1981.

167 British Library, Add. MS 3983. The engraving is in the British Museum Department of Prints and Drawings.

168 Prerogative Court of Canterbury, Pykering 1, 1574.

169 *The Loseley Manuscripts*, ed. A. J. Kempe, London, 1836, p. 304. Hatfield, CP 143, p. 33.

170 Hatfield, CP 143, pp. 41, 42, 50. The Burghley elevation is amongst the unattributed drawings in the Drawings Collection of the Royal Institute of British Architects. These are not listed in the published catalogue.

171 John Strype, *The Life of the Learned Sir Thomas Smith* [1698], Oxford, 1820, pp. 274–81.

172 Essex Record Office, D/DSH/F17/1.

173 *Letters from Sir Robert Cecil to Sir George Carew*, ed. John MacLean, Camden Society, London, 1864, p. 144; Marquess of Newcastle to his son, Viscount Mansfield, 15 November 1659, printed in Historical Manuscripts Commission, *The Manuscripts of His Grace of Portland, Preserved at Welbeck Abbey*, vol. II, London, 1893, p. 143: 'I believe you and I are not such good architects as your worthy grandfather'.

174 *Girouard, *Smythson*, p. 184, quoting Historical Manuscripts Commission, *Calendar of the Manuscripts of the Most Honourable the Marquess of Salisbury . . . Preserved at Hatfield House, Hertfordshire*, 24 vols, London, 1883–1976, vol. XIX, pp. 120–21.

175 *Smythson Drawings*, II/10, 11.

176 Anon. [attributed to W. Anderson and P. Heylin], *Aulicus Coquinariae; or, A vindication in answer to a pamphlet entitled the Court and Character of King James*, London, 1650, p. 66. *Royal Works*, vol. IV, p. 324, quoting Dudley Carleton to John Chamberlain, 16 September 1607, SP 14/28/5.

177 The plan was at Petworth, but has been lost; East Sussex Record Office and Courtauld Institute of Art, Witt Library, have photographs.

178 John Shute, *The First and Chief Groundes of Architecture by John Shute Paynter and*

Archytecte First Printed in 1563, facsimile edn with introduction by Lawrence Weaver, London, 1912, A ii v.

179 Ibid., B ii v; preface by Dee in H. Billingsley, *The Elements of Geometrie* [1570], printed in Frances A. Yates, *Theatre of the World*, London, 1969, Appendix A, p. 192.

180 Shute, *The First and Chief Groundes of Architecture*, facsimile edn, B iii v. Vitruvius, *De Architectura* I.i: 'Itaque architecti, qui sine literis contendant, ut manibus essent exercitati, non potuerunt officere ut haberent pro laboribus auctoritatem; qui autem ratiocinationibus et literis solis confisi fuerunt, umbram non rem persecuti videntur. At qui utrumque perdidicerunt, uti omnibus armis ornati citius cum auctoritate, quod fuit propositum, sunt adsecuti.'

181 Leon Battista Alberti, *De Re Aedificatoria* IX.x. Alberti does not refer to Vitruvius by name, but only as 'a certain author'.

182 Dee in Yates, *Theatre of the World*, pp. 194–5, translating Alberti, *De Re Aedificatoria*, I.i.

183 Dee in Yates, *Theatre of the World*, p. 196.

184 Henry Wotton, *The Elements of Architecture*, London, 1624, pp. 10–12.

185 Essex Record Office, D/DSH/F17/1; for Smith, see pp. 175–7 below.

186 John Baret, *An Alvearie or Quadruple Dictionarie*, 1581. His *An Alvearie or Triple Dictionarie*, with only occasional Greek, had been published *circa* 1574.

187 John Summerson, *Architecture in Britain, 1530 to 1830*, Harmondsworth, 1991, p. 55, giving no source.

188 'Description of a Masque' for the Somerset–Howard marriage, published in *Campion's Works*, ed. Vivian, p. 150 (de Servi). Grosart, ed., *Lismore Papers*, vol. V, p. 64 (de Caox). For Glover, see *ODNB*; no architectural work by him has been identified. For Cecil and 'My Lord', see pp. 55–6 below.

189 Stephen Harrison, *The Arch's of Triumph*, London, 1604. See full entry in Harris and Savage, *British Architectural Books and Writers*, pp. 229–31; Christine Stevenson, 'Occasional Architecture in Seventeenth-century London', *Architectural History*, 49 (2006), pp. 35–74. In fact, the arch erected by the Netherlandish merchants was designed by Conrad Jansen.

190 Bentley called 'architectus peritissimus' on his monument (destroyed; see *Colvin, entry for Akroyd); Scampion, 'architectus', in the Parish Register, Montgomery (ibid.);

Holt, 'architectus', on churchyard monument (destroyed; ibid.); Leminge, 'architect', in Blickling Paris Register; Robert Smythson, 'architecter', on his monument in Wollaton church; John Smythson 'Architecter', will, Prerogative Court of Canterbury, Seager 110; Morgan, 'architector', inventory, Bristol Record Office, Inventory 1635/63; Stickells, 'artichect', in John Stow, *Summarie of Englyshe Chronicles*, London, 1598, *sub* 1595.

Chapter 2   Catering for a Lifestyle

1 The section that follows is mainly a compressed version of my *Life in the English Country House* (New Haven and London, 1978), especially chapter 4: 'The Elizabethan and Jacobean House'.

2 Thomas Campion, 'Entertainment of the Queen at Caversham House, 1613', quoted in J. Nichols, *The Progresses, Processions and Magnificent Festivities of King James the First*, 4 vols, London, 1828, vol. II, p. 636.

3 At Trinity College, Cambridge, the central grate or brazier has been moved to the Senior Combination Room, and adapted as a coffee or drinks table. It had remained in use until 1866; the brazier at Trinity Hall until 1742; at Gonville Hall until 1792; at St John's College until 1865 (*Willis and Clark, *Cambridge*, vol. III, p. 356).

4 Somerset House: *Thorpe Drawings*, T88, pl. 41. At Syon House the hall, possibly as built by the Duke of Somerset, is still shown without a chimneypiece in an early seventeenth-century plan in the Northumberland archives, and remains without a chimneypiece today, as redecorated by Robert Adam. Although Burghley and Theobalds are both shown by Thorpe with wall fireplace openings (ibid., T57, pl. 27; T245, pl. 113) and the Elizabethan chimneypiece survives in the hall at Burghley, remains of a hall louvre were found during recent repairs to the roof at Burghley (information John Culverhouse) and a design for the hall louvre at Theobalds is at Hatfield (CP 143/35), and reproduced on p. 425 below. It is possible that fireplaces were installed shortly after building, or even that the halls had both wall and central hearths. At Staple Hall, Holborn (1581), a nineteenth-century drawing shows a central stove, the replacement of

the original hearth, combined with a post-Elizabethan wall chimneypiece.

5 John Smyth, *The Lives of the Berkeleys* [1618], ed. J. Maclean, 3 vols, Gloucester, 1883–5, vol. II, p. 363.

6 For English galleries, see Rosalys Coope, 'The Long Gallery', *Architectural History*, 29 (1986), pp. 43–72. The earliest example of the term 'long gallery' that I know of is in Thorpe's plan of Northampton (later Northumberland) House, London: *Thorpe Drawings*, T275, pl. 123, 'the long galere'.

7 *Royal Works*, vol. IV, pp. 19–20 and pl. 10.

8 The length of Gorhambury gallery has to be surmised from a plan of *circa* 1820 redrawn in *The Victoria History of the County of Hertford*, ed. William Page, vol. II, London, 1908, p. 395, and reproduced (together with external views) in Nick Hill, 'Conservation and Decay: Two Centuries at Old Gorhambury', *Transaction of the Association for Studies in the Conservation of Historic Buildings*, 21 (1996), pp. 36–48. The plan is only of the ground floor.

9 A gallery is shown filling most of the north range of Longleat on the Elizabethan plan of Longleat, Hatfield, CPM 1/16–17, but the plan in *Vitruvius Britannicus*, vol. II, London, 1717, pls 68–9, shows a gap in the range where the gallery should be. A gallery is listed in an inventory of March 1574 (Thynne papers, Box 3, vol. 50, fol. 204), but not in those of 1594 (Box 6, vol. 53, fol. 204) and 1639 (Box 32, vol. 79, fol. 40). For Hunsdon House, see *The Parish of Hackney*, Survey of London, vol. XXVIII, London, 1960, especially plan and reconstructed view, pp. 27–8. For Copped Hall, see John Newman, 'Copthall, Essex', in *The Country Seat: Studies in the History of the British Country House Presented to John Summerson*, ed. Howard Colvin and John Harris, London, 1970, pp. 18–29. Newman dates the gallery to the 1560s, but on stylistic grounds a later date is more likely. For Worksop Manor, see *Girouard, *Smythson*, pp. 110–15.

10 *Girouard, *Smythson*, p. 113, quoting Talbot Papers, College of Arms, L. fol. 122.

11 Dimensions surmised from *Thorpe Drawings*, T105–6, pl. 49, and related plans T81–2, pl. 39, and T101–2, pl. 48. These are the only known plans of or for Buckingham's Burley, and it is by no means certain that they were executed or even accepted.

12 Hatfield, CP 3370.

13 *Of Household Stuff: The 1601 Inventories of Bess of Hardwick*, National Trust, London, 2001, pp. 48–50. David N. Durant, *Bess of Hardwick: Portrait of an Elizabethan Dynast*, London, 1977, pp. 205–7.

14 The *Heptameron* was republished in 1593 as *Aurelopia: A Paradise of Pleasure*. There is no modern edition, but see T. C. Izard, *George Whetstone: Elizabethan Man of Letters*, New York, 1942.

15 See Roy Strong in 'Sir Henry Unton and his Portrait: An Elizabethan Memorial Picture and its History', *Archaeologia*, 99 (1965), pp. 53–76. Strong does not accept the often-repeated theory that the depiction is of the Untons' marriage feast.

16 Nichols, *The Progresses . . . of King James the First*, vol. II, pp. 145–52; Girouard, *Life in the English Country House*, New Haven and London, 1978, p. 88.

17 Maidstone, Kent County Archives, Sackville MSS 269/F38. See Marion O'Connor, 'Rachel Fane's May Masque at Apethorpe, 1627', English Literary Renaissance, vol. 36, no. 1, winter 2006, pp. 90–113; I owe this reference to Emily Cole.

18 *The Autobiography of Thomas Whythorne*, ed. J. M. Osborn, Oxford, 1961, passim. The autobiography is written in a phonetic spelling, not difficult but somewhat irritating to read. A version with modernised spelling was published in 1962.

19 John Maynard, *The Twelve Wonders of the World*, 1611. On the title page he describes himself as 'Lutenist at the most famous Schoole, St Julians, in Hertfordshire'. He dedicates the work to 'Lady Joane Thynne of Cause-Castle in Shropshire', and writes in the dedication that 'This poore play-worke of mine had its prime originall and birth wrights in your own house when by nearer service I was obliged yours', and also acknowledges 'The powerfull persuasion of that nobly-disposed Gentlewoman Mrs Dorothy Thynne, your vertuous Daughter, whose breast is possest with an admirable hereditary love of music, and who once laboured mee to that effect'. Joan Thynne was married to Sir John Thynne, son of the builder of Longleat. He inherited from his father in 1580, and died in 1604, when his widow (d. 1612) went to live in Caus Castle, which she had inherited from her father. The lutenist must have been one of two John Maynards: (1) John Maynard, baptised in 1577, the third son of Ralph Maynard, of St Julians, Hertfordshire; or (2) John Maynard, baptised in Frome in 1581, the second son of Alan Maynard (see pp. 163–5, 201 below), the French master mason at Longleat, living since *circa* 1573 as tenant of a Thynne farm at Woodlands, near Frome. The *ODNB* identifies him with the first of these two, but in spite of the St Julians connection, this John Maynard seems socially a level too high: he was the nephew of Sir Henry Maynard, Burghley's chief secretary and builder of Easton Lodge (see p. 5 above, Fig. 8); his father owned the converted medieval hospital of St Julian, and he was to inherit it, so that it seems curious that he should describe himself as 'Lutenist at the most famous schoole', etc. The language and background of the dedication fits better with Alan Maynard's son, whose employment by a family of the same name could be a coincidence.

20 His will is Prerogative Court of Canterbury, I Dorset, 1608.

21 *Girouard, Smythson*, p. 145, and Durant, *Bess of Hardwick*, pp. 192–3.

22 The party is described, but its members not named, in Sir John Harington, *The Metamorphosis of Ajax*, 1596, part 3. Harington's own manuscript notes on the copy now in the Folger Museum, Washington, DC, identify the place as Wardour, and name the participants as Harington himself, Sir Matthew Arundell of Wardour, his son Thomas Arundell and his wife, the Earl of Southampton and Sir Henry Danvers. See *A New Discourse of a Stale Subject, Called 'The Metamorphosis of Ajax'*, ed. E. S. Donno, London, 1962, pp. 174–5, 232. For Walter Ralegh at Wolfeton, see British Library, Harleian MS 6345, fols 185–6, 190, and E. A. Strathmann, *Sir Walter Ralegh: A Study in Elizabethan Skepticism*, New York, 1951, pp. 46–52.

23 Hassel Smith, 'Concept and Compromise: Sir Nicholas Bacon and the Building of Stiffkey Hall', *East Anglia's History*, ed. C. Harper-Bill, C. Rawcliffe and R. G. Wilson, Norwich, 2002, pp. 159–87, with redrawing of the original plan (Norfolk Record Office, MS Raynham 6/50), p. 169.

24 Staffordshire Record Office, Paget Papers. I am grateful to Nicholas Cooper for sending me copies of this, and related, plans, together with his extensive analysis of them.

25 The structure of the entrance archway makes clear that the Tower of the Orders is an addition.

26 The hall and engravings of the exterior before Victorian remodelling are illustrated in *Country Life*, 34 (19 July 1913), pp. 90–94. The hall was subdivided horizontally and the panelling removed by the University of York in the 1960s.

27 *Thorpe Drawings*, T175, pl. 80.

28 For Eastington, see p. 267 below, and Nicholas Kingsley, *The Country Houses of Gloucestershire, vol. I: 1500–1660*, Chichester, 2001, pp. 88–9 and pl. 72; for Barlborough and Heath, see *Girouard, Smythson*, pp. 120–25. Kingsley thinks that Eastington is 'much later' than the date of 1578 given in Ralph Bigland's *Historical, Monumental and Genealogical Collections Relative to the County of Gloucester*, 1789, but I see no reason not to accept it.

29 *Smythson Drawings*, II/2–3, I/2.

30 Malcolm Airs, *The Tudor and Jacobean Country House: A Building History*, Stroud, 1995, p. 124.

31 For Holdenby, see pp. 191–4 below. An eighteenth-century plan of Toddington is redrawn in James Boutwood, 'A Vanished Elizabethan Mansion', *Country Life*, 129 (23 March 1961), pp. 638–40.

32 The plans of Mount Edgcumbe are reproduced in *Girouard, Smythson*, p. 101, pl. 2. For Wollaton, see pp. 209, 213–14, 242–5 below. For the ingenious entry to the hall at Fountains Hall, Yorkshire, similar to that at Wollaton, see *Girouard, Smythson*, pp. 192, 194, and Figs 14, 15.

33 *Girouard, Smythson*, p. 306, n. 47; ibid., p. 102, pls 56–7; and D. N. Durant, 'Wollaton Hall: A Rejected Plan', *Transactions of the Thoroton Society*, 75 (1972), pp. 13–16.

34 For Blackwell in the Peak, see *Smythson Drawings*, I/1; for Renishaw, see *Country Life*, 82 (7 and 14 May 1938), pp. 476–80, 506–11; for Tissington, see *Country Life*, 160 (15, 22 and 29 July 1960), pp. 158–61, 214–17, 286–9, with plan on p. 289; for Constable Burton, see bird's-eye view in J. Kip and L. Knyff, *Britannia Illustrata*, 1707; for Sandbeck, see *Country Life*, 138 (7 October 1965), pp. 880–83, suggesting that the present eighteenth-century house is the remodelling and enlargement of a Jacobean one; for Manor Lodge, see *Girouard, Smythson*, pp. 131–3, with plans on p. 131, fig. 5.

35 See chapter 7, note 54.

36 *Thorpe Drawings*, T182, pl. 84, inscribed 'Holdenby banquet h'. This has been identified, by me amongst others (*Girouard, *Smythson*, p. 153, and p. 312, n. 12; Girouard, 'Reconstructing Holdenby', in *Town and Country*, New Haven, 1992, pp. 205–6), with the building shown to the south-east of the house in Ralph Treswell's survey of 1587 (Northamptonshire Record Office, Finch-Hatton MSS; Girouard, *Town and Country*, p. 207, pl. 187). On this site the Parliamentary Survey of 1650 described 'a goodly fabrick . . . consisting of many fair large rooms'; this was the house in which the widow of Sir Christopher Hatton's nephew and ultimate heir Sir Christopher Hatton junior lived on after her husband's death in 1619. But Treswell's survey suggests a smaller and simpler building; I now think it more likely that Christopher Hatton's banqueting house was rebuilt by his nephew *circa* 1608, but retained the old name. This would place it chronologically in the same group as Tresham's other Palladian plans, instead of dating it twenty years or so earlier.

37 For Easton Lodge, see *Thorpe Drawings*, T92, pl. 42, and see p. 5 above; for Worcester Lodge, see *Smythson Drawings*, I/17.

38 The plan of Verulam has to be deduced from the description and crude drawing in John Aubrey's *Brief Lives*, ed. Anthony Powell, London, 1949, pp. 194–5, and Aubrey's sketch in the manuscript from which this derives (Bodleian Library, MS Aubrey 6, fol. 72v). The drawing is reproduced in Paula Henderson, *The Tudor House and Garden*, New Haven and London, 2005, fig. 202. For Little Walden Hall, see Nicholas Cooper, *Houses of the Gentry, 1480–1680*, New Haven and London, 1999, p. 111, pl. 100.

39 *Thorpe Drawings*, T189 and T190, both pl. 87. The latter may relate to Lulworth Castle, Dorset, for which see pp. 445–6 below.

40 *Thorpe Drawings*, T98 and T97, pl. 345. Plans for a timber-framed house, annotated 'Hix' and 'Mr Hix'. Summerson surmised that they were unexecuted designs for Campden House, Kensington, made for Baptist Hicks or Hickes; but it seems more likely that they were for his brother, Michael Hickes, who lived at Rusholt Hall, Essex, where James I visited and knighted him in 1604 (Alan G.

R. Smith, *Servant of the Cecils*, London, 1977, p. 169). For Thorpe's work for other Cecil servants, see p. 412 below.

41 For Holland House, see pp. 413 below and *Thorpe Drawings*, T93 and pl. 43; for Wothorpe, pp. 415–17 below and ibid., T56, pl. 26. Westwood is securely dated 1613 by a carpenter's contract made with Thomas and Richard Bridgen in that year (Pakington Papers, Worcestershire Record Office; this was no. 478267 when papers were in Birmingham Reference Library). I am grateful to Howard Colvin for drawing this to my attention. Andor Gomme did not know of it when he surmised a date in the 1590s in 'Redating Westwood', *Architectural History*, 44 (2001), pp. 310–21, and much of the argument in his article is not sustainable; he redates it to 'begun 1612' in Gomme and Alison Maguire, *Design and Plan in the Country House*, New Haven and London, 2008, pp. 61–3 and plan 29. Barningham is dated 1612 on the porch; it is possible that its centrally entered hall is original, rather than the result of alterations by J. A. Repton, who worked there in 1807 (*Colvin).

42 For Whitehall, see Cooper, *Houses of the Gentry*, pp. 143–4, with plan; Andor Gomme, 'Hall into Vestibule', in *The Renaissance Villa in Britain, 1500–1700*, ed. Malcolm Airs and Geoffrey Tyack, Reading, 2007; and Gomme and Maguire, *Design and Plan in the Country House*, pp. 199–203, with revised plan based on survey of house when under alteration.

43 Robin Thornes and J. T. Leach, 'Buxton Hall', *Derbyshire Archaeological Journal*, 114 (1994), pp. 25–53. This establishes that the original fabric of Buxton Old Hall, described as rebuilt in Charles Cotton, *Wonders of the Peak*, London, 1681, in fact substantially survives behind a later façade.

44 *Thorpe Drawings*, T135–6, pl. 612, plans of ground and first floors. Summerson only 'probably' identifies the plans as of Fowler's house, but his identification seems irrefutable. Fowler died in 1595.

45 *Thorpe Drawings*, T18, pl. 6.

46 *Thorpe Drawings*, T17, pl. 6, T18, pl. 6 ['for the cytty']; T28, pl. 11 [Dowsby?]; T47, pl. 13; T35, pl. 15; T43, pl. 20; T110, pl. 50; T135–6, pl. 61 [Fowler house]; T176, pl. 80 ['Mr Panton']; T195–6, pl. 90; T225–6, pl. 105 ['Mr Tayler at potters bar', 1596?].

47 Cooper, *Houses of the Gentry*, pp. 146–7 with plan. Gomme and Maguire, *Design and Plan in the Country House*, pp. 129–30 [Dowsby], pp. 210–12 [Red Hall], with plans.

48 For Boyton, see *Country Life*, 28 (20 August 1910), pp. 262–8; for Over Court, see Kingsley, *The Country Houses of Gloucestershire, vol. I*, pp. 155–6.

49 Cooper, *Houses of the Gentry*, pp. 169–73.

50 The subject of this section is treated much more fully in Paula Henderson, *The Tudor House and Garden*, New Haven and London, 2005.

51 *Smythson Drawings*, I/25 (1), and see p. 243 below.

52 *Country Life*, 64 (14 and 21 July 1928), pp. 50–57, 94–100; Andor Gomme, 'Redating Westwood', dates the wings to 1617–20, but I suspect a later date.

53 *Thorpe Drawings*, T32, pl. 22, but not listed as Brockhall in the catalogue; the identification is established by the modern plan in John Heward and Robert Taylor, *The Country Houses of Northamptonshire*, Royal Commission on the Historical Monuments of England, Swindon, 1996, fig. 137, and the drawing by Peter Tillemans, 1721, reproduced in John Harris, *The Artist and the Country House*, London, 1979, p. 231, pl. 248, which shows the courtyard ranges, since demolished. Another possible Thorpe connection is provided by the entrance door, originally to one side of the porch, as shown in the Thorpe drawing, but re-erected in a central position, probably in the eighteenth century. This is almost identical to a doorway at the base of the main staircase at Kirby Hall, Northamptonshire, which has masons' marks identified in Jennifer S. Alexander and Kathryn A. Morrison, 'Apethorpe Hall and the Workshop of Thomas Thorpe, Mason of King's Cliffe: A Study in Masons' Marks', *Architectural History*, 50 (2007), pp. 59–94, as belonging to the Thorpe workshop.

54 Unlike the ranges at Blickling and Stratfield Saye, no trace of the Wothorpe ranges survives.

55 *Of Household Stuff: The 1601 Inventories of Bess of Hardwick*, p. 57.

56 Royal Commission on the Historical Monuments of England, *An Inventory of the Historical Monuments in Herefordshire, vol. III: North-West*, London, 1934, pp. 87–8 and pl. 119.

57 A drawing in the possession of Alexander Waugh shows that the two-storey gatehouse was originally a storey higher; a second fine chimneypiece may have been removed from the upper storey. I am grateful to Richard Windsor-Clive for photographs and information.

58 The gatehouse at Leighton Bromswold is shown in the plan of the house in *Thorpe Drawings*, T65–6, pl. 31.

59 In 1634 'The territ in the garden' at Donington Park, Leicestershire, was 'where Edward Bromhead the gardiner lies'; 'the other territ in the garden' was 'where Mr Jackson lies' – probably an upper servant (inventory in Huntington Library, California, Huntingdon Papers L5/BI).

60 *Of Household Stuff: The 1601 Inventories of Bess of Hardwick*, p. 24: 'the Rownde turret'.

61 *Girouard, *Smythson*, p. 46.

62 Montacute banqueting house described in inventory of 1667, quoted in Malcolm Rogers, *Montacute House*, National Trust Guide, London, 1991, pp. 58–9; the Wimbledon one is shown on John Smythson's survey plan of Wimbledon, in *Smythson Drawings*, I/24; *Of Household Stuff: The 1601 Inventories of Bess of Hardwick*, pp. 29–30.

63 Inventory in Cholmondeley papers, Cheshire Record Office.

64 Swarkestone (now Landmark Trust) is dated in accounts for 'Bowl-alley house', quoted in *Colvin, entry for Richard Shepherd.

65 J. A. Gotch, *The Old Halls and Manor Houses of Northamptonshire*, London, 1936, p. 69 and pl. 124; T. F. Dibdin, *Aedes Althorpianae*, 2 vols, London, 1822, vol. I, pp. xvii–xviii, with engraving.

66 Peter Hansell and Jean Hansell, *Doves and Dovecotes*, Bath, 1988, p. 202 with illustration.

67 Rodminster Lodge is shown on a sixteenth-century survey of Longleat in the park to the east of the house. I am grateful to Michael McGarvie for this information.

68 For Portington, see *Girouard, *Smythson*, p. 133. He supplied commendatory verses to the first part of Robert Greene's *Mamillia*, 1580 or 1583, and the second part, 1583 or 1593, is dedicated to him and Robert Lee.

69 See chapter 1, note 158, and this chapter, p. 89–90 and note 38.

70 Thomas Fuller, *Worthies of England*, under Northamptonshire. Fuller had been working on the *Worthies* since the mid-1640s, but it was first published after his death in 1661.

71 Aubrey, *Brief Lives*, ed. Powell, p. 256.

72 Durant, *Bess of Hardwick*, p. 147.

73 *The Countess of Pembroke's Arcadia*, ed. A. Feuillerat, Cambridge, 1912, p. 20.

74 Girouard, *Life in the English Country House*, p. 76.

75 *Country Life*, 65 (23 March 1929), pp. 400–08.

76 *Girouard, *Smythson*, pp. 110–15 and passim.

77 Ibid., pp. 137–40. Doddington is clearly influenced by Worksop, and I would like to attribute this fine house to Robert Smythson, as I did in my monograph on him, but I now have doubts about it; the prominent placing of chimney stacks in the outside walls on all but the entrance front is untypical of his planning. At most it seems possible that he provided a 'plott' for the entrance front.

78 *Royal Works*, vol. III, pp. 349–50, with plan at fig. 13.

79 Ibid., vol. IV, pp. 196–200, with plan at fig. 18.

80 Ibid., vol. IV, pp. 14–15, and plan at fig. 2; the project is there assigned to Henry VIII, but I think Philip and Mary more likely.

81 Ibid., vol. IV, pp. 150–53, with plan redrawn as fig. 15.

82 Girouard, *Life in the English Country House*, p. 110, quoting Thomas Platter, *Travels in England* [1599], ed. Clare Williams, London, 1937, pp. 193–5. A similar ceremony seems to be described in 1600 at Whitehall; see Leslie Hotson, *The First Night of Twelfth Night*, London, 1954, quoted in *The Diary of Baron Waldstein*, trans. G. W. Groos, London, 1981, p. 80 n. 135.

83 J. Summerson, 'The Building of Theobalds, 1564–1585', *Archaeologia*, 97 (1959), pp. 107–26, with Hawthorne plan reproduced on pl. xxva, from Hatfield, CP 143/31–32.

84 Ibid., p. 120. Summerson does not, however, comment on the intended provision of two state apartments and the omission of one of them.

85 The two great chambers are distinguished as North and South Great Chamber in inventories of 1596 and 1599; the room off the South Great Chamber is the 'best chamber'. In an inventory of 1609, following a visit by Queen Anne and Prince Henry in 1603, the 'best chamber' has become 'the princes chamber' and the equivalent chamber in the north lodgings 'the queens chamber'. Inventories printed in Pamela Marshall, *Wollaton Hall: An Archaeological Survey*, Nottingham, 1996, pp. 100–09.

86 Hatfield, CPM I/16–17 (fols 20, 21), reproduced in *Girouard, *Smythson*, p. 43, pl. 19.

87 The equivalent rooms are called in the inventory of 1601 (*Of Household Stuff: The 1601 Inventories of Bess of Hardwick*) 'high great Chamber', 'with drawing Chamber', 'best bed Chamber' and 'Pearl Bed Chamber'.

88 D. N. Durant, *Arbella Stuart: A Rival to the Queen*, London, 1978, p. 36.

89 Ibid., pp. 54, 61, 68–9.

90 The visit of 1619 is recorded in the account-book Hardwick MS 29, fol. 581. It is possible that Prince Charles spent the night as well, but my reading of the accounts suggests that he did not.

91 See Emily Cole, 'The Uses of Elizabethan and Jacobean State Apartments with Reference to Apethorpe Hall, Northamptonshire', in *Apethorpe Hall, Apethorpe, Northamptonshire: Survey, Research and Analysis*, vol II, appendix 10, English Heritage Research Department Report Series, no. 82, 2 vols, Cambridge, 2006; this is a by-product of her ongoing doctoral studies into state aartments.

92 Hatfield, CP 211/1. Two similar plans annotated 'for Amptell'. *Thorpe Drawings*, T267–8, T271–2, pls 120, 121. These are among the very few plans signed by Thorpe.

93 See Girouard, *Life in the English Country House*, p. 115 and fig. 4. It is interesting that Robert Cecil, unlike his father, was content with providing sequences of three, rather than four, royal rooms. This may reflect the desires of James himself.

94 For Audley End, see especially P. J. Drury, 'No other palace in the kingdom will compare with it: The Evolution of Audley End, 1605–1745', *Architectural History*, 23 (1980), pp. 1–39 and pls 1–27. The house was magnificently depicted, with plans, in a set of folio engravings published by Henry Winstanley *circa* 1688–95.

95 *Thorpe Drawings*, T101–2, T105–6, and possibly T81–2, pls 48, 49 and 39.

96 Hatfield, CPM II/8 (17); facsimile British Library, MSS Facs. 372. And see M. Girouard, 'Designs for a Lodge at Ampthill', in *The Country Seat*, ed. Colvin and Harris, pp. 13–17. I would not now agree with my ten-

tative attribution (pp. 15–16) of the designs to Simon Basil.

97 For example, the change of room names at Wollaton; see note 85.

98 For Works artificers at Knole, see chapter 1, note 51. The bedroom at the end of the potential royal lodgings is called the 'Queens chamber' in an inventory of 1645 (Centre for Kentish Studies, U269/O10/1–2, printed in C. J. Phillips, *History of the Sackville Family*, 2 vols, London, *circa* 1901, vol. 1, pp. 353 et seq.), but has become the 'King's Chamber' in an inventory of 1687 (U269 E2/3), and has kept that or a similar name up to the present. Presumably a queen, probably Henrietta Maria, slept in it before 1645, and a king, probably Charles II, between 1645 and 1687, but no record is known of either visit.

99 See useful account in *The English Court*, ed. David Starkey, London, 1987: 'The Revival of the Entourage', especially p. 180.

100 See chapter 1, note 128.

101 See plans in Heward and Taylor, *The Country Houses of Northamptonshire*, p. 247, fig. 323, and in Lucy Worsley, *Kirby Hall*, English Heritage Guide, 2000, endpapers.

102 Ibid., pp. 58–69, with plans at figs 71–2; *Apethorpe Hall, Apethorpe, Northamptonshire: Survey, Research and Analysis*, English Heritage Research Department Report Series, no. 82, 2 vols, Cambridge, 2006.

103 Heward and Taylor, *The Country Houses of Northamptonshire*, pp. 129–38; *Country Life*, 179 (30 January 1986), pp. 248–52, but neither of these discuss the possibility of new grand apartments on the second floor. The parapets are dated 1624 and (on a turret) 1635; the great room at the south end of the east range (now the Old Library) cannot from its heraldry be later than 1630; payments were made in 1635–6 for 'worke begun on the King's Bedchamber, privy chamber on the east side of the house'. Charles I visited for four days in 1634. The Old Library could have been the presence chamber of otherwise remodelled king's lodgings. The drawback to suggesting a matching queen's lodgings in the west range is that the grand door-case at the head of the staircase leads into the middle of the room sequence rather than one end. A possible explanation is that it led into an antechamber between matching new apartments for the earl and countess, as possibly

in the entrance range at Godolphin (*circa* 1630) and at Chatsworth in the late seventeenth century; in this case the queen's lodgings would have been on the first floor of the east range, under the king's.

Chapter 3 Learning a Language

1 Names extracted from the alphabetical list in *Letters of Denization and Acts of Naturalization for Aliens in England, 1509–1603*, ed. William Page, Huguenot Society, VIII, Lymington, 1893.

2 Arthur Oswald, *Country Houses of Dorset*, 2nd edn, London, 1959, pp. 21–2, pls 1–4, 5–6, 56; J. Newman and N. Pevsner, *Buildings of England: Dorset*, Harmondsworth, 1972, pp. 42–4.

3 For Henry VIII's tomb, see Edward Chaney, 'Early Tudor Tombs', in his *The Evolution of the Grand Tour: Anglo-Italian Cultural Relations since the Renaissance*, London, 1998, pp. 45–52, with references.

4 Toto has a useful biographical entry with references in E. Croft-Murray, *Decorative Painting in England, 1537–1837*, 2 vols, London, 1962–70, vol. 1, pp. 164–5, and ibid., pp. 17–18.

5 Erna Auerbach, *Tudor Artists*, London, 1954, pp. 56–7, and see **Royal Works*, vol. III, pp. 43–5, for a concise account of Italian artificers in royal service.

6 British Library, MS Cotton Augustus I/1/5.

7 Henry Peacham, *The Art of Drawing with the Pen*, London, 1606, chapter 13: 'Of Antique'.

8 Historical Manuscripts Commission, *The Manuscripts of His Grace of Rutland, GCB, Preserved at Belvoir Castle*, 4 vols, London, 1888–1905, vol. IV, pp. 317, 341.

9 For Nonsuch, see **Royal Works*, vol. IV, pp. 179–205; S. Thurley, *The Royal Palaces of Tudor England*, New Haven and London, 1993, pp. 60–65.

10 William Camden, *Britain*, trans. P. Holland, London, 1610, p. 299 or p. 287 (the pagination is confused).

11 Monique Chatenet, *La Cour de France au XVIème siècle*, Paris, 2002, p. 37.

12 Reproduced in John Summerson, *Architecture in Britain, 1530 to 1830*, 8th rev. edn, Harmondsworth, 1991, p. 35, fig. 11; Thurley, *The Royal Palaces of Tudor England*, p. 217, pl. 284.

13 **Royal Works*, vol. IV, pp. 195–6. His work for Somerset is recorded in British Library, Egerton MS 2815.

14 In a return of aliens quoted in *Huguenot Society Publications*, vol. X, part 2, 1902, p. 114. For Cure, see pp. 59–60 above, and 311–12 below.

15 For Bellin, see Martin Biddle, 'Nicholas Bellin of Modena', *Journal of the British Archaeological Association*, 3rd series, 29 (1966); **Royal Works*, vol. IV, especially pp. 23–4, 193–5. Payment (no date) to eight 'Frenche men workyng upon the Fronte of the Chemnaye For the prevye Chamber', British Library, MS Royal 14 B.IV.A., quoted in C. Gapper, 'Plasterers and Plasterwork in City, Court and Country, *c.* 1530–*c.* 1640', PH.D thesis, University of London (Courtauld Institute of Art), 1998, p. 131. One of the eight may have been Bellin himself.

16 For the three assistants, Nicholas Goose and Symon Moynowe, smith and joiner, both of Normandy, and Maryn or Martyn Sasshey or Sashoy, a joiner, place of origin not given; see *Letters of Denization*, ed. Page, pp. 108, 175, 215.

17 Albert Feuillerat, *Documents Relating to the Revels in the Time of King Edward VI and Queen Mary*, Louvain, 1914, pp. 6–7 and nn. p. 257.

18 *The Diary of Henry Machyn: Citizen and Merchant-Taylor of London, from AD 1550 to AD 1563*, ed. J. G. Nichols, Camden Society, London, 1848; **House of Commons, Elizabeth*, *sub* Cawarden.

19 Feuillerat, *Documents Relating to the Revels in the Time of King Edward VI and Queen Mary*, and Feuillerat, *Documents Relating to the Offices of the Revels in the Time of Queen Elizabeth*, Louvain, 1908, both passim. Denization of 'John Carowne from parish of Breme-juxta-aide, Picardy', 16 March 1536; of 'John Caron. From France. Married to an alien woman. In England 12 years', 14 April 1541 (*Letters of Denization*, ed. Page). For Trunquet, who claimed that Bellin was his 'master', see pp. 134–5 in this chapter.

20 Bellin's New Year gift is recorded in John Nichols, *The Progresses and Public Processions of Queen Elizabeth*, 3 vols, London, 1823, vol. III, p. 19.

21 See Karen Hearn, ed., *Dynasties: Painting in Tudor and Jacobean England, 1530–1630*, Tate Gallery catalogue, 1995, pp. 50–52,

for a full entry and discussion of this portrait and reproduction of the School of Fontainebleau print (also reproduced in *Wells-Cole, *Decoration*, p. 38, pl. 42), on which the surround is closely based.

22 For plasterwork, see especially Gapper, 'Plasterers and Plasterwork in City, Court and Country'.

23 See M. Biddle, 'A "Fontainebleau" Chimneypiece at Broughton Castle', in *The Country Seat: Studies in the History of the British Country House Presented to John Summerson*, ed. Howard Colvin and John Harris, London, 1970, pp. 9–12.

24 British Library, Add. Charter 1262*, summarised in *Royal Works*, vol. III, pp. 44–5, omitting, however, the references to Leicester and 'worshipfull personages'. The petition is not dated, but is likely to have been made soon after the death of Bellin in 1569, in which case the work claimed to have been done for Leicester 'at Killingworthe against your ma.ties repaire thether' would have been for her visits in 1566 or 1568.

25 For Trunquet, see Feuillerat, *Documents Relating to the Revels in the Time of King Edward VI and Queen Mary*, and Feuillerat, *Documents Relating to the Offices of the Revels in the Time of Queen Elizabeth*, passim. In his denization, 24 July 1549, he is described as 'From the dominion of the emperor' (see *Letters of Denization*, ed. Page; Arras was then in the Low Countries, not France). His freedom of Bristol, as 'Robertus Trunqueth Joiner', is recorded in Bristol City Archives, Burgess roll, 13 May 1562, on payment of 44s. 6d.

26 John Evelyn, *Diaries*: 21 August 1655: 'The chimney-piece in the great chamber, carved in wood, was of Henry VIII, and was taken from a house of his in Bletchingley.' Bletchingley was part of the dowry settled by Henry VIII on Anne of Cleves; she surrendered her interest to Cawarden in 1547, in return for an annual payment.

27 *House of Commons,. Elizabeth, sub Cawarden.

28 Daniel Defoe, *A Tour through the Whole Island of Great Britain, 1724–1727*, 2 vols, London, 1927, vol. II, p. 501.

29 For example, the great chamber described in George Whetstone, *An Heptameron of Civill Discourses*, 1582, 'the roof wherof was Allablaster plaister' (quoted on p. 73); and the inscription on an anonymous design for plasterwork, *circa* 1580–1601, in Longleat

archives: 'It shall shew as fayre in whitwork as in alabaster'.

30 See Chaney, *The Evolution of the Grand Tour*, especially chapters 3 and 6. A biographical dictionary of English visitors to Italy in the two centuries previous to those covered by John Ingamells and Brinsley Ford, *The Dictionary of British and Irish Travellers in Italy, 1701–1800*, New Haven and London, 1997, remains a desideratum. Permissions for visits were much harder to obtain after Pius V excommunicated Elizabeth in 1570, but became easier under James I.

31 'A booke of the travaile and lief of me, Thomas Hoby', ed. Edgar Powell, in *Camden Miscellany*, vol. X, London, 1902, and see Chaney, *The Evolution of the Grand Tour*, pp. 45–6, 62–6 and 90, n. 22, and passim. For Bisham Abbey, see *Country Life*, 89 (12, 19 and 26 April 1941), pp. 320–24, 342–6, 364–8.

32 Camden, *Britain*, trans. Holland, p. 594. For more on Moreton Corbet and the suggestion that the influence was anyway from Antwerp rather than Italy, see pp. 196–9 and notes.

33 His will is Prerogative Court of Canterbury, Pykering 1, 1574. The legacy is described in J. W. Burgon, *The Life and Times of Sir Thomas Gresham*, 2 vols, London, 1839, vol. II, p. 459, quoting from the will. I owe this important reference to Claire Gapper and Paula Henderson.

34 A useful account of such publications is Vaughan Hart and Peter Hicks, eds, *Paper Palaces: The Rise of the Renaissance Architectural Treatise*, New Haven and London, 1998.

35 Thomas Smith, John Dee, Thomas Knyvett, Thomas Tresham and Robert Cecil certainly had them; see pp. 52–3 above. For Elizabethan and Jacobean architectural libraries, see the appendix 'Books on Art, Perspective and Architecture in English Renaissance Libraries, 1580–1630', in Lucy Gent, *Picture and Poetry, 1560–1620* Leamington Spa, 1981.

36 Female terms on Serlio's Ionic and Corinthian chimneypieces, Book IV, chapter 7, fol. 43, and Book IV, chapter 8, fol. 58. The male and female characters of the various columns are described in Vitruvius, *De Architectura* IV.i.1–9. Serlio refers to this (though not naming Vitruvius) in the introduction to his Fourth Book, and again in the

sections on Ionic and Corinthian in the same chapter (Vaughan Hart and Peter Hicks, *Serlio on Architecture*, New Haven and London, 1996, pp. 254, 338, 363). Shute, in his preliminary 'Discourse', p. B. II, refers to 'writers' on the orders having 'resembled and lykned' them 'to sertain feyned Goddes and Goddesses', clearly drawing on Vitruvius and Serlio, but also, unlike them, including Atlas and Pandora as expressing the qualities of Tuscan and Composite; his sources for these, if any, have not been identified.

37 Hart and Hicks, 'On Sebastiano Serlio: Decorum and the Art of Architectural Invention', in *Paper Palaces*, especially pp. 146–57.

38 See *Bibliographia Serliana: Catalogue des editions imprimées des livres de traité d'architecture de Sebastiano Serlio*, ed. Magali Vène, Paris, 2006; Hart and Hicks, *Serlio on Architecture*, vol. I, Appendix, pp. 470–71.

39 Others in the group include Gulielmus Paludanus or Van den Broecke, Martin von Heemskerk, Lambert van Noort, Sebastiaan van Noyen, Jan Gossaert, Lambertus Suavius or Zutman, Jacques Dubroencoff and Dirk Grabeth of Gouda. For Coecke as architectural publisher and writer, see Krista De Jonge in *Unity and Discontinuity: Architectural Relationships between the Southern and Northern Low Countries, 1530–1700*, ed. De Jonge and Konrad Ottenheym, Architectura Moderna, vol. V, Turnhout, Belgium, 2007, especially pp. 42–9. For his important work as a designer of tapestries (for Henry VIII amongst others), see Thomas P. Campbell, *Tapestry in the Renaissance: Art and Magnificence* [Metropolitan Museum of Art catalogue], New Haven and London, 2002, especially pp. 379–91 and cat. nos. 45–9.

40 *The First Booke of Architecture made by Sebastian Serly, entreating of Geometrie. Translated out of Italian into Dutch, and Dutch into English. London Printed for Robert Peake . . .* [1611]. Bound in with this, or issued at the same time, were translations of the Books II–V, the Second, Fourth and Fifth with title pages also dated 1611. Facsimile edition, New York and London, 1982 [Dover Publications]. See also Eileen Harris and Nicholas Savage, *British Architectural Books and Writers*, Cambridge, 1990, pp. 414–17. The First and Second Books were reprinted

in 1657, but otherwise there were no later editions. Peake added a dedication to Henry, Prince of Wales, a general address 'To the Lovers of Architecture' and introductions to the Third and Fourth Books. The language of the dedication suggests that the actual translation was not by Peake.

41 See Maurice Howard, 'A Drawing by "Robertus Pyte" for Henry VIII', *Architectural History*, 44 (2001), pp. 22–8. 'Henry Pytt gunfounder', who made and cast 'modells for two terms' for Lord Burghley in 1582, may have been related (Hatfield, CP 143/70).

42 *Royal Works*, vol. IV, pp. 301–2, 313, suggesting *circa* 1548 as a possible date.

43 British Library, Egerton MS 2815, payments to Bellin, Gering, Cure and Lovell. The payment to Revell is in National Archives, SP 3/51/408. I owe this reference to Simon Thurley.

44 Letter (from Longleat MSS) printed in M. Girouard. 'The Development of Longleat House between 1546 and 1572', *Architectural Journal*, 116 (1959), p. 210.

45 Cornelius Grapheus, *De Seer wonderlujke schoone, Triumphelijcke Incompst . . .*, Antwerp, 1550. The arch erected by the English merchants (and possibly other arches) was destroyed by the Antwerp painter Lambert van Noort; see W. Kuyper, *The Triumphant Entry of Renaissance Architecture into the Netherlands*, Alphen aan den Rijn, 1994, pp. 58–60. Kuyper's book treats of the arches in detail, in the context of contemporary building.

46 See Paul Davies and David Hemsoll, 'Renaissance Balusters and the Antique', *Architectural History*, 26 (1983), pp. 1–23.

47 Dormer's will, Prerogative Court of Canterbury, 26 Powell, made 20 June 1552, directs only 'my bodye to be buried where yt shall please Almighty god', and it is unlikely that the monument could have been erected within the same year. One of the engraved brass inscriptions set under coats of arms in the wall above the tomb chest refers to Sir Robert's granddaughter as wife of the Duke of Feria, a title conferred on her husband in 1567. But the black-letter inscriptions are stylistically so different from the monument that they seem likely to be a later insertion into a monument put up some time after Sir Robert's death. Apart from

the date of 1552, there are no inscriptions or arms on the tomb chest or canopy, though they had clearly been intended: on the pedestal of the north-east Corinthian column is a blank frame for a coat of arms, stylistically a variant on the coats of arms at the end of Serlio's Fourth Book, and two blank tablets for inscriptions. I am not convinced by the argument that the canopy was erected subsequently to the tomb chest, as put forward by Lawrence Butler in 'The Monument to Sir Robert Dormer (d. 1552) at Wing, Buckinghamshire: A New Hypothesis', *Church Monuments*, 21 (2006), pp. 130–40. The two seem splendidly all of a piece.

48 See Howard Colvin, 'Pompous Entries and English Architecture', in *Essays on English Architectural History*, New Haven and London, 1999, pp. 70–71, 90–91, quoting from a description by an Italian visitor, G. R. Rosso of Ferrara, published as *I Successi d'Inghilterra dopo la morte di Odoardo sesto . . .*, Ferrara, 1560.

49 For Shute's *Architecture*, see Harris and Savage, *British Architectural Books and Writers*, pp. 418–22. It was published in facsimile, London, 1912, with an introduction by Lawrence Weaver, including some biographical details and the text of the inscription on his (demolished) monument, which gives the date of his death, 25 September 1563. His will, if any, has not been located. For his miniatures, see Auerbach, *Tudor Artists*, pp. 185–6; Richard Haydocke, in his 1598 translation of Lomazzo's *Trattato*, referred to 'Shoote' as a precursor to Hilliard. For his masque, see *Malone Society Collections*, 3 (1954), p. 41.

50 In his 'Defence of the Earl of Leicester', in *Miscellaneous Prose of Sir Philip Sidney*, ed. K. Duncan-Jones and J. van Dorsten, Oxford, 1973, pp. 134–9.

51 I am grateful to Howard Colvin for sending me a photocopy of such a sarcophagus in the Capitoline Museum, Rome.

52 John Heward and Robert Taylor, *The Country Houses of Northamptonshire*, Royal Commission on the Historical Monuments of England, Swindon, 1996, p. 158, fig. 198.

53 For Dingley, ibid., pp. 170–74 and fig. 38. My attribution to Thorpe is on stylistic grounds only. The crest of the Griffins of Dingley features in the decoration of Kirby Hall, where the Thorpe family were certainly involved (see p. 179 in this chapter). Its pres-

ence there suggests a family connection between the Griffins and the Staffords of Kirby, which I have not been able to establish. The remarkable Griffin monument in Braybrooke church is presumably by the same mason.

54 For Melford, see *Country Life*, 82 (31 July and 7 August 1937), pp. 116–21, 142–7.

55 The sixteenth-century porch at Longleat is shown in the plans at Hatfield, illustrated in *Girouard, Smythson*, pl. 19. The worn inscription below the male bust on the entrance front of the Holbein porch appears to be 'Apolonius Prince of Tier'. It and the extremely elaborate quarterings on the coat of arms suggest a reference to a mythical ancestry, in need of elucidation. Ruth Guilding has pointed out to me that the porch shows traces of original colouring.

56 For Charlecote, see *Country Life*, 111 (11 and 18 April 1952), pp. 1080–83, 1164–7.

57 For Loseley, see *Country Life*, 146 (2 and 9 October 1969), pp. 802–5, 894–8 [articles by Marcus Binney].

58 *Wells-Cole, Decoration*, pp. 25, 35, 387, figs 17–19, 43.

59 'Gyllane', described as a 'freemason', 'Perowe' and 'Brykleton' feature in the accounts of 1563–6 for Loseley, paid wages for one year (£4), two years (£9) and one year (£1 12s. 4d, as an apprentice), respectively, with extra for livery and meat and drink. In addition, 'one frencheman that hewed stone XXVIII dayes' was paid 14s. A relationship can be surmised with 'Guillaume Guillain, maitre des oeuvres de maconnerie de la ville de Paris', working at the Louvre and elsewhere *circa* 1548–68, and Antoine Perrault 'maistre macon' paid for work at the Louvre, 1556. 'Harvey Perrowse, joyner, Frenchman' was listed as an alien in the city and liberties of Westminster in 1568; 'Richard Brickleton, born in Brabant' was listed as a joiner in 1583. A 'joiner' could be a carver, working in stone as well as wood (Loseley MSS; L. de Laborde, *Comptes des Bâtiments du Roi, 1528–71*, Paris, 1877–80, vol. I, p. 295; R. E. G. Kirk and E. F. Kirk, eds, *Returns of Aliens Dwelling in the City and Suburbs of London*, Huguenot Society, VIII, Aberdeen, 1900–08, part 3, p. 399; part 2, p. 369. The manuscripts at Loseley, originally reported on by A. J. Kempe, *The Loseley Manuscripts*, London, 1836, with extracts from the building accounts, and then in *Seventh Report of the*

Royal Commission on Historical Manuscripts, London, 1879, pp. 596–681, are now mainly distributed between the Folger Library, Washington, DC, and the Surrey History Centre, Woking. William More's account-books are Folger L.b.550, with microfilm in British Library, M/437). A pair of matching chimneypieces from Loseley were for a time at Scarsdale House, South Kensington, and are now at Dyffryn House, Glamorgan (*Kensington Square to Earl's Court*, Survey of London, vol. XLII, London, 1986, p. 103 and pls 64–5; John Harris, *Moving Rooms: The Trade in Architectural Salvages*, New Haven and London, 2007, p. 72 and pls 64–5). They were from the wing added to Loseley in the early seventeenth century, containing a long gallery from which they probably came (*Thorpe Drawings*, T39–40 and pl. 18). Edward Cecil Curzon, their Scarsdale House owner, added Curzon mottoes and probably made other alterations.

60 For Gorhambury, see especially Nick Hill, 'Conservation and Decay: Two Centuries at Old Gorhambury', *Transactions of the Association for Studies in the Conservation of Historic Buildings*, 21 (1996).

61 London, Lambeth Palace Library, Bacon MS 647, fol. 54.

62 University of Chicago Library, Bacon MS 4091, transcribed in *Proceedings of the Suffolk Institute of Archaeology*, 24 (1961), p. 28.

63 *White, Dictionary*, including attributions, pp. 37–9, 45, 47–8.

64 John Bayliss, 'The Decline of the Marblers' Company', *Monumental Brass Society Bulletin*, 33 (June 1983), pp. 41–2.

65 Ibid., p. 42, where 'Masons'' appears to be a misprint for 'Marblers''.

66 See chapter 1, note 121.

67 British Library, Royal MS 17A.XXIII, and see John Aubrey, *Brief Lives and Other Selected Writings*, ed. Anthony Powell, London, 1949, p. 196. Jane Lumley's translations, British Library, Royal MSS 15A I, II, IX.

68 There are biographies of all four sisters and their father in *ODNB. For Anne Bacon's translation, see C. S. Lewis, *English Literature in the Sixteenth Century, Excluding Drama*, Oxford, 1954, p. 307.

69 *White, Dictionary*, p. 37. The inscription on the Hoby monument reveals that it was set up by Thomas Hoby's widow, Elizabeth.

70 My source for this important letter of May 1509 has been mislaid.

71 For a discussion of the proportions and possible background of the Gate of Honour, see Lorna MacNear, 'The Gate of Honour in its Setting', *The Caian* [Cambridge] (1996–7), pp. 103–8. See also Tom Nickson, 'Moral Edification at Gonville and Caius College, Cambridge', *Architectural History*, 48 (2005), pp. 49–68. Caius did not originate the concept; a 'Porta honoris' is shown on a plan of Trinity College, probably dating from the 1550s, reproduced in *Willis and Clark, *Cambridge*, between pp. 465 and 466.

72 On the Gothic elements, see p. 438 below.

73 Like too many Elizabethan artificers, little is known about Theodore Haveus. The one full reference to him is in Thomas Legge's continuation of Caius's Latin *Annales Collegii de Goneville et Caius*, in reference to the columns and elaborate hexecontahedron sundial set up in Caius Court of the College in 1576, and made by 'Theodoreus Haveus Cleviensis, artifex egregius et insignis architecturae professor'. 'Cleviensis' can be taken to mean 'from Cleves' in Germany. 'Theodore and others' were paid £33 16s. 5d 'for carving' the monument of Caius in the college chapel in the years 1573–5 (originally on the ground, but elevated to its present wall position in 1637). 'Theodore' also appears in 1575, carving and colouring the still-in-position College coat of arms and its pilastered surround over the hall entrance in Queens' College. His alleged portrait, with compasses and polyhedron, is at Caius. The Cambridge Theodore is perhaps the same as the 'Theodoric Hake, from the dominion of the Kings of Spain' who took out denization on 9 March 1562 (he could have come from Cleves to England by way of the Low Countries).

74 See *ODNB.

75 The early history of Longleat is dealt with in detail in M. Girouard, 'The Development of Longleat House between 1546 and 1572', *Architectural Journal*, 116 (1969), pp. 200–22. For Thynne, see *House of Commons, Elizabeth and *ODNB.

76 See Girouard, 'The Development of Longleat House', pp. 206, 216; *Girouard, Smythson*, p. 40.

77 'John Carowne from parish of Breme-juxta-Aide Picardy' is reported in England on 16 March 1536, and 'John Caron. From France. Married to an alien woman. In England 12

years' was granted denization in 1541. In 1547 he was one of the large body of artificers working on the 'mount' made for Edward VI's coronation festivities (see p. 131 below). From 1550 till his death early in 1575 there are constant payments to him in the Revels accounts, as 'carver' or 'property master', including 'past and cement molded work'.

78 For Maynard, see Girouard, 'The Development of Longleat House', pp. 216–18; *Girouard, Smythson*, pp. 62–5, 70–76 and passim; *Wells-Cole, Decoration*, pp. 137, 139–40. His denization as Alenus Maynard 'from the dominion of the King of France', on 12 February 1566, is in Patent Rolls, 8 Elizabeth, 6/35. From about 1573 he was living in a tenement belonging to Thynne at Woodlands, or West Woodlands, between Longleat and Frome (Longleat archives). Frome Parish Register (see chapter 1, note 58) records the baptism, between 1573 and 1585, of his children Rachel, Judith, Samuel, Adrian, John and Alice, and his burial on 4 April 1598. His will has not been traced. In the Longleat archives are his elevation of an unidentified façade (1560s?), his elevation of a portion of the final façade of Longleat (*circa* 1572), a little plan and elevation dated 1585 and annotated 'Allan Maynards draft for Rodmister Lodge', and various sketch designs for cartouches and parapet details. Works attributed to Maynard and/or his workshop are:

Chimneypieces
Longleat: in hall (*circa* ?1575–80), and two, original position unknown, re-erected on first floor and in basement.

Woodlands Manor, Mere, Wiltshire (*circa* ?1570): two on ground and first floors, the latter now at Barton Abbey, near Banbury.

?Wiston Hall, Sussex (*circa* 1575): one on first floor (photograph sent to me by Maurice Howard), portions of at least two re-erected on north façade (*Wells-Cole, Decoration*, pp. 140–42, pls 212–18).

Upper Upham, Wiltshire (*Country Life*, 51, 1 July 1922, pp. 888–95): in hall and on first floor (1590s?).

?Probably from Bristol, re-erected in Broomwell House, Bristol (demolished, shown in drawing by W. H. Bartle of *circa* 1825 in Brackenridge Collection, City of Bristol Art Gallery). this might also be by

Thomas Collins; see chapter 6, note 24, section A

Apparent portion of chimneypiece, probably from Sapperton Manor, Gloucestershire, re-erected in church as part of eighteenth-century monument of Sir Robert Atkyns.

Church monuments

Nunney, Somerset (to member of Paulet family?).

Bishop's Canning, Wiltshire, to John Ernele (d. 1571).

St Peter's, Bristol, to member of Newton family (demolished; *Wells-Cole, *Decoration*, p. 140 and pl. 209).

Sherborne Abbey, Dorset, to John Leweston (d. 1584) and his wife (d. 1579).

Others

Wolfeton house, Dorset: stone staircase and doorcase (*circa* ?1590).

For a suggested connection with William Arnold, with the gatehouse at Clifton Maybank, Dorset, and with the Hall, Bradford-on-Avon, see chapter 7, note 36; for Chalcot House, Wiltshire, see note 79.

79 *Wells-Cole, *Decoration*, pp. 136–7 and pls 201–3, reproducing the two Du Cerceau designs. The aedicule window frames of the designs suggest that Maynard may have had a hand in the much-altered façade of Chalcot House, Wiltshire (*Girouard, *Smythson*, p. 63 and pl. 26).

80 Smythson was working on one of them in 1569 (*Girouard, *Smythson*, p. 46). They feature in a specification (undated, but it must be of 1567 or 1568), reprinted in Girouard, 'The Development of Longleat House', pp. 213–14: 'all the starres to Ryse above the howse and to be typed and iiii to have lytle starres wonne from the roofe so as they may serve as banketting howses'. The window design is *Smythson Drawings, 1/16.

81 Girouard, 'The Development of Longleat House', pp. 205–6, 210–12 [Chapman]; pp. 206–10, 212–16 [Spicer]; pp. 206, 216, 218 [Lewis], and for his work at Middle Temple Hall, see p. 345 below; David N. Durant, *Bess of Hardwick: Portrait of an Elizabethan Dynast*, London, 1977, pp. 27, 47. John Fortune is paid as a freemason in the Longleat building accounts from February 1568 to June 1569, always linked with John Moore, probably the same as the John Moore active

in Bath from 1575 to 1595. He is listed in a way that suggests that he was not one of the artificers who came with Robert Smythson in March 1568. 'The two Fortunes' occur alongside Merryman in the accounts for Grafton Manor in 1568–9; their work included John Talbot's coat of arms and 'sylinge and freating the new great chamber'. John Humphreys, 'The Elizabethan Estate Book of Grafton Manor', *Birmingham Archaeological Society Transactions*, 44/i (1919). The Estate Book covers 1568–9. Further building accounts for 1576–7 are now in British Library, Add. MS 46461, fols 40 et seq., but nothing survives for the intervening years. The chronology and the stylistic distinction of the work at Grafton suggest that one of the two Grafton Fortunes was John from Longleat, in which case he would have been a 'carver', prepared to work in several materials.

82 In his introduction Floris claims that the inspiration for his designs came from Italy.

83 The direct quotation from Serlio, an extended Ionic volute over a window, deriving from one of his Ionic chimneypieces in his Fourth Book, is reproduced by Krista De Jonge in 'Vitruvius, Alberti and Serlio: Architectural Treatises in the Low Countries, 1530–1620', in *Paper Palaces*, ed. Hart and Hicks, p. 289. De Jonge refers to it, p. 286, as 'the only surviving clear-cut reference in the Low Countries to Serlio in actual, three-dimensional architecture', a description that will read surprisingly to English historians. For a similar adaptation at Wollaton, see pp. 305–6 below.

84 The Town Hall must have been well known to the many Englishmen visiting or trading in Antwerp. In addition, it was twice engraved in 1565 (engravings reproduced in Piet Lombaerde, ed., *Hans Vredeman de Vries and the *Artes Mechanicae* Revisited*, Turnhout, 2005, pp. 198, 209).

85 Ibid., p. 67, and engraving, p. 68. For Paesschen's and Daem's contribution to the Town Hall, ibid., p. 144.

86 For the Royal Exchange, see Burgon, *The Life and Times of Sir Thomas Gresham*, vol. II, pp. 115, 177–8, 255; Anne Saunders, *The Royal Exchange*, London Topographical Society, no. 52, 1997. On 19 November 1568 Hendryk von Paesschen's wife Marie appeared for her husband before magistrates in Antwerp, 'he of necessity being in England making

and building there the Bourse of the merchants of London' (Certificatiboek 28 [1568], Stadsarchief Antwerp, fol. 34r, quoted in Saunders, *The Royal Exchange*, pt I, section IV, pp. 40–41).

87 Richard Clough to Thomas Gresham, Antwerp, 1 December 1566: '. . . for the tochestone you send me [for], I cannot write you answer by this my letter; for that both Henryke and Florys are both out of town. But and if they will deliver them in London, redy hewed at 2s. the foote, it wolde not be dear; as by my next I wyll', quoted in Burgon, *The Life and Times of Sir Thomas Gresham*, vol. II, pp. 177–8. 'Floris' could, of course, have been one of numerous other Florises, including Cornelis's brother Frans; but the stylistic resemblance between the Town Hall, the Hanseatenhuis and the Royal Exchange make identification with Cornelis tempting.

88 See pp. 185, 191 in this chapter.

89 For Bachecraig, see Burgon, *The Life and Times of Sir Thomas Gresham*, vol. II, pp. 310–12; Girouard, 'Bachecraig, Denbighshire', in *The Country Seat*, ed. Colvin and Harris, pp. 30–32 (written in the belief that the house had been completely demolished); Peter Howell, 'Country Houses in the Vale of Clwyd, I', *Country Life*, 162 (22 December 1977), pp. 1906–7, including photographs of the remaining wing. Howell dismisses the tradition that the Crown Hotel in Ruthin was Corbet's town house.

90 Quoted in Burgon, *The Life and Times of Sir Thomas Gresham*, vol. II, p. 312.

91 Amsterdam weigh-house illustrated in De Jonge in *Unity and Discontinuity*; engraving of château of Oudenhove in Antonius Sanderus, *Chorographia Sacra Brabantiae*, Brussels, 1659–69. The high dormered roof of the royal hunting lodge at Mariemont, which made it so like a grander version of Bachegraig, was not added to the original building of 1545–9 until 1605 (De Jonge in *Unity and Discontinuity*, pp. 69–70).

92 See the wide spacing of the arcade on the south front, and on the west side of the courtyard, both altered later, as shown in *Thorpe Drawings*.

93 Boswell's *Life of Johnson*, ed. G. B. Hill and L. F. Powell, Oxford, 1934–64, vol. IV, p. 436.

94 See Randall Davies, *Chelsea Old Church*, 1904, pp. 220–23, with illustration.

95 Thomas Mason's tomb is discussed in Martin Biddle, 'Early Renaissance at Winchester', in *Winchester Cathedral: Nine Hundred Years, 1093–1993*, ed. John Crook, Chichester, 1993, pp. 286–92. The style of the low-relief panels on the Mason and Gervoise monuments suggests the same hand at work.

96 I am grateful to Nicholas Cooper for communicating his typescript report on Bassingthorpe, made for the RCHM, with plans and reproductions of an inventory of 1564. See also Edmund Turner, 'Extracts from the Household-Book of Thomas Cony', Society of Antiquaries, 1792; *Lincolnshire Notes and Queries*, 1 (1889), pp. 113–18, 132–3, 164–6, 198–9, 230–33.

97 For Sissinghurst, see Edward Hasted, *History of the County of Kent, 1778–1799*, Canterbury, vol. III, p. 48; *Country Life*, 92 (28 August and 4 September 1942), pp. 410–14, 458–62.

98 Windows designed as ornamental features, at least; Roman windows were, perhaps invariably, plain unmoulded openings punched in the wall, filled (if glazed at all) with wooden-framed glazing, which had disappeared long before the sixteenth century.

99 A copy of one of the plans in it is in the Middleton (Wollaton) archives, and had an influence on the plan of Wollaton. Illustrated in *Girouard, Smythson*, p. 102, pl. 56; and see D. N. Durant, 'Wollaton Hall: A Rejected Plan', *Transactions of the Thoroton Society*, 76 (1972), pp. 13–16.

100 Paragraph 4 of the section on the Doric order, translated from the French edition of 1577; the 'Architecta' are listed later on in the paragraph, and commended for 'scavoir d'accomoder l'art a la situation et necessite du pais, pluys queoncque a este besoing aux Anciens'.

101 See Lombaerde, ed., *Hans Vredeman de Vries*, pp. 14, 144. There were tensions, too, between painters who were members of the Antwerp guild and outsiders, of whom Vredeman was one. Ibid., p. 12.

102 See pp. 48–9 above.

103 For Smith, see John Strype, *The Life of the Learned Sir Thomas Smith* [1698], Oxford, 1820; M. Dewar, *Sir Thomas Smith: A Tudor Intellectual in Office*, London, 1964; *ODNB*.

104 For Hill Hall, see Paul Drury, 'The Development of Hill Hall, Essex, 1557–81', *Journal of the British Archaeological Association*, 136 (1983), pp. 98–123. His monograph on Hill Hall will be publishd by the Society of Antiquaries in 2009.

105 Hatfield papers, August 1568. Cecil to Sir Henry Norris, ambassador in Paris. 'At Sir Thomas Smith's' could refer either to Hill Hall or to Smith's house in London.

106 List printed by Strype, *The Life of the Learned Sir Thomas Smith*, pp. 274–81.

107 Two generations of Richard Kirbys appear in the City of London Carpenters' Company records. The elder was made free of the Company in February 1544 (*Records of the Worshipful Company of Carpenters*, ed. B. March, London, 1913–37, vol. III, p. 10), his son in October 1569 (ibid., p. 201). Smith's Richard must be the son. He married Elizabeth, the daughter of Smith's brother George, in 1577, and died in 1600 (Drury, 'The Development of Hill Hall'). He was probably involved only with the 1572–3 portion of the work.

108 *Thorpe Drawings*, pp. 2, 81–8, pls 62–3. There has been a good deal of discussion about the date and raison d'être of Thorpe's two plans (of the ground and first floors); they may have been made *circa* 1600, to show suggested additions and alterations projected by the Hatton family.

109 For Kirby, see Heward and Taylor, *The Country Houses of Northamptonshire*, pp. 245–56; Lucy Worsley, *Kirby Hall*, English Heritage Guide, 2000.

110 Examples listed in R. B. MacKerrow and F. S. Ferguson, *Title-Page Borders Used in England and Scotland, 1485–1640*, London, 1932, pp. 97–9, pl. 110.

111 Serlio, Book IV, chapter 9 ('Of the Composite Order'). But according to Hart and Hicks, *Serlio on Architecture*, p. 453 n. 302, the capital was in the Temple of Minerva in the Forum of Nerva (also called Forum Transitorium).

112 Engraving reproduced in *Les Plus Excellents Bastiments de France par J.-A. du Cerceau*, ed. David Thomson, trans. Catherine Ludet, Paris, 1988, pp. 214–15. The Charleval façade (published in the second volume (1579) of the original edition) has a Doric order.

113 The possibility of another artificer being involved cannot be ruled out, for there is no evidence in the sixteenth century of any of the Thorpe family being 'carvers', though this is certainly not impossible. In the early seventeenth century a 'Thorpe', possibly John's brother Henry, was paid for supplying carved detail for the Trinity College fountain; see *Willis and Clark, Cambridge*, vol. II, pp. 628–9.

114 Illustrated in Nikolaus Pevsner, *Buildings of England: Northamptonshire*, Harmondsworth, 1961, pl. 33.

115 'A Booke of the Travaile and life of me Thomas Hoby', ed. Powell, Royal Historical Society, *Camden Miscellany*, vol. X, London, 1902, pp. 19, 24; Feuillerat, *Documents Relating to the Revels in the Time of King Edward VI and Queen Mary*, pp. 59, 60, and footnotes; *DNB*, entry for Thomas Stafford; SP Dom. 1, pp. 28, 80, 82; SP Foreign, Mary, pp. 264, 282; Elizabeth, vol. I, p. 1589, vol. IV, p. 354; vol. VIII, pp. 1386, 2550. *Acts of the Privy Council*, n.s. VII (1893), p. 348. In the pedigree of Stafford of Grafton and Blatherwick, British Library, Harleian 6128, fol. 90, 'Rogerus miles' features as the uncle of Humfrey, the builder of Kirby. Since no Sir Roger Stafford ('miles' signifies a knight) is recorded, and Robert and Roger can be used interchangeably, the identification seems reasonable. He married Jane, the sister of Sir Thomas Gorges of Longford (manuscript pedigree of Gorges affixed to copy of Raymond Gorges, *The Story of a Family*, Boston, 1944, Somerset County Record Office, Taunton).

116 For the final remodelling of Longleat, see *Girouard, Smythson*, pp. 46–54. The Maynard elevation (ibid., pl. 22) is in the Longleat archives.

117 For example, in the untitled set of engravings by Vredeman de Vries. Dedicated by Hieronymus Cock to Cardinal Granville, 1562.

118 The *Booke of Five Columns*, 1601, section H: 'The setting of the Columnes one upon the top of the other', etc. The English version is in fact a considerable expansion on the equivalent passage in the original edition of 1550.

119 The letter is printed in full in *Girouard, Smythson*, pp. 295–6.

120 Jill Husselby, 'Architecture at Burghley House: The Patronage of William Cecil, 1553–1598', 3 vols, PH.D thesis, University of Warwick, 1996, is the best analysis and discussion of the building to date.

121 It is never clear whether references to work

supplied by Henryk in this period was for Burghley, Theobalds or London.

122 Historical Manuscripts Commission, *Calendar of the Manuscripts of the Most Honourable the Marquess of Salisbury . . . Preserved at Hatfield House, Hertfordshire*, 24 vols, London, 1883–1976, vol. III, pp. 27–277 [27 August 1587]: 'Your lordship's buildings go on very fast this year, and I hope by Michaelmas they will be ready to cover with lead; the next year it will be some comfort if your lordship can get leave to see the perfection of your long and costly buildings, wherein your posterity I hope will be thankful unto your lordship for it, as myself must think myself most bound, who of all others receiveth the most use of it.' The central feature of the north front is inscribed 1587.

123 A. G. R. Smith, ed., *The 'Anonymous Life' of William Cecil, Lord Burghley*, Leweston, New York, 1990, p. 93; Francis Peck, *Desiderata Curiosa*, London, 1779, p. 25. Peck first published the 'Life' as anonymous; Smith's identification of the biographer as Sir Michael Hicks has been widely accepted.

124 The Thorpe plans show a much simpler porch, with coupled columns on the ground floor only, corresponding to the rear portion of the porch that is there today. Peter Kemp to William Cecil, 26 May 1573, had reported 'yor mason is in hande, wt yor porche so spedely as he can' (Hatfield MSS).

125 *Thorpe Drawings*, p. 61; T57 and T58, pl. 27.

126 Reproduced in M. Girouard, 'Burghley House, Lincolnshire, I', *Country Life*, 191 (23 April 1992), p. 56.

127 The motif figures prominently on the triumphal arch erected (but not designed) by the English merchants at Antwerp in 1549, illustrated in Grapheus, *De Seer wonderlujke schoone*, and dsigned by Sebastiaan van Noyen; see note 45 above

128 Husselby, 'Architecture at Burghley House'.

129 *ODNB*, entry for Rhys ap Thomas.

130 Waldstein (*The Diary of Baron Waldstein*, trans. G. W. Gross, London, 1981, p. 112) describes how, in 1600, 'going up the stairs you see the names, and coats-of-arms, of some of the Garter Knights'. The rooms on the first floor in the south front are described as the 'George rooms' in payments for their decoration in the years 1690–97 (Croft-Murray, *Decorative Painting in England*, vol. II, p. 236); since at that date no

member of the family had the Garter or was likely to receive it, it is possible that the rooms had been so described since the sixteenth century.

131 For Hawthorne, see *Royal Works*, vol. III, p. 85, and for his work at Windsor, ibid., pp. 325–6; National Archives, SP 12/114/11, 12; and W. H. St J. Hope, *Windsor Castle*, 1913, pl. I, especially pp. 274–8. His Windsor designs are reproduced in Hope, *Windsor Castle*, *Plans* volume, Plan 7. A letter of September 1575 from Peter Kempe to Lord Burghley shows that preparations were being made for new building work at Burghley; on 17 September he asked for the 'upright of the face' of the intended new building, because the workmen were almost at a standstill for the want of it. What was involved was almost certainly the new west range (the vaulting of the gatehouse is dated 1577), and the author of the 'upright' was probably Hawthorne.

132 For Symonds, see John Summerson. 'Three Elizabethan Architects', *John Rylands Library Bulletin* (September 1959), pp. 209–16, and (his will, Prerogative Court of Canterbury, Cobham 61), pp. 222–5. 'Symons plat of Burghley hall' is the endorsement on a letter from Thomas Fowler to Burghley of 9 September 1578: 'It maie please your Lordship I have ssent you the Platt from John Symons According as you gave him order' (Hatfield, CP 143/99). There is nothing in the letter to show whether the 'platt' was for the whole hall or for details – screen, chimneypiece, bay window or roof? Symonds was employed in 1583 to add a bay, incorporating two bay windows and another bay of the open timber roof, to the south of the fifteenth-century hall of Lincoln's Inn: the oriels and new roof section duplicated the fifteenth-century detail (J. Summerson, in *Transactions of the Ancient Monument Society*, new series, 28, 1984, pp. 10–11). A fire back dated 1575 and said to be 'the original one placed in the great dining-hall of Burghley House by Elizabeth's minister, whose arms are upon it' was in 'The Pryor's Bank', Fulham, described in T. Crofton Croker, *A Walk from London to Fulham*, ed. T. F. D. Croker, London, 1860, p. 121.

133 For the Cure family, see pp. 59–60 above, and notes 63 and 65 in this chapter; and pp. 311–12 below. The doorway and chimneypiece designs attributed to him, both anno-

tated by Lord Burghley, are at Hatfield, CP 141/73 and CPM 11/55; the chimneypiece design is dated 1586. Similar coffered vaults feature prominently also in the monument to Sir William Cordell at Long Melford, Suffolk, attributed to him, and in his documented monument to Mary, Queen of Scots of 1605. Burghley got him the post of Master Mason in the Works in 1596, and was described as his 'master' in 1587 (Arnold Oldsworth to Sir Charles Morison, August 1587, British Library, Add. MS 40629, fols 75–6, quoted in *White, Dictionary*, p. 40, n. 5).

134 So John Norden in his *Hertfordshire*, 1598: 'To speak of the beauty of this most stately house at large as it deserveth for curious buildings, delightful walks, and pleasant conceits within and without, and other things very glorious and elegant to be seen, would challenge a great portion of this little treatise, and therefore, lest I should come short of that due commendation that it deserveth, I leave it, as indeed it is, a Princely Seat.' But Ben Jonson, who thought himself not well enough entertained on a visit there, denigrated it as a 'proud ambitious heep' in his 'To Penshurst'.

135 The foundation for all more recent work on Theobalds is John Summerson, 'The Building of Theobalds, 1564–1585', *Archaeologia*, 97 (1959), pp. 107–26, reproducing site plans and all the relevant sixteenth-century plans and drawings, and including a 'sketch reconstruction . . . from the South-West' (p. 119), and a modern plan with annotations, based on Thorpe. More recently, James H. Sutton, *Materializing Space at an Early Modern Prodigy House: The Cecils at Theobalds, 1564–1607*, Aldershot, 2004, offers an interesting analysis of the way rooms, spaces, gardens and decorations were used. See also contributions by Malcolm Airs, Paula Henderson and J. M. Sutton in *Patronage Culture and Power: The Early Cecils, 1558–1612*, ed. Pauline Croft, New Haven and London, 2002.

136 *Thorpe Drawings*, T243, T245–6, pls 112–13. Although Summerson inclined to date these to 1606, when Thorpe is known to have surveyed the house, there is little doubt that they were made before Burghley's death in 1598. The plans are on ink over scorer, with minimal pencil shading, in Thorpe's earlier manner; the basement plan

lists 'ye Qs wyne sellor' and 'my Lo: wyne sellor'; the main staircase rises round a solid newel and the open timber staircase now at Herstmonceux (see note 137) is not shown.

137 The open timber staircase, which has come to Herstmonceux Castle, Sussex, by way of Crew's Hill House, Enfield, and the nineteenth-century Theobalds Park (Summerson, 'The Building of Theobalds', p. 123 and pl. XXXI), must, on stylistic and technological grounds, date from the last days of the ownership of Robert Cecil or the first of James I; it perhaps replaced the original solid newel staircase at the same time as the great chamber was redecorated, and the panelling drawn by John Smythson in 1618 (*Smythson Drawings, 111/13) was installed. In 1592 a German visitor made a sketch of the design of ceiling decoration in an unspecified room (reproduced, as redrawn, Summerson, 'The Building of Theobalds', p. 124). A portion of a stone chimneypiece, incorporating a panel said to have shown 'Minerva, driving away Discord, overthrowing idolatry, and restoring true religion', came by way of Forty Hill, Enfield, in Middlesex, to J. B. Nichols's house, The Chancellor's, Hammersmith, where it was in 1836, according to the Gentleman's Magazine (May 1836), p. 154. The Chancellor's has been demolished, but the chimneypiece may resurface one of these days.

138 British Library, Lansdowne MS 43, fol. 14.

139 See M. Cappouillex, 'Historique et description des châteaux de Boussu, Binche et Mariemont', in Jacques Du Broeucq, sculpteur et architecte de la Renaissance, exhibition catalogue, Brussels, 1985, pp. 177–90.

140 For Holdenby, see M. Girouard, 'Reconstructing Holdenby', in his Town and Country, New Haven, 1992, pp. 197–210 (based on articles in Country Life, 18 and 25 October 1979), with reconstructed bird's-eye view of the south front by the author. I concluded that the main rooms were on the second floor, as at Hardwick and elsewhere, with impressive effect on the south (garden) front. My main reason was that the chapel, shown in Thorpe's plan of the ground floor, would almost certainly, in a house of that importance, have been two storeys in height, necessitating the placing of the great chamber, which was clearly above it, on the second floor; but a not impossible alternative arrangement could have been

that the lower storey of the chapel was in the basement. I also now think it probable (see chapter 2 note 36) that the 'Holdenby banquet h[ouse]', as shown in Thorpe's plan and elevation T182, dated from the early seventeenth century rather than the 1580s. Sophia Hartshorne, Memorials of Holdenby, 1867, reproduces much contemporary documentation in the State Papers and elsewhere. No building accounts survive.

141 *Thorpe Drawings, T183–4 and pl. 85.

142 Distinctive detailing on the screen is identical to that on the Saunders monument in Harington church nearby, which Jon Bayliss convincingly attributes to Garret Hollemans. See his 'A Dutch carver: Garret Hollemans I in England', Church Monuments, 8 (1993), pp. 46–55. The Sanders family was closely related to the Hattons.

143 For Hugh Hall's somewhat shadowy work and identity, see references in Paula Henderson, The Tudor House and Garden, New Haven and London, 2005, pp. 225 and 252, nn. 199–200; *DNB and *ODNB, entries for Edward Arden.

144 British Library, Add. MS 15891, fol. 32, quoted in Hartshorne (Memorials of Holdenby), pp. 15–16.

145 Tresham to Hatton, 1 October 1583. Historical Manuscripts Commission, Report on Manuscripts in Various Collections, vol. III, London, 1904, p. 33.

146 Printed in full, ibid., p. XXXIX.

147 Sampson Erdeswicke, A Survey of Staffordshire [1598], ed. Revd Thomas Harwood, London, 1844, pp. 68–70, assigns the gatehouse to Sir Walter and the house to his father, Sir Thomas. Both are illustrated in Robert Plot, Natural History of Staffordshire, Oxford, 1686. The pediments now on the side elevations are later replacements of chimney stacks. The Aston archives do not appear to survive, and little has been published about the gatehouse. The Tixall property descended to the Clifford Constables of Burton Constable and was sold in 1845. The gatehouse was acquired by the Landmark Trust in 1968 and restored. The Trust have got together a useful typescript album of history, extracts, reproductions of numerous views, and photographs, etc., for the information of tenants; I am grateful to Caroline Stanford for supplying me with a copy.

148 For Moreton Corbet Castle, see Elizabeth

Corbet, The Family of Corbet: Its Life and Times, 2 vols, London, 1914–20; Barbara Coulton, 'Moreton Corbet Castle: A House and its Family', Shropshire History and Archaeology: Transactions of the Shropshire Archaeological and Historical Society, 70 (1955), p. 185; and especially Elain Harwood, 'Moreton Corbet Castle', English Heritage Historical Review, 1 (2006), pp. 37–45. This reproduces the eighteenth-century drawings of the castle belonging to Shrewsbury School, and quotes extensively from the description of it in the Court Book of 1588, now Shrewsbury, Shropshire Archives, 322, Box 2.

149 Corbet, The Family of Corbet, p. 293.

150 A circular pediment and the beginning of a straight one survive on the north-west corner of the south range. Drawings reproduced by Harwood, 'Moreton Corbet Castle', figs 2 and 8, show that the alternation continued across the rest of the façade, and that there were four gables.

151 A single giant Corinthian column is shown in a mid-eighteenth-century painting incorporated in the overmantel of Swan Hill Court, Shrewsbury (photograph NMR Y877/1, Harwood, 'Moreton Corbet Castle', n. 28). A watercolour (ibid., fig. 7) appears to show two Tuscan pilasters; a pen-and-ink drawing (ibid., fig. 6) shows no order at all.

152 Especially in the detail, wrongly identified by Serlio as the Basilica del Foro Transitorio (Hart and Hicks, Serlio on Architecture, p. 175; Peake edn [1611], Book III, chapter 4, fol. 39).

153 In the Corinthian section of Serlio Book IV (Hart and Hicks, Serlio on Architecture, p. 349; Peake edn [1611], Book IV, chapter 8, fol. 50). In books by Du Cerceau, passim, but, for example, in the so-called Petites Habitations (circa 1545), Château B. Alternating pediments incorporated in a continuous entablature are found at Chalcot, see chapter three, note 79

154 The freemason John Richmond is described as 'of Aston Clinton' in contemporary documents.

155 For Corsham, see Frederick J. Ladd, Architects at Corsham Court, Bradford-on-Avon, 1978, chapter I; *Girouard, Smythson, pp. 65–6. Nothing Elizabethan of any significance survives inside the house.

156 *Girouard, Smythson, pp. 66–8. The interior was largely redecorated by the 1st Duke of

157 Sherborne House is in need of more research, but see Nicholas Kingsley, *The Country Houses of Gloucestershire, vol. 1: 1500–1660*, Chichester, 2001, pp. 171–7, and *Girouard, *Smythson*, p. 309, n. 41. The house was rebuilt in the years 1829–39, but the new entrance façade was based on that of its predecessor, as shown in the watercolour reproduced in *Country Life*, 120 (25 October 1956), p. 954, and repeated the difference in detail between the two halves. Dutton bought the property in 1551; Elizabeth visited him there on progress in 1574. Thomas Gresham's illegitimate daughter Anne married Sir Nathaniel Bacon of Stiffkey in 1569; her mother married Gresham's factor Thomas Dutton, probably after her birth, *circa* 1550. See A. Hassell Smith, 'The Papers of Nathaniel Bacon of Stiffkey', vol. 1, *Norfolk Record Society*, 46 (1978 and 1979), pp. xvi, 290 n. 18, 291 n. 50, and G. Leveson-Gower, *Genealogy of the Family of Gresham*, London, 1883.

158 See note 78.

159 For Sudeley, see Kingsley, *The Country Houses of Gloucestershire, vol. 1*, pp. 202–4. A chimneypiece, probably of the 1570s, survives much later alteration, but is not in the Longleat manner. William Spicer, writing to Leicester in July, probably 1571 (Longleat, Dudley Papers, 11, fol. 321), refers to 'my absence for this weeke I have spent apone my Lord Shandoes bylldinge', that is, Lord Chandos of Sudeley. I owe this refence to Eizabeth Goldring.

160 For Wardour, see *Girouard, *Smythson*, pp. 78–82.

161 For Lumley, see *Country Life*, 27 (18 June 1910), pp. 896–904; Kathryn Barron, 'Classicism and Antiquarianism in Elizabethan Patronage: The Case of John, Lord Lumley', MA dissertation, Oxford, 1995, pp. 77–87, and for the chimneypiece, p. 84. Its lower half is now submerged behind a platform erected for medieval-style banquets.

162 For Corpus Christi chapel, see *Willis and Clark, *Cambridge*, vol. 1, pp. 289–97. The drawing is in the College archives. John Osborne witnessed the agreement to build the chapel, made between Bacon and the College (College Treasury, Drawer 26, n. 11). For Osborne's work for Bacon at Stiffkey,

see chapter 1, p. 60 and note 151. There is no documentary evidence to link him with the Gorhambury loggia, but his connections with Bacon make it probable. For John Osborne of the Porticus and Haynes Grange Room, see pp. 306–10 below.

163 For the Lumley Inventory, and the suggestion that the drawings in it may be by Cornelius Cure, see chapter 1, p. 40, and note 121. For the Nonsuch gardens, see Martin Biddle, 'The Gardens of Nonsuch', *Garden History*, 27 (1999), pp. 145–83; for the Spanish ambassador's comment, ibid., p. 165. The fountain in the courtyard is described in Anthony Watson's Latin account of Nonsuch, *circa* 1582 (Trinity College, Cambridge, MS R.7.22, para. 14), and illustrated in the Lumley Inventory, fol. 35r. The drum has the same motif of ox-masks linked by swags as the Dormer tomb chest at Wing, suggesting the possibility of common craftsmen.

164 For fountains, see Henderson, *The Tudor House and Garden*, pp. 181–95 and illustrations. In addition, other vanished Elizabethan fountains include one supplied to Petworth House, Sussex, by 'Mr Delafolla', London merchant, *circa* 1577 (G. Batho, 'The Percies at Petworth, 1574–1632', *Sussex Archaeological Collections*, 95, 1957, pp. 9–11); in the inner courtyard of Chatsworth (shown in the Elizabethan embroidery of the house, now at Chatsworth); at Worksop Manor, illustrated in Robert Thoroton, *The Antiquities of Nottinghamshire*, London, 1677; before Chartley, Staffordshire, illustrated in Plot, *The Natural History of Staffordshire*, 1686. The remains of a fountain bowl with carved masks for water ejection have been excavated at Glentworth Hall, Lincolnshire. The Wilton fountain and the great fountain in the courtyard at Trinity College, Cambridge, are rare survivals of what was once a sizeable group. Since fountains are relatively easy to move, others may be awaiting identification in gardens or other locations around the world.

165 The 'Queens seat of freestone' in the garden, listed in a valuation for *circa* 1603–7 (quoted in H. Knowles, *The Castle of Kenilworth*, Warwick, 1872), can probably be identified as the little building attached to the since-demolished castle outer wall, shown in the plan in Dugdale's *Warwickshire*, 1656, reproduced in M. W. Thomp-

son, *Kenilworth Castle*, HMSO and English Heritage, 1982, etc., p. 9. Leicester wrote to Burghley on 17 May 1575: 'Perceiving by Hen. Hawthorn that your L. is pleased to help me that I may have some [stone] toward the making a lytle banquett-house in my garden' (John Nichols, *The Progresses and Public Processions of Queen Elizabeth*, 3 vols, London, 1823, vol. 1, pp. 524–5).

166 Engraving reproduced in *Wells-Cole, *Decoration*, pl. 53, p. 51. The carver may be William Gregory, mason, who was living at Taynton, where Harman owned the quarry, from 1579 and perhaps from 1560 (Elizabeth Gregory, parents not named, baptised there 1560, numerous children of William Gregory from 1579). In his will (Oxford Probate Registry, Oxfordshire Record Office, 196/134) of 6 August 1615, he leaves 'the lease of Taynton quarry and all my working tooles' to his sons William and Simon; but no books, drawings or drawing instruments are mentioned in the will or accompanying inventory (Oxfordshire Record Office, b669, fol. 11). His son Simon's property was appraised by Timothy Strong in 1632; Strong had been in the parish by 1607, when his daughter Anne was baptised. He and his descendants took over the quarries; it is possible that he married a Gregory.

167 For Cuckfield House, see *Country Life*, 45 (1919), pp. 278, 310. 'Flynte' could possibly be identifiable with the William Flynte who was servant to John Rogers, the eminent early Tudor freemason, in 1558 (*Royal Works*, vol. III, p. 259).

168 M. Girouard, 'Renaissance Splendour in Decay: The Ruins of Slaugham Place', *Country Life*, 135 (9 January 1964), p. 70; *Thorpe Drawings*, T239–40, pls 109–11. For the possibility of Longleat craftsmen working at Wiston, see chapter 3, note 78. I have benefited from the tyescript 'Slaugham Place: A Brief History' by Arthur Shopland (1996), kindly communicated to me by Alan Urwick.

169 Heward and Taylor, *The Country Houses of Northamptonshire*, pp. 325–7 [Winwick], pp. 152–65 [Deene].

170 For Trerice, see *Country Life*, 192 (29 October 1992), pp. 62–5. The arms of Henry FitzAlan, 12th Earl of Arundel (d. 1580), are under the cove at one end of the great chamber; as Sir John Arundell, the builder

of Trerice, was only distantly connected with him, the likely explanation for their presence there is that he was, or had been, in Arundel's household, or retained by him.

171 See Rick Turner, *Plas Mawr Conwy*, CADW: Welsh Historic Monuments, 1997; and for Robert Wynn's possible service under Hoby, see A. D. Carr, 'The Affairs of Robert Wynn', *Transactions of the Caernarvonshire Historical Society*, 49 (1988), pp. 151–72.

172 See Howard Colvin, 'Herms, Terms and Caryatids in English Architecture', in *Essays in English Architectural History*, New Haven and London, 1999, p. 116 and pls 90–91.

173 Jonathan Edis, 'Beyond Thomas Kirby: Monuments of the Mordaunt Family and their Circle, 1567–1618', *Church Monuments*, 16 (2001), pp. 30–43.

174 *Wells-Cole, *Decoration*, p. 49, pls 49–50.

175 Similar Vriesian ornament is found on the soffits of the arches in the centrepiece of the north front, dated 1587.

176 *Smythson Drawings*, 1/25 (1).

177 The first catalogue of the library at Wollaton dates from the late seventeenth or early eighteenth century. The bulk of the library was sold at Christie's, 15 June 1925. According to the descriptions in the sale catalogue, many of the books, including a large number of architectural ones, carried the name of Sir Francis Willoughby's great-great-grandson, Thomas Willoughby, who inherited from his brother in 1688, and was created Lord Middleton in 1712; he died in 1729. Since there is no record that he was a bibliophile, or interested in architecture, the probability is that Francis Willoughby was the buyer of architectural books at Wollaton published before his death in 1596.

178 For Wollaton, see *Girouard, *Smythson*, pp. 81–108; Alice T. Friedman, *House and Household in Elizabethan England*, Chicago, 1989; Pamela Marshall, *Wollaton Hall: An Archaeological Survey*, Nottingham, 1996. The last reprints all the relevant surviving inventories and includes a room-by-room analysis, with many measured drawings by D. Taylor.

Chapter 4   Speaking Buildings

1 Karen Hearn, *Marcus Gheeraerts II: Elizabethan Artist*, London, 2002, pp. 36–7, pl. 27.

Roy Strong, 'My Weeping Stagg I Crowne: The Persian Lady Reconsidered', in *The Tudor and Stuart Monarchy: Vol. 2: Elizabethan*, Woodbridge, 1995, pp. 303–24. Strong suggested Frances Walsingham, Countess of Essex, as the sitter. The painting is now at Hampton Court.

2 See pp. 308–10 below.

3 For the Northampton House inscriptions, see Manolo Guerci, 'The Strand Palaces of the Early Seventeenth Century: Salisbury House and Northumberland House', PH.D thesis, University of Cambridge, 2007, pp. 118–20. Those at Trentham are shown in the engraving in Robert Plot, *The Natural History of Staffordshire*, Oxford, 1686. The rest are still *in situ*.

4 Richard Williams, 'A Catholic Sculpture in Elizabethan England: Sir Thomas Tresham's Reredos at Rushton Hall', *Architectural History*, 44 (2001), pp. 221–7.

5 The Chatsworth relief was moved to the Withdrawing Chamber at Hardwick in the early nineteenth century. It must originally have been in the 'Muses Chamber', a description used in the inventory of 1601 as an alternative either for the High Great Chamber or the Withdrawing Chamber to the Earl of Leicester's Chamber. *Of Household Stuff: The 1601 Inventories of Bess of Hardwick*, National Trust, London, 2001, p. 24. The Toddington Relief is now in the Victorian and Albert Museum, London; there is no documentary evidence as to its location at Toddington.

6 See chapter 3, note 137. Diana, personifying Elizabeth, would seem more suitable.

7 For Great Binnall, see Madge Moran, *Vernacular Buildings of Shropshire*, Logaston, Herefordshire, 2003, p. 346, with illustrations. The Weston panel has been reset in a cupboard in the house.

8 *Wells-Cole, *Decoration*, p. 184. Burton Agnes is discussed and illustrated at length with source engravings reproduced, pp. 172–84.

9 Ibid., *Decoration*, chapter 15, pp. 247–95: 'The Decoration of Elizabethan Chatsworth and Hardwick', especially p. 292.

10 Gerard Legh, The *Accedens of Armorie*, 1562, 1568, 1572, 1591, 1597, 1612; John Bossewell, *Workes of Armorie*, 1572, 1597; William Segar, *The Booke of Honor and Armes*, 1590; William Wyrley, *The True Use of Armorie*, 1592; Edmund Bolton, *The Elements of Armories*,

1610; John Guillim, *A Display of Heraldrie*, 1610 and numerous later editions.

11 See Hugh Murray, *The Great Chamber at Gilling Castle*, St Laurence Papers VIII, York, 1996.

12 M. W. Greenslade, 'Staffordshire', in *A Guide to English County Histories*, ed. C. R. J. Currie and C. P. Lewis, Stroud, 1997, p. 355.

13 Edward Hasted, *History of the County of Kent*, 1778–1799, vol. 11, Canterbury, 1782, pp. 656–7, quoting John Johnstone, *Iter Plantarum Investigationis ergo susceptum anno 1629*.

14 Account of the visit of the Duke of Stettin-Pomerania to England, 1602, written by his secretary, F. Gerschow, printed in translation in *Transactions of the Royal Historical Society*, new series, 6 (1892). The decoration is briefly described in a lodgings schedule of 1583, quoted in John Nichols, *The Progresses and Public Processions of Queen Elizabeth*, 3 vols, London, 1823, vol. 11, p. 402.

15 It is curious that to the best of my knowledge the significance of the Cavendish snake and motto has never been discussed.

16 The literature of emblems is overwhelming. I have found especially helpful Rosemary Freeman, *English Emblem Books*, London, 1948, and Michael Bath, *Speaking Pictures: English Emblem Books and Renaissance Culture*, London, 1994. See also *Emblem Studies in Honor of Peter M. Daly*, ed. Michael Bath et al., Baden-Baden, 2002.

17 William Drummond, *The Works* [1711], reprinted 1970, pp. 228–9: 'A short Discourse upon Impresas and Anagrams', addressed to the Earl of Perth.

18 *Royal Works*, vol. IV, p. 303, quoting 'Journey through England of L. von Wedel, 1584–5', *Transactions of the Royal Historical Society*, new series, IX (1895), p. 236.

19 Historical Manuscripts Commission, *The Manuscripts of His Grace of Rutland, GCB, Preserved at Belvoir Castle*, 4 vols, London, 1888–1905, vol. IV, pp. 494, 508.

20 Listed in his library catalogue, British Library, Add. MS 39830, fols 155v–214r. For his library, portions of which survive at St John's College, Oxford, and Deene Park, Northamptonshire, see Nicholas Barker and David Quentin, *The Library of Thomas Trsham and Thomas Brudenell*, introduction by John Martin Robinson, The Roxburgh Club, 2006.

21 John Newman, 'The Jacobean House', in *Blickling Hall*, National Trust, 1987, pp. 20–

22. A photocopy of *Minerva Britannia* is, or was, on sale in the house, together with a key to the library ceiling.

22 The panels were moved to Hardwick House, Suffolk, bought from there in 1924 by Ipswich Borough Council, and installed in Christchurch Mansion. See *A Guide to the Hawstead Panels at Christchurch Mansion, Ipswich*, published by the Friends of the Ipswich Museums, 2006.

23 Newman, 'The Jacobean House', p. 20. Hobart's reference to 'my word' is in his will, National Archives, PROB/11/148, proved 7 March 1626.

24 British Library, Add. MS 39831, fol. 7v. The opinion is given in Tresham's long explanation of the meanings of his decoration of his rooms when in prison in Ely.

25 Krista De Jonge in *Unity and Discontinuity: Architectural Relationships between the Southern and Northern Low Countries, 1530–1700*, ed. De Jonge and Konrad Ottenheym, Architectura Moderna, vol. 5, Turnhout, Belgium, 2007, p. 46 and pl. 20. I am grateful to Gerard Kilroy for sending me the typescript of his forthcoming 'Sir Thomas Tresham: His Emblem', which discusses the engraved portrait of Tresham (British Museum, Department of Prints and Drawings, O.5–143) and goes into his symbolism and his numerical and geomeric codes in greater depth than I have done.

26 The building accounts are in British Library, Add. MSS 39832 and 39836. Extracts were printed in Historical Manuscripts Commission, *Report on Manuscripts in Various Collections*, vol. III, London, 1904, pp. xxxvi–xli (introduction by Mrs S. C. Lomas). J. A. Gotch, *A Complete Account of . . . the Buildings Erected in Northamptonshire by Sir Thomas Tresham*, Northampton, 1883, contains plans and excellent measured drawings.

27 D. Stocker and M. Stocker, 'Sacred Profanity: The Theology of Rabbit Breeding and the Symbolic Landscape of the Warren', *World Archaeology*, 28/ii (1996), pp. 265–72, suggests that Tresham may have contemplated the activities of rabbits as symbolic of the human condition.

28 *Willis and Clark, *Cambridge*, vol. II, p. 482 n. 5, p. 487 n. 1. Andrew Downes, Regius Professor of Greek at Cambridge, wrote to Tresham on 20 April (no year, but probably 1593), recommending Fletcher 'for the

mathematics, he is ready to come at any time when you will, if your work be such as he can skill of. Mary, if it be architecture, he doubteth he shall not be so well able to deal with it, anything else he dare undertake' (Historical Manuscripts Commission, *Report on Manuscripts in Various Collections*, vol. III, p. 59). There are payments in Add. MS 39832, fols 13r, 83r, in 1593–4: 'To Browne going to Cambridge with Mr Fletcher for the globes, etc.' and for 'bringinge thinges from Mr Fletcher from Cambridge'; and in 1596 for 'Bartles . . . his charges for goeing to Cambridge with Mr Fletchers books'. Fletcher, who was a Fellow of Caius, 1587–1613, also had a reputation as an astrologer. See John Venn, *Biographical History of Gonville and Caius College*, vol. I: *1349–1713*, Cambridge, 1897, p. 95.

29 The main building accounts for Lyveden New Bield are missing. There are a few payments for the early stages in Add. MS 39828, and some relevant letters in Add MSS 39828–9. John Summerson established that the plan and elevation, Add. MS 39832, fol. 34, incorrectly described in Historical Manuscripts Commission, *Report on Manuscripts in Various Collections*, as for the demolished Hawkfield Lodge at Rushton, are for an intended cupola or lantern at Lyveden New Bield (Summerson, 'Three Elizabethan Architects', *John Rylands Library Bulletin*, September 1959, pp. 218–19). There is a survey plan of basement, ground and first floors, *circa* 1600, in *Thorpe Drawings*, T215–16, pl. 100.

30 The plan of the lantern clearly shows that it was to span a gallery running across the centre, which could have been only on an intended second floor.

31 Paris certainly made designs for the Doric metopes; these are commented on by Tresham in letters to his steward George Levens on 6 and 7 December 1596. But Tresham also refers to 'a carver whom I intend to use also in yt worke', who would work quicker than Paris. The quality of the carving suggests the hand of Paris.

32 'Striceles' supplied 'moulds' for the Doric order accompanied by a letter to Tresham, British Library, Add. MS 39829, fol. 194. The letter is signed Rol Sticiles; the drawings for the cupola are initialled RS; a letter from Tresham to his steward George Levens, 1604, Add. MS 39829, fols 130–31, refers to a

'Roland' or 'Roeland', whom he directs should be present when bargains are being made with the freemasons for that year's work. Mrs Lomas in Historical Manuscripts Commission, *Report on Manuscripts in Various Collections*, vol. III, identified drawings, letter and reference as all applying to a Roland Sticiles or Stickles. Summerson assigned drawings and letter to Robert Stickles, but the signature of the letter is incontrovertibly for 'Rol', not 'Rob'.

33 According to a printed catalogue of the picture collection of the Earl of Radnor at Longford *circa* 1910, 'the date on the keystone of the centre arch in front of the house is 1591'.

34 A selection of the drawings and plans by Thorpe and Thacker are reproduced in Christopher Hussey's two articles on Longford: *Country Life*, 70 (12 and 19 December 1931), pp. 648–55, 696–702, along with extracts from the manuscript history of Longford by Henry Pelate, and Lord Coleraine's verse description of the house of 1694 (both Longford Castle archives). The entrance front as it was in 1808 is engraved in John Britton, *Architectural Antiquities of Great Britain*, 1805–18, vol. II. The courtyard was filled in during the nineteenth century; Anthony Salvin restored the entrance front to something approaching its original appearance, but with considerable variations. This front is discussed on pp. 300–02 below.

35 *Thorpe Drawings*, T155–6, pl. 72. Probably a copy of a first, unexecuted design. A rough ink and pen elevation of part of the garden front as built has been added. Thorpe's elevation of part of the entrance front, as built, is T158; an unfinished plan of the entrance range, as built, is T157. The drawing of the entrance front (Longford Castle archives) reproduced in Nikolaus Pevsner, *Buildings of England: Wiltshire* [1963], 2nd edn, rev. Bridget Cherry, London, 1975, is a crude copy of (or just possibly a preliminary sketch for) Thacker's engraving.

36 *Thorpe Drawings*, T161, pl. 75.

37 Gorges's Swedish trip is documented in *Calendar of State Papers, Foreign*, May to December 1582. He was at Uppsala on 28 July and Gripsholm before 6 August. He returned by way of Paris, where he was on 3 September. Gripsholm (started 1537) has three squat round towers irregularly grouped round an irregular hexagon.

38 Pamela Marshall, *Wollaton Hall: An Archae-ological Survey*, Nottingham, 1996, p. 97.

39 The possibility was discussed at greater length in M. Girouard, 'Solomon's Temple in Nottinghamshire', in *Town and Country*, New Haven, 1992, pp. 187–96.

40 The reconstructions had first been made by Nikolaus de Lyra and published in his biblical commentary *Prologus Primus* in 1481; they were then incorporated in the Latin Bible printed by Anton Koberger, first published in 1487 and frequently reprinted.

41 See chapter 3, note 178.

42 It is worth mentioning the design for a Protestant temple in Jacques Perret's *Des Fortifications et Artifices*, 1620, between text pages C and D. There is no evidence that Perret ever came to England or had an English contact, but the design is clearly inspired by Wollaton, and also appears to aim to relate a Protestant place of worship to the Jerusalem Temple, though with a single-storey central space. Perret is described in the book as 'Gentilhomme Savoysien' and 'de Chambery'.

43 I am grateful to Arnold Pacey for background information about Margaret Clifford. She has a short entry in *ODNB*, but has never received the attention given to her daughter.

44 The full epitaph is given in Daniel Lyson, *The Environs of London*, 2nd edn, London, 1811, vol. II, part 2, p. 426.

45 Richard Cavendish or Candish has a short entry in *ODNB*, but is in need of further research. The passage on Layfield's skill in architecture is from Jeremy Collier, *An Ecclesiastical History of Great Britain*, 9 vols, London, 1840–41, vol. VII, p. 337, citing no source. A part-autobiographical letter to him from Margaret Clifford is published in G. C. Williamson, *George Clifford, Earl of Cumberland*, 1920, pp. 285–8.

46 John Aubrey, *Brief Lives and Other Selected Writings*, ed. Anthony Powell, London, 1949, p. 33.

47 For Elizabethan and Jacobean architectural libraries, see the appendix 'Books on Art, Perspective and Architecture in English Renaissance Libraries, 1580–1630', in Lucy Gent, *Picture and Poetry, 1560–1620* Leamington Spa, 1981.

48 Architectural (as opposed to theatrical) historians have steered clear of the London theatres. The classic monograph is E. K. Chambers, *The Elizabethan Stage*, 2 vols, Oxford, 1923; revised 1951; it prints all the few relevant documents. The standard recent histories are John Durrell, *The Human Stage: English Theatre Design, 1567–1640*, Cambridge, 1988, and Andrew Gurr, *The Shakespearean Stage*, Cambridge, 1985. Frances A. Yates, coming from outside both disciplines, related the London theatre to contemporary Renaissance thought in her *Theatre of the World*, London, 1969; she may have exaggerated the influence of John Dee and Robert Fludd, but it remains a stimulating and fascinating book. The remarkable drawings reproduced in Joy Hancox, *The Byrom Collection*, London, 1992, appear to date from the late seventeenth or early eighteenth century, and her claim that they include original plans for the London theatres is not convincing.

49 *The Diary of Baron Waldstein*, trans. G. W. Gross, London, 1981, p. 37 and n. 34. Waldstein does not identify the theatre. De Witt's famous drawing of the Swan (in fact a copy of it by Arend van Buchell), with accompanying Latin annotations and description, is in the University Library, Utrecht, MS 842, fol. 132r. In a revisionist article in *From Script to Stage in Early Modern England*, ed. P. Holland and S. Orgel, London, 2005, pp. 11–31, R. A. Foakes casts doubt on the value of the drawing; but it is all we have.

50 Leon Battista Alberti, *De Re Aedificatoria* VIII.viii. John Aubrey, in his *Natural History of Wiltshire*, says that Longford was built 'after the fashion of one of the King of Sweden's palaces'. Henry Pelate, in his manuscript history of 1678 (Longford Castle archives), to which Thacker's engravings were an accompaniment, said that it was built 'according to the modell of a Castle (whether it was Uraniborg or some other I cannot distinctly tell, but one said to be contrived by the noble Tycho Brahe'). Both men were presumably retailing tradition, but nearly a century after the house was built, and after it had changed ownership. Tycho Brahe's famous observatory at Uraniborg, on the island of Hveen off the coast of Denmark, was built on an elaborate geometric plan, but bore little resemblance to Longford.

51 For example, Peter Street, who re-erected The Theatre as the Globe, in 1600, and built the Fortune Theatre in the same year, was Warden of the Carpenters' Company, 1598–9.

52 See pp. 28, 54 above. One of the editions was almost certainly Cesariano's.

53 Full contract given in Chambers, *The Elizabethan Stage* [1923], vol. II, n. 48, pp. 436–9, and Yates, *Theatre of the World*, pp. 198–200.

54 Yates, *Theatre of the World*, p. 131, n. 24, quoting Malone's *Variorum* edition of Shakespeare, London, 1821, vol. III, pp. 66–7.

55 For Chilham, see *Country Life*, 55 (24 and 31 May 1924), pp. 812–19, 858–65.

56 The plan (once attributed to Inigo Jones) is reproduced in ibid., p. 816. It is among the unattributed drawings in the Drawings Collection of the Royal Institute of British Architects and does not feature in the printed catalogue.

57 According to the register (quoted in ibid.), 'Simon Rennet one of the workmen under Mr Smith in Sir Dudley Digges his work was buried here the 28th of August 1616'. For William Smith, see Edward Conder, *Records of the Hole Craft and Fellowship of Masons*, London, 1894, pp. 166, 294. He was Warden of the Masons' Company in 1631, and Master in 1640.

58 There is an Elizabethan plan of Queenborough Castle at Hatfield, CPM 11/20.

59 Sir Dudley Digges was a prominent shareholder in the East India Company (*ODNB*). A remarkable collection of some 154 pieces of oriental porcelain is listed in an inventory of Wardour Castle of 1605 (Arundell of Wardour Archives, Wiltshire Record Office).

60 *Thorpe Drawings*, T30, T50, pl. 23.

61 See Arthur Oswald, *Country Houses of Dorset*, 2nd edn, London, 1959, p. 97.

62 *Richard Carew of Antony: The Survey of Cornwall*, ed. F. E. Halliday, London, 1953, pp. 175–6 and plan p. 319.

63 Hatfield, CPM 1/7–8; J. A. du Cerceau *De Architectura*, 1559, plan XLIII.

64 For Wothorpe, see pp. 306–7 below. The 'Tempio quadrato in croce' in Serlio's Fifth Book is a possible source for the plan. Thomas Cecil's son, William Cecil, later 2nd Earl, had travelled in Italy in 1609 and before; see p. 414 below.

65 For Star Castle, see *Royal Works*, vol. IV, pp. 592–3, fig. 51. For Spur Royal Castle, see Alistair Rowan, *Buildings of Ireland: North*

West Ulster (Augher, Co. Tyrone), Harmondsworth, 1979, pp. 113–14 and pl. 38. The builder was Sir Thomas Ridgeway, later Lord Ridgeway and Earl of Londonderry, who came from Tormohan (now in Torquay), Devon.

66 Philip Sidney, *The Countess of Pembroke's Arcadia*, ed. Albert Feuillerat, Cambridge, 1912, p. 91. The Hvězda or Star Pavilion (Letohrádek Hvězda) just outside Prague was built by Archduke Ferdinand, Viceroy of Bohemia, who laid the foundation stone in 1555. Its plan is a six-pointed star, unlike the Star and Spur castles, which have eight points.

67 Henry Wotton, *The Elements of Architecture*, London, 1624, pp. 19–20.

Chapter 5   Towers of Glass

1 The verses are in the Sherborne Castle archives. I am grateful to Mrs Anne Smith, the Curator and Archivist there, for communicating them to me, and to John Wingfield-Digby and Sherborne Castle Estates for permission to reproduce them.

2 The Bishop of Salisbury, under pressure from the queen, granted Walter Ralegh a ninety-nine-year lease of the castle in January 1592. Ralegh gave instructions to cut down oaks for work on it on 28 August of the same year (letter quoted in *Calendar of State Papers, Domestic*, vol. III, 1867, p. 263). On 2 May 1594 a deputation travelling from Cornwall to London about the renewal of Duchy of Cornwall leases stopped at Sherborne and were shown round 'the new buildings' by Ralegh's half-brother Adrian Gilbert (R. Trevelyan, *Sir Walter Raleigh*, London, 2002, p. 212). In a lawsuit (Enys Papers, Cornwall Record Office, Truro) in 1601 (text communicated by Anne Smith), Ralegh stated that the castle was entirely ruinous when he took on the lease, that he first repaired an 'old tower', almost certainly the keep, then two towers on the curtain wall and 'sithence . . . to his very great charge hath begun to build and finished a good parte of the said Castell for himself to dwell in'.

3 The Lodge, the Castle of today, was built by Ralegh in or soon after 1600 (see p. 11, Fig. 13). According to the *Survey of Dorset* (long attributed to Robert Coker, but in fact written by Thomas Gerard [1593–1634] about 1625), Ralegh 'beganne very fairelie to builde the Castell, but altering his purpose he built, in a park adjoineing to it out of the grounde a most fine house' (1732 edn, p. 124). One can wonder if, rather than 'altering his purpose', Ralegh intended the Lodge to be an appendage to his main residence, as Wothorpe was to Burghley and Verulam to Gorhambury; but Gerard was writing close enough to the event to deserve to be taken seriously.

4 Tristram Risdon's *Choreographical Description or Survey of Devon*, written 1605–30, but first adequately published in 1811, suggests that the north wing of Berry Pomeroy was built by Sir Edward Seymour, 1st Bart, who inherited in 1593 and died in 1613. This was confirmed by extensive archaeological investigations, carried out in the years 1980–96 and published in Stewart Brown, *Berry Pomeroy Castle*, a full issue of *Devon Archaeological Society Proceedings*, no. 54 (1996). This placed its building 'in the period around 1600' (see especially pp. 164–83, and reconstructed plan and elevation, fig. 52). H. Gordon Slade's thesis that the wing was built by Protector Somerset *circa* 1548–51, first put forward in 1986, was accepted in Bridget Cherry and Nikolaus Pevsner, *Buildings of England: Devon*, 2nd edn, London, 1989, and other publications, but cannot be maintained.

5 No building accounts survive for the Hall. A manuscript 'petegre for hall of Bradford truly derived from the xth year of Edward the first', in the Hall Pierrepont papers, British Library, Egerton MS 3653, fol. 17, ends with 'John Hall seised of the man. of Portishead married Dorothy daughter and eyer of Anthony Rogers, of Bradford, Es., but did not benefit'. An addition in a different hand states that 'Son John married Eliz the da of Hy Bruine Es. bought Bath estate and built Bradford House'. The elder John died in 1597. By the Elizabethan period, at least, the Halls were a gentry rather than, as sometimes stated, a clothier family.

6 The saying first featured as 'Hardwick Hall more window than wall', according to Mary S. Lovell, *Bess of Hardwick: First Lady of Chatsworth*, London, 2005, p. 410.

7 For engravings by George Vertue, see **Royal Works*, vol. III, pls 3B, 24, 25.

8 The chronology is as follows: Henry VII tower, Windsor, 1500; Henry VII's Lady Chapel, 1503–*circa* 1510; Thornbury Castle, *circa* 1510, left incomplete 1521; Hengrave window, dated 1538. A fifth example was the complex bay window of the old Hall at Trinity College, Cambridge, probably 1547 (*Willis and Clark, *Cambridge*, vol. II, p. 468, figs 10 and 11). The first windows may have been designed by Robert Janyns, junior, one of the leading masons in the King's Works, who was involved in both the Windsor tower and Henry VII's Lady Chapel; John Harvey, *English Mediaeval Architects: A Biographical Dictionary Down to 1550*, 2nd edn, Gloucester, 1984, suggests that their 'star-polygon form undoubtedly derived from the contemporary Mozarabic designs at Saragossa by way of the embassies exchanged with Ferdinand and Isabella'.

9 See **Royal Works*, vol. IV, pp. 224–5. S. Thurley, *The Royal Palaces of Tudor England*, New Haven and London, 1993, thinks that the lodgings were conditioned by incorporating an earlier building.

10 Thurley, *The Royal Palaces of Tudor England*, p. 42, pl. 59; Thurley, *Hampton Court*, New Haven and London, 2003, pp. 29–30, pls 27, 29. In fact, Henry VIII seems never to have occupied the upper-floor lodgings, which were assigned to his queen.

11 Skelton, *Colin Clout*, quoted in Thurley, *Hampton Court*, p. 27.

12 *The Faerie Queene*, 1.10.56–58.

13 Built *circa* 1538–44. See **Royal Works*, vol. IV, p. 209, fig. 21, pl. 16.

14 For numerous examples, demolished or surviving, at Bruges, see Luc Devliegher, *Les Maisons à Bruges: inventoire descriptif*, Amsterdam, 1975, pls 6, 48, 110–12, 280, 282, 332, 426–30, 820–22, 862, 874, 1061, 1077.

15 For Melbury, see Royal Commission on the Historical Monuments of England, *Ancient and Historical Monuments in Dorset*, vol. I: *West*, London, 1952, pp. 164–7. Arthur Oswald, *Country Houses of Dorset*, 2nd edn, London, 1959, pp. 118–22; for Lacock, *Country Life*, 53 (3 May 1923), pp. 280–87.

16 See Royal Commission on the Historical Monuments of England, *An Inventory of the Historical Monuments in Essex*, vol. III: *North-East*, London, 1922, pp. 198–204.

17 John Stow, 'The Singularities of the City of London', in *The Survey of London* [1598], ed. Henry B. Wheatley, London, [1912], p. 121,

under Tower Street Ward. John Champneys was Lord Mayor in 1534, and died in
1556. But Stow's passage is ambiguous; the
tower may have been added by his predecessor Angell Dun, who originally built the
house.

18 Freston Tower was described in 1561 as
'built within these twelve years' (Nikolaus
Pevsner, *Buildings of England: Suffolk*, Harmondsworth, 1961).

19 'God is Al in Al Thikng: This windous
Whire made by William Moreton in the
yeare of oure Lorde M.D. LIX. Richard Dale
Carpeder made theies windous by the grac
of God'.

20 Reproduced in Nick Hill, 'Conservation
and Decay: Two Centuries at Old Gorhambury', *Transactions of the Association for
Studies in the Conservation of Historic Buildings*, 21 (1996), fig. 3. And see *St Albans and
Hertfordshire Architectural and Archaeological
Society Transactions* (1936), pp. 30–32.

21 See J. C. Ward and K. Marshall, *Old Thorndon Hall*, Essex Record Office Publication
61, 1972.

22 The front of Dunham Massey, long-since
rebuilt, is shown in J. Kip's and L. Knyff's
view in *Britannia Illustrata*, 1707. It was built
by Sir George Booth (1566–1652), who inherited as a minor in 1579. In his compendium
of family and estate accounts (John
Rylands Library, EGR3/3/3/2), he states that
'he builded three parts of Dunham House',
plus barns, mills, gardens, stables, etc. The
courtyard was closed with a fourth range by
his son, *circa* 1655.

23 Laneham's (alternatively Langham's) account, published in 1575, is printed in John
Nichols, *The Progresses and Public Processions
of Queen Elizabeth*, 3 vols, London, 1823, vol.
1, and was edited, with notes, by R. J. P.
Kuin, *A Letter*, Leiden, 1983. It has been
argued that the account was actually by
William Patten, satirising Laneham. For a
summary of the arguments for and against,
see *ODNB*, entry for Robert Langham.
The construction of 'Leicester's Building' at
Kenilworth was well underway by June/
July 1571, when William Spicer, who was in
charge of the building and probably designed it, wrote two letters to Leicester,
now in the Longleat archives (ROB III, p. 161,
Dudley Papers, II, fol. 321). For an earlier,
unexecuted scheme of *circa* 1565, for which
a plan survives, also at Longleat (200, 01/

01/1570), see Richard K. Morris, 'A Plan for
Kenilworth Castle at Longleat', *English Heritage Historical Review* 2 (2007), pp. 23– 35.
Morris attributes the plan to Henry
Hawhorne. See also chapter 8, note 70
below, and Nicholas A. D. Molyneux, 'Kenilworth Castle in 1563', *English Heritage Historical Review*, vol 3, 2008, pp. 47–61.

24 Whetstone, *Heptameron of Civil Discourses*,
1582: 'First Day'.

25 See T. C. Izard, *George Whetstone: Elizabethan Man of Letters*, New York, 1942, and
ODNB.

26 See *Girouard, *Smythson*, p. 309 n. 41 [Sher-
borne]; Nicholas Kingsley, *The Country
Houses of Gloucestershire, vol. I: 1500–1660*,
Chichester, 2001, pp. 88–9 [Eastington]; pp.
169–70 [Sapperton]; pp. 190–94 [Stanway].
Hilary Spurling, *Elinor Fettiplace's Receipt
Book*, London, 1986, pp. 2–4. But I incline to
earlier dates than those suggested by
Kingsley. He questions, for instance, the
date of *circa* 1578 given for Eastington in
Ralph Bigland, *Historical, Monumental and
Genealogical Collections Relative to a History of
Gloucestershire*, 2 vols, London, 1791–2, vol. 1,
p. 375, but I see no reason not to accept it,
and suspect a Maynard/Smythson involvement; the banded pilasters of the central
feature of the entrance front are repeated in
the basement doors at Wollaton (Pamela
Marshall, *Wollaton Hall: An Archaeological
Survey*, Nottingham, 1996, p. 35, fig. 27). The
likely builder of Sapperton is Sir Guy Poole
(d. 1589), who had been in the household of
Sir John Thynne, and whose stepdaughter
was Thynne's second wife; what are clearly
portions of chimneypieces built into the
Atkyns monument at Sapperton relate to
Longleat work (see chapter 3, note 78). The
south front at Stanway is dated *circa* 1620–
37 (Kingsley, *The Country Houses of Gloucestershire, vol. I*), *circa* 1630–40 (David Verey,
*Buildings of England: Gloucestershire, The Cots-
wolds*, Harmondsworth, 1970) and *circa* 1630
(*Architectural History*, 41, 1998, p. 254), but
the two solid-newel staircases in this wing
make a date of *circa* 1600 more likely.

27 See D. J. Cathcart King and J. Clifford
Perks, 'Carew Castle, Pembrokeshire', *Archaeological Journal*, 119 (1962), pp. 270–307,
especially p. 273 and pp. 294–5. Perrot seems
to have started to build the wing when he
returned from serving as Lord Deputy in
Ireland in 1588; he was tried and convicted

for high treason in 1592, but died before sentence could be carried out. According to a
survey of 1631–2 (National Archives, E178/
5866), the range 'was set up though not finished and covered with lead by the said Sir
John Perrot'.

28 *Thorpe Drawings*, T234, pl. 119, and see
chapter 2, note 31.

29 An early nineteenth-century engraving of
the interior shows the date 1600 in the plasterwork of the overmantel (information
Clare Gapper).

30 They are shown in a number of related
early eighteenth-century bird's-eye views,
perhaps deriving from a lost seventeenth-
century original. See Kingsley, *The Country
Houses of Gloucestershire, vol. 1*, pp. 62–6 and
pl. 52.

31 *Thorpe Drawings*, T201, T205, pl. 92, and see
Oliver Fairclough, 'John Thorpe and Aston
Hall', *Architectural History*, 32 (1989), pp. 30–
51.

32 For example, vignettes of house fronts in
the borders of Jacobus Millerd's plan of
Bristol, 1673, and Joseph Gilmore's plan of
Bath, 1694; Jean Manco, 'Bath and the
Great Rebuilding', *Bath History*, 4 (1992),
pp. 25–31.

33 See Manolo Guerci, 'The Strand Palaces of
the Early Seventeenth Century: Salisbury
House and Northumberland House', PH.D
thesis, University of Cambridge, 2007.

34 The unaltered north (entrance) façade is
shown in a painting by Balthazar Nabot of
1738, now in Buckinghamshire County Museum. An engraving of it in W. H. Smyth,
Aedes Hartwellianae, 2 vols, London, 1851–
64, is based on the Nabot painting. Sculptures and architectural detail removed from
the north front and elsewhere during the
eighteenth-century alterations were re-
erected in the form of a triumphal arch on
either side of a road bridge in the grounds
(and portions of panelling were assembled
in the Old Dairy). The arch has been carefully restored, necessitating, however, the
replacement of a good deal of stonework.
I am grateful to Eric Throssel for information and drawings, including his careful
measured reconstruction of the north front.
For the 'Nine Worthies' staircase, see pp.
223–4.

35 *Of Household Stuff: The 1601 Inventories of
Bess of Hardwick*, National Trust, London,
2001, p. 53.

36 Gervase Markham, *The English Husband-man*, London, 1613, sig. A4–B.

37 British Library, Add. MS 15891, fol. 32, quoted in Hartshorne (*Memorials of Holdenby*), pp. 15–16.

38 Thorpe's centralised perspective drawings are T37A [a demonstration of perspective, probably based on Serlio's Second Book], T71, T74, T86, T148, T160, T174, T265. Slightly off-centre are T49 [Wollaton], T85 and T182. Only T50 (the house based on his initials, probably using the perspective system in J. A. du Cerceau, *Leçons de Perspective Positive*, Paris, 1576) is taken from a viewpoint well to the right of the building depicted. The Wollaton drawing (T49) is likely to date from 1596 or earlier (it is inscribed 'Sir Francis Willoughby', who died in that year). It is drawn in very incorrect perspective, and must be the earliest in the series. It was perhaps in the year immediately before or after 1600 that Thorpe first studied Serlio and Du Cerceau, the latter to the extent of translating him into English; his undated translation of *Leçons de Perspective Positive*, together with his copy of the book, is now in the Bodleian Library, Oxford (LL23* Art. Seld.). Robert Smythson's perspective elevation of Wollaton is *Smythson Drawings*, I/25 (3).

39 For the arguments that the top floor of Chatsworth was an addition of *circa* 1570, see M. Girouard, 'The Ghost of Elizabethan Chatsworth', in *Town and Country*, 1992, pp. 211–20. For Castle Ashby, see chapter 2, p. 124 and note 103 above. Opinions differ as to whether the long gallery at Little Moreton Hall was integral with the south wing, was added during the course of construction, or was an afterthought. That it was an addition was first suggested by H. A. Tipping in *Country Life*, 66 (December 1929), pp. 798–808; C. F. Stell in *Archaeological Journal*, 120 (1963), p. 274, was sceptical; the current National Trust guide, 1995, does not commit itself. For Bramhall Hall, see George Ormerod, *History of the County Palatinate and City of Chester*, 3 vols, London, 1819, vol. III, pp. 400–02. For Worksop, see *Girouard, Smythson*, p. 114. At Raglan, William Somerset, Earl of Worcester, raised the height of the hall and added the gallery over the adjacent medieval chapel and adjoining rooms, *circa* 1573 (see the current CADW guide).

40 It is shown in its original state in an early nineteenth-century watercolour in the Hall.

41 *Smythson Drawings*, I/19 (unexecuted design for Slingsby Castle, Yorkshire), II/2, II/3. For Verulam, long since demolished, see John Aubrey, *Brief Lives and Other Selected Writings*, ed. Anthony Powell, London, 1949, pp. 12–13, with rough drawing by Aubrey. For Kiplin, built *circa* 1620, see *Country Life*, 174 (28 July and 4 August 1983), pp. 202–5, 278–81.

42 See Guerci, 'The Strand Palaces of the Early Seventeenth Century'.

43 *Thorpe Drawings*, T91–2, pl. 42; T95–6, pl. 44.

44 The house, before it was largely rebuilt in the eighteenth and nineteenth centuries, was engraved in Philip Morant, *History and Antiquities of the County of Essex*, 2 vols, London, 1768, vol. II, p. 431. Henry Maynard, secretary to William Cecil, was granted the property in 1590.

45 The identification was made by John Summerson (ed., *The Book of Architecture of John Thorpe*, p. 72). Campden House was built by Sir Baptist Hicks about 1612, on land bought from Sir Walter Cope. In an eighteenth-century painting it is shown as a brick-built house; but Summerson saw sufficient resemblance between this house and the timber-framed T95–6, and between the plan of the latter's hall and a description of the hall in Campden House in 1820, to suggest that the original timber-framed house, as shown by Thorpe, had later been encased in brick. But the resemblances do not seem sufficiently close to make his theory convincing; and against it must be set the fact that the known houses of any importance at this period in the north-western suburbs are of brick or stone, not timber-framed; and that the lions so prominent on the façade had no known connection with Baptist Hicks or Walter Cope.

46 See Hugh Murray, *The Great Chamber at Gilling Castle*, St Laurence Papers VIII, York, 1996.

47 Hugh Murray, 'The Restoration of the Heraldic Window at Fountains Hall', *Apollo*, 145 (April 1997), pp. 40–42.

48 Gilbert Talbot to the Earl and Countess of Shrewsbury, 28 February 1578/9. College of Heralds, Talbot Papers P929 (also transcribed in Edmund Lodge, *Illustration of British History*, 2nd edn, 3 vols, London, 1838, vol. II, p. 144).

49 William Jones to the Earl of Shrewsbury, 9 May 1579. London, Lambeth Palace, Shrewsbury Papers 697, fol. III.

50 Francis Bacon, 'Of Building', in *The Essayes or Counsells, Civill and Morall*, ed. Michael Kiernan, Oxford, 1985, p. 137. The reference to 'Faire Houses so full of glass' is on the same page. 'Of Building' was first published in the 1624 edition of the *Essayes*.

51 Letter quoted in Joseph Hunter, *Hallamshire: History and Topography of the Parish of Sheffield in the County of York . . .*, ed. Alfred Gatty, Sheffield, 1869, p. 87.

52 See David N. Durant, *Bess of Hardwick: Portrait of an Elizabethan Dynast*, London, 1977, p. 206.

53 Quoted in Harris Nicolas, *Memoirs of the Life and Times of Sir Christopher Hatton*, London, 1847, p. 126.

54 For example, the plaster ceilings at Cartmel Priory, Lancashire, installed by George Preston, *circa* 1618–22, and removed in the late nineteenth century. They are illustrated in early nineteenth-century engravings, reproduced in Eric Rothwell, *Cartmel Priory*, n. d. [*circa* 1990?], guide on sale in church. The plaster ceilings installed by the rector, Christopher Wren (father of the architect), *circa* 1639 at East Knoyle, Wiltshire, and by Bishop Montagu at Bath Abbey, have similarly been removed, though at East Knoyle the elaborate wall decorations were retained. Plaster ceilings survive at Axbridge and East Brent, Somerset, of 1636 and 1637 respectively (illustrated in Nikolaus Pevsner, *Buildings of England: North Somerset and Bristol*, Harmondsworth, 1958).

55 A Gedde design is used for a ceiling at Nutcombe Manor, Devon, illustrated in *Wells-Cole, Decoration*, pl. 188.

56 The original state of the great hall as a complete Elizabethan room is shown in *Country Life*, 34 (19 July 1913), pp. 90–97. The chimneypiece and almost all of the panelling have been removed, and a staircase and mezzanine floor inserted. 'The new staircase is entirely modern and suits the hall excellently' (Nikolaus Pevsner, *Buildings of England: Yorkshire: York and the East Riding*, Harmondsworth, 1972).

57 For Oxwich, see *Inventory of the Ancient Monuments of Glamorgan*, vol. IV, part I: *The Greater House*, Cardiff, 1981, pp. 63–76.

58 For Bramhall, see note 39.

59 *The Diary of Baron Waldstein*, trans. G. W. Gross, London, 1981, p. 113.

60 Chatsworth arch. Hardwick MS 29, *circa* fol. 600: 'Given by My Lady to . . . the Musicians that came from Court XI IIIs. More given to them playing at my La: Chamber window vs.'. This is likely to have been on the loggia roof outside 'My Lady's withdrawing chamber', today the drawing room.

61 Aubrey, *Brief Lives*, ed. Powell, p. 195.

62 For Brereton Hall, see *Country Life*, 25 (18 September 1909), pp. 388–94, reproducing an engraving of the cupolas still in position.

63 *The Diary of Baron Waldstein*, trans. Gross, p. 84.

64 Nicholas Tyacke, ed., *A History of the University of Oxford*, vol. IV, Oxford, 1997, p. 382.

65 Historical Manuscripts Commission, *Report on the Manuscripts of Lord Middleton*, London, 1911, p. 534, quoting from Cassandra Willoughby's history of the family, which incorporated material from many letters, etc., now lost.

66 Francis Bacon, *The Advancement of Learning* [1605], Book I, in *Philosophical Works*, ed. J. Spedding, vol. III, 1887, p. 294.

67 Christopher Marlowe, *Tamburlaine the Greate*, Part 2 [written *circa* 1588], 1606, ll. 4090–92 (Act 4, Scene 3).

Chapter 6   Serlio or Vredeman?

1 See especially *Wells-Cole, *Decoration*, pp. 43–4.

2 Serlio's second Doric (Vaughan Hart and Peter Hicks, *Serlio on Architecture*, New Haven and London, 1996, p. 319; Sebastiano Serlio, *The Five Books of Architecture* [1611], Peake edn, Book IV, chapter 6, fol. 32) and second Composite (Hart and Hicks, *Serlio on Architecture*, p. 369; Peake edn [1611], Book IV, chapter 12, fol. 62).

3 British Library, Add. MS 39828. Tresham to George Levens, 6 December 1596: 'In ye paynm [pagan?] freeses weer platters in one metopp and ox hedds garlanded, as they wer sacrificed to their idols'. He lists three possible Christian alternatives, but 'I am not wedded to my owne devyse, but am reddy to follow ye beste'.

4 For Peter Osborne, see *ODNB* and Mark Girouard, 'The Haynes Grange Room', in *Town and Country*, New Haven, 1992, pp. 171–86, especially pp. 184–5.

5 See Manolo Guerci, 'John Osborne, the Salisbury House Porticus and the Haynes Grange Room', *Burlington Magazine*, 148 (January 2006), pp. 15–24. The porticus specification is National Archives, SP 14/57, fols 70–74 (abstract in *Calendar of State Papers, Domestic*). Guerci gives the full text. The elevation is at Hatfield, CPM, Supplementary 89. It was discovered in 2004 by Joseph Friedman, among eighteenth-century drawings for estate development on Cecil property in London.

6 Pula theatre in Serlio, Peake edn (1611), Book III, chapter 4, fol. 24; Hart and Hicks, *Serlio on Architecture*, p. 143. Athenian council chamber in Serlio, Peake edn, Book IIII, chapter 4, fol. 44; Hart and Hicks, *Serlio on Architecture*, p. 191. Serlio does not identify it; its identification as the council chamber or Bouleterion is in George Hersey, *Pythagorean Palaces: Magic and Architecture in the Italian Renaissance*, Ithaca, New York, and London, 1976, pp. 57–8.

7 Girouard, 'The Haynes Grange Room', pp. 184–6, surmised that the panelling and ceiling came from the room known as the Pigeon Gallery, at Chicksands, and not, as previously accepted, from nearby Houghton House, Bedfordshire, when it was dismantled in the late eighteenth century. But I did not then know of John Osborne's porticus design, and suggested that the room had been commissioned by his father, Peter, *circa* 1575–80. Guerci, 'John Osborne, the Salisbury House Porticus and the Haynes Grange Room', p. 23, has found payments in the Osborne (today Osborn) papers, now in Bedfordshire County Record Office, that show that the room was in Haynes Grange in 1754. This conclusively refutes the Houghton theory, for Houghton was not dismantled until 1794. The room was probably moved to Haynes Grange *circa* 1714, when John Osborne, son and heir of Sir John Osborne or Osborn of Chicksands went to live there (ibid., p. 23). He died in 1719, a year before his father.

8 Osborn MSS, Bedfordshire County Record Office, O/4–5; *The Victoria County History of the County of Bedford*, 3 vols, Westminster, 1904–14, vol. II, pp. 271–3, 341–3. The lawyer employed by the Osbornes in their lawsuit with the Snowes, from whom they bought Chicksands, was Thomas Owen, later the builder of Condover Hall, Shropshire.

9 There are all too many available John Osbornes. Hassel Smith, 'Concept and Compromise: Sir Nicholas Bacon and the Building of Stiffkey Hall', in *East Anglia's History*, ed. C. Harper-Bill, C. Rawcliffe and R. G. Wilson, Norwich, 2002, identifies Bacon's servant with John Osborne of Harkstead, Suffolk, who was born *circa* 1544, granted arms in 1578, bought Wattisfield Hall, Suffolk, *circa* 1592, and died in 1619. The Chicksands John Osborne was already working in the Treasury in 1576, and may have continued as an auditor there till he succeeded his father as Lord Treasurer's Remembrancer in 1592; there are problems in reconciling this with possible work for Bacon. But the subject needs further research. In 1582 a John Osborne dedicated a manuscript translation of Demosthenes' oration against Leptinos to Sir Christopher Hatton, acknowledging 'your particular goodness towarde my selfe' (British Library, Add. MS 10059).

10 See pp. 59–60 above; p. 188 above.

11 The chimneypiece in the withdrawing chamber (Reynolds Room) at Knole; *Wells-Cole, *Decoration*, illustrates the detail and its source, p. 40, pls 45–6.

12 For Ightham Court, see *Country Life*, 123 (26 June 1958), pp. 1424–7; Nicholas Cooper, *Houses of the Gentry, 1480–1680*, New Haven and London, 1999, p. 118, pls 112–13. The Tower of the Orders was part of additions to a small earlier building made by Thomas Willoughby, whose son Percival was to marry the daughter and heiress of Sir Francis Willoughby of Wollaton.

13 According to Robert Surtees, *The History and Antiquities of the County Palatine of Durham*, 4 vols, 1816–40, vol. III, p. 316, Walworth Castle was built by Thomas Jenison (Comptroller of Works at Berwick, see p. 9 above), who died in 1586. The Elizabethan work at Stoneyhurst was built in the years before the death of its owner, Sir Richard Shireburn, who left it unfinished on his death in 1592, according to his will. See *Country Life*, 28 (15 October 1910), pp. 534–42; reference to will p. 537.

14 See the two comparative illustrations in 'Bramshill, II', *Country Life*, 178 (10 October 1985), p. 1095. There is a close copy of one of the milder Dietterlin doorways at Wentworth Woodhouse, West Yorkshire, of *circa* 1630 (*Wells-Cole, *Decoration*, pls

27–8); for John Smythson derivations, see *Girouard, Smythson*, pls 181–4, 188–9. The hall chimneypiece and doorway to the chapel at the Charterhouse, London, are clearly influenced by Dietterlin, though his style is toned down by the London artificer.

15 *Les Plus Excellents Bastiments de France par J.-A. du Cerceau*, ed. David Thomson, trans. Catherine Ludet, Paris, 1988, pp. 264–5 (original edition, vol. 2, 1579).

16 Ibid., p. 267 [Anet chapel]; pp. 274–5 [Ecouen].

17 Jon Bayliss, 'A Dutch Carver: Garret Hollemans I in England', *Church Monuments*, 8 (1993), pp. 46–56, with lists of attributed monuments on pp. 54–5. For Hollemans at Kyre Park, see Mrs Baldwyn-Childe, 'The Building of Kyre Park', *Antiquary*, 21 (1890), pp. 262–3, drawing on an account-book then at Kyre, now British Library, Add. MS 62674.

18 See pp. 192–4 above.

19 For Richard Whalley or Whaley (*circa* 1499–1583), see *ODNB* and *House of Commons, Elizabeth*. His widow (and third wife) married Edward Burnell in 1581; his son Thomas and William Whalley, probably Thomas's brother, were each described as 'servant to the Earl of Rutland' (Historical Manuscripts Commission, *The Manuscripts of His Grace of Rutland, GCB, Preserved at Belvoir Castle*, 4 vols, London, 1888–1905, vol. I, p. 230).

20 Jon Bayliss ('A Dutch Carver') assigns the four monuments to one workshop, and suggests Henry Kinder of Newark-on-Trent as possible carver. If one accepts that the carver could also work in wood, and recognises the Manners connection, another possibility is John Fletcher, who worked as 'joyener' at Belvoir in 1587, and was paid £6 in part payment for providing 'fret worke to be maide in his Lo. galery' (Historical Manuscripts Commission, *The Manuscripts of His Grace of Rutland*, vol. IV, pp. 391–2). Neither suggestion is in the least conclusive.

21 As Timothy Mowl (*Elizabethan and Jacobean Style*, London, 1993, p. 31) perceptively comments: 'The Earl appears to have taken his best dining table and lent it to the alabaster worker . . . to serve as a model'.

22 So dated in Nikolaus Pevsner, *Buildings of England: Leicestershire and Rutland*, Harmondsworth, 1960, following Gordon Nares, *Country Life*, 112 (20 June 1952), pp.

1908–11. In fact, investigation of the woodwork made when the paint had been stripped in the 1970s showed the main chimneypiece and panelling to be of oak, with additions made in softwood when it was reset in the eighteenth century (Report kindly shown to me by Mrs Pam Clarke of Baggrave).

23 See chapter 7, note 5, for the dating of this.

24 Dating and locating these Bristol chimneypieces is a tricky business, partly because of their migratory history, partly because even when they were in Bristol, they may have been moved from house to house, and their successive owners certainly added later dates and initials to them, and may have changed their heraldry. They are much in need of a separate study, but a provisional list follows, which could certainly be added to. The *Transactions of the Bristol and Gloucestershire Archaeological Society* (here *TBGAS*) feature numerous articles on the chimneypieces.

A. Chimneypiece attributed to Thomas Collins, *circa* 1570–93.

1. Dating from the ?1570s. Was in 'Colston's House', Small Street, part re-erected in the Assize Courts, where it remains. Photographed *circa* 1860, when still in Small Street (reproduced in Reece Winston, *Bristol as It Was, 1873–87*, Bristol, *circa* 1966, fig. 12). As shown in the old photograph, the row of anthemion ornament, still in position today, was the base of a vanished overmantel, but the photograph is puzzling: it suggests something not in its original position, and perhaps made up out of more than one chimneypiece. Colston's House was the residence of the Colston family in the seventeenth century and possibly later; it may be that Edward Colston, the great philanthropist, moved the chimneypiece or chimneypieces from Sir John Young's 'great house' (erected *circa* 1568–74) on St Augustine's Quay when he converted it for use as Colston's School in the early eighteenth century.

2. Dating from the 1570s. Single stage, with terms. Very grand in scale.

Installed by G. W. Braikenridge in the library of Broomwell House, Brislington. Shown in a pencil drawing of the library by W. H. Wartlett (Braikenridge Collection, City of Bristol Museum and Art Gallery; reproduced in Sheena Stoddard, *Mr Braikenridge's Bristol*, published by the Gallery, 1981, p. 32, pl. 26, and by John Harris, *Moving Rooms: The Trade in Architectural Salvages*, New Haven and London, 2007, pl. 33). According to Braikenridge's notes, it had been bought *circa* 1818 from a fire-damaged house in Small Street, in which Charles I had been entertained. This must have been Colston's House (see previous entry), where William Colston, father of the philanthropist, had entertained the king in 1643, and it is possible that this chimneypiece, too, came from Sir John Young's house. The room in Broomwell House was moved in the 1850s to Claremont Villa, Highdale Road, Clevedon, where it survives, but apparently without the chimneypiece (Stoddard, *Mr Braikenridge's Bristol*, pp. 41, 50).

3. Dating from the 1580s. Red Lodge. See notes 26 and 27 below.

B. Chimneypieces attributed to Collins or the Fryndes (also Frynd, Frind[e], Ferend[e]), *circa* 1590–1605.

4. Was in John Whitson mansion, Small Street, now in Red Maids' School, Westbury-on-Trym. Coupled Corinthian on Ionic. Dated 1629 (the date of Whitson's death), but with arms of Queen Elizabeth. *TBGAS*, 49 (1927), p. 208 and pl. IV.

5. Was at 7 Small Street. Removed to Bristol Water Works Office by 1927. Coupled Corinthian and Ionic. Inscribed 1700, and E, A, M, for Abraham and Mary Elton, who then owned it. *TBGAS*, 27 (1904), p. 338; 49 (1927), p. 204 and pl. II.

C. Chimneypieces attributed to the Frynde workshop, *circa* 1605–30.

6. Was at 11 (later 36) Corn Street. Advertised for sale, *Country Life*,

175 (29 March 1984). Present location unknown. Two-stage, single terms on both stages, central relief of angels with scales. Bristol Record Society 48, p. 61, no. 36b. Braikenridge Coll. M2482.

7. The *Five Senses* chimneypiece. Was at 15 Small Street. Now in Cincinnati Art Museum, Ohio (Harris, *Moving Rooms*, p. 185). Two stages. Single terms on both stages. Central coat of arms framed by Corinthian columns. Relief panels of the *Five Senses*, more crudely carved than the terms. Achievements of military arms in the lower stage above opening. Probably erected by Humphrey Brown, Captain of Bristol Trained Bands by 1623. *TBGAS*, 49 (1927), p. 203, pl. 1.

8. Formerly in St Werburgh's Chambers, Small Street; by 1927 in New Post Office. Lower stage without columns or terms, upper with three consoles under Ionic capitals, strapwork panels in between. *TBGAS*, 30 (1907), pp. 163–4; 49 (1927), pl. 3. Destroyed in the war of 1939–45.

9. Chimneypiece from house of John Langton, Welsh Back, Bristol. Moved to New Place, Shedfield, Hampshire, *circa* 1906. Coupled terms above coupled Ionic columns, central Stuart coat of arms framed by further terms, with figures of *Charity* and (?)*Justice*. Perhaps dating from year of Langton's mayoralty, 1628, The most elaborate of surviving Bristol chimneypieces. *Country Life*, 17 (13 May 1905), p. 664 (when still in Bristol); 27 (1910), p. 522 [New Place].

10. Formerly in house of John Aldworth, off St Peter Street, later St Peter's Hospital, reconstruction of earlier house by Aldworth, dated 1612, destroyed in war of 1939–45. Overmantel only, above late medieval chimneypiece. Single Corinthian columns with fretted drums, as at S. Wraxall, figures of *Charity* and (?) *Justice*, Stuart royal arms. *TBGAS*, 29 (1906), pp. 29–30. (The

monument to John Aldworth, d. 1634, and his wife Elizabeth, d. 1619, in St Peter's Church, also destroyed in the Second World War, was clearly from the same workshop. *TBGAS*, 32, 1909, p. 293.)

11. Chimneypiece originally at Piercefield Park, Monmouthshire, bought for William Randolph Hearst, 1925 (illus. in Harris, *Moving Rooms*, p. 228).

D. Chimneypiece attributed to Frynde or, more probably, to Bird (also Bird[e], Byrd[e]) workshop.

    12. Illustrated in Rothery, *English Chimneypieces*, London, 1927. With Frynde-type chimneypiece opening, but clearly related to no. 12. Present location unknown.

E. Chimneypieces attributed to Bird workshop.

    13, 14. Chimneypieces formerly at 8 Broad Quay, sold to USA by Charles of Brook Street, London, *circa* 1909. *TBGAS*, 32 (1909), p. 326. (For Charles, see note 68.)

    15. Chimneypiece bearing Cordwainer's Arms, formerly at Mary-le-Port Street, sold by Charles of Brook Street, London, to New York, *circa* 1922. *TBGAS*, 44 (1922), p. 90 and pl. 11.

    16. Chimneypiece now in lower dining room of Gore Hotel, Queensgate, London.

    17. Chimneypiece 'from a merchant's house at Bristol'; was moved in 1930s to Lake House, Wiltshire. The *chef-d'œuvre* of this workshop. Upper stage with terms framing panels of strapwork and oval relief of *St George and the Dragon*. Illustrated in *Country Life*, 81 (3 April 1937), p. 353.

25 For Collins, see chapter 1, notes 99 and 141; Bristol Burgess Rolls (microfiches, Bristol Record Office) and Bristol Apprentice Books (1566–93, transcribed and indexed by Margaret McGregor, Bristol and Avon Family History Society, 4 vols, 1922–4).

26 Young bought the site of Red Lodge in

April 1578 (J. F. Nicholls and J. Taylor, *Bristol Past and Present*, 3 vols, Bristol, 1880–81, vol. 1, p. 259). Bath stone was being delivered to him in 1581, probably for use in the Lodge, and perhaps for the chimneypiece there (Bath Chamberlain Accounts, Bath Record office). He died in 1589, leaving a son and heir who was a minor; the Red Lodge was sold in 1605 to Sir Hugh Smyth, to whom, on stylistic grounds, the ceiling in the great room there can be attributed.

27 The coat of arms on the chimneypiece derives from a Vredeman de Vries set of engravings, dated 1555. A related set, of the same year, was used for the cartouche enclosing the arms of the Earl of Pembroke, on the east façade of the east gatehouse at Wilton House, Wiltshire. The arms, with an earl's coronet, but not Garter, must be those of the 2nd Earl, and date from 1570–75, before he was given the Garter. The cartouche is set in a frame with nearly identical mouldings to those on the surrounds of the fireplace openings of the Red Lodge and Assize Court chimneypieces. William Herbert of Wilton, 1st Earl of Pembroke, was Constable of Bristol Castle and Steward of Bristol. It was probably he who obtained for Young the position of Collector of Customs in Bristol in 1559 (*House of Commons, Elizabeth*). He died in March 1570. It would make sense if Collins came from London to work at Wilton in the 1560s, and then moved on to Bristol in the early 1570s, perhaps to work on William Young's house. Collins became a freeman of Bristol in 1571.

28 The acanthus frieze and low-relief vases in the side panels seem to derive from one of Serlio's Composite chimneypieces, and from ceiling designs at the end of his Fourth Book, the sprays under the coat of arms perhaps from one of his Corinthian drawings. The Serlio façade design is also in the Fourth Book (Peake edn [1611], chapter 6, fol. 28; Hart and Hicks, *Serlio on Architecture*, p. 309). Although the present dentilled cornice may be a later replacement, Millard's late seventeenth-century Bristol maps show the lodge with a horizontal roofline and no gables.

29 See list in note 24. John and Anthony Frynde were not brothers, though they may have been related. John was apprenticed to Thomas Collins in 1579, Anthony to John Bird in 1583 (Apprentice Books).

30 See note 24 above. The Bristol Corporation records show that the Birds did much more work for the corporation than the Fryndes. This does not mean that they were more successful; the corporation did little of much importance at this period, and the more interesting work was for private patrons. For Thomas Bird's work on enlarging Bristol High Cross, in 1633–4, see p. 432 below and Fig. 575.

31 The plasterwork in the South Wraxall great chamber has written on it the signature 'John Sweetman, 1612' (kindly communicated to me by Bob Louden, who discovered it). The Langton chimneypiece may date from 1628; see entry C9 in note 24 above.

32 For the decoration and chimneypieces at South Wraxall, see *Country Life*, 15 (26 March 1904), pp. 450–58, and especially *Wells-Cole, *Decoration*, p. 142, and pls 220–24.

33 I am grateful to Adam White for sending me the entry on Samuel Baldwin, with illustrated list of documented (only two) or attributed church monuments, from his thesis 'Church Monuments in Britain, *c*.1560–*c*.1660' (Courtauld Institute of Art, University of London, 1991), pp. 60–74. See also Irvine Gray, 'A "Forgotten Sculptor" of Stroud', *Transactions of the Bristol and Gloucestershire Archaeological Society*, 83 (1964), p. 149; John Broome, 'Samuel Baldwin: Carver of Gloucester', *Church Monuments*, 10 (1995), pp. 37–54. White disagrees with some of his attributions.

34 See Gray, 'A "Forgotten Sculptor" of Stroud'. The Berkeley contract (in fact an acquittance) is in the Berkeley Castle archives.

35 The Ampney chimneypiece was first attributed to Baldwin in *Wells-Cole, *Decoration*, p. 113. It is quite clearly from the same workshop as the monuments.

36 *Wells-Cole, *Decoration*, pls 172–3.

37 There seems a convincing progress in design from Ampney to the equally distinctive but simpler chimneypieces at Lasborough Manor, formerly at Prinknash Park, and at Misarden Park, all in Gloucestershire (Nicholas Kingsley, *The Country Houses of Gloucestershire, vol. I: 1500–1660*, Chichester, 2001, p. 28, pl. 23; p. 167, pl. 132; colour pl. XI (he does not attribute them to Baldwin)). The device, found at Prinknash and Misarden, of a coat of arms surrounded by a circular wreath, is also found on the entrance façade of Westwood Park in Worcestershire.

38 *Girouard, *Smythson*, p. 124, pl. 70 [Heath Old Hall]; p. 146, pl. 84, with related Serlio designs, pl. 83 [Hardwick].

39 For Giles de Witt, see his entry in *White, *Dictionary*. This lists the documentation, discusses the reasons for giving the chimneypieces to him, and also attributes to him a small group of church monuments, mostly in Kent. See also J. Bayliss, 'Giles de Witt "Marbeler"', *Monumental Brass Society Bulletin*, 55 (October 1990), pp. 465–6. De Witt is documented as living and working in Bruges from 1576 to 1585, when he moved to London. In 1593 he was described as 'marbeler'. In 1601 he was negotiating prices for two chimneypieces at Cobham. There is a lack of other documentation, but it is stylistically convincing to assign to him most of the Cobham chimneypieces, and the elaborate two-stage frontispiece on the north side of the north wing.

40 See note 44.

41 See chapter 1, p. 33 and note 91.

42 Quenby is dated 1621 on the rainwater heads; Fountains was described as 'newly built' about 1625 (*Girouard, *Smythson*, p. 314, n. 49); the Canons Ashby chimneypiece is perhaps *circa* 1590 (John Heward and Robert Taylor, *The Country Houses of Northamptonshire*, Royal Commission on the Historical Monuments of England, Swindon, 1996, p. 118). For Hatfield, see C. Gapper, J. Newman and A. Ricketts, 'Hatfield: A House for a Lord Treasurer', in *Patronage, Culture and Power: The Early Cecils, 1558–1612*, ed. Pauline Croft, New Haven and London, 2002, pp. 62–95.

43 Illustrated in *Country Life*, 177 (17 October 1985), p. 1097.

44 Payments and references to Maximilian Colt in the Cecil papers are just for three chimneypieces, location not named. Two of these are generally accepted as being those in the Book Room (now the private dining room) and the King's Great Chamber (now King James Drawing Room); there is disagreement about the third: it may be the one now in the library, though this has been altered, and the early seventeenth-century mosaic portrait of Robert Cecil is a later insertion. See *White, *Dictionary*, entry for Stone, and Gapper, Newman and Ricketts, 'Hatfield', in *Patronage, Culture and Power*, ed. Croft, pp. 62–95. In his notebooks Stone records: 'in February 1656 I took a tombe and a chemney-pieces of Ser Henry Bellasess to be set up at Yorke, for which I had well payed 150 £' (*The Note-Book and Account-Book of Nicholas Stone*, ed. W. L. Spiers, Walpole Sociey VII, Oxford, 1919, p. 42). This might have been moved from York to Newburgh Priory, but stylistically the Newburgh chimneypiece suggests a later date.

45 See *White, *Dictionary*, entries for Colt and Stone.

46 The Hatfield chimneypiece is said to have come from Robert Cecil's other house at Quixwood, Hertfordshire, though Newman (Gapper, Newman and Ricketts, 'Hatfield', in *Patronage, Culture and Power*, ed. Croft, p. 83) argues that it is the third Colt chimneypiece, and has always been at Hatfield. The Cobham chimneypiece is not one of those I would attribute to Giles de Witt (see note 39).

47 The authorship of these Apethorpe chimneypieces lacks documentation. Emily Cole and Kathryn A. Morrison (*Apethorpe Hall, Apethorpe, Northamptonshire: Survey, Research and Analysis*, English Heritage Research Department Report Series, no. 82, 2 vols, Cambridge, 2006) argue for the workshop of Thomas Thorpe; Adam White surmises a London workshop, and tentatively suggests that of Gerard Christmas (Report: 'Sculpture at Apethorpe Hall' made for the Royal Commission on the Historic Monuments of England, 2006, and published, but without the illustrations, in vol. II of *Apethorpe Hall, Apethorpe*. I am not convinced by either ascription and suspect an idiosyncratic and unidentified carver, based in the Midlands. The chimneypieces are clearly influenced by the monument to Sir Anthony and Lady Grace Mildmay in the church at Apethorpe which is attributed to Maximilian Colt, but the sculpture is not of equivalent quality. For their iconography, see Adam White, 'The Iconography of the State Apartment at Apethorpe Hall', *English Heritage Historical Review*, vol. 3, 2008, pp. 63–85.

48 *Wells-Cole, *Decoration*, pp. 185–96, pls 304–45.

49 Ibid., pp. 172–84, pls 278–303.

50 Ibid., p. 113, pls 168–71.

51 Stephen Harrison, *The Arch's of Triumph*

erected in honor of . . . James . . . King of England, London, 1604.

52 Drawing in Essex County Record Office, reproduced in John Newman, 'Copthall, Essex', in *The Country Seat: Studies in the History of the British Country House Presented to John Summerson*, ed. Howard Colvin and John Harris, London, 1970, p. 23. The chimneypiece carries the arms and crests of Sir Thomas Heneage and his first wife, Anne Poyntz, and must have been erected before the death of the latter in 1593.

53 Illustrated in *Country Life*, 18 (2 December 1905), pp. 777–8 [Langleys]; 114 (3 September 1953), pp. 694, 697 [Aston].

54 Diary of Henry Ferrers of Baddesley Clinton, 2 March 1628/9 (Oxford, Bodleian Library, MS Rawl. D676, fol. 42v): 'I went to the Radcliffs being at woork in the great chamber who have finished and set up the chimneypiece'. The reference has been taken to be to a wooden chimneypiece at Baddesley Clinton, but the stone Serlian one is more likely.

55 John Stow, *The Survey of London*, ed. Henry B. Wheatley, London, [1912], p. 353.

56 *Country Life*, 27 (15 January 1910), p. 93 [Seckford; the screen was sold in the 1920s]; p. 28 above [Bowringsleigh]; *Country Life*, 109 (15 June 1951), p. 1801 [Parham]; *Country Life*, 45 (22 March 1919), pp. 310–11 [Cuckfield]; *Wells-Cole, Decoration*, p. 170, pl. 277 [Grey's Inn].

57 *Wells-Cole, Decoration*, p. 170.

58 Ibid., p. 170 and pl. 275.

59 *The Records of the Honourable Society of Lincoln's Inn: The Black Books*, ed. J. Douglas Walker, London, 1897–1902, vol. II, p. 253; H. L. Phillips *Annals of the Joiners' Company*, London, 1915, p. 17.

60 For Buck, see Lawrence Stone, 'The Building of Hatfield House', *Archaeological Journal*, 112 (1955), p. 121, etc.; *Royal Works, vol. IV, p. 259, n. 3. He also worked for Cecil at his London house (Manolo Guerci, 'The Strand Palaces of the Early Seventeenth Century: Salisbury House and Northumberland House', PH.D thesis, University of Cambridge, 2007, p. 53).

61 *Girouard, Smythson, p. 62.

62 *Willis and Clark, Cambridge, vol. II, pp. 491–2, and for Carter's career in general, see *Colvin.

63 Sir Thomas Graham Jackson, *Wadham College, Oxford*, Oxford, 1893, pp. 177–8, drawing on the building accounts in Wadham College archives.

64 Petre papers, Essex County Record Office, passim.

65 For Sizergh, see Ian Goodall, 'Privacy, Display and Over-extension: Walter Strickland's Rebuilding of Sizergh', *Antiquaries Journal*, 82 (2002), pp. 197–245.

66 See p. 28 above. But though Baggett died in 1619, the screen at Penheale, Cornwall (*Country Life*, 62, 4 April 1925, pp. 524–5), which from the heraldry seems to date from 1637 or later, is sufficiently close to that at Bowringsleigh to suggest that his workshop or his influence survived him.

67 *Country Life*, 14 (26 December 1903), pp. 926–30. For Bradfield and Bradninch, see *Wells-Cole, Decoration*, p. 172. For The Grange, see *Country Life*, 16 (30 July 1904), pp. 162–6, and *Wells-Cole, Decoration*, p. 25. Wells-Cole, p. 25, relates their joinery to a room from an unidentified house near Exeter (now V&A: 4870–8v–1856), which draws on Vredeman's *Der Erste Buch* and engravings by Cornelis Floris and Abraham de Bruyn.

68 Photograph of King's Lynn, chimneypiece, National Monuments Record [NMR], BB 89/969; photo of Rotherwas, Hereford City Library, BB 57/10343. The latter is now in Mead Art Museum, Amherst College, Massachusetts. The entire interior of Rotherwas was sold by 'Charles of London', or 'Charles of Brook Street', the trade name of Charles Joe Duveen, whose famous brother paid him $25,000 a year not to use the Duveen name (Harris, *Moving Rooms*, n. 65, p. 102, and n. 11, pp. 196–7). The whereabouts of the King's Lynn chimneypiece is not known.

69 Edmund Bolton, *Elements of Armories*, 1610, in 'table of hard words' at end.

70 V&A: 4239–1856. H. Borggrefe et al., *Hans Vredeman de Vries und die Renaissance in Norden* (catalogue of exhibition in Weserrenaissance-Museum Schloss Brake and Kininklijk Museum voor Schone Kunsten Antwerp 2002), pp. 306–7, p. 305 (cat. no. 146) and illustrations, pp. 306–7, dating it 1580. Similar marquetry is illustrated on pp. 258–60, including a cupboard (cat. no. 91) inscribed HS. 1565.

71 Listed in Girouard, 'The Ghost of Elizabethan Chatsworth', in *Town and Country*, pp. 217–18.

72 B. Stallybrass, 'Bess of Hardwick's Buildings and Building Accounts', *Archaeologia*, 64 (1923), pp. 347–98.

73 Information John Harris.

74 See pp. 135–7 above; pp. 354–61 below.

75 *Wells-Cole, Decoration*, pp. 260–71 and pls.

76 D. N. Durant and P. Riden, eds, *The Building of Hardwick Hall. Part 2: The New Hall, 1591–98*, Derbyshire Record Society IX, Chesterfield, 1984, pp. LXIV, LXVI.

77 C. Gapper, 'Plasterers and Plasterwork in City, Court and Country, c. 1530–c. 1640', PH.D thesis, University of London (Courtauld Institute of Art), 1998, p. 200. The name of the plasterer is not recorded in the relevant accounts.

78 See chapter 1, pp. 27–8, and note 51. Dungan is paid for unlocated plasterwork and materials in the fragment of accounts that survives.

79 See C. Stanley-Millson and J. Newman, 'Blickling Hall: The Building of a Jacobean Mansion', *Architectural History*, 29 (1986), pp. 11–12.

80 *Royal Works, vol. IV, pp. 322–4.

81 *Patronage, Culture and Power*, ed. Croft, pp. 82–3. Lee (or Leigh) was also responsible for the ceilings of the rooms built for Anne of Denmark at Somerset House in 1610–11 (*Royal Works, vol. IV, p. 257).

82 J. Imrie and J. G. Dunbar, *Accounts of the Masters of Works for Building and Repairing Royal Palaces and Castles*, 2 vols, Edinburgh, 1957–82, vol. II, pp. 47–111; Gapper, 'Plasterers and Plasterwork in City, Court and Country', p. 167. Cobb and Robert Whitehead and their English plasterer went to install plasterwork in Holyrood Palace, Edinburgh, for the visit of James I in 1617. For plasterwork in Scotland at this period, see Charles McKean, *The Scottish Château: The Country House of Renaissance Scotland*, Stroud, 2001, especially pp. 199–202, pls 10.10, 10.11, 11.17–19, 11.22, colour pl. 20. The plasterer employed at Winton House, *circa* 1628, was John White.

83 See previous pages.

84 John Ferris, 'Herringston: The Prince of Wales Connexion', *Notes and Queries for Somerset and Dorset* (March 2001), pp. 21–3.

85 For Easton at Chantmarle, see p. 29 above. For the Abbots, see K. French and C. French, 'Devonshire Plasterwork', *Transactions of the Devonshire Association*, vol. 89, 1957, pp. 124–40, and *Wells-Cole, Decora-

tion, pp. 159–63, pls 254–64. The earliest known payment to an Abbot is in 1667; and the celebrated 'patternbook' (Devon County Record Office, Exeter, MS 404 M/BI), which had been accepted as 'handed down from generation to generation' of Abbots (John, 1565–1635; Richard, b. 1612; John, 1639–1727), can be shown by the watermarks to date from the 1650s, and to be, in all probability, the work of the younger John only (Michael Bath, 'The Sources of John Abbot's Pattern-book', *Architectural History*, 41, 1998, pp. 49–66). If, however, as is possible, John as an apprentice or young man was copying engraved designs in possession of his family or master, his drawings are still of value as showing some of what had been available for use by earlier generations. Wells-Cole has identified engravings by Vredeman de Vries, the Italian Benedetto Battini and the German George Pencz; Bath adds George Withers's *Emblems* (1635) and Edward Tapsell's *Historie of Four-footed Beastes* (1607). The Barnstaple ceiling, with its prominent Vredeman-style cartouches and menageries of animals, could well have drawn on these, and Frithelstock is only a few miles from Barnstaple. For Lanhydrock, see Paul Holden, ' "Situation, Contrivance, Receipt, Strength and Beauty": The Building of Lanhydrock House, 1620–51', *Journal, Royal Institution of Cornwall*, volume for 2005, especially pp. 40–41.

86 Panelling and glass were bought by Hearst, in 1929, but kept in packing cases until bought back for Gilling in 1952. See Hugh Murray, *The Great Chamber at Gilling Castle*, St Laurence Papers VIII, York, 1996, pp. 37–41. The part played by Father James Forbes of Ampleforth Abbey in bringing about its return deserves recognition.

87 Printed in *Archaeologia*, 48 (1885), pp. 123–36. Original in Winn MSS, West Yorkshire Archives Service, Leeds.

88 See Murray, *The Great Chamber at Gilling Castle*, pp. 4–7.

89 *Country Life*, 175 (5 July 1984), pp. 22–3, pls 8–10.

90 See Adam White, 'The Booke of Monuments Reconsidered: Maximilian Colt and William Wright', *Church Monuments*, 9 (1994), pp. 62–7.

91 Gapper, 'Plasterers and Plasterwork in City, Court and Country', pp. 139–40.

92 Ibid., p. 141.

93 *Smythson Drawings*, III/1 (2–3).

94 See chapter 5, p. 287 and note 48.

95 Rutland MSS, Belvoir, book 76 (Receipts and Payments, 1586–8).

96 *Royal Works*, vol. III, p. 410.

97 For Barningham, see *Country Life*, 27 (5 February 1910), pp. 198–203. The date 1612 is over the porch.

98 For Intwood, see J. W. Burgon, *The Life and Times of Sir Thomas Gresham* (London, 1839), p. 102. The engraving he reproduces is said to be 'from an old oil-painting in the possession of J. Salusbury Muskett, Esqre', which I have not been able to locate. There is a print of better quality of the same view in the Norwich Museum picture archive.

99 E. R. Sandeen, 'The Building of Redgrave Hall, 1545–1554', thesis, University of Chicago (copy in Bodleian Library), part published in *Proceedings of the Suffolk Institute of Archaeology and History*, 29 (1961). A. L. Baggs, 'Cannons Hall', *Norfolk Archaeology*, 39/i (1966), pp. 9–12. Richard Garnier, 'Merton Hall', *Georgian Group Journal*, 14 (2004), pp. 131–66. Merton Hall, dated 1613 on the rainwater heads, was in the local style, but in the gatehouse, dated 1620, Blickling-type gables have arrived; Garnier surmises a direct input from Robert Leminge.

100 According to W. A. Copinger, *The Manors of Suffolk*, 7 vols, London, 1905–11, vol. IV, pp. 47–9, the Manor of Thorpe Hall with Wotton, Horham, appears to have been sold in 1572 to Ralph Roberts (Fine, Trin 14 Eliz) and by 1609 had passed to Sir Edward Coke. One can surmise that the house originally had just a newel staircase in the rear projection, and that the present staircase was a later insertion.

101 *Thorpe Drawings*, T67–8, pl. 32 and pp. 65–6. Unusually for the date, the house was buttressed, which one would have thought might have prevented collapse; but the Thorpe plan suggests the presence of ovens and privy shafts in the thickness of the external angles, which would certainly have weakened the structure.

102 The projected Lyveden ceiling is shown in the plan by 'RS' (see chapter 4, note 29). For Wollaton, see Pamela Marshall, *Wollaton Hall: An Archaeological Survey*, Nottingham, 1996, pp. 12–14 and ill. 8. The roofing system is illustrated in Serlio's First Book (Peake edn [1611], Book 1, chapter 1, fol. 12; Hart and Hicks, *Serlio on Architecture*, p. 31). As Marshall puts it, 'conventional tie beams would have served to counteract the outward thrust in the central tower walls', but the Serlian system had no such quality. Strengthening buttresses had to be added at the corners between 1677 and 1695. Marshall surmises: 'one cannot help suspecting that Smythson was seduced by the opportunity to try out an innovative scheme'.

103 Christ's Hospital papers, Guildhall MSS 12819 and 12848.

104 I am grateful to the staff of Atherley School, which now occupies Grove Place, for showing me the house and staircase, sending me photographs of the (very authentic looking) 1576 inscribed in the plaster of a room in the west wing and communicating Helen Comley's 'Grove Place: A Record of the Historic Building', April 1998.

105 '. . . the stairs rest on a solid centre composed of oak uprights, bolted together, with the interstices filled in with plaster panels. But inside this centre, which is square, is a service lift, which was used to take up the food etc., to the long gallery at the top of the house. There is a small doorway on each of the floors, and the bottom of the lift is close to the itchen. It was probably worked by a simple pulley and carrier'. *Country Life*, 16 (26 November 1904), p. 778.

106 *Thorpe Drawings*, T113–14, pl. 54. The date of 1588 is recorded by John Aubrey, *The Natural History and Antiquities of Surrey*, 5 vols, London, 1718–19, vol. 1, p. 15.

107 The two Audley End staircases have been much altered (P. J. Drury, 'No other palace in the kingdom will compare with it: The Evolution of Audley End, 1605–1745', *Architectural History*, 23, 1980, pp. 8–9), but the system of continuous newels seems original. Both would have been subsidiary to a great staircase that was never built. For Cranborne, see Royal Commission on the Historical Monuments of England, *Ancient and Historical Monuments in Dorset*, vol. 1: *West*, London, 1952; for Chilham, *Country Life*, 55 (24 and 31 May 1924), pp. 812–19, 858–65.

108 In the surviving fragment of accounts (see chapter 1, note 51), Portington is just paid for providing timber and wainscot for Knole, but it is likely that he was responsible for the staircases.

109 *Royal Works*, vol. IV, p. 354.

110 Stone, 'The Building of Hatfield House', p. 121; *Royal Works, vol. IV, p. 259, n. 3.

111 In the surviving Knole accounts (see chapter 1, note 51), 0269 A1/1, he is paid on 4 March 1608 for 'painting and guilding worke to be by him done and performed in yor 10: Gallery at Knoll', but this is likely to have been preceded by the painting of the staircases.

112 *Country Life*, 27 (26 March 1910), pp. 450–58.

113 For Treowen, see *Country Life*, 128 (27 October 1960), pp. 920–24. The hall screen is dated 1627. Similar impressive, undecorated ground-floor-to-attics staircases are found at Reaside Manor, Shropshire, and Fawley Manor, South Fawley, Oxfordshire.

Chapter 7   Three Architects

1 The section on Robert Smythson is based on my *Robert Smythson and the Elizabethan Country House*, new edn, New Haven and London, 1983, and I have not footnoted it, except for new material or changed judgements since its publication.

2 According to Richard Hall, writing to Sir William Dugdale about a herald's visitation of Derbyshire in 1668: 'There is one Mr Smithson at Boulsover who says they have Armes belonging to his family of Westmorland, but being left yong knows them not' (Adrian Woodhouse, 'In Search of Smythson', *Country Life*, 190, 19 December 1991, pp. 56–8). The only Westmorland Smythsons whom Woodhouse could trace were interrelated families of Crosthwaite and Crosby Ravensworth, the latter tenant farmers of the Bellinghams of Gaythorne. There is no evidence that these Smythsons were ever armigerous.

3 Of buildings attributed, sometimes tentatively, to Robert Smythson in my *Robert Smythson and the Elizabethan Country House*, I now have doubts about Doddington (see chapter 2, note 77), Chastleton, the Hall, Bradford-on-Avon, and Lulworth Castle.

4 In my catalogue of the Smythson drawings (*Smythson Drawings*), I distinguished two handwritings, the first (especially to be found in the records of a visit of 1609, mostly to London) I assigned to Robert, the second (found in the records of a similar visit in 1619) to John. Adrian Woodhouse ('A Newly Identified Estate Plan by John Smythson', *Transactions of the Thoroton Society*, 103, 1999, pp. 125–30) argued, on the basis of a survey of 1608 of Carbarton, near Welbeck, carrying John's signature, that the earlier handwriting is also John's. He is certainly correct; a list of 'glass measured' at Wollaton made and signed by Robert in 1588 (Nottingham University Library, MI 5/165/129) is in a quite different hand. The difference between the handwritings of 1609 and 1619 must represent the chronological development of one man.

The bulk of the more important original designs in the Smythson drawings are uninscribed. Only two are inscribed in a hand I take to be Robert Smythson's: the plan of Wollaton and its outbuildings (1/25 [1]) and the plans of four storeys of an unidentified courtyard house (11/2 [1–4]). The drawings that I assigned to Robert, but which I now believe to be inscribed by John, include: plans of Blackwell in the Peak (1/1 [1–2]), plan of Burton Agnes (1/2), plans for a house for Lord Sheffield (1/18 [1–2]), survey plan of Warwick Castle (1/21), screen elevation for Worksop Manor (1/26), plans, perhaps for Kirkby in Ashfield (11/4 [1–2]), designs for a closet (11/13), designs for round window in round wall, 1599 (11/33).

The Worksop screen elevation is curious. The design must have been made in or (probably) before 1585 (*Girouard, Smythson*, p. 115), but the inscription is in John's hand. It is scarcely conceivable that he was inscribing or making drawings so early. Two explanations seem possible: either the design was made by Robert but inscribed by John at a later date; or it, and possibly others of the more elaborately finished drawings, were drawn subsequent to the date of the original design, perhaps as show drawings to present to prospective clients.

5 The Haddon long gallery wing is usually assigned (e.g., Nikolaus Pevsner, *Buildings of England: Derbyshire*, London, 1953) to the early seventeenth century. But armorial stained glass in one of the windows is dated 1589, and although stained glass can be moved in from elsewhere, the late 1580s is a more likely date. At that period Sir John Manners of Haddon was the right-hand man in the north Midlands of the 6th Earl of Shrewsbury, of Worksop (*House of Commons, Elizabeth*). Haddon is not discussed in *Girouard, Smythson*.

6 I have unfortunately mislaid the name of the correspondent who kindly sent me a drawing of the foundations of Kirkby as revealed by aerial photographs and excavation. These show a plan two-thirds or so of which closely resemble the Smythson drawing; the other third is different, suggesting a possible rebuilding to Smythson's plan of something earlier, which was never completed.

7 Another recent ascription not in *Girouard, Smythson*. The gatehouse design is *Smythson Drawings*, 11/12.

8 Churchwarden Accounts, Charlton Musgrove (Somerset County Record Office, Taunton).

9 The many members of the family recorded in the Charlton Musgrove Parish Registers (Somerset County Record Office, 2/1/1) are always just Goverson up till 1629, with the exception of 'Edward Arnold', born January 1561. From 1629 they are usually 'Goverson alias Arnold' or 'Arnold alias Goverson'. In the churchwardens' accounts they appear just as Goverson until references to John Arnold in 1614, and William and Godfrey Arnold in 1622. In surviving references outside Charlton Musgrove, William, Gabriel, Thomas and Edmund/Edward are always just 'Arnold', starting with 'Godfrey Arnold' working as a mason at Lulworth in 1603. A William Arnold was vicar of Blandford in 1594 (Rachel Lloyd, *Dorset Elizabethans*, London, 1967, p. 261).

10 He was paid for 'seling doors and cubberds in the gallery', 'new crests in the old seling', 'wainscot and seling in the hall' and 'a new door' (Longleat archives, Accts 1554–9, Box LXXXV).

11 They were always at or towards the bottom of lists of rates raised from landowners in the parish, e.g., in 1622: 'James ffarewell Es. 8s., John Ewens gent 3s., Hierome debin, gent. 4s. 2d., Roger Numan 4s., Godfrey Arnold 10d., William Arnold 12d.'.

12 Letter quoted in Nancy Briggs, 'The Foundation of Wadham College, Oxford', *Oxoniensia*, 21 (1956), p. 63. For the foundation of the college, see also C. S. L. Davies, 'A Woman in the Public Sphere: Dorothy Wadham and the Foundation of Wadham College, Oxford', *English Historical Review*, 118 (2003), pp. 883–911.

13 Ibid., p. 64.

14 Ibid., pp. 66–8. Dorothy Wadham's man of

business was called John Arnold, but is unlikely to have been related to William (ibid., p. 63, n. 6).

15 All Wadham College building accounts in College archives. The accounts are drawn on and widely quoted in Sir Thomas Graham Jackson, *Wadham College, Oxford*, Oxford, 1893, pp. 29–51.

16 Joseph and Daniell Rowe, described as 'of Hambdon Hill' by Sir John Strode when he employed them at Chantmarle in Dorset (see p. 29 above). The Rowes were not in the original batch of masons at Wadham, but came as part of a small additional group somewhat later.

17 H. C. Maxwell Lyte, *A History of Dunster and the Families of Mohun and Luttrell*, 2 vols, London, 1909, vol. II, p. 366.

18 For Dunster, see *Country Life*, 182 (16 and 23 July 1987), pp. 102–5, 124–7, reproducing drawings, etc., of the castle before extensive alterations by Salvin.

19 Sebastiano Serlio, *The Five Books of Architecture* [1611], Peake edn, Book III, chapter 4, fol. 19v; Vaughan Hart and Peter Hicks, *Serlio on Architecture*, New Haven and London, 1996, p. 134 [Bramante's Tempietto]; Peake edn, Book III, chapter 4, fol. 48; Hart and Hicks, *Serlio on Architecture*, p. 193 [Janus Quadrifons, Forum Boarium]; Peake edn, Book IV, chapter 8, fol. 50; Hart and Hicks, *Serlio on Architecture*, p. 349 [Corinthian façade, with alcoves on two levels and of two types, normal shells below, reversed above].

20 *Wells-Cole, *Decoration*, p. 152, pls 235–6.

21 Arthur Oswald, *Country Houses of Dorset*, 2nd edn, London, 1959, pp. 123–7; Royal Commission on the Historical Monuments of England, *Ancient and Historical Monuments in Dorset*, vol. V: *East Dorset*, London, 1975, pp. 7–12.

22 For original setting and garden design at Cranborne, see Paula Henderson, *The Tudor House and Garden*, New Haven and London, 2005, p. 107, pls 129–30; Henderson, 'Maps of Cranborne Manor in the 17th Century', *Architectural History*, 44 (2001), pp. 358–64.

23 See chapter 3, note 151, in connection with the similar rustication at Moreton Corbet. It is also found inside the porch at Old Beaupre (see p. 312 above).

24 Henderson, *The Tudor House and Garden*, p. 107, pls 129–30.

25 Oswald, *Country Houses of Dorset*, p. 101 and pl. 110.

26 John Hutchins, *The History and Antiquities of the County of Dorset*, 2 vols, London, 1774, vol. II, p. 461 [1st edn]; reproduced in Oswald, *Country Houses of Dorset*, pl. 66.

27 Oswald, *Country Houses of Dorset*, pls 10 and 12.

28 For Warmwell, see ibid., pp. 93–4, pl. 97; Royal Commission on the Historical Monuments of England, *Ancient and Historical Monuments in Dorset*, vol. II: *South-East*, 3 parts, London, 1970, pt 2, pp. 327–9.

29 For Wolfeton, see Oswald, *Country Houses of Dorset*, pp. 60–66, pls 8, 14, 50–53; *Country Life*, 212 (1 August 2002), pp. 56–60.

30 Oswald, *Country Houses of Dorset*, pl. 13 [Stockton]; pp. 94–6, pls 98–100 [Hanford]; pp. 88–9, pls 88–9 [Herringston]; pls 73–7 [Mapperton]; pp. 92–3, pls 94–6 [Poxwell]; *Country Life*, 132 (11, 18 and 25 October 1962), pp. 840–44, 900–04, 1020–23 [Hall, Bradford-on-Avon]; Henderson, *The Tudor House and Garden*, p. 155, pl. 177 [Edington]. The shell-alcoves at Edington are set in the north front of the north transept of the church, which must then have abutted on the garden.

31 See *Colvin, entry for William Arnold.

32 They are shown in a watercolour by C. J. Richardson, illustrated in the National Trust guidebook to Montacute.

33 See illustrations in John Newman and Nikolaus Pevsner, *Buildings of England: Dorset*, Harmondsworth, 1972, pl. 33; Royal Commission on the Historical Monuments of England, *Ancient and Historical Monuments in Dorset*, vol. III: *Central Dorset*, 2 parts, London, 1970, part 1, pp. 126–7. The *Buildings of England* is undecided as to whether the screen dates from *circa* 1610, when Sir Thomas Freke made alterations and additions to the church, or *circa* 1654, the date of his monument behind the screen. The earlier date is more likely. The screen can be compared with that in the chapel at Wadham College, carved by John Bolton.

34 For the church, see John Hutchins, *The History and Antiquities of the County of Dorset* [1774], 3rd edn, ed. W. Shipp and J. W. Hodson, 4 vols, London, 1861–73, vol. IV, pp. 182–5. An inscription at the beginning of the Parish Register reads: 'Folke Register, new written in the year 1628, in which year the church was new built', and an early entry is to 'Helena Taylor, the first that was buried in the new church', 29 December 1628. This

would suggest that 1628 is the date of the completion of the 'new building', which was perhaps commenced *circa* 1625. Bampfield Chafin, Lord of the Manor, who probably paid for or largely contributed to the re-building, was the stepson of Sir George Trenchard, of Wolfeton.

35 For Leweston, see Hutchins, *The History*, ed. Shipp and Hodson, vol. IV, pp. 128–32; Royal Commission on the Historical Monuments of England, *Ancient and Historical Monuments in Dorset*, vol. I: *West*, London, 1952, pp. 132–3. Heraldry in the chapel gable is dated 1616. Sir John Fitz-James had inherited Leweston from his stepfather, John Leweston, in 1584; it was he who erected the monument to Leweston and his wife in Sherborne Abbey, attributed to Alan Maynard, in the chapel that he had purchased from the vicar and churchwardens as a family burial place (Hutchins, *The History*, ed. Shipp and Hodson, vol. IV, p. 129, giving no date). The present Leweston House dates from the 1770s; Hutchins laments that 'the noble mansion at Leweston has been to the regret of many admirers of ancient grandeur, entirely pulled down', apparently without record. He quotes Coker as saying that it had been 'much beautified' by Fitz-James, and refers to a coat of arms on the house (as recorded British Library, Harleian MS 1437, fol. 43), quartering Fitz-James and Leweston and dated 1600.

36 The relationships can be worked out in the detailed family trees printed in Hutchins, *The History*, ed. Shipp and Hodson, e.g., Trenchard, vol. III, pp. 326–7; Leweston and Fitz-James, vol. IV, pp. 129–30.

Because I cannot sufficiently substantiate it, I must leave to a footnote my suspicion of a relationship between William Arnold and Alan Maynard (perhaps working together on the gatehouse at Clifton Maybank), and of the possibility that Arnold had worked under Maynard and inherited his connections. Combinations of Maynard-style and Arnold-style work are found at the Hall, Bradford-on-Avon, possibly at Stockton House, at Sherborne Abbey and Leweston (for Sir John Fitz-James), and at Wolfeton House.

37 Inscribed in one of the south windows of the chapel is the following: 'Johannes Fitzjames me struxit in honorem Stae Trinitatis pro antiqua capella dilapidata per multos annos'.

38 The derivations are as follows (all references to *Thorpe Drawings*):

Serlio: T37–8, pls 16–17, explanatory perspective drawing based on Serlio's Second Book; T127, pl. 59, sketch from the Tragic Scene in Second Book.

Vredeman de Vries: T24, pl. 9, 'house for a nobleman, 1600', façade based on *Architectura*; T26, pl. 10, gable from *Variae Architecturae Formae*; T60, pl. 28, term from *Caryatidum*.

Du Cerceau: T71, pl. 34, house in perspective, based on *Leçons de Perspective Positive*, 1576; T75–6, pl. 36: *Plus Excellents Bastiments*, I (1576) [Ancy le France]; T77–8, pl. 37, ibid. [Château de Madrid]; T165, pl. 76, ibid. [Saint-Germain-en-Laye].

Blum: T13–14, pl. 5, the Five Orders, based on *Quinque Columnarum* (1550, and numerous subsequent editions).

Palladio: see note 54.

39 Hans Blum, *The Book of Five Columns of Architecture . . . Translated out of Latine into English by I. T.*, London, 1601; 2nd edn, 1608. Thorpe's redrawing of Blum (see note 38) makes it highly probable that I. T. stands for Iohannes Thorpe.

40 Thorpe's copy of Du Cerceau's *Leçons de Perspective Positive* (Paris, 1576), together with his translation, is in the Bodleian Library, Oxford (LL 23*Art. Seld). See article by K. J. Hoeltgen in *England and the Continental Renaissance*, ed. E. Chaney and P. Mack, Woodbridge, 1990.

41 Summerson's 'The Life of John Thorpe', in *Thorpe Drawings*, pp. 5–6.

42 *Thorpe Drawings*, pp. 1–2.

43 Thorpe's visit seems a reasonable deduction from the combination of Nevill's letter (see note 44) and Thorpe's plan of the Parisian house of Sebastian Zamet, annotated 'Monsieur Jammet in Paris his howse 1600' (*Thorpe Drawings*, T163, pl. 78). The plan is not known to have been engraved, and Thorpe's annotations suggest he had visited it in person. Plans of the Palais du Luxembourg in Paris (T123–4, T127–8, pls 58–9), dated 1 November 1621, suggest a second visit.

44 *Thorpe Drawings*, p. 4, quoting from Historical Manuscripts Commission, *Calendar of the Manuscripts of the Most Honourable the Marquess of Salisbury . . . Preserved at Hatfield House, Hertfordshire*, 24 vols, London, 1883–1976, vol. X, p. 140.

45 *Thorpe Drawings*, p. 6.

46 The payments are in the Rutland archive, Belvoir Castle, account-book no. 144, and elevation. Belvoir, map 164 (*Colvin, entry for John Thorpe). The work involved (long since demolished) was a new gallery on the south front between the Rosse and Stanton towers, on the first floor with central access to a 'Balcone' supported on pillars. (I am grateful to Howard Colvin for sending me his sketch of this plan.)

47 See note 38.

48 The second edition of the Blum translation was published by Woutmeel's widow in 1608 (Eileen Harris and Nicholas Savage, *British Architectural Books and Writers*, Cambridge, 1990, p. 121).

49 *Thorpe Drawings*, T225–6, pl. 105.

50 Ibid., T235–6, pl. 108 [Condover]; T207–10, T90, pls 94–5 [Babraham]; T229, T231–2, pls 106–107, T213–14, T119, T219, pls 98–9 [related].

51 See *Victoria History of the Counties of England: A History of Shropshire*, vol. VIII, ed. A. T. Gaydon, London, 1968, pp. 39–40, based on building accounts, etc., in Corbet papers, now in Shrewsbury Archive. John Richmond, of Acton Reynold, Shropshire, contracted with Owen to build a house at Condover in 1589, but this may not have been to the Thorpe design. In 1592 Lawrence Shipway, a mason who had worked on the church at Standish in Lancashire, and on the Shire Hall in Stafford, was paid for visits to Condover 'to sett forward the worke' (Malcolm Airs, 'Lawrence Shipway, Freemason', *Architectural History*, 27, 1984, pp. 368–73). By then Richmond had disappeared, and the principal mason seems to have been Walter Hancock. The house was still unfinished in 1598, when Owen died, and left his son Roger 'all my provysons for building' in his will (Prerogative Court of Canterbury, 15 Kidd, 1599).

52 For Palavicino and Babraham, see Lawrence Stone, *An Elizabethan: Sir Horatio Palavicino*, Oxford, 1956, pp. 271–6, and especially the detailed manuscript description of the Elizabethan house by the antiquary William Cole, who was born and brought up nearby (British Library, Add. MS 5819, fols 176–8). This clearly identifies Thorpe's plans T207–10 and T90 as for Babraham; Summerson had unconvincingly identified them as of Hinchingbrooke, Huntingdonshire. But the grand semicircular window at Hinchingbrooke, dated 1602, was probably built in emulation of the similar window shown in Thorpe's plan of Babraham; Sir Oliver Cromwell, who built it, married Palavicino's widow, and his son and heir married Palavicino's daughter.

53 In 1595 Francis Newport, when suggesting Walter Hancock as the builder for Shrewsbury Market Hall, wrote: 'Mr Justice Owen would recommend him' (Shropshire Archives, 3365/2621/9).

54 Directly from Palladio, *I Quattro Libri dell'Architettura*, Venice, 1570; *Thorpe Drawings*, T34, pl. 14 (Palladio, Book II, p. 52); T141, pl. 64 (Palladio, Book II, p. 59). Related: T85, T86, pl. 40; T152, pl. 70; T182, pl. 84 [Holdenby banqueting house]; T178, pl. 81; T202, pl. 96 [Somerhill]; T254, pl. 116; possibly T257, pl. 117.

55 For Ashley Park, see M. Blackman, 'Ashley Park Building Accounts, 1602–1607', *Surrey Record Society*, 29 (1977).

56 *Thorpe Drawings*, T29, pl. 12. The elevation is inscribed 'Sir Fraunces Willoughby', and is drawn in ink on scored lines; Willoughby died in 1596.

57 For Plas Teg, see Peter Smith in *Flintshire Historical Society Publications*, 18 (1960), pp. 157–62; Smith, *Houses of the Welsh Countryside*, London, 1975; *Country Life*, 132 (19 July 1962), pp. 134–7. Its plan was inspired by that of Ashley Park, a plan of which is among the Trevor Papers in West Sussex County Record Office (Nicholas Cooper, *Houses of the Gentry, 1480–1680*, New Haven and London, 1999, pl. 135 and caption to pl. 156). The Trevor Papers show that Sir John Trevor had an interest in the property by 1609; there is no documentation for the erection of the house; one could guess *circa* 1615. The centre of the entrance front, with its distinctive broken and curved pediments, has been considered a later rebuild, but there is a similar motif on the early seventeenth-century tomb of Trevor's father, also John, in Gresford Church, Denbighshire (illustrated in *Country Life*, 132, 12 July 1962, p. 80).

58 For Eagle House, see Cooper, *Houses of the Gentry*, p. 136 and pls 133–4, including plans of the ground and first floors. It was probably built in 1613, for Robert Bell, one of the founders of the East India Company.

59 For Charlton House, see *Country Life*, 25

(1 and 8 May 1909), pp. 630–38, 666–75; Cooper, *Houses of the Gentry*, p. 136 and pls 136–7, including plans of the ground and second floors. The house was built by Adam Newton, tutor to Prince Henry, who was married to the daughter of the wealthy Lord Keeper Sir John Puckering (1544–1596). He acquired the manor, jointly with his wife, in May 1607 (John G. Smith, *Charlton*, privately printed, 1970), but the house may not have been started until a few years later. The chapel was consecrated in 1616 (Daniel Lysons, *The Environs of London*, 2nd edn, London, 1811, citing papers in the possession of Lady Wilson, the then owner). Lysons says it was built 'about the year 1612', giving no source.

60 See pp. 5–6 above.

61 See p. 93 above.

62 For Leighton Bromswold, see catalogue entry in *Thorpe Drawings*, pp. 64–5. The house has been demolished; the gatehouse survives.

63 Holland House is widely thought of as having been gutted or largely destroyed in the war of 1939–45 ('destroyed by fire as a result of enemy action in 1941'; *Thorpe Drawings*, p. 71), but photographs taken in the early 1950s (photographic collection, Kensington Public Library) show it with some damage to the roof and upper storey, but otherwise complete and eminently restorable. Apart from the pathetic survival of the restored and partially rebuilt east wing, and portions of the lower façades, it was demolished in the years 1955–7.

64 For Cope Castle, later Holland House, see references in *Northern Kensington*, Survey of London, vol. XXXVII, London, 1973, pp. 25, 55n. But the volume deliberately excluded a full account of Holland House, with unrealised hopes that it 'may form the subject of a separate monograph at a later date' (ibid., p. 101n). The complicated early history of Sir Walter Cope's land purchases and building in Kensington is still in need of clarification. He originally lived in another house there, where he had the 'cabinet of curiosities' remarked on by travellers. Although he had bought the area known as West Town, on which Cope Castle was to be built, in 1591, it was subject to an existing lease, and he seems not to have got possession of it until some unspecified date in the early seventeenth century. The small rectangular lodge with northern staircase turret that

appears from Thorpe's plan to have been the core of the house may have been built by a previous owner or leaseholder, but if so it was embellished by Cope, first with bay windows, porch and east and west extensions ending in identical staircase turrets, then by further long eastern and western wings and south and east loggias. Thorpe's plan T93 is not a survey, but a project for demolishing the staircase turrets and adding the final wings (drawing inscribed 'Sr Walter Coap at Kensington pfected p me JT'). The design was largely carried out, except that the turrets were retained and incorporated in the extended house, which as a result was slightly wider than projected in Thorpe's drawing. In writing about a visit to 'Cope Castle' on 7 July 1608, John Chamberlain wrote: 'We had the honor to see all, but touch nothing so much as a cherry which are dailie preserved for the Quenes comming'. This sounds like a first viewing of Cope's stage 1. James I stayed there in November 1612, and, according to Chamberlain, again: 'The King was quickly wearie of Kensington, because he saide the wind blew through the walles that he could not lie warme in his bed'. Could this have been because stage two was not quite completed? (John Chamberlain, *The Letters*, 2 vols, ed. N. E. McClure, Philadelphia, 1939, vol. 1, pp. 258, 390–91.) Cope died in 1614.

65 For Aston Hall, see Oliver Fairclough, 'John Thorpe and Aston Hall', *Architectural History*, 32 (1989), pp. 30–51.

66 See chapter 4, note 64.

Chapter 8 Gothic

1 G. Vasari, *The Lives of the Painters, Sculptors and Architects* [1550], trans. Gaston de Vere, ed. D. Ekserdjian, 2 vols, London, 1996 [Everyman edn], vol. 1, p. 43.

2 The earliest example I know of is Henry Wotton, fresh back from Italy in 1624, urging his countrymen to abandon pointed arches to 'their first inventors, the Goths, or Lumbards, amongst other reliques of that barbarous age' (Henry Wotton, *The Elements of Architecture*, London, 1624, p. 51). Though intervening examples no doubt exist, the next I have come across are John Aubrey, probably in the 1670s, writing on how Roman architecture degenerated 'into what we call Gothick by the inundation of

the Goths . . . this barbarous fashion continued till Henry 7th of England . . .' (*Chronologia Architectonica*, quoted in H. M. Colvin, 'Aubrey's *Chronologia Architectonica*', in *Concerning Architecture: Essays on Architectural Writers and Writing Presented to Nikolaus Pevsner*, London, 1968, p. 4), and Roger North: 'In the whole the Gothick manner looks great at first and the more you are acquainted with it the more you despise it', and 'a mode introduced by a barbarous sort of people that first distrest then dissolved the Roman Empire' (from 'Architecture' [*circa* 1690], and 'Of Building' [*circa* 1696], in *Of Building: Roger North's Writings on Architecture*, ed. Howard Colvin and John Newman, Oxford, 1981, pp. 108, 110).

3 John Nichols, *The Progresses and Public Processions of Queen Elizabeth*, 3 vols, London, 1823, vol. 1, p. 163.

4 William Camden, *Britain*, trans. P. Holland, London, 1610, p. 487 [King's College, Cambridge]; p. 429 [Henry VII's Lady Chapel]; p. 248 [Salisbury cathedral]; p. 539 [Lincoln cathedral].

5 Edward Hubbard, *Buildings of Wales: Clwyd*, Harmondsworth, 1986, pp. 145–6; Laurence Butler, 'Leicester's Church, Denbigh: An Experiment in Puritan Worship', *Journal of the British Archaeological Association*, vol. 37, 1974, pp. 40–62.

6 See Malcolm Airs, 'Lawrence Shipway, Freemason', *Architectural History*, 27 (1984), pp. 368–73.

7 For new or rebuilt churches and enlarged churches in the period, see Maurice Howard, *The Building of Elizabethan and Jacobean England*, New Haven and London, 2007, pp. 61–71.

8 Inscription given by Thomas Clifford, *Topographical and Historical Description of the Parish of Tixall* (1817), quoting the manuscript Thomas Loxdale *Parochial Antiquities of Staffordshire*. The top portions of two Gothic windows, one with tracery, are shown in the engraving of Tixall in Robert Plot, *The Natural History of Staffordshire*, Oxford, 1686. A fine drawing of 1838, drawn from inside the ruins of the Hall and depicting the former of these windows in its entirety, is reproduced in the Landmark Trust's excellent *Album* on Tixall; I am most grateful to Caroline Stanford of the Trust for sending me a photocopy of the *Album*.

9 The windows of Harlaxton Old Hall are shown in drawings made by James Deeson

for Anthony Salvin in 1831 (Drawings Collection of the Royal Institute of British Architects) and in an oil painting (?early nineteenth century) belonging to the Welby family, but in 1978 on loan to Harlaxton. These are reproduced in Russell Read, *Harlaxton*, Grantham, 1978. An engraving is reproduced in *Harlaxton Manor*, by Pamela Tudor-Craig and others, Norwich, n. d., published for Harlaxton College, the British campus of the University of Evansville, Indiana. For Steane, see John Heward and Robert Taylor, *The Country Houses of Northamptonshire*, Royal Commission on the Historical Monuments of England, Swindon, 1996, pp. 309–11, reproducing a drawing of the main front by Peter Tillemans (British Library, Add. MS 32467, fol. 235).

10 I am grateful to John Goodall for pointing this out to me. But the conoids at Lacock are left plain; perhaps they were originally painted with tracery, or painting was intended.

11 The vault features in Lord Coleraine's verse description of Longford, written *circa* 1690:

Ten polisht Columns hold up roof and all,
Whose Pendant Centre is of massy Stone
Which for this hundred years uncrackt
   hangs down
Pointing at hard tasks to Architects
Than the Pantheon's open round detects.

(Quoted in *Country Life*, 70, 19 December 1931, p. 702.)

12 For Burghley, see pp. 185–90 above. For Castle Ashby and Drayton, see Heward and Taylor, *The Country Houses of Northamptonshire*, pp. 129–39, 175–88.

13 The valuation of the castle made *circa* 1606 listed 'a chimney pece & pells of tuchestone in ye presence with one of Allablaster curiously wrought in ye privy chamber, & one other of freestone in the great chamber'. The three together valued at £50 (British Library, Cotton MS Tiberius E VIII, fol. 212v). The chimneypiece now in the gatehouse was probably the second of these.

14 Hatfield, CP 143/35: 'Platt of ye upper sylyg of my tower at Thebalds'.

15 Quoted in G. W. O. Addleshaw and Frederick Etchells, *The Architectural Setting of Anglican Worship*, London, 1948, pp. 30–31.

16 John Stow, 'The Singularities of the City of London', in *The Survey of London* [1598], ed. Henry B. Wheatley, London, [1912], pp. 238–9.

17 'Arminian' is a convenient term, used at the time, for the High Church movement of the period, and does not imply an exact correlation with the teaching of the Dutch theologian Jacobus Arminius (or Harmenszoon). There is much disagreement, and a great deal written, about the context, importance and influence of English Arminianism; for one view and a statement of (and attack on) opposing views, see Nicholas Tyacke, 'Anglican Attitudes: Some Recent Writings on English Religious History, from the Reformation to the Civil War', in his *Aspects of English Protestantism, c. 1530–1700*, Manchester, 2001, pp. 172–200.

18 Illustrated in P. J. Drury, 'No other palace in the kingdom will compare with it: The Evolution of Audley End, 1605–1745', *Architectural History*, 23 (1980), pp. 1–39. For private chapels in general, see Annabel Ricketts, *The English Country House Chapel: Building a Protestant Tradition*, Reading, 2007.

19 For work in Oxford University in this period, see especially John Newman, 'The Architectural Setting', in *The History of the University of Oxford*, vol. IV: *Seventeenth-century Oxford*, ed. Nicholas Tyacke, Oxford, 1997, pp. 135–77; for Lincoln's Inn chapel, see *The Records of the Honourable Society of Lincoln's Inn: The Black Books*, ed. J. Douglas Walker, London, 1897–1902, vol. II, pp. 209, 243, 246–9. For Peterhouse chapel, see *Willis and Clark, Cambridge*, vol. I, pp. 40–50. It was originally built of brick, but was refaced with ashlar and more fittings, including stained glass, introduced by John Cosin, who succeeded Wren as Master in 1635. Only the impressive east window, depicting the *Crucifixion*, survives of the glass. The pretty four-centred arcades, with Gothic windows above to either side of the chapel, as shown in Loggan's engraving, were rebuilt in conventional classical style in 1709.

20 C. Gapper, J. Newman and A. Ricketts, 'The Chapel and Antechamber to the Chapel at Hatfield: A Reconstruction of Their Interiors', in *Patronage, Culture and Power: The Early Cecils, 1558–1612*, ed. Pauline Croft, New Haven and London, 2002, pp. 88–93.

21 The side windows February to April 1612, the east window May to September 1612. Sir Thomas Graham Jackson, *Wadham College, Oxford*, Oxford, 1893, pp. 161–71, quoting agreement with Van Ling(e) 'of Emden in East Freesland'.

22 For the Van Linge family, see Michael Archer, 'English Painted Glass in the Seventeenth Century: The Early Work of Abraham van Linge', *Apollo*, 101 (January 1975), pp. 26–30.

23 East window, Wadham College chapel, Oxford, 1621–2. Mildmay-Fane chapel, parish church, Apethorpe, Northamptonshire, dated 1621. Chapel, Easton Lodge, Essex, *circa* 1621. Possibly chapel (later parish church), Low Ham, Somerset, chapel endowed 1622. See note 25 below. Chapel, Buckden Palace, Huntingdonshire, 1620s. Lincoln College chapel, Oxford, 1626–30. Peterhouse College chapel, Cambridge, *circa* 1632. Queen's College chapel, Oxford, 1635. The window depicting the *Ascension* at Abbey Dore, Herefordshire, dated 1634, seems the earliest surviving east window of this period in a parish church depicting a scene from the life of Christ.

24 See Sherfield entry in *ODNB*. Tyacke, 'Anglican Attitudes', pp. 150, 195.

25 The deed of endowment of the chapel is dated 10 June 1622. Hext's will, dated 10 November 1623, proved 11 May 1624, laid down that he 'is to be buried in the North Isle of the Chapple of Netherham under a tomb which I have caused to be made there' (G. D. Stawell, *A Quantock Family: The Stawells of Cothelstone and their Descendants . . .*, Taunton, 1910, pp. 472–3; *Abstracts of Somersetshire Wills, etc., Copied from the Manuscript Collections of the Late Rev. Frederick Brown*, ed. F. A. Crisp, 6 vols, [London], 1887–90, vol. II, p. 57). The stained glass in the east window, depicting the *Crucifixion*, dates from 1669; perhaps it replaces a Jacobean *Crucifixion* destroyed under the Commonwealth. It is uncertain whether its distinctive tracery (illustrated in Nikolaus Pevsner, *Buildings of England: South and West Somerset*, Harmondsworth, 1958, p. 21) is of the date of the glass or the original build. The chapel was clearly completed by the time of Hext's death; the inscription recorded in John Collinson, *The History and Antiquities of the County of Somerset*, 3 vols, Bath, 1791, vol. III, p. 445, must refer to

post-Restoration or Commonwealth refurbishment in the 1660s.

26 See Arthur Oswald, *Country Houses of Dorset*, 2nd edn, London, 1959, p. 97.

27 Philip Morant, *The History and Antiquities of the County of Essex*, 2 vols [1762–8]; reprinted 1816 and 1978, vol. II, p. 431, and engraving. Two short undated poems by Robert Aylet, on the consecration of the chapel, are in his collected *Divine and Moral Speculations in Metrical Numbers*, 1654, last section, pp. 90–93. One is dedicated to William, Lord Maynard:

> The Father built the Palace in his days
> But leaves God's house unto his prudent Son,
> Who Numa-like now plants Religion,
> Where Romulus the first Foundation lays . . .

28 See Nikolaus Pevsner, *Buildings of England: Cumberland and Westmorland*, Harmondsworth, 1967, pp. 61–2; 2nd edn, rev. Bridget Cherry, 2000, pls 41 and 43, entry for Arthuret and Warwick, Whoof House.

29 For St Katherine Cree and other London churches of this period, see John Newman, 'Laudian Literature and the Interpretation of Caroline Churches in London', in *Art and Patronage in the Caroline Courts: Essays in Honour of Sir Oliver Millar*, ed. David Howarth, Cambridge, 1993, pp. 176–80; J. F. Merritt, 'Puritans, Laudians and the Phenomenon of Church-Building in Jacobean London', *Historical Journal*, 41 (1998), pp. 935–60; Thomas Cocke, 'Le Gothique anglais sous Charles I', *Revue de l'Art*, 30 (1975), pp. 21–30; Peter Lake, *The Boxmaker's Revenge: 'Orthodoxy', 'Heterodoxy' and the Politics of the Parish in Early Stuart London*, Manchester, 2001, pp. 298–311. Lake calls it 'the epitome of a new model Laudian Church'. The earlier church at St Giles-in-the-Fields (1623–5, rebuilt 1731–3) was similar in style and liturgical background to St Katherine Cree; the two churches were consecrated by Laud in the same year.

30 For St Nicholas, Rochester, see John Newman, *Buildings of England: Kent, West Kent and the Weald*, Harmondsworth, 1969, pp. 469–70.

31 See J. E. Stocks, 'The Church of St John the Evangelist, New Briggate, Leeds', *Publications of the Thoresby Society*, 24 (1919), appendix, p. 217. The joiner and plasterer was Francis Gunby, who had also worked at Gawthorpe (see chapter 1, p. 34 and note 96), and carved the choir screen in Wakefield cathedral, pp. 163–5.

32 See Nikolaus Pevsner, *Buildings of England: Northamptonshire*, Harmondsworth, 1961.

33 Terrington St Clement, in Nikolaus Pevsner, *Buildings of England: Norfolk, North-West and South*, Harmondsworth, 1962. Langley Marish, discussed and illustrated by John Harris in 'A Rare and Precious Room: The Kederminster Library, Langley, Buckinghamshire', *Country Life*, 162 (1 December 1977), pp. 1576–8.

34 See Canon Eric Rothwell, *The Misericords and Screen in Cartmel Priory*, 1997, and *Cartmel Priory*, n. d., guides on sale in the church, using material from James Stockdale, *Annales Caermoclenes; or, Annals of Cartmel*, 1872. *Cartmel Priory* illustrates two early nineteenth-century engravings showing the ceilings.

35 See John Harington to Burghley, 1595, printed in Harington, *Nugae Antiquae*, vol. I, London, 1804, p. 185. 'Our work at the Bathe dothe go on *haud passibus aequis* . . . but it seemeth more like a church than it has aforetime'; Harington to Thomas Sutton, 13 June 1608: 'The tower, the quire, the two isles, are all ready finished by Master Billet executor to the worthie Lord Treasurer Burghleigh; the walls are up ready for covering'; Harington to Sutton, 5 September 1608: 'Saynt Billet the benefactor of this church' (N. E. McClure, ed., *The Letters and Epigrams of Sir John Harington*, Philadelphia, 1930, pp. 130–31, 134–5); J. Ede and R. Symons, *Heraldry in the Vault of Bath Abbey*, n. d., on sale in church; 'Great Church Accot: A Brife of Mr Walter Chapmans accompt for the greate churche worke in Bath' (in Bath Chamberlains Account, No. 6, Bath Record Office), apparently an abstract of expenditure under Bishop Montagu, 1608–19, including 'paid to Yarrington for vatting the tower' £8 10s., and £80 10s. 'to the plaisterer', regrettably not named. Engravings showing the nave with its plasterwork ceiling are reproduced in James Lees-Milne and David Ford, *Images of Bath*, Richmond upon Thames, 1982, Gallery nos. 95, 97, 100–04.

36 For Carfax, see *Colvin, entry for John Clarke, and *Wells-Cole, *Decoration*, p. 149 and figs 241–2, reproducing the engraving. Wells-Cole attributes Carfax to William Arnold; but Clarke's work is fully documented, and Carfax was built well after Arnold had left Oxford. For the Bristol cross, see Bristol Record Office, Bristol audit Book F/AD/I/21.

37 For all this work, see Newman, 'The Architectural Setting', and *Colvin, entry for Akroyd.

38 This reference has been mislaid.

39 See J. Newman, 'Oxford Libraries before 1800', *Archaeological Journal*, 135 (1978), pp. 248–57; Howard Colvin, *The Canterbury Quadrangle: St John's College, Oxford*, Oxford, 1988, pp. 56–78.

40 *Willis and Clark, *Cambridge*, vol. II, pp. 263–71. Nikolaus Pevsner, *Buildings of England: Cambridgeshire*, 2nd edn, Harmondsworth, 1970, pp. 148–9. Henry Man, a carpenter and builder active in Cambridge *circa* 1615–34, was paid seven guineas in 1624 'for drawing of Plots for the Librarie, and his jorneyes to London and Northampton' (*Willis and Clark, *Cambridge*, vol. II, p. 267). 'Ashly' (possible Thomas Thorpe's nephew John Ashly, see *Thorpe Drawings*, p. 9 and n. 6) was paid in September 1624 'for his pt in working a tracery window' (*Willis and Clark, *Cambridge*, vol. II, p. 267).

41 Williams also paid for the richly furnished new chapel at Lincoln College, Oxford, 1631. But he was not an Arminian, was no friend to Laud, and wrote against east-end altars in churches; John Newman suggested that the Broadway chapel in Westminster, 1635–42, was built auditorium-fashion under his influence as an anti-Laudian model (Newman, 'Laudian Literature and the Interpretation of Caroline Churches in London'; and see Peter Guillery, 'Suburban Models, or Calvinism and Continuity in London's Seventeenth-century Church Architecture', *Architectural History*, 48, 2005, especially pp. 72–82).

42 See Colvin, *The Canterbury Quadrangle*, Appendix VI, p. 119: 'The Porch at St Mary's Church, Oxford'. Jackson had worked on the completion of the Canterbury Quad at St John's. Charles Stoakes claimed that the porch had been 'desind and built' by his uncle, Nicholas Stone. No supporting evidence has come to light, and the porch was certainly 'built' by Jackson.

The chapel at Burford Priory, Oxfordshire, built in a similar classical-Gothic mix, was consecrated in 1662; but since no religious buildings were consecrated under the Commonwealth, it is worth surmising whether it could have been built, or at least started, in the late 1640s.

43 Illustrated in Andor Gomme and Alison Maguire, *Design and Plan in the Country House*, New Haven and London, 2008, fig. 52.

44 *Willis and Clark, *Cambridge*, vol. 1, p. 95, dates the east range, in which the gatehouse is incorporated, but gives no individual payment for the vault.

45 Anthony Wood, *The History and Antiquities of the Colleges and Halls in the University of Oxford*, ed. John Gutch, Oxford, 1786–90, p. 456; John Peshall, *The Antient and Present State of the City of Oxford* (based on Wood), London, 1773, p. 126.

46 So Christopher Potter, Provost of Queen's College, as reported in *The Diary of Thomas Crosfield*, ed. F. S. Boas, London, 1935, p. 7, entry for 13 December 1634: 'The Deane of Christ Church knew not how to have proceeded but for him'.

47 Colvin, *The Canterbury Quadrangle*, pp. 6–7.

48 Ibid., pp. 44–5.

49 See probate account by his widow Mary, 4 August 1635 (Oxford, Bodleian Library, MS HYP B9/86–7). He died intestate. I am grateful to Howard Colvin for abstracting the acount for me. See also my 'Smith and the Hall Staircase', in *Christ Church Oxford: A Portrait of the House*, ed. Christopher Butler, London, 2006, pp. 49–51.

50 Oswald, *Country Houses of Dorset*, p. 97 and pp. 58–60.

51 See John Heward and Robert Taylor, *The Country Houses of Northamptonshire*, Royal Commission on the Historical Monuments of England, Swindon, 1996, pp. 109–11, and for the identification of the Thorpe plan, chapter 2, note 53. The entrance door at Brockhall is a virtual duplicate of the door at the base of the main staircase at Knole, which has the Thorpe mason's mark. Brockhall is built of local ironstone, not Kingscliffe oolite, but this need not have precluded Henry Thorpe acting as surveyor.

52 For Stapleford, see *Country Life*, 56 (23 August 1924), pp. 288–90.

53 Robert Withington, *English Pageantry: An Historical Outline*, 2 vols, Cambridge, Massachusetts, 1918–20, vol. 1, p. 113.

54 Abigail Wheatley, *The Idea of the Castle in Medieval England*, York, 2004, p. 103.

55 Ibid., pp. 94–8.

56 For Neville, see *ODNB. He was the second son of Sir Richard Neville, 2nd Baron Latimer (1468–1530).

57 Withington, *English Pageantry*, vol. 11, p. 198.

58 Roger Ascham, *The Schoolmaster* [1570], 1934 edn, p. 74.

59 Henry Goldwyn's contemporary description of the Triumph is given in full in Katherine Duncan-Jones, ed., *Sir Philip Sidney: A Critical Edition of the Major Works*, Oxford, 1989, Appendix A, pp. 299–311.

60 The pioneering studies are Frances A. Yates, 'Elizabethan Chivalry: The Romance of the Accession Day Tilts', *Journal of the Warburg and Courtauld Institutes*, 20 (1957), pp. 4–25; and Roy C. Strong, 'The Popular Celebration of the Accession Day of Queen Elizabeth I', *Journal of the Warburg and Courtauld Institutes*, 21 (1958), pp. 86–103.

61 The tilts are listed in Stephen Orgel and Roy Strong, *Inigo Jones: The Theatre of the Stuart Court*, 2 vols, London, Berkeley and Los Angeles, 1973, vol. 1, pp. 179–80.

62 Sir Philip Sidney, *The Countess of Pembroke's Arcadia*, ed. A. Feuillerat, Cambridge, 1912, pp. 282–8.

63 Quoted in G. C. Williamson, *George, Third Earl of Cumberland*, Cambridge, 1920, pp. 108–9.

64 Shown in the well-known depiction of the event, now at Hampton Court.

65 Shown in the engraving accompanying the contemporary description of the event, reproduced in Nichols, *The Progresses and Public Processions of Queen Elizabeth*, vol. III, pp. 101–21; *Girouard, *Smythson*, pl. 137. An earlier edition of the description showed a different design of castle, perhaps surmise on the part of the engraver.

66 Orgel and Strong, *Inigo Jones*, pp. 216–18, pls 63–4.

67 British Library, Royal MS 17 CXXXV: 'A description of the severall fireworks . . .' with illustrations.

68 Shown in the engraving is the celebration of the games *Annalia Dubrensia*, ed. M. Walbancke, London, 1636, reprinted 1700, 1877, 1878; C. Whitfield, *Robert Dover and the Cotswold Games*, London, 1962, p. 68.

69 Orgel and Strong, *Inigo Jones*, pp. 208–9.

70 For the widespread belief that keeps in English castles were built by Julius Caesar, or at least of Roman origin, see, for example, Willyam Slatyer's marginal note in his verse *History of Great Britanie*, 1621, sg L3: 'They say Caesar built the Castles of Dover, Canterbury and Rochester, and the Tower of London, though the Roman storie maketh no mention thereof.' The Tower of London had been assigned to Caesar since at least the fourteenth century, and is twice so ascribed by Shakespeare (see Homer Nearing, Jr, 'Local Caesar Traditions in Britain', *Speculum*, 24, 1949, pp. 218–27. I am grateful to Clare Gapper for bringing this article and related Roman and Caesar material to my notice). The keep at Kenilworth was known as Caesar's Tower by the 1570s, when Laneham referred to it: 'the Castle hath one auncient strong and large Keep that is called Ceazarz Tour, rather (az I have good cauz to think) for that it iz square and high foormed than that ever he bylt it' (quoted in Nichols, *The Progresses and Public Processions of Queen Elizabeth*, vol. 1, p. 428, with a footnote reference to William of Malmesbury, Book 1). Camden, in *Britannia*, referred to the tradition and dismissed it.

The Leicester Building forms a lantern tower, balancing but contrasting with the keep. Spicer's letter (Longleat, Dudley Papers, 11, fol. 321; see chapter 5, note 23) also refers to the keep at 'Seseres toure', and shows that the relationship was carefully considered, in contrast to the earlier scheme (see also chapter 5, note 23), which masked the keep with the new building. I am grateful to Elizabeth Goldring for bringing this letter to my attention.

71 Notably the inconspicuous façades of Hawthorne's gallery wing. See W. H. St J. Hope, *Windsor Castle*, vol. 1 (1913), pp. 276–8.

72 For Wardour, see *Girouard, *Smythson*, pp. 78–82; *Country Life*, 189 (14 and 21 February 1991), p. 44–9, 76–9.

73 The façade, including the Tower of the Orders, is usually assigned to the early part of the seventeenth century (Nikolaus Pevsner, *Buildings of England: Northumberland*, Harmondsworth, 1957; *Country Life*, 33, 18 March 1913, p. 346), but a date in the 1590s is at least as likely. Lord Burghley was in friendly correspondence with the owner of the time, Sir Ralph Grey.

74 For Lulworth, see J. Manco, D. Greenhalf and M. Girouard, 'Lulworth Castle in the

Seventeenth Century', *Architectural History*, 33 (1990), pp. 29–53. The Bindon quote is in a letter to Robert Cecil (July 1608: Historical Manuscripts Commission, *Calendar of the Manuscripts of the Most Honourable the Marquess of Salisbury . . . Preserved at Hatfield House, Hertfordshire*, 24 vols, London, 1883–1976, vol. XIX, p. 310). For Gerard, see chapter five, note 3. The fragments of building accounts are now in Dorset Record Office, D/WLC.E2.

75　For Ruperra, see Royal Commission on Historical Monuments (Wales), *An Inventory of the Ancient Monuments in Glamorgan*, vol. IV: *Domestic Architecture from the Reformation to the Industrial Revolution*, pt I: *The Greater Houses*, Cardiff, 1981, pp. 262–8, and Thomas Morgan's entry in *House of Commons, Elizabeth*. The gabled dormers are shown in a drawing by Thomas Dyneley, reproduced in Dyneley, *The Account of the Progress of His Grace, Henry, the First Duke of Beaufort through Wales*, ed. R. Banks, London, 1888.

76　John Aubrey, *The Natural History of Wiltshire*, ed. John Britton, London, 1847, p. 88.

77　See John Collinson, *The History and Antiquities of the County of Somerset*, 3 vols, Bath, 1791, vol. III, pp. 169–70. He calls it 'Walton Castle or Lodge'.

78　Drawing of Audley End garden wall reproduced in Drury, 'No other palace', p. 21, pl. 22A. For Hazelbury, see *Country Life*, 59 (20 and 27 February 1926), pp. 274–81, 306–12, with illustrations of walls, p. 279.

79　Described in John Chamberlain, *The Letters*, 2 vols, ed. N. E. McClure, Philadelphia, 1939, vol. I, p. 235.

80　*Smythson Drawings*, III/16, and see Pete Smith, 'The Sundial Garden and House-Plan Mount: Two Gardens at Wollaton Hall, Nottinghamshire, by Robert and John Smythson', *Garden History*, 31/i (2003), pp. 1–28.

81　Reproduced in Erna Auerbach, *Nicholas Hilliard*, London, 1961, p. 118, plate 94.

82　See pp. 43–5 above.

83　The fountain is shown in front of the house in an early eighteenth-century painting by Peter Tillemans, reproduced in 'Newstead Abbey', *Country Life*, 155 (9 May 1974), p. 1123. There and elsewhere it is attributed to the early sixteenth century, but an early seventeenth-century date is much more likely. No contemporary documentation has come to light.

84　*Smythson Drawings*, III/i (9), III/25. The former is close to the fountain as it was erected, though it does not show the statue. The busts in the surrounding alcoves were later removed, but new busts have been placed in them in recent years.

85　For the architecture of Bolsover, see *Girouard, Smythson*, pp. 206–10, 234–45, 260–69; Lucy Worsley, *Bolsover Castle*, English Heritage, 2000; John Goodall in *Country Life*, 212 (5 December 2002), pp. 98–101.

86　Printed as 'The Bolsover Castle Building Account, 1613', ed. with introduction, Douglas Knoop and G. P. Jones, in *Ars Quatuor Coronatorum*, 49 (1936), pp. 3–56.

87　See Rosamond Meredith, *Farms and Families of Hathersage Outseats*, vol. I, Sheffield, 1981, pp. 8–21; *Girouard, Smythson*, pp. 125–6; Maxwell Craven and Michael Stanley, *The Derbyshire Country House*, Derby, 1982.

88　For Carlton Hall, later Towers, see *Girouard, Smythson*, p. 277 and p. 317, n. 37; *Country Life*, 141 (26 January 1967), pp. 176–80, reproducing a drawing by Buck (British Library, Lansdowne MS 914, fol. 41), showing it before nineteenth-century remodelling. For Stydd and Tupton, see *Girouard, Smythson*, p. 277, and p. 317, n. 38; Craven and Stanley, *The Derbyshire Country House*, p. 65 [Stydd only].

89　Charles Cavendish has no entry in the *DNB* and the *ODNB*, and his entry in *House of Commons, Elizabeth* is not concerned with his building activities.

90　Letter (Historical Manuscripts Commission, *Calendar of the Manuscripts of the Marquess of Salisbury*, vol. XIX, pp. 120–21), part quoted in *Girouard, Smythson*, pp. 184–5.

91　*Smythson Drawings*, III/i (3).

92　British Library, Harleian MS 4955, fol. 67v. The whole poem is reproduced in facsimile as the endpapers of *Girouard, Smythson*.

93　*Girouard, Smythson*, p. 232, quoting from the diary of Archbishop Laud, 1624, and a list of those required to tilt in 1618 (J. Nichols, *The Progresses, Processions and Magnificent Festivities of King James the First*, 4 vols, London, 1828, vol. III, pp. 969, 472–3).

94　In a talk, 'The Lascivious Beasts of Bolsover', given *circa* 2000. Repeated in her *Cavalier: The Biography of A Seventeenth Century Household*, London, 2007, p. 95. 'Is it a fountain of Love . . . or of Lust . . . ?' (ibid., p. 96).

95　The masque, and the accompanying king's 'Entertainment at Welbeck', are printed in Ben Jonson, *Works*, vol. VII, ed. C. H. Herford, Percy Simpson and Evelyn Simpson, Oxford, 1941, pp. 787, 806.

96　*Smythson Drawings*, III/15 (5), III/2 [Clifton].

607　An enthusiast photographs the chimneypiece formerly in the upper gallery at Knole.

Index
and
Photograph
Acknowledgements

Index compiled by Meg Davies
(Fellow of the Society of Indexers)

References in the photograph acknowledgements below are to figure numbers.

National Trust © NTPL / Andreas von Einsiedel: 1, 2, 367, 442, 451, 476; Northampton Museum and Art Gallery: 4; Author: 3 (Devonshire Collection, Chatsworth), 5, 15, 16, 21, 28, 36, 48, 54, 57, 58, 64, 77, 91, 94, 95, 99, 103, 105, 110, 116, 132a, 136, 161, 164, 172, (collection of the Earl of Scarborough), 173 (collection of the Marquess of Salisbury, Hatfield House), 178, 180, 185, 191, 193, 194, 214, 219, 220, 224, 225, 227, 233, 234, 240, 241, 275, 282, 306, 307, 313, 320, 321, 342, 345, 356, 357, 358, 364, 366, 377, 380, 382, 385, 386, 396, 398 (collection of the Marquess of Salisbury, Hatfield House), 413, 414, 417, 424, 425, 427, 428, 447, 461, 466, 467, 469, 472, 477, 480, 486, 491, 493, 522, 527, 530, 531, 532, 533, 534, 536, 539, 550, 560, 561, 562 (collection of the Marquess of Salisbury, Hatfield House), 563, 569, 575, 585, 589, 590, 598, 604, 605; © Martin Charles: 6, 7, 11, 12, 24, 56, 65, 68, 69, 73, 100, 117, 137, 142, 143, 144, 145, 146, 156, 158, 159, 162, 163, 165, 166, 168, 169, 170, 174, 175, 198, 199, 200, 202, 203, 208, 216, 217, 218, 226, 231, 232, 238, 239, 243, 247, 248, 249, 252, 254, 262, 263, 268, 288, 305, 309, 315, 319, 328, 334, 338, 339, 347, 354, 355, 359, 360, 363, 393, 402, 403, 405, 407, 409, 411, 412, 416, 419, 422, 434, 439, 440, 441b, 443, 444, 445, 446, 457, 459, 460, 463, 465, 468, 473, 478, 479, 481, 482, 484, 489, 490, 494, 495, 496, 510, 516, 517, 518, 519, 520, 524, 529, 548, 555, 572, 578, 580, 583; © Georg-Philipp Pezold: 9, 30, 102, 104, 109, 135, 260, 317, 371, 431, 432, 492, 543, 568; © Bodleian Library, University of Oxford, 2008: 10 (530.32.A.2 (FOL)), 37, 42, 53 (Gough Land. 145), 96 (Douce Prints A.24, p. 65), 125 (B.2.4 Art), 152 (K.413 (2) Art, f. LV verso), 195 (Gough Kent 37, opp. p. 48), 258 (530.32 A.2 (FOL)), 296 (Auct. 2. R.2.7, p. 44), 303 (Gough Dorset 4, p. 283), 312 (G.A. Surrey B.8–10, p. 786), 314 (530.32 A.2 (FOL)), 318 (DH. R top 564/2, p. 28), 349, 372 (Arch. AA. B.3, opp. p. 48), 415 (B 2.4 Art, p .131), 512 (Vet. A3b.22, p. 324/5), 528 (Gough Dorset 4, p. 461), 565 (Arch. Antiq. A 11. 14, ref xiii); Sherborne Castle Estates: 13; Wiltshire Heritage Museum, Devizes: 14; Local Studies Collection, Lincoln City Library, by courtesy of Lincolnshire County Council: 17; Mark Watson Photography: 18, 72, 106, 108, 221, 274, 341, 373, 404, 556, 557, 566, 567, 576, 581; © Edward Piper: 19, 101, 111, 119, 130,

154, 230, 362, 368, 369, 370, 374, 379, 387, 497, 501, 502, 603; Norwich Castle Museum and Library: 20; © Juliane Batthyany: 22; © English Heritage. NMR: 23, 25, 131, 155, 184, 222, 223, 236, 244, 256, 264, 273, 276, 277, 278, 279, 280, 316, 337, 350, 423, 433, 470, 471, 487, 564, 574, 584, 591, 600; Carpenters' Company of London: 26, 27; Drake Eboracam: 29; Harland Walshaw: 31, 112, 123, 406; The Royal Collection © 2008, Her Majesty Queen Elizabeth II: 32, 587; © RIBA: 33, 39, 50, 51, 71, 82, 292, 335, 336, 455, 485, 506, 507, 508, 524, 554, 595, 597; National Trust © NTPL / Brenda Norrish: 34, 267, back jacket; © The Marquess of Salisbury / Hatfield House: 35, 41, 127, 132b, 134, 346, 397; © The Trustees of Sir John Soane's Museum, London: 38, 150, 207, 352, 353, endpapers; Courtauld Institute of Art, London: 40, 250, 310; Courtesy Conway Library, Courtauld Institute of Art, London / © The Trustees of Sir John Soane's Museum, London: 44, 83, 85, 86, 89a, 89b, 133, 149, 207b, 285, 286a, 286b, 287, 322, 325, 331, 332, 378, 538b, 540a, 540b, 542, 545a, 545b, 546, 549, 551, 552, 553; National Trust © NTPL / Angelo Hornak: 43; © British Library Board. All rights reserved: 45, 47, 97, 138, 284 (Add. MS 39831, ff. 3–4), 290, 291, 293, 514, 559, 588; Corpus Christi College, Cambridge: 46; © RIBA (photo: A. C. Cooper): 49, 300, 344, 505; West Sussex Record Office: 52; National Portrait Gallery, London: 55, 141; Country Life Picture Library: frontispiece, 59, 120, 210, 436, 453, 483; National Trust © NTPL / Nadia Mackenzie: 61, 271; Essex Record Office: 66, 450; Harland Walshaw and Peter Burton: 92, 107, 122, 245, 294, 343, 361, 498, 504, 509, 535, 537, 573, 596; John Piper: 114; Landmark Trust: 115, 295; John Schofield: 121; Lucinda Lambton: 124; Ashmolean Museum, Oxford: 140; © Courtauld Images / The Trustees of Sir John Soane's Museum, London: 150, 207a, 302, 538a; Crown Copyright. NMR: 151, 153; Lark Gilmer: 171; Thomas Pakenham: 181, 182, 205, 206; © The Trustees of the British Museum: 186, 187, 281; National Library of Sweden / Andrea Davis Kronlund: 188; National Library of Wales: 189, 190; National Trust © NTPL / David Dixon: 196; Burghley House Collections: 209; © Peter Moyse: 211; Bibliothèque royale de Belgique: 213; The Paul Mellon Centre for Studies in British Art, London: 215; Bristol Museums and Art Gallery: 228; Majed Najjar: 237; National Trust

© NTPL J. Whitaker: 253; National Trust © NTPL / Paul Wakefield: 255; National Trust © NTPL / Rupert Truman: 257; V&A Images / Victoria and Albert Museum, London: 259; National Trust © NTPL / John Hammond: 261; © Robert Thrift. Courtesy of Anthony Wells-Cole: 265; © Fred J. Maroon: 269; Tankerdale Workshop: 270; Colchester and Ipswich Museum Services: 272; National Trust © NTPL / Paul Harris: 283; Mary Evans Picture Library: 297; Tessa Wheeler: 299; © Historic Royal Palaces: 311; Society for the Protection of Ancient Buildings: 323; Eric Throssell: 329; National Trust © NTPL / Graham Challifour: 333, 500, front jacket; Nicholas Kingsley: 340; Alnwick Castle Archive: 351; Cadw: 365; Kiplin Hall Trust: 375; John Bethell: 376; Courtesy of Manolo Guerci: 391; Courtesy of Knight Frank: 399; Cincinnati Art Museum, Ohio: 426; Red Maids' School, Bristol: 430; Gloucestershire County Library: 435; © Patricia Payne / English Heritage: 448; Courtesy of Michael Mitchell Publications Ltd: 474; © National Trust / Condé Nast (Photo: Antony Crolla): 475; Angus McBean: 488; © Andor Gomme and Alison Maguire: 503; National Trust © NTPL / Fay Godwin: 515; Devonshire Collection, Chatsworth: 526; Kensington and Chelsea Public Library: 547; Deborah Howard: 579; National Maritime Museum, Greenwich, London: 586; © Jan Teagle. Courtesy of John Thorneycroft: 592; Somerset Archaeological and Natural History Society: 593; Renishaw Hall Archive: 599, 601, 602; © Richard Einzig / Arcaid: 606

Gemma Bryant drew the plans reproduced in figures 74a-b, 76, 78, 79a-d, 88a-d, 90a-d, 128a-e, 129 and 304, and Daphne Ford, that in figure 311.

In addition to those mentioned above or in the author's acknowledgements on page viii, the publisher thanks the following for their help with providing or obtaining photographic material: Jonathan Butler (English Heritage), Geoffrey Fisher (Conway Library, Courtauld Institute of Art), Anna Harrison (National Trust), Nikita Hooper (National Trust), Gerard Kilroy, Susan Palmer (Sir John Soane's Museum), Victoria Perry (Hatfield House), Jeffrey Tabberner, Nigel Wilkins (English Heritage).

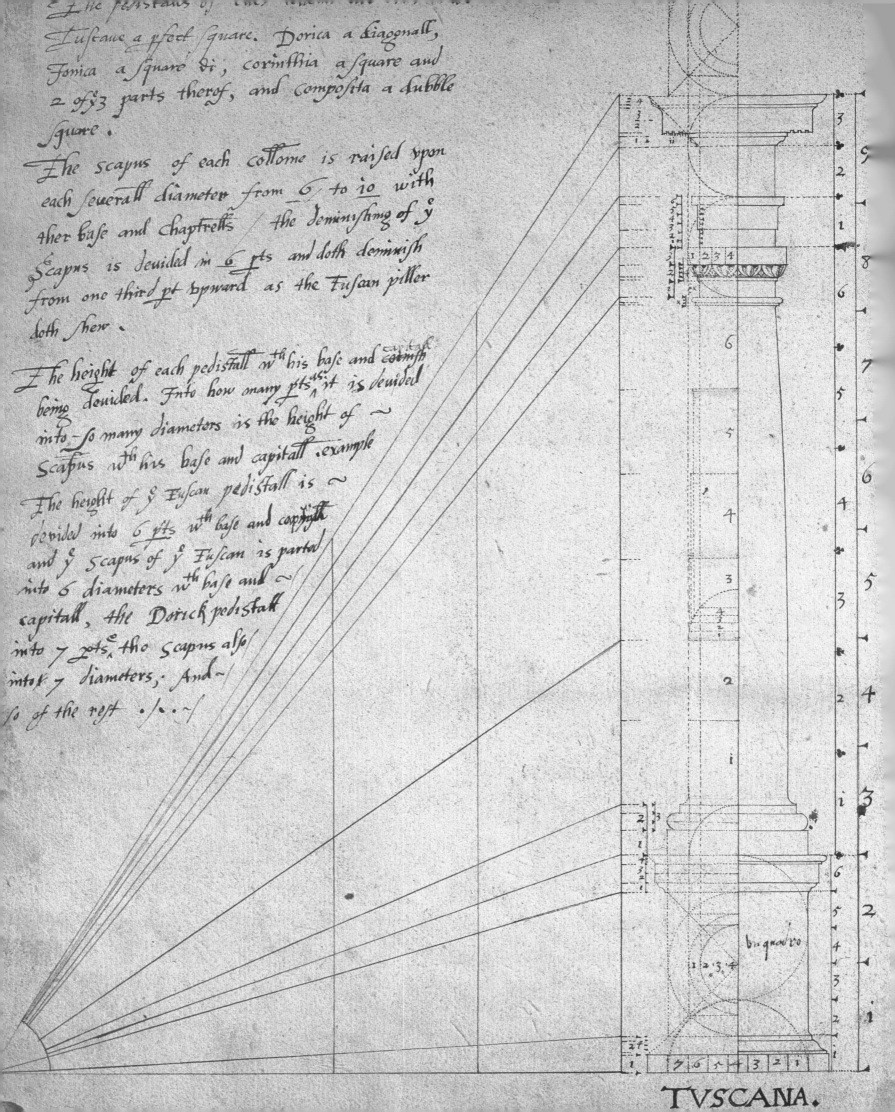

The resistans of the... tenem and...

Tuscane a pfect square. Dorica a diagonall,
Jonica a square di, corinthia a square and
2 of y³ parts therof, and Composita a dubble
square.

The scapus of each collome is raised ypon
each seuerall diameter from 6 to 10 with
ther base and chaptrells / the deminishing of y
scapns is deuided in 6 pts and doth deminish
from one third pt vpward as the Fuscan piller
doth shew.

The height of each pedistall wth his base and capitall corinsh
being deuided. Into how many pts as it is deuided
into so many diameters is the height of ~
Scapus wth his base and capitall. example
The height of y Fuscan pedistall is ~
deuided into 6 pts wth base and copright
and y Scapus of y Fuscan is parted
into 6 diameters wth base and ~
capitall, the Dorick pedistall
into 7 pts tho Scapus also
intox 7 diameters: And ~
so of the rest .:.~

bis quadro

TVSCANA.